English Fiction, 1900-1950

AMERICAN LITERATURE, ENGLISH LITERATURE, AND WORLD LITERATURES IN ENGLISH: AN INFORMATION GUIDE SERIES

Series Editor: Theodore Grieder, Curator, Division of Special Collections, Fales Library, New York University, New York, New York

Associate Editor: Duane DeVries, Associate Professor, Polytechnic Institute of New York, Brooklyn, New York

Other books on English literature in this series:

AUTHOR NEWSLETTERS AND JOURNALS—*Edited by Margaret Patterson**

ENGLISH DRAMA TO 1660 (EXCLUDING SHAKESPEARE)—*Edited by Frieda Elaine Penninger*

ENGLISH DRAMA, 1660-1800—*Edited by Frederick M. Link*

ENGLISH DRAMA AND THEATRE, 1800-1900—*Edited by L.W. Conolly and J.P. Wearing*

ENGLISH DRAMA, 1900-1950—*Edited by E.H. Mikhail*

ENGLISH FICTION, 1660-1800—*Edited by Jerry C. Beasley*

ENGLISH FICTION, 1800-1850—*Edited by Duane DeVries**

ENGLISH NOVEL, 1851-1900—*Edited by Robert Schweik and Albert Dunn**

ENGLISH FICTION, 1900-1950 (volume 2)—*Edited by Thomas Jackson Rice**

CONTEMPORARY FICTION IN AMERICA AND ENGLAND, 1950-1970—*Edited by Alfred F. Rosa and Paul A. Echholz*

OLD AND MIDDLE ENGLISH POETRY TO 1500—*Edited by Walter H. Beale*

ENGLISH POETRY, 1900-1950—*Edited by Emily Ann Anderson**

ENGLISH PROSE, PROSE FICTION, AND CRITICISM TO 1660—*Edited by S.K. Heninger, Jr.*

ENGLISH PROSE AND CRITICISM IN THE NINETEENTH CENTURY—*Edited by Harris W. Wilson and Diane Long Hoeveler*

ENGLISH PROSE AND CRITICISM, 1900-1950—*Edited by Christopher C. Brown and William B. Thesing**

ENGLISH LITERARY JOURNAL TO 1900—*Edited by Robert B. White, Jr.*

ENGLISH LITERARY JOURNAL, 1900-1950—*Edited by Michael N. Stanton**

ENGLISH LITTLE MAGAZINES, 1950-1975—*Edited by B.C. Bloomfield**

*in preparation

The above series is part of the
GALE INFORMATION GUIDE LIBRARY

The Library consists of a number of separate series of guides covering major areas in the social sciences, humanities, and current affairs.

General Editor: Paul Wasserman, Professor and former Dean, School of Library and Information Services, University of Maryland

Managing Editor: Denise Allard Adzigian, Gale Research Company

English Fiction, 1900-1950

General Bibliography and Individual Authors: Aldington to Huxley

A GUIDE TO INFORMATION SOURCES

Volume 1 of a 2 Volume Set

Volume 20 in the American Literature, English Literature, and World Literatures in English Information Guide Series

Thomas Jackson Rice

Associate Professor of English
University of South Carolina
Columbia

Gale Research Company
Book Tower, Detroit, Michigan 48226

Library of Congress Cataloging in Publication Data

Rice, Thomas Jackson.
English fiction, 1900-1950.

(American literature, English literature, and world literatures in English ; v. 20) (Gale information guide library)
Includes indexes.
1. English fiction—20th century—Bibliography.
I. Title.
Z2014.F4R5 [PR881] 016.823'9 73-16989
ISBN 0-8103-1217-4

VITA

Thomas Jackson Rice is currently associate professor of English at the University of South Carolina where he teaches courses in fiction, nineteenth- and twentieth-century English literature, and contemporary literature. He received his B.A. degree from the University of Delaware, and his M.A. and Ph.D. degrees from Princeton University. Academic honors awarded him include a Woodrow Wilson Fellowship.

Rice is the author of several articles on nineteenth- and twentieth-century English novelists, and is working on a study of the English historical novel and an analysis of Joseph Conrad's major fiction.

CONTENTS

Contents

ACKNOWLEDGMENTS

I should like to thank Theodore Grieder, Duane DeVries, Joel A. Myerson, Trevor Howard-Hill, Matthew J. Bruccoli, A. Walton Litz, G. Ross Roy, James T. Boulton, S. Ashley Brown, and Gordon Lindstrand for their several suggestions, loans of materials, and helpful advice throughout the preparation of this guide. To my research assistants, who typed and searched, I owe a special debt: Michael Barrett, Deborah Boogaarde, Glenn Ellen Jones, Brent Kendrick, Joseph McNally, and David Pitre. I am also grateful for the cheerful cooperation of the interlibrary loan librarians of the McKissick and Cooper Libraries of the University of South Carolina, and for the kindness shown me by the staffs of the Firestone Library of Princeton University, the Morris Library of the University of Delaware, the Perkins Library of Duke University, the Louis Round Wilson Library of the University of North Carolina, the Princeton Theological Seminary Library, the New York Public Library, and the Library of Congress.

To my teacher, colleague and friend, Calhoun Winton, who first suggested this project to me, I owe more than I can possibly acknowledge. And for the patience and support of my wife, Diane, I owe a debt I can never repay.

ABBREVIATIONS OF AUTHORS' NAMES

The following abbreviations of authors' names are used only in the General Bibliography annotations (to indicate those writers considered in the work annotated), within the author's own section of the guide, and in the index. An author's name is not abbreviated when he appears as the author or editor of a work, or as part of a title, or within an annotation in a section dealing with another writer. Adjectival forms of an author's name are not abbreviated (e.g., "Conradian," not "JCian"). In all cases where an abbreviation might cause unnecessary confusion, the author's name is given in full.

RA: Richard Aldington

MB: Max Beerbohm

AB: Arnold Bennett

EB: Elizabeth Bowen

GKC: G.K. Chesterton

IC: Ivy Compton-Burnett

JC: Joseph Conrad

ND: Norman Douglas

RF: Ronald Firbank

FMF: Ford Madox Ford

EMF: E.M. Forster

JG: John Galsworthy

HG: Henry Green

LPH: L.P. Hartley

AH: Aldous Huxley

JJ: James Joyce

DHL: D.H. Lawrence

RL: Rosamond Lehmann

CSL: C.S. Lewis

WL: Wyndham Lewis

RM: Rose Macaulay

KM: Katherine Mansfield

SM: Somerset Maugham

HHM: H.H. Munro ("Saki")

LHM: L.H. Myers

GO: George Orwell

JCP: J.C. Powys

TFP: T.F. Powys

DR: Dorothy Richardson

FR: Frederick Rolfe

EW: Evelyn Waugh

RW: Rebecca West

HGW: H.G. Wells

CW: Charles Williams

VW: Virginia Woolf

JOURNAL ABBREVIATIONS

The following abbreviations of journal titles conform to the MLA INTERNATIONAL BIBLIOGRAPHY Master List and Table of Abbreviations. Journals not in the Master List are given in full when cited in this text. The abbreviations in this list are used consistently throughout this guide, except when the journal itself is the main entry. That is, special issues are classified as "essay collections" and entered alphabetically, by the name of the journal.

AI	AMERICAN IMAGO
AntigR	ANTIGONISH REVIEW
AR	ANTIOCH REVIEW
ArQ	ARIZONA QUARTERLY
ASch	AMERICAN SCHOLAR
AUMLA	JOURNAL OF THE AUSTRALASIAN UNIVERSITIES LANGUAGE AND LITERATURE ASSOCIATION
AusQ	AUSTRALIAN QUARTERLY
BB	BULLETIN OF BIBLIOGRAPHY
BC	BOOK COLLECTOR
BJA	BRITISH JOURNAL OF AESTHETICS
BNYPL	BULLETIN OF THE NEW YORK PUBLIC LIBRARY
BSUF	BALL STATE UNIVERSITY FORUM
BuR	BUCKNELL REVIEW
BUSE	BOSTON UNIVERSITY STUDIES IN ENGLISH
CalR	CALCUTTA REVIEW
C&L	CHRISTIANITY AND LITERATURE
CathW	CATHOLIC WORLD
CCC	COLLEGE COMPOSITION AND COMMUNICATION

Journal Abbreviations

CE	COLLEGE ENGLISH
CEA	COLLEGE ENGLISH ASSOCIATION CRITIC
CentR	CENTENNIAL REVIEW
ChiR	CHICAGO REVIEW
CimR	CIMARRON REVIEW
CL	COMPARATIVE LITERATURE
CLAJ	COLLEGE LANGUAGE ASSOCIATION JOURNAL
CLJ	CORNELL LIBRARY JOURNAL
CLQ	COLBY LIBRARY QUARTERLY
CLS	COMPARATIVE LITERATURE STUDIES
ConL	CONTEMPORARY LITERATURE (supersedes WSCL)
ConnR	CONNECTICUT REVIEW
ContempR	CONTEMPORARY REVIEW
CR	CRITICAL REVIEW
Crit	CRITIQUE: STUDIES IN MODERN FICTION
CritQ	CRITICAL QUARTERLY
CSLBull	BULLETIN OF THE NEW YORK C.S. LEWIS SOCIETY
DHLR	D.H. LAWRENCE REVIEW
DR	DALHOUSIE REVIEW
EA	ETUDES ANGLAISES
E&S	ESSAYS AND STUDIES BY MEMBERS OF THE ENGLISH ASSOCIATION
EDH	ESSAYS BY DIVERS HANDS
EFT	ENGLISH FICTION IN TRANSITION (now ELT)
EIC	ESSAYS IN CRITICISM
EJ	ENGLISH JOURNAL (COLLEGE EDITION)
ELH	JOURNAL OF ENGLISH LITERARY HISTORY
ELN	ENGLISH LANGUAGE NOTES
ELT	ENGLISH LITERATURE IN TRANSITION (1880-1920) (supersedes EFT)
EM	ENGLISH MISCELLANY
EngR	ENGLISH RECORD
ES	ENGLISH STUDIES

ESA	ENGLISH STUDIES IN AFRICA
EWN	EVELYN WAUGH NEWSLETTER
FMod	FILOLOGIA MODERNA
GaR	GEORGIA REVIEW
HAB	HUMANITIES ASSOCIATION BULLETIN
HJ	HIBBERT JOURNAL
HLB	HARVARD LIBRARY BULLETIN
HSL	HARTFORD STUDIES IN LITERATURE
HudR	HUDSON REVIEW
HUSL	HEBREW UNIVERSITY STUDIES IN LITERATURE
JAAC	JOURNAL OF AESTHETICS AND ART CRITICISM
JAmS	JOURNAL OF AMERICAN STUDIES
JASt	JOURNAL OF ASIAN STUDIES
JEGP	JOURNAL OF ENGLISH AND GERMANIC PHILOLOGY
JGE	JOURNAL OF GENERAL EDUCATION
JHI	JOURNAL OF THE HISTORY OF IDEAS
JJQ	JAMES JOYCE QUARTERLY
JML	JOURNAL OF MODERN LITERATURE
JNT	JOURNAL OF NARRATIVE TECHNIQUE
KanQ	KANSAS QUARTERLY
KR	KENYON REVIEW
L&P	LITERATURE AND PSYCHOLOGY
LCrit	LITERARY CRITERION
LCUT	LIBRARY CHRONICLE OF THE UNIVERSITY OF TEXAS
LFQ	LITERATURE/FILM QUARTERLY
LHY	LITERARY HALF-YEARLY
LQHR	LONDON QUARTERLY AND HOLBORN REVIEW
MD	MODERN DRAMA
MFS	MODERN FICTION STUDIES
MHRev	MALAHAT REVIEW
MLN	MODERN LANGUAGE NOTES
MLQ	MODERN LANGUAGE QUARTERLY
MLR	MODERN LANGUAGE REVIEW
ModA	MODERN AGE

Journal Abbreviations

MP	MODERN PHILOLOGY
MQ	MIDWEST QUARTERLY
MR	MASSACHUSETTS REVIEW
N&Q	NOTES AND QUERIES
NCF	NINETEENTH-CENTURY FICTION
NDQ	NORTH DAKOTA QUARTERLY
NLH	NEW LITERARY HISTORY
NS	DIE NEUEREN SPRACHEN
NYTBR	NEW YORK TIMES BOOK REVIEW
NZSJ	NEW ZEALAND SLAVONIC JOURNAL
OhR	OHIO REVIEW (supersedes OUR)
OL	ORBIS LITTERARUM
OUR	OHIO UNIVERSITY REVIEW (now OhR)
OW	ORIENT/WEST
PBSA	PAPERS OF THE BIBLIOGRAPHICAL SOCIETY OF AMERICA
Person	PERSONALIST
PLL	PAPERS ON LANGUAGE AND LITERATURE
PMASAL	PAPERS OF THE MICHIGAN ACADEMY OF SCIENCE, ARTS, AND LETTERS
PMLA	PUBLICATIONS OF THE MODERN LANGUAGE ASSOCIATION OF AMERICA
PolR	POLISH REVIEW
PQ	PHILOLOGICAL QUARTERLY
PR	PARTISAN REVIEW
PrS	PRAIRIE SCHOONER
PSQ	POLITICAL SCIENCE QUARTERLY
PsyR	PSYCHOANALYTIC REVIEW
PULC	PRINCETON UNIVERSITY LIBRARY CHRONICLE
QFRT	QUARTERLY OF FILM, RADIO AND TELEVISION
QQ	QUEEN'S QUARTERLY
QR	QUARTERLY REVIEW
REL	REVIEW OF ENGLISH LITERATURE (now ARIEL)
RES	REVIEW OF ENGLISH STUDIES

RLV	REVUE DES LANGUES VIVANTES
RMS	RENAISSANCE AND MODERN STUDIES
RomN	ROMANCE NOTES
RR	ROMANIC REVIEW
RS	RESEARCH STUDIES
RusR	RUSSIAN REVIEW
SAB	SOUTH ATLANTIC BULLETIN
SAQ	SOUTH ATLANTIC QUARTERLY
SatR	SATURDAY REVIEW (NEW YORK)
SatR (London)	SATURDAY REVIEW (LONDON)
SB	STUDIES IN BIBLIOGRAPHY
SEEJ	SLAVIC AND EAST EUROPEAN JOURNAL
SEER	SLAVONIC AND EAST EUROPEAN REVIEW
SEL	STUDIES IN ENGLISH LITERATURE, 1500-1900
SEL (Tokyo)	STUDIES IN ENGLISH LITERATURE (TOKYO)
SFS	SCIENCE FICTION STUDIES
ShawR	SHAW REVIEW
SHR	SOUTHERN HUMANITIES REVIEW
SLitI	STUDIES IN THE LITERARY IMAGINATION
SNL	SATIRE NEWSLETTER
SNNTS	STUDIES IN THE NOVEL (NORTH TEXAS STATE UNIVERSITY)
SoR	SOUTHERN REVIEW
SP	STUDIES IN PHILOLOGY
SR	SEWANEE REVIEW
SSF	STUDIES IN SHORT FICTION
STC	STUDIES IN THE TWENTIETH CENTURY
SWR	SOUTHWEST REVIEW
TamR	TAMARACK REVIEW
TCL	TWENTIETH CENTURY LITERATURE
TLS	[LONDON] TIMES LITERARY SUPPLEMENT
TQ	TEXAS QUARTERLY
TSE	TULANE STUDIES IN ENGLISH
TSL	TENNESSEE STUDIES IN LITERATURE
TSLL	TEXAS STUDIES IN LITERATURE AND LANGUAGE

UKCR	UNIVERSITY OF KANSAS CITY REVIEW (later UR)
UR	UNIVERSITY REVIEW (supersedes UKCR)
UTQ	UNIVERSITY OF TORONTO QUARTERLY
VQR	VIRGINIA QUARTERLY REVIEW
VS	VICTORIAN STUDIES
VWQ	VIRGINIA WOOLF QUARTERLY
WascanaR	WASCANA REVIEW
WHR	WESTERN HUMANITIES REVIEW
WR	WESTERN REVIEW: A JOURNAL OF THE HUMANITIES
WSCL	WISCONSIN STUDIES IN CONTEMPORARY LITERATURE (now ConL)
WVUPP	WEST VIRGINIA UNIVERSITY PHILOLOGICAL PAPERS
XUS	XAVIER UNIVERSITY STUDIES
YES	YEARBOOK OF ENGLISH STUDIES
YR	YALE REVIEW
YULG	YALE UNIVERSITY LIBRARY GAZETTE
ZRL	ZAGADNIENIA RODZAJOW LITERAKICH

INTRODUCTION
THE SCOPE AND FORMAT OF THIS GUIDE

AUTHORS REPRESENTED

Three criteria have been used for determining who among the scores of British writers of fiction, flourishing during the years 1900-1950, would be represented in this research guide. Included are (1) all generally acknowledged "major" novelists--Conrad, Joyce, Lawrence, and Woolf (indeed, the critical literature on these writers alone has assumed "industrial" proportions)--and those one might call the "second echelon" of major-minor novelists--Bennett, Ford, Forster, Galsworthy, Huxley, Maugham, Orwell, Waugh, and Wells; (2) all major men of letters who, though they may be better known for their achievements in other fields, have made a significant contribution to modern fiction--Aldington, Beerbohm, Chesterton, C.S. Lewis, and Wyndham Lewis; and (3) all so-called minor writers who have, nonetheless, attracted a significant amount of bibliographical, biographical, or critical commentary, and who have contributed significantly to the development of modern long and short fiction in Britain--Bowen, Compton-Burnett, Douglas, Firbank, Hartley, Lehmann, Macaulay, Mansfield, Munro, Myers, J.C. and T.F. Powys, Richardson, Rolfe, West, and Williams.

Guides to Graham Greene, Neil Gunn, Rudyard Kipling, Sean O'Faolain, Liam O'Flaherty, J.R.R. Tolkien, and others who might legitimately have been included, are to be found in companion volumes in this Gale Information Guide Series.

THE GENERAL BIBLIOGRAPHY

The first part of this guide consists of an annotated, general bibliography for the study of English fiction, 1900-1950. Throughout the individual author guides which follow, reference will be made, by short title and reference number, to the general works listed in this opening section. Within the general bibliography, works cited are arranged under eight headings, often with internal subdivisions. These eight parts reflect the three major purposes of this general listing: parts 1-2 (Bibliography and Literary History) offer general, introductory research materials; parts 3-6 (Critical Studies of Modern English Fiction, Theory of Fiction,

Studies of the Short Story, and Studies of Major Types) list the most important studies of fiction; and parts 7-8 (Histories and Memoirs and Related Arts) offer useful background materials for a more informed study of English fiction, 1900-1950. While many of the works so classified might easily fit into more than one category, I have attempted to list these items either in the most appropriate section, or, when such discrimination is impossible, into the first appropriate section. Headnotes are used extensively throughout the general bibliography to explain the nature and selectivity of the individual sections. The annotations are intended to give the user some sense of an item's thesis, pertinence, and value (self-explanatory titles are often not annotated). Asterisks are used, as in the individual author sections of this guide, to indicate the most important works.

INDIVIDUAL AUTHOR SECTIONS

The guides to research for individual authors are divided into two general parts: the primary and the secondary bibliographies, each with internal subdivisions.

(1) The Primary Bibliography

The primary bibliography is usually divided into four main sections:

(1.1) Fiction: A comprehensive bibliography. Includes title, editor (if applicable, place of first publication (British and American, in the order of first publication--and foreign, only if first edition), publisher, and date for all novels, novellas, and story collections (first collected publication). Also included are all collaborations, if any, in a further subsection. All "textual" editions are described in the annotations. Each title is briefly annotated to give the reader a general idea of the nature of the work.

(1.2) Miscellaneous Writings: A selective bibliography. Includes volumes of poetry, drama, criticism, essays, histories, and so on, listed in the same format as the fiction section. With some of the more prolific authors this section is necessarily quite selective. In each case, however, the criteria for inclusion are the intrinsic significance of the work and the relevance of the nonfiction for the student of the author's fiction. Annotations are provided, as above, to give the user a general idea of the work's nature. In those rare cases when the author considered has published no nonfiction, this fact is noted.

(1.3) Collected and Selected Works: A selective bibliography. Includes all major editions (if any) and anthologies of the author's works, listed in the same format as the previous sections. Annotations give the user a brief account of the contents of the titles. If there are no collections or selections of the author's works, this fact is so noted.

(1.4) Letters: A selective bibliography. Includes all book and periodical publications containing a substantial number of letters by the author, listed in the same format as the previous sections, unless they have been absorbed into larger, collected editions of correspondence. A headnote is usually added to this section to cross-reference biographical or critical materials which include some correspondence, or which comment on the author as letterwriter. Annotations usually note the number of letters involved and briefly describe the relationship of the author and his correspondent. If the author's letters have not been published, this fact is noted.

(1.5) Concordances: A comprehensive bibliography. In a few cases the primary bibliography is expanded to include concordances, listed in the same format as the previous sections. Within the secondary section of the author's guide, cross-references are made to these listings under the work indexed, in the section Studies of Individual Works. Annotations note format, limitations, and methodology of the concordances.

Throughout the primary bibliography the abbreviation used for the work's title, if any, is added to the main entry for that work. This abbreviation will be used only within the individual author's section. Also, where applicable, the symbol "(P)" is added to the main entry to indicate whether the work is available in American paperback reprint. Headnotes are used throughout to indicate important forthcoming work (e.g., textual editions in progress).

(2) The Secondary Bibliography

The secondary bibliography is divided into five main sections, described below. A headnote to this part of the individual author's guide will list all author-centered journals (active and inactive) and, occasionally, describe forthcoming research of significance. As in the General Bibliography, asterisks are used throughout to indicate items of special importance.

(2.1) Bibliographies: A selective list. Includes all major primary and secondary bibliographies, checklists, and annual updates of criticism, specifically devoted to the author. Unpublished dissertations are omitted, as well as those bibliographies that have become obsolete, that are needless duplications (e.g., most of the end-bibliographies in critical books), or that have been incorporated into later publications already noted. Occasionally a distinguished essay-survey of the author's critical reception is included, although such items are not bibliographies as such. Annotations generally describe the nature, scope, reliability, and usefulness of the item.

(2.2) Biographies, Memoirs, Reminiscences, Interviews: A selective list. Includes book-length items as well as periodical articles and sections from books. Annotations describe the substance and value of the work and, where applicable, the nature and duration of the memoirist's relationship with the author.

(2.3) Book-Length Critical Studies and Essay Collections: By far the most inclusive section of the secondary bibliography, omitting only unpublished dissertations, most student outline-guides (e.g., "Cliff's Notes" and "Monarch Outlines"), and foreign-language studies (see note on foreign-language publications below). Also included here are special issues of periodicals, character indexes, glossaries, and pamphlets. Annotations for this section are more expansive than elsewhere, generally including a brief summary of the critic's thesis, or describing the complexion of the essay collection and noting the individual works considered. The studies are also frankly evaluated for their persuasiveness and quality. A headnote to this section refers the user to book-length critical studies and essay collections devoted to individual works, which are entered in section 2.5, Studies of Individual Works.

(2.4) General Critical Articles, or Chapters: A selective list. Includes all truly general essays on the author, commentaries on specific themes, techniques, or other aspects of his works, and studies of more than two of his individual works. Annotations suggest the subject and value of the item. In rare cases, the annotation is omitted when the title is self-explanatory.

(2.5) Studies of Individual Works: A selective list. Includes all books, essay collections, articles, and chapters devoted to (i) the author's fiction, alphabetically by title, or (ii) his nonfiction (general, heterogeneous list). Annotations, as in the previous sections, suggest the subject and value of the item. A headnote to this section lists all previously cited books, collections, and general articles which provide significant work-by-work commentaries on the individual works. With one author, Joyce, the format of this section is altered to accommodate the extensive and unique varieties of scholarship on his individual works. In rare cases, this section is omitted entirely when there exists no significant commentary on the author's individual works. Self-explanatory titles are not annotated.

CROSS-REFERENCES

All items in this guide are numbered for cross-reference. By far the greatest portion of these cross-references will appear within the individual authors' sections, to refer to works listed in the opening, general bibliography. The entry format is modified to include only a short title (with page references) and the cross-reference number. Items to be found in the General Bibliography are designated by a "G" prefix, followed by a four-digit reference number. The first two digits indicate the appropriate division and subdivision of the General Bibliography. For example, William York Tindall's FORCES IN MODERN BRITISH LITERATURE has the reference number G2122: G--General Bibliography; 21--section 2: Literary History, subsection 1: General; 22--item number 22 in that subsection. Cross-references to other works within an author's section are occasionally simplified, in favor of "see above" or "see below." However, since this method is sometimes unwieldy, and can prove confusing, a five-digit cross-reference number, keyed to the divisions of the section and without the "G" prefix is generally used.

FOREIGN-LANGUAGE PUBLICATIONS

Translations of authors' works and critical material appearing in foreign languages are omitted from this guide, unless their significance demands inclusion. In a few cases, works originally written by the author in a foreign language, and not translated by him into English, are included (e.g., Conrad's LETTRES FRANCAISES).

ABBREVIATIONS, REFERENCE TERMS, AND SPECIAL SYMBOLS

Abbreviations are used throughout this guide for selected journal titles (see list below) and, in specific circumstances, for authors' names (see list below). Major works are also abbreviated, within the individual author's guide, and are so noted in the primary bibliography section of each author section. The most frequently used, and perhaps unfamiliar, reference terms are passim ("throughout the work" or "here and there"); cf. (within parentheses--indicates a comparison made by the author of the book or article annotated). When the first edition date differs from the date of the edition being cited, the first edition date follows the main title, preceding the facts of publication. An asterisk (*) denotes an item of special importance. "(P)" denotes availability of a work in recent American paperback reprint, and is used in primary bibliographies only.

DATES OF COVERAGE

The terminal date for the general bibliography and individual authors' guide (in volume one), is January 1977. Major publications appearing through 1977 have been included and annotated when accessible.

GENERAL BIBLIOGRAPHY

G1. BIBLIOGRAPHY

1.1 PRIMARY BIBLIOGRAPHIES

Several of the research guides listed in the following sections also contain brief primary bibliographies. Also see G6101, G6414, and G6423.

G1101 BRITISH NATIONAL BIBLIOGRAPHY. London: Council of the British National Bibliography, 1950-- .

Full primary and secondary bibliography of books published in Great Britain (with good coverage of American publications). Organized by the Dewey decimal classification system (e.g., 823.91: Modern Fiction in English), with an author index. Since this compilation begins with 1950, its primary listings of English novels must be supplemented by the ENGLISH CATALOGUE OF BOOKS (G1106).

*G1102 Bufkin, E.C., comp. THE TWENTIETH-CENTURY NOVEL IN ENGLISH: A CHECKLIST. Athens: Univ. of Georgia Press, 1967.

An impressive, if flawed, list of novels in English by over 400 writers.

G1103 Burns, Landon C., comp. "A Cross-Referenced Index of Short Fiction and Author-Title Listing." SSF, 7 (1970), 1-218.

Useful guide to reprinted short fiction and anthologies.

G1104 CONTEMPORARY AUTHORS: A BIO-BIBLIOGRAPHICAL GUIDE TO CURRENT WRITERS IN FICTION, GENERAL NONFICTION, POETRY, JOURNALISM, DRAMA, MOTION PICTURES, TELEVISION AND OTHER FIELDS. Detroit: Gale, 1962-- .

Alphabetical listing and "bio-bibliographical" guides to current authors, published semiannually, and revised and consolidated periodically. Cumulative index to volumes

1-64 published following volume 64 in 1976. A new, "permanent" series (begun 1975) will recompile entries for authors who have died or ceased publishing.

G1105 Cook, Dorothy E., and Isabel S. Monroe, comps. THE SHORT STORY INDEX. New York: Wilson, 1953.

A primary listing of over 60,000 short story titles. Supplements for more recent publications appeared in 1956, 1960, 1965, 1969, and 1974.

G1106 ENGLISH CATALOGUE OF BOOKS, 1801-1965. London: S. Low, 1864-1901; Publishers' Circular, 1906-66.

Annual author and title listings of books published in Great Britain.

1.2 ANNUAL SECONDARY BIBLIOGRAPHIES (which include sections on modern English fiction and individual novelists)

G1201 ANNUAL BIBLIOGRAPHY OF ENGLISH LANGUAGE AND LITERATURE. Cambridge, Engl.: Modern Humanities Research Association, 1920-- .

Generally less comprehensive than the MLA bibliography, below.

*G1202 MLA INTERNATIONAL BIBLIOGRAPHY. New York: Modern Language Association of America, 1969-- . Formerly "Annual Bibliography" and "International Bibliography," PMLA, 34 (1919)-83 (1968).

Originally appeared as the May issue of PMLA and, since 1969, as a separate volume. Most pertinent entries appear under "Types" of literature, or under the general twentieth-century British literature classification. Individual author listings included. A separate volume of abstracts was compiled for the years 1971-75.

G1203 THE YEAR'S WORK IN ENGLISH STUDIES. London: English Association, 1919-- .

Both a bibliography and a review of studies.

1.3 GENERAL SELECTIVE BIBLIOGRAPHIES (primary and secondary)

*G1301 Altick, Richard D., and Andrew Wright, comps. SELECTIVE BIBLIOGRAPHY FOR THE STUDY OF ENGLISH AND AMERICAN LITERATURE. 1960. 5th ed. New York: Macmillan, 1975.

An excellent general research guide.

G1302 Bateson, F.W., ed. A GUIDE TO ENGLISH LITERATURE. 1965. 2nd ed. Garden City, N.Y.: Doubleday, 1968.

Another fine, selective handbook for research.

*G1303 Kennedy, Arthur G., Donald B. Sands, and William E. Colburn, eds. A CONCISE BIBLIOGRAPHY FOR STUDENTS OF ENGLISH. 1940. 5th ed. Stanford, Calif.: Stanford Univ. Press, 1972.

Excellent guide for initial research. Includes sections on general literary study, the novel, and "The Modern Period" (pp. 139-65), but no bibliographies of individual authors.

*G1304 Watson, George, ed. THE CONCISE CAMBRIDGE BIBLIOGRAPHY OF ENGLISH LITERATURE. 1958. 2nd ed. Cambridge: At the Univ. Press, 1965.

A quite selective, but useful section on modern British literature.

1.4 BIBLIOGRAPHIES OF MODERN ENGLISH LITERATURE, THE NOVEL, AND FICTION CRITICISM

Also see G6409 and G8019.

*G1401 "Annual Review Number." JML, 1 (1971)-- .

Bibliographical listings, and reviews of major studies of modern literature. Issued annually.

G1402 Beebe, Maurice, comp. "Selected Bibliography on Theories of Modernism and Post-Modernism." JML, 3 (1974), 1080-84.

An important topical checklist.

G1403 Bell, Inglis F., and Donald Baird, comps. THE ENGLISH NOVEL, 1578-1956: A CHECKLIST OF TWENTIETH-CENTURY CRITICISMS. Denver, Colo.: Swallow, 1959.

*G1404 "Bibliography, News, and Notes." EFT [now ELT] 1 (1957) through 18 (1975).

Annotated bibliographies of individual authors (floruit 1880-1920). Updated annually; suspended 1975.

G1405 Booth, Bradford A. "The Novel." In CONTEMPORARY LITERARY SCHOLARSHIP: A CRITICAL REVIEW. Ed. Lewis Leary. New York: Appleton, 1958. Pp. 259-88.

A general bibliographical essay, now somewhat dated.

*G1406 "Current Bibliography." TCL, 1 (1954)-- .

Annotated bibliography of current critical literature appearing in American and foreign periodicals. Listings arranged alphabetically by author considered or by topical classifications. Appears quarterly.

G1407 Daiches, David. THE PRESENT AGE IN BRITISH LITERATURE. Bloomington: Indiana Univ. Press, 1958.

Critical survey and brief primary and secondary bibliographies for an impressive number of writers.

*G1408 Dyson, A.E., ed. THE ENGLISH NOVEL: SELECT BIBLIOGRAPHICAL GUIDES. London: Oxford Univ. Press, 1974.

Bibliographical essays on twenty-two major novelists, including JC, EMF, JJ, and DHL.

G1409 Lauterbach, Edward S., and W. Eugene Davis, comps. THE TRANSITIONAL AGE IN BRITISH LITERATURE, 1880-1920. Troy, N.Y.: Whitston, 1973.

A research guide with selective bibliographies for 177 writers of the period. Includes MB, AB, GKC, JC, EMF, FMF, JG, DHL, RM, KM, SM, HHM, DR, FR, HGW.

*G1410 "Modern Fiction Newsletter." MFS, 1 (1955) through 14 (1968).

Biannual bibliographical essays covering modern fiction criticism and individual author studies.

G1411 Palmer, Helen H., and Anne J. Dyson, comps. ENGLISH NOVEL EXPLICATION: CRITICISMS TO 1972. Hamden, Conn.: Shoe String Press, 1973.

Arranged by authors studied. Lists over 4,800 items. Addenda and supplement through 1975, issued 1976.

G1412 Pownall, David E., comp. ARTICLES ON TWENTIETH-CENTURY LITERATURE: AN ANNOTATED BIBLIOGRAPHY, 1954 TO 1970. Millwood, N.Y.: Kraus-Thomson, 1973. Vols. 1-3.

First three volumes (A-I) of a proposed seven-volume compilation of articles on modern writers. Brief annotations. Arranged alphabetically by authors studied. Drawn from the "Current Bibliography" of TCL (see G1406).

G1413 Putnam, Margaret, et al., comps. "Textual Studies in the Novel: A Selected Checklist, 1950-1974." SNNTS, 7 (1975), 445-71.

Lists general textual studies and studies of individual authors.

G1414 Souvage, Jacques, comp. "A Systematic Bibliography for the Study of the Novel." In AN INTRODUCTION TO THE STUDY OF THE NOVEL. New York: Humanities, 1965. Pp. 103-254.

Topically organized checklist of over 2,300 items. Also see G4085.

G1415 Stallman, Robert W., comp. "A Selected Bibliography of Criticism of Modern Fiction." In CRITIQUES AND ESSAYS ON MODERN FICTION. Ed. J.W. Aldridge. New York: Ronald, 1952. Pp. 553-610. See G3001.

Useful, though now dated.

G1416 Stevick, Philip, comp. "Selected Bibliography." In his THE THEORY OF THE NOVEL. Ed. P. Stevick. New York: Free Press, 1967. Pp. 407-28. See G4091.

Excellent listing of general and theoretical studies.

G1417 Temple, Ruth Z., and Martin Tucker, comps. TWENTIETH CENTURY BRITISH LITERATURE: A REFERENCE GUIDE AND BIBLIOGRAPHY. New York: Ungar, 1968.

A general research guide, with brief summary bibliographies for over 400 modern British writers.

G1418 Walker, Warren, comp. TWENTIETH-CENTURY SHORT STORY EXPLICATION: INTERPRETATIONS, 1900-1975, OF SHORT FICTION SINCE 1800. 1961. 3rd ed. Hamden, Conn.: Shoe String Press, 1977.

*G1419 Wiley, Paul L., comp. THE BRITISH NOVEL: CONRAD TO THE PRESENT. Northbrook, Ill.: AHM, 1973.

Secondary checklists on individual authors, prefaced by a selective general bibliography.

*G1420 Willison, I.R., ed. THE NEW CAMBRIDGE BIBLIOGRAPHY OF ENGLISH LITERATURE. VOL. 4, 1900-1950. Cambridge: At the Univ. Press, 1972.

Encyclopedic listing of primary and secondary materials.

1.5 BIBLIOGRAPHIES OF BIBLIOGRAPHIES

G1501 Howard-Hill, Trevor H., comp. BIBLIOGRAPHY OF BRITISH LITERARY BIBLIOGRAPHIES. Oxford: Clarendon, 1969. Supplement: SHAKESPEARIAN BIBLIOGRAPHY AND TEXTUAL CRITICISM: A BIBLIOGRAPHY. Oxford: Clarendon, 1971. Pp. 179-322.

General and subject listings, plus bibliography of individual author bibliographies. Although curiously bound with a Shakespearian bibliography, the supplement is a general bibliography of bibliographies.

G1502 Mellown, Elgin W., comp. A DESCRIPTIVE CATALOGUE OF THE BIBLIOGRAPHIES OF 20TH CENTURY BRITISH WRITERS. Troy, N.Y.: Whitston, 1972.

Lists book-length primary and secondary bibliographies, as well as major bibliographies and checklists which have appeared in periodicals or as appendixes to books.

1.6 BOOK REVIEW INDEXES

G1601 BOOK REVIEW DIGEST. New York: Wilson, 1905-- .

Brief reviews and indexes of reviews. Cumulated annually.

*G1602 BOOK REVIEW INDEX. Detroit: Gale, 1965-- .

Cumulated annually. Lists reviews of scholarly publications, alphabetically by author reviewed.

G1603 INDEX TO BOOK REVIEWS IN THE HUMANITIES. Detroit: Thomson, 1960-- .

Annual. Similar to index cited above.

G2. LITERARY HISTORY

2.1 GENERAL

G2101 Batho, E.C., and Bonamy Dobree. INTRODUCTION TO ENGLISH LITERATURE, VOL. 4: THE VICTORIANS AND AFTER (1830-1914). 1938. 3rd ed. London: Cresset, 1962.

General literary and historical background essay, plus a series of brief bibliographies. "Novels and Short Stories" (pp. 266-321).

G2102 Bergonzi, Bernard, ed. THE TWENTIETH CENTURY. London: Barrie and Jenkins, 1970.

Essays by several hands on major figures and modern movements. Includes G3011 and G3153.

G2103 Cazamian, Louis, and Raymond Las Vergnas. "Modern Times (1660-1963)." In A HISTORY OF ENGLISH LITERATURE. Ed. Emile H. Legouis, Cazamian, and Las Vergnas. 1924. Rev. ed. New York: Macmillan, 1964. Bibliographies by Donald Davie and Pierre Legouis.

A fine "history of ideas" survey.

*G2104 Chew, Samuel E., and Richard D. Altick. "The Nineteenth Century and After (1789-1939)." In A LITERARY HISTORY OF ENGLAND. Ed. Albert C. Baugh et al. 1948. 2nd ed. New York: Appleton, 1967. Pp. 1111-1605.

A broad historical survey of recent literature. Also separately published.

G2105 Collins, Arthur S. ENGLISH LITERATURE OF THE TWENTIETH CENTURY. 1951. 4th ed. London: University Tutorial Press, 1961.

Guide to "major writers and main tendencies of our century."

G2106 Cunliffe, J.W. ENGLISH LITERATURE IN THE TWENTIETH CENTURY. New York: Macmillan, 1934.

Brief critiques and bibliographies of major authors and groups.

G2107 Daiches, David. A CRITICAL HISTORY OF ENGLISH LITERATURE. 2 vols. 1960. 2nd ed. New York: Ronald, 1970.

Includes chapter on the twentieth-century novel (pp. 1152-78).

*G2108 _____. THE PRESENT AGE IN BRITISH LITERATURE. Bloomington: Indiana Univ. Press, 1958.

Historical and critical essays with extensive bibliographies.

G2109 Evans, B. Ifor. A SHORT HISTORY OF ENGLISH LITERATURE. 1940. Rev. ed. Baltimore: Penguin, 1968.

Brief historical overview of the modern period.

*G2110 Ford, Boris, ed. THE MODERN AGE. 1961. 3rd ed. Baltimore: Penguin, 1973.

Excellent, heterogeneous collection of essays on intellectual backgrounds, literary movements, and individual writers of the modern period (JC, EMF, JJ, DHL, LHM, EW). Includes G2301, G2323, G2325, G2327, G2332, G2339, G2340, G2370.

G2111 Fraser, G.S. THE MODERN WRITER AND HIS WORLD. 1953. Rev. ed. London: Deutsch, 1964.

Discusses the ideological backgrounds to "modernity" and surveys the genres of modern literature ("Fiction," pp. 73-187).

G2112 Gaunt, William. THE MARCH OF THE MODERNS. London: Cape, 1949.

Modernism in music, art, and literature.

G2113 Gillie, Christopher. MOVEMENTS IN ENGLISH LITERATURE, 1900-1940. Cambridge: At the Univ. Press, 1975.

Account of the main literary movements and figures of the period.

G2114 Harvey, Paul, comp. THE OXFORD COMPANION TO ENGLISH LITERATURE. 1932. 4th ed. Oxford: Clarendon Press, 1967.

A reader's encyclopedia.

G2115 Lehmann, John, ed. THE CRAFT OF LETTERS IN ENGLAND: A SYMPOSIUM. London: Crescent, 1956.

Thirteen essays on the state of various literary activities in England. Includes biography, novel, and other genres. Includes G2215 and G2310.

G2116 Moody, William Vaughan, Robert M. Lovett, and Fred B. Millett. A HISTORY OF ENGLISH LITERATURE. 1902. 8th ed. New York: Scribner's, 1964.

Competent historical survey.

G2117 Phelps, Robert, and Peter Deane, eds. THE LITERARY LIFE: A SCRAPBOOK ALMANAC OF THE ANGLO-AMERICAN LITERARY SCENE FROM 1900 TO 1950. New York: Farrar, Straus and Giroux, 1968.

An interesting year-by-year chronicle of major publications and literary events, spiced with anecdotes, quotations, and illustrations.

G2118 Robson, W.W. MODERN ENGLISH LITERATURE. London: Oxford Univ. Press, 1970.

A capable overview of modern British writing, focusing selectively on individual authors and groups.

G2119 Routh, Harold V. ENGLISH LITERATURE AND IDEAS IN THE TWENTIETH CENTURY. 1935. 3rd ed. London: Methuen, 1950.

Trends of modern humanism and continuities among modern writers.

*G2120 Sampson, George, and R.C. Churchill. THE CONCISE CAMBRIDGE HISTORY OF ENGLISH LITERATURE. 1941. 3rd ed. Cambridge: At the Univ. Press, 1970.

The best contemporary literary history.

G2121 Scott-James, Rolfe A. FIFTY YEARS OF ENGLISH LITERATURE, 1900-1950; WITH A POSTSCRIPT 1951-1955. London: Longmans, 1956.

Survey of modern English literary movements and figures.

*G2122 Tindall, William York. FORCES IN MODERN BRITISH LITERATURE, 1885-1956. New York: Knopf, 1956.

Excellent, thematically organized literary history.

G2123 Ward, Alfred C. TWENTIETH-CENTURY ENGLISH LITERATURE, 1900-1960. London: Methuen, 1964.

Brief literary history. "Novelists" (pp. 25-89) concentrates on the continuing realistic tradition.

G2124 _____, comp. LONGMAN COMPANION TO TWENTIETH CENTURY LITERATURE. 1970. 2nd ed. London: Longmans, 1975.

Encyclopedia of writers, their works, literary terms, and other aspects of literature. Useful brief biographies.

2.2 HISTORIES OF THE NOVEL

G2201 Allen, Walter. THE ENGLISH NOVEL: A SHORT CRITICAL HISTORY. New York: Dutton, 1954.

An excellent history by a professional novelist.

G2202 _____. THE MODERN NOVEL IN BRITAIN AND THE UNITED STATES. New York: Dutton, 1964. English title: TRADITION AND DREAM: A CRITICAL SURVEY OF BRITISH AND AMERICAN FICTION FROM THE 1920'S TO THE PRESENT DAY. Harmondsworth, Engl.: Penguin, 1965.

Contains more detailed considerations of recent writers than his earlier general history, above.

*G2203 Baker, Ernest A. THE HISTORY OF THE ENGLISH NOVEL. Vol. 10. YESTERDAY. New York: Barnes and Noble, 1939.

Primarily historical. Includes extended discussions of AB, JC, JG, and DHL. Also see G2212.

G2204 Church, Richard. GROWTH OF THE ENGLISH NOVEL. London: Methuen, 1961.

A broad survey.

G2205 Edgar, Pelham. THE ART OF THE NOVEL: FROM 1700 TO THE PRESENT TIME. New York: Macmillan, 1933.

Critical history.

G2206 Gerould, Gordon Hall. THE PATTERNS OF ENGLISH AND AMERICAN FICTION: A HISTORY. Boston: Heath, 1942.

Thematic historical survey.

G2207 Knight, Grant C. THE NOVEL IN ENGLISH. New York: Smith, 1931.

Includes sections on the novel c. 1914. Includes AB, JC, JG, HGW.

G2208 Leavis, Q.D. FICTION AND THE READING PUBLIC. London: Chatto and Windus, 1932.

Social and economic history of novel publishing.

G2209 Lovett, Robert M., and Helen S. Hughes. THE HISTORY OF THE NOVEL IN ENGLAND. Boston: Houghton Mifflin, 1932.

Popular history. Final chapters devoted to moderns. Includes AB, JC, EMF, JG, AH, JJ, DHL, DR, HGW, VW.

G2210 Neill, S. Diana. A SHORT HISTORY OF THE ENGLISH NOVEL. 1951. Rev. ed. New York: Collier, 1964.

Competent historical introduction.

*G2211 Stevenson, Lionel. THE ENGLISH NOVEL: A PANORAMA. Boston: Houghton Mifflin, 1960.

A useful and readable history of English fiction from Elizabethan times to the present. Good bibliography and "chronological summary."

*G2212 _____. THE HISTORY OF THE ENGLISH NOVEL. Vol. 11. YESTERDAY AND AFTER. New York: Barnes and Noble, 1967.

Continues and supplements Baker's history to the early 1960's. Should be read together with volume 10 (G2203) for a full picture of the twentieth-century English novel.

G2213 West, Paul. THE MODERN NOVEL. Vol. 1. ENGLAND AND FRANCE. 1963. Rev. ed. London: Hutchinson, 1965.

History, with penetrating critical commentary.

G2214 Weygant, Cornelius. A CENTURY OF THE ENGLISH NOVEL. New York: Century, 1925.

History of the novel from Scott to the 1920's, with some perceptive criticisms. Includes AB, JC, JG, HGW.

G2215 Wyndham, Francis. "Twenty-Five Years of the Novel." In THE CRAFT OF LETTERS IN ENGLAND. Ed. John Lehmann. Pp. 44-59. See G2115.

Competent brief survey, 1930-55.

2.3 IDEOLOGICAL BACKGROUNDS, PERIODS, SPECIAL THEMES, AND LITERARY GROUPS

G2301 Bantock, G.H. "The Social and Intellectual Background." In THE MODERN AGE. Ed. Boris Ford. Pp. 13-48. See G2110.

Introduction to the modern British cultural situation.

G2302 Barrett, William. TIME OF NEED: FORMS OF IMAGINATION IN THE TWENTIETH CENTURY. New York: Harper, 1972.

Distinguished analyses of the prevailing philosophic nihilism of modern writers.

*G2303 Becker, George J., ed. DOCUMENTS OF MODERN LITERARY REALISM. Princeton, N.J.: Princeton Univ. Press, 1963.

Anthology of manifestos and critical commentaries on realism and naturalism. Excellent historical introduction by Becker: "Modern Realism as a Literary Movement" (pp. 3-38).

G2304 Beebe, Maurice. "Introduction: What Modernism Was." JML, 3 (1974), 1065-84.

Essay definition.

G2305 Bell, Clive. OLD FRIENDS: PERSONAL RECOLLECTIONS. New York: Harcourt, 1957.

Personal reminiscences of the Bloomsbury Circle. Includes VW.

*G2306 Bell, Quentin. BLOOMSBURY. Pageant of History Series. New York: Basic Books, 1968.

Introductory study of the members and ideas of pre- and post-war Bloomsbury. Includes DHL, HGW, VW, among others.

G2307 Bentley, Eric, ed. THE IMPORTANCE OF "SCRUTINY": SELECTIONS FROM "SCRUTINY": A QUARTERLY REVIEW, 1932-1948. New York: Stewart, 1948.

Includes reprinted essays by the SCRUTINY critics (Leavis et al.), on "modern culture" and recent writers. Includes EMF, JJ, DHL, VW.

*G2308 Bergonzi, Bernard. HEROES' TWILIGHT: A STUDY OF THE LITERATURE OF THE GREAT WAR. New York: Coward-McCann, 1965.

Reflections of the impact of World War I in English and American poetry, autobiography, and fiction. Includes RA, EMF, DHL, WL, HGW, among others.

G2309 _____. THE TURN OF THE CENTURY: ESSAYS ON VICTORIAN AND MODERN ENGLISH LITERATURE. New York: Barnes and Noble, 1973.

Reprinted essays on modern themes and figures. Includes GKC, FMF, JG, AH, WL, HGW.

G2310 Bloomfield, Paul. "The Bloomsbury Tradition and English Literary Criticism." In THE CRAFT OF LETTERS IN ENGLAND. Ed. John Lehmann. Pp. 160-82. See G2115.

From Strachey and Woolf to Cyril Connolly.

G2311 Brander, Laurence. "The Long Weekend." ARIEL, 3 (1972), 74-82.

British fiction between the wars.

G2312 Brewster, Dorothy. EAST-WEST PASSAGE: A STUDY IN LITERARY RELATIONSHIPS. London: Allen and Unwin, 1954.

The influences and reception of Russian literature in England and America. Many moderns mentioned in passing. Includes ND, SM, HHM, VW.

G2313 Bridgwater, Patrick. NIETZSCHE IN ANGLOSAXONY: A STUDY OF NIETZSCHE'S IMPACT ON ENGLISH AND AMERICAN LITERATURE. Leicester, Engl.: Leicester Univ. Press, 1972.

Nietzsche's influence on several moderns, including DHL, JCP, HGW.

G2314 Campos, Christophe. "The Salon (Bloomsbury)." In THE VIEW OF FRANCE FROM ARNOLD TO BLOOMSBURY. New York: Oxford Univ. Press, 1965. Pp. 208-37.

Draws particularly from the views of Bell, Fry, and Strachey.

G2315 Chapple, J.A.V. DOCUMENTARY AND IMAGINATIVE LITERATURE, 1880-1920. New York: Barnes and Noble, 1970.

Thematically organized literary history. Includes AB, JC, EMF, JG, JJ, DHL, HGW.

G2316 Chiari, Joseph. THE AESTHETICS OF MODERNISM. London: Vision, 1970.

Philosophic discussion of realism, existentialism, and modern literary trends.

G2317 Colum, Mary. FROM THESE ROOTS: THE IDEAS THAT HAVE MADE MODERN LITERATURE. New York: Columbia Univ. Press, 1937.

A good layman's introduction to the philosophic backgrounds of modern world literature.

G2318 Coveney, Peter. THE IMAGE OF CHILDHOOD. THE INDIVIDUAL AND SOCIETY: A STUDY OF THE THEME IN ENGLISH LITERATURE. 1957. Rev. ed. Baltimore: Penguin, 1967.

Includes chapter on JJ, DHL, VW. Originally entitled: POOR MONKEY.

G2319 Davie, Donald, ed. RUSSIAN LITERATURE AND MODERN ENGLISH FICTION: A COLLECTION OF CRITICAL ESSAYS. Chicago: Univ. of Chicago Press, 1965.

Includes essays by FMF and DHL, and articles on JG and DHL.

G2320 Ellmann, Richard. "Two Faces of Edward." In his EDWARDIANS AND LATE VICTORIANS. Pp. 188-210. See below.

The transitional character of the Edwardian period.

*G2321 _____, ed. EDWARDIANS AND LATE VICTORIANS. New York: Columbia Univ. Press, 1960.

An important collection of seven essays on the <u>fin de siecle</u> and Edwardian period in literature.

*G2322 Ellmann, Richard, and Charles Feidelson, Jr., eds. In THE MODERN TRADITION: BACKGROUNDS OF MODERN LITERATURE. New York: Oxford Univ. Press, 1965.

An outstanding anthology of major statements on themes and topics central to the study of modern literature (e.g., symbolism, realism, the unconscious, and myth). Each section includes editorial introductions and commentaries. Selections are drawn chiefly from modern artists and from influential philosophers (from Vico to Tillich). An indispensible handbook for any student of modernism.

G2323 Enright, D.J. "The Literature of the First World War." In THE MODERN AGE. Ed. Boris Ford. Pp. 154-69. See G2110.

Brief general survey, concentrating on poetry.

G2324 Evans, B. Ifor. ENGLISH LITERATURE BETWEEN THE WARS. London: Methuen, 1948.

Survey of writers and movements of the twenties and thirties. Includes EMF, AH, JJ, DHL, VW.

G2325 Freyer, Grattan. "The Irish Contribution." In THE MODERN AGE. Ed. Boris Ford. Pp. 196-208. See G2110.

Introductory essay on modern Irish literary movements.

G2326 Friedman, Melvin J., and John B. Vickery, eds. THE SHAKEN REALIST: ESSAYS IN MODERN LITERATURE IN HONOR OF FREDERICK J. HOFFMAN. Baton Rouge: Louisiana State Univ. Press, 1970.

Festschrift devoted to figures (includes VW) and themes of modern literature. Some excellent contributions.

G2327 Furbank, P.N. "The Twentieth-Century Best-Seller." In THE MODERN AGE. Ed. Boris Ford. Pp. 429-41. See G2110.

Brief history of the best-seller in Britain.

*G2328 Fussell, Paul. THE GREAT WAR AND MODERN MEMORY. New York: Oxford Univ. Press, 1975.

Excellent study of the social and literary impact of World War I.

G2329 Gadd, David. THE LOVING FRIENDS: A PORTRAIT OF BLOOMSBURY. New York: Harcourt, 1974.

Biographical history of the personalities of the Bloomsbury group, with passing reference to their work. Includes VW.

G2330 Gill, Richard. HAPPY RURAL SEAT: THE ENGLISH COUNTRY HOUSE AND THE LITERARY IMAGINATION. New Haven, Conn.: Yale Univ. Press, 1972.

The English country house as a symbol of tradition, stability, and values in modern fiction. Includes EB, FMF, EMF, JG, HG, AH, DHL, EW, HGW, VW.

G2331 Glicksberg, Charles I. THE SELF IN MODERN LITERATURE. University Park: Pennsylvania State Univ. Press, 1963.

The origins and contemporary expressions of the theme of alienation from the self in modern literature.

G2332 Gomme, Andor. "Criticism and the Reading Public." In THE MODERN AGE. Ed. Boris Ford. Pp. 350-76. See G2110.

T.S. Eliot, F.R. Leavis, and modern critical trends.

G2333 Green, Martin. CHILDREN OF THE SUN: A NARRATIVE OF "DECADENCE" IN ENGLAND AFTER 1918. New York: Basic Books, 1975.

Literary history of the postwar decadent generation. Includes EW.

G2334 Gross, John. THE RISE AND FALL OF THE MAN OF LETTERS: A STUDY OF THE IDIOSYNCRATIC AND THE HUMANE IN MODERN LITERATURE. New York: Macmillan, 1969.

The decline of the critic-reviewer literary journalist, traced into the twentieth century.

G2335 Hampshire, Stuart N. MODERN WRITERS, AND OTHERS ESSAYS. New York: Knopf, 1970.

Includes EMF, JJ, VW.

G2336 Heilbrun, Carolyn G. "The Bloomsbury Group." In TOWARDS ANDROGYNY: ASPECTS OF MALE AND FEMALE IN LITERATURE. London: Gollancz, 1973. Pp. 115-67.

Sees Bloomsbury as the center of rebellion against the "establishment" values of its day, the first example of the androgynous life "in practice."

G2337 Hepburn, James G. THE AUTHOR'S EMPTY PURSE AND THE RISE OF THE LITERARY AGENT. London: Oxford Univ. Press, 1968.

History of the literary agent and the relationships among authors, agents, and publishers.

*G2338 Hoffman, Frederick J. FREUDIANISM AND THE LITERARY MIND. 1945. 2nd ed. Baton Rouge: Louisiana State Univ. Press, 1957.

The standard study of Freud's influence on literature. Includes JJ, DHL.

G2339 Hoggart, Richard. "Mass Communications in Britain." In THE MODERN AGE. Ed. Boris Ford. Pp. 442-57. See G2110.

Cultural impact of the modern mass media in Britain.

*G2340 Holloway, John. "The Literary Scene." In THE MODERN AGE. Ed. Boris Ford. Pp. 51-100. See G2110.

Excellent brief history of the movements in modern British literature.

G2341 Holroyd, Michael. LYTTON STRACHEY AND THE BLOOMSBURY GROUP. HIS WORK, THEIR INFLUENCE. Baltimore: Penguin, 1971.

Backgrounds and literary relationships of Bloomsbury (including EMF, VW), centering upon Strachey. A revision of Holroyd's earlier biography.

*G2342 Howarth, Herbert. THE IRISH WRITERS, 1880-1940: LITERATURE UNDER PARNELL'S STAR. London: Rockliff, 1958.

Cultural and political backgrounds to the Irish literary revival. Includes JJ.

*G2343 Howe, Irving. "Introduction: The Idea of the Modern." In THE IDEA OF THE MODERN. Ed. Howe. Pp. 11-40. See below.

Fine attempt to classify and characterize the "elusive and protean" literary movement of modernism.

*G2344 _____, ed. THE IDEA OF THE MODERN IN LITERATURE AND THE ARTS. New York: Horizon, 1967.

Excellent anthology of reprinted materials. Contains eleven critical essays on the nature of modernism and the avant-garde, two modernist "manifestos" (on futurism and revolutionary literature), seven essays on modern movements (e.g., symbolism, surrealism), and seven studies of figures (including Eliot and Yeats).

G2345 Hynes, Samuel. EDWARDIAN OCCASIONS: ESSAYS ON ENGLISH WRITING IN THE EARLY TWENTIETH CENTURY. London: Routledge, 1972.

Reprinted essays. Includes AB, JC, GKC, FMF, EMF, HGW, VW.

*G2346 _____. THE EDWARDIAN TURN OF MIND. Princeton, N.J.: Princeton Univ. Press, 1968.

Informative and entertaining social and literary history of the transitional Edwardian period, concentrating on the shifting views of "politics, science, the arts, and the relations between men and women." One of the rare "indispensable" books for students of modern British literature.

G2347 Jackson, Holbrook. THE EIGHTEEN NINETIES: A REVIEW OF ART AND IDEAS AT THE CLOSE OF THE NINETEENTH CENTURY. 1913. New York: Putnam's, 1966.

Still useful, early study of the movements and personalities of _fin de siecle_ "decadence." Valuable as immediate background to the modern period.

*G2348 Johnstone, J.K. THE BLOOMSBURY GROUP: A STUDY OF E.M. FORSTER, LYTTON STRACHEY, VIRGINIA WOOLF, AND THEIR CIRCLE. New York: Noonday, 1954.

The backgrounds, values, and works of the Bloomsbury circle.

G2349 Kaplan, Morton, and Robert Kloss. "Psychoanalysis and Literary Criticism." In THE UNSPOKEN MOTIVE: A GUIDE TO PSYCHOANALYTIC LITERARY CRITICISM. New York: Free Press, 1973. Pp. 3-43.

Defends and defines the Freudian analysis of "unconscious motive" in literary criticism. Includes JC.

*G2350 Kenner, Hugh. THE POUND ERA. Berkeley and Los Angeles: Univ. of California Press, 1971.

An impressively learned intellectual and cultural history, pivoting upon Pound, but dealing widely with the modernist movement.

G2351 Leavis, Frank R., ed. A SELECTION FROM "SCRUTINY." 2 vols. Cambridge: At the Univ. Press, 1968.

Reprinted essays and reviews with emphasis on modern literary movements and figures. Includes EMF, DHL, WL, DR, VW.

G2352 Lester, John A., Jr. JOURNEY THROUGH DESPAIR, 1880-1914: TRANSFORMATIONS IN BRITISH LITERARY CULTURE. Princeton, N.J.: Princeton Univ. Press, 1968.

The emotional, intellectual, and imaginative responses to the modern crisis of despair in literature, science, and the arts.

*G2353 Nicholson, Norman. MAN AND LITERATURE. London: Macmillan, 1943.

Attempt to define the "assumptions as to the nature and purpose of Man which underlie much of modern writing," from the Wellsian "liberal" man and the Lawrencean "natural" man, to the Christian "imperfect" man. Includes RA, AB, EB, EMF, JG, AH, JJ, DHL, TFP, HGW.

G2354 Nowell-Smith, Simon H., ed. EDWARDIAN ENGLAND, 1901-1914. London: Oxford Univ. Press, 1964.

Collects "15 essays on various aspects of Edwardian life."

G2355 O'Connor, William Van. "Toward a History of Bloomsbury." SWR, 40 (1955), 36-52.

On the various literary histories of Bloomsbury.

G2356 Ray, Paul C. THE SURREALIST MOVEMENT IN ENGLAND. Ithaca, N.Y.: Cornell Univ. Press, 1971.

On the nature of and the growth of interest in surrealism in England, culminating in the native English surrealist movement of the late thirties. Includes FMF, JJ, WL.

G2357 Rogers, Katherine M. "The Fear of Mom: The Twentieth Century." In THE TROUBLESOME HELPMATE: A HISTORY OF MISOGYNY IN LITERATURE. Seattle: Univ. of Washington Press, 1966. Pp. 226-64.

The post-Freudian "debunking of romantic idealization of women." Principally concerned with American writers, and DHL.

*G2358 Rosenbaum, Stanford P., ed. THE BLOOMSBURY GROUP: A COLLECTION OF MEMOIRS, COMMENTARY, AND CRITICISM. Toronto: Univ. of Toronto Press, 1975.

Useful collection of comments on and memoirs of the Bloomsbury group and its individual figures from within (45 items), criticisms of Bloomsbury from without (13 essays), and documentation of various Bloomsbury controversies (involving DHL and WL among others). Editorial introductions are provided for each section. Also includes EMF and VW.

G2359 ______, ed. ENGLISH LITERATURE AND BRITISH PHILOSOPHY: A COLLECTION OF ESSAYS. Chicago: Univ. of Chicago Press, 1971.

Contains several pertinent essays. Includes DHL, VW.

G2360 Slochower, Harry. NO VOICE IS WHOLLY LOST...: WRITERS AND THINKERS IN WAR AND PEACE. New York: Creative Age Press, 1945.

A rather confused Marxist sociological-political-literary study of the chaos of disbelief and displacement in the post-World War I culture. Includes AH, JJ, DHL.

G2361 Smith, Warren S. THE LONDON HERETICS, 1870-1914. New York: Dodd, Mead, 1968.

Fine survey of the various religious and secular movements, from Roman Catholicism to theosophy, and representative figures in those movements who responded to the crisis of faith in late Victorian and Edwardian England.

G2362 Starkie, Enid. FROM GAUTIER TO ELIOT: THE INFLUENCE OF FRANCE ON ENGLISH LITERATURE, 1851-1939. London: Hutchinson, 1960.

Cross-cultural literary history. Includes RA, JJ, VW, among others.

G2363 Swinnerton, Frank. "Bloomsbury: Bertrand Russell, Roger Fry and Clive Bell, Lytton Strachey, Virginia Woolf." In his THE GEORGIAN LITERARY SCENE. Pp. 265-94. See below.

Surveys the Bloomsbury reputation and the achievements of its members.

G2364 ______. THE GEORGIAN LITERARY SCENE, 1910-1935. 1934. 2nd ed. London: Hutchinson, 1969.

A literary history which touches on virtually every figure of importance during the period.

G2365 Symons, Arthur. THE SYMBOLIST MOVEMENT IN LITERATURE. 1899. Rev. ed. New York: Dutton, 1919.

Classic study of French symboliste writers which deeply influenced the symbolic experiments of modern British authors.

G2366 Symons, Julian. THE THIRTIES: A DREAM REVOLVED. London: Cresset, 1960.

Surveys the political and social context of the literature of the thirties. Most illustrations are drawn from the poetry of the period.

G2367 Taylor, Estella R. THE MODERN IRISH WRITERS. Lawrence: Univ. of Kansas Press, 1954.

Introduction to the Irish mind, character, and literature. Includes JJ.

G2368 Temple, Ruth Z. "Truth in Labelling: Pre-Raphaelitism, Aestheticism, Decadence, Fin-de-Siecle." ELT, 17 (1974), 201-22.

The "general misuse and misapprehension" of labels in literary history.

G2369 Thale, Jerome. "The Making of the Edwardian Age." MOSAIC, 7, No. 2 (1974), 25-43.

The "myth" of the Edwardian Age.

G2370 Tomlin, E.W.F. "The Prose of Thought." In THE MODERN AGE. Ed. Boris Ford. Pp. 231-44. See G2110.

Brief introduction to the major works of nonfiction prose in modern Britain.

G2371 Vickery, John B. THE LITERARY IMPACT OF THE GOLDEN BOUGH. Princeton, N.J.: Princeton Univ. Press, 1973.

Traces the "intellectual, thematic and formal" impact of Frazer's anthropological studies on the myths and myth-making propensities of modern writers. Includes JJ, DHL.

G2372 Walsh, William. THE USE OF THE IMAGINATION: EDUCATIONAL THOUGHT AND THE LITERARY MIND. London: Chatto and Windus, 1959.

Surveys literary expression of ideas on and attitudes toward education.

G2373 Ward, Alfred C. THE NINETEEN-TWENTIES: LITERATURE AND IDEAS IN THE POST-WAR DECADE. London: Methuen, 1930.

A "review of literature in the nineteen-twenties and a free fantasia on contemporary themes." Includes interesting commentary on thrillers, detective fiction, and humorous writing of the period. Includes AB, JG, AH, DHL, RM, DR, HGW, VW.

G2374 Wees, William C. VORTICISM AND THE ENGLISH AVANT-GARDE, 1910-1915. Toronto: Univ. of Toronto Press, 1972.

Important survey of English avant-garde literary movements, focusing on the vorticist movement. Includes FMF, WL.

G2375 Wilson, Edmund. CLASSICS AND COMMERCIALS: A LITERARY CHRONICLE OF THE FORTIES. New York: Farrar, Straus and Giroux, 1950.

Collected reviews and essays. Includes MB, RF, AH, JJ, EW.

G2376 _____. THE SHORES OF LIGHT: A LITERARY CHRONICLE OF THE TWENTIES AND THIRTIES. New York: Farrar, Straus and Giroux, 1952.

Collected reviews and essays. Includes ND, RF, DHL, VW.

G2377 Wimsatt, William K., Jr., and Cleanth Brooks. LITERARY CRITICISM: A SHORT HISTORY. New York: Vintage, 1957.

An excellent, standard history.

G3. CRITICAL STUDIES OF MODERN ENGLISH FICTION

This section includes articles, essay collections, and book-length studies wholly or in part concerned with the themes, techniques, and backgrounds of modern British fiction. Many of the titles, as noted, contain sections on individual novelists and their work(s) which are annotated in the individual author section of this guide. For additional related titles, also see G2.3 above ("Ideological Backgrounds, Periods, Special Themes, and Literary Groups"), and the subsequent subdivisions of this General Section.

G3001 Aldridge, John W., ed. CRITIQUES AND ESSAYS ON MODERN FICTION: 1920-1951. New York: Ronald, 1952.

> Twenty-nine reprinted essays on fictional techniques and individual writers. Includes JC, EMF, AH, JJ, DHL, VW. Includes G1415.

G3002 Allen, Walter. READING A NOVEL. 1949. Rev. ed. New York: Hilary House, 1963.

> Introduction to the genre and discussion of several recent works.

G3003 Atkins, John. SIX NOVELISTS LOOK AT SOCIETY. London: Calder, 1977.

> The reflection of "certain social attitudes, preoccupations and realities" in six representative recent novelists. Includes EB, LPH, RL.

G3004 Beach, Joseph Warren. THE TWENTIETH-CENTURY NOVEL: STUDIES IN TECHNIQUE. New York: Appleton, 1932.

> Developments toward and away from the "well-made novel." Includes AB, JC, JG, AH, JJ, DHL, DR, VW.

*G3005 Beebe, Maurice. IVORY TOWERS AND SACRED FOUNTS: THE ARTIST AS HERO IN FICTION FROM GOETHE TO JOYCE. New York: New York Univ. Press, 1964.

Excellent study of the hieratic and demotic traditions in fiction. Includes JC, AH, JJ, DHL.

G3006 Beja, Maurice. EPIPHANY IN THE MODERN NOVEL. Seattle: Univ. of Washington Press, 1971.

The symbolic moment. Includes JJ, VW.

G3007 Bellamy, William. THE NOVELS OF WELLS, BENNETT, AND GALSWORTHY: 1890-1910. New York: Barnes and Noble, 1971.

Of general interest to the student of the realist tradition into the twentieth century.

G3008 Benedikz, B.S., ed. ON THE NOVEL: A PRESENT FOR WALTER ALLEN ON HIS 60TH BIRTHDAY FROM HIS FRIENDS AND COLLEAGUES. London: Dent, 1971.

Essays on JJ and VW, among others.

G3009 Bentley, Phyllis. THE ENGLISH REGIONAL NOVEL. London: Allen and Unwin, 1941.

Pamphlet-definition of the sub-genre of the regional novel, with wide reference to English regionalists. Includes AB.

G3010 Bergonzi, Bernard. THE SITUATION OF THE NOVEL. Pittsburgh: Univ. of Pittsburgh Press, 1970.

Assessment of the state of modern British fiction, emphasizing the cultural backgrounds and social contexts of the works discussed.

G3011 Bradbury, Malcolm. "The Novel in the 1920's." In THE TWENTIETH CENTURY. Ed. Bernard Bergonzi. Pp. 180-221. See G2102.

History and criticism.

G3012 ______. POSSIBILITIES: ESSAYS ON THE STATE OF THE NOVEL. New York: Oxford Univ. Press, 1973.

Critical and theoretical study of realism and "modernism" in the novel, from Fielding to Fowles. Includes FMF, EMF, AH, WL, EW, VW, and others.

G3013 ______. THE SOCIAL CONTEXT OF MODERN ENGLISH LITERATURE. New York: Schocken, 1971.

The social, economic, and cultural milieu of the modern arts.

G3014 Brewster, Dorothy, and Angus Burrell. MODERN FICTION. New York: Columbia Univ. Press, 1934.

Critical essays on several major novelists, and modern literary movements. Includes AB, JC, AH, JJ, DHL, KM, SM, VW.

*G3015 Brown, Edward K. RHYTHM IN THE NOVEL. Toronto: Univ. of Toronto Press, 1950.

Explores the Forsterian idea of "rhythmic" form. Includes AB, EMF, VW.

G3016 Brumm, Ursula. "Symbolism and the Novel." PR, 25 (1958), 329-42.

G3017 Buckley, Jerome H. "Autobiography in the English Bildungsroman." In THE INTERPRETATION OF NARRATIVE. Ed. Morton W. Bloomfield. Pp. 93-104. See G4011.

G3018 Bullett, Gerald. MODERN ENGLISH FICTION. London: Jenkins, 1926.

Critical appreciations and surveys of selected novelists. Includes AB, JC, EMF, JG, HGW.

G3019 Burgess, Anthony. THE NOVEL NOW: A GUIDE TO CONTEMPORARY FICTION. London: Faber, 1967.

Thematic essays grouping over 200 American, English, and foreign novelists. Brief, inaccurate bibliographies.

G3020 Burgum, Edwin B. THE NOVEL AND THE WORLD'S DILEMMA. New York: Oxford Univ. Press, 1947.

The impact of social forces on modern European, British, and American writers. Includes JG, AH, JJ, VW.

G3021 Charques, R.D. CONTEMPORARY LITERATURE AND SOCIAL REVOLUTION. London: Secker, 1933.

Modern literature in the light of postwar political and social changes (Marxist).

G3022 Chattopadhyaya, Sisir [also Sisir Chatterjee]. THE TECHNIQUE OF THE MODERN ENGLISH NOVEL. Calcutta: Mukhopadhyay, 1959.

General essays on the Jamesian tradition in modern fiction. Includes JC, JJ, VW.

G3023 Chevalley, Abel. THE MODERN ENGLISH NOVEL. Trans. B.R. Redman. New York: Knopf, 1927.

Brief critical surveys. Includes AB, JC, JG, DHL, HGW.

G3024 Church, Margaret. TIME AND REALITY: STUDIES IN CONTEMPORARY FICTION. Chapel Hill: Univ. of North Carolina Press, 1963.

The influence of durational concepts of time (via Bergson and Proust) on several modern writers. Includes AH, JJ, VW.

G3025 Connolly, Cyril. ENEMIES OF PROMISE. 1938. Rev. ed. New York: Macmillan, 1948.

An "enquiry into the nature of contemporary prose style" (c. 1900-1938) and an exercise in autobiography.

G3026 Cook, Albert S. THE MEANING OF FICTION. Detroit: Wayne State Univ. Press, 1960.

The "content" of novels rather than their form, from Cervantes to the present. Includes JC, JJ, DHL.

G3027 Cooper, Frederic Taber. SOME ENGLISH STORY TELLERS: A BOOK OF THE YOUNGER NOVELISTS. New York: Holt, 1912.

Frequently perceptive early assessments. Includes AB, JC, JG.

G3028 Cox, C.B. THE FREE SPIRIT: A STUDY OF LIBERAL HUMANISM IN THE NOVELS OF GEORGE ELIOT, E.M. FORSTER, VIRGINIA WOOLF, ANGUS WILSON. London: Oxford Univ. Press, 1963.

Philosophic implications in fiction.

G3029 Cross, Wilbur J. FOUR CONTEMPORARY NOVELISTS. New York: Macmillan, 1930.

Supplements his DEVELOPMENT OF THE ENGLISH NOVEL, 1899. Includes AB, JC, JG, HGW.

*G3030 Daiches, David. THE NOVEL AND THE MODERN WORLD. 1939. Rev. ed. Chicago: Univ. of Chicago Press, 1960.

The impact of modern civilization on the twentieth-century novel. Includes JJ, DHL, VW. Original edition (1939) had chapters on JG, AH, KM.

G3031 Davis, Edward. READINGS IN MODERN FICTION. Cape Town: Simondium, 1964.

Essays concentrating on the love themes in modern novels. Includes JC, JJ, DHL, VW.

G3032 Davis, Robert M. "Introduction: The Imagination of Defeat." In MODERN BRITISH SHORT NOVELS. Ed. R.M. Davis. Pp. 1-8. Glenview, Ill.: Scott, Foresman, 1972.

Valuable defense of the traditionalism of recent British fiction.

G3033 _____. "The Shrinking Garden and New Exits: The Comic-Satiric Novel in the Twentieth Century." KanQ, 1, No. 3 (1969), 5-16.

G3034 Dobree, Bonamy. MODERN PROSE STYLE. 1935. 2nd ed. Oxford: Clarendon Press, 1964.

General consideration, with analyses of the varieties of traditional and innovative prose styles.

G3035 Drew, Elizabeth A. THE MODERN NOVEL: SOME ASPECTS OF CONTEMPORARY FICTION. New York: Harcourt, 1926.

General essays on types of modern fiction, plus chapters on individual novelists. Includes AB, JC, JG, HGW.

G3036 _____. THE NOVEL: A MODERN GUIDE TO FIFTEEN ENGLISH MASTERPIECES. New York: Dell, 1963.

Gathering of essays which includes studies of JC, JJ, DHL, and VW.

G3037 Dyson, A.E. THE CRAZY FABRIC: ESSAYS IN IRONY. London: Macmillan, 1965.

On the ironic, from Swift to the present day. Includes AH, GO, EW.

G3038 Eaglestone, Arthur A. [Roger Dataller]. THE PLAIN MAN AND THE NOVEL. London: Nelson, 1940.

A survey of the forms of popular fiction (e.g., detective novel, historical novel, rural novel).

G3039 Eagleton, Terry. EXILES AND EMIGRES: STUDIES IN MODERN LITERATURE. New York: Schocken, 1970.

The literature of alienation, and the alienated writers of modern England. Includes JC, EMF, JJ, DHL, GO, EW, VW.

G3040 Ellis, Geoffrey U. TWILIGHT ON PARNASSUS: A SURVEY OF POST-WAR FICTION AND PRE-WAR CRITICISM. London: Michael Joseph, 1939.

Impact of English Victorian criticism of fiction and continental literary movements on the development of the modern British novel. Includes AH, JJ, DHL, EW, HGW, VW.

G3041 Fiedler, Leslie. "No! In Thunder." In NO! IN THUNDER: ESSAYS ON MYTH AND LITERATURE. Boston: Beacon Press, 1960. Pp. 1-18.

G3042 Fleishman, Avrom. THE ENGLISH HISTORICAL NOVEL: WALTER SCOTT TO VIRGINIA WOOLF. Baltimore: Johns Hopkins Univ. Press, 1971.

Critical study. Includes JC, VW.

G3043 Follett, Helen Thomas, and Wilson Follett. SOME MODERN NOVELISTS: APPRECIATIONS AND ESTIMATES. New York: Holt, 1918.

Generally appreciative, rather than critical. Includes AB, JG, HGW.

G3044 Freund, Philip. THE ART OF READING THE NOVEL. 1947. Rev. ed. New York: Macmillan, 1965.

"A Search for Amateur Criticism" which succeeds. Originally published in 1947 as HOW TO BECOME A LITERARY CRITIC.

*G3045 Friedman, Alan W. THE TURN OF THE NOVEL. New York: Oxford Univ. Press, 1966.

The movement toward open fictional structures. Includes JC, EMF, JJ, DHL.

G3046 _____, ed. FORMS OF MODERN BRITISH FICTION. Austin: Univ. of Texas Press, 1975.

Seven critical and historical essays on the evolution of the modern British novel. Includes EB, JC, JG, HG, JJ, DHL, VW, among others.

*G3047 Frierson, William C. THE ENGLISH NOVEL IN TRANSITION, 1885-1940. Norman: Univ. of Oklahoma Press, 1942.

Excellent study of the evolving modern novel, with emphasis on philosophic and social backgrounds. Includes most modern novelists of significance.

G3048 Garrett, Peter K. SCENE AND SYMBOL FROM GEORGE ELIOT TO JAMES JOYCE: STUDIES IN CHANGING FICTIONAL MODE. New Haven, Conn.: Yale Univ. Press, 1969.

Study which concentrates on the varying symbolic uses of realistic fictional detail. Includes JC, JJ, DHL.

G3049 Gindin, James. HARVEST OF A QUIET EYE: THE NOVEL OF COMPASSION. Bloomington: Indiana Univ. Press, 1971.

Definition and examination of the tradition of compassion, or humanistic skepticism in fiction, which touches on AB, EMF, JJ, DHL, and VW.

G3050 Glicksberg, Charles I. MODERN LITERARY PERSPECTIVISM. Dallas: Southern Methodist Univ. Press, 1970.

Thematic study of the varieties of internal and external (e.g., mythic, utopian, Marxist) perspectives in recent literature. Includes AH, DHL, HGW.

G3051 _____. THE SEXUAL REVOLUTION IN MODERN ENGLISH LITERATURE. The Hague: Martinus Nijhoff, 1973.

Traces the reaction against the "Victorian ethos" and the emergence of a "New Sex Morality" in modern writers, from Hardy to the present. Includes AH, JJ, DHL, SM, HGW.

G3052 Goldberg, Gerald Jay. "The Artist-Novel in Transition." EFT [now ELT], 4, No. 4 (1961), 12-27.

G3053 Goldknopf, David. "Realism in the Novel." In THE LIFE OF THE NOVEL. Chicago: Univ. of Chicago Press, 1972. Pp. 177-98.

On the mystical, psychological realism of modern writers. Includes JJ and DHL.

G3054 Goodheart, Eugene. THE CULT OF THE EGO: THE SELF IN MODERN LITERATURE. Chicago: Univ. of Chicago Press, 1968.

Images of the self in literature from Rousseau to Joyce.

G3055 Gordon, Caroline. HOW TO READ A NOVEL. New York: Viking, 1957.

General approach, from a professional novelist's perspective, to the critical problems of reading fiction.

G3056 Gorsky, Susan. "The Gentle Doubters: Images of Women in English Women's Novels, 1840-1920." In IMAGES OF WOMEN IN FICTION: FEMINIST PERSPECTIVES. Ed. Susan K. Cornillon. Bowling Green, Ohio: Bowling Green Univ. Popular Press, 1972. Pp. 28-54.

G3057 Gould, Gerald. THE ENGLISH NOVEL OF TODAY. London: Castle, 1924.

Thematic study of the varieties of modern fiction. Several lesser writers discussed.

G3058 Grabo, Carl. THE TECHNIQUE OF THE NOVEL. New York: Scribner's, 1928.

Introductory survey of plot, point of view, conduct of narrative, and "actualism" (i.e., realism and naturalism) in fiction. Includes JC, JJ, DHL, DR, VW.

G3059 Gregor, Ian, and Brian Nicholas. THE MORAL AND THE STORY. London: Faber, 1962.

Morality and fiction. Includes DHL.

G3060 Gregory, Horace. SPIRIT OF TIME AND PLACE: COLLECTED ESSAYS. New York: Norton, 1973.

Includes essays on JJ, DHL, WL, HGW, VW.

G3061 Hall, James. THE TRAGIC COMEDIANS: SEVEN MODERN BRITISH NOVELISTS. Bloomington: Indiana Univ. Press, 1963.

Modern tragicomedy. Includes EMF, HG, LPH, AH, EW.

G3062 Hardy, Barbara. THE APPROPRIATE FORM: AN ESSAY ON THE NOVEL. London: Univ. of London Press, 1964.

Fictional structure and its relation to the novelist's "moral or metaphysical views." Includes EMF, DHL.

*G3063 Hardy, John Edward. MAN IN THE MODERN NOVEL. Seattle: Univ. of Washington Press, 1964.

Quests for identity in modern novels. Includes JC, EMF, JJ, DHL, EW, VW.

G3064 Harper, Howard M., and Charles Edge, eds. THE CLASSIC BRITISH NOVEL. Athens: Univ. of Georgia Press, 1972.

Includes essays on JC, JJ, DHL, VW.

G3065 Harris, Wendell V. "Molly's 'Yes': The Transvaluation of Sex in Modern Fiction." TSLL, 10 (1968), 107-18.

Sex as an affirmation of life in AB, JG, AH, JJ, DHL, SM.

G3066 Hartley, L.P. THE NOVELIST'S RESPONSIBILITY. London: Hamilton, 1967.

An eclectic collection of essays, touching at points on the novelist's responsibility (commitment) as illustrated by a number of writers.

G3067 Henderson, Philip. THE NOVEL TODAY: STUDIES IN CONTEMPORARY ATTITUDES. London: Lane, 1936.

Staunchly Marxist division of modern fiction into two factions: the effete romantics (including EMF, JG, AH, JJ, DHL, HGW, VW), and the vigorous revolutionaries (few read today; see below).

G3068 ______. "The Proletarian Novel in Britain: Alec Brown, John Sommerfield, Lewis Grassic Gibbon." In his THE NOVEL TODAY, pp. 258-87. See above.

English revolutionary novelists favorably considered in the study above.

G3069 Hoare, Dorothy M. SOME STUDIES IN THE MODERN NOVEL. London: Chatto and Windus, 1938.

Lecture essays. Includes EMF, JJ, DHL, KM, VW.

G3070 Hoffman, Frederick J. THE MORTAL NO: DEATH AND THE MODERN IMAGINATION. Princeton, N.J.: Princeton Univ. Press, 1964.

Metaphors of death and rebirth in modern secular contexts. Includes JC, EMF, JJ, DHL, GO, HGW, VW.

G3071 Hough, Graham. IMAGE AND EXPERIENCE: STUDIES IN A LITERARY REVOLUTION. Lincoln: Univ. of Nebraska Press, 1960.

The modern revolution and its romantic and Victorian antecedents.

G3072 Hughes, D.J. "Character in Contemporary Fiction." MR, 3 (1962), 788-95.

G3073 James, Henry. "The New Novel, 1914." In NOTES ON NOVELISTS AND SOME OTHER NOTES. New York: Scribner's, 1914. Pp. 314-61.

Briefly comments on AB, JC, DHL, HGW, among others.

G3074 Jameson, Storm. THE GEORGIAN NOVEL AND MR. ROBINSON. London: Heinemann, 1929.

Lecture, justifying the technical experimentations of recent fiction to a hypothetical common reader, Mr. Robinson. Includes AB, AH, VW, among others.

G3075 ______. PARTHIAN WORDS: AN ANALYSIS OF THE NOVEL. London: Collins, 1970.

Discursive critical essays on various topics related to fiction (e.g. language, the new novel).

G3076 Johnson, Reginald Brimley. SOME CONTEMPORARY NOVELISTS (MEN). London: Parsons, 1922.

Includes EMF, DHL. General assessments.

G3077 ______. SOME CONTEMPORARY NOVELISTS (WOMEN). London: Parsons, 1920.

Includes RM, DR, VW. Similar to above.

G3078 Kantra, Robert A. "The Fiction of Orthodox and Apostate Satire." KanQ, 1, No. 3 (1969), 78-88.

G3079 Kaplan, Harold J. THE PASSIVE VOICE: AN APPROACH TO MODERN FICTION. Athens: Ohio Univ. Press, 1966.

Solipsism and moral passivity in the modern novel. Includes JC, JJ, DHL.

G3080 Kaplan, Sydney Janet. FEMININE CONSCIOUSNESS IN THE MODERN BRITISH NOVEL. Urbana: Univ. of Illinois Press, 1975.

Discusses RL, DR, VW.

G3081 Karl, Frederick R. A READER'S GUIDE TO THE CONTEMPORARY ENGLISH NOVEL. 1962. Rev. ed. New York: Noonday, 1972.

Brief essays on EB, IC, HG, GO, EW, among others.

G3082 Karl, Frederick R., and Marvin Magalaner. A READER'S GUIDE TO GREAT TWENTIETH-CENTURY ENGLISH NOVELS. New York: Noonday, 1959.

Biographies and criticisms of JC, EMF, AH, JJ, DHL, VW.

G3083 Kenner, Hugh. GNOMON: ESSAYS ON CONTEMPORARY LITERATURE. New York: McDowell, Obelensky, 1958.

Essays and reviews. Includes JC, FMF, WL.

G3084 Kermode, Frank. CONTINUITIES. New York: Random House, 1968.

Essays and reviews (1962-67) on modernism, modern themes, and individual writers. Includes DHL.

G3085 ______. "The English Novel, circa 1907." In TWENTIETH-CENTURY LITERATURE IN RETROSPECT. Ed. Reuben A. Brower. Cambridge, Mass.: Harvard Univ. Press, 1971. Pp. 45-64.

1907 a year of transition.

G3086 ______. PUZZLES AND EPIPHANIES, ESSAYS AND REVIEWS 1958-1961. New York: Chilmark, 1962.

Includes EMF, JJ, EW.

G3087 ______. THE ROMANTIC IMAGE. London: Routledge, 1957.

Continuities between romanticism and modernism (primarily poetry).

*G3088 Kettle, Arnold. AN INTRODUCTION TO THE ENGLISH NOVEL. Vol. 2. HENRY JAMES TO THE PRESENT. London: Hutchinson, 1951.

Criticism with a Marxist flavor. Includes AB, IC, JC, EMF, JG, HG, AH, JJ, DHL, HGW, VW.

G3089 Krieger, Murray. THE TRAGIC VISION: VARIATIONS ON A THEME IN LITERARY INTERPRETATION. Chicago: Univ. of Chicago Press, 1966.

The "unconscious" existentialism of several modern writers. Includes JC, DHL.

G3090 Leavis, Frank R. THE COMMON PURSUIT. New York: Stewart, 1952.

Reprinted essay-reviews. Includes EMF, DHL, WL.

*G3091 ______. THE GREAT TRADITION. London: Chatto and Windus, 1948.

Important and influential discussion of the moral and technical continuity among Austen, Eliot, James, and Conrad.

G3092 Levin, Harry. SYMBOLISM AND FICTION. Charlottesville: Univ. of Virginia Press, 1956.

A plea for moderation in symbol hunting and a sober definition of the role of symbols in fiction. A pamphlet.

G3093 Liddell, Robert. A TREATISE ON THE NOVEL. London: Cape, 1947.

General inquiry into the elements of the novel and the nature of the novelist.

G3094 Lindsay, Jack. AFTER THE THIRTIES: THE NOVEL IN BRITAIN AND ITS FUTURE. London: Lawrence and Wishart, 1956.

Survey of trends in the development of the contemporary English novel from 1930 and critique of the elements of recent fiction.

G3095 McCormick, John. CATASTROPHE AND IMAGINATION: AN INTERPRETATION OF THE RECENT ENGLISH AND AMERICAN NOVEL. London: Longmans, 1957.

The transformation in fictional matter and manner since 1914. Background essay and thematic surveys. Includes RA, EB, RF, FMF, LPH, AH, DHL, RL, WL, GO, EW, VW.

G3096 McCullough, Bruce. REPRESENTATIVE ENGLISH NOVELISTS: DEFOE TO CONRAD. New York: Harper, 1946.

Includes essays on AB, JC, and JG.

*G3097 Mack, Maynard, and Ian Gregor, eds. IMAGINED WORLDS: ESSAYS ON SOME ENGLISH NOVELS AND NOVELISTS IN HONOUR OF JOHN BUTT. London: Methuen, 1968.

Excellent collection of essays treating novels from Congreve to the *nouveau roman*. Includes JC, JJ, DHL, EW. Also includes G4074.

G3098 MacNeice, Louis. "The Contemporary World: Prose Narrative." In VARIETIES OF PARABLE. New York: Cambridge Univ. Press, 1963. Pp. 128-51.

Historical and critical study of the narrative form.

G3099 Marcus, Steven. "The Novel Again." PR, 29 (1962), 171-95.

On the current state of the novel.

G3100 Markovic, Vida E. THE CHANGING FACE: DISINTEGRATION OF PERSONALITY IN THE TWENTIETH-CENTURY BRITISH NOVEL, 1900-1950. Carbondale: Southern Illinois Univ. Press, 1970.

Character studies, from Conrad to Cary. Includes EB, JJ, DHL, RL, EW, VW.

G3101 Marsh, John L. "The Doughboy Novelists of Flanders Fields." GENRE, 3 (1970), 242-53.

G3102 Maurois, Andre. PROPHETS AND POETS. Trans. Hamish Miles. New York: Harper, 1935.

Appreciations and criticisms of modern English novelists. Includes GKC, JC, AH, DHL, KM, HGW.

G3103 Melchiori, Giorgio. THE TIGHTROPE WALKERS: STUDIES OF MANNERISM IN MODERN ENGLISH LITERATURE. London: Routledge, 1956.

Movement toward fictional forms of "greater stability." Includes HG, JJ, DHL, VW, among others.

G3104 Meyerhoff, Hans. TIME IN LITERATURE. Berkeley and Los Angeles: Univ. of California Press, 1955.

Varieties of time consciousness in literature.

G3105 Meyers, Jeffrey. PAINTING AND THE NOVEL. Manchester: Manchester Univ. Press, 1975.

Examines the use of paintings as "aesthetic models" for symbolism, character, and theme in selected novels, from Hawthorne to Mann. Includes EMF, DHL.

G3106 Miller, J. Hillis. POETS OF REALITY: SIX TWENTIETH-CENTURY WRITERS. Cambridge, Mass.: Harvard Univ. Press, 1965.

The antiromantic transcendence of nihilism in modern literature. Includes JC.

G3107 Mizener, Arthur. THE SENSE OF LIFE IN THE MODERN NOVEL. Boston: Houghton Mifflin, 1964.

Study of the modern novel of manners which touches on British, but concentrates on American fiction.

G3108 Monroe, Nellie Elizabeth. THE NOVEL AND SOCIETY: A CRITICAL STUDY OF THE MODERN NOVEL. Chapel Hill: Univ. of North Carolina Press, 1941.

Emphasis on women novelists. Includes VW.

G3109 Moynahan, Julian. "Pastoralism as Culture and Counter-Culture in English Fiction, 1800-1928 (from a View to a Death)." NOVEL, 6 (1972), 20-35.

G3110 Muir, Edwin. TRANSITION: ESSAYS ON CONTEMPORARY LITERATURE. New York: Viking, 1926.

Includes studies of AH, JJ, DHL, VW.

G3111 Muller, Herbert J. MODERN FICTION: A STUDY OF VALUES. New York: Funk and Wagnalls, 1937.

The vision of life and moral values of modern fiction.

G3112 Myers, Walter L. THE LATER REALISM: A STUDY OF CHARACTERIZATION IN THE BRITISH NOVEL. Chicago: Univ. of Chicago Press, 1927.

Experimentation with and refinement of realistic methods of characterization from the mid-nineteenth century into the modern period. Includes AB, JG, DR, HGW.

G3113 Newby, Percy H. THE NOVEL, 1945-1950. London: Longmans, 1951.

Brief critical assessment of the recent British novel. Includes EB, IC, HG, LPH, among others.

*G3114 O'Connor, William Van, ed. FORMS OF MODERN FICTION: ESSAYS COLLECTED IN HONOR OF JOSEPH WARREN BEACH. Minneapolis: Univ. of Minnesota Press, 1948.

Theoretical essays on fiction and six studies of individual authors. Includes EMF, AH, JJ, DHL, VW.

G3115 O'Donovan, Michael [Frank O'Connor]. THE MIRROR IN THE ROADWAY: A STUDY OF THE MODERN NOVEL. New York: Knopf, 1956.

The realistic tradition (reflection of life) in English and European fiction, from Austen to Joyce. Also includes DHL.

G3116 O'Faolain, Sean. THE VANISHING HERO: STUDIES IN NOVELISTS OF THE TWENTIES. London: Eyre and Spottiswoode, 1956.

Ambivalence and detachment in several "vanishing" novelists. Includes EB, AH, JJ, EW, VW.

G3117 Pascal, Roy. "The Autobiographical Novel and the Autobiography." EIC, 9 (1959), 134-50.

Discusses JJ, DHL.

G3118 Paterson, John. THE NOVEL AS FAITH: THE GOSPEL ACCORDING TO JAMES, HARDY, CONRAD, JOYCE, LAWRENCE AND VIRGINIA WOOLF. Boston: Gambit, 1973.

Critical introductions to and assessments of the moral dimensions of the novelists considered.

G3119 Pendry, E.D. THE NEW FEMINISM OF ENGLISH FICTION: A STUDY IN CONTEMPORARY WOMEN-NOVELISTS. Tokyo: Kenkyusha, 1956.

Argues the emergence of a distinct feminine "culture" (in Eliot's sense) in modern British fiction. Includes general chapters on the social context and characteristics of feminine fiction, plus studies of EB, IC, RL, and VW.

G3120 Phelps, Gilbert. THE RUSSIAN NOVEL IN ENGLISH FICTION. London: Hutchinson, 1956.

Influence chiefly of Turgenev and Tolstoy on selected modern English novelists. Includes AB, JC, JG, DHL, KM, VW.

*G3121 _____, ed. LIVING WRITERS: BEING CRITICAL STUDIES BROADCAST IN THE B.B.C. THIRD PROGRAMME. London: Sylvan Press, 1947.

Broadcast lectures by several critics on EB, IC, EMF, AH, WL, GO, TFP, EW.

G3122 Phelps, William L. THE ADVANCE OF THE ENGLISH NOVEL. New York: Dodd, Mead, 1916.

Critical survey of fiction in English, from Defoe to the twentieth century. Largely appreciations. Includes AB, JC, JG, HGW.

G3123 Pratt, Annis. "Women and Nature in Modern Fiction." ConL, 13 (1972), 476-90.

G3124 Prescott, Orville. IN MY OPINION: AN INQUIRY INTO THE CONTEMPORARY NOVEL. Indianapolis: Bobbs-Merrill, 1952.

Opinionated survey of the post-World War II generation of American and British novelists. Includes EB, IC, HG, LHM, GO, EW.

G3125 Pritchett, Victor S. THE LIVING NOVEL AND LATER APPRECIATIONS. New York: Random House, 1964.

Gathering of brief, appreciative essays on American, British, and European fiction. Includes JC, FMF, EMF, JG, DHL, HHM, HGW.

G3126 Raban, Jonathan. TECHNIQUE OF MODERN FICTION: ESSAYS IN PRACTICAL CRITICISM. Notre Dame, Ind.: Notre Dame Univ. Press, 1969.

Exercises in the critical analysis of selected passages from post-1945 fiction. Includes GO.

G3127 Raleigh, John Henry. TIME, PLACE, AND IDEA: ESSAYS ON THE NOVEL. Carbondale: Southern Illinois Univ. Press, 1968.

Heterogeneous collection of commentaries on American, German, and British novels of the nineteenth and twentieth centuries.

G3128 Reed, Henry. THE NOVEL SINCE 1939. London: Longmans, 1946.

Brief critical comments on selected contemporaries. Includes EB, IC, HG, LPH, AH, RL, SM, EW, VW.

G3129 Savage, Derek S. THE WITHERED BRANCH: SIX STUDIES IN THE MODERN NOVEL. London: Eyre and Spottiswoode, 1950.

General critical essays on EMF, AH, JJ, VW.

G3130 Scholes, Robert. ELEMENTS OF FICTION. New York: Oxford Univ. Press, 1968.

Quite useful, elementary consideration of the aspects of fiction, plus three stories (by deMaupassant, JJ, and Borges), with illustrative "commentaries."

*G3131 Schorer, Mark. THE WORLD WE IMAGINE: SELECTED ESSAYS. New York: Farrar, Straus and Giroux, 1968.

Important collection of Schorer's essays on novels and fictional theory. Includes G4081 and G4082.

*G3132 ______, ed. MODERN BRITISH FICTION. New York: Oxford Univ. Press, 1961.

Twenty-six outstanding essays on modern fiction (including two by DHL and VW) and on individual novelists (including JC, FMF, EMF, JJ, DHL, VW).

G3133 Seward, Barbara. "The Contemporary Symbol." In THE SYMBOLIC ROSE. New York: Columbia Univ. Press, 1960. Pp. 118-55.

Rose symbolism in several modern novels. Includes EMF, JJ, DHL, CW, VW.

G3134 Shapiro, Charles, ed. TWELVE ORIGINAL ESSAYS ON GREAT ENGLISH NOVELS. Detroit: Wayne State Univ. Press, 1960.

Includes JC, EMF, JJ, DHL.

G3135 Spender, Stephen. THE CREATIVE ELEMENT: A STUDY OF VISION, DESPAIR, AND ORTHODOXY AMONG SOME MODERN WRITERS. London: Hamilton, 1953.

Creative and orthodox reactions against the extreme individualist's despair in modern literature. Includes EMF, GO, EW, among others.

G3136 _____. THE DESTRUCTIVE ELEMENT: A STUDY OF MODERN WRITERS AND BELIEFS. London: Cape, 1935.

The moral and political rejection of degenerate modern society among recent writers ("the destructive element"), and their search within for belief. Includes DHL.

G3137 _____. "English Threnody, American Tragedy: Novelists of Poetry and of Saturation." In LOVE-HATE RELATIONS: ENGLISH AND AMERICAN SENSIBILITIES. New York: Random House, 1974. Pp. 205-22.

"Poetic" and realistic novelists in early twentieth-century England.

G3138 _____. THE STRUGGLE OF THE MODERN. Berkeley and Los Angeles: Univ. of California Press, 1963.

Discursive essays on the nature of modernism and modern movements in the arts.

G3139 _____. "Two Landscapes of the Novel." In THE MAKING OF A POEM. New York: Norton, 1962. Pp. 73-94.

Comparison of the modern realistic and symbolic trends in fiction. Several authors mentioned passim.

G3140 Stade, George, ed. SIX MODERN BRITISH NOVELISTS. New York: Columbia Univ. Press, 1974.

Collects the "Columbia Essays on Modern Writers" pamphlets on AB (John Wain), JC (Robert S. Ryf), FMF (Grover Smith), EMF (Harry T. Moore), EW (David Lodge) and VW (Carl Woodring).

G3141 Stanton, Robert. AN INTRODUCTION TO FICTION. New York: Holt, 1965.

Introduction to the reading and critical study of fiction.

G3142 Stewart, Douglas H. THE ARK OF GOD: STUDIES IN FIVE MODERN NOVELISTS. London: Carey Kingsgate Press, 1961.

Distinguished analyses of the varying responses to the modern negation of God. Includes AH, JJ, RM.

*G3143 Stewart, J.I.M. EIGHT MODERN WRITERS. Oxford: Clarendon Press, 1963.

Includes JC, JJ, DHL. Biographies, bibliographies, and general critical surveys.

G3144 Swinden, Patrick: UNOFFICIAL SELVES: CHARACTER IN THE NOVEL FROM DICKENS TO THE PRESENT DAY. London: Macmillan, 1973.

Varieties of realistic characterization. Includes AB, FMF, DHL.

G3145 Tillyard, E.M.W. THE EPIC STRAIN IN THE ENGLISH NOVEL. London: Chatto and Windus, 1963.

Epic elements in fiction. Includes AB, JC, JJ.

G3146 Tindall, William York. THE LITERARY SYMBOL. New York: Columbia Univ. Press, 1955.

Definition, history, and technical study of the role of symbolism in literature. Extensive application to modern fiction.

G3147 Troy, William. SELECTED ESSAYS. Ed. Stanley E. Hyman. New Brunswick, N.J.: Rutgers Univ. Press, 1967.

Includes JJ, DHL, VW.

G3148 Unterecker, John, ed. APPROACHES TO THE TWENTIETH CENTURY NOVEL. New York: Crowell, 1965.

Six critical essays. Includes JC, JJ, DHL.

*G3149 Van Ghent, Dorothy. THE ENGLISH NOVEL: FORM AND FUNCTION. New York: Rinehart, 1953.

Critical essays on several novels from Cervantes to Joyce, with an appendix on "Problems for Study and Discussion." Also includes JC, DHL.

G3150 Verschoyle, Derek, ed. THE ENGLISH NOVELISTS: A SURVEY OF THE NOVEL BY TWENTY CONTEMPORARY NOVELISTS. London: Chatto and Windus, 1936.

Essays by several professional novelists on English authors, from Chaucer to Joyce. Includes JC, EMF, AH, JJ, DHL, VW.

G3151 Wagenknecht, Edward. CAVALCADE OF THE ENGLISH NOVEL. New York: Holt, 1954.

Critical and historical survey. Important sections on AB, JC, JG, JJ, DHL, DR, HGW, and VW.

G3152 Wain, John. "The Conflict of Forms in Contemporary English Literature." In ESSAYS IN LITERATURE AND IDEAS. London: Macmillan, 1963.

G3153 Wall, Stephen. "Aspects of the Novel 1930-1960." In THE TWENTIETH CENTURY. Ed. Bernard Bergonzi. Pp. 222-76. See G2102.

History and criticism.

G3154 Webster, Harvey Curtis. AFTER THE TRAUMA: REPRESENTATIVE BRITISH NOVELISTS SINCE 1920. Lexington: Univ. Press of Kentucky, 1970.

Impact of the postwar disillusionment on a number of significant recent novelists. Includes IC, LPH, AH, EW.

*G3155 Williams, Raymond. CULTURE AND SOCIETY, 1780-1950. New York: Columbia Univ. Press, 1958.

The social, political, and economic impact on the development of England's sense of its own culture. Excellent studies of individual writers from Burke to Orwell. Also includes DHL.

G3156 _____. THE ENGLISH NOVEL FROM DICKENS TO LAWRENCE. London: Chatto and Windus, 1970.

Social change and the development of the modern English novel. Includes AB, JC, JG, JJ, DHL, HGW, VW.

G3157 _____. "Realism and the Contemporary Novel." PR, 26 (1959), 200-213.

G3158 Wilson, Angus. "Evil in the English Novel." KR, 29 (1967), 167-94.

Discusses IC, JC, and others.

G3159 Wilson, Colin. THE STRENGTH TO DREAM: LITERATURE AND THE IMAGINATION. Boston: Houghton Mifflin, 1962.

Existentialist study of the modern literary imagination, concerned principally with fiction. Includes AH, DHL, EW, HGW.

*G3160 Wilson, Edmund. AXEL'S CASTLE: A STUDY OF THE IMAGINATIVE LITERATURE OF 1870-1930. New York: Scribner's, 1931.

Symbolism in French and English literature. Includes JJ.

G3161 Winegarten, Renee. "The Phase of Aesthetic Nihilism." In WRITERS AND REVOLUTION: THE FATAL LURE OF ACTION. New York: New Viewpoints, 1974. Pp. 214-328.

On the continental, British, and American responses to the romantic idea and the act of revolution.

*G3162 Zabel, Morton Dauwen. CRAFT AND CHARACTER: TEXTS, METHODS, AND VOCATION IN MODERN FICTION. New York: Viking, 1957.

A collection of essays on the novelist's craft and the character of his fiction from Dickens to Hemingway. Includes JC, FMF, EMF.

G4. THEORY OF FICTION

The following section includes essays, collections, and book-length studies. While it is not intended as a comprehensive bibliography, the editor has attempted a fairly inclusive representation of philosophic considerations of fictional theory, primarily theoretical essays on the elements of fiction, and genre studies which have a theoretical slant. Several but not all of the works listed make direct reference to modern English fiction.

G4001 Allott, Miriam, ed. NOVELISTS ON THE NOVEL. New York: Columbia Univ. Press, 1959.

Useful collection of statements by novelists on their art.

G4002 Ames, Van Meter. AESTHETICS OF THE NOVEL. Chicago: Univ. of Chicago Press, 1928.

A philosophic inquiry into the novel genre.

G4003 ______. "The Novel: Between Art and Science." KR, 5 (1943), 34-48.

*G4004 Auerbach, Erich. MIMESIS: THE REPRESENTATION OF REALITY IN WESTERN LITERATURE. Trans. Willard R. Trask. Princeton, N.J.: Princeton Univ. Press, 1953.

Several of the later chapters deal with the development of realism in fiction.

G4005 Baker, Joseph. "Aesthetic Surface in the Novel." TROLLOPIAN [now NCF], 2 (1947), 91-106.

G4006 Barnes, Hazel E. "Modes of Aesthetic Consciousness in Fiction." BuR, 12 (1964), 82-93.

G4007 Becker, George J. "Realism: An Essay in Definition." MLQ, 10 (1949), 184-97.

Theory of Fiction

G4008 Bentley, Phyllis E. SOME OBSERVATIONS ON THE ART OF NARRATIVE. New York: Macmillan, 1947.

A concise pamphlet introduction to the basic characteristics of fiction.

G4009 Blackmur, R.P. "Between the Numen and the Moha: Notes Towards a Theory of Literature." In THE LION AND THE HONEYCOMB: ESSAYS IN SOLICITUDE AND CRITIQUE. New York: Harcourt, 1955. Pp. 289-309.

Emphasis on the novel.

G4010 Bland, D.S. "Endangering the Reader's Neck: Background Description in the Novel." CRITICISM, 3 (1961), 121-39.

G4011 Bloomfield, Morton W., ed. INTERPRETATION OF NARRATIVE: THEORY AND PRACTICE. Cambridge, Mass.: Harvard Univ. Press, 1970.

More "practical" than theoretical essays. Includes G3017.

*G4012 Booth, Wayne C. THE RHETORIC OF FICTION. Chicago: Univ. of Chicago Press, 1961.

Important study of narrative techniques.

*G4013 Bowen, Elizabeth. "Notes on Writing a Novel." 1945. In COLLECTED IMPRESSIONS. New York: Knopf, 1950. Pp. 249-63.

Excellent, concise statement of the professional novelist's view of the elements of fiction. First published in 1945.

G4014 Bowling, L.E. "What is the Stream of Consciousness Technique?" PMLA, 65 (1950), 333-45.

G4015 Bradbury, Malcolm. "Towards a Poetics of Fiction: 1) An Approach Through Structure." NOVEL, 1 (1967), 45-52.

*G4016 Calderwood, James, and Harold E. Toliver, eds. PERSPECTIVES ON FICTION. Oxford: Oxford Univ. Press, 1968.

Twenty-five theoretical essays on the elements of fiction. Good collection. Includes G4059.

G4017 Cohn, Dorrit. "Narrated Monologue: Definition of a Fictional Style." CL, 18 (1966), 97-112.

G4018 Crane, Ronald S. "The Concept of Plot and the Plot of TOM JONES." In his CRITICS AND CRITICISM, ANCIENT AND MODERN. Chicago: Univ. of Chicago Press, 1952. Pp. 616-47.

Classic consideration of plot in fiction.

G4019 Davis, Robert G. "The Sense of the Real in English Fiction." CL, 3 (1951), 200-217.

G4020 Davis, Robert M., ed. THE NOVEL: MODERN ESSAYS IN CRITICISM. Englewood Cliffs, N.J.: Prentice-Hall, 1969.

A collection of twenty theoretical essays on fiction, plus editorial comments.

G4021 Edel, Leon. THE MODERN PSYCHOLOGICAL NOVEL. 1955. Rev. ed. New York: Grosset and Dunlap, 1964.

Technique and forms of psychological fiction.

G4022 Elliott, George P. "A Defense of Fiction." HudR, (1963), 9-48.

G4023 Fasel, Ida. "Spatial Form and Spatial Time." WHR, 16 (1962), 223-34.

G4024 Ferrara, Fernando. "Theory and Model for the Structural Analysis of Fiction." NLH, 5 (1974), 245-68.

*G4025 Forster, E.M. ASPECTS OF THE NOVEL. New York: Harcourt, 1927.

Emphasis on plot and rhythm, rather than narrative technique.

*G4026 Frank, Joseph. "Spatial Form in Modern Literature." 1945. In THE WIDENING GYRE: CRISIS AND MASTERY IN MODERN LITERATURE. New Brunswick, N.J.: Rutgers Univ. Press, 1963. Pp. 3-62.

The concept of aesthetic form in modern poetry and fiction.

G4027 Freedman, Ralph. THE LYRICAL NOVEL: STUDIES IN HERMANN HESSE, ANDRE GIDE, AND VIRGINIA WOOLF. Princeton, N.J.: Princeton Univ. Press, 1963.

Good general definition of lyrical fiction.

G4028 Friedman, Melvin J. STREAM OF CONSCIOUSNESS: A STUDY IN LITERARY METHOD. New Haven, Conn.: Yale Univ. Press, 1955.

The philosophic, psychological and technical characteristics of the stream of consciousness method and its use by several authors.

*G4029 Friedman, Norman. FORM AND MEANING IN FICTION. Athens: Univ. of Georgia Press, 1975.

An intelligent introduction to the pluralistic criticism of fiction, i.e., the employment of several discrete approaches to the study of fiction "to solve different critical problems." Includes theoretical chapters and practical analyses (including JC, VW). Absorbs several previously published essays on plot, structure, point of view, the short story, and other aspects of fiction.

*G4030 Frye, Northrop. "Specific Continuous Forms (Prose Fiction)." In his ANATOMY OF CRITICISM: FOUR ESSAYS. Princeton, N.J.: Princeton Univ. Press, 1957. Pp. 303-14.

Theoretical definition of the genre.

G4031 Glicksberg, Charles I. "Fiction and Philosophy." ArQ, 13 (1957), 5-17.

G4032 ______. "The Numinous in Fiction." ArQ, 15 (1959), 305-13.

G4033 Gold, Herbert. "The Mystery of Personality in the Novel." PR, 24 (1957), 453-62.

G4034 ______. "Truth and Falsity in the Novel." HudR, 8 (1955), 410-22.

G4035 Grossvogel, David I. LIMITS OF THE NOVEL: EVOLUTIONS OF A FORM FROM CHAUCER TO ROBBE-GRILLET. Ithaca, N.Y.: Cornell Univ. Press, 1968.

Opaquely written theoretical inquiry into the emotional and intellectual responses to fiction ("appreciation" and "belief").

*G4036 Halperin, John, ed. THE THEORY OF THE NOVEL: NEW ESSAYS. New York: Oxford Univ. Press, 1974.

Excellent collection of eighteen theoretical essays, with emphasis on approaches to modern and contemporary fiction.

G4037 Handy, William J. "The Formalist Approach to the Criticism of Fiction." In MODERN FICTION: A FORMALIST APPROACH. Carbondale: Southern Illinois Univ. Press, 1971. Pp. 1-28.

Defends the search for "meaning through form" in fiction criticism (i.e., the use of the critical tools applicable to a lyric poem).

G4038 Harris, Wendell V. "Style and the Twentieth-Century Novel." WHR, 18 (1964), 127-40.

*G4039 Harvey, William J. CHARACTER AND THE NOVEL. Ithaca, N.Y.: Cornell Univ. Press, 1965.

A theoretical definition and defense of the realistic character in fiction.

G4040 Honig, Edwin. DARK CONCEIT: THE MAKING OF ALLEGORY. Evanston, Ill.: Northwestern Univ. Press, 1959.

The nature and significance of the allegorical mode in fiction (Melville-Kafka).

G4041 Humphrey, Robert. STREAM OF CONSCIOUSNESS IN THE MODERN NOVEL. Berkeley and Los Angeles: Univ. of California Press, 1954.

Theoretical definition and technique study.

*G4042 James, Henry. THE ART OF THE NOVEL: CRITICAL PREFACES. Ed. R.P. Blackmur. New York: Scribner's, 1934.

The prefaces constitute "a fairly exhaustive reference book on the technical aspects of the art of fiction" (Blackmur).

G4043 _____. THEORY OF FICTION: HENRY JAMES. Ed. James E. Miller, Jr. Lincoln: Univ. of Nebraska Press, 1972.

Reprints James's important essays and comments on novel theory. Miller supplies an important introduction, "A Theory of Fiction in Outline" (pp. 1-26).

G4044 Jessup, Bertram E. "On Fictional Expressions of Cognitive Meaning." JAAC, 23 (1965), 481-86.

G4045 Kermode, Frank. THE SENSE OF AN ENDING: STUDIES IN THE THEORY OF FICTION. New York: Oxford Univ. Press, 1967.

The impact of apocalyptic endings on the patterns and structures of the novelist.

G4046 _____. "The Structure of Fiction." MLN, 84 (1969), 891-915.

G4047 Kohler, Dayton. "Time in the Modern Novel." CE, 10 (1948-49), 15-24.

G4048 Kumar, Shiv K. BERGSON AND THE STREAM OF CONSCIOUSNESS NOVEL. New York: New York Univ. Press, 1963.

Bergsonian theories of time and consciousness related to modern fiction.

G4049 Langer, Susanne K. FEELING AND FORM: A THEORY OF ART. New York: Scribner's, 1953.

A general philosophic inquiry into the nature of art.

G4050 Leggett, H.W. THE IDEA IN FICTION. London: Allen and Unwin, 1934.

Introductory critical survey of the traditional characteristics of fiction (e.g., structure, narration).

G4051 Lesser, Simon O. FICTION AND THE UNCONSCIOUS. Boston: Beacon Press, 1957.

A psychoanalytic approach to the reading of, and response to, fiction.

G4052 Levin, Harry. THE GATES OF HORN: A STUDY OF FIVE FRENCH REALISTS. New York: Oxford Univ. Press, 1963.

Contains important statements on the nature of realism in fiction.

G4053 _____. "Toward a Sociology of the Novel." JHI, 26 (1965), 148-54.

*G4054 Lodge, David. LANGUAGE OF FICTION: ESSAYS IN CRITICISM AND VERBAL ANALYSIS OF THE ENGLISH NOVEL. New York: Columbia Univ. Press, 1966.

Theoretical statement on the role of language in the novel, plus several illustrative essays. Includes HGW.

G4055 _____. THE NOVELIST AT THE CROSSROADS, AND OTHER ESSAYS ON FICTION AND CRITICISM. Ithaca, N.Y.: Cornell Univ. Press, 1971.

A gathering of theoretical and critical essays on recent fictional trends (criticism, catholicism, modernism, and utopianism).

*G4056 Lubbock, Percy. THE CRAFT OF FICTION. London: Cape, 1921.

Still valuable Jamesian study of point of view.

G4057 Lukacs, Georg. THEORY OF THE NOVEL. Trans. A. Bostock. London: Merlin, 1971.

A philosophic and historical theory of the novel form (Marxist).

G4058 Lutwack, Leonard. "Mixed and Uniform Prose Styles in the Novel." JAAC, 18 (1960), 350-57.

G4059 MacDonald, Margaret. "The Language of Fiction." 1954. In PERSPECTIVES ON FICTION. Ed. James Calderwood and Harold E. Toliver. Pp. 55-70. See G4016.

G4060 Mann, Thomas. "The Art of the Novel." In THE CREATIVE VISION: MODERN EUROPEAN WRITERS ON THEIR ART. Ed. Haskell M. Block and Herman Salinger. Gloucester, Mass.: P. Smith, 1960. Pp. 84-96.

G4061 Martin, Harold C., ed. STYLE IN PROSE FICTION. New York: Columbia Univ. Press, 1959.

Theory of and exercises in stylistic analysis.

G4062 Mellard, James M. "Solipsism, Symbolism, and Demonism: The Lyrical Mode in Fiction." SHR, 7 (1973), 37-52.

*G4063 Mendilow, A.A. TIME AND THE NOVEL. New York: Humanities, 1952.

Standard statement of the theoretical and practical significance of time in fiction.

G4064 Miller, James E., Jr., ed. MYTH AND METHOD: MODERN THEORIES OF FICTION. Lincoln: Univ. of Nebraska Press, 1960.

A basic collection of nine important statements on the art of fiction.

G4065 Muir, Edwin. THE STRUCTURE OF THE NOVEL. London: Hogarth Press, 1928.

Surveys the principles of fictional structure, such as action, character, time, and space.

G4066 Nin, Anais. THE NOVEL OF THE FUTURE. New York: Macmillan, 1968.

Dream qualities in the novel.

G4067 Noon, Rev. William T. "Modern Literature and the Sense of Time." THOUGHT, 33 (1958), 571-603.

*G4068 Ortega y Gasset, Jose. MEDITATIONS ON QUIXOTE. Trans. Evelyn Rugg and Diego Marin. New York: Norton, 1961.

A philosophic and theoretical essay on fiction.

G4069 Overton, Grant. THE PHILOSOPHY OF FICTION. New York: Appleton, 1928.

Historical and technical study of plot, character, and realism in fiction. Includes AB, JC, EMF.

G4070 Page, Norman. SPEECH IN THE ENGLISH NOVEL. London: Longmans, 1973.

A linguistic analysis of speech and its impact on character and dialogue in fiction.

G4071 Pascal, Roy. "The Autobiographical Novel and the Autobiography." EIC, 9 (1959), 134-50.

G4072 ______. "Form and Novel." MLR, 57 (1962), 1-11.

G4073 Paul, David. "Time and the Novelist." PR, 21 (1954), 636-49.

G4074 Price, Martin. "The Other Self: Thoughts about Character in the Novel." In IMAGINED WORLDS. Ed. Maynard Mack and Ian Gregor. Pp. 279-99. See G3097.

G4075 Rahv, Philip. "Fiction and the Criticism of Fiction." In THE MYTH AND THE POWERHOUSE. New York: Farrar, Straus and Giroux, 1965. Pp. 33-60.

Attack on overly symbolic readings of fiction.

G4076 Roberts, Thomas J. WHEN IS SOMETHING FICTION? Carbondale: Southern Illinois Univ. Press, 1972.

Worthwhile essay in theoretical definition.

G4077 Romberg, Bertil. STUDIES IN THE NARRATIVE TECHNIQUE OF THE FIRST-PERSON NOVEL. Trans. M. Taylor and H. Borland. Stockholm: Almquist and Wiksell, 1962.

A comprehensive review of the first-person novel, in theory and in practice.

G4078 Said, Edward W. "Molestation and Authority in Narrative Fiction." In ASPECTS OF NARRATIVE: SELECTED PAPERS FROM THE ENGLISH INSTITUTE. Ed. J. Hillis Miller. New York: Columbia Univ. Press, 1971. Pp. 47-68.

*G4079 Scholes, Robert, ed. APPROACHES TO THE NOVEL: MATERIALS FOR A POETICS. 1961. Rev. ed. San Francisco: Chandler, 1966.

Outstanding collection of important theoretical essays on fictional modes, realism, and technique (with editorial commentaries).

*G4080 Scholes, Robert, and Robert Kellogg. THE NATURE OF NARRATIVE. London: Oxford Univ. Press, 1966.

A historical survey of the development of narrative forms and a theoretical definition of the elements of fiction.

*G4081 Schorer, Mark. "Fiction and the 'Matrix of Analogy.'" 1949. In his THE WORLD WE IMAGINE. Pp. 24-45. See G3131.

*G4082 ______. "Technique as Discovery." 1948. In his THE WORLD WE IMAGINE. Pp. 3-23. See G3131.

Both Schorer essays are widely available in a variety of critical anthologies.

G4083 Seltzer, Alvin J. CHAOS IN THE NOVEL/THE NOVEL IN CHAOS. New York: Schocken, 1974.

Studies the breakdown of form in recent fiction and theorizes on the relationship between chaotic vision and various fictional structures. Includes JC, VW.

G4084 Shroder, Maurice Z. "The Novel as a Genre." MR, 4 (1963), 291-308.

G4085 Souvage, Jacques. AN INTRODUCTION TO THE STUDY OF THE NOVEL. New York: Humanities, 1965.

A broad essay (pp. 3-100) on fictional theory, organized into thirty brief topics. For note on Souvage's bibliography (pp. 103-254), see G1414.

G4086 Spencer, Sharon. SPACE, TIME AND STRUCTURE IN THE MODERN NOVEL. Chicago: Swallow, 1971.

A provocative study of the various technical innovations of modern and experimental fiction.

G4087 Springer, Mary Doyle. FORMS OF THE MODERN NOVELLA. Chicago: Univ. of Chicago Press, 1975.

Theoretical and critical study of the novella form. Includes DHL.

G4088 Stanzel, Franz K. NARRATIVE SITUATIONS IN THE NOVEL. Trans. J.P. Pusack. Bloomington: Indiana Univ. Press, 1971.

On the relationship between narrative structure and content in the novel.

G4089 Stevick, Philip. "Fictional Chapters and Open Ends." JGE, 17 (1966), 261-72.

G4090 _____. "The Theory of Fictional Chapters." WHR, 20 (1966), 231-41.

*G4091 _____, ed. THE THEORY OF THE NOVEL. New York: Free Press, 1967.

An excellent anthology of more than fifty reprinted essays and commentaries on novel theory, arranged by topics such as genre, technique, perspective, plot, and style. Includes a useful section of comments by novelists. Fine bibliography (see G1416). Includes G4090.

G4092 Tate, Allen. "Techniques of Fiction." SR, 52 (1944), 210-25.

G4093 Theobald, D.W. "Philosophy and Fiction: The Novel as Eloquent Philosophy." BJA, 14 (1974), 17-25.

G4094 Tillyard, E.M.W. "The Novel as Literary Kind." E&S, 9 (1956), 73-86.

*G4095 Trilling, Lionel. THE LIBERAL IMAGINATION: ESSAYS ON LITERATURE AND SOCIETY. New York: Viking, 1950.

Several important theoretical essays included (e.g., "Freud and Literature," "Art and Neurosis," "Manners, Morals, and the Novel").

G4096 Turnell, Martin. "The Language of Fiction." In THE NOVEL IN FRANCE. New York: New Directions, 1951. Pp. 3-23.

An important concentration on language and style.

G4097 Vickery, John B., ed. MYTH AND LITERATURE: CONTEMPORARY THEORY AND PRACTICE. Lincoln: Univ. of Nebraska Press, 1966.

Many theoretical essays pertinent to modern fiction.

G4098 Walcutt, Charles Child. "From Scientific Theory to Aesthetic Fact: The 'Naturalistic' Novel." QUARTERLY REVIEW OF LITERATURE, 3 (1946), 167-79.

*G4099 Watt, Ian. THE RISE OF THE NOVEL. Berkeley and Los Angeles: Univ. of California Press, 1957.

Excellent theoretical definition of realism. Individual studies limited to eighteenth-century novelists.

G4100 Wellek, Rene, and Austin Warren. "The Nature and Modes of Narrative Fiction." In THEORY OF LITERATURE. 1948. 3rd ed. New York: Harcourt, 1956. Pp. 212-25.

Surveys the theoretical "ground-rules" for fiction.

G4101 White, John J. MYTHOLOGY IN THE MODERN NOVEL: A STUDY OF PREFIGURATIVE TECHNIQUES. Princeton, N.J.: Princeton Univ. Press, 1971.

Theoretical approach to the roles of myth and archetype in fiction.

G4102 Wilson, Colin. THE CRAFT OF THE NOVEL. London: Gollancz, 1975.

*G4103 Woolf, Virginia. "Mr. Bennett and Mrs. Brown." 1923. In her COLLECTED ESSAYS. London: Hogarth, 1966. I, 319-37.

Important modern reaction against Edwardian realistic fiction.

G5. STUDIES OF THE SHORT STORY

This brief listing includes only the most significant essays devoted exclusively to the short story. Most of the theoretical studies described above (G4) are equally concerned with the short form, and several of the studies of modern British fiction (G3) have sections on the short story. Much additional material may also be culled from the short fiction studies in the individual author bibliographies. Also see G1103, G1105, and G1418.

G5001 Bates, Herbert E. THE MODERN SHORT STORY: A CRITICAL SURVEY. New York: Nelson, 1943.

An appreciative commentary on the short story form, from Gogol and Poe to Lawrence.

G5002 Beachcroft, Thomas O. THE ENGLISH SHORT STORY (II). London: Longmans, 1964.

Brief critical survey of modern English short story.

*G5003 _____. THE MODEST ART: A SURVEY OF THE SHORT STORY IN ENGLISH. New York: Oxford Univ. Press, 1968.

An excellent study of the short-story genre, from its origins to recent times. Expands his earlier pamphlet essays.

G5004 Bowen, Elizabeth. "The Faber Book of Modern Short Stories." 1936. In COLLECTED IMPRESSIONS. New York: Knopf, 1950. Pp. 38-46.

Preface-introduction to the genre.

G5005 Current-Garcia, Eugene, and Walton R. Patrick, eds. WHAT IS THE SHORT STORY? 1961. Rev. ed. Glenview, Ill.: Scott, Foresman, 1974.

Anthology, containing a large prefatory collection (pp. 3-136) of major critical commentaries on the short story as a genre. Includes Poe, Hawthorne, James, Frank O'Connor.

Studies of the Short Story

G5006 Grabo, Carl. THE ART OF THE SHORT STORY. New York: Scribner's, 1913.

Extended study of the techniques of short fiction, intended primarily for the writer rather than the critic.

G5007 Hagopian, John V., and Martin Dolch, eds. INSIGHT II: ANALYSES OF MODERN BRITISH LITERATURE. Frankfurt, Germany: Hirschgraben, 1964.

Essays on short stories and novellas, with plot summaries and study questions. Includes EB, GKC, JC, EMF, JG, AH, JJ, DHL, KM, SM, HHM, GO, HGW, VW.

G5008 O'Donovan, Michael [Frank O'Connor]. THE LONELY VOICE: A STUDY OF THE SHORT STORY. Cleveland: World, 1963.

A fine critical and historical essay on the short story form.

G5009 O'Faolain, Sean. "On Keeping the Lines Clear." In THE SHORT STORY. New York: Devin-Adair, 1951. Pp. 3-32.

Anthology introduction to the genre.

G5010 Ward, Alfred C. ASPECTS OF THE MODERN SHORT STORY: ENGLISH AND AMERICAN. London: Univ. of London Press, 1924.

"Analytical survey of representative short stories by certain modern writers who have combined literary merit with a popular appeal." Includes JC, KM, HGW.

G5011 West, Ray B., and Robert W. Stallman, eds. THE ART OF MODERN FICTION. New York: Rinehart, 1949.

Anthology of modern short fiction and novellas, with appended analyses and study questions.

G6. STUDIES OF MAJOR TYPES: CRIME FICTION—POLITICAL FICTION—RELIGIOUS FICTION—SCIENCE FICTION, FANTASY, AND UTOPIAN FICTION

These four broad generic "types" have not been chosen arbitrarily for special consideration here. Rather, they represent four fields in which British novelists (1900-1950) have been particularly active and which have, in turn, received a considerable amount of critical attention as discrete forms of fiction. The four subsection checklists which follow are very selective, but provide a basic introduction to the major critical and historical studies of each type.

6.1 CRIME FICTION

G6101 Barzun, Jacques, and Wendell H. Taylor. A CATALOGUE OF CRIME. 1971. 2nd ed. New York: Harper, 1974.

Critical survey of crime and detective fiction (over 3,000 publications noted).

G6102 Haycraft, Howard. MURDER FOR PLEASURE: THE LIFE AND TIMES OF THE DETECTIVE STORY. New York: Appleton, 1941.

Fine critical history, from Poe to the 1930's.

*G6103 ______, ed. THE ART OF THE MYSTERY STORY: A COLLECTION OF CRITICAL ESSAYS. New York: Simon and Schuster, 1946.

Excellent large anthology of criticism.

G6104 Murch, Alma E. THE DEVELOPMENT OF THE DETECTIVE NOVEL. New York: Philosophical Library, 1958.

Most scholarly introduction to and history of the genre. Little literary analysis.

G6105 Symons, Julian. BLOODY MURDER: FROM THE DETECTIVE STORY TO THE CRIME NOVEL, A HISTORY. London: Faber, 1972. Published as MORTAL CONSEQUENCES. New York: Harper, 1972.

Popular history.

6.2 POLITICAL FICTION

G6201 Blotner, Joseph I. THE POLITICAL NOVEL. Garden City, N.Y.: Doubleday, 1955.

Written for students of political science. Surveys British, American, and foreign fiction, and tentatively suggests types of political novels. Includes JC, EMF, AH, GO, HGW passim.

G6202 Harrison, John. THE REACTIONARIES: YEATS, LEWIS, POUND, ELIOT, LAWRENCE: A STUDY OF THE ANTI-DEMOCRATIC INTELLIGENTSIA. New York: Schocken, 1967.

Traces the sympathetic views of fascism and authoritarianism among the intelligentsia, and the impact of their views on their work.

*G6203 Howe, Irving. POLITICS AND THE NOVEL. New York: Horizon Press, 1957.

Impact of political ideology on the European, English, and American novel. Includes JC, GO. Considers novels "political" in a broad sense of the term.

G6204 Howe, Susanne. NOVELS OF EMPIRE. New York: Columbia Univ. Press, 1949.

Survey of the imperialistic fiction of Britain, France, and Germany.

G6205 Killam, G.D. AFRICA IN ENGLISH FICTION, 1874-1939. Ibadan, Nigeria: Ibadan Univ. Press, 1968.

Traces African and imperial themes in British fiction, passim.

G6206 Meyers, Jeffrey. FICTION AND THE COLONIAL EXPERIENCE. Totowa, N.J.: Rowman and Littlefield, 1973.

JC and EMF, along with Kipling, Cary, and Greene, as colonial novelists.

*G6207 Panichas, George A., ed. THE POLITICS OF TWENTIETH-CENTURY NOVELISTS. New York: Hawthorne Books, 1971.

"The effect of politics on fiction and fiction on public affairs in the life and work of contemporary writers." Essays on several figures. Includes EMF, AH, DHL, WL, GO, HGW.

G6208 Raskin, Jonah. THE MYTHOLOGY OF IMPERIALISM: RUDYARD KIPLING, JOSEPH CONRAD, E.M. FORSTER, D.H. LAWRENCE, AND JAMES JOYCE. New York: Random House, 1971.

Imperial themes discussed from a Marxist perspective.

*G6209 Speare, Morris E. THE POLITICAL NOVEL: ITS DEVELOPMENT IN ENGLAND AND IN AMERICA. New York: Oxford Univ. Press, 1924.

Still the standard definition of the genre and history of its development, from Disraeli to the 1920's.

G6210 Viswanatham, Kalive. INDIA IN ENGLISH FICTION. Waltair: Andhra Univ. Press, 1971.

Indian themes in fiction, 1800-- .

G6211 Wagner, Geoffrey. "The Novel of Empire." EIC, 20 (1970), 229-42.

Includes JC, EMF, GO.

6.3 RELIGIOUS FICTION

Also see Muller (G3111), Paterson (G3118), and Stewart (G3142), above.

G6301 Davies, Horton. A MIRROR OF THE MINISTRY IN MODERN NOVELS. New York: Oxford Univ. Press, 1959.

The modern clerical novel. Includes SM.

G6302 Eliot, T.S. AFTER STRANGE GODS: A PRIMER OF MODERN HERESY. London: Faber, 1934.

Attacks the "lack of moral criteria--at bottom of course religious criteria--in the criticism of modern literature."

G6303 Gardiner, Harold C. NORMS FOR THE NOVEL. 1953. Rev. ed. New York: Hanover House, 1960.

Consideration of morality in fiction from a Christian perspective.

*G6304 Hopper, Stanley R., ed. SPIRITUAL PROBLEMS IN CONTEMPORARY LITERATURE: A SERIES OF ADDRESSES AND DISCUSSIONS. New York: Institute for Religious and Social Studies, 1952.

Important collection of eighteen essays on religion and the artist's situation, means, and beliefs.

G6305 Huttar, Charles A., ed. IMAGINATION AND THE SPIRIT: ESSAYS IN LITERATURE AND THE CHRISTIAN FAITH PRESENTED TO CLYDE S. KILBY. Grand Rapids, Mich.: Eerdmans, 1971.

Includes CSL.

G6306 Jones, W.S. Handley. THE PRIEST AND THE SIREN, AND OTHER LITERARY STUDIES. London: Epworth, 1953.

Religious themes in modern writers. Includes an essay entitled "Religion in Literature" and studies of AB, GKC, EMF, JG, AH, DHL, HGW.

G6307 Killinger, John. THE FAILURE OF THEOLOGY IN MODERN LITERATURE. New York: Abingdon, 1963.

Failure of modern writers to represent "with genuine consequence, the total pattern of Christian theology, or even the total impact of it."

G6308 Moorman, Charles. THE PRECINCTS OF FELICITY: THE AUGUSTINIAN CITY OF THE OXFORD CHRISTIANS. Gainesville: Univ. of Florida Press, 1966.

Includes CSL, CW.

*G6309 Moseley, Edwin M. PSEUDONYMS OF CHRIST IN THE MODERN NOVEL. Pittsburgh: Univ. of Pittsburgh Press, 1962.

Critical survey of the Christ symbol in modern fiction. Includes JC, EMF, DHL.

G6310 Mueller, William R. CELEBRATION OF LIFE: STUDIES IN MODERN FICTION. New York: Sheed and Ward, 1972.

A personal search for Christian affirmation in modern novelists. Includes JC, JJ, DHL, GO, VW.

G6311 O'Donnell, Donat [Conor Cruise O'Brien]. MARIA CROSS: IMAGINATIVE PATTERNS IN A GROUP OF MODERN CATHOLIC WRITERS. New York: Oxford Univ. Press, 1952.

The "imaginative worlds" of eight Catholic writers, viewed in light of their religion. Includes EW.

*G6312 Panichas, George A., ed. MANSIONS OF THE SPIRIT: ESSAYS IN LITERATURE AND RELIGION. New York: Hawthorn, 1967.

Essays on the "theory and aesthetic" of religion in literature, and applied criticism in recent literature. Includes AH, DHL.

G6313 Reilly, Robert J. ROMANTIC RELIGION: A STUDY OF BARFIELD, LEWIS, WILLIAMS AND TOLKIEN. Athens: Univ. of Georgia Press, 1971.

Study of the romantic literary "manner" applied to "religious matter" among modern writers.

G6314 Scott, Nathan A. REHEARSALS OF DISCOMPOSURE: ALIENATION AND RECONCILIATION IN MODERN LITERATURE. New York: King's Crown Press, 1952.

Relation between theology and literature. Includes DHL.

G6315 Tennyson, G.B., and Edward E. Ericson, eds. RELIGION AND MODERN LITERATURE: ESSAYS IN THEORY AND CRITICISM. Grand Rapids, Mich.: Eerdmans, 1974.

Collects seventeen theoretical essays on "Relationships Between Religion and Literature" (including T.S. Eliot, CSL, Auden and others) and on "Religious Backgrounds of Modern Literature," with fifteen articles on the "Religious Dimensions" of selected moderns (including JC, DHL).

G6316 Turnell, Martin. MODERN LITERATURE AND CHRISTIAN FAITH. London: Darton, Longman and Todd, 1961.

Three lectures on the problems of faith in modern poetry and fiction. Includes EMF, DHL, and VW passim, as questers of "transcendental experience."

G6317 Urang, Gunnar. SHADOWS OF HEAVEN: RELIGION AND FANTASY IN THE WRITINGS OF C.S. LEWIS, CHARLES WILLIAMS, AND J.R.R. TOLKIEN. Philadelphia: Pilgrim Press, 1971.

Critical studies with a theological slant.

G6318 Wicker, Brian. THE STORY-SHAPED WORLD: FICTION AND METAPHYSICS: SOME VARIATIONS ON A THEME. Notre Dame, Ind.: Univ. of Notre Dame Press, 1975.

Theoretical and critical study of the modern novelist's manipulation or rejection of metaphoric style and the metaphysical world view it implies. Includes JJ, DHL, EW.

6.4 SCIENCE FICTION, FANTASY, AND UTOPIAN FICTION

Note: Two journals are devoted exclusively to the theory, criticism and bibliography of science fiction. See EXTRAPOLATION, 1958-- , and SCIENCE FICTION STUDIES, 1973-- .

*G6401 Aldiss, Brian. BILLION YEAR SPREE: THE TRUE HISTORY OF SCIENCE FICTION. Garden City, N.Y.: Doubleday, 1973.

Fine historical study.

G6402 Amis, Kingsley. NEW MAPS OF HELL: A SURVEY OF SCIENCE FICTION. New York: Harcourt, 1960.

Interesting discussion of themes and types (Verne to mid-twentieth century).

G6403 Atkins, John. TOMORROW REVEALED. New York: Roy, 1956.

Fantasy-critique of speculative fiction of our time, written by a credulous "new Herodotus" in 3750 A.D. Includes AH, CSL, GO, HGW, CW passim.

G6404 Bailey, James O. PILGRIMS THROUGH SPACE AND TIME: TRENDS AND PATTERNS IN SCIENTIFIC AND UTOPIAN FICTION. New York: Argus, 1947.

Popular history, with some analysis.

G6405 Berneri, Marie L. JOURNEY THROUGH UTOPIA. London: Routledge, 1950.

History of utopian literature. Includes AH, HGW.

G6406 Biles, Jack I., ed. "Aspects of Utopian Fiction." SLitI, 6, No. 2 (1973), v-xii, 1-145.

Collects ten original essays on the theory and technique of utopian fiction. Includes GO, HGW.

G6407 Bloomfield, Paul. IMAGINARY WORLDS, OR THE EVOLUTION OF UTOPIA. London: Hamilton, 1932.

Surveys utopian fiction, from More to Huxley. Includes AH, HGW.

*G6408 Bretnor, Reginald, ed. MODERN SCIENCE FICTION: ITS MEANING AND ITS FUTURE. New York: Coward-McCann, 1953.

Still valuable essays on science fiction as literature and on the sociological significance of science fiction. Eleven essays by separate hands.

*G6409 Clareson, Thomas D. SCIENCE FICTION CRITICISM: AN ANNOTATED CHECKLIST. Kent, Ohio: Kent State Univ. Press, 1972.

*G6410 _____, ed. SF: THE OTHER SIDE OF REALISM: ESSAYS ON MODERN FANTASY AND SCIENCE FICTION. Bowling Green, Ohio: Bowling Green Univ. Popular Press, 1971.

Twenty-six essays on technique, individual works, and critical history of science fiction, the film "SF," and related topics.

G6411 Davenport, Basil. INQUIRY INTO SCIENCE FICTION. London: Longmans, 1955.

Theoretical and historical essay in definition.

G6412 DelRey, Lester. SCIENCE FICTION, 1926-1976. New York: Garland, 1976.

Comprehensive critical history and introduction to the "Garland Library of Science Fiction" (45 vols.).

G6413 Elliott, Robert C. THE SHAPE OF UTOPIA: STUDIES IN A LITERARY GENRE. Chicago: Univ. of Chicago Press, 1970.

The literary utopia, from Thomas More's UTOPIA to Huxley's ISLAND. Also includes HGW.

*G6414 Gerber, Richard. UTOPIAN FANTASY: A STUDY OF ENGLISH UTOPIAN FICTION SINCE THE END OF THE NINETEENTH CENTURY. London: Routledge, 1955.

Broad definition and historical survey of the "utopian imagination and view of life" in modern British fiction. Includes AH, CSL, GO, HGW. Includes "Appendix: An Annotated List of English Utopian Fantasies 1901-1951."

G6415 Hillegas, Mark R. THE FUTURE AS NIGHTMARE: H.G. WELLS AND THE ANTI-UTOPIANS. New York: Oxford Univ. Press, 1964.

The anti-utopian phenomenon in modern fantasy and science fiction. Includes EMF, AH, CSL, GO, HGW.

G6416 _____, ed. SHADOWS OF IMAGINATION: THE FANTASIES OF C.S. LEWIS, J.R.R. TOLKIEN, AND CHARLES WILLIAMS. Carbondale: Southern Illinois Univ. Press, 1969.

Twelve essays, equally divided among the three authors.

G6417 Irwin, W.R. THE GAME OF THE IMPOSSIBLE: A RHETORIC OF FANTASY. Urbana: Univ. of Illinois Press, 1976.

Historical and critical study of the modes and techniques of fantasy. Includes GKC, ND, RF, EMF, CSL, HGW, CW.

G6418 Moore, Patrick. SCIENCE AND FICTION. London: Harrap, 1957.

A good historical and critical introduction to science fiction.

G6419 Moskowitz, Sam. EXPLORERS OF THE INFINITE: SHAPERS OF SCIENCE FICTION. Cleveland: World, 1963.

A history of science fiction from the seventh century through the 1930's.

G6420 Penzoldt, Peter. THE SUPERNATURAL IN FICTION. New York: Humanities, 1952.

Study of supernatural themes in the English short story.

*G6421 Philmus, Robert M. INTO THE UNKNOWN: THE EVOLUTION OF SCIENCE FICTION FROM FRANCIS GOODWIN TO H.G. WELLS. Berkeley and Los Angeles: Univ. of California Press, 1970.

Excellent definition and analysis of the genre, stressing the relationships between scientific discovery, man's mythmaking, and science fiction.

G6422 Rabkin, Eric S. THE FANTASTIC IN LITERATURE. Princeton, N.J.: Princeton Univ. Press, 1976.

Attempts to define fantasy and the fantastic, and their role in fairy tales, science fiction, detective stories, religious allegory, and traditional literature.

G6423 Reginald, R. SCIENCE FICTION AND FANTASY LITERATURE: A CHECKLIST; WITH CONTEMPORARY SCIENCE FICTION AUTHORS II. Detroit: Gale, 1976.

Bibliographical guide and author index.

G6424 Scarborough, Dorothy. THE SUPERNATURAL IN MODERN ENGLISH FICTION. London: Putnam, 1917.

G6425 Scholes, Robert. STRUCTURAL FABULATION: AN ESSAY ON FICTION OF THE FUTURE. Notre Dame, Ind.: Notre Dame Univ. Press, 1975.

Four lectures. Especially valuable for Scholes's theoretical consideration of science fiction as genre.

G6426 Schwartz, Sheila. "Science-Fiction as Humanistic Study." EngR, 22 (1971), 49-55.

G6427 ______. "The World of Science-Fiction." EngR, 21 (1971), 27-40.

G6428 Suvin, Darko. "On the Poetics of the Science Fiction Genre." CE, 34 (1972), 372-82.

G7. HISTORIES AND MEMOIRS

7.1 HISTORIES

G7101 Branson, Noreen. BRITAIN IN THE NINETEEN TWENTIES. History of British Society Series. London: Weidenfeld and Nicolson, 1975.

Social history.

G7102 Branson, Noreen, and Margot Heinemann. BRITAIN IN THE 1930'S. London: Weidenfeld and Nicolson, 1971.

Social and economic history.

G7103 Briggs, Asa, comp. THEY SAW IT HAPPEN: AN ANTHOLOGY OF EYE-WITNESS ACCOUNTS OF EVENTS IN BRITISH HISTORY. Vol. 4. 1897-1940. Oxford: Blackwell, 1960.

G7104 Cecil, Robert. LIFE IN EDWARDIAN ENGLAND. New York: Putnam's, 1969.

Social history.

*G7105 Cox, C.B., and A.E. Dyson, eds. THE TWENTIETH-CENTURY MIND: HISTORY, IDEAS, AND LITERATURE IN BRITAIN. 3 vols. New York: Oxford Univ. Press, 1972.

Essays on social, intellectual, economic, and political history.

G7106 Ensor, Robert. ENGLAND: 1870-1914. Oxford: Clarendon Press, 1936.

The standard history.

G7107 Graves, Robert, and Alan Hodge. THE LONG WEEK-END: A SOCIAL HISTORY OF GREAT BRITAIN, 1918-1939. London: Faber, 1940.

Entertaining and informative popular history.

G7108 Halevy, Elie. IMPERIALISM AND THE RISE OF LABOUR (1895-1905); THE RULE OF DEMOCRACY (1905-1914). Trans. E.I. Watkin. New York: Barnes and Noble, 1951, 1952.

Concluding volumes of a distinguished HISTORY OF THE ENGLISH PEOPLE IN THE NINETEENTH CENTURY.

G7109 Judd, Denis. THE LIFE AND TIMES OF GEORGE V. London: Weidenfeld and Nicolson, 1973.

Pictorial history, 1865-1936.

G7110 Martin, Christopher. THE EDWARDIANS. London: Wayland, 1975.

Illustrated social history of English life.

G7111 _____. ENGLISH LIFE IN THE FIRST WORLD WAR. London: Wayland, 1975.

Continuation of above. Also see Yass below (G7125).

G7112 Marwick, Arthur. BRITAIN IN THE CENTURY OF TOTAL WAR: WAR, PEACE AND SOCIAL CHANGE, 1900-1967. Boston: Little, Brown, 1968.

G7113 _____. THE DELUGE: BRITISH SOCIETY AND THE FIRST WORLD WAR. Boston: Little, Brown, 1965.

Excellent social history.

G7114 Nowell-Smith, Simon H., ed. EDWARDIAN ENGLAND, 1901-1914. London: Oxford Univ. Press, 1964.

Fine collection of historical essays on the many facets of the Edwardian era.

G7115 Pearsall, Ronald. EDWARDIAN LIFE AND LEISURE. London: David, 1973.

Social history.

G7116 Pelling, Henry. MODERN BRITAIN, 1885-1955. New York: Norton, 1960.

G7117 Priestley, John B. THE EDWARDIANS. London: Heinemann, 1970.

Pictorial history.

G7118 Read, Donald. EDWARDIAN ENGLAND, 1901-1915. SOCIETY AND POLITICS. London: Harrap, 1972.

G7119 Seaman, Lewis C.B. POST-VICTORIAN BRITAIN, 1902-1951. London: Methuen, 1966.

*G7120 Taylor, A.J.P. ENGLISH HISTORY, 1914-1945. Oxford: Clarendon Press, 1965.

Fine comprehensive survey.

*G7121 ______, ed. HISTORY OF WORLD WAR I. London: Octopus Books, 1974.

Excellent introductory history, by a team of historians. Illustrated.

G7122 Thomson, David. ENGLAND IN THE TWENTIETH CENTURY (1914-63). Baltimore: Penguin, 1965.

Brief and concise.

G7123 Winter, Gordon. THE GOLDEN YEARS, 1903-1913. London: David, 1975.

Illustrated social history of pre-war England.

*G7124 Woodward, Ernest Llewellyn. GREAT BRITAIN AND THE WAR OF 1914-1918. New York: Barnes and Noble, 1967.

Outstanding historical study.

G7125 Yass, Marion. BRITAIN BETWEEN THE WORLD WARS. London: Wayland, 1975.

Illustrated social history of English life. See Martin entries above (G7110, G7111).

7.2 MEMOIRS, REMINISCENCES, BIOGRAPHIES

This highly selective bibliography of memoirs and biographies of literary relevance does not list the autobiographies and reminiscences of the individual novelists included elsewhere in this volume. Readers should take particular note of the works by Bennett (JOURNALS), Ford, and Wells in the individual author bibliographies. For a more complete, slightly annotated list of "Autobiographies, Diaries, Memoirs, Reminiscences," see TWENTIETH CENTURY BRITISH LITERATURE, comp. Temple and Tucker, pp. 26-44 (G1417).

G7201 Bell, Clive. OLD FRIENDS: PERSONAL RECOLLECTIONS. New York: Harcourt, 1957.

Memoirs of Strachey, Keynes, Fry, Woolf, and T.S. Eliot, among others.

G7202 Goldring, Douglas. THE NINETEEN TWENTIES: A GENERAL SURVEY AND SOME PERSONAL MEMORIES. London: Nicholson and Watson, 1945.

*G7203 Graves, Robert. GOODBYE TO ALL THAT. London: Cape, 1929.

Excellent chronicle of pre-war idyllic England, the war from the trenches, and the post-war disillusionment.

G7204 Heilbrun, Carolyn G. THE GARNETT FAMILY. New York: Macmillan, 1961.

Good study of the three generations of the Garnetts.

G7205 Lehmann, John. IN MY OWN TIME: MEMOIRS OF LITERARY LIFE. Boston: Little, Brown, 1969.

Autobiography. Touches importantly on literary movements and figures of the twenties and thirties.

G7206 Morrell, Ottoline. MEMOIRS OF LADY OTTOLINE MORRELL. Vol. 1. A STUDY IN FRIENDSHIP, 1873-1915. Vol. 2. OTTOLINE AT GARSINGTON. Ed. Robert Gathorne-Hardy. London: Faber, 1964, 1974.

Lady Ottoline was a close associate of the Bloomsbury group, Bertrand Russell and, for a time, D.H. Lawrence. Also includes AH, KM, VW.

*G7207 Russell, Bertrand. THE AUTOBIOGRAPHY OF BERTRAND RUSSELL. Vols. 1-2. 1872-1914; 1914-1944. Boston: Little, Brown, 1961, 1968. Vol. 3. 1944-1969. New York: Simon and Schuster, 1969.

Personal responses to nearly a century of intellectual, social, and cultural change.

G7208 _____. PORTRAITS FROM MEMORY, AND OTHER ESSAYS. New York: Simon and Schuster, 1956.

Includes JC, DHL, HGW.

*G7209 Sassoon, Siegfried. COMPLETE MEMOIRS OF GEORGE SHERSTON. London: Faber, 1937.

Collects MEMOIRS OF A FOX-HUNTING MAN, 1928; MEMOIRS OF AN INFANTRY OFFICER, 1930; and SHERSTON'S PROGRESS, 1936. Important, slightly fictionalized reminiscences of pre-war England and the catastrophe of World War I.

G7210 _____. THE OLD CENTURY, AND SEVEN MORE YEARS. London: Faber, 1938.

Semifictional memoir of the idyllic pre-war England of the author's first twenty-one years.

G7211 _____. SIEGFRIED'S JOURNEY, 1916-1920. London: Faber, 1946.

Memoir of literary friends and activities.

G7212 Spender, Stephen. WORLD WITHIN WORLD. London: Hamilton, 1951.

Autobiography of the years 1928-39.

G7213 Swinnerton, Frank. BACKGROUND WITH CHORUS: A FOOTNOTE TO CHANGES IN ENGLISH LITERARY FASHION BETWEEN 1901 AND 1917. New York: Farrar, Straus and Cudahy, 1956.

G7214 _____. FIGURES IN THE FOREGROUND: LITERARY REMINISCENCES, 1917-1940. London: Hutchinson, 1963.

Sequel to above memoirs and commentaries.

G7215 Wilson, Angus. FOR WHOM THE CLOCHE TOLLS: A SCRAPBOOK OF THE TWENTIES. London: Secker and Warburg, 1973.

G7216 Woolf, Leonard. AUTOBIOGRAPHY. 4 vols. SOWING (1880-1904); BEGINNING AGAIN (1911-18); DOWNHILL ALL THE WAY (1919-39); THE JOURNEY, NOT THE ARRIVAL MATTERS (1939-69). London: Hogarth, 1961, 1964, 1967, 1969.

Memoirs of the husband of Virginia Woolf, associate of several prominent literary figures, and founder of the Hogarth Press.

G7217 Yeats, William B. AUTOBIOGRAPHY. New York: Macmillan, 1938.

Particularly informative on the Edwardian literary scene.

G8. RELATED ARTS: ART, FILM, AND MUSIC

The following checklist of introductions to and studies of modern art, film, and music is highly selective. The works have been chosen for the student of modern British fiction who might wish to pursue correspondences in the developments of related arts in Britain or in the evolving movements in the modern arts generally. Only a few of the works directly explore the correspondences between literature and the arts (see Brown [G8003], Eisenstein [G8006], Fell [G8007], "Literature and Film" [G8019], Richardson [G8032], and Ross [G8033]), but all relate significantly to the narrative tradition of the modern novel or to the cultural world of the modern novelist.

G8001 Arnason, H. Harvard. A HISTORY OF MODERN ART: PAINTING, SCULPTURE, ARCHITECTURE. Englewood Cliffs, N.J.: Prentice-Hall, 1968.

From French Revolution to 1967.

G8002 Austin, William W. MUSIC IN THE TWENTIETH CENTURY: FROM DEBUSSY THROUGH STRAVINSKY. New York: Norton, 1966.

Brief chapters on English music.

*G8003 Brown, Calvin S. MUSIC AND LITERATURE: A COMPARISON OF THE ARTS. Athens: Univ. of Georgia Press, 1948.

Thorough comparative study.

G8004 Collaer, Paul. A HISTORY OF MODERN MUSIC. Trans. Sally Abeles. Cleveland: World, 1961.

French perspective.

*G8005 Demuth, Norman. MUSICAL TRENDS IN THE 20TH CENTURY. London: Rockliff, 1952.

Six chapters on English composers.

*G8006 Eisenstein, Sergei. "Dickens, Griffith and the Film Today." In FILM FORM. Trans. and ed. Jay Leyda. New York: Harcourt, 1949. Pp. 195-255.

The great Russian director's classic statement of the technical relationships between film and fiction.

*G8007 Fell, John L. FILM AND THE NARRATIVE TRADITION. Norman: Univ. of Oklahoma Press, 1974.

G8008 Gifford, Denis, comp. THE BRITISH FILM CATALOGUE, 1895-1970; A GUIDE TO ENTERTAINMENT FILMS. London: David and Charles, 1973.

G8009 Hamilton, G.H. PAINTING AND SCULPTURE IN EUROPE, 1880-1940. Pelican History of Art series. Baltimore: Penguin, 1967.

G8010 Hammacher, A.M. MODERN ENGLISH SCULPTURE. New York: Abrams, 1967.

*G8011 Hansen, Peter. AN INTRODUCTION TO TWENTIETH CENTURY MUSIC. 1961. 3rd ed. Boston: Allyn and Bacon, 1971.

Particularly good on backgrounds and experimental movements.

G8012 Hauser, A. THE SOCIAL HISTORY OF ART. Vol. 4. NATURALISM, IMPRESSIONISM, THE FILM AGE. New York: Knopf, 1951.

G8013 Hitchcock, Henry-Russell. ARCHITECTURE: NINETEENTH AND TWENTIETH CENTURIES. Pelican History of Art series. Baltimore: Penguin, 1969.

G8014 Hofmann, W. TURNING POINTS IN TWENTIETH-CENTURY ART, 1890-1917. Trans. Charles Kessler. New York: Braziller, 1969.

Considers the rapid and radical changes in the period of the transition to modernism.

G8015 Hutchings, Arthur. "Music in Britain: 1918-1960." In THE MODERN AGE, 1890-1960. Ed. Martin Cooper. Vol. 10 of The New Oxford History of Music. Gen. ed. J.A. Westrup et al. London: Oxford Univ. Press, 1974. Pp. 503-68.

Survey, by composer.

G8016 Jackson, A. THE POLITICS OF ARCHITECTURE: A HISTORY OF MODERN ARCHITECTURE IN BRITAIN. Toronto: Univ. of Toronto Press, 1970.

G8017 Janson, H.W. HISTORY OF ART: A SURVEY OF THE MAJOR VISUAL ARTS FROM THE DAWN OF HISTORY TO THE PRESENT DAY. 1962. Rev. ed. New York: Abrams, 1969.

A standard history.

G8018 Jencks, Charles. MODERN MOVEMENTS IN ARCHITECTURE. Garden City, N.Y.: Doubleday, 1973.

Modern British and American architecture related to social history.

*G8019 "Literature and Film: Narrative Art." STYLE, 9 (1975), 451-609.

Important special issue on the theory and practice of the study of film as literature. Includes valuable annotated bibliographical checklists: "Literature as Film" (articles) and "Literature Into Film" (books).

G8020 Low, Rachel, and Roger Manvell. HISTORY OF THE BRITISH FILM. 3 vols. London: Allen and Unwin, 1948-50.

Covers 1896-1918.

G8021 Mackerness, E.D. A SOCIAL HISTORY OF ENGLISH MUSIC. London: Routledge, 1964.

G8022 Mast, Gerald. A SHORT HISTORY OF THE MOVIES. New York: Pegasus, 1971.

British film industry discussed passim.

*G8023 Mast, Gerald, and Marshall Cohen, eds. FILM THEORY AND CRITICISM. New York: Oxford Univ. Press, 1974.

Essay collection. Includes essays on film as a narrative art.

*G8024 Mellers, Wilfred. CALIBAN REBORN: RENEWAL IN TWENTIETH-CENTURY MUSIC. London: Gollancz, 1968.

Search for "incarnation," or unity of being, in music comparable to modern literary themes.

G8025 Neumeyer, Alfred. THE SEARCH FOR MEANING IN MODERN ART. Englewood Cliffs, N.J.: Prentice-Hall, 1964.

Historical and theoretical study.

G8026 Pearsall, Ronald. EDWARDIAN POPULAR MUSIC. London: David and Charles, 1975.

Social history of music.

*G8027 Poggioli, R. THE THEORY OF THE AVANT-GARDE. Trans. Gerald Fitzgerald. Cambridge, Mass.: Harvard Univ. Press, 1968.

Avant-gardism (elitism and alienation) in the arts. Surveys trends.

G8028 Read, Herbert. ART AND ALIENATION: THE ARTIST IN SOCIETY. New York: Horizon, 1967.

G8029 _____. CONTEMPORARY BRITISH ART. 1951. Rev. ed. Harmondsworth, Engl.: Penguin, 1964.

G8030 _____. PHILOSOPHY OF MODERN ART. New York: Horizon, 1953.

Realism, surrealism, abstraction, and other aspects of modern art. Includes chapter on English art.

G8031 Rehrauer, George, comp. CINEMA BOOKLIST. Metuchen, N.J.: Scarecrow Press, 1972.

Bibliography of studies of the film.

*G8032 Richardson, Robert D. LITERATURE AND FILM. Bloomington: Indiana Univ. Press, 1972.

Theoretical study.

*G8033 Ross, T.J. FILM AND THE LIBERAL ARTS. New York: Holt, 1970.

G8034 Rothenstein, John. BRITISH ART SINCE 1900: AN ANTHOLOGY. London: Phaidon, 1962.

G8035 _____. MODERN ENGLISH PAINTERS. 3 vols. London: Eyre and Spottiswoode, 1952-74.

*G8036 Salzman, Eric. TWENTIETH-CENTURY MUSIC: AN INTRODUCTION. 1967. 2nd ed. Englewood Cliffs, N.J.: Prentice-Hall, 1974.

Valuable introduction to modern themes and techniques.

G8037 Shattuck, Roger. THE BANQUET YEARS: THE ARTS IN FRANCE, 1885-1918. New York: Harcourt, 1958.

Useful background to emerging British and continental avant-garde movements in the arts.

G8038 Slonimsky, Nicolas. MUSIC SINCE 1900. 1937. 4th ed. New York: Scribner's, 1971.

G8039 Sternfeld, F.W., ed. A HISTORY OF WESTERN MUSIC. Vol. 5. MUSIC IN THE MODERN AGE. London: Weidenfeld and Nicolson, 1973.

Historical essays on the international music scene in the last century.

G8040 Stuckenschmidt, H.H. TWENTIETH CENTURY MUSIC. New York: McGraw-Hill, 1969.

G8041 Walker, Ernest. A HISTORY OF MUSIC IN ENGLAND. 1907. 3rd ed. Oxford: Clarendon Press, 1952.

Last three chapters especially pertinent.

G8042 Webb, Michael. ARCHITECTURE IN BRITAIN TODAY. Feltham, Engl.: Country Life, 1969.

G8043 Young, Percy M. A HISTORY OF BRITISH MUSIC. New York: Norton, 1967.

INDIVIDUAL AUTHOR GUIDES

Each of the following author guides is divided into two major parts: the primary bibliography and the secondary bibliography. These parts are further subdivided in the following manner:

Primary bibliography:

1.1 Fiction

1.2 Miscellaneous Writings

1.3 Collected and Selected Works

1.4 Letters

1.5 Concordances (if any)

Secondary bibliography:

2.1 Bibliographies

2.2 Biographies, Memoirs, Reminiscences, Interviews

2.3 Book-Length Critical Studies and Essay Collections

2.4 General Critical Articles, or Chapters

2.5 Studies of Individual Works (subclassified by work considered)

The principles of arrangement, selection, numbering, and cross-referencing, are fully described in the introduction to this volume.

RICHARD ALDINGTON (1892-1962)

1. PRIMARY BIBLIOGRAPHY

Books available in recent paperback printings are denoted by "(P)."

1.1 Fiction

All works are novels unless otherwise noted.

11001 ALL MEN ARE ENEMIES. London: Chatto and Windus; Garden City, N.Y.: Doubleday, Doran, 1933.

English-Austrian love affair which bridges the war.

11002 THE COLONEL'S DAUGHTER. London: Chatto and Windus; Garden City, N.Y.: Doubleday, Doran, 1931.

Satiric novel, set among fox hunting colonels, industrialists, and empire builders.

11003 DEATH OF A HERO. Abridged. London: Chatto and Windus; New York: Covici-Friede, 1929. Unexpurgated ed. London: Consul Books, 1965.

RA's best known novel, a savage indictment of the war.

11004 LAST STRAWS. [Story]. Paris: Hours Press, 1930.

Short story, included in the American, but not the English edition of SOFT ANSWERS (see 11009).

11005 REJECTED GUEST. London: Heinemann; New York: Viking, 1939.

Serio-comic fortunes of David Norris, illegitimate child of a World War I romance, who loves and loses in the shadow of the second war.

11006 ROADS TO GLORY. [Stories]. London: Chatto and Windus; Garden City, N.Y.: Doubleday, Doran, 1930.

Thirteen stories, dealing variously with the war and its impact.

11007 THE ROMANCE OF CASANOVA. London: Heinemann; New York: Duell, Sloan, and Pearce, 1946.

Historical tale of Casanova's one true love.

11008 SEVEN AGAINST REEVES: A COMEDY-FARCE. London: Heinemann; Garden City, N.Y.: Doubleday, Doran, 1938.

Comedy, in the manner of Wodehouse.

11009 SOFT ANSWERS. [Stories]. London: Chatto and Windus; Garden City, N.Y.: Doubleday, Doran, 1932.

Five tales. American edition also includes a sixth story "Last Straws" (see 11004).

11010 VERY HEAVEN. London: Heinemann; Garden City, N.Y.: Doubleday, 1937.

A tormented and embittered young idealist faces the sterility of the modern world.

11011 WOMEN MUST WORK. London: Chatto and Windus; Garden City, N.Y.: Doubleday, 1934.

Rather opinionated story of a new woman finding independence in the London business world.

1.2 Miscellaneous Writings

It would be impractical to list here the large number of nonfictional publications by RA. See Kershaw's bibliography (21003) for full descriptions of RA's activities as a biographer not listed here (T.E. Lawrence, Voltaire, Charles Waterton, the Duke of Wellington), or as a translator, editor, and travel writer. RA's literary essays, biographies, and memoirs are noted here for their direct relevance to his life and career as a novelist.

12001 A.E. HOUSMAN AND W.B. YEATS: TWO LECTURES. Hurst, Berkshire, Engl.: Peacock Press, 1955.

12002 ARTIFEX: SKETCHES AND IDEAS. London: Chatto and Windus, 1935; Garden City, N.Y.: Doubleday, 1936.

Sixteen "miscellaneous papers," including several fictional sketches.

12003 D.H. LAWRENCE. London: Chatto and Windus, 1930.

Brief critical appreciation (43 pp. pamphlet).

12004 EZRA POUND AND T.S. ELIOT: A LECTURE. Hurst, Berkshire, Engl.: Peacock Press, 1954.

12005 FOUR ENGLISH PORTRAITS, 1801-1851. London: Evans Brothers, 1948.

Includes biographical sketches of Dickens and Disraeli.

12006 FRENCH STUDIES AND REVIEWS. London: Allen and Unwin; New York: Dial Press, 1926.

Twenty-two essays on French literature, from the medieval to the modern.

12007 "Introduction." In THE PORTABLE OSCAR WILDE. Ed. Richard Aldington. New York: Viking, 1946. Pp. 1-45. (P).

Biography and criticism.

12008 INTRODUCTION TO MISTRAL. London: Heinemann, 1956; Carbondale: Southern Illinois Univ. Press, 1960.

Biographical and critical study of the nineteenth-century Provencal poet.

12009 JANE AUSTEN. Pasadena, Calif.: Ampersand Press, 1948.

RA's introduction to Austen, from the "Chawton edition" (London: Wingate, 1948).

12010 LIFE FOR LIFE'S SAKE: A BOOK OF REMINISCENCES. New York: Viking, 1941.

Memoirs, through 1939. Much anecdotal material on the London and Paris literary scenes.

12011 LIFE OF A LADY: A PLAY. Garden City, N.Y.: Doubleday, Doran, 1936.

Adaptation (with Derek Patmore) of RA's story "Now Lies She There," from SOFT ANSWERS.

12012 LITERARY STUDIES AND REVIEWS. London: Allen and Unwin; New York: Dial Press, 1924.

Twenty-one essays, principally on French literature. Includes studies of Joyce and Eliot.

12013 PINORMAN: PERSONAL RECOLLECTIONS OF NORMAN DOUGLAS, PINO ORIOLI, AND CHARLES PRENTICE. London: Heinemann, 1954.

Continental memories of Douglas and Orioli, and critical attack on Douglas for his "editing" of Orioli's tales.

12014 PORTRAIT OF A GENIUS, BUT...(THE LIFE OF D.H. LAWRENCE, 1885-1930). London: Heinemann; New York: Duell, Sloan and Pearce, 1950. (P).

Biographical and critical attempt to present a balanced, objective view of Lawrence.

12015 PORTRAIT OF A REBEL: THE LIFE AND WORK OF ROBERT LOUIS STEVENSON. London: Evans, 1957.

Literary biography.

12016 REMY DE GOURMONT: A MODERN MAN OF LETTERS. Seattle: Univ. of Washington Book Store, 1928.

Critical appreciation (41 pp. pamphlet).

1.3 Collected and Selected Works

13001 THE COMPLETE POEMS OF RICHARD ALDINGTON. London: Wingate, 1948.

Most complete collection of RA's poetry, drawn from fourteen of the individual volumes (1915-37).

13002 SELECTED CRITICAL WRITINGS, 1928-1960. Ed. Alister Kershaw. Carbondale: Southern Illinois Univ. Press, 1970.

Collects ten essays on literary figures (including Huxley, D.H. Lawrence, Wyndham Lewis, and Maugham).

13003 "Uncollected Poems." Ed. Norman T. Gates. In THE POETRY OF RICHARD ALDINGTON. Pp. 169-336. See 23001.

1.4 Letters

Also see Gates (21001), Lawrence (22006) and Moore (22008), below.

14001 "Nine for Reeves: Letters from Richard Aldington." Ed. Miriam J. Benkovitz. BNYPL, 69 (1965), 349-74.

Nine letters from RA to James Reeves (1930-33). Excellently annotated.

14002 A PASSIONATE PRODIGALITY: LETTERS TO ALAN BIRD FROM RICHARD ALDINGTON, 1949-1962. Ed. Miriam J. Benkovitz. New York: New York Public Library, 1976.

One hundred forty-seven letters (1949-62) to the "distinguished educator, writer, and lecturer on literature and art," Alan Bird. Scrupulously annotated.

14003 "Richard Aldington's Letters to Herbert Read." Ed. David S. Thatcher. MHRev, No. 15 (1970), pp. 5-44.

Thirty-six letters (1919-61), with brief annotations and an introductory commentary on the Read-Aldington friendship.

2. SECONDARY BIBLIOGRAPHY

Since there are so few commentaries on individual works by RA, the following listing omits section 2.5, Studies of Individual Works. Articles and chapters on specific works are so noted and included in section 2.4, General Critical Articles.

2.1 Bibliographies

21001 Gates, Norman T., comp. A CHECKLIST OF THE LETTERS OF RICHARD ALDINGTON. Carbondale: Southern Illinois Univ. Press, 1977.

Alphabetical listing of RA's letters by recipients, with present locations. Several indexes and an expansive biographical introduction (see 22001).

21002 Harrington, Frank G., comp. RICHARD ALDINGTON: 1892-1962. Philadelphia: Temple Univ. Library, 1973.

Catalog of the Harrington collection of RA and Hilda Doolittle. Includes listings of RA's separately published writings, and contributions to books and periodicals, with lists of materials concerning RA, "HD," and the imagists.

*21003 Kershaw, Alister, ed. A BIBLIOGRAPHY OF THE WORKS OF RICHARD ALDINGTON, FROM 1915 TO 1948. London: Quadrant Press, 1950.

Lists, with title-page collations, all editions of RA's work through 1948, including translations, and works edited by or with an introduction by RA.

21004 Schlueter, Paul, comp. "A Chronological Check List of the Books by Richard Aldington." RICHARD ALDINGTON: AN INTIMATE PORTRAIT. Ed. Alister Kershaw and Frederic-Jacques Temple. Pp. 175-86. See 22004.

Supplements Kershaw's bibliography after 1948.

2.2 Biographies, Memoirs, Reminiscences, and Interviews

Also see RA's memoirs, LIFE FOR LIFE'S SAKE, above (12010).

*22001 Gates, Norman T. "Introduction." In A CHECKLIST OF THE LETTERS OF RICHARD ALDINGTON. Comp. Gates. Pp. 1-52. See 21001.

Best available summary of RA's life.

22002 ______. "Richard Aldington and the Clerk's Press." OhR, 13, No. 1 (1971), 21-27.

RA's unique relations during wartime with a small Cleveland-based publishing firm.

22003 Kenner, Hugh. THE POUND ERA. Pp. 55-58, 177-78, and passim. See G2350.

RA and Pound.

*22004 Kershaw, Alister, and Frederic-Jacques Temple, eds. RICHARD ALDINGTON: AN INTIMATE PORTRAIT. Carbondale: Southern Illinois Univ. Press, 1965.

Twenty-two memoirs and appreciations by a distinguished list of contributors, including T.S. Eliot, Lawrence Durrell, Henry Miller, Herbert Read, and C.P. Snow.

22005 Kittredge, Selwyn. "Richard Aldington's Challenge to T.S. Eliot: The Background of Their James Joyce Controversy." JJQ, 10 (1973), 339-41.

Eliot wrote his famous defense of ULYSSES at RA's suggestion.

22006 Lawrence, D.H. THE LETTERS OF D.H. LAWRENCE. Ed. Aldous Huxley. New York: Viking, 1932. Passim.

Several references to "old friends" RA and "HD" (his first wife, Hilda Doolittle).

22007 Moore, Harry T. THE PRIEST OF LOVE: A LIFE OF D.H. LAWRENCE. New York: Farrar, Straus and Giroux, 1974. Passim.

RA's friendship with Lawrence.

22008 ______. "Richard Aldington in His Last Years." TQ, 6, No. 3 (1963), 60-74.

Meetings, conversations and correspondence with a by-no-means embittered RA (1958-62).

22009 Morgan, Louise. "Richard Aldington." In WRITERS AT WORK. London: Chatto and Windus, 1931. Pp. 10-16.

Interview-discussion of RA's writing habits.

2.3 Book-Length Critical Studies

23001 Gates, Norman T. THE POETRY OF RICHARD ALDINGTON: A CRITICAL EVALUATION AND AN ANTHOLOGY OF UNCOLLECTED POEMS. University Park: Pennsylvania State Univ. Press, 1974.

Developed from a doctoral dissertation. Gates's "evaluation" of RA's poetry consumes eleven of the nearly four hundred pages of this volume. The balance is given to an exhaustive survey of RA's critical reception as a poet, and an edition of the uncollected poems. Of peripheral value to the student of RA's fiction. Includes 13003.

*23002 McGreevy, Thomas. RICHARD ALDINGTON: AN ENGLISHMAN. London: Chatto and Windus, 1931.

First full critical study of RA, limited by its date of composition to the discussion of the poetry of the imagist period and the early fiction. McGreevy perceptively discusses DEATH OF A HERO, ROADS TO GLORY and THE COLONEL'S DAUGHTER.

23003 Smith, Richard Eugene. RICHARD ALDINGTON. Boston: Twayne, 1977.

Full survey of RA's life and work, including an expansive biographical chapter, several chapters on the poetry and fiction, and briefer accounts of RA's related literary activities (biography, translation, and criticism). Good general introduction.

23004 Snow, C.P. RICHARD ALDINGTON: AN APPRECIATION. London: Heinemann, [1938].

Publisher's advertising pamphlet (26 pp.). Critical essay by Snow, with list of RA's works.

2.4 General Critical Articles, or Chapters on RA

RA's poetry has received by far the most critical attention, as the following selection of articles will attest. Those studies which note RA's career as a novelist rarely discuss any of the fiction in depth.

24001 Baum, Paull F. "Mr. Richard Aldington." SAQ, 28 (1929), 201-8.

RA illustrates the strengths and weaknesses of modern poetry.

*24002 Bergonzi, Bernard. HEROES' TWILIGHT. Pp. 182-86 and passim. See G2308.

Impact of the war in RA's fiction (DEATH OF A HERO).

24003 Bouyssou, Roland. "Dulce et Decorum est pro Patria Mori." CALIBAN 3, No. 2 (1967), 115-24.

24004 Coffman, Stanley K., Jr. IMAGISM: A CHAPTER FOR THE HISTORY OF MODERN POETRY. Norman: Univ. of Oklahoma Press, 1951. Pp. 164-70 and passim.

RA's interpretation of "imagism" and relations with the imagists.

24005 Frierson, William C. THE ENGLISH NOVEL IN TRANSITION. Pp. 290-92 and passim. See G3047.

Very brief summary of RA's fiction (to 1937).

24006 Gates, Norman T. "Richard Aldington and F.S. Flint: Poet's Dialogue." PLL, 8 (1972), 63-69.

RA's friendship with Flint and its impact on his poetry.

24007 ______. "Richard Aldington's 'Personal Notes on Poetry.'" TQ, 17, No. 1 (1974), 107-13.

Commentary upon and first publication of RA's brief essay (c. 1920).

24008 Harmer, J.B. VICTORY IN LIMBO: IMAGISM, 1908-1917. London: Secker and Warburg, 1975. Pp. 66-72 and passim.

RA's relationship to the imagist poets, and his poetry.

24009 Howarth, Herbert. NOTES ON SOME FIGURES BEHIND T.S. ELIOT. Boston: Houghton Mifflin, 1964. Passim.

Eliot's personal and literary relationships with RA.

24010 Hughes, Glenn. "Richard Aldington: The Rebel." In IMAGISM AND THE IMAGISTS: A STUDY IN MODERN POETRY. Stanford, Calif.: Stanford Univ. Press, 1931. Pp. 85-108.

Essence of RA's character and poetry is rebellion.

24011 Knightley, Phillip. "Aldington's Enquiry Concerning T.E. Lawrence." TQ, 16, No. 4 (1973), 98-105.

RA's exposure of the Lawrence legend, "created by modern publicity," and the reverberations among the Lawrence cult (re: T.E. LAWRENCE, A BIOGRAPHICAL ENQUIRY, 1955).

24012 McCormick, John. CATASTROPHE AND IMAGINATION. Pp. 214-17. See G3095.

DEATH OF A HERO more "unoriginal" than RA knew or intended.

*24013 Moore, Harry T. "Preface." In RA's SOFT ANSWERS. Carbondale: Southern Illinois Univ. Press, 1967. Pp. v-xxii.

Asserts RA's lack of "bitterness" in his later years (despite the opinion of the English press) and briefly describes the satiric quality of SOFT ANSWERS.

24014 Moore, T. Sturge. "Richard Aldington." In SOME SOLDIER POETS. New York: Harcourt, 1920. Pp. 95-105.

Brief critical review of RA's poetry, with extensive quotation.

24015 Morris, John. "Richard Aldington and DEATH OF A HERO--or Life of an Anti-Hero?" In THE FIRST WORLD WAR IN FICTION. Ed. Holger Klein. London: Macmillan, 1976. Pp. 183-92.

Bitterness, cynicism, and sense of betrayal in RA's life and fiction.

24016 Nicholson, Norman. MAN AND LITERATURE. Pp. 103-6. See G2353.

RA's fiction caters to a "middlebrow" taste for the unscrupulous "natural" man.

24017 Palmer, Herbert. POST-VICTORIAN POETRY. London: Dent, 1938. Pp. 325-30.

Although fewer than half of RA's poems are imagistic, he has become the center of the imagist group.

24018 Rosenfeld, Paul. "The Importance of Richard Aldington." In BY WAY OF ART. New York: Coward-McCann, 1928. Pp. 236-49.

RA the first Englishman to recognize and absorb the experimentation of American poets.

*24019 Rosenthal, Sidney. "Richard Aldington and the Excitement of Reason: A Defense." In TWENTY-SEVEN TO ONE. Ed. B. Broughton. Ogdensburg, N.Y.: Ryan Press, 1970. Pp. 133-43.

RA not a sentimentalist (see Swinnerton, 24024), rather a writer of "passionate intensity." He intended to "defy the very depersonalization or dissolution of self which was to be a central theme in his fiction." Concentrates analysis on DEATH OF A HERO and SOFT ANSWERS.

24020 Ross, Robert H. THE GEORGIAN REVOLT, 1910-1922: RISE AND FALL OF A POETIC IDEAL. Carbondale: Southern Illinois Univ. Press, 1965. Pp. 46-50 and passim.

RA's and the imagists' role in the "pre-war poetic revolt."

24021 Silkin, Jon. OUT OF BATTLE: THE POETRY OF THE GREAT WAR. London: Oxford Univ. Press, 1972. Pp. 187-91.

RA's mixture of the war subject and the imagist technique (cf. Herbert Read).

24022 Sisson, G.H. ENGLISH POETRY, 1900-1950: AN ASSESSMENT. London: Hart-Davis, 1971. Pp. 60-64.

RA as an imagist.

24023 Starkie, Enid. FROM GAUTIER TO ELIOT. Pp. 157-61. See G2362.

RA among the imagist poets.

24024 Swinnerton, Frank. THE GEORGIAN LITERARY SCENE. Pp. 349-52. See G2364.

RA a sentimentalist.

24025 Tindall, William York. FORCES IN MODERN BRITISH LITERATURE. Pp. 98-99 and passim. See G2122.

RA's relation to modern literary movements, in poetry and fiction.

Katherine Mansfield Beauchamp. See Katherine Mansfield in vol. 2.

MAX BEERBOHM (1872-1956)

1. PRIMARY BIBLIOGRAPHY

Books available in recent paperback printings are denoted by "(P)."

1.1 Fiction

While the three titles below suggest a very slight fictional output, an argument could be made for the inclusion of many of MB's parodies, sketches, and satires under this heading as a sort of hybrid-fiction (see AND EVEN NOW, A CHRISTMAS GARLAND, SEVEN MEN, and A VARIETY OF THINGS in section 1.2 below). Whatever the proper classification of these works, MB deserves the attention of the student of modern English fiction for his classic ZULEIKA DOBSON, "one of the best novels of our time" (W.Y. Tindall--see G2122).

11001 THE DREADFUL DRAGON OF HAY HILL. [Story]. London: Heinemann, 1928. No separate Amer. ed.

Fantasy, set c. 39,000 B.C., illustrating man's unchanging quarrelsome nature. Also published in A VARIETY OF THINGS (12007).

11002 THE HAPPY HYPOCRITE: A FAIRY TALE FOR TIRED MEN. [Story]. London and New York: Lane, 1897.

Ironic fantasy tale of a hyprocritical rake's progress toward maturity. One of MB's most popular works.

11003 ZULEIKA DOBSON; OR AN OXFORD LOVE STORY. London: Heinemann; New York: Lane, 1911.

The beautiful, frigid Zuleika drives the Oxford undergraduates to mass suicide during "Eights week."

1.2 Miscellaneous Writings

MB's careers as literary parodist, broadcaster, essayist, and dramatic critic are reflected in the following selection of his nonfiction prose. Limitation of space forbids a complete listing of MB's caricatures. Hart-Davis's CATALOGUE OF THE CARICATURES OF MAX BEERBOHM (21004) should be examined for a complete list of MB's subjects, and Gallatin's bibliographies (21002, 21003) for information on their publication. The most important collections of MB's caricatures are A BOOK OF CARICATURES (1907); CARICATURES BY MAX, FROM THE COLLECTION OF THE ASHMOLEAN MUSEUM (1958); CARICATURES OF TWENTY-FIVE GENTLEMEN (1896); FIFTY CARICATURES (1913); MAX'S NINETIES: DRAWINGS, 1892-1899 (1958); OBSERVATIONS (1925); THE POETS' CORNER (1904); A SURVEY (1921); and THINGS NEW AND OLD (1923).

12001 AND EVEN NOW. London: Heinemann, 1920. New York: Dutton, 1921.

Twenty essays, satires, and fantasies (1910-20). Includes a memoir of a childhood visit with Swinburne.

12002 AROUND THEATRES. 2 vols. London: Heinemann, 1924. New York: Knopf, 1930.

Selected drama criticism from MB's twelve years as columnist for the SATURDAY REVIEW (1898-1910). Also published as vols. 8-9 of WORKS. See 13010.

12003 A CHRISTMAS GARLAND. London: Heinemann; New York: Dutton, 1912.

Seventeen delightful and penetrating parodies of modern novelists, supplemented in later editions. Includes Bennett, Chesterton, Conrad, Galsworthy, and Wells.

12004 MAINLY ON THE AIR. London: Heinemann, 1946. New York: Knopf, 1947.

Six essays and six broadcasts. Second "enlarged" edition (1958) adds eight additional essays and talks.

12005 MORE. London and New York: Lane, 1899.

Twenty essays on art, music, drama, popular entertainment, and travel.

12006 SEVEN MEN. London: Heinemann, 1919. New York: Knopf, 1920.

Six semifictional, satiric sketches of MB himself (number "seven"), at various stages of his life. Reprinted with additional material as SEVEN MEN AND TWO OTHERS (London, 1950; New York, 1959).

12007 A VARIETY OF THINGS. London: Heinemann; New York: Knopf, 1928.

Eleven essays, fairy tales, memoirs, and fictional sketches.

12008 WORKS OF MAX BEERBOHM. London: Lane; New York: Scribner's, 1896.

Seven early essays on the English scene. Also published as vol. 1 of WORKS (see 13010), and in a combined edition with MORE (1930). Not a collected edition, despite its facetious title.

12009 YET AGAIN. London: Chapman and Hall, 1909. New York: Lane, 1910.

Twenty-two essays and nine impressionistic word pictures.

1.3 Collected and Selected Works

13001 THE BODLEY HEAD MAX BEERBOHM. Ed. David Cecil. London: Bodley Head, 1970.

Collects THE HAPPY HYPOCRITE, four sketches, a selection from ZULEIKA DOBSON, thirteen essays, six parodies, and six critical essays on the drama. Excellent anthology. See 24004.

13002 THE INCOMPARABLE MAX: A COLLECTION OF WRITINGS OF SIR MAX BEERBOHM. New York: Dodd, 1962. (P).

Thirty-three essays, sketches, parodies, criticisms, broadcasts, and THE HAPPY HYPOCRITE (complete). Good representative selection. See 24017.

13003 LAST THEATRES, 1904-1910. London: Hart-Davis; New York: Taplinger, 1970.

Completes the publication of MB's uncollected drama criticism. See MORE THEATRES, below.

13004 MAX BEERBOHM: SELECTED ESSAYS. Ed. N.L. Clay. London: Heinemann, 1958.

13005 MAX IN VERSE: RHYMES AND PARODIES. Ed. J.G. Riewald. Brattleboro, Vt.: Stephen Greene, 1963. (P).

Collects and annotates MB's verse and sonnets.

13006 MORE THEATRES, 1898-1903. London: Hart-Davis; New York: Taplinger, 1969.

Previously uncollected drama criticism by MB from the SATURDAY REVIEW. See LAST THEATRES, above.

13007 A PEEP INTO THE PAST, AND OTHER PROSE PIECES. Ed. Rupert Hart-Davis. London: Heinemann; Brattleboro, Vt.: Stephen Greene, 1972.

Reprints MB's essays on Oscar Wilde, A PEEP INTO THE PAST (1893), and twenty-seven previously uncollected prose pieces.

13008 SELECTED PROSE. Ed. David Cecil. Boston: Little, Brown, 1971.

13009 A SELECTION FROM AROUND THEATRES. Garden City, N.Y.: Doubleday, 1960.

13010 WORKS. 10 vols. London: Heinemann, 1922-28.

Limited edition, prepared with MB's assistance. Includes ZULEIKA DOBSON, plus four volumes of essays, two of parodies and satires, two of drama criticism, and one of caricatures.

1.4 Letters

Also see Cecil (22003).

14001 LETTERS TO REGGIE TURNER. Ed. Rupert Hart-Davis. London: Hart-Davis, 1964. Published MAX BEERBOHM'S LETTERS TO REGGIE TURNER. Philadelphia: Lippincott, 1965.

Two hundred letters (1891-1938) to MB's Oxford classmate and close friend. Annotated. See 22006.

14002 MAX AND WILL: MAX BEERBOHM AND WILLIAM ROTHENSTEIN, THEIR FRIENDSHIP AND LETTERS, 1893-1945. Ed. Mary M. Lago and Karl Beckson. Cambridge: Harvard Univ. Press, 1975.

Collects, annotates, and introduces 130 letters to and from MB. See 22009.

2. SECONDARY BIBLIOGRAPHY

2.1 Bibliographies

21001 CATALOGUE OF THE LIBRARY AND LITERARY MANUSCRIPTS OF THE LATE SIR MAX BEERBOHM. London: Sotheby, 1960.

Auction catalog.

21002 Gallatin, A.E., comp. SIR MAX BEERBOHM: BIBLIOGRAPHICAL NOTES. Cambridge: Harvard Univ. Press, 1944.

Lists numerous uncollected and unpublished works not included in the Gallatin and Oliver bibliography below.

21003 Gallatin, A.E., and L.M. Oliver, comps. A BIBLIOGRAPHY OF THE WORKS OF MAX BEERBOHM. Cambridge: Harvard Univ. Press, 1952.

Primary descriptive bibliography of MB's collected and separately published works, with an appendix listing Harvard's manuscript holdings, association items, and other MB-related items.

21004 Hart-Davis, Rupert, comp. A CATALOGUE OF THE CARICATURES OF MAX BEERBOHM. Cambridge: Harvard Univ. Press, 1972.

Classification and catalog of over 2,000 caricatures, plus 100 plates. Excellently indexed by title, publication, and owner.

*21005 Riewald, J.G., comp. "Bibliography." In his SIR MAX BEERBOHM, MAN AND WRITER. Pp. 213-343. See 23004.

More complete primary bibliography than Gallatin and Oliver above. Lists first appearances of all collected items, and catalogs an enormous number of uncollected and unpublished works. Riewald also supplies a secondary checklist of over 300 writings about MB (most items transient reviews and incidental mentions), and a list of portraits of MB.

2.2 Biographies, Memoirs, Reminiscences, and Interviews

*22001 Behrman, S.N. PORTRAIT OF MAX: AN INTIMATE MEMOIR OF SIR MAX BEERBOHM. New York: Random House, 1960. Published as CONVERSATION WITH MAX: SIR MAX BEERBOHM. London: Hamilton, 1960.

Remembered conversations with MB (often on literary topics) and portrait of MB in his last years, originally published as a series of magazine articles. Miscellaneous in nature, but a useful supplement to the standard biography. Extract reprinted in 23005.

22002 Bottome, Phyllis. "Max Beerbohm." In FROM THE LIFE. London: Faber, 1944. Pp. 32-46.

Visits and literary conversations with MB in Italy (1930's).

*22003 Cecil, David. MAX: A BIOGRAPHY. Boston: Houghton Mifflin, 1964.

The standard biography, commissioned and authorized by MB's widow. Cecil quotes extensively from MB's works and correspondence throughout, but avoids critical commentary altogether. Slight index.

22004 Davies, William H. LATER DAYS. New York: Doran, 1926. Pp. 196-204.

Insinuating attack on MB as an unscrupulously vicious gossip and calumniator.

22005 Frere-Reeves, A.S. "A Visit to Max." LIVING AGE, 332 (1927), 340-43.

Visit and conversation with MB in Italy (1926).

22006 Hart-Davis, Rupert. "Introduction." In MB's LETTERS TO REGGIE TURNER. Pp. 7-19. See 14001.

Brief biographical sketch of Turner and commentary on his friendship with MB.

22007 Huneker, James G. "Mid-Victorian Max." In STEEPLEJACK. New York: Scribner's, 1921. II, 251-56.

Huneker's involvement in critical controversy with MB and G.B. Shaw.

22008 Knox, Collie. "Sir Max Beerbohm." In PEOPLE OF QUALITY. London: MacDonald, 1947. Pp. 154-64.

Visit and conversation with MB in Italy, recounted by his step-nephew.

22009 Lago, Mary M. "Introduction." In MAX AND WILL. Ed. Lago and Karl Beckson. Pp. 3-16, 67-79. See 14002.

Two-part introduction tracing the friendship of MB and William Rothenstein, to 1911 and after.

22010 MacCarthy, Desmond. "Max Beerbohm." In MEMORIES. New York: Oxford Univ. Press, 1953. Pp. 192-98.

Memories of MB, from the late nineties, and comments on his skills as caricaturist and mimic.

22011 Mix, Katherine L. MAX AND THE AMERICANS. Brattleboro, Vt.: Stephen Greene Press, 1974.

Documents MB's ambivalence toward America, an undertaking hardly worthy of book-length development, or publication.

22012 ______. "Max on Shaw." ShawR, 6 (1963), 100-104.

MB's ambivalent views of Shaw, in his comments and caricatures. Reprinted in 23005.

22013 Rothenstein, William. MEN AND MEMORIES. 3 vols. New York: Coward-McCann, 1931, 1932, 1939. I, 131-47, 272-78. II-III, passim.

Considerable reference throughout to MB and the art world of the nineties and after, by a distinguished painter.

22014 Waugh, Evelyn. "Max Beerbohm: A Lesson in Manners." ATLANTIC MONTHLY, 198 (Sept. 1956), 75-76.

Brief memoir of MB's gentlemanly kindness to Waugh. Reprinted in 23005.

22015 Weintraub, Stanley. REGGIE: A PORTRAIT OF REGINALD TURNER. New York: Braziller, 1965. Pp. 38-45.

MB's relations with Turner, at Oxford, as fellow-writers of the nineties, and in later years.

22016 West, Rebecca. "Notes on the Effect of Women Writers on Mr. Max Beerbohm." In ENDING IN EARNEST: A LITERARY LOG. Garden City, N.Y.: Doubleday, Doran, 1931. Pp. 66-74.

Anecdotes of meetings with MB, presenting MB as a dandified museum piece, in appearance and opinions.

*22017 Wilson, Edmund. "A Miscellany of Max Beerbohm." In THE BIT BETWEEN MY TEETH: A LITERARY CHRONICLE OF 1950-1965. New York: Farrar, Straus and Giroux, 1965. Pp. 41-62.

Meetings and conversations with MB (1954), recollections of his likes (e.g., James) and dislikes (Shaw), and reproduction of his notes for an unwritten essay on men's clothes. Reprinted in 23005.

2.3 Book-Length Critical Studies and Essay Collections

*23001 Felstiner, John. THE LIES OF ART: MAX BEERBOHM'S PARODY AND CARICATURE. New York: Knopf, 1972.

A well-illustrated criticism and interpretation of MB as visual and literary artist, which assumes some familiarity with the biography. Felstiner organizes his study upon MB's developing views of the artist's role, emphasizing, as his title suggests, MB's "masked" detachment of the nineties. Extract reprinted in 23005.

23002 Lynch, J.G. Bohun. MAX BEERBOHM IN PERSPECTIVE. London: Heinemann, 1921.

Two-part study of MB, as writer and artist, which nevertheless argues that the "caricatures and writings are not manifestations of two arts, but of one." Lynch traces the career and comments generally on the style, quality, and materials of the parodies, essays, fiction, and other writing. Still valuable.

23003 McElderry, Bruce R. MAX BEERBOHM. New York: Twayne, 1972.

Principally an introduction to MB's life and the cultural milieu of the nineties and early twentieth century. McElderry includes brief chapters on the writings, the caricatures, and an "evaluation," but offers little original comment (the critiques are mostly summary with some explication). Brief bibliography.

*23004 Riewald, J.G. SIR MAX BEERBOHM: MAN AND WRITER. A CRITICAL ANALYSIS WITH A BRIEF LIFE AND A BIBLIOGRAPHY. The Hague: Nijhoff, 1953.

Brief biography, character sketch, and useful critical commentaries on and surveys of MB as essayist, fantasist, parodist, critic, and stylist. Although Riewald is overly concerned with classifying and enumerating works and techniques, he offers the only extended discussion of MB as prose writer. Riewald's bibliography alone (described above, 21005) would make this a valuable book. Extract reprinted in 23005.

*23005 ______, ed. THE SURPRISE OF EXCELLENCE: MODERN ESSAYS ON MAX BEERBOHM. Hamden, Conn.: Archon, 1974.

Collects twenty previously published essays on MB in various roles, such as friend, novelist, essayist, and caricaturist, by a distinguished list of contributors (e.g., Auden, Harold Nicolson, John Rothenstein, John Updike, Evelyn Waugh, Edmund Wilson. Includes: 22012, 22014, 22017, 24002, 24003, 24004, 24009, 24013, 24018, 24020, 24022, 24023, 24028, 24030, 25002, 25005, 25016; and extracts from the following books: 22001, 23001, and 23004.

2.4 General Critical Articles, or Chapters on MB

24001 Acton, Harold. "Max Beerbohm: Dandy Among English Classics." EDH, 38 (1975), 1-14.

General, appreciative critique.

*24002 Auden, W.H. "One of the Family." In FOREWORDS AND AFTERWORDS. New York: Random House, 1973. Pp. 367-83.

Graceful and witty overview of MB's life and work. Reprinted in 23005.

24003 Boas, Guy. "The Magic of Max." BLACKWOOD'S MAGAZINE, 260 (1946), 341-50.

MB a genial, "elfin" artist. Contains appreciations of MB's drawings and essays. Reprinted in 23005.

24004 Cecil, David. "Introduction." In THE BODLEY HEAD MAX BEERBOHM. Pp. 7-18. See 13001.

MB a consummate entertainer, a comic genius, often with a serious message. Reprinted in 23005.

*24005 Cross, Wilbur J. "The Humor of Max Beerbohm." YR, 13 (1924), 209-27.

Distinguished theoretical and critical discussion of the qualities of MB's humor.

24006 Gorman, Herbert S. "'The Incomparable Max.'" In THE PROCESSION OF MASKS. Boston: Brimmer, 1923. Pp. 57-71.

MB an ironist, more than a humorist, whose prose deserves as close critical attention as his drawing.

*24007 Hillebrand, Harold N. "Max Beerbohm." JEGP, 19 (1920), 254-69.

MB the heir in prose to the "crown of Oscar Wilde." Intelligent survey of MB's criticism and theories of art, his parodies, and his fiction.

24008 Jackson, Holbrook. "The Incomparable Max." In his THE EIGHTEEN NINETIES. Pp. 117-25 and passim. See G2347.

MB epitomizes the posing, dandyism, and comic spirit of the nineties. (Jackson's book is dedicated to MB.)

*24009 Kronenberger, Louis. "Max Beerbohm." 1947. In THE REPUBLIC OF LETTERS. New York: Knopf, 1955. Pp. 224-35.

The benign personality of the "perfect trifler" animates MB's work, but "form and finish . . . go far toward preserving it." Examines several essays and ZULEIKA DOBSON. Reprinted in 23005.

24010 Langbaum, Robert. "Max and Dandyism." VICTORIAN POETRY, 4 (1966), 121-26.

MB the perfectly detached dandy in his work (cf. Wilde).

24011 Littell, Philip. "An Immortal Writer." In BOOKS AND THINGS. New York: Harcourt, 1919. Pp. 201-7.

Impressionistic praise of MB's literary style.

24012 Lynd, Robert. "Mr. Max Beerbohm." In BOOKS AND AUTHORS. London: Cobden-Sanderson, 1922. Pp. 153-67.

MB a perfectionist, most successful in his sketches and parodies. Finds MB's works of the early twenties among his best.

24013 McElderry, Bruce R. "Max Beerbohm: Essayist, Caricaturist, Novelist." In ON STAGE AND OFF: EIGHT ESSAYS IN ENGLISH LITERATURE. Ed. J.W. Ehrstine, J.R. Elwood, and R.C. McLean. Pullman: Washington State Univ. Press, 1968. Pp. 76-86.

Brief appreciative commentaries on MB's essays (principally the drama criticism), caricatures (slight), and ZULEIKA DOBSON. Reprinted in 23005.

*24014 Moers, Ellen. "Epilogue: Sir Max Beerbohm." In THE DANDY: BRUMMELL TO BEERBOHM. London: Secker and Warburg, 1960. Pp. 315-30.

Considers MB as "dandy," as well as his writings on and caricatures of dandyism.

24015 Muddiman, Bernard. THE MEN OF THE NINETIES. London: Danielson, 1920. Pp. 110-17.

Among the "appallingly serious" artists of the nineties, MB and Beardsley alone have an ironic sense of humor.

24016 Riewald, J.G. "Introduction." In his THE SURPRISE OF EXCELLENCE. Pp. vii-xiii. See 23005.

The "uniqueness" and strengths of MB's work. Introduces an anthology of critical essays.

24017 Roberts, Sidney C. "Introduction." In THE INCOMPARABLE MAX. Pp. xi-xviii. See 13002.

MB's skills as essayist, satirist, and parodist.

24018 _____. "Max Beerbohm." In DR. JOHNSON AND OTHERS. Cambridge: At the Univ. Press, 1958. Pp. 156-76.

Brief survey of MB's essays, criticism, parodies, and fiction. Reprinted in 23005.

24019 Robson, W.W. MODERN ENGLISH LITERATURE. Pp. 43-45. See G2118.

Traces MB's career from "dandy" of the nineties to popular broadcaster in the forties.

24020 Rothenstein, John. "'Max.'" In MB's THE POET'S [sic] CORNER. London: Penguin, 1943. Pp. 5-13.

MB's appeal to a limited but "influential and fervently admiring public." Reprinted in 23005.

24021 Smith, Logan Pearsall. "Sir Max Beerbohm." ATLANTIC MONTHLY, 170 (Nov. 1942), 88-90.

MB's "mocking detachment [and] ironical disdain of the world's opinion" the keynote to his life and work.

24022 Stanford, Derek. "The Writing of Sir Max Beerbohm." MONTH, 13 (1955), 352-65.

MB as a critic of his own work, a commentator on "things in general," and a parodist of the talented. Reprinted in 23005.

24023 Stevenson, David. "Irony and Deception." In THE SURPRISE OF EXCELLENCE. Ed. J.G. Riewald. Pp. 65-76. See 23005.

The stylistic techniques of MB's irony, from simple comparisons to complex, deceptive hoaxes.

24024 Swinnerton, Frank. THE GEORGIAN LITERARY SCENE. Pp. 192-94. See G2364.

MB's "sweetness" of humor.

24025 ______. "The Special Genius of Sir Max." SatR, 2 Aug. 1958, pp. 13-14.

MB a "cockney" ironist and master of the art of gentle ridicule.

24026 Thompson, Edward R. [E.T. Raymond]. "Henry James and Max Beerbohm." In PORTRAITS OF THE NEW CENTURY (THE FIRST TEN YEARS). Garden City, N.Y.: Doubleday, Doran, 1928. Pp. 282-99.

MB carries on the "torch" of James's "literary dandyism," with the added "alien strain of humour."

24027 Tindall, William York. FORCES IN MODERN BRITISH LITERATURE. P. 115 and passim. See G2122.

MB's relations to and comments upon modern literary movements.

24028 Updike, John. "Beerbohm and Others"; "Rhyming Max." In ASSORTED PROSE. New York: Knopf, 1965. Pp. 241-56; 256-63.

MB's embrace of the "total personality" of his parodees (discussed in a review of a parody-anthology). Second essay praises MB's frequently ignored light verse, but mocks the academic apparatus of Riewald's edition (see 13005). "Rhyming Max" reprinted in 23005.

24029 Ward, Alfred C. TWENTIETH-CENTURY ENGLISH LITERATURE. Pp. 197-201. See G2123.

Survey, stressing MB's maturation and loss of artificiality.

*24030 Wilson, Edmund. "An Analysis of Max Beerbohm." In CLASSICS AND COMMERCIALS. Pp. 431-41. See G2375.

The complexity of MB's point of view in his works (e.g., his frequent juxtaposition of the exotic and the British) and the distinction of his criticism. Reprinted in 23005.

2.5 Studies of Individual Works

The following section is subdivided into two parts: (i) Fiction (alphabetically by title), and (ii) Miscellaneous Writings and Caricatures. Each of the five book-length critical studies listed in section 2.3, above, contains commentaries on individual works. Also several of the critical essays in section 2.4, above, discuss individual works in passing.

i. FICTION

THE HAPPY HYPOCRITE (1897)

25001 Squire, John C. [Solomon Eagle]. "Mr. Max Beerbohm's Idyll." In BOOKS IN GENERAL. SECOND SERIES. New York: Knopf, 1920. Pp. 262-68.

MB's pastoral idyll, THE HAPPY HYPOCRITE, a work which permanently delights.

ZULEIKA DOBSON (1911)

*25002 Dupee, F.W. "Max Beerbohm and the Rigors of Fantasy." 1966. In THE SURPRISE OF EXCELLENCE. Ed. J.G. Riewald. Pp. 175-91. See 23005.

Enlarged version of previously published critical essay on the quality of MB's fantasy in ZULEIKA DOBSON ("the process of comic literalization").

25003 Forster, E.M. ASPECTS OF THE NOVEL. Pp. 116-19. See G4025.

ZULEIKA DOBSON "the most consistent achievement of fantasy in our time."

25004 Hackett, Francis. "Introduction." In ZULEIKA DOBSON. New York: Dodd, Mead, 1924. Pp. 1-5.

MB's skill as a caricaturist in fiction.

25005 Nicolson, Harold. "ZULEIKA DOBSON--A Revolution." LISTENER, 38 (1947), 521-22.

Analysis of novel's characterization and style, emphasizing MB's tone of "intimacy." Reprinted in 23005.

25006 Ray, Cyril. "Max Beerbohm's ZULEIKA DOBSON." WORLD REVIEW, Apr. 1947, pp. 65-67.

25007 Scott, Dixon. "Beau Beerbohm." In MEN OF LETTERS. New York: Hodder and Stoughton, 1916. Pp. 179-83.

Praise for the delicacy and polish of MB's style in ZULEIKA DOBSON.

25008 Stevenson, Lionel. THE HISTORY OF THE ENGLISH NOVEL. XI, 155-56. See G2212.

The "brief masterpiece" ZULEIKA DOBSON a prototype of the elegant wit and cynical satire in modern fiction.

ii. MISCELLANEOUS WRITINGS AND CARICATURES

25009 Braybrooke, Patrick. "Max Beerbohm, Swinburne, and Other Things." In PEEPS AT THE MIGHTY. Philadelphia: Lippincott, 1927. Pp. 43-58.

Delightful simplicity and "unselfishness" of MB's essays.

25010 Bross, Addison C. "Beerbohm's 'The Feast' and Conrad's Early Fiction." NCF, 26 (1971), 329-36.

MB's parody (in A CHRISTMAS GARLAND) exploits several of Conrad's early works, not just HEART OF DARKNESS.

*25011 Felstiner, John. "Changing Faces in Max Beerbohm's Caricature." PULC, 33 (1972), 73-88.

Salient remarks on the relationship between aesthetic and moral vision in the art of caricature. Discusses and publishes several new caricatures.

25012 Grushow, Ira. "The Chastened Dandy: Beerbohm's 'Hilary Maltby and Stephen Braxton.'" PLL, 8, supplement (1972), 149-64.

Autobiographical dimensions of two of the SEVEN MEN.

25013 Guedalla, Philip. "An Old Master." In MASTERS AND MEN. New York: Putnam's, 1923. Pp 65-69.

MB has ennobled the art of caricature.

25014 Hammerton, John A. "Max Beerbohm." In HUMORISTS OF THE PENCIL. London: Hurst and Blackett, 1905. Pp. 68-73.

MB as caricaturist.

25015 Hart-Davis, Rupert. "Introduction." In his A CATALOGUE OF THE CARICATURES OF MAX BEERBOHM. Pp. 9-15. See 21004.

"Writing was always a labour to Max. . . . Drawing, on the other hand, was always his delight." Describes scope and format of the catalog.

25016 Huss, Roy. "The Aesthete as Realist." In THE SURPRISE OF EXCELLENCE. Ed. J.G. Riewald. Pp. 113-22. See 23005.

MB's realistic criteria in his drama criticism.

25017 Lancaster, Osbert. "Introduction." In MAX'S NINETIES: DRAWINGS, 1892-1899. Philadelphia: Lippincott, 1958. Pp. 7-10.

MB an "English phenomenon" belonging essentially to the nineties.

25018 Lynch, J.G. Bohun. "Mr. Beerbohm's Caricatures." FORTNIGHTLY REVIEW, 117 (1925), 794-803.

MB's skill and wit as a satirist in caricature. Surveys publications and exhibitions.

25019 Shand, John. "Max." In NINETEENTH CENTURY AND AFTER, 132 (1942), 84-87.

MB's even-tempered drama criticism.

25020 Tuell, Anne K. "The Prose of Mr. Beerbohm." In A VICTORIAN AT BAY. Boston: Jones, 1932. Pp. 81-94.

Reviews MB's "more serious work," his personal essays.

ARNOLD BENNETT (1867-1931)

1. PRIMARY BIBLIOGRAPHY

Abbreviations of titles used in this bibliography (if any) are noted at the end of the entry. Books available in recent paperback printings are designated by "(P)."

1.1 Fiction

This section is divided into two parts: (i.) Novels and Story Collections; and (ii.) Collaborations. All works are novels unless otherwise noted. AB's ninety-nine short stories are not itemized here. Emery's bibliography (see 21001) should be consulted for the contents of AB's story collections. The descriptive terms used here (e.g., "sensational," "humorous," "serious") are AB's own.

i. NOVELS AND STORY COLLECTIONS (first collected publication)

11001 ACCIDENT. Garden City, N.Y.: Doubleday, Doran, 1928. London: Cassell, 1929.

"Sensational" novel based on a train wreck.

11002 ANNA OF THE FIVE TOWNS: A NOVEL. London: Chatto and Windus; New York: Doran, 1902.

AB's first novel of "Potteries" life. See 13013.

11003 THE BOOK OF CARLOTTA. See SACRED AND PROFANE LOVE (11039).

11004 BURIED ALIVE: A TALE OF THESE DAYS. London: Chapman and Hall, 1908. Garden City, N.Y.: Doubleday, n.d. [c.1908].

Possibly the best of AB's "humorous" novels. See 13009.

11005 THE CARD: A STORY OF ADVENTURE IN THE FIVE TOWNS. London: Methuen, 1911. Published as DENRY THE AUDACIOUS. New York: Dutton, 1911.

A successful, "humorous" novel. See 22011.

11006 THE CITY OF PLEASURE: A FANTASIA ON MODERN THEMES. London: Chatto and Windus; New York: Doran, 1907.

AB's best "sensational" novel, dealing with a great amusement park.

11007 CLAYHANGER. London: Methuen; New York: Dutton, 1910. (P).

First novel in the Clayhanger trilogy (with HILDA LESSWAYS and THESE TWAIN).

11008 DENRY THE AUDACIOUS. See THE CARD (11005).

11009 "DREAM OF DESTINY: AN UNFINISHED NOVEL" AND "VENUS RISING FROM THE SEA." London: Cassell, 1932. Published as "STROKE OF LUCK" AND "DREAM OF DESTINY: AN UNFINISHED NOVEL." Garden City, N.Y.: Doubleday, Doran, 1932.

AB's last fragment and a novella. VENUS RISING FROM THE SEA also published separately in a limited edition in 1931.

11010 ELSIE AND THE CHILD: A TALE OF RICEYMAN STEPS AND OTHER STORIES. [Stories]. London: Cassell; New York: Doran, 1924.

Collects thirteen stories.

11011 THE GATES OF WRATH: A MELODRAMA. London: Chatto and Windus, 1903. New York: Doran, n.d. [c. 1903].

A "sensational" novel.

11012 THE GHOST: A FANTASIA ON MODERN THEMES. London: Chatto and Windus; Boston: Turner, 1907.

AB's exploitation of occult themes.

11013 THE GLIMPSE: AN ADVENTURE OF THE SOUL. London: Chapman and Hall; New York: Appleton, 1909.

Another occult novel: "simply theosophy, nothing else."

11014 THE GRAND BABYLON HOTEL: A FANTASIA ON MODERN THEMES. London: Chatto and Windus, 1902. Published as T. RACKSOLE AND DAUGHTER. New York: New Amsterdam, 1902. (P).

The great hotel as microcosm. Melodramatic adventure.

11015 A GREAT MAN: A FROLIC. London: Chatto and Windus, 1904. New York: Doran, n.d. [c.1904].

AB's first try at "humorous" fiction.

11016 THE GRIM SMILE OF THE FIVE TOWNS. [Stories]. London: Chapman and Hall, 1907. No Amer. ed.

Collects thirteen stories, including AB's highly-regarded "Death of Simon Fugue" (1907). Also see 11027.

11017 HELEN WITH THE HIGH HAND: AN IDYLLIC DIVERSION. London: Chapman and Hall; New York: Doran, 1910.

A weak, "humorous" novel.

11018 HILDA LESSWAYS. London: Methuen; New York: Dutton, 1911. (P).

Second novel in the Clayhanger trilogy (with CLAYHANGER and THESE TWAIN).

11019 HUGO: A FANTASIA ON MODERN THEMES. London: Chatto and Windus; New York: Buckles, 1906.

Inside view of a great department store.

11020 IMPERIAL PALACE. London: Cassell; Garden City, N.Y.: Doubleday, Doran, 1930.

AB returns to the use of the hotel as microcosm (see GRAND BABYLON HOTEL). Important late novel.

11021 LEONORA: A NOVEL. London: Chatto and Windus, 1903. New York: Doran, n.d. [c. 1903].

A "serious" Five Towns novel.

11022 LILIAN. London: Cassell; New York: Doran, 1922.

A slight "potboiler."

11023 THE LION'S SHARE. London: Cassell; New York: Doran, 1916.

A "light" novel dealing with woman's suffrage.

11024 THE LOOT OF CITIES: BEING THE ADVENTURES OF A MILLIONAIRE IN SEARCH OF JOY (A FANTASIA). [Stories]. London: Rivers, 1905. No Amer. ed.

Six connected fantastic stories. Three additional unrelated stories added to later editions.

11025 LORD RAINGO. London: Cassell; New York: Doran, 1926.

Successful political roman a clef.

11026 A MAN FROM THE NORTH. London and New York: Lane, 1898.

AB's first novel.

11027 THE MATADOR OF THE FIVE TOWNS, AND OTHER STORIES. [Stories]. London: Methuen; New York: Doran, 1912.

Twenty-two stories. The considerably different American edition actually collects a selection of sixteen stories, drawn from the English edition of MATADOR as well as from GRIM SMILE and TALES OF THE FIVE TOWNS.

11028 MR. PROHACK. London: Methuen; New York: Doran, 1922.

A slight comic novel, later successfully dramatized.

11029 THE NIGHT VISITOR, AND OTHER STORIES. [Stories]. London: Cassell; Garden City, N.Y.: Doubleday, 1931.

Seventeen stories.

11030 THE OLD ADAM. See THE REGENT (11036).

11031 THE OLD WIVES' TALE: A NOVEL. London: Chapman and Hall, 1908. New York: Doran, 1911. Abbreviated as OWT.

AB's "masterpiece." AB added a Preface for the American edition which has been retained in most later editions.

11032 THE OLD WIVES' TALE BY ARNOLD BENNETT: REPRODUCED IN FACSIMILE FROM THE AUTHOR'S MANUSCRIPT. London: Benn; New York: Doran, 1927.

A rare facsimile edition of the original manuscript (only 500 copies printed).

11033 "PICCADILLY": STORY OF THE FILM. London: Readers Library, 1929. No Amer. ed.

Film scenario in book form.

11034 THE PRETTY LÁDY: A NOVEL. London: Cassell; New York: Doran, 1918.

Novel of wartime England.

11035 THE PRICE OF LOVE: A TALE. London: Methuen; New York: Harper, 1914.

A "serious" Five Towns novel.

11036 THE REGENT: A FIVE TOWNS STORY OF ADVENTURE IN LONDON. London: Methuen, 1913. Published as THE OLD ADAM: A STORY OF ADVENTURE. New York: Doran, 1913.

"Humorous" sequel to THE CARD (11005).

11037 RICEYMAN STEPS: A NOVEL. London: Cassell; New York: Doran 1923.

This superb later novel is testimony to AB's enduring powers.

11038 THE ROLL-CALL. London: Hutchinson; New York: Doran, 1918.

Related to, but not part of the Clayhanger trilogy (history of Hilda Lessway's son).

11039 SACRED AND PROFANE LOVE: A NOVEL IN THREE EPISODES. London: Chatto and Windus, 1905. Rev. ed. Published as THE BOOK OF CARLOTTA. New York: Doran, 1911.

"Serious" study of a modern woman. See 13013.

11040 THE STRANGE VANGUARD. See THE VANGUARD (11046).

11041 STROKE OF LUCK. See DREAM OF DESTINY (11009).

11042 TALES OF THE FIVE TOWNS. [Stories]. London: Chatto and Windus, 1905. No Amer. ed.

Thirteen stories. Also see 11027.

11043 TERESA OF WATLING STREET: A FANTASIA ON MODERN THEMES. London: Chatto and Windus, 1904. No Amer. ed.

AB's abortive try at detective fiction.

11044 THESE TWAIN. New York: Doran, 1915. London: Methuen, 1916. (P).

Third novel in the Clayhanger trilogy (with CLAYHANGER and HILDA LESSWAYS).

11045 T. RACKSOLE AND DAUGHTER. See GRAND BABYLON HOTEL (11014).

11046 THE VANGUARD: A FANTASIA. New York: Doran, 1927. Published as THE STRANGE VANGUARD: A FANTASIA. London: Cassell, 1928.

A weak tale of a millionaire's adventures.

11047 VENUS RISING FROM THE SEA. See DREAM OF DESTINY (11009).

11048 WHOM GOD HATH JOINED. London: Nutt; New York: Doran, 1906.

A serious polemic against the English divorce law.

11049 THE WOMAN WHO STOLE EVERYTHING, AND OTHER STORIES. [Stories]. London: Cassell; New York: Doran, 1927.

Collects thirteen stories.

ii. COLLABORATIONS

11050 DOUBLOONS. See THE SINEWS OF WAR, below.

11051 THE SINEWS OF WAR: A ROMANCE OF LONDON AND THE SEA (with Eden Phillpotts). London: Laurie, 1906. Published as DOUBLOONS. New York: McClure, Phillips, 1906.

"Sensational" novel.

11052 THE STATUE (with Eden Phillpotts). London: Cassell, 1908. Published as THE STATUE: A STORY OF INTERNATIONAL INTRIGUE AND MYSTERY. New York: Moffat, Yard, 1908.

"Sensational" novel.

1.2 Miscellaneous Writings

Although AB is chiefly remembered for his fiction, he had long and productive careers as a playwright, travel writer, librettist, literary critic, and popular philosopher. What follows is a selection of AB's nonfiction which reflects his critical attitudes, and his most important autobiographical papers. A full listing of AB's miscellaneous writings is to be found in Emery's bibliography (see 21001).

12001 THE AUTHOR'S CRAFT. London: Hodder and Stoughton; New York: Doran, 1914.

Reprinted essays on the art of fiction.

12002 BOOKS AND PERSONS: BEING COMMENTS ON A PAST EPOCH, 1908-1911. London: Chatto and Windus; New York: Doran, 1917.

Collects AB's journalistic essays from the NEW AGE, 1908-1911.

12003 FAME AND FICTION: AN ENQUIRY INTO CERTAIN POPULARITIES. London: Richards; New York: Dutton, 1901.

Drawn from AB's journalistic essays in ACADEMY, 1898-1901.

12004 THE FEAST OF ST. FRIEND. London: Hodder and Stoughton; New York: Doran, 1911.

An agnostic's view of Christmas.

12005 FLORENTINE JOURNAL, 1ST APRIL-25TH MAY 1910. Ed. Dorothy Cheston Bennett. London: Chatto and Windus, 1967. No Amer. ed.

Recently released section of the journals.

12006 HOW TO BECOME AN AUTHOR: A PRACTICAL GUIDE. London: Pearson, 1903. No Amer. ed.

Literary handbook for aspiring writers.

12007 JOURNAL, 1929. London: Cassell, 1930. Published as JOURNAL OF THINGS NEW AND OLD. Garden City, N.Y.: Doubleday, Doran, 1930.

12008 THE JOURNALS OF ARNOLD BENNETT. Ed. Newman Flower. 3 vols. London: Cassell, 1932-33. Slightly altered ed. 3 vols. New York: Viking, 1932-33.

Covers 1896-1928. Selected from AB's still largely unpublished journal volumes.

12009 LITERARY TASTE: HOW TO FORM IT; WITH DETAILED INSTRUCTIONS FOR COLLECTING A COMPLETE LIBRARY OF ENGLISH LITERATURE. London: New Age, 1909. New York: Doran, 1927.

The only one of AB's many books of self-improvement which deals significantly with literature and criticism.

12010 THINGS THAT HAVE INTERESTED ME. Series 1-3. London: Chatto and Windus; New York: Doran, 1921, 1923, 1926.

Eclectic collections of AB's journalism (121, 68, and 39 essays, respectively).

12011 THE TRUTH ABOUT AN AUTHOR. Westminster, Engl.: Constable, 1903. New York: Doran, 1911.

Autobiography. First English edition published anonymously.

1.3 Collected and Selected Works

13001 ARNOLD BENNETT: THE JOURNALS. Ed. Frank Swinnerton. Harmondsworth, Engl.: Penguin, 1971.

A selection from the collected editions of the JOURNALS (1896-1929), supplemented with newly published fragments (1906-7) and the FLORENTINE JOURNAL (1910). See 22025.

13002 THE ARNOLD BENNETT OMNIBUS BOOK. London: Cassell, 1931.

Includes RICEYMAN STEPS, "Elsie and the Child," LORD RAINGO, and ACCIDENT.

13003 "THE AUTHOR'S CRAFT," AND OTHER CRITICAL WRITINGS OF ARNOLD BENNETT. Ed. Samuel Hynes. Lincoln: Univ. of Nebraska Press, 1968. (P).

Anthology of AB's critical journalism. See 25038.

13004 THE CLAYHANGER FAMILY. London: Methuen, 1925.

Includes the Clayhanger trilogy: CLAYHANGER, HILDA LESSWAYS, and THESE TWAIN.

13005 THE COLLECTED WORKS OF ARNOLD BENNETT. 91 vols. Plainview, N.Y.: Books for Libraries Press, 1975.

Includes the novels, collaborations, drama, nonfiction, and journals, reprinted from their various original editions (mostly the first American editions). Intended and priced for libraries.

13006 ESSAYS OF TO-DAY AND YESTERDAY. London: Harrap, 1926.

Collects eight representative literary and "philosophical" essays.

13007 THE "EVENING STANDARD" YEARS: "BOOKS AND PERSONS," 1926-1931. Ed. Andrew Mylett. London: Chatto and Windus, 1974.

Some of AB's latest journalism.

13008 HOW TO LIVE: CONTAINING, "HOW TO LIVE ON TWENTY-FOUR HOURS A DAY"; "THE HUMAN MACHINE"; "MENTAL EFFICIENCY"; "SELF AND SELF-MANAGEMENT." Garden City, N.Y.: Garden City, 1925.

Collects AB's four most successful "pocket philosophies."

13009 MILESTONES (with E. Knoblock); THE GREAT ADVENTURE. London: Methuen, 1926.

Two of AB's most successful plays (1912, 1913). THE GREAT ADVENTURE is an adaption of BURIED ALIVE (11004).

13010 THE MINERVA EDITION OF THE WORKS OF ARNOLD BENNETT. 7 vols. London: Library Press, 1926.

Includes ANNA OF THE FIVE TOWNS, TERESA OF WATLING STREET, A GREAT MAN, WHOM GOD HATH JOINED, BURIED ALIVE, THE CARD, and THE REGENT.

13011 SHORT STORIES OF TO-DAY AND YESTERDAY. [Stories]. London: Harrap, 1928.

Recollects ten stories from earlier story collections.

13012 TALES OF THE FIVE TOWNS, INCLUDING "THE GRIM SMILE OF THE FIVE TOWNS." London: Chatto and Windus, 1964.

Combines two of AB's story collections (11042, 11016).

13013 THREE PLAYS. London: Chatto and Windus, 1931.

Includes THE BRIGHT ISLAND (1924), CUPID AND COMMONSENSE (1909--an adaptation of ANNA OF THE FIVE TOWNS), and SACRED AND PROFANE LOVE (1919--an adaptation of the novel of the same name).

1.4 Letters

Also see Davis (23003), Farmer (22008), and Harris (22013), below.

14001 ARNOLD BENNETT: A PORTRAIT DONE AT HOME. Comp. Dorothy Cheston Bennett. New York: Kendall and Sharp, 1935. Pp. 163-350.

Reprints 170 letters from AB as an appendix to a memoir. See 22003.

14002 ARNOLD BENNETT AND H.G. WELLS: A RECORD OF A PERSONAL AND A LITERARY FRIENDSHIP. Ed. Harris Wilson. Urbana: Univ. of Illinois Press, 1960.

See 22028.

14003 ARNOLD BENNETT IN LOVE: ARNOLD BENNETT AND HIS WIFE MARGUERITE SOULIE: A CORRESPONDENCE. Ed. and trans. George and Jean Beardmore. London: Bruce and Watson, 1972.

14004 ARNOLD BENNETT'S LETTERS TO HIS NEPHEW. Ed. Richard Bennett. London: Heinemann, 1936.

14005 LETTERS OF ARNOLD BENNETT. Ed. James G. Hepburn. London and New York: Oxford Univ. Press, 1966-- .

To be completed in four volumes: I, LETTERS TO J.B. PINKER (1966); II, 1889-1915 (1968); III, 1916-1931 (1970); and IV, letters to family (in preparation). Absorbs the other editions and printings of AB's letters.

2. SECONDARY BIBLIOGRAPHY

Note: ARNOLD BENNETT NEWSLETTER (1975--) is a new journal devoted to bibliographical, biographical, and critical materials related to AB and his associates (especially H.G. Wells).

2.1 Bibliographies

*21001 Emery, Norman, comp. ARNOLD BENNETT (1867-1931): A BIBLIOGRAPHY. Hanley, Stoke-on-Trent, Engl.: Central Library, 1967.

A primary bibliography of AB's novels, stories, plays, "pocket philosophies," literary criticism, and other writings. Usefully subdivided by subject matter, with appendixes for cross-references. The bibliographical information is, however, frequently limited to English publication data.

21002 Farmer, David R. "The Bibliographical Potential of a 20th Century Literary Agent's Archives: The Pinker Papers." LCUT, 2 (Nov. 1970), 27-35.

Describes papers of importance on AB and others recently acquired by the Univ. of Texas.

*21003 Gordan, John D. ARNOLD BENNETT: THE CENTENARY OF HIS BIRTH: AN EXHIBITION IN THE BERG COLLECTION. New York: New York Public Library, 1968. From BNYPL, 72 (1968), 72-122.

Detailed chronology of AB's career and survey of the Berg collection of manuscripts, early editions, and letters. Provides considerable useful background information on AB's immense variety of works.

21004 Hepburn, James G., comp. "Arnold Bennett Manuscripts and Rare Books: A List of Holdings." EFT [now ELT] 1, No. 2 (1958), 23-29.

A census of public and private holdings.

21005 Hepburn, James G., et al., comps. "Arnold Bennett." EFT [now ELT] 1, No. 1 (1957), 8-12 and continuing.

Annotated secondary bibliography, supplemented regularly. See G1404.

*21005a Miller, Anita, ed. ARNOLD BENNETT: AN ANNOTATED BIBLIOGRAPHY, 1887-1932. New York: Garland, 1976.

Full descriptive primary bibliography. Miller provides extensive information on all AB's publications, including his heretofore uncataloged contributions to English and American periodicals, and a lengthy introduction surveying AB's critical reputation.

21006 Riemer, Werner W., comp. "Arnold Bennett: A Check List of Secondary Literature." BNYPL, 77 (1974), 342-57.

Lists 412 items in three categories: books and pamphlets, articles and chapters in books, and dissertations. No annotation.

21007 Wiley, Paul L., comp. "Arnold Bennett (1867-1931)." In his THE BRITISH NOVEL. Pp. 17-19. See G1419.

Brief primary and secondary checklist.

2.2 Biographies, Memoirs, Reminiscences

22001 Atkins, John B. INCIDENTS AND REFLECTIONS. London: Christophers, 1947. Pp. 174-82.

Memories of friendship with AB in Paris.

22002 Barker, Dudley. WRITER BY TRADE: A VIEW OF ARNOLD BENNETT. London: Allen and Unwin, 1966.

A commercial biography of little value. Although Barker tells the story of AB pleasantly enough, he has litte to contribute to the information already available in Pound's biography (see 22019). Moreover, Drabble's biography (see 22007) more effectively creates the portrait of AB's private life. As do the other biographers, Barker avoids critical judgment of AB's work.

*22003 Bennett, Dorothy Cheston. ARNOLD BENNETT: A PORTRAIT DONE AT HOME. New York: Kendall and Sharp, 1935.

A personal portrait of AB by his second wife, covering the years 1922-31. Mrs. Bennett, AB's "private analyzer," emphasizes the psychological complexities of AB's personality. The second half of her book collects 170 letters from AB to her, with some slight annotation (see 14001).

22004 Bennett, Marguerite. ARNOLD BENNETT. New York: Adelphi, 1925.

Largely an account of AB's personal habits by his first wife. Informal, anecdotal, and, in light of its publishing circumstances, often in bad taste (at the time of its writing AB had left Marguerite, fallen in love with Dorothy Cheston, and been denied a divorce).

22005 ______. MY ARNOLD BENNETT. New York: Dutton, 1932.

Similar to above. The first Mrs. Bennett's possessiveness of her husband (evident in her chosen title) and contempt for his frailties of character suffuse her narrative. Their years of separation are glossed over with scarce mention.

22006 Doran, George H. "The Old Friend's Tale." In CHRONICLES OF BARABBAS, 1884-1934. FURTHER CHRONICLES AND COMMENT, 1952. New York: Rinehart, 1952. Pp. 125-48.

Memoirs of AB's chief American publisher and personal friend.

*22007 Drabble, Margaret. ARNOLD BENNETT: A BIOGRAPHY. New York: Knopf, 1974.

A useful supplement to Pound's standard biography (see 22019, below). Drabble, like Pound, reviews the facts of AB's career in her narrative and generally avoids critical commentary, but her emphasis falls on his "background, his childhood and origins, for they are very similar to my own." AB emerges as a complex figure, deeply affected by his lower middle class, Methodist, "potteries" upbringing, who achieved stability and adjustment, as well as literary triumph. Drabble's strengths are her gifted style (she is herself a novelist of distinction), her sympathy for her subject, and her enthusiasm for his work.

22008 Farmer, A.J. "Arnold Bennett Seen Through His Correspondence." EA, 25 (1972), 395-407.

Appreciative review of AB generally, and of Hepburn's edition of the letters (see 14005).

22009 Flower, Newman. JUST AS IT HAPPENED. London: Cassell, 1950. Pp. 157-68.

Brief reminiscences by AB's friend and sometime publisher.

22010 Ford, J.R., et al. ARNOLD BENNETT CENTENARY, 1867-1967. Stoke-on-Trent, Engl.: City of Stoke-on-Trent, 1967.

Pamphlet brochure issued by AB's home town on the occasion of his centenary celebrations. Includes photographs, a calendar of events, a summary of AB's career, and four brief essays on AB.

22011 Hales, Harold K. THE AUTOBIOGRAPHY OF "THE CARD." London: Low, Marston, 1936.

Memoir of AB's childhood friend and self-proclaimed model for THE CARD. Some views of AB in early youth and at school.

22012 Haresnape, Geoffrey. "Pauline Smith and Arnold Bennett." ESA, 6 (1963), 144-48.

Smith's dependent relationship with AB. See 22024.

22013 Harris, Frank. FRANK HARRIS TO ARNOLD BENNETT: FIFTY-EIGHT LETTERS, 1908-1910. Merion Station, Pa.: Privately Printed [by American Autograph Shop], 1936.

Pamphlet collection which documents the Harris-Bennett relationship.

*22014 Hepburn, James G. "Introduction." In LETTERS OF ARNOLD BENNETT. Vol. 1. LETTERS TO J.B. PINKER. Pp. 1-28. See 14005.

Good introduction to AB's letters, his early career, and his relationship with Pinker (his agent).

22015 Hunt, Viola. "Arnold Bennett in Paris." BOOKMAN (New York), 75 (1932), 345-48.

Brief, equivocal memoir.

22016 Mackenzie, Norman, and Jeanne Mackenzie. H.G. WELLS: A BIOGRAPHY. New York: Simon and Schuster, 1973. Passim.

AB's literary and personal relationships with Wells.

22017 Marriott, Frederick. MY ASSOCIATION WITH ARNOLD BENNETT. Staffordshire, Engl.: Univ. of Keele, 1967.

Centenary issue of the previously unpublished memoir (c. 1931) of a life-long friend. Contains interesting comments on AB's early years as a writer, his working methods, and his character.

22018 Maugham, W. Somerset. "Some Novelists I Have Known." In THE VAGRANT MOOD: SIX ESSAYS. Garden City, N.Y.: Doubleday, 1953. Pp. 229-43.

Generally fond memories of AB in Paris, with praise for OWT and some contempt for AB's "commonness."

*22019 Pound, Reginald. ARNOLD BENNETT: A BIOGRAPHY. London: Heinemann, 1952.

The standard, scholarly biography of AB. Pound excellently describes the rise to fame and the public years of AB as journalist, social lion and man of letters. Pound is most valuable for his correction of AB's reputation as a methodical, businessman-novelist. Rather, AB is seen as a somewhat harried journalist, a driven man, of more psychological complexity than generally assumed. For a useful supplementary perspective on AB, also see Drabble, 22007, above.

22020 Ravenscroft, Arthur. "Pauline Smith." REL, 4, No. 2 (1963), 55-66.

Brief biographical sketch of a close acquaintance of AB.

22021 Roberts, R. Ellis. "Arnold Bennett." NINETEENTH CENTURY AND AFTER, 109 (1931), 613-24.

Obituary tribute and memoir of a one-year acquaintance.

22022 Roberts, Thomas R. ARNOLD BENNETT'S FIVE TOWNS ORIGINS. Stoke-on-Trent, Engl.: Libraries, Museums, and Information Committee, 1961.

Pamphlet account of AB's family background (from 1624) and early childhood.

22023 Sitwell, Osbert. "Arnold Bennett." In NOBLE ESSENCES. Boston: Little, Brown, 1950. Pp. 317-34.

Memoir of meetings with AB (1918 and after).

22024 Smith, Pauline. A.B., " . . . A MINOR MARGINAL NOTE." London: Cape, 1933.

Memoir by a longtime friend and protege.

22025 Swinnerton, Frank. "Introduction." In ARNOLD BENNETT: THE JOURNALS. Pp. 5-15. See 13001.

Brief biographical summary.

22026 Warrilow, E.J.D. ARNOLD BENNETT AND STOKE-ON-TRENT. Stoke-on-Trent, Engl.: Etruscan Publications, 1966.

Photographic guide to the "Bennett country" and identifications of the landmarks in several of the Five-Towns fictions. Frequently careless in detail and poorly organized, but informative.

22027 Wells, H.G. EXPERIMENT IN AUTOBIOGRAPHY. New York: Macmillan, 1934. Pp. 533-40.

Reminiscences and critique of AB. Wells knew AB well from the 1890's on.

22028 Wilson, Harris. "Introduction." In ARNOLD BENNETT AND H.G. WELLS. Pp. 11-31. See 14002.

A summary of the Bennett-Wells personal and literary relationship, from 1897 on.

2.3 Book-Length Critical Studies and Essay Collections

23001 Allen, Walter. ARNOLD BENNETT. Denver: Swallow, 1949.

A brief biographical summary and critical study. Allen considers OWT AB's masterpiece--a stylistic, imaginative, and technical triumph, a "tremendous feat." CLAYHANGER is a fine novel of adolescent development (cf. THE WAY OF ALL FLESH) but HILDA LESSWAYS and THESE TWAIN are a "comparative failure."

23002 Darton, F.J. Harvey. ARNOLD BENNETT. New York: Holt, 1915.

Early "writers of the day" critique. Darton's commonplace assumption that a novelist "must reveal himself willy-nilly" in his work often reduces his commentaries to biographical remarks, although he does occasionally offer fine critical observations. Includes bibliography of AB's works to 1914.

23003 Davis, Oswald H. THE MASTER: A STUDY OF ARNOLD BENNETT. London: Johnson, 1966.

Originally written c. 1945. The only study of AB which comments at length on the criticism, pocket philosophies, journals, journalism, collaborations, and drama. Davis, nonetheless, reserves most of his space, and admiration, for the fiction. AB is praised for his mastery of technique (from a Jamesian perspective). Davis argues valuably against the prevalent decline theory for AB's career (see Geoffrey West below), asserting that the late works, though weaker, are "expressions of his fecund versatility." Prefaced by a memoir of a visit to AB and twelve letters to Davis from AB.

23004 Follett, Helen Thomas, et al. ARNOLD BENNETT: APPRECIATIONS. WITH A GUIDE TO THE AUTHOR OF THE FIVE TOWNS. New York: Doran, n.d. [c. 1924].

Includes an essay by Grant Overton ("The Phenomenon of Arnold Bennett"), excerpts from the studies of J.W. Cunliffe and Helen and Wilson Follett (see 24018 and 24028), and a brief annotated list of AB's works.

*23005 Hall, James. ARNOLD BENNETT: PRIMITIVISM AND TASTE. Seattle: Univ. of Washington Press, 1959.

Important assessment of AB's place in the tradition of modern fiction. Hall sees AB, like Mann, Forster, the early Lawrence, Conrad, and R.P. Warren, as a novelist preoccupied by the divisions between the two worlds of aristocratic and primitive values, who is "intensely desirous of reconciling the two by taking the best from both." In his most successful fiction (OWT and the Clayhanger trilogy--the works chiefly studied here), AB employs an archetype of exile and return (the Joseph myth) in an attempt to mediate between the "aspiration to aristocracy" and the "appreciation of middle-class vitality." Excellent thesis, well supported and convincingly argued.

*23006 Hepburn, James G. THE ART OF ARNOLD BENNETT. Bloomington: Indiana Univ. Press, 1963.

The most important single study of AB's fiction. Hepburn argues persuasively against the traditional view of AB as a realist, asserting that his "main task was [not] to describe the social scene." Rather, AB is "equally a psychological realist, a symbolist, an allegorist . . . a discoverer of beauty." Hepburn ranges widely among the works of demonstrate AB's "Psychological Realism," his uses of "Symbol, Image and Reality" (and their vital interrelationship), his use of the allegorical mode, and other literary devices. This thesis is excellently illustrated throughout by intelligent and sensitive analyses of the novels. Hepburn includes two valuable appendixes: "The Supposed Unevenness of Bennett's Work"; and "Gestation and Composition; Chronology of Composition" as well as an extremely useful primary and secondary bibliography.

23007 Johnson, L.G. ARNOLD BENNETT OF THE FIVE TOWNS. London: Daniel, 1924.

Study of the "Five Towns" novels and stories, with special emphasis on ANNA OF THE FIVE TOWNS, the Clayhanger Trilogy, and OWT. AB is seen as a realist and provincial novelist, consumed with the faithful record of detail and local color, who nevertheless achieves, in his finest fiction, the universality of art. Still a useful book.

*23008 Lafourcade, Georges. ARNOLD BENNETT: A STUDY. London: Muller, 1939.

Highly admiring critical study of AB as a modern "classicist," representative of the continued high regard for AB among the French. ANNA OF THE FIVE TOWNS, LEONORA, WHOM GOD HATH JOINED, the "Aeschylean" Clayhanger trilogy, RICEYMAN STEPS, THE PRETTY LADY, LORD RAINGO, and IMPERIAL PALACE are all regarded as nearly equal and at times superior to OWT. AB is neither a romantic "wearing a mask," nor a realist, but is firmly within the classical tradition (e.g., Racine, Pope, Voltaire) as a "highly rational and selective artist." Although occasionally overly enthusiastic, Lafourcade offers a highly persuasive defense of AB's conscious artistry. A valuable study of the source materials for OWT and a useful primary bibliography are added as appendixes.

*23009 Lucas, John. ARNOLD BENNETT: A STUDY OF HIS FICTION. London: Methuen, 1974.

A full, chronological study of AB's fiction, reserving considerable space for analysis and evaluation of the major novels. Lucas attributes AB's mixed critical reputation to the difficulty of discussing his fictional achievement. AB defies easy analysis as a realist, a formalist, a naturalist, or a symbolist, for example, because his philosophy and his technique are subordinated, when successful, to his subject matter: "It is life itself" (quoting James on Turgenev). With qualifications, Lucas finds AB's "best work" in ANNA OF THE FIVE TOWNS, WHOM GOD HATH JOINED, OWT, THE CARD, THE PRICE OF LOVE, the Clayhanger trilogy (although HILDA LESSWAYS is weaker than CLAYHANGER and THESE TWAIN), RICEYMAN STEPS, LORD RAINGO, and IMPERIAL PALACE. Intelligent, judicious, and often perceptive readings.

23010 Roby, Kinley E. A WRITER AT WAR: ARNOLD BENNETT, 1914-1918. Baton Rouge: Louisiana State Univ. Press, 1972.

Literary history and biographical account of AB's activities (1914-18), arguing, along with Davis (see 23003), a revaluation of AB's work after 1914. AB's career follows a pattern of achievement (OWT, 1908), crisis (the war), and renewed distinction (e.g., RICEYMAN STEPS and LORD RAINGO, 1923, 1926), which is paralleled in his personal life by the break-up of his marriage, his nearly fatal illnesses, and his revival of powers. Although Roby offers little critical interpretation of the work, his book has much value as a concentrated view of a climatic period in AB's career.

23011 Simons, J.B. ARNOLD BENNETT AND HIS NOVELS: A CRITICAL STUDY. Oxford: Blackwell, 1936.

Highly admiring critical assessment of AB's novels and short fiction together with an expansive survey of his literary heritage (French, Russian, and English) and his critical reputation. Simons's commentaries are weakened by his too ready assumption that AB's works are autobiographical or "self-revealing," yet he offers several critiques of works that are now largely ignored.

23012 Swinnerton, Frank. ARNOLD BENNETT. 1950. Rev. ed. London: Longmans, 1961.

Pamphlet critique. Swinnerton traces the Staffordshire "spirit" in AB's life and work: "Pride of craft, pride in uncommon wisdom, pride in prosperity, gave the whole county an assurance of being and making the best there was in England." Includes a brief annotated primary and secondary bibliography.

*23013 Tillier, Louis. STUDIES IN THE SOURCES OF ARNOLD BENNETT'S NOVELS. Paris: M. Didier, 1969.

Important discussion of sources in AB's experience and reading for twelve of the novels, "to reach a more exact estimate of his originality and gain a closer insight into the creative processes of his imaginiation." Tillier is most valuable for his exhaustive studies of the evolution of OWT ("original idea," "French literary influences," "The Siege of Paris"), the "sociological research" behind CLAYHANGER, the "genesis" of RICEYMAN STEPS, and the roman-a-clef elements of LORD RAINGO.

23014 Wain, John. ARNOLD BENNETT. New York: Columbia Univ. Press, 1967.

Highly admiring pamphlet critique. Wain, a distinguished novelist himself, supports the traditional view of AB as a consummate realist working within the tradition of Continental (especially French) fiction. Wain's essay (together with Allen's book and Drabble's biography noted in section 2.2 above) testifies to AB's enduring significance as a novelist's novelist and as a strong influence upon recent British fiction. Includes bibliographical checklist.

23015 West, Geoffrey [Geoffrey Wells]. THE PROBLEM OF ARNOLD BENNETT. London: Joiner and Steele, 1932.

Investigates the dual reputation of AB and seeks to account for the "absolute gulf between the best, and the rest, of his work." West dates AB's decline from the war, after which his genius was "incapable of further growth or even of sustaining itself alive." After OWT, AB was content to concentrate on the externals of technique, the surfaces of things. An articulate early statement of the AB "problem."

23016 West, Rebecca. ARNOLD BENNETT HIMSELF. New York: Day, 1931.

Pamphlet obituary tribute, praising AB's craft and his novels' celebration of life.

23017 Wright, Walter F. ARNOLD BENNETT: ROMANTIC REALIST. Lincoln: Univ. of Nebraska Press, 1971.

Study of AB's fiction, nonfiction, and personal philosophy, governed by the thesis that AB's temperamental attraction toward the romantic view of life exists in conflict with his intellectual acceptance of the bleaker, realistic vision he inherited from his French and Russian masters. Wright's first four chapters expound this thesis and explore its implications for his literary criticism and own "Practice of His Craft." The last two chapters classify and summarily discuss the romantic and realistic fictions.

23018 Young, Kenneth. ARNOLD BENNETT. London: Longmans, 1976.

Introduction to the "writer and his work." (Pamphlet--not seen.)

2.4 General Critical Articles, or Chapters on AB

24001 Allen, Walter. THE ENGLISH NOVEL. Pp. 381-88 and passim. See G2201.

Survey of AB at his best, as a regional novelist (e.g., OWT, Clayhanger trilogy).

24002 Baker, Ernest A. THE HISTORY OF THE ENGLISH NOVEL. X, 288-318. See G2203.

Balanced survey and assessment of AB's career, stressing his craftsmanship and his businesslike approach to art.

24003 Beach, Joseph Warren. "Variations: Bennett." In his THE TWENTIETH-CENTURY NOVEL. Pp. 231-45. See G3004.

AB's techniques, form, and style.

24004 Beerbohm, Max. "Scruts, by Arn*ld B*nn*tt." In A CHRISTMAS GARLAND. London: Heinemann, 1912. Pp. 85-99.

Amusing parody of AB's five-towns "sagas."

*24005 Bellamy, William. THE NOVELS OF WELLS, BENNETT, AND GALSWORTHY. Pp. 71-87, 144-64, and passim. See G3007.

The transition from fin de siecle fiction, which concerns itself largely with the "post-Darwinian cultural crisis" (AB's MAN FROM THE NORTH), to the "utopianization" of experience in the Edwardian fiction. Wells, AB, and Galsworthy emerge, rather strangely, as modern existentialists who have assimilated Darwinism, "learning to live with human animality" (AB's OWT and CLAYHANGER).

24006 Bentley, Phyllis. THE ENGLISH REGIONAL NOVEL. Pp. 29-33 and passim. See G3009.

AB the "most complete" regional novelist.

24007 Braybrooke, Patrick. "Arnold Bennett." In his PHILOSOPHIES IN MODERN FICTION. London: Daniel, 1929. Pp. 23-28.

AB's philosophical "sadness" nears despair.

24008 Bullett, Gerald. "Arnold Bennett." In his MODERN ENGLISH FICTION. Pp. 34-45. See G3018.

Brief critical survey.

24009 Byrne, M. St.-Claire. "Arnold Bennett and His Critics." NATIONAL REVIEW, 96 (1931), 702-6.

Disputes Woolf (24083) and supports AB's conception of the novelist's art.

*24010 Campos, Christophe. "Watch the Woman (Arnold Bennett)." In THE VIEW OF FRANCE FROM ARNOLD TO BLOOMSBURY. New York: Oxford Univ. Press, 1965. Pp. 193-207.

AB's views of France (Paris) from his journals, memoirs, and OWT.

24011 Chesterton, G.K. "The Mercy of Mr. Arnold Bennett." In FANCIES VERSUS FADS. London: Methuen, 1923. Pp. 86-92.

AB's "mercy," or dogmatic dismissal of dogmatism, actually an abdication of moral responsibility.

24012 Chevalley, Abel. "Arnold Bennett." In his THE MODERN ENGLISH NOVEL. Pp. 166-75. See G3023.

General overview.

24013 Collins, Arthur S. "Arnold Bennett." In ENGLISH LITERATURE OF THE TWENTIETH CENTURY. Pp. 155-62. See G2105.

General survey.

24014 Conacher, W.M. "Arnold Bennett and the French Realists." QQ, 56 (1949), 409-17.

AB's style less "French" than his analyses of thought and feeling in character (e.g., CLAYHANGER).

24015 Cooper, Frederic Taber. "Arnold Bennett." In his SOME ENGLISH STORY TELLERS. Pp. 206-31. See G3027.

Interesting mid-career assessment.

24016 Cox, Sidney H. "Romance in Arnold Bennett." SR, 28 (1920), 358-66.

Despite the "dreary world" of his novels, AB reflects the attitudes and language of romance in his fiction.

24017 Cross, Wilbur J. "Arnold Bennett." In his FOUR CONTEMPORARY NOVELISTS. Pp. 63-98. See G3029.

AB's multiple personalities, from businessman and journalist to innovative novelist.

24018 Cunliffe, J.W. "Arnold Bennett (1867-1931)." In his ENGLISH LITERATURE IN THE TWENTIETH CENTURY. Pp. 185-200. See G2106.

Critical survey and brief bibliography. Extract reprinted in 23004.

24019 Curtin, Frank D. "Arnold Bennett, and After." In IF BY YOUR ART. Ed. Agnes Starrett. Pittsburgh: Univ. of Pittsburgh Press, 1948. Pp. 117-36.

AB's masterpieces testify to the validity of his documentary realism (contra Virginia Woolf).

24020 Decker, Clarence R. THE VICTORIAN CONSCIENCE. New York: Twayne, 1952. Pp. 164-67.

Influence of French naturalism on AB, via Zola.

24021 Downs, Brian W. "Arnold Bennett." NORTH AMERICAN REVIEW, 219 (1924), 71-81.

AB's "catholicity and tolerance of outlook" (surveys works).

*24022 Drew, Elizabeth A. "Arnold Bennett." In her THE MODERN NOVEL. Pp. 199-219. See G3035.

Praises AB's craftsmanship.

24023 Dutton, George B. "Arnold Bennett, Showman." SR, 34 (1952), 64-72.

AB's flair for melodrama.

24024 Eagleton, Terry. EXILES AND EMIGRES. Pp. 71-76. See G3039.

AB as a middle-brow, provincial novelist.

24025 Edgar, Pelham. "Arnold Bennett." In his THE ART OF THE NOVEL. Pp. 238-43. See G2205.

AB's Englishness remains, despite his deep immersion in the continental tradition.

24026 Elwin, Malcolm. "Arnold Bennett: The Card of Genius." In OLD GODS FALLING. New York: Macmillan, 1939. Pp. 329-62.

Biographical and critical survey, praising both AB's serious fiction and his "brilliant" entertainments.

24027 Ervine, St. John G. "Arnold Bennett." In SOME IMPRESSIONS OF MY ELDERS. New York: Macmillan, 1922. Pp. 61-89.

Finds in AB an "ineradicable desire for romance," despite his "hard and fact-ridden style."

24028 Follett, Helen Thomas, and Wilson Follett. "Arnold Bennett." In their SOME MODERN NOVELISTS. Pp. 206-32. See G3043.

Despite his weaknesses, AB does successfully convey his philosophy of life: that experience is the "only teacher of meaning in life." Surveys work. Extract reprinted in 23004.

*24029 Frierson, William C. "Arnold Bennett." In his THE ENGLISH NOVEL IN TRANSITION. Pp. 149-58. See G3047.

AB an objective naturalist, chronicling man's inhumanity to man.

24030 Goldring, Douglas. "The Gordon Selfridge of English Letters." In REPUTATIONS: ESSAYS IN CRITICISM. New York: Seltzer, 1920. Pp. 147-56.

AB the most successful "big businessman" of modern writers. Condescending.

24031 Guedalla, Philip. "Mr. Arnold Bennett." In A GALLERY. New York: Putnam's 1924. Pp. 70-76.

Facetious appreciation. AB's critical reputation has suffered from his popularity.

24032 Harding, J.N. "The Puritanism of Arnold Bennett." ContempR, 180 (1951), 107-12.

AB's best fiction unconsciously reflects the puritan heritage he rejected.

24033 Hepburn, James G. THE AUTHOR'S EMPTY PURSE AND THE RISE OF THE LITERARY AGENT. Pp. 56-65, 89-92, 95-98, and passim. See G2337.

AB's various relations with literary agents, especially his long-time association with G.B. Pinker.

24034 Hoffmann, Richard. "Proportion and Incident in Joseph Conrad and Arnold Bennett." SR, 32 (1924), 79-92.

AB's naturalistic use of detail compared to Conrad's impressionism.

*24035 Howells, William Dean. "Speaking of Mr. Bennett." HARPER'S, 122 (1911), 633-36.

Early recognition of AB's paradoxical dual nature: "Apparently there are two selves of the one novelist who are simultaneously writing fiction entirely opposed in theory and practice."

24036 Hughes, Dorothea P. "The Novels of Mr. Arnold Bennett and Wesleyan Methodism." ContempR, 110 (1916), 602-10.

AB's hatred of Methodism distorts his perspective.

*24037 Hynes, Samuel. "The Whole Contention Between Mr. Bennett and Mrs. Woolf." In his EDWARDIAN OCCASIONS. Pp. 24-38. See G2345.

The public and personal quarrel between AB and Woolf reflects the conflict between popular and coterie art.

24038 James, Henry. NOTES ON NOVELISTS. London: Dent, 1914. Pp. 317-39.

AB's weaknesses with technique, not matter. AB considered together with Wells, Gilbert Cannan, and others among the "new novelists."

24039 Jones, W.S. Handley. "The Card from the Five Towns." In his THE PRIEST AND THE SIREN. Pp. 79-95. See G6306.

AB an artful "show-off" and a "vulgar writer," yet a serious moralist in his best fiction.

24040 Kennedy, James G. "Arnold Bennett: Kunstler and Burger." EFT [now ELT], 5, No. 2 (1962), 1-20.

AB's two roles: artist and businessman novelist.

*24041 ______. "Reassuring Facts in THE PRETTY LADY, LORD RAINGO, and Modern Novels." ELT, 7 (1964), 131-42.

AB uses facts from his own experience to reassure the reader of the reality of his fiction (e.g., PRETTY LADY, LORD RAINGO).

*24042 ______. "Voynich, Bennett, and Tressell: Two Alternatives for Realism in the Transition Age." ELT, 13 (1970), 254-86.

The meaning and validity of the "epithets" of "realism" and "naturalism."

24043 Knight, Grant C. THE NOVEL IN ENGLISH. Pp. 326-32. See G2207.

Survey and brief critique.

24044 Lovett, Robert M., and Helen S. Hughes. "Arnold Bennett (1867-1931)." In their THE HISTORY OF THE NOVEL IN ENGLAND. Pp. 388-93. See G2209.

Brief summary of career.

24045 MacCarthy, Desmond. "Bennett, Wells and Trollope." In MEMORIES. New York: Oxford Univ. Press, 1953. Pp. 21-30.

Comparison of three businessmen novelists whose reputations have suffered similar declines.

24046 ______. "The Popularity of Mr. A.B." LIVING AGE, 291 (1916), 251-54.

AB "one of the few good novelists who is really popular" (cf. Wells).

24047 McIntyre, Carla F. "Arnold Bennett and Old Age." Person, 4 (1923), 31-38.

AB's obsession with the passage of time and the "horrors of growing old."

24048 Martin, Wallace. "THE NEW AGE" UNDER ORAGE: CHAPTERS IN ENGLISH CULTURAL HISTORY. New York: Barnes and Noble, 1967. Passim.

AB a critic and arbiter of taste in his NEW AGE "Books and Persons" columns (1908-11).

24049 Mencken, H.L. "Arnold Bennett." In PREJUDICES: FIRST SERIES. New York: Knopf, 1919. Pp. 36-51.

AB's consistent irony and "unmitigated" skepticism. Selective appreciation.

24050 Muir, Edwin. "Arnold Bennett." In SCRUTINIES. Ed. Edgell Rickword. London: Wishart, 1928. I, 16-27.

General critical estimate.

24051 Muller, Herbert J. "Realism of the Center: Arnold Bennett." In his MODERN FICTION: A STUDY OF VALUES. Pp. 226-32. See G3111.

Most of AB's works can be dismissed, although OWT is a masterpiece of literary realism.

24052 Munro, John M. "'Byzantium' or the Imperial Palace?: Ultimate Vision or Variable Compromise?" VENTURE, 5 (Apr. 1968), 93-105.

Compares Yeats's ideal of the reconciled, unity of being, and AB's ideal of compromise.

24053 Myers, Walter L. THE LATER REALISM. Passim. See G3112.

AB's experimentation with and refinement of realistic methods of characterization into the modern period.

*24054 Nicholson, Norman. "Arnold Bennett." In his MAN AND LITERATURE. Pp. 40-48. See G2353.

AB's fiction "one of the best products of a materialist age--honest, accurate, vivid, detailed, and made with that joy in reproducing the appearance of reality which is found also in the painting of the Impressionists."

24055 Nishimura, Shigeshi. "On the Misers in Arnold Bennett's Novels." SEL (Tokyo), 13 (1933), 527-38.

AB's misers seen in the light of William James's theories of the character type.

24056 Overton, Grant. "Audacious Mr. Bennett." In WHEN WINTER COMES TO MAIN STREET. New York: Doran, 1922. Pp. 133-51.

AB's audacious attempts to portray the truths of modern life (e.g., love and marriage in LILIAN and MR. PROHACK).

24057 Phelps, Gilbert. THE RUSSIAN NOVEL IN ENGLISH FICTION. Pp. 110-12 and passim. See G3120.

Influence of Russians, especially Turgenev, on AB.

24058 Phelps, William L. THE ADVANCE OF THE ENGLISH NOVEL. Pp. 156-59. See G3122.

Condescending notice of AB's industriousness.

24059 Pilkington, Frederick. "Methodism in Arnold Bennett's Novels." ContempR, 189 (1956), 109-15.

AB's warped views of Methodism.

*24060 Priestley, John B. "Mr. Arnold Bennett." In FIGURES IN MODERN ENGLISH LITERATURE. London: Lane, 1924. Pp. 3-30.

Important, balanced assessment of AB, taking into account his "more than fifty" books to date.

24061 Pritchett, Victor S. "The Five Towns." In his THE LIVING NOVEL AND LATER APPRECIATIONS. Pp. 169-75. See G3125.

AB an unimaginative realist.

24062 Roby, Kinley E. "Arnold Bennett: Shaw's Ten O'Clock Scholar." ShawR, 13 (1970), 96-104.

AB's relations with Shaw and their views of each other's drama.

*24063 ______. "Arnold Bennett's Social Conscience." MFS, 17 (1971), 513-24.

AB's social commentary during the war.

*24064 Scarfe, Francis. "Arnold Bennett: 'A Synthetic Impressionist.'" EA, 25 (1972), 408-11.

The oversimplification and ambiguities of AB's critical reputation.

24065 Scott-James, Rolfe A. "Arnold Bennett." In PERSONALITY IN LITERATURE: 1913-1931. New York: Holt, 1932. Pp. 77-95.

Critical assessment (and comparison with Wells), based chiefly on OWT, CLAYHANGER, and HILDA LESSWAYS.

24066 ______. "Bennett and Galsworthy." In his FIFTY YEARS OF ENGLISH LITERATURE. Pp. 34-46. See G2121.

AB and Galsworthy, unlike Wells, both concerned with the craft of their fiction.

24067 Shaw, George Bernard. "Arnold Bennett Thinks Playwriting Easier than Novel Writing." In PEN PORTRAITS AND REVIEWS. London: Constable, 1932. Pp. 43-52.

Shaw rewrites the final scene of MACBETH in the manner of AB.

24068 Sherman, Stuart P. "The Realism of Arnold Bennett." In ON CONTEMPORARY LITERATURE. New York: Holt, 1917. Pp. 102-19.

AB a humanist, rather than a naturalist.

24069 Stevenson, Lionel. THE ENGLISH NOVEL. Pp. 436-37, 447-50 and passim. See G2211.

AB among the turn-of-the-century realists as an analyst of modern society.

24070 Swinden, Patrick. "Time and Motion: English Realism. Ford. Bennett. V.S. Naipaul." In UNOFFICIAL SELVES. Pp. 120-57. See G3144.

Impressionism (e.g., Ford) versus naturalism (e.g., AB) in modern fiction, with a decided preference for the former.

24071 Swinnerton, Frank. "ARNOLD BENNETT." SatR, 9 (1932), 301-2.

Biographical sketch and admiration, occasioned by the publication of the JOURNALS.

24072 ______. THE GEORGIAN LITERARY SCENE. Pp. 144-53 and passim. See G2364.

Brief biographical summary and critique.

24073 Tindall, William York. FORCES IN MODERN BRITISH LITERATURE. Pp. 132-36 and passim. See G2122.

AB a "superior" disciple of the French realist tradition of Zola.

24074 Wagenknecht, Edward. "Novelist of Being: Arnold Bennett." In his CAVALCADE OF THE ENGLISH NOVEL. Pp. 441-57. See G3151.

Useful, but primarily historical overview of AB's career.

*24075 Wain, John. "The Quality of Arnold Bennett." In PRELIMINARY ESSAYS. London: Macmillan, 1957. Pp. 121-56.

Important, favorable assessment of AB's humanism, realism, and craftsmanship.

24076 Ward, Alfred C. "Arnold Bennett." In his TWENTIETH-CENTURY ENGLISH LITERATURE. Pp. 34-41. See G2123.

AB as a detached, dispassionate naturalist in the tradition of Zola.

24077 ______. "Wells; Bennett; Galsworthy." In his THE NINETEEN-TWENTIES. Pp. 30-37. See G2373.

"Between 1920 and 1930 the three senior English novelists published little that is likely to take a permanent place in literature."

*24078 West, Rebecca. "Uncle Bennett." In THE STRANGE NECESSITY. Garden City, N.Y.: Doubleday, Doran, 1928. Pp. 215-31.

AB (with Galsworthy, Shaw, and Wells) seen as a generous "Uncle of the English-speaking world." AB praised especially for his embodiment of the "Protestant" distrust of pretension, in art and in life.

24079 Weygant, Cornelius. "Of Arnold Bennett, Hard Work and Beauty." In A CENTURY OF THE ENGLISH NOVEL. Pp. 415-29. See G2214.

AB a "most successful tradesman of letters" and, in four books (OWT and Clayhanger trilogy), "as much of a genius as an infinite capacity for hard work can make any man."

24080 Wheatley, Elizabeth D. "Arnold Bennett's Trifles: His Novels for the Gay Middle-Aged." SR, 42 (1934), 180-89.

The virtues of AB's lighter work.

24081 Wilson, Angus. "Arnold Bennett's Novels." LONDON MAGAZINE, 1, No. 9 (1954), 59-67.

AB due respect among younger writers as the "last of the old-time school of novelists."

24082 Wilson, Edmund. "Post-War Shaw and Pre-War Bennett." NEW REPUBLIC, 71 (1932), 92-94.

AB an artificial Socialist, a "glorifier of the commercial and organizational side of capitalism."

*24083 Woolf, Virginia. "Mr. Bennett and Mrs. Brown." 1924. In her COLLECTED ESSAYS. Ed. L. Woolf. London: Hogarth, 1966-67. I, 319-37.

Woolf's rejection of Edwardian realistic techniques.

2.5 Studies of Individual Works

The following section is subdivided into two parts: (i.) Fiction (alphabetically by title) and (ii.) Miscellaneous Writings. Many of the full-length studies of AB consider the major works in detail, and often comment significantly on the lesser novels and miscellaneous writings. See in section 2.3, above: Allen (23001), Darton (23002), Davis (23003), Hall (23005), Hepburn (23006), Johnson (23007), Lafourcade (23008), Lucas (23009), Roby (23010), Tillier (23013), and Wright (23017). None of the biographical studies (section 2.2) offers considerable critical commentary.

Arnold Bennett

i. FICTION

ANNA OF THE FIVE TOWNS (1902)

25001 Heywood C. "D.H. Lawrence's THE LOST GIRL and Its Antecedents by George Moore and Arnold Bennett." ES, 47 (1966), 131-34.

Slight similarities among Lawrence's novel, ANNA OF THE FIVE TOWNS, and a novel by Moore (A MUMMER'S WIFE).

THE CARD (1911)

25002 Scott, Dixon. "The Commonsense of Mr. Arnold Bennett." In MEN OF LETTERS. New York: Hodder and Stoughton, 1916. Pp. 119-32.

THE CARD a comic "skylarking" novel which lacks the distinction of OWT or CLAYHANGER.

"Clayhanger Trilogy"--including CLAYHANGER (1910), HILDA LESSWAYS (1911), and THESE TWAIN (1915)

25003 Ball, David. "Some Sources for Bennett's CLAYHANGER Trilogy." ENGLISH, 21 (1972), 13-17.

AB's "direct" and "free" borrowings from various sources in his life and reading.

25004 Harris, Wendell V. "Molly's 'Yes': The Transvaluation of Sex in Modern Fiction." TSLL, 10 (1968), 107-18.

Sex an affirmation of life (e.g., CLAYHANGER, among others).

*25005 Kreutz, Irving. "Mr. Bennett and Mrs. Woolf." MFS, 8 (1962), 103-15.

Contradicts Woolf's analysis of AB's characterization, drawing illustration from HILDA LESSWAYS and Woolf's MRS. DALLOWAY.

25006 Muir, Edwin. THE STRUCTURE OF THE NOVEL. Pp. 116-24. See G4065.

The chronicle, or period, novel "not essentially an aesthetic form" (Clayhanger trilogy, among others).

25007 Swinnerton, Frank. "Introduction." In AB's CLAYHANGER. Harmondsworth, Engl.: Penguin, 1954. Pp. 9-13.

Brief comments on AB's conception of CLAYHANGER and the following novels in the trilogy.

DREAM OF DESTINY (1932)

25008 Bennett, Dorothy Cheston. "Arnold Bennett's Unfinished Novel." BOOKMAN (New York), 75 (1932), 497-500.

Discusses AB's intentions for the finished novel.

THE GRAND BABYLON HOTEL (1902)

25009 Swinnerton, Frank. "Introduction." In AB's THE GRAND BABYLON HOTEL. Harmondsworth, Engl.: Penguin, 1954. Pp. 7-11.

Spontaneous origin of AB's serial-writing career.

IMPERIAL PALACE (1930)

*25010 Munro, John M. "The Case for Compromise: Arnold Bennett's IMPERIAL PALACE." ARIEL, 2, No. 4 (1971), 18-29.

Compromise of ideals the subject of the novel and a significant influence on its techniques.

LORD RAINGO (1926)

*25011 Hepburn, James G. "Manuscript Notes for LORD RAINGO." EFT [now ELT], 5, No. 1 (1962), 1-5.

AB's own notes for LORD RAINGO indicate that he did not plan the book as a roman-a-clef.

A MAN FROM THE NORTH (1898)

25012 Braybrooke, Patrick. "Arnold Bennett and an Early Book." In PEEPS AT THE MIGHTY. Philadelphia: Lippincott, 1927. Pp. 147-58.

AB's potential evident as early as his first novel.

25013 Swinnerton, Frank. "Introduction." In AB's A MAN FROM THE NORTH. London: Hamilton, 1973. Pp. vii-xii.

Summarizes the conditions surrounding the publication of AB's first novel.

THE OLD WIVES' TALE (1908)

25014 Bland, D.S. "'Too Many Particulars.'" EFT [now ELT], 2, No. 1 (1959), 36-38.

Asserts significance of setting and environment in the portrayal of character (contra Virginia Woolf), illustrating with a model analysis of a passage from OWT.

*25015 Booth, Wayne C. THE RHETORIC OF FICTION. Pp. 144-47. See G4012.

On AB's narrative technique in OWT.

25016 Brewster, Dorothy, and Angus Burrell. "Time Passes: Bennett." In their MODERN FICTION. Pp. 94-101. See G3014.

AB's effective handling of time in OWT.

25017 Brown, Edward K. RHYTHM IN THE NOVEL. Pp. 16-18. See G3015.

AB's use of "emphatic repetition" creates moving effects in OWT.

25018 Jameson, Storm. THE GEORGIAN NOVEL AND MR. ROBINSON. Pp. 15-19. See G3074.

Brief, but perceptive comments on OWT as an example of the transition of the modern novelist's concern from story (e.g., Dickens), to character (e.g., AB), to the "inner" character (e.g., Woolf).

*25019 Kettle, Arnold. "Arnold Bennett: THE OLD WIVES' TALE." In his AN INTRODUCTION TO THE ENGLISH NOVEL. II, 85-89. See G3088.

OWT falls short of true greatness by virtue of its provinciality. AB fails to universalize his characters or realize the full extent of the broad social changes they experience.

25020 McCullough, Bruce. "Realism and the Spirit of Compromise: Arnold Bennett: THE OLD WIVES' TALE." In REPRESENTATIVE ENGLISH NOVELISTS. Pp. 303-19. See G3096.

Survey of the life and brief critique of OWT, noting AB's limited sensibility as well as his lack of "imaginative intensity or subtlety of feeling."

25021 Overton, Grant. "Arnold Bennett: THE OLD WIVES' TALE." In THE PHILOSOPHY OF FICTION. Pp. 148-61. See G4069.

Character, "personal or familial or racial," the subject of OWT.

25022 Priestley, John B. "Introduction." In AB's THE OLD WIVES' TALE. New York: Harper, 1950. Pp. vii-xiv.

AB a compassionate novelist with a comic sense and a pessimistic outlook (a "grim smile").

25023 Siegel, Paul N. "Revolution and Evolution in Bennett's THE OLD WIVES' TALE." CLIO, 4 (1975), 159-72.

AB's tale of his characters' gradual evolution through time, in tension with the novel's backdrop of scientific and political revolutions.

25024 Sillitoe, Alan. "Introduction." In AB's THE OLD WIVES' TALE. London: Pan Books, 1964. Pp. 9-20.

*25025 Tillyard, E.M.W. "Middlemarch and Bursley." In his THE EPIC STRAIN IN THE ENGLISH NOVEL. Pp. 168-86. See G3145.

Important general analysis of OWT stressing AB's handling of the provincial atmosphere.

25026 Wain, John. "Afterword." In AB's THE OLD WIVES' TALE. New York: New American Library, 1963. Pp. 568-82.

AB's note of "stoical resignation," his craft, and his French antecedents.

*25027 Williams, Orlo. "THE OLD WIVES' TALE." NATIONAL REVIEW, 99 (1932), 387-97.

The formal excellence of OWT. Perceptive critique.

RICEYMAN STEPS (1923)

25028 Durkin, Brian. "Some New Lights on RICEYMAN STEPS." ELT, 10 (1967), 66-80.

AB's comic intentions missed in the emphasis on the novel's sober realism.

25029 Flory, Evelyn A. "RICEYMAN STEPS: The Role of Violet and Elsie." ELT, 14 (1971), 93-102.

The two women of the novel are equally central to AB's intentions.

*25030 Hepburn, James G. "The Notebook for RICEYMAN STEPS." PMLA, 78 (1963), 257-61.

A close examination of AB's working notebook demonstrates his primary concern was for the psychology of his characters, not for the careful ordering of external, realistic detail.

*25031 ______. "Some Curious Realism in RICEYMAN STEPS." MFS, 8 (1962), 116-26.

The symbolism within AB's reputed "note-taking" realism.

25032 Sillitoe, Alan. "Introduction." In AB's RICEYMAN STEPS. London: Pan Books, 1964. Pp. 9-20.

ii. MISCELLANEOUS WRITINGS

25033 Agate, James. "A Happy Commentator." In ALARUMS AND EXCURSIONS. New York: Doran, 1922. Pp. 259-64.

Light-hearted praise for AB's AUTHOR'S CRAFT.

25034 Banerjee, Srikumar, and C.B. Nath. COMPLETE STUDY OF "THE ADMIRABLE CRICHTON," "MILESTONES," "THE GREAT ADVENTURE." Bombay: Shahani, 1930.

Surveys THE ADMIRABLE CRICHTON, by J.M. Barrie, and two plays by AB (1912, 1913). Not seen.

25035 Brown, Ivor. "Arnold Bennett." In CRITICS WHO HAVE INFLUENCED TASTE. London: Bles, 1965. Pp. 79-81.

AB a lively, tasteful and enormously well-read critic.

25036 Dunkel, Wilbur D. "The Genesis of MILESTONES." CE, 13 (1952), 375-78.

AB as a collaborator. (MILESTONES, 1912, was a dramatic collaboration with Edward Knoblock.)

*25037 Gross, John. THE RISE AND FALL OF THE MAN OF LETTERS. Pp. 211-18. See G2334.

AB for the most part a popular journalist, yet around 1910 he produced his most creative fiction and most distinguished literary criticism.

*25038 Hynes, Samuel. "Introduction." In "THE AUTHOR'S CRAFT," AND OTHER CRITICAL WRITINGS OF ARNOLD BENNETT. Pp. ix-xx. See 13003.

AB's attempts in criticism and in practice to raise the novel to the status of art.

25039 Lynd, Robert. "Arnold Bennett as Critic." 1945. In BOOKS AND WRITERS. London: Dent, 1952. Pp. 257-61.

AB's critical judgments (c. 1905) readable and generally sound forty years later.

25040 ______. "Mr. Arnold Bennett Confesses." In BOOKS AND AUTHORS. London: Cobden-Sanderson, 1922. Pp. 168-74.

AB a connoisseur, man of genius and "tipster" in his THINGS THAT HAVE INTERESTED ME.

25041 MacCarthy, Desmond. "A Question of Standards." In HUMANITIES. New York: Oxford Univ. Press, 1954. Pp. 194-97.

AB's literary criticism pernicious when he flaunts his "insensibility."

Eric Arthur Blair. See "George Orwell" in vol. 2.

ELIZABETH BOWEN (1899-1973)

1. PRIMARY BIBLIOGRAPHY

Books available in recent paperback printings are denoted by "(P)."

1.1 Fiction

All works are novels unless otherwise noted. For itemized contents of the story collections, see Sellery's "Elizabeth Bowen: A Check List" (21002), below.

11001 ANN LEE'S, AND OTHER STORIES. [Stories]. London: Sidgwick and Jackson; New York: Boni and Liveright, 1926.

Eleven stories.

11002 THE CAT JUMPS, AND OTHER STORIES. [Stories]. London: Gollancz, 1934. No Amer. ed.

Twelve stories. See 11015.

11003 THE DEATH OF THE HEART. London: Gollancz, 1938. New York: Knopf, 1939. (P)

EB's most praised novel, a study of an innocent young girl's confrontation with the world of "experience" in London.

11004 THE DEMON LOVER, AND OTHER STORIES. [Stories]. London: Cape, 1945. Published as IVY GRIPPED THE STEPS. New York: Knopf, 1946.

Twelve stories, many dealing with the impact of the war.

11005 ENCOUNTERS. [Stories]. London: Sidgwick and Jackson, 1923. New York: Boni and Liveright, 1925.

Fourteen stories. EB's first book.

11006 EVA TROUT, OR CHANGING SCENES. New York: Knopf, 1968. London: Cape, 1969.

The isolation in a world of fantasy of the traumatized central character, Eva. EB's last completed novel.

11007 FRIENDS AND RELATIONS. London: Constable; New York: Dial Press, 1931.

Subtle study of two related marriages and the frustrated love of sister-in-law and brother-in-law.

11008 THE HEAT OF THE DAY. London: Cape; New York: Knopf, 1949.

The conflicting loves of the heroine, against the background of wartime London.

11009 THE HOTEL. London: Constable, 1927. New York: Dial Press, 1928.

Friendships and loves at a Riviera hotel.

11010 THE HOUSE IN PARIS. London: Gollancz, 1935. New York: Knopf, 1936. (P)

Unsentimental story of a romance in Paris.

11011 IVY GRIPPED THE STEPS. See THE DEMON LOVER (11004).

11012 JOINING CHARLES, AND OTHER STORIES. [Stories]. London: Constable; New York: Dial Press, 1929.

Eleven stories.

11013 THE LAST SEPTEMBER. London: Constable; New York: Dial Press, 1929.

Decorous Anglo-Irish family life, against the background of the Irish uprisings (c. 1913-1916).

11014 THE LITTLE GIRLS. London: Cape; New York: Knopf, 1964.

The decision of three women to recover a box of mementoes after fifty years, and its impact upon them.

11015 LOOK AT ALL THOSE ROSES. [Stories]. London: Gollancz; New York: Knopf, 1941.

English (fourteen stories) and American editions (nineteen stories) differ substantially, the American including seven stories from THE CAT JUMPS and dropping two titles from the English edition.

11016 TO THE NORTH. London: Gollancz, 1932. New York: Knopf, 1933.

Developing romances among two couples.

11017 A WORLD OF LOVE. London: Cape; New York: Knopf, 1955.

Discovery of a cache of love letters has far-reaching effects on an Anglo-Irish household.

1.2 Miscellaneous Writings

EB's autobiographical writings, criticism, and comments on the novel are listed here for their value to the student of her fiction. For a full list of EB's nonfiction, periodical essays, and other miscellaneous pieces, see Sellery's bibliographical "Check List" (21002), below.

12001 AFTERTHOUGHT: PIECES ABOUT WRITING. London: Longmans, 1962. Published as AFTERTHOUGHTS: PIECES ABOUT WRITING [with SEVEN WINTERS]. New York: Knopf, 1962. See 13005.

Collects nine prefaces, two broadcasts, four reviews, a travel essay and six reflections. American edition reprints SEVEN WINTERS (12009).

12002 BOWEN'S COURT. London: Longmans; New York: Knopf, 1942.

History of the Bowen family and the family's estate "Bowen's Court" (1776--), in the context of Irish history.

12003 COLLECTED IMPRESSIONS. London: Longmans; New York: Knopf, 1950.

Collects five prefaces, thirty-four reviews, and twelve miscellaneous pieces. Includes ANTHONY TROLLOPE: A NEW JUDGMENT (1946), a broadcast, and "Notes on Writing a Novel" (1945).

12004 ENGLISH NOVELISTS. London: Collins, 1942.

Brief critical overview of the English novel.

12005 "Jane Austen." In THE ENGLISH NOVELISTS. Ed. Derek Verschoyle. Pp. 99-110. See G3150.

Interesting study of a novelist to whom EB has herself often been compared.

12006 "A Novelist and His Characters." EDH, 36 (1970), 19-23.

Brief consideration of the novelist's relationship to his creations.

12007 "A Passage to E.M. Forster." In ASPECTS OF E.M. FORSTER. Ed. Oliver Stallybrass. New York: Harcourt, 1969. Pp. 1-12.

12008 PICTURES AND CONVERSATIONS: CHAPTERS OF AN AUTOBIOGRAPHY WITH OTHER COLLECTED WRITINGS. London: Lane; New York: Knopf, 1975.

Contains chapters and an outline of an unfinished autobiography, a fragment of an unfinished short novel (THE MOVE-IN), a critical essay on Proust, a nativity play and a reprint of "Notes on Writing a Novel" (1945). See 24005.

12009 SEVEN WINTERS: MEMORIES OF A DUBLIN CHILDHOOD. Dublin: Cuala Press, 1942. London: Longmans, 1943. Published with AFTERTHOUGHTS. New York: Knopf, 1962. See 13005.

Fragment of an autobiography.

12010 THE SHELBOURNE: A CENTER IN DUBLIN LIFE FOR MORE THAN A CENTURY. London: Harrap, 1951. Published as THE SHELBOURNE HOTEL. New York: Knopf, 1951.

History of the Shelbourne (1824--) in the context of Irish history.

12011 A TIME IN ROME. London: Longmans; New York: Knopf, 1960.

Travel essays, history, and impressions.

12012 WHY DO I WRITE? AN EXCHANGE OF VIEWS BETWEEN ELIZABETH BOWEN, GRAHAM GREENE, AND V.S. PRITCHETT. London: Marshall, 1948.

Letters commenting on the novelist's role.

1.3 Collected and Selected Works

13001 THE COLLECTED EDITION OF THE WORKS OF ELIZABETH BOWEN. 14 vols. London: Cape, 1948-65.

Uniform publication of the novels and principal story collections.

13002 A DAY IN THE DARK, AND OTHER STORIES. London: Cape, 1965.

Twenty stories selected by EB, fifteen from earlier published collections (ENCOUNTERS, JOINING CHARLES, THE CAT

JUMPS, LOOK AT ALL THOSE ROSES, and THE DEMON LOVER) and five previously uncollected tales.

13003 EARLY STORIES. New York: Knopf, 1951.

Collects twenty-five stories originally published in ENCOUNTERS and ANN LEE'S.

13004 SELECTED STORIES. London: Fridberg, 1946.

Eleven stories, drawn from JOINING CHARLES, THE CAT JUMPS, and LOOK AT ALL THOSE ROSES.

13005 "SEVEN WINTERS: MEMORIES OF A DUBLIN CHILDHOOD" AND "AFTERTHOUGHTS: PIECES ABOUT WRITING." New York: Knopf, 1962.

First American printing of SEVEN WINTERS combined with slightly rearranged text of AFTERTHOUGHTS.

13006 STORIES BY ELIZABETH BOWEN. New York: Knopf, 1959.

Eighteen stories, selected by EB from earlier volumes: ENCOUNTERS, ANN LEE'S, THE CAT JUMPS, LOOK AT ALL THOSE ROSES, and THE DEMON LOVER.

1.4 Letters

EB's letters have not been published. See, however, 12012 above, and 22003 below.

2. SECONDARY BIBLIOGRAPHY

2.1 Bibliographies

A full bibliography of EB's major work, with modified treatment of her periodical and broadcast contributions, manuscript descriptions and locations, and lists of her correspondence, has been announced for publication in 1978 by the Humanities Research Center of the University of Texas at Austin (edited by J'nan Sellery and William O. Harris).

21001 Davis, Robert M., comp. "Contributions to NIGHT AND DAY by Elizabeth Bowen, Graham Greene, and Anthony Powell." SNNTS, 3 (1971), 401-4.

Lists EB's contributions as drama critic for NIGHT AND DAY (1937).

*21002 Sellery, J'nan, comp. "Elizabeth Bowen: A Check List." BNYPL, 74 (1970), 219-74.

Excellent listing of EB's works: "Books and Pamphlets" (31 items, with itemized contents and reviews), "Contributions to Books" (59), "Contributions to Periodicals" (615), "Translations" (49), and "Manuscripts" (69 items, described and located). Second part of bibliography lists ninety-four books, chapters, and articles about EB. Invaluable.

21003 Wiley, Paul L., comp. "Elizabeth Bowen (1899--)." In his THE BRITISH NOVEL. Pp. 19-20. See G1419.

Brief primary and secondary checklist.

2.2 Biographies, Memoirs, Interviews

The full-length critical studies of Austin, Heath, and Kimmey, listed in section 2.3 below contain important biographical information on EB. Also see Spencer C. Brown's "Foreword" to PICTURES AND CONVERSATIONS (24005) below, and EB's own autobiographical writings.

22001 Bowen, Elizabeth. "How I Write My Novels." In HOW I WRITE MY NOVELS. Ed. Ted Jones. London: Spearman, 1948. Pp. 8-12.

Interview discussion.

22002 Breit, Harvey. "Talk with Miss Bowen." NYTBR, 26 Mar. 1950, p. 27.

Interview discussion of the state of modern English fiction.

22003 Glendinning, Victoria. ELIZABETH BOWEN. London: Weidenfeld and Nicolson, 1977.

Biography, drawing new information from EB's correspondence and from recollections of her friends. Not seen.

22004 Moss, Howard. "Elizabeth Bowen, 1899-1973." NYTBR, 8 Apr. 1973, pp. 2-3.

An "anecdotal and nostalgic" obituary memoir.

2.3 Book-Length Critical Studies

23001 Austin, Allan E. ELIZABETH BOWEN. New York: Twayne, 1971.

Good introduction to EB's fiction. Austin briefly discusses

EB's biography and major themes and summarizes, with some critical commentary, the ten novels and major stories. Austin particularly admires EB's prose style ("authentic art") and her two most distinguished works, THE DEATH OF THE HEART and THE HEAT OF THE DAY, while he finds her remaining fiction (except for a few stories) less satisfactory. Includes a brief survey of EB criticism.

23002 Blodgett, Harriet. PATTERNS OF REALITY: ELIZABETH BOWEN'S NOVELS. The Hague: Mouton, 1975.

Critical study of EB's themes and techniques, stressing her personal faith in life's divine meaning. Two survey-chapters on seven of the novels and the autobiographical writings bracket close readings of the three chief works: THE HOUSE IN PARIS, THE DEATH OF THE HEART, and THE HEAT OF THE DAY.

23003 Brooke, Jocelyn. ELIZABETH BOWEN. London: Longmans, 1952.

Critical essay on the stories and novels, stressing the visual powers of EB's art, as distinguished from the novel of pure subjectivity or "sensibility" (cf. landscape painting). A 32 page pamphlet.

*23004 Heath, William. ELIZABETH BOWEN: AN INTRODUCTION TO HER NOVELS. Madison: Univ. of Wisconsin Press, 1961.

Full critical study of the first eight novels and the stories, with occasional reference to the essays and autobiography. Heath considers EB above all a "literary" novelist, a writer so thoroughly imbued by the narrative tradition that she sees "life through literature," achieving a "subtle position from which she can present life in literary terms." In her novels, EB shares with the reader "their mutual awareness that this is an art." Heath's analyses of EB's literary antecedents and of the matter, style, technique, and self-conscious artistry of her works are consistently rewarding.

23005 Kenney, Edwin J. ELIZABETH BOWEN. Lewisburg, Pa.: Bucknell Univ. Press, 1974.

Critical commentary on the novels, stressing EB's preoccupation with her central theme, the fall from innocence, and its biographical relevance (EB's sense of betrayal by her parents and her Anglo-Irish heritage of insecurity). While Kenney relates the life and the fiction too forcibly at times, many of his interpretations deserve attention.

2.4 General Critical Articles, or Chapters on EB

24001 Allen, Walter. THE MODERN NOVEL. Pp. 191-95 and passim. See G2202.

The innocent's confrontation with experience in EB's fiction (cf. James). High praise for THE DEATH OF THE HEART.

24002 Atkins, John. "Elizabeth Bowen: Connoisseur of the Individual." SIX NOVELISTS LOOK AT SOCIETY. Pp. 48-76. See G3003.

EB's reflection of various social themes and attitudes (e.g., class, snobbery, homes, and speech patterns).

*24003 Beachcroft, Thomas O. THE MODEST ART. Pp. 182-85 and passim. See G5003.

EB's brilliance of observation, arresting imagery and sensitivity to impressions (cf. Mansfield). Examines "Easter Egg Party," "Tears Idle Tears," and "Joining Charles."

24004 Brooke-Rose, Christine. "Lady Precious Stream." LONDON MAGAZINE, 4 (May 1964), 83-86.

EB's sentimental, overwrought, and affected style.

*24005 Brown, Spencer C. "Foreword." In EB's PICTURES AND CONVERSATIONS. Pp. vii-xlii. See 12008.

Reminiscences and valuable comments on EB's work by her literary executor, derived from conversations with EB.

24006 Burgess, Anthony. THE NOVEL NOW. Pp. 119-21. See G3019.

The exquisite texture of EB's style (cf. James).

24007 Coles, William. "The Pattern of Responsibility in the Novels of Elizabeth Bowen." HARVARD ADVOCATE, 137 (Dec. 1952), 20-22, 37-40.

24008 Collins, Arthur S. ENGLISH LITERATURE OF THE TWENTIETH CENTURY. Pp. 257-61. See G2105.

Survey and comparison with Virginia Woolf.

*24009 Daiches, David. "The Novels of Elizabeth Bowen." EJ, 38 (1949), 305-13.

EB a "great British novelist" in the "tradition of subtle inquiry into phases of human sensibility" (cf. James and Mansfield). Brief survey of first six novels, through THE HEAT OF THE DAY (1949).

24010 Davenport, Gary T. "Elizabeth Bowen and the Big House." SHR, 8 (1974), 27-34.

EB's symbolic exploration of "houses and rooms" in her fiction related to her Irish national heritage.

24011 Frierson, William C. THE ENGLISH NOVEL IN TRANSITION. Pp. 314-18 and passim. See G3047.

In theme and technique, EB shows many of the virtues of James and Woolf, and few of their faults.

24012 Gill, Richard. HAPPY RURAL SEAT. Pp. 181-91 and passim. See G2330.

The country house as symbol in EB.

24013 Gindin, James. "Ethical Structures in John Galsworthy, Elizabeth Bowen, and Iris Murdoch." In FORMS OF MODERN BRITISH FICTION. Ed. Alan W. Friedman. Pp. 15-41. See G3046.

Discusses the continuity of traditional fiction with a social and "ethical focus," rather than an individual and metaphysical orientation, in Galsworthy, EB, and Murdoch.

24014 Greene, George. "Elizabeth Bowen: Imagination as Therapy." PERSPECTIVE, 14 (1965), 42-52.

Discusses THE DEATH OF THE HEART, THE HEAT OF THE DAY, A WORLD OF LOVE, and THE LITTLE GIRLS.

*24015 Hall, James. "The Giant Located: Elizabeth Bowen." In THE LUNATIC GIANT IN THE DRAWING ROOM: THE BRITISH AND AMERICAN NOVEL SINCE 1930. Bloomington: Indiana Univ. Press, 1968. Pp. 17-55.

EB "one of the few radical explorers in the recent novel." Discusses THE HOUSE IN PARIS and THE DEATH OF THE HEART in particular.

24016 Hardwick, Elizabeth. "Elizabeth Bowen's Fiction." PR, 16 (1949), 1114-21.

Argues EB's fiction overvalued. EB a "romantic feminist who serves up a perennial dish," the impossible romance.

24017 Hawkins, Desmond. "Contemporaries: I. Elizabeth Bowen." CRITERION, 18 (1938), 90-93.

EB's preoccupation with the "aborted pursuit of romantic love." Brief survey, through THE HOUSE IN PARIS (1935).

24018 Karl, Frederick R. "The World of Elizabeth Bowen." In his A READER'S GUIDE TO THE CONTEMPORARY ENGLISH NOVEL. Pp. 107-30. See G3081.

Despite its condescending view of EB's "limitation of range," a useful introduction and critical survey, concentrating on THE HOUSE IN PARIS, THE DEATH OF THE HEART, and THE HEAT OF THE DAY.

24019 Kiely, Benedict. MODERN IRISH FICTION: A CRITIQUE. Dublin: Golden Eagle Books, 1950. Pp. 151-59.

Patterns of betrayal and the search for stability in EB's writings stem from her Anglo-Irish heritage.

24020 McCormick, John. CATASTROPHE AND IMAGINATION. Passim. See G3095.

EB a minor novelist of manners. Patronizing.

24021 Mitchell, Edward. "Themes in Elizabeth Bowen's Short Stories." Crit, 8, No. 3 (1966), 41-54.

Thematic patterns and variations among the stories (especially "innocence and experience").

24022 Newby, Percy H. THE NOVEL, 1945-1950. Pp. 19-20. See G3113.

EB as traditionalist.

*24023 O'Faolain, Sean. "Elizabeth Bowen, or 'Romance Does Not Pay.'" In his THE VANISHING HERO. Pp. 169-90. See G3116.

EB's detachment from English life (through her Irish heritage) lends a "nice ambivalence" of sentiment and malice to her work.

*24024 Parrish, Paul A. "The Loss of Eden: Four Novels of Elizabeth Bowen." Crit, 15, No. 1 (1973), 86-100.

The awakening to life and love of the innocent young girl in THE LAST SEPTEMBER, THE HOUSE IN PARIS, THE DEATH OF THE HEART, and EVA TROUT.

*24025 Pendry, E.D. "Elizabeth Bowen." In her THE NEW FEMINISM OF ENGLISH FICTION. Pp. 120-52. See G3119.

EB "the most feminine of contemporary novelists," the greatest successor to Woolf. Intelligent survey of the fiction and nonfiction through A WORLD OF LOVE (1955).

24026 Prescott, Orville. IN MY OPINION. Pp. 101-5. See G3124.

EB praised for her "authentic talent" and verbal dexterity, despite her limited "coterie" appeal.

24027 Reed, Henry. THE NOVEL SINCE 1939. Passim. See G3128.

Discusses EB's stories passim.

24028 Rule, Jane. "Elizabeth Bowen." In LESBIAN IMAGES. Garden City, N.Y.: Doubleday, 1975. Pp. 115-25.

EB's use of the lesbian relationship in her fiction.

24029 Rupp, Richard Henry. "The Post-War Fiction of Elizabeth Bowen." XUS, 4 (1965), 55-67.

The deterioration of EB's fiction after THE DEATH OF THE HEART (1938).

*24030 Sackville-West, Edward. "Ladies Whose Bright Pens. . . ." In INCLINATIONS. London: Secker and Warburg, 1949. Pp. 78-103.

Extended comparison of EB and Ivy Compton-Burnett, two novelists who know their limitations and turn them to account.

24031 Saul, George Brandon. "The Short Stories of Elizabeth Bowen." ArQ, 21 (1965), 53-59.

The stories debilitated by their aura of self-conscious professionalism.

24032 Scott-James, Rolfe A. FIFTY YEARS OF ENGLISH LITERATURE. Pp. 182-85. See G2121.

EB's strengths in conveying passion and feeling.

*24033 Seward, Barbara. "Elizabeth Bowen's World of Impoverished Love." CE, 18 (1956), 30-37.

Although EB's novels and stories create sympathy for the disillusioned idealist, they present, in fact, a critique of the ideals themselves.

24034 Sharp, Sister M. Corona. "The House as Setting and Symbol in Three Novels by Elizabeth Bowen." XUS, 2 (1963), 93-103.

House symbolism in THE LAST SEPTEMBER, THE HOUSE IN PARIS, and THE DEATH OF THE HEART.

24035 Snow, Lotus. "The Uncertain 'I': A Study of Elizabeth Bowen's Fiction." WHR, 4 (1950), 299-310.

EB's chief theme the search for a "personal identity." Survey, through THE HEAT OF THE DAY (1949).

24036 Stevenson, Lionel. THE HISTORY OF THE ENGLISH NOVEL. XI, 288-97 and passim. See G2212.

EB a novelist of "acute sensibility and a fastidious style," yet her works defy simple classification. Surveys through THE LITTLE GIRLS (1964).

24037 Stokes, Edward. "Elizabeth Bowen--Pre-Assumptions or Moral Angle?" AUMLA, No. 11 (1959), pp. 35-47.

24038 Strickhausen, H. "Elizabeth Bowen and Reality." SR, 73 (1965), 158-65.

Admiring and perceptive review essay (LITTLE GIRLS, LAST SEPTEMBER, STORIES BY ELIZABETH BOWEN, and SEVEN WINTERS).

*24039 Strong, Leonard A.G. "Elizabeth Bowen." In PERSONAL REMARKS. New York: Liveright, 1953. Pp. 132-45.

EB's "precision of awareness and of expression." Admiring defense of EB against such charges as introversion, abstraction, and specialized vision.

24040 Sullivan, Walter. "A Sense of Place: Elizabeth Bowen and the Landscape of the Heart." SR, 84 (1976), 142-49.

General, memorial overview of EB's career, noting a decline in her later works.

24041 Tindall, William York. FORCES IN MODERN BRITISH LITERATURE. Pp. 207-9. See G2122.

EB in relation to modern literary movements.

2.5 Studies of Individual Works

The book-length critical studies by Austin (23001), Blodgett (23002), Heath (23004) and Kenney (23005) (section 2.3, above) and several of the general critical essays (especially Beachcroft (24003), Daiches (24009), Davenport (24010), Greene (24014), Hall (24015), Karl (24018), Mitchell (24021), Parrish (24024) and Sharp (24034), section 2.4, above) draw their illustrations from one or more of the novels and stories. There are no extended commentaries of EB's nonfiction.

"The Cat Jumps" (1934)

25001 Perry, John Oliver. "'The Cat Jumps.'" In INSIGHT II. Ed. John V. Hagopian and Martin Dolch. Pp. 21-28. See G5007.

Summary, critique, and study questions.

THE DEATH OF THE HEART (1938)

25002 Bogan, Louise. "The Pure in Heart." 1939. In SELECTED CRITICISM: PROSE, POETRY. New York: Noonday, 1955. Pp. 125-28.

THE DEATH OF THE HEART "too packed, too brilliant for its own good."

25003 Coles, Robert. "Youth: Elizabeth Bowen's THE DEATH OF THE HEART." In IRONY IN THE MIND'S LIFE: ESSAYS ON NOVELS BY JAMES AGEE, ELIZABETH BOWEN, AND GEORGE ELIOT. Charlottesville: Univ. Press of Virginia, 1974. Pp. 107-53.

Novel's thematic variations upon innocence and adolescence. Detailed, though often derivative, summary and critique.

*25004 Harkness, Bruce. "The Fiction of Elizabeth Bowen." EJ, 44 (1955), 499-506.

THE DEATH OF THE HEART epitomizes EB's work in its concern for place, its theme of betrayal, and its nonexperimental style.

25005 Heinemann, Alison. "The Indoor Landscape in Bowen's THE DEATH OF THE HEART." Crit, 10, No. 3 (1968), 5-12.

EB a modern romantic, concerned with the emotional significance of objects in an "indoor," rather than a natural, landscape.

25006 Van Duyn, Mona. "Pattern and Pilgrimage: A Reading of THE DEATH OF THE HEART." Crit, 4, No. 2 (1961), 52-66.

Close study of the novel's structure, its formal "patterning of characters, setting, narrative organization, and prose style."

"The Demon Lover" (1941)

25007 Hughes, Douglas A. "Cracks in the Psyche: Elizabeth Bowen's 'The Demon Lover.'" SSF, 10 (1973), 411-13.

Story a study of "psychological delusion," not a parapsychological thriller.

THE HEAT OF THE DAY (1949)

25008 Dorenkamp, Angela G. "'Fall or Leap': Bowen's THE HEAT OF THE DAY." Crit, 10, No. 3 (1968), 13-21.

Close reading of the novel's "hesitant, tortured, and ambivalent" style, symbolism, and meaning.

25009 Markovic, Vida E. "Stella Rodney." In his THE CHANGING FACE. Pp. 112-22. See G3100.

Study of the disintegrating character of Stella in THE HEAT OF THE DAY.

THE HOUSE IN PARIS (1935)

25010 Greene, Graham. "The Dark Backward: A Footnote." LONDON MERCURY, 32 (1935), 562-65.

Style and technique a novelist's means for disguising an inability to describe the passage of time (e.g., EB's THE HOUSE IN PARIS).

"Ivy Gripped the Steps" (1945)

25011 Davis, Robert M. "On Bowen." In his MODERN BRITISH SHORT NOVELS. Glenview, Ill.: Scott, Foresman, 1972. Pp. 260-64.

Penetrating commentary on the "genesis and execution" of the story, with brief bibliography.

A WORLD OF LOVE (1955)

25012 Wagner, Geoffrey. "Elizabeth Bowen and the Artificial Novel." EIC, 13 (1963), 155-63.

EB most successful as a social critic and least satisfying as an experimental, Jamesian prose-poet (e.g., A WORLD OF LOVE).

GILBERT KEITH CHESTERTON (1874-1936)

1. PRIMARY BIBLIOGRAPHY

Books available in recent paperback printings are denoted by "(P)."

1.1 Fiction

All works are novels unless otherwise noted.

11001 THE BALL AND THE CROSS. New York: Lane, 1909. London: Gardner, Darton, 1910.

Fantasy tale of an ongoing debate and a frustrated duel between a Catholic and an atheist.

11002 THE CLUB OF QUEER TRADES. [Stories]. London and New York: Harper, 1905. (P).

Six long short stories centering on a group of individuals who have developed unique professions ("queer trades").

11003 THE FLYING INN. [Stories]. London: Methuen; New York: Lane, 1914.

Twenty-five loosely related fantasies.

11004 FOUR FAULTLESS FELONS. [Stories]. London: Cassell; New York: Dodd, Mead, 1930.

Collects four comic novellas: THE MODERATE MURDERER (previously published 1929), THE HONEST QUACK (1929), THE ECSTATIC THIEF (1930), and THE LOYAL TRAITOR.

11005 THE INCREDULITY OF FATHER BROWN. [Stories]. London: Cassell; New York: Dodd, Mead, 1926. (P).

Eight detective stories.

11006 THE INNOCENCE OF FATHER BROWN. [Stories]. London: Cassell; New York: Lane, 1911. (P).

Twelve detective stories.

11007 MANALIVE. London: Nelson; New York: Lane, 1912.

Witty parable attacking modern man's convenient assumptions and pretensions.

11008 THE MAN WHO KNEW TOO MUCH, AND OTHER STORIES. [Stories]. London: Cassell; New York: Harper, 1922.

Twelve tales. Includes "The Five of Swords," which GKC describes as his "best story."

11009 THE MAN WHO WAS THURSDAY: A NIGHTMARE. London: Simpkin, Marshall, Hamilton, Kent; New York: Dodd, Mead, 1908. (P).

Grotesque fantasy revolving around a group of seven anarchists (code-named for days of the week), most of whom are in fact detectives incognito.

11010 THE NAPOLEON OF NOTTING HILL. London and New York: Lane, 1904.

Political fantasy dealing with a twenty-first-century rebellion of the Notting Hill district of London (in part, an allegory of the Boer War).

11011 THE PARADOXES OF MR. POND. [Stories]. London: Cassell; New York: Dodd, Mead, 1937.

Eight mystery tales.

11012 THE POET AND THE LUNATICS: EPISODES IN THE LIFE OF GABRIEL GALE. [Stories]. London: Cassell; New York: Dodd, Mead, 1929.

Eight connected mystery stories.

11013 THE RETURN OF DON QUIXOTE. New York: Dood, Mead, 1926. London: Chatto and Windus, 1927.

Fantasy of the rebirth of chivalry and medieval values in modern England.

11014 THE SCANDAL OF FATHER BROWN. [Stories]. London: Cassell; New York: Dodd, Mead, 1935.

Seven detective stories.

11015 THE SECRET OF FATHER BROWN. [Stories]. London: Cassell; New York: Harper, 1927. (P).

Ten detective stories.

11016 THE SWORD OF WOOD. [Story]. London: Mathews and Marrot, 1928.

Separately published story, later collected in STORIES, ESSAYS AND POEMS (1935). See 13019.

11017 TALES OF THE LONG BOW. [Stories]. London: Cassell; New York: Dodd, Mead, 1925.

Eight fantasy satires, two of which were also separately published in America as THE EXCLUSIVE LUXURY OF ENOCH OATES AND THE UNTHINKABLE THEORY OF PROFESSOR GREEN (New York: Dodd, Mead, 1925).

11018 THE WISDOM OF FATHER BROWN. [Stories]. New York: Macaulay, 1912. London: Cassell, 1914. (P).

Twelve detective tales.

1.2 Miscellaneous Writings

What follows is a very partial selection from the volumes of essays collected or supervised by GKC, on topics as diverse as temperence, eugenics, travel, Christian apologetics, and Roman roads, and from the ten poetry collections, fourteen biographies and critical studies, three plays, and uncounted pamphlets, introductions, contributions to books, and periodical essays (see Sullivan's bibliography, 21004 below, for a more thorough, though incomplete listing). The works included here have been chosen for their direct bearing on GKC as novelist and literary critic.

12001 ALL IS GRIST: A BOOK OF ESSAYS. London: Methuen, 1931. New York: Dodd, Mead, 1932.

Thirty-eight essays. Includes discussions of Dante, Mencken, Shaw, and Trollope.

12002 "ALL I SURVEY": A BOOK OF ESSAYS. London: Methuen; New York: Dodd, Mead, 1933.

Forty-four essays, several on literary figures (including Scott, Stevenson, and Swift).

12003 APPRECIATIONS AND CRITICISMS OF THE WORKS OF CHARLES DICKENS. London: Dent; New York: Dutton, 1911.

Collects twenty-three introductions to Dickens' works, written by GKC for the Everyman Library editions.

12004 AS I WAS SAYING: A BOOK OF ESSAYS. London: Methuen; New York: Dodd, Mead, 1936.

Thirty-six essays. Includes commentaries on Coleridge, Meredith, Morris, and Voltaire.

12005 AUTOBIOGRAPHY. London: Hutchinson, 1936. Published as THE AUTOBIOGRAPHY OF G.K. CHESTERTON. New York: Sheed and Ward, 1936.

Important biographical document.

12006 AVOWALS AND DENIALS: A BOOK OF ESSAYS. London: Methuen, 1934. New York: Dodd, Mead, 1935.

Thirty-six essays. Includes discussions of Blake, Shaw and Wordsworth.

12007 CHARLES DICKENS. London: Methuen, 1906. Published as CHARLES DICKENS, A CRITICAL STUDY. New York: Dodd, Mead, 1906. (P).

Biographical and critical study.

12008 CHAUCER. London: Faber; New York: Farrar and Rinehart, 1932.

Critical commentary on Chaucer's art, age, and religion.

12009 THE COLOURED LANDS. London and New York: Sheed and Ward, 1938.

Includes much previously unpublished or uncollected verse, prose, drawings, and juvenilia. See 24083.

12010 THE DEFENDANT. London: Johnson, 1901. New York: Dodd, Mead, 1902.

Sixteen essays, including "A Defence of Detective Stories."

12011 FANCIES VERSUS FADS. London: Methuen; New York: Dodd, Mead, 1923.

Thirty essays, including several on literary subjects (e.g., Shakespeare, Milton, and Bennett).

12012 GENERALLY SPEAKING: A BOOK OF ESSAYS. London: Methuen, 1928. New York: Dodd, Mead, 1929.

Forty-two articles. Includes essays on detective novels, Byron, and Hardy.

12013 GEORGE BERNARD SHAW. London and New York: Lane, 1909. (P).

Critical commentary on Shaw's art and ideas.

12014 G.K.'S WEEKLY. 1-23, Nos. 1-587 (1925-36).

Journal of the "Distributist" political league, edited by, and containing numerous contributions from, GKC. Superseded the NEW WITNESS (1911-25), founded by Belloc and edited by GKC's brother Cecil, and later by GKC (1916-23).

12015 HERETICS. London and New York: Lane, 1905.

Twenty essays on the writers of the nineties, several questioning the "false prophets" of the time (including Kipling, Shaw, and Wells).

12016 ORTHODOXY. London and New York: Lane, 1908.

The most important of GKC's writings on Christian apologetics, a companion volume to his literary essays in HERETICS.

12017 ROBERT BROWNING. London and New York: Macmillan, 1903.

Biographical and critical study.

12018 ROBERT LOUIS STEVENSON. London: Hodder and Stoughton, 1927. New York: Dodd, Mead, 1928.

Biography with critical commentary.

12019 SIDELIGHTS ON NEW LONDON AND NEWER YORK, AND OTHER ESSAYS. London: Sheed and Ward; New York: Dodd, Mead, 1932.

Twenty-eight light essays, several on literary topics. Includes essays on Dickens, Shakespeare, Shaw, "The Spirit of the Age in Literature," and "Magic and Fantasy in Fiction."

12020 TWELVE TYPES. London: Humphreys, 1902. Published as VARIED TYPES. New York: Dodd, Mead, 1903.

Twelve critical essays on literary and historical figures, including Byron, Pope, Stevenson, and Tolstoy. American edition collects eight additional essays.

12021 THE USES OF DIVERSITY: A BOOK OF ESSAYS. London: Methuen, 1920. New York: Dodd, Mead, 1921.

Thirty-five articles, several on literary types (e.g., detective and historical fiction) and figures (e.g., Dickens, Meredith, and Tennyson).

12022 VARIED TYPES. See TWELVE TYPES (12020).

12023 THE VICTORIAN AGE IN LITERATURE. London: Williams and Norgate, 1912. New York: Holt, 1913. (P).

Still valuable critical study of the Victorian period.

12024 WILLIAM BLAKE. London: Duckworth; New York: Dutton, 1910.

Brief biography and criticism of Blake's poetry, art, and ideas.

1.3 Collected and Selected Works

What follows is a selective list of the more important anthologies and selections of GKC's work, and posthumous volumes of previously uncollected essays.

13001 THE APOSTLE AND THE WILD DUCKS, AND OTHER ESSAYS. Ed. Dorothy Collins. London: Elek, 1975.

Previously uncollected essays.

13002 "Chesterton Continued." Comp. John Sullivan. In CHESTERTON CONTINUED: A BIBLIOGRAPHICAL SUPPLEMENT. Pp. 85-113. See 21003.

Reprints twelve uncollected essays, poems, and letters (1900-1936).

13003 CHESTERTON ON SHAKESPEARE. Ed. Dorothy Collins. Beaconsfield, Engl.: Finlayson; Chester Springs, Pa.: Dufour, 1971.

Reprints from various sources thirty-two of GKC's essays on Shakespeare's works, his age, and his critical reputation.

13004 THE COLLECTED POEMS OF G.K. CHESTERTON. London: Palmer, 1927. New York: Dodd, Mead, 1932.

First American and subsequent British and American editions contain additional material.

13005 THE COMMON MAN. London and New York: Sheed and Ward, 1950.

Forty-four previously uncollected essays, articles, and introductions. Includes studies of James, Johnson, and Tolstoy.

13006 THE FATHER BROWN STORIES. London: Cassell, 1929. Published as THE FATHER BROWN OMNIBUS. New York: Dodd, Mead, 1933.

Collected issue of the Father Brown detective story volumes: THE INCREDULITY OF FATHER BROWN (1926), THE INNOCENCE OF FATHER BROWN (1911), THE SECRET OF FATHER BROWN (1927), and THE WISDOM OF FATHER BROWN (1912). Later editions add THE SCANDAL OF FATHER BROWN (1935), in 1947, and the last story, "The Vampire of the Village" (1936), in 1953.

13007 G.K.C. AS M.C.: BEING A COLLECTION OF THIRTY-SEVEN INTRODUCTIONS BY G.K. CHESTERTON. Ed. J.P. De Fonseka. London: Methuen, 1929.

Critical introductions to works by diverse authors including Austen, Belloc, Dickens, and Housman. See 24021.

13008 G.K. CHESTERTON OMNIBUS. London: Methuen, 1932.

Collects three novels: THE NAPOLEON OF NOTTING HILL (1904), THE MAN WHO WAS THURSDAY (1908), and THE FLYING INN (1914).

13009 G.K. CHESTERTON: SELECTIONS FROM HIS NON-FICTIONAL PROSE. Ed. W.H. Auden. London: Faber, 1970.

Thirty-six essays, divided between twenty-four literary and twelve philosophic topics. See 25013.

13010 THE GLASS WALKING-STICK, AND OTHER ESSAYS FROM "THE ILLUSTRATED LONDON NEWS," 1905-1936. Ed. Dorothy Collins. London: Methuen, 1955.

Forty miscellaneous essays. Includes studies of Fielding, Shakespeare, and the essay genre.

13011 A HANDFUL OF AUTHORS: ESSAYS ON BOOKS AND WRITERS. Ed. Dorothy Collins. New York: Sheed and Ward, 1953.

Thirty-seven of GKC's previously uncollected critical essays and articles.

13012 LUNACY AND LETTERS. Ed. Dorothy Collins. London and New York: Sheed and Ward, 1958.

Thirty-eight previously uncollected essays (1901-11), several on literary subjects.

13013 THE MAN WHO WAS CHESTERTON: THE BEST ESSAYS, STORIES, POEMS AND OTHER WRITINGS OF G.K. CHESTERTON. Ed. Raymond T. Bond. New York: Dodd, Mead, 1937.

Collects ninety-five essays, a selection of poems, nine stories.

13014 THE MAN WHO WAS ORTHODOX: A SELECTION FROM THE UNCOLLECTED WRITINGS OF G.K. CHESTERTON. Comp. A.L. Maycock. London: Dobson, 1963.

Anthology, ordering and arranging extracts from ninety-eight previously uncollected articles (1891-1936), chiefly on religious themes. See 24060.

13015 THE MINERVA EDITION OF THE WORKS OF G.K. CHESTERTON. 9 vols. London: Library Press, 1926.

Seven previously published volumes of essays and criticism (including CHARLES DICKENS), poetry, and a novel (THE FLYING INN).

13016 SELECTED ESSAYS. Ed. Dorothy Collins. London: Methuen, 1949.

Sixty-one essays. Excellent representative selection. See 25015.

13017 SELECTED STORIES. Ed. Kingsley Amis. London: Faber, 1972.

Thirteen tales. A good, highly selective collection. See 24003.

13018 THE SPICE OF LIFE, AND OTHER ESSAYS. Ed. Dorothy Collins. Beaconsfield, Engl.: Finlayson, 1964.

Previously uncollected essays. Includes sections on general literature and on particular books and writers.

13019 STORIES, ESSAYS AND POEMS. London: Dent, 1935.

Everyman Library anthology.

1.4 Letters

There has been no collected publication of GKC's letters, although some correspondence may be found in several of the memoirs and biographies listed below. Maisie Ward's two biographical volumes, G.K. CHESTERTON and RETURN TO CHESTERTON, reprint a large number of letters to and from GKC; see 22019 and 22020 below. Also see 21003.

2. SECONDARY BIBLIOGRAPHY

Note: THE CHESTERTON REVIEW (1974--), the newsletter of the GKC Society, publishes bibliographical, biographical, and critical articles on GKC and his work.

2.1 Bibliographies

21001 Sullivan, John. "The Trials of Bibliography." MANCHESTER REVIEW, 8 (1959), 331-38.

Chiefly concerns Sullivan's work with GKC.

21002 _____, ed. "Chesterton Bibliography Continued." CHESTERTON REVIEW, 2 (1975-76), 94-98 and continuing.

Corrigenda and addenda to Sullivan's book-length bibliographies (below).

*21003 _____. CHESTERTON CONTINUED: A BIBLIOGRAPHICAL SUPPLEMENT. London: Univ. of London Press, 1968.

Addenda and supplement (1956-66) to Sullivan's G.K. CHESTERTON: A BIBLIOGRAPHY (below). Also reprints twelve uncollected essays, poems, and letters (see 13002).

*21004 _____. G.K. CHESTERTON: A BIBLIOGRAPHY. London: Univ. of London Press, 1958.

Descriptive bibliography of GKC's books and pamphlets (114 items, few American editions noted), with checklists of GKC's contributions to books (over 200 items), articles (arranged by periodical source), illustrations, collections, translations, and miscellaneous GKC materials. The article listings are limited to essays of special merit or writings which were later collected into book form. Although Sullivan's cross-referencing system is unwieldy and his index scanty, his bibliography is very useful for most research tasks. Also includes a chronological list of 138 books and articles about GKC.

21005 _____. G.K. CHESTERTON, 1874-1974: AN EXHIBITION OF BOOKS, MANUSCRIPTS, DRAWINGS, AND OTHER MATERIAL RELATING TO G.K. CHESTERTON. London: National Book League, 1974.

Exhibition catalog of GKC's books and pamphlets, contributions to books and periodicals, drawings, notebooks, manuscripts, and letters. Generously annotated and illustrated.

2.2 Biographies, Memoirs, Reminiscences

Note: GKC's AUTOBIOGRAPHY (see 12005 above) should be consulted for preliminary biographical information.

*22001 Barker, Dudley. G.K. CHESTERTON: A BIOGRAPHY. London: Constable, 1973.

Well-written biography of GKC which manages to comment in some detail on most of the major works. Barker deals less with GKC's personality than Ward (22019 below), but gives a competent, concise account of GKC's ideas and literary relationships.

22002 Bentley, Edmund C. THOSE DAYS. London: Constable, 1940.

Memoir. Includes considerable material on the close friendship of GKC and Bentley (author of TRENT'S LAST CASE).

22003 Braybrooke, Patrick. I REMEMBER G.K. CHESTERTON. Epsom, Engl.: Dorling, 1938.

Miscellaneous anecdotes and reminiscences of a Pickwickian GKC (c. 1900-1930s).

22004 Chesterton, Ada E. THE CHESTERTONS. London: Chapman and Hall, 1941.

Memories of GKC, his wife Frances, and his brother Cecil, by his sister-in-law, chiefly concentrating on their political and journalistic activities. Factually unreliable, and distorted in perspective by an evident dislike of Frances.

22005 Chesterton, Lilian. "My Cousin Chesterton; Further Recollections; Chesterton's First Canadian Visit." MARK TWAIN QUARTERLY, 5, No. 3 (1943), 13-16; 5, No. 4 (1943), 19-20, 24; 6, No. 1 (1943), 9-11.

Memories of GKC (1900-1920) by his cousin's daughter.

22006 Chisholm, Joseph. G.K. CHESTERTON AND HIS BIOGRAPHER. Webster Groves, Mo.: International Mark Twain Society, 1945.

General survey of the works and brief biographical summary, with special praise for Maisie Ward's biography (22019). Pamphlet (27 p.).

22007 Clemens, Cyril, comp. CHESTERTON AS SEEN BY HIS CONTEMPORARIES. Webster Groves, Mo.: International Mark Twain Society, 1939.

First-hand accounts of GKC as schoolboy, friend, literary apprentice, public figure, traveler, poet, critic, and in other roles, compiled from extensive interviews and correspondence with GKC's acquaintances.

22008 Collins, Dorothy. "Recollections." In G.K. CHESTERTON. Ed. John Sullivan. Pp. 156-67. See 23019.

Memories of GKC during the last ten years of his life (1926-36) by his secretary and literary executrix.

22009 Heseltine, G.C. "G.K. Chesterton--Journalist." In G.K. CHESTERTON. Ed. John Sullivan. Pp. 125-40. See 23019.

Uninspired account of GKC's "Fleet Street" career, with personal memoir (1915 and after).

22010 McCorkell, E.J. "Chesterton in Canada." CHESTERTON REVIEW, 2 (1975-76), 39-54.

Account of GKC's two Canadian visits.

22011 MARK TWAIN QUARTERLY. I, No. 3 (1937), 1-24.

A "Chesterton Memorial Number" containing brief essays, impressions, memoirs, and extracts from books by eighteen hands.

22012 O'Connor, John [Father Brown]. FATHER BROWN ON CHESTERTON. London: Muller, 1937.

Memories of GKC by the original of Father Brown. Monsignor O'Connor, GKC's friend (from 1904) and spiritual counselor, formally received him into the Roman Catholic church in 1922.

22013 ———. "G.K. Chesterton: Recognita Decennalia." NINETEENTH CENTURY AND AFTER, 139 (1946), 301-7.

Memoir and appreciation on the tenth anniversary of GKC's death.

22014 Pearson, Hesketh. "G.K. Chesterton." In LIVES OF THE WITS. London: Heinemann, 1962. Pp. 302-18.

Anecdotal biographical sketch of a Falstaffian GKC.

22015 Sewell, Brocard. "Devereux Nights: A Distributist Memoir." In G.K. CHESTERTON. Ed. John Sullivan. Pp. 141-55. See 23019.

Reminiscences of the Secretary of the Distributist League, "office boy and general factotum to G.K.'S WEEKLY."

22016 Sieverking, Lance. "'Mr. Tame Lion': Reminiscences of G.K. Chesterton." LISTENER, 57 (1957), 24-25.

Brief memoir of acquaintance with GKC (1900-1936).

22017 Titterton, W.R. G.K. CHESTERTON: A PORTRAIT. London: Ouseley, 1936.

Memoirs of GKC by his journalistic companion at the DAILY NEWS, and his assistant editor at the NEW WITNESS and G.K.'S WEEKLY.

22018 Valentine, Ferdinand. "Father Vincent and Gilbert Chesterton." In FATHER VINCENT MCNABB, O.P. London: Burns, Oates, 1955. Pp. 264-80 and passim.

Documents Fr. McNabb's friendship with GKC with ample quotation from correspondence to GKC, his wife, and his associates.

*22019 Ward, Maisie. G.K. CHESTERTON. New York: Sheed and Ward, 1943.

The best full biography of GKC (supplemented by RETURN TO CHESTERTON, below). Ward has compiled a generous amount of memoir material from GKC's friends and acquaintances to form an appealing composite picture of his life and personality. Similarly, she documents the growth of GKC's ideas with wide reference to his published works and unpublished notebooks. An appendix is devoted to correcting some of the grosser distortions in Ada E. Chesterton's THE CHESTERTONS (22004, above).

22020 ______. RETURN TO CHESTERTON. New York: Sheed and Ward, 1952.

Compilation of GKC's "unpublished letters, verses, and *jeux d'espirit*," of several memoirs, "fresh stories" and additional materials, intended as a supplement to Ward's biography (above), in lieu of a revision.

2.3 Book-Length Critical Studies and Essay Collections

Also see the book-length studies of GKC's miscellaneous writings, by Keane and White (25025, 25036, below). Prof. Denis Conlon has announced the forthcoming publication (c. 1977) of a two-volume anthology of GKC criticism, to appear in the Antwerp Studies in English Literature series. Volume one will reprint selected reviews and assessments (1900-1937), and volume two will collect major critiques (1936-74). Also see 24047.

23001 Belloc, Hilaire. ON THE PLACE OF GILBERT CHESTERTON IN ENGLISH LETTERS. New York: Sheed and Ward, 1940.

Brief study (84 p.) of GKC's work, emphasizing his preoccupations with "social philosophy" and religion, and his characteristics as a writer: nationalism, precision of thought, allegorical imagination, historical perspective, charity, and faith.

23002 Bogaerts, Anthony M.A. CHESTERTON AND THE VICTORIAN AGE. Hilversum, Netherlands: Rozenbeek en Veneman, 1940.

Essays defining the Victorian age and assessing GKC's critical studies of the period (THE VICTORIAN AGE IN LITERATURE) and its writers (Dickens, Browning, and Stevenson). Bogaerts also includes a brief chapter on GKC "as a literary critic" (noting his preference for "healthy, optimistic and interesting literature"). A good introduction to GKC's view of Victorianism and his impact on modern critical perspectives.

*23003 Boyd, Ian. THE NOVELS OF CHESTERTON: A STUDY IN ART AND PROPAGANDA. New York: Barnes and Noble, 1975.

The best critical study of the longer fiction (the Father Brown stories and other story collections omitted). Boyd sees the novels primarily as allegorical embodiments of GKC's political and social views and carefully relates his readings to their topical contexts and GKC's developing ideas. The inseparability of GKC's art and propaganda is convincingly demonstrated. Extract originally published in 23019.

23004 Braybrooke, Patrick. G.K. CHESTERTON. 1922. 2nd ed. London: Chelsea, 1926.

Chapter-by-chapter survey of GKC's works, with considerable summary and occasional critical comment. Includes chapters entitled "The Essayist," "The Poet," "The Playwright," and "The Novelist."

23005 _____. THE WISDOM OF G.K. CHESTERTON. London: Palmer, 1929.

A sequel to, rather than a revision of, the above study. Braybrooke again examines GKC's works under several headings (e.g. "The Critic," "The Novelist," "The Essayist"), yet provides considerably more critical comment, and less summary. His chapter on the novels examines THE NAPO-

LEON OF NOTTING HILL, THE MAN WHO WAS THURSDAY, MANALIVE, THE FLYING INN, and THE RETURN OF DON QUIXOTE.

23006 Bullett, Gerald. THE INNOCENCE OF G.K. CHESTERTON. London: Palmer, 1923.

Admiring survey of GKC's many roles, from "controversialist" and "defender of the faith" to "laughing philosopher" and "creator of fantasy." Bullett dismisses GKC's fiction as an unsuccessful "blend of the modern novel and the fairy tale" and concentrates his study on GKC's achievements in nonfiction.

23007 Cammaerts, Emile. THE LAUGHING PROPHET. THE SEVEN VIRTUES AND G.K. CHESTERTON. London: Methuen, 1937.

Sentimental portrait of GKC's "philosophy of life" (in light of the seven virtues), waging an "eternal fight against the vices of civilization."

23008 Carol, Sister M. G.K. CHESTERTON: THE DYNAMIC CLASSICIST. Delhi: Motilal Banarsidass, 1971.

General reading of GKC's works, loosely bound by the thesis that GKC's "sensibility as a writer intimately fuses the romantic and the classic elements" of fancy and dogmatism. Individual chapters survey "themes" and "ideas" in the short fiction and the novels.

23009 [Chesterton, Cecil]. G.K. CHESTERTON--A CRITICISM. London: Alston Rivers, 1908.

Interesting and still valuable early assessment of GKC as a propagandist, written and published anonymously by his brother. The book deals at length with the origins of GKC thought and considers individual aspects of his work in several chapters, including "A Teller of Tales" on the fiction, pages 196-221.

*23010 Clipper, Lawrence J. G.K. CHESTERTON. New York: Twayne, 1974.

Admirable survey and general introduction to GKC as a man of ideas. Much of Clipper's book is devoted to the clarification of GKC's political and social views and to brief accounts of his literary criticism and religious essays, although he devotes his final two chapters to the poetry and fiction. The novels and stories, seen as "romances," are "continuing skirmishes in the social, political, and intellectual battles" of the nonfictional writings. Brief annotated bibliography.

23011 Evans, Maurice. G.K. CHESTERTON. Cambridge: At the Univ. Press, 1939.

GKC presented as a writer for the common man who, paradoxically, retained his popularity while "denouncing" the age in which he lived. GKC's opinions are ruled throughout by his sense of the "permanent facts of human nature" and orthodox moral values. Includes separate chapters on GKC's religious and political views and on his novels, essays, poems, and style.

*23012 Furlong, William B. GBS/GKC: SHAW AND CHESTERTON, THE METAPHYSICAL JESTERS. University Park: Pennsylvania State Univ. Press, 1970.

Detailed account of the literary and personal relationship of Shaw and GKC, from the time of their meeting (c. 1901) to GKC's death in 1936. Furlong describes the controversies surrounding GKC's brilliant critical study of Shaw, their great public debates on politics and religion (with copious quotation from the scarce documentation), and their written challenges to one another's philosophies (a discarded act from BACK TO METHUSELAH figures importantly), yet stresses throughout the bond of personal affection which united the two writers despite their "metaphysical" differences. A valuable book for readers of GKC and Shaw alike.

23013 Hollis, Christopher. G.K. CHESTERTON. London: Longmans, 1950.

Fine short introduction (27 p.) to GKC's work and thought which concentrates on the nonfiction for illustration, although the Father Brown stories are briefly considered. The selected bibliography, but not the text, was revised in 1964.

*23014 ____. THE MIND OF CHESTERTON. London: Hollis and Carter, 1970.

Excellent, full study of GKC's religion and its influence on his social and political ideas as they are revealed in his writings. Hollis necessarily deals at length with the nonfiction, GKC's chief medium, but not to the total exclusion of the novels and short fiction.

*23015 Kenner, Hugh. PARADOX IN CHESTERTON. New York: Sheed and Ward, 1947.

Distinguished, controversial reading of GKC as a (humorless) modern philosopher, in the scholastic tradition of Aquinas. GKC's several failings as an artist--"he merely did not polish what he made"--are redeemed by the essential rightness of his message and his brilliant use of the Thomistic idea of analogy: "His especial gift was his metaphysical intuition of being; his especial triumph was his exploitation of paradox to embody that intuition."

23016 LasVergnas, Raymond. CHESTERTON, BELLOC, BARING. Trans. C.C. Martindale. New York: Sheed and Ward, 1938.

Separate essays on the three Anglo-Catholic men of letters and Christian apologists. LasVergnas's commentary on GKC (pp. 1-49) is limited to a general summary of GKC's ideas and an impressionistic appreciation of his qualities. The translator's Appendix (134-53) takes issue with several of the author's judgments, of GKC especially.

23017 Reckitt, Maurice B. G.K. CHESTERTON: A CHRISTIAN PROPHET FOR ENGLAND TO-DAY. London: S.P.C.K., 1950.

Two lectures on GKC as a spokesman for orthodoxy and, in his works, "an emanation of Christian Joy." A 40-page pamphlet.

23018 Sprug, Joseph W., ed. AN INDEX TO G.K. CHESTERTON. Washington, D.C.: Catholic Univ. of America Press, 1966.

Subject index of GKC's ideas, keyed to nearly one hundred books, pamphlets collections, and other writings. Purpose and value of this compilation questionable.

*23019 Sullivan, John, ed. G.K. CHESTERTON: A CENTENARY APPRAISAL. London: Elek, 1974.

Excellent collection of fourteen original essays reevaluating GKC's "achievement" (seven), GKC "the man" (three) and GKC's "relevance" (four). Includes items 22008, 22009, 22015, 23003 (extract), 24002, 24005, 24014, 24022, 24030, 24062, 24063, 24078, 25004, and 25014.

23020 Virginia, Sister Marie. G.K. CHESTERTON'S EVANGEL. New York: Benziger, 1937.

Intelligent reading of GKC from an interesting but narrowly religious point of view. GKC's works and personal philosophy are consistently seen in a semimystical light as influenced by the "Sacred Mysteries" of Catholicism and the miracle of the Incarnation.

23021 West, Julius. G.K. CHESTERTON: A CRITICAL STUDY. London: Secker, 1915.

Interesting, balanced, and still-valuable mid-career assessment, viewing GKC both as reacting against and being a product of the literary decadence of the nineties. Includes chapters on GKC as novelist ("Romancer"), dramatist, critic, poet, politician, and Christian apologist.

23022 Wills, Gary. CHESTERTON: MAN AND MASK. New York: Sheed and Ward, 1961.

Thorough chronological reading of GKC's works and commentary on his ideas. Wills finds the reputation and the reality of GKC oftentimes contradictory and attempts to resolve his portrait in arguing that GKC adopted a variety of "masks" throughout his career. Wills's commentaries are useful, though his thesis remains unconvincing.

2.4 General Critical Articles, or Chapters on GKC

24001 Agar, Herbert. "A Great Democrat." SoR, 3 (1937), 95-105.

Admiring obituary survey.

*24002 Amis, Kingsley. "Four Fluent Fellows: An Essay on Chesterton's Fiction." In G.K. CHESTERTON. Ed. John Sullivan. Pp. 28-39. See 23019.

Four characteristics of GKC as novelist: polemicist, buffoon, melodramatist, and impressionist. Good brief commentaries on the novels and story collections.

24003 ______. "Introduction." In his GKC'S SELECTED STORIES. Pp. 11-21. See 13017.

General critical assessment of GKC as storyteller, noting his antiprogressivist message and technique.

*24004 Baker, Ernest A. THE HISTORY OF THE ENGLISH NOVEL. X, 271-87. See G2203.

GKC's fiction essentially "the expression of philosophic ideas in the artistic form of a story." Fine survey of GKC's techniques and literary relationships (cf. Butler and Shaw).

24005 Barker, Dudley. "A Brief Survey of Chesterton's Work." In G.K. CHESTERTON. Ed. John Sullivan. Pp. 3-15. See 23019.

Comments on several books chosen from the more than one hundred published works.

24006 Batchelor, John. "Chesterton as an Edwardian Novelist." CHESTERTON REVIEW, 1 (1974), 23-35.

GKC's fantasy novels quite representative of the "aesthetic and intellectual climate" of the Edwardian period.

24007 Belloc, Hilaire. "Gilbert Chesterton." 1940. In ONE THING AND ANOTHER. London: Hollis and Carter, 1955. Pp. 171-76.

The unique relationship between GKC's style and meaning. Essay largely absorbed into Belloc's study of GKC (see 23001).

24008 Bishop, John. "G.K. Chesterton: Man of Letters and Defender of the Faith." LQHR, 173 (1948), 149-55.

GKC's greatness and his unashamed Christianity.

*24009 Borges, Jorge Luis. "On Chesterton." In OTHER INQUISITIONS, 1937-1952. Trans. Ruth L.C. Simms. Austin: Univ. of Texas Press, 1964. Pp. 82-85.

GKC rejected the extravagant in his opinions and his art (cf. Poe or Kafka) to affirm the simple "solutions of this world."

24010 Bradbrook, B.R. "The Literary Relationship between G.K. Chesterton and Karl Capek." SEER, 39 (1960), 327-38.

Not seen.

24011 Braybrooke, Patrick. "G.K. Chesterton." PHILOSOPHIES IN MODERN FICTION. London: Daniel, 1929. Pp. 29-33.

GKC's admirable combination of Catholic dogma and humanistic toleration.

24012 Bridges, Horace J. "Mr. G.K. Chesterton as Theologian." In CRITICISMS OF LIFE: STUDIES IN FAITH, HOPE AND DESPAIR. Boston: Houghton Mifflin, 1915. Pp. 42-76.

Notes GKC's haste, irresponsibility, and incoherence, despite fundamental agreement with his orthodoxy.

24013 Brome, Vincent. "G.K. Chesterton versus Bernard Shaw." In SIX STUDIES IN QUARRELLING. London: Cresset, 1958.

Brief account of the Chesterton-Shaw controversies. See Furlong's book, GBS/GKC (23012 above), for a fuller study.

*24014 Cahill, Patrick. "Chesterton and the Future of Democracy." In G.K. CHESTERTON. Ed. John Sullivan. Pp. 182-205. See 23019.

Analysis of GKC's social ideas, developing the relationship between "Distributism" and democracy.

24015 Churchill, R.C. "The Man Who Was Sunday: G.K. Chesterton, 1874-1936." ContempR, 224 (1974), 12-15.

GKC's "supreme" gifts as storyteller.

*24016 Clarke, Margaret. "Chesterton the Classicist." DUBLIN REVIEW, 229 (1955), 51-67.

Influence of GKC's classical training on his fiction, essays, and Christian apologetics.

24017 Compton-Rickett, Arthur. "Three Social Critics: Wells, Chesterton, Shaw." In PORTRAITS AND PERSONALITIES. London: Selwyn and Blount, 1937. Pp. 47-54.

On the "Big Three" social critics, Wells the futurist, Chesterton the medievalist, and Shaw the palatable idealogue.

24018 Corrin, Jay P. "The Formation of the Distributist Circle." CHESTERTON REVIEW, 1 (1975), 52-83.

In-depth account of the origins of the Distributist political movement in GKC, Belloc, and others.

24019 Cunningham, Lawrence S. "Chesterton as Mystic." AMERICAN BENEDICTINE REVIEW, 26 (1975), 16-24.

Central correspondences, in GKC's thought, to traditional mystic themes.

24020 Day, A.E. "The Story of G.K.'S WEEKLY." LIBRARY REVIEW, 24 (1974), 209-12.

Account of the origins and conduct of GKC's periodical.

24021 De Fonseka, J.P. "Preface." In G.K.C. AS M.C. Pp. ix-xx. See 13007.

GKC's catholicity of taste as a critic.

24022 d'Haussy, Christiane. "Chesterton in France." In G.K. CHESTERTON. Ed. John Sullivan. Pp. 206-18. See 23019.

Surveys French criticism of GKC and GKC's impact on French writers.

24023 Donaghy, Henry J. "Chesterton on Shaw's Views of Catholicism." ShawR, 10 (1967), 108-16.

GKC thought Shaw misunderstood Catholicism because he was unable to understand paradox.

24024 Eaker, J. Gordon. "G.K. Chesterton among the Moderns." GaR, 13 (1959), 152-60.

GKC's attacks upon the ideas and spokesmen of modernism fueled by his optimistic confidence in reason and common sense.

24025 Edwards, Dorothy. "G.K. Chesterton." In SCRUTINIES. Comp. Edgell Rickword. London: Wishart, 1928. I, 30-40.

GKC "far worse than a liar," a writer who "cannot distinguish between symbols and facts."

24026 Ervine, St. John G. "G.K. Chesterton." In SOME IMPRESSIONS OF MY ELDERS. New York: Macmillan, 1922. Pp. 90-112.

GKC's characteristics (e.g., for the common man, anti-modern, nationalistic).

24027 Feeney, Leonard. "The Metaphysics of Chesterton." THOUGHT, 17 (1942), 22-36.

GKC's fascination with "being as being, with thing as thing," a "metaphysical" statement in the truest sense of the word.

24028 Firkins, O.W. "G.K. Chesterton." FORUM, 48 (1912), 597-607.

GKC's extraordinary powers of argument and brilliant writing style.

24029 Freeman, John. "A Canterbury Pilgrim." In ENGLISH PORTRAITS AND ESSAYS. London: Hodder and Stoughton, 1924. Pp. 1-32.

GKC's "natural piety" in his work.

24030 Furbank, P.N. "Chesterton the Edwardian." In G.K. CHESTERTON. Ed. John Sullivan. Pp. 16-27. See 23019.

GKC the archetypal Edwardian prophet, an excellent "teacher and entertainer combined."

24031 Gilkes, A.N. "G.B.S., G.K.C. and Paradox." FORTNIGHTLY REVIEW, 168 (1950), 266-70.

Similarities and distinctions between Shaw's and GKC's use of paradox.

24032 Green, V.H.H. "G.K. Chesterton." THEOLOGY, 43 (1941), 93-101, 150-55.

GKC's "eminent place in the rehabilitation of Christian thought and laughter at the beginning of this century." Defines GKC's theology.

24033 Guedalla, Philip. "Mr. G.K. Chesterton." In MASTERS AND MEN. New York: Putnam's, 1923. Pp. 125-28.

Attacks GKC's ignorant responses to the Zionist movement.

24034 Hamilton, Robert. "The Rationalist from Fairyland." QR, 305 (1967), 444-53.

GKC's great sensibility and "unique power of imaginative reason" (i.e., creative association of ideas).

24035 Hardie, W.F.R. "The Philosophy of G.K. Chesterton." HJ, 29 (1931), 449-64.

GKC's "impulse to find reasons for his beliefs." Surveys GKC's ideas.

*24036 Hart, Jeffrey. "In Praise of Chesterton." YR, 53 (1963), 49-60.

Essay in revaluation, attacking misconceptions about GKC's social, religious, and political beliefs.

24037 Hetzler, Leo A. "Chesterton and the Man in the Forest." CHESTERTON REVIEW, 1 (1974), 11-18.

GKC's themes of "primal intuition and mystical insights."

24038 _____. "Chesterton's Teen-Age Writings." CHESTERTON REVIEW, 2 (1975-76), 65-77.

Description and evaluation of GKC's unpublished juvenilia.

*24039 Hynes, Samuel. "Chesterton." In his EDWARDIAN OCCASIONS. Pp. 80-87. See G2345.

Perceptive critique of the works, finding continuity in GKC's "allegorical imagination" which repeatedly affirms "the intelligible order of existence."

24040 Irvine, William. "Shaw and Chesterton." VQR, 23 (1947), 273-81.

Fundamental similarity of purpose in the friendly antagonists. Brief account of their relations.

24041 Irwin, W.R. THE GAME OF THE IMPOSSIBLE. Pp. 132-34. See G6417.

The "innocence" of GKC's fantasies.

24042 Jago, David. "The Metaphysician as Fiction-Writer: G.K. Chesterton's Narrative Techniques." AntigR, No. 22 (1975), pp. 85-99.

GKC's search for a "suitable form" most successful in the Father Brown stories. Brief comments on the major fiction.

24043 John, V.V. "The Chestertonian Style." CathW, 184 (1957), 369-74.

Appreciation (but no analysis) of GKC's style.

24044 Jones, W.S. Handley. "G.K. Chesterton and the Discovery of Christianity." In his THE PRIEST AND THE SIREN. Pp. 13-29. See G6306.

GKC's religion the "vitalizing root" of his thinking.

24045 Kirk, Russell. "Chesterton, Madmen, and Madhouses." In MYTH, ALLEGORY, AND GOSPEL: AN INTERPRETATION OF J.R.R. TOLKIEN, C.S. LEWIS, G.K. CHESTERTON, CHARLES WILLIAMS. Ed. John W. Montgomery. Minneapolis: Bethany Fellowship, 1974. Pp. 33-51.

Theme of lunacy and parabolic use of madness in GKC's fiction.

24046 Knox, Ronald A. "G.K. Chesterton." 1936. In LITERARY DISTRACTIONS. London: Sheed and Ward, 1958. Pp. 153-69.

GKC's use of fantasy, dream, and romance as vehicles for his political and religious ideas.

*24047 Lea, Frank A. "G.K. Chesterton." In MODERN CHRISTIAN REVOLUTIONARIES. Ed. Donald Attwater. New York: Devin-Adair, 1947. Pp. 89-157.

Excellent brief introduction to the "life and thought" of GKC. Earlier published separately as A WILD KNIGHT OF BATTERSEA: G.K. CHESTERTON (1945).

24048 Lewis, C.S. "Notes on the Way." TIME AND TIDE, 27 (1946), 1070-71.

GKC's imaginative work transcends its period quality.

24049 Lodge, David. "The Chesterbelloc and the Jews." In THE NOVELIST AT THE CROSSROADS. Pp. 145-58. See G4055.

Anti-Semitism of GKC and Belloc exaggerated by their critics, but not unsubstantiated.

*24050 ______. "Dual Vision: Chesterton as a Novelist." MONTH, 7 (1974), 579-82, 584.

"Idea of Metaphysical duality" central to GKC's early, successful fiction, but incompatible with GKC's later orthodox Catholicism.

24051 Lowther, F.H. "G.K. Chesterton: The Man and His Work." LQHR, 168 (1943), 335-41.

Strong autobiographical elements in GKC's writing (especially his faith).

24052 Lynd, Robert. "Mr. G.K. Chesterton and Mr. Hilaire Belloc." In OLD AND NEW MASTERS. London: Unwin, 1919. Pp. 25-41.

Ambivalent response to GKC, Belloc and "Chester-Belloc."

24053 MacCallum, R.B. "Mr. Chesterton as a Democrat." BOOKMAN (London), 81 (1931), 14-15.

GKC's idiosyncratic political views.

24054 MacDonald, Gregory. "The Other Face: Chesterton's Later Journalism." CHESTERTON REVIEW, 1 (1975), 84-99.

Controversial "clarification" of several misconceptions about GKC's work with G.K.'S WEEKLY (see several responses, 2 [1975-76], 102-28).

24055 McLuhan, H. Marshall. "Introduction." In Hugh Kenner's PARADOX IN CHESTERTON. Pp. xi-xxii. See 23015.

GKC not a literary artist, but a distinguished "metaphysical moralist."

24056 ______. "The Origins of Chesterton's Medievalism." CHESTERTON REVIEW, 1 (1975), 49-50.

GKC's medievalism derived from Pre-Raphaelites (brief note).

*24057 Mason, Michael. THE CENTRE OF HILARITY: A PLAY UPON IDEAS ABOUT LAUGHTER AND THE ABSURD. London: Sheed and Ward, 1959. Pp. 174-88 and passim.

GKC's natural holism and Christian affirmation an ideological synthesis of the controversy between the representative "earnest" moderns, Lawrence and Eliot.

24058 _____. "Chesterbelloc." TWENTIETH CENTURY, 177-78 (1968-69), 84-87.

General introduction to the Chesterton-Belloc relationship.

24059 Maurois, Andre. "G.K. Chesterton." In PROPHETS AND POETS. Pp. 141-74. See G3102.

GKC as optimist, democrat, and reactionary (surveys life and works).

*24060 Maycock, A.L. "Introduction." In THE MAN WHO WAS ORTHODOX. Ed. Maycock. Pp. 13-80. See 13014.

Expansive introduction to this anthology of GKC, which summarizes his journalistic career in detail and assesses the development of his thought (with special emphasis on his religious views).

24061 Maynard, Theodore. "Some Chesterbellocian Controversies." CathW, 120 (1924), 19-27.

The love of argument, and its style, in GKC and Belloc.

*24062 Medcalf, Stephen. "The Achievement of G.K. Chesterton." In G.K. CHESTERTON. Ed. John Sullivan. Pp. 81-121. See 23019.

Portrait of GKC as a deeply divided personality, both revealing and sublimating his "shadow self" in his work through his compulsive defenses against consciousness, mysticism and symbolism, nightmare and despair.

24063 Milward, Peter. "Chesterton in Japan." In G.K. CHESTERTON. Ed. John Sullivan. Pp. 219-38. See 23109.

Surveys GKC's critical reputation in Japan.

24064 Morton, Arthur Leslie. "Chesterton: Man of Thermidor." In LANGUAGE OF MEN. London: Cobbett Press, 1945. Pp. 72-77.

GKC's limitations as historian and social critic.

24065 Murch, Alma E. THE DEVELOPMENT OF THE DETECTIVE NOVEL. Pp. 199-202. See G6104.

GKC "one of the first distinguished men of letters to champion detective fiction." Brief review.

24066 Murray, Henry. "G.K. Chesterton." BOOKMAN (London), 38 (1910), 63-69.

Early critical overview of GKC as novelist, essayist, stylist, and man of "genius" (several fascinating illustrations).

24067 Noyes, Alfred. "The Centrality of Chesterton." QR, 291 (1953), 43-50.

Among the moderns, GKC's originality attributed to his rediscovery of the "laws of God and nature."

24068 Orage, Alfred R. "Mr. G.K. Chesterton." In THE ART OF READING. New York: Farrar and Rinehart, 1930. Pp. 242-45 and passim.

GKC's clever, sparkling style, frequently inappropriate to his subject matter (e.g., his polemical essays).

24069 Pfleger, Karl. "Chesterton, the Adventurer of Orthodoxy." In WRESTLERS WITH CHRIST. Trans. E.I. Watkin. New York: Sheed and Ward, 1936. Pp. 159-81.

Humorless portrait of GKC as "bard," prophet, and vanquisher of infidels, in defense of orthodoxy.

24070 Purnell, George. "The Humor of Chesterton." CHESTERTON REVIEW, 2 (1975-76), 1-21.

Characterizes and describes GKC's humor.

24071 Scott-James, Rolfe A. "Chesterton and Other Essayists." In his FIFTY YEARS OF ENGLISH LITERATURE. Pp. 47-53. See G2121.

Surveys the development of GKC's (and others') style and ideas as an essayist.

24072 ____. "Gilbert Chesterton." In PERSONALITY IN LITERATURE: 1913-1931. New York: Holt, 1932. Pp. 96-105.

GKC's philosophy "a sort of sublimated public opinion minus the opinion of the intellectuals."

*24073 Sewell, Elizabeth. "G.K. Chesterton: The Giant Upside-Down." THOUGHT, 30 (1955), 555-76.

GKC a decadent (cf. Wilde), protecting himself from himself, through "nonsense." An instrumental attempt to describe GKC's "darker" side.

*24074 Shaw, George Bernard. PEN PORTRAITS AND REVIEWS. London: Constable, 1932. Pp. 71-104.

Collects four reviews and commentaries, on GKC and Belloc (in which Shaw coins the name "Chesterbelloc"), GKC's critical study of Shaw himself, GKC's SHORT HISTORY OF ENGLAND (1917), and GKC's EUGENICS AND OTHER EVILS (1922). Witty and perceptive.

24075 Shuster, George N. "The Adventures of a Journalist: G.K. Chesterton." In THE CATHOLIC SPIRIT IN MODERN ENGLISH LITERATURE. New York: Macmillan, 1922. Pp. 229-48.

Mid-career estimate, noting GKC's diversity and strengths as well as his many imperfections (affectation, haste, and "stubbornness of opinion").

24076 Slosson, Edwin E. "G.K. Chesterton." In SIX MAJOR PROPHETS. Boston: Little, Brown, 1917. Pp. 129-89.

GKC a spokesman for the great "inarticulate" masses in his defense of orthodoxy and "all forms of ritualism and medievalism." Surveys GKC's views.

24077 Smith, Mary C. "The Rightness of G.K. Chesterton." CathW, 113 (1921), 163-68.

GKC achieves spiritual "rightness" through paradox and contradictions.

24078 Sullivan, John. "A Liberal Education." In G.K. CHESTERTON. Ed. John Sullivan. Pp. 171-81. See 23019.

Recounts the course of Sullivan's reading of GKC (with a prediction of a GKC revival).

24079 Swinnerton, Frank. THE GEORGIAN LITERARY SCENE. Pp. 72-82. See G2364.

GKC and Belloc as Catholic "liberals."

24080 Symons, Julian. BLOODY MURDER. Pp. 81-84 and passim. See G6105.

Brief review of GKC's detective stories and his comments on the genre.

24081 Versfeld, M. "Chesterton and St. Thomas." ESA, 4 (1961), 128-46.

GKC's Thomistic "vision of reality."

24082 Ward, Leo R. "The Innocence of G.K. Chesterton." ModA, 19 (1975), 146-56.

Centennial appreciation and brief commentary on GKC's orthodox beliefs.

24083 Ward, Maisie. "Introduction." In GKC's THE COLOURED LANDS. Pp. 9-16. See 12009.

Fantasy in GKC not an escape from reality, but "an extension of reality," a recognition of the magic in the world.

24084 Ward, Wilfred P. "Mr. Chesterton among the Prophets." In MEN AND MATTERS. London: Longmans, 1914. Pp. 105-44.

GKC's "thought" classed with Burke, Butler, and Coleridge. Principal emphasis on ORTHODOXY.

24085 Waring, Hubert. "G.K. Chesterton: Prince of Essayists." FORTNIGHTLY REVIEW, 142 (1937), 588-95.

General estimate and obituary tribute.

24086 Wells, H.G. "About Chesterton and Belloc." In AN ENGLISHMAN LOOKS AT THE WORLD. London: Cassell, 1914. Pp. 175-82.

Wells's fundamental agreement with GKC, in spirit, and antipathy toward Belloc.

2.5 Studies of Individual Works

The following section is subdivided into two parts: i. Fiction (alphabetically by title and ii. Miscellaneous Writings. Several studies of GKC contain commentaries on the individual works. For discussions of the fiction, in particular, consult the books by Boyd (23003), Braybrooke (23004, 23005), Clipper (23010), West (23021), and Wills (23022), in section 2.3,above.

i. FICTION

The "Father Brown" Stories

25001 Gillespie, Robert. "Detections: Borges and Father Brown." NOVEL, 7 (1974), 220-30.

Technical and philosophic similarities between GKC's and Borges's detective fiction.

25002 Haycraft, Howard. MURDER FOR PLEASURE. Pp. 74-77. See G6102.

GKC's best detective stories found in the first two "Father Brown" volumes.

25003 Knox, Ronald A. "Father Brown." In LITERARY DISTRACTIONS. London: Sheed and Ward, 1958. Pp. 170-79.

Humanity and simplicity of GKC's detective: "There is nothing of the mystic about him." (Also printed as introduction to the Oxford World's Classics anthology of Father Brown stories, 1955).

25004 Robson, W.W. "Father Brown and Others." In G.K. CHESTERTON. Ed. John Sullivan. Pp. 58-72. See 23019.

Revised version of essay below, arguing that the Father Brown stories transcend their detective genre and Catholic themes.

*25005 ______. "G.K. Chesterton's 'Father Brown' Stories." SoR, 5 (1969), 611-29.

GKC's detective stories both the "most ingenious" ever written and distinguished works of literary art. Excellent survey of their general characteristics.

*25006 Routley, Erik. "The Mystery of Iniquity; The Fairy Tale and the Secret: Father Brown." In THE PURITAN PLEASURES OF THE DETECTIVE STORY. London: Gollancz, 1972. Pp. 89-116.

Two essays on the implicit moral allegory in the stories. "Father Brown is the Catholic Church impersonated as the church of the common man."

25007 Ryan, Alvan S. "The Blue Cross." In INSIGHT II. Ed. John V. Hagopian and Martin Dolch. Pp. 43-47. See G5007.

Story summary, critique, and study questions. "The Blue Cross" is the first of the Father Brown stories (in THE INNOCENCE OF FATHER BROWN).

25008 Scott, Dixon. "The Guilt of Mr. Chesterton." In MEN OF LETTERS. New York: Hodder and Stoughton, 1916. Pp. 184-90.

THE INNOCENCE OF FATHER BROWN collection transforms at midpoint from fantasy to sinister nightmare.

THE MAN WHO WAS THURSDAY (1908)

25009 Amis, Kingsley. "Speaking of Books: THE MAN WHO WAS THURSDAY." NYTBR, 13 Oct. 1968, p. 2.

Continued appeal of GKC's archaic melodrama.

25010 Waugh, Evelyn. "The Jesuit Who Was Thursday: Villians by Mrs. Trollope, Chesterton, and Koestler." COMMONWEAL, 45 (1947), 558-61.

GKC's obsolete confidence in the resilience of the social and moral order.

*25011 Wills, Gary. "Introduction." In THE MAN WHO WAS THURSDAY: A NIGHTMARE. London: Sheed and Ward, 1975. Pp. vii-xxx.

Excellent full reading of the "dream novel."

THE NAPOLEON OF NOTTING HILL (1904)

25012 Hamilton, Kenneth M. "G.K. Chesterton and George Orwell: A Contrast in Prophecy." DR, 31 (1951), 198-205.

Two contrasting futuristic novels, set in 1984: GKC's NAPOLEON OF NOTTING HILL and Orwell's "1984."

ii. MISCELLANEOUS WRITINGS

25013 Auden, W.H. "Foreword." In G.K. CHESTERTON: SELECTIONS FROM HIS NON-FICTIONAL PROSE. Ed. Auden. Pp. 11-18. See 13009.

Strengths and weaknesses of GKC's journalism. Reprinted several times.

25014 _____. "The Gift of Wonder." In G.K. CHESTERTON. Ed. John Sullivan. Pp. 73-80. See 23019.

Brief appreciation of GKC's poetry.

25015 Bentley, Edmund C. "Introduction." In GKC's SELECTED ESSAYS. Ed. Dorothy Collins. Pp. v-x. See 13016.

GKC's gifts as journalist and essayist. "He could not be a novelist."

25016 Bergonzi, Bernard. "Chesterton and/or Belloc." 1959. · In his THE TURN OF THE CENTURY. Pp. 124-33. See G2309.

GKC's miscellaneous prose his only lasting achievement.

25017 Braybrooke, Patrick. "Chesterton and Some History." In PEEPS AT THE MIGHTY. Philadelphia: Lippincott, 1927. Pp. 77-94.

Critique of GKC's SHORT HISTORY OF ENGLAND (1917), particularly his handling of the medieval period.

25018 Chambers, Leland H. "Gide, Santayana, Chesterton, and Browning." CLS, 7 (1970), 216-28.

GKC's study of Browning (1903) significantly influenced Gide's enthusiasm for the poet.

25019 Churchill, R.C. "Chesterton on Dickens: The Legend and the Reality." DICKENS STUDIES NEWSLETTER, 5 (1974), 34-38.

GKC the best Dickens critic of his time (also see responses, 6 [1975], 14-16).

25020 Cunningham, Lawrence S. "Chesterton Reconsidered." THOUGHT, 47 (1972), 271-79.

Continuing vitality and importance of GKC's theological writings.

25021 Derus, David L. "Chesterton as Literary Critic." RENASCENCE, 25 (1973), 103-12.

GKC's dogmatism and failure to achieve a consistent point of view as a critic.

25022 Evans, David. "The Making of G.K. Chesterton's HERETICS." YES, 5 (1975), 207-13.

Several of the essays in HERETICS derived from periodical essays in the DAILY NEWS (1901-4).

*25023 Gross, John. THE RISE AND FALL OF THE MAN OF LETTERS. Pp. 219-26 and passim. See G2334.

Excellent assessment of GKC's strengths and weaknesses as a literary critic.

25024 Hagiwara, Kyohei. "Mr. G.K. Chesterton as Poet." SEL (Tokyo), 14 (1934), 571-81.

GKC the humorous "mortal enemy" of the New Poetry.

25025 Keane, Janus M. THE MARIOLOGY OF G.K. CHESTERTON'S POETRY. Rome: International Marian Commission, 1952.

Marian themes in the poetry.

25026 Lunn, Arnold. "G.K. Chesterton." In ROMAN CONVERTS. London: Chapman and Hall, 1924. Pp. 211-65.

GKC an effective critic of modern thought and other people's creeds (e.g., HERETICS and ORTHODOXY).

25027 Marcus, Steven. "Introduction." In CHARLES DICKENS. New York: Schocken, 1965. Pp. vii-xviii.

GKC's significant role in the twentieth-century revaluation of Dickens. Introduces the reissue of GKC's 1906 essay.

25028 Maynard, Theodore. "G.K. Chesterton: The Wild Knight on Crusade." In OUR BEST POETS: ENGLISH AND AMERICAN. New York: Holt, 1922. Pp. 3-16.

GKC's excellent but "unfinished" poetry.

25029 Miller, L.G. "The Wild Knight: Chesterton, the Poet." CathW, 155 (1942), 68-74.

GKC's grand theme, the wonder of common things.

25030 Palmer, Herbert. "G.K. Chesterton and His School." In POST-VICTORIAN POETRY. London: Dent, 1938. Pp. 158-67.

The "robustiousness, rapture," and Catholicism of the "Modern School of the Medieval Elizabethans."

25031 Petitpas, Harold M. "Chesterton's Metapoetics." RENASCENCE, 23 (1971), 137-44.

Jargon-laden assessment of GKC's contribution to poetic theory.

25032 Reilly, Joseph J. "Chesterton as Poet." In OF BOOKS AND MEN. New York: Messner, 1942. Pp. 60-76.

General critical survey of GKC's poetry.

25033 Scott, William T. "Chesterton as Writer and Critic; Chesterton as a Religious Writer." In CHESTERTON AND OTHER ESSAYS. Cincinnati: Jennings and Graham, 1912. Pp. 11-39, 43-75.

Appreciative reviews of and commentary on GKC as a champion of Christianity.

25034 Semper, I.J. "The Quintessence of Chesterton." CathW, 156 (1942), 40-45.

Critique of GKC's play MAGIC (1913).

25035 Sheed, Wilfrid. "Introduction." In GKC's ESSAYS AND POEMS. Baltimore: Penguin, 1958. Pp. 9-20.

GKC gifted with an original fund of ideas and a felicitous style as light essayist (principally on his essays).

25036 White, Albert C. [Alan Handsacre]. AUTHORDOXY: BEING A DISCURSIVE EXAMINATION OF MR. G.K. CHESTERTON's "ORTHODOXY." London: Lane, 1921.

Point-by-point response to GKC's arguments in ORTHODOXY (1908), by one whom he has failed to convert.

25037 Williams, Charles. "G.K. Chesterton." In POETRY AT PRESENT. Oxford: Clarendon, 1930. Pp. 97-113.

GKC's preoccupation with war, battle, and debate.

IVY COMPTON-BURNETT (1884-1969)

1. PRIMARY BIBLIOGRAPHY

IC's career as a writer is doubly unique: unlike most of the other authors in this guide, who have been active in many different forms, IC has published no essays, drama, travel literature, or other "miscellaneous" writings. Therefore, this primary section is limited to two of the standard four divisions: Fiction and Collected Works. Further, IC's unique formula-novels defy individual annotation. As Charles Burkhart observes: "the titles of her books are so alike . . . within the books the conventions are as severe as in any other classical artist: the novels are ninety percent dialogue, concern power, secrets, jealousy, illegitimacy, incest, money, and death, take place in a late-Victorian or Edwardian house in the country, have a tyrant, a choric and inquisitive neighboring family, and a plot whose external features are the detritus of Victorian melodrama used with almost contemptuous arbitrariness . . . but whose internal feature may be a strong and organic image which the title itself often suggests" (THE ART OF IVY COMPTON-BURNETT, ed. Burkhart, p. 159; see 23003 below).

1.1 Fiction

All works are novels.

11001 BROTHERS AND SISTERS. London: Cranton; New York: Harcourt, 1929.

11002 BULLIVANT AND THE LAMBS. See MANSERVANT AND MAIDSERVANT (11013).

11003 DARKNESS AND DAY. London: Gollancz; New York: Knopf, 1951.

11004 DAUGHTERS AND SONS. London: Gollancz, 1937. New York: Norton, 1938.

11005 DOLORES. Edinburgh: Blackwood, 1911. No Amer. ed.

IC's first novel, later dismissed by her as a juvenile work.

11006 ELDERS AND BETTERS. London: Gollancz, 1944. No Amer. ed.

11007 A FAMILY AND A FORTUNE. London: Gollancz, 1939. Published as "A FAMILY AND A FORTUNE" AND "MORE WOMEN THAN MEN." New York: Simon and Schuster, 1965.

11008 A FATHER AND HIS FATE. London: Gollancz, 1957. New York: Messner, 1958.

11009 A GOD AND HIS GIFTS. London: Gollancz, 1963. New York: Simon and Schuster, 1964.

11010 A HERITAGE AND ITS HISTORY. London: Gollancz, 1959. New York: Simon and Schuster, 1960.

11011 A HOUSE AND ITS HEAD. London: Heinemann, 1935. No Amer. ed.

11012 THE LAST AND THE FIRST. London: Gollancz; New York: Knopf, 1971.

11013 MANSERVANT AND MAIDSERVANT. London: Gollancz, 1947. Published as BULLIVANT AND THE LAMBS. New York: Knopf, 1949.

11014 MEN AND WIVES. London: Heinemann; New York: Harcourt, 1931.

11015 THE MIGHTY AND THEIR FALL. London: Gollancz, 1961. New York: Simon and Schuster, 1962.

11016 MORE WOMEN THAN MEN. London: Heinemann, 1933. Published as "A FAMILY AND A FORTUNE" AND "MORE WOMEN THAN MEN." New York: Simon and Schuster, 1965.

11017 MOTHER AND SON. London: Gollancz; New York: Messner, 1955.

11018 PARENTS AND CHILDREN. London: Gollancz, 1941. No Amer. ed.

11019 PASTORS AND MASTERS: A STUDY. London: Cranton, 1925. No Amer. ed.

11020 THE PRESENT AND THE PAST. London: Gollancz; New York: Messner, 1953.

11021 TWO WORLDS AND THEIR WAYS. London: Gollancz; New York: Knopf, 1949.

1.2 Miscellaneous Writings

See opening note to this section.

1.3 Collected and Selected Works

13001 NOVELS. 19 vols. London: Gollancz, 1972.

Collects the nineteen novels, from PASTORS AND MASTERS (1925) to THE LAST AND THE FIRST (1971). The early novel DOLORES (1911) is omitted from this edition, though it has been recently reprinted (see 25002).

1.4 Letters

See Greig, 22003 below.

2. SECONDARY BIBLIOGRAPHY

2.1 Bibliographies

21001 Burkhart, Charles, comp. "Bibliography." In his IVY COMPTON-BURNETT. Pp. 135-37. See 23002.

21002 Wiley, Paul L., comp. "Ivy Compton-Burnett (1892 [sic]-1969)." In THE BRITISH NOVEL. Comp. Wiley. Pp. 23-24. See G1419.

Brief primary and secondary checklist.

2.2 Biographies, Memoirs, Reminiscences, Interviews

22001 "A Conversation between Ivy Compton-Burnett and M. Jourdain." In ORION: A MISCELLANY. London: Nicholson and Watson, 1945. I, 20-28.

Interview discussion of IC's books. Source of her often quoted claim: "I do not feel that I have any real or organic knowledge of life later than about 1910." Reprinted in 23003.

22002 Dick, Kay. IVY & STEVIE: IVY COMPTON-BURNETT AND STEVIE SMITH: CONVERSATIONS AND REFLECTIONS. London: Duckworth, 1971.

Interview discussion of IC's early life, beliefs, and methods of composition, bound with a memoir of meetings with IC from 1950 to her last years, and two similar pieces on Stevie Smith. Several interesting domestic sidelights on the novelist. ("Stevie" Smith, i.e., Florence Margaret Smith, was an English poet and novelist, and mutual friend of the author and IC.)

22003 Greig, Cicely. IVY COMPTON-BURNETT: A MEMOIR. London: Garnstone Press, 1972.

Reminiscences of IC's friend and manuscript typist, covering the years 1946-69, and generously documented with a number of letters by IC.

22004 Kermode, Frank. "The House of Fiction: Interviews with Seven English Novelists." PR, 30 (1963), 61-82.

IC (pp. 70-74) defends the need for form in fiction and her use of dialogue.

22005 [Millgate, Michael]. "Interview with Miss Compton-Burnett." REL, 3, No. 4 (1962), 96-112.

Discussion of IC's techniques of composition and views of her own work. Reprinted in 23003.

22006 Sprigge, Elizabeth. THE LIFE OF IVY COMPTON-BURNETT. London: Gollancz, 1973.

Biography of IC, written by a close friend. Although lacking the scrupulous academic documentation of Spurling's larger biography, Sprigge's account of the life is frequently enlivened by her personal recollections of IC.

*22007 Spurling, Hilary. IVY WHEN YOUNG: THE EARLY LIFE OF IVY COMPTON-BURNETT, 1884-1919. London: Gollancz, 1974.

First volume of a two-part biography. Spurling exhaustively details the early years of IC leading up to the dividing line of the world war, the crucial experience in the novelist's development. Since this biography is an attempt "to suggest some of the uses to which [IC] put the experiences of her first thirty-five years in the nineteen novels written during the next fifty," Spurling devotes considerable space to tracing prototypes of the characters and situations of the novels in IC's personal life. Includes an extended discussion of DOLORES (1911).

22008 Webster, Harvey Curtis. "A Visit with Ivy Compton-Burnett." SatR, 2 Mar. 1957, pp. 14-15.

Brief impressions of IC's character, but no account of her conversation.

2.3 Book-Length Critical Studies and Essay Collections

23001 Baldanza, Frank. IVY COMPTON-BURNETT. New York: Twayne, 1964.

Useful biographical and critical introduction. After a survey of IC's life, to the early sixties, Baldanza analyzes the novels, through A GOD AND HIS GIFTS (1963), under several general thematic headings. Baldanza's final chapter assesses IC's critical reputation. Brief bibliography.

*23002 Burkhart, Charles. IVY COMPTON-BURNETT. London: Gollancz, 1965.

Excellent critical discussion of IC's themes and techniques with analyses of the novels through A GOD AND HIS GIFTS (1963). Burkhart defines his view of IC as an "eccentric" novelist and examines in particular her ultimately unconventional manipulation of conventions, her use of secrets ("the search for truth"), her characters (tyrants, children, fools), and her tragic, religious, and cynical perspectives. The novels are individually surveyed in Burkhart's lengthy, final chapter. Bibliography.

*23003 ______, ed. THE ART OF IVY COMPTON-BURNETT: A COLLECTION OF CRITICAL ESSAYS. London: Gollancz, 1972.

Excellent collection of interviews, reviews, critical articles, obituaries, and a speech. Major items listed separately: see 22001, 22005, 24007, 24010, 24014, 24020, 24028, 24034, 24035, and 24042.

23004 Grylls, R. Glynn, and Ian Scott-Kilvert. IVY COMPTON-BURNETT. London: Longmans, 1971.

Pamphlet introduction briefly tracing the "dominant theme" of vanity in several of the novels.

23005 Johnson, Pamela Hansford. IVY COMPTON-BURNETT. London: Longmans, 1951.

Early pamphlet-summary of IC's characteristics (amorality, flat characters, melodrama) and critique of the novels to DARKNESS AND DAY (1951).

*23006 Liddell, Robert. THE NOVELS OF IVY COMPTON-BURNETT. London: Gollancz, 1955.

The first critical book on IC, a highly enthusiastic defense of the novelist from her detractors (and from some of her admirers). Liddell chiefly attacks the charges of stereotypical characterization and artificial "happenings" in the novels, sensibly arguing the subtlety of IC's characters and, less reasonably, documenting the plausibility of her plots. Liddell's final chapter is an excellent analysis of IC's fictional techniques, especially her use of dialogue. Liddell's comparison of her art with that of the classical tragedians has been influential.

23007 Nevius, Blake. IVY COMPTON-BURNETT. New York: Columbia Univ. Press, 1970.

Adequate novel-by-novel introduction to IC's fiction, to A GOD AND HIS GIFTS (1963). This work consolidates much of the critical opinion on IC's plotting, characterization, dialogue, and other literary techniques.

23008 Powell, Violet. A COMPTON-BURNETT COMPENDIUM. London: Heinemann, 1973.

A cultist's brief plot summaries of the twenty novels, with occasional asides on related topics (e.g., houses, professions). An unnecessary book.

2.4 General Critical Articles, or Chapters on IC

24001 Allen, Walter. THE MODERN NOVEL. Pp. 188-91. See G2202.

The closed, very small world and the tightly knit style of IC's fiction.

24002 Amis, Kingsley. "One World and Its Way." TWENTIETH CENTURY, 158 (1955), 168-75.

Objections to the critical adulation of IC, with a left-handed tribute (deplores IC's repetitiveness, admires her comic sense).

24003 Balutowa, Bronislawa. "The Group Dynamics in the Plots of Ivy Compton-Burnett." ZRL, 13, No. 1 (1970), 75-94.

Not seen.

24004 _____. "Type versus Character in the Novels of Ivy Compton-Burnett." KWARTALNIK NEOFILOLOGICZNY, 17 (1970), 377-98.

Not seen.

24005 Bland, D.C. "T.S. Eliot's Case-Book." MLN, 75 (1960), 23-26.

Influence of IC's fiction on Eliot's play THE FAMILY REUNION.

24006 Bogan, Louise. "Ivy Compton-Burnett." In SELECTED CRITICISM: PROSE, POETRY. New York: Noonday, 1955. Pp. 189-90.

IC "fixed permanently at the emotional level of childhood's 'knowing' and disabused stage."

*24007 Bowen, Elizabeth. "Ivy Compton-Burnett." In her COLLECTED IMPRESSIONS. New York: Knopf, 1950. Pp. 82-91.

Two review essays, discussing IC's "formalized" use of characters (e.g., in PARENTS AND CHILDREN) and her completion of the task, neglected by the Victorians and declined by the Edwardians, of describing the emotional "battle for power that goes on in every unit of English middle-class life" (e.g., in ELDERS AND BETTERS). Reprinted in 23003.

24008 Bradbury, Malcolm. "Unhappy Families Are All Alike: New Views of Ivy Compton-Burnett." ENCOUNTER, 41 (July 1973), 71-74.

Review article and commentary on the "pleasure of exposing" and the moral passion of the irony in IC's work.

24009 Burgess, Anthony. THE NOVEL NOW. Pp. 115-17. See G3019.

The tension between upper-class formality and the nature of unspoken desires in IC's fiction.

*24010 Burkhart, Charles. "Ivy Compton-Burnett: The Shape of a Career." In THE ART OF IVY COMPTON-BURNETT. Ed. Burkhart. Pp. 158-71. See 23003.

Valuable novel-by-novel survey and search for patterns, from DOLORES (1911) to THE LAST AND THE FIRST (1971).

24011 Cranston, Maurice. "Ivy Compton-Burnett." Trans. R. Villoteau. LETTRES NOUVELLES, 6 (1958), 425-40.

General survey of IC's themes and techniques.

24012 Curtis, Mary M. "The Moral Comedy of Miss Compton-Burnett." WSCL, 5 (1964), 213-21.

Because of her serious, "ultimately classical moral outlook," critics have overlooked IC's savage, bitterly ironic, and very funny comic technique.

24013 Gill, Brendan. "Ivy Compton-Burnett and the Gift of Gab." NEW YORKER, 19 June 1948, pp. 77-78, 81.

IC is "about as fastidious and detached as a writer can become." Examines two novels, MANSERVANT AND MAIDSERVANT and PARENTS AND CHILDREN.

24014 Ginger, John. "Ivy Compton-Burnett." LONDON MAGAZINE, 9 (Jan. 1970), 58-71.

Self-effacement and sacrifice central to IC's (nonreligious) morality. Reprinted in 23003.

24015 Gold, Joseph. "Exit Everybody: The Novels of Ivy Compton-Burnett." DR, 42 (1962), 227-38.

The disappearance of authorial perspective in IC's dialogue-fiction, and the resultant lack of moral or comic vision to support her satire. Equivocal survey.

24016 Hansen, Marlene R. "The 'Victorianism' of Ivy Compton-Burnett." ES, 55 (1974), 516-22.

Asserts the significance of the late-Victorian social, intellectual, and political backgrounds for IC's fiction.

24017 Jefferson, D.W. "A Note on Ivy Compton-Burnett." REL, 1, No. 2 (1960), 19-24.

IC's self-conscious "spareness" and "dryness" ironically reflect the modern age "which drives the artist to such disciplines to avoid banality."

24018 Johnson, Pamela Hansford. "Three Novelists and the Drawing of Character: C.P. Snow, Joyce Cary and Ivy Compton-Burnett." E&S, 3 (1950), 82-99.

The social dimension, variety, and typicality of IC's characters (pp. 94-99).

24019 Karl, Frederick R. "The Intimate World of Ivy Compton-Burnett." In A READER'S GUIDE TO THE CONTEMPORARY ENGLISH NOVEL. Pp. 201-19. See G3081.

Survey of the novels, with special attention to MANSERVANT AND MAIDSERVANT and TWO WORLD AND THEIR WAYS, stressing the predatory law of the jungle in IC's vision of family life and IC's fictional techniques (e.g., in "recognition" scenes and dialogue).

*24020 Liddell, Robert. "The Novels of Ivy Compton-Burnett." In A TREATISE ON THE NOVEL. Pp. 146-63. See G3093.

Excellent critical summary of IC's fiction (to MANSERVANT AND MAIDSERVANT), emphasizing her relationship with Jane Austen. Reprinted in 23003.

24021 McCabe, Bernard. "Ivy Compton-Burnett: An English Eccentric." Crit, 3, No. 2 (1960), 47-63.

IC's "concentrated examination of moral relationships" within the microcosm of the family. General survey and critique, to A HERITAGE AND ITS HISTORY (1959).

*24022 McCarthy, Mary. "The Inventions of Ivy Compton-Burnett." ENCOUNTER, 27 (Nov. 1966), 19-31.

IC's novels "subversive packets," radically attacking injustice. Excellent balanced survey of IC's chief themes and techniques.

24023 MacSween, Roderick J. "Ivy Compton-Burnett: Merciless Understanding." AntigR, No. 7 (1971), 38-46.

IC's "merciless" dissection of personality.

24024 Newby, Percy H. THE NOVEL, 1945-50. Pp. 29-31. See G3113.

Brief, highly favorable appreciation.

24025 Page, Norman. SPEECH IN THE ENGLISH NOVEL. Pp. 17-19. See G4070.

The "unlifelike elegance and pointedness" of IC's dialogue.

24026 Pendry, E.D. "Ivy Compton-Burnett." In her THE NEW FEMINISM OF ENGLISH FICTION. Pp. 90-119. See G3119.

The peculiar blend of anachronism and modernity in both IC's fiction and her views of woman. Critical of IC's formula-writing.

24027 Phelps, Gilbert. "The Novel Today." In THE MODERN AGE. Ed. Boris Ford. Pp. 475-95. See G2110.

IC (pp. 478-81) finds her strength in her conscious limitations of her material. Her wit and her consistent and credible world reminiscent of Austen.

24028 Praz, Mario. "The Novels of Ivy Compton-Burnett." 1955. In THE ART OF IVY COMPTON-BURNETT." Ed. Charles Burkhart. Pp. 123-28. See 23003.

IC's vision of an "inferno that rages behind the respectable facades of many a bourgeois house of the late Victorian period."

24029 Prescott, Orville. IN MY OPINION. Pp. 98-101. See G3124.

Praises IC's satiric brilliance, despite her limited appeal.

24030 Preston, John. "'The Matter in a Word.'" EIC, 10 (1960), 348-56.

IC's novels, through their sense of language as a social form, a "linguistic rather than a psychological scrutiny of human experience."

24031 Reed, Henry. THE NOVEL SINCE 1939. Pp. 18-20. See G3128.

Brief appreciation, noting the developing sense of the sinister in IC's novels.

24032 Rule, Jane. "Ivy Compton-Burnett." In LESBIAN IMAGES. Garden City, N.Y.: Doubleday, 1975. Pp. 105-14.

IC's "asexuality" a latent form of lesbianism.

24033 Sackville-West, Edward. "Ivy Compton-Burnett." In LIVING WRITERS. Ed. Gilbert Phelps. Pp. 79-93. See G3121.

General survey of IC's qualities as novelist.

24034 ______. "Ladies Whose Bright Pens. . . ." In INCLINATIONS. London: Secker and Warburg, 1949. Pp. 78-103.

Extended comparison of IC and Elizabeth Bowen, two novelists who know their limitations and turn them to account. Reprinted in 23003.

*24035 Sarraute, Nathalie. THE AGE OF SUSPICION: ESSAYS ON THE NOVEL. Trans. Maria Jolas. New York: Braziller, 1963. Pp. 112-17.

IC artfully locates her dialogue on the "fluctuating frontier that separates conversation from sub-conversation." Reprinted in 23003.

24036 Snow, Lotus. "'Good Is Bad Condensed': Ivy Compton-Burnett's View of Human Nature." WHR, 10 (1956), 271-76.

Characters in IC's fiction are true to their own natures, doing what "does them good, some sensitively, some cruelly."

24037 Stevenson, Lionel. THE HISTORY OF THE ENGLISH NOVEL. XI, 265-72 and passim. See G2212.

Literary historian's selective survey of the fiction, stressing IC's determinism (cf. Hardy) and her irony (cf. Radcliffe).

24038 Strachey, Richard. "The Works of Ivy Compton-Burnett." LIFE AND LETTERS, 12 (1935), 30-36.

Defends IC against critical charges of artificiality and plotlessness.

*24039 Webster, Harvey Curtis. "Ivy Compton-Burnett: Factualist." In his AFTER THE TRAUMA. Pp. 51-71. See G3154.

Despite their consciously Edwardian atmosphere, IC's novels reflect the fundamental assumptions about human character and experience of the post-war generation. Fine critical survey.

24040 West, Anthony. "Ivy Compton-Burnett." In PRINCIPLES AND PERSUASIONS. New York: Harcourt, 1957. Pp. 225-32.

Unable to accept IC's mannered style and manipulated action.

24041 Wilson, Angus. "Evil in the English Novel." KR, 29 (1967), 167-94.

Discusses IC, among others.

*24042 ______. "Ivy Compton-Burnett." LONDON MAGAZINE, 2 (July 1955), 64-70.

IC exceptional among modern novelists as an experimental traditionalist. Reprinted in 23003.

2.5 Studies of Individual Works

All of the book-length critical studies (section 2.3, above) and many of the general critical articles (section 2.4, above) offer significant commentaries on the individual novels. Also see 22007.

BROTHERS AND SISTERS (1929)

25001 Benveniste, Asa. AN INTRODUCTION TO "BROTHERS AND SISTERS." New York: Zero Press, 1956.

The family to IC "a situation as closed, terrible and fraught with violence as Hell itself." Pamphlet (10 pp.) introduction to reissue of BROTHERS AND SISTERS.

DOLORES (1911)

25002 Burkhart, Charles. "Introduction." In IC's DOLORES. Edinburgh: Blackwood, 1971. Pp. v-xvii.

The "interesting immaturity" of IC's disowned first novel, especially its indebtedness to George Eliot.

ELDERS AND BETTERS (1944)

25003 Pittock, Malcolm. "Ivy Compton-Burnett's Use of Dialogue." ES, 51 (1970), 43-46.

Close analysis of a passage from ELDERS AND BETTERS to illustrate the characteristics of IC's dialogue.

A FAMILY AND A FORTUNE (1939)

25004 Kettle, Arnold. "Ivy Compton-Burnett: A FAMILY AND A FORTUNE." In his AN INTRODUCTION TO THE ENGLISH NOVEL. II, 184-90. See G3088.

Despite her wit and exposure of the false standards and values of society, IC's fiction limited as a social criticism.

A HERITAGE AND ITS HISTORY (1959)

25005 Cosman, Max. "Manners and Morals." COMMONWEAL, 71 (1960), 525-27.

General critique of IC's methods and themes, with a review of A HERITAGE AND ITS HISTORY.

*25006 Iser, Wolfgang. "Dialogue of the Unspeakable: Ivy Compton-Burnett: A HERITAGE AND ITS HISTORY." In THE IMPLIED READER: PATTERNS OF COMMUNICATION IN PROSE FICTION FROM BUNYAN TO BECKETT. Baltimore: Johns Hopkins Univ. Press, 1974. Pp. 234-56.

IC's separation of technique and reality (especially in dialogue) paradoxically creates a higher sense of reality.

THE LAST AND THE FIRST (1971)

25007 Burkhart, Charles. " A Critical Epilogue." In IC's THE LAST AND THE FIRST. London: Gollancz, 1971. Pp. 151-59.

Critical essay on IC's posthumous novel, noting its weaknesses as well as its strengths.

25008 Sprigge, Elizabeth. "Foreword: A Book in the Making." In IC's THE LAST AND THE FIRST. London: Gollancz, 1971. Pp. 7-12.

Brief account of IC's last years and the survival of the manuscript of THE LAST AND THE FIRST.

PASTORS AND MASTERS: A STUDY (1925)

*25009 Greenfield, Stanley B. "PASTORS AND MASTERS: The Spoils of Genius." CRITICISM, 2 (1960), 66-80.

Critical analysis, stressing the themes of parasitism and exploitation.

"JOSEPH CONRAD" (1857-1924)

[Jozef Teodor Konrad Nalecz Korzeniowski]

1. PRIMARY BIBLIOGRAPHY

Abbreviations of titles used in this bibliography (if any) are noted at the end of the entry. Books available in recent paperback printings are designated by "(P)."

Note: A variorum edition of the complete works of JC is currently being prepared for publication by Cambridge University Press under the general editorship of Bruce Harkness, Marion Michael, and Norman Sherry.

1.1 Fiction

This section is divided into two parts: i. Novels and Story Collections, and ii. Collaborations. All works are novels unless otherwise noted.

i. NOVELS AND STORY COLLECTIONS (first collected publication)

11001 ALMAYER'S FOLLY: A STORY OF AN EASTERN RIVER. London: Unwin; New York: Macmillan, 1895. (P). Abbreviated as AF.

> JC's first novel. The multiple "follies" of a Dutch outcast in the East.

11002 THE ARROW OF GOLD: A STORY BETWEEN TWO NOTES. London: Unwin; Garden City, N.Y.: Doubleday, Page, 1919. (P). Abbreviated as AG.

> Romantic adventure story of initiation "into the life of passion," set among Carlist revolutionaries in southern France.

11003 CHANCE: A TALE IN TWO PARTS. London: Methuen; Garden City, N.Y.: Doubleday, Page, 1913. (P). Abbreviated as Ch.

Technically complex tale of a betrayed young woman, narrated by Marlow.

11004 "Heart of Darkness." Abbreviated as HD. See YOUTH: A NARRATIVE AND TWO OTHER STORIES (11024).

11005 LORD JIM: A TALE. Edinburgh and London: Blackwood, 1900. Subtitle changed to A ROMANCE. New York: Doubleday, McClure, 1900. (P). Abbreviated as LJ.

Idealistic English sailor's self-betrayal and questionable redemption, also narrated by Marlow. Textual edition: LORD JIM: AN AUTHORITATIVE TEXT. Ed. Thomas C. Moser. New York: Norton, 1968. Pp. 1-253. See 25145.

11006 THE NIGGER OF THE "NARCISSUS." London: Heinemann, 1897. Published as THE CHILDREN OF THE SEA. New York: Dodd, Mead, 1897. (P). Abbreviated as NN.

Near catastrophic voyage of initiation.

11007 NOSTROMO: A TALE OF THE SEABOARD. London and New York: Harper, 1904. (P). Abbreviated as N.

Tale of self-betrayals set against a background of political unrest in South America ("Costaguana").

11008 AN OUTCAST OF THE ISLANDS. London: Unwin; New York: Apleton, 1896. (P). Abbreviated as OI.

Companion novel to AF, telling the earlier story of passion, fraud, and betrayal in Sambir.

11009 THE RESCUE: A ROMANCE OF THE SHALLOWS. London: Dent; Garden City, N.Y.: Doubleday, Page, 1920. (P).

Sentimental and melodramatic tale of self-betrayal (through passion), again set in the East.

11010 THE ROVER. London: Unwin; Garden City, N.Y.: Doubleday, Page, 1923. (P). Abbreviated as Rov.

"Valedictory," historical novel of an aged mariner's heroism during the French Revolution.

11011 THE SECRET AGENT: A SIMPLE TALE. London: Methuen; New York: Harper, 1907. (P). Abbreviated as SA.

Political novel dealing with complex personal and political repercussions of an anarchist bombing attempt.

11012 "The Secret Sharer." Abbreviated as SS. See 'TWIXT LAND AND SEA (11019).

11013 A SET OF SIX. [Stories]. London: Methuen, 1908; Garden City, N.Y.: Doubleday, Page, 1915.

Contains "Gaspar Ruiz" (1906), "The Informer" (1906), "The Brute" (1906), "An Anarchist" (1906), "The Duel" (1908), "Il Conde" (1908).

11014 THE SHADOW LINE: A CONFESSION. London: Dent; Garden City, N.Y.: Doubleday, Page, 1917. (P). Abbreviated as SL.

Tale of a young captain's initiation into the unknown perils of command. Largely autobiographical.

11015 THE SISTERS. [Novel fragment]. New York: Crosby, Gaige, 1928.

See Ford's comments on this fragment, 25340 below.

11016 SUSPENSE: A NAPOLEONIC NOVEL. [Unfinished]. London: Dent; Garden City, N.Y.: Doubleday, Page, 1925.

Romantic historical novel.

11017 TALES OF HEARSAY. [Stories]. London: Unwin; Garden City, N.Y.: Doubleday, Page, 1925.

Contains "The Warrior's Soul" (1917), "Prince Roman" (1911), "The Tale" (1917), "The Black Mate" (1908).

11018 TALES OF UNREST. [Stories]. London: Unwin; New York: Scribner's, 1898.

Contains "Karain: A Memory" (1897), "The Idiots" (1896), "An Outpost of Progress" (1897), "The Return" (1898), "The Lagoon" (1897).

11019 'TWIXT LAND AND SEA: THREE TALES. [Stories]. London: Dent; New York: Hodder, Stoughton and Doran, 1912.

Contains "A Smile of Fortune" (1911), "The Secret Sharer" (1910) (abbreviated SS), "Freya of the Seven Isles" (1912). SS, one of JC's best known stories, develops the theme of the young captain's initiation. Textual edition of SS: CONRAD'S "SECRET SHARER" AND THE CRITICS. Ed. Bruce Harkness. Belmont, Calif.: Wadsworth, 1962. Pp. 3-36. See 25317.

11020 TYPHOON AND OTHER STORIES. [Stories]. London: Heinemann, 1903. Garden City, N.Y.: Doubleday, Page, 1923. (P).

Contains "Typhoon" (1902), "Amy Foster" (1901), "Falk: A Reminiscence" (1903), "To-morrow" (1902).

11021 UNDER WESTERN EYES. London: Methuen; New York: Harper, 1911. (P). Abbreviated as UWE.

Political novel of Russian radicalism and emigre Russians in Geneva.

11022 VICTORY: AN ISLAND TALE. London: Methuen; Garden City, N.Y.: Doubleday, Page, 1915. (P). Abbreviated as V.

The idyllic island paradise and idealism of the passive central character (Heyst) are corrupted by malignant forces.

11023 WITHIN THE TIDES: TALES. [Stories]. London: Dent, 1915. Garden City, N.Y.: Doubleday, Page, 1916.

Contains "The Planter of Malata" (1914), "The Partner" (1911), "The Inn of the Two Witches" (1913), "Because of the Dollars [or, Laughing Anne]" (1914).

11024 YOUTH: A NARRATIVE, AND TWO OTHER STORIES. [Stories]. Edinburgh and London: Blackwood, 1902. New York: McClure, Phillips, 1903. (P).

Contains "Youth" (1898), "Heart of Darkness" (1899), (abbreviated HD), "The End of the Tether" (1902). "Youth" and HD, both using the same narrator Marlow, are especially effective studies of initiation and maturation. Textual edition of HD: "HEART OF DARKNESS": AN AUTHORITATIVE TEXT. Ed. Robert Kimbrough. New York: Norton, 1963. Pp. 3-79. See 25068.

ii. COLLABORATIONS

11025 THE INHERITORS: AN EXTRAVAGANT STORY (with F.M. Ford). London: Heinemann; New York: McClure, Phillips, 1901.

First collaboration with Ford.

11026 THE NATURE OF A CRIME (with F.M. Ford). London: Duckworth; Garden City, N.Y.: Doubleday, Page, 1924.

Short novel originally published serially in 1909.

11027 ROMANCE: A NOVEL (with F.M. Ford). London: Smith, Elder, 1903. New York: McClure, Phillips, 1904.

Most important (and successful) of their collaborations.

1.2 Miscellaneous Writings

For more information on JC's uncollected essays, prefaces and introductions, pamphlets, drama, and other writings, see the bibliographies compiled by Ehrsam (21005), Lohf and Sheehy (21008), and Wise (21013).

12001 JOSEPH CONRAD'S DIARY OF HIS JOURNEY UP THE CONGO. Ed. R. Curle. London: Privately printed, 1926.

Raw materials eventually used in HD. See 25047. Reprinted in 25039, 25051, and 25063.

12002 LAST ESSAYS. London: Dent; Garden City, N.Y.: Doubleday, Page, 1926.

Nineteen essays on several literary and maritime topics.

12003 THE MIRROR OF THE SEA: MEMORIES AND IMPRESSIONS. London: Methuen; New York: Harper, 1906.

Memoir of JC's "relation with the sea."

12004 NOTES ON LIFE AND LETTERS. London: Dent; Garden City, N.Y.: Doubleday, Page, 1921.

Thirteen literary essays and thirteen essays on "life" (politics and other aspects).

12005 A PERSONAL RECORD: SOME REMINISCENCES. New York: Harper, 1912. Published as SOME REMINISCENCES. London: Nash, 1912.

Memoir of JC's early (preliterary) life.

1.3 Collected and Selected Works

The large number of editions and anthologies of JC's works precludes their full listing here. Only the most important editions and best collections are noted. For a fuller checklist see the Lohf and Sheehy bibliography, 21008 below.

13001 THE COLLECTED EDITION OF THE WORKS OF JOSEPH CONRAD. 21 vols. London: Dent, 1946-54. Rev. ed. 1974-- .

The principal British edition, presently being reissued (some volumes newly annotated).

13002 THE COLLECTED WORKS OF JOSEPH CONRAD. 21 vols. Garden City, N.Y.: Doubleday, Page, 1925.

This American collected edition has appeared in a variety of formats since 1925.

13003 CONRAD'S MANIFESTO: PREFACE TO A CAREER. THE HISTORY OF THE "PREFACE" TO "THE NIGGER OF THE 'NARCISSUS'" WITH FACSIMILES OF THE MANUSCRIPTS. Ed. David R. Smith. Northhampton, Mass.: Gehenna Press, 1966.

Preface plus introduction and notes. See 25424.

13004 CONRAD'S PREFACES TO HIS WORKS. Ed. Edward Garnett. London: Dent, 1937.

JC's prefaces are notoriously unreliable documents. See 24046.

13005 THE GREAT SHORT WORKS OF JOSEPH CONRAD. New York: Harper and Row, 1966. (P).

Includes three short stories, three novellas ("Youth," HD, "Typhoon") and a full-length novel (NN).

13006 JOSEPH CONRAD ON FICTION. Ed. Walter F. Wright. Lincoln: Univ. of Nebraska Press, 1964. (P).

Anthology of principal critical writings and comments. See 25428.

13007 THE PORTABLE CONRAD. 1947. Rev. ed. Ed. Morton D. Zabel. New York: Viking Press, 1969. (P).

Includes short stories, three novellas (same as in 13005), one full-length novel (NN), and selected letters and essays. See 24168.

13008 THREE PLAYS: LAUGHING ANNE; ONE DAY MORE; AND THE SECRET AGENT. London: Methuen, 1934.

Dramatic adaptations of the fiction.

13009 THE WORKS OF JOSEPH CONRAD. 20 vols. London: Heinemann, 1921-27.

The last edition supervised by JC.

1.4 Letters

A collected edition of JC's correspondence is currently in progress, under the editorship of Frederick Karl and Zdzislaw Najder (see Karl, 24071 below). Also see Karl (22025, 22026, 24069), Krzyzanowski (22027), Randall (22032), Said (23057), and Symons (23068).

14001 CONRAD'S POLISH BACKGROUND: LETTERS TO AND FROM POLISH FRIENDS. Ed. Zdzislaw Najder. Trans. Halina Carroll. London: Oxford Univ. Press, 1964.

One-hundred-four letters by JC and seventy-three by other hands, with additional Polish documents. See 22031.

14002 CONRAD TO A FRIEND. Ed. Richard Curle. Garden City, N.Y.: Doubleday, Doran, 1928.

Contains 150 letters to Curle, 1912-24.

14003 JOSEPH CONRAD: LETTERS TO WILLIAM BLACKWOOD AND DAVID S. MELDRUM. Ed. William Blackburn. Durham, N.C.: Duke Univ. Press, 1958.

Two-way correspondence, including over 230 letters by JC to his publisher. See 22008.

14004 JOSEPH CONRAD: LIFE AND LETTERS. Ed. G. Jean-Aubry. 2 vols. Garden City, N.Y.: Doubleday, Page, 1927.

Both biography and correspondence. See 22005.

14005 JOSEPH CONRAD'S LETTERS TO HIS WIFE. London: Privately printed, 1927.

14006 JOSEPH CONRAD'S LETTERS TO R.B. CUNNINGHAME GRAHAM. Ed. Cedric T. Watts. London: Cambridge Univ. Press, 1969.

Eighty-one letters, 1897-1923. See 22039.

14007 LETTERS FROM JOSEPH CONRAD, 1895-1924. Ed. Edward Garnett. Indianapolis, Ind.: Bobbs-Merrill, 1928.

Contains 219 letters, most concentrated in the period of JC's close relations with the Garnetts (1895-1900). See 22021.

14008 LETTERS OF JOSEPH CONRAD TO MARGUERITE PORADOWSKA, 1890-1920. Trans. and ed. John A. Gee and Paul J. Sturm. New Haven, Conn.: Yale Univ. Press, 1940.

JC's correspondence with his Polish-Belgian confidante. See 22022.

14009 LETTRES FRANCAISES. Ed. G. Jean-Aubry. Paris: Gallimard, 1929. In French.

Contains 166 miscellaneous items (1889-1924) to numerous correspondents (in JC's peculiar French).

1.5 Concordances

15001 Bender, Todd K., J.W. Parins, and Robert J. Dilligan, comps. A CONCORDANCE TO CONRAD'S "LORD JIM." New York: Garland, 1975.

Not seen.

15002 Jacobson, Sibyl C., Robert J. Dilligan, and Todd K. Bender, comps. A CONCORDANCE TO JOSEPH CONRAD'S "HEART OF DARKNESS." Carbondale: Southern Illinois Univ. Press, 1973. Microfiche--2 cards.

Reprints text for reference and indexes all words except "the." Unfortunately omits surrounding context of entries.

2. SECONDARY BIBLIOGRAPHY

Note: CONRADIANA (1968--) is the chief journal devoted entirely to bibliographical, biographical, and critical materials related to JC. A British periodical, JOURNAL OF THE JOSEPH CONRAD SOCIETY [formerly JOSEPH CONRAD SOCIETY (U.K.) NEWSLETTER], (1973--), and an American journal, JOSEPH CONRAD TODAY (the newsletter of the Joseph Conrad Society of America [1976--]), also publish Joseph Conrad research.

2.1 Bibliographies

Also see 25291 below.

*21001 Beebe, Maurice, comp. "Criticism of Joseph Conrad: A Selected Checklist." MFS, 10 (1964), 81-106.

Judicious selection of important materials. Supersedes his earlier checklist, MFS, 1, No. 1 (1955), 30-45. See 23040 and 23041.

21002 Bojarski, Edmund A., and Henry T. Bojarski, comps. JOSEPH CONRAD: A BIBLIOGRAPHY OF MASTERS' THESES AND DOCTORAL DISSERTATIONS, 1917-1963. Lexington: Univ. of Kentucky Libraries, 1964.

Lists about 350 items.

*21003 Chapple, J.A.V. "Conrad." In THE ENGLISH NOVEL. Ed. A.E. Dyson. Pp. 300-313. See G1408.

Bibliographical essay on JC studies and a selected checklist.

21004 "Conrad Bibliography: A Continuing Checklist." CONRADIANA, 2 (1969), and following.

Compiled by several hands. Supplements available bibliographies. Updated annually.

21005 Ehrsam, Theodore G., ed. A BIBLIOGRAPHY OF JOSEPH CONRAD. Metuchen, N.J.: Scarecrow, 1969.

Primary and secondary. Scarce annotation.

21006 Keating, George T., ed. A CONRAD MEMORIAL LIBRARY: THE COLLECTION OF GEORGE T. KEATING. Garden City, N.Y.: Doubleday, Doran, 1929.

Primary bibliographical descriptions and appreciative essays. Also see 23034, below.

21007 Lindstrand, Gordon, comp. "A Bibliographical Survey of the Literary Manuscripts of Joseph Conrad." CONRADIANA, 2, Nos. 1-2 (1970), 23-32, 105-14.

Indispensible for locating JC's manuscripts.

*21008 Lohf, Kenneth A., and Eugene P. Sheehy, eds. JOSEPH CONRAD AT MID-CENTURY: EDITIONS AND STUDIES, 1895-1955. Minneapolis: Univ. of Minnesota Press, 1957.

Now somewhat dated, but still useful compilation of secondary materials. Primary bibliography is cursory.

21009 Nowak, Jadwiga, comp. THE JOSEPH CONRAD COLLECTION IN THE POLISH LIBRARY IN LONDON. London: Polish Library, 1970.

Lists 399 primary and secondary items in English and in Polish.

21010 Sherry, Norman. "Introduction." In CONRAD: THE CRITICAL HERITAGE. Ed. Sherry. Pp. 1-44. See 23063.

Fine survey of JC's critical reputation.

*21011 Teets, Bruce E., and Helmut Gerber, eds. JOSEPH CONRAD: A BIBLIOGRAPHY OF WRITINGS ABOUT HIM. DeKalb: Northern Illinois Univ. Press, 1971.

Abstracts for over 1,900 publications on JC. Entries arranged chronologically rather than by subject. An indispensable research aid.

21012 Wiley, Paul L., comp. "Joseph Conrad (1857-1924)." In THE BRITISH NOVEL. Comp. Wiley. Pp. 24-32. See G1419.

Brief primary and secondary checklists.

*21013 Wise, Thomas J., ed. A CONRAD LIBRARY. A CATALOGUE OF PRINTED BOOKS, MANUSCRIPTS AND AUTOGRAPH LETTERS BY JOSEPH CONRAD, COLLECTED BY THOMAS JAMES WISE. London: Privately printed, 1928.

Still the best primary bibliography, though not generally available.

2.2 Biographies, Memoirs, Reminiscences

22001 Adams, Elbridge L. CONRAD THE MAN [with "A Burial in Kent," by John S. Zelie]. New York: Rudge, 1925.

Pamphlet, including a brief sketch of JC's personality, notes on his American visit, and a detailed account (by Zelie) of his funeral and burial.

22002 Allen, Jerry. THE SEA YEARS OF JOSEPH CONRAD. Garden City, N.Y.: Doubleday, 1965.

Biography and source of study of JC's maritime career, largely superseded by Sherry's CONRAD'S EASTERN WORLD and CONRAD'S WESTERN WORLD. See below (23061, 23062).

22003 ______. THE THUNDER AND THE SUNSHINE: A BIOGRAPHY OF JOSEPH CONRAD. New York: Putnam's, 1958.

Inept, semifictional biography of JC's early years.

22004 Allen, Vio. "Memories of Joseph Conrad." REL, 8, No. 2 (1967), 77-90.

JC's last years.

22005 Aubry, Georges Jean-. JOSEPH CONRAD: LIFE AND LETTERS. 2 vols. Garden City, N.Y.: Doubleday, Page, 1927.

Incomplete and often inaccurate biography, but a fine collection of letters. Extract reprinted in 25063.

22006 _____. THE SEA DREAMER: A DEFINITIVE BIOGRAPHY OF JOSEPH CONRAD. Trans. Helen Sebba. Garden City, N.Y.: Doubleday, 1957.

Outdated and definitely not "definitive."

*22007 Baines, Jocelyn. JOSEPH CONRAD: A CRITICAL BIOGRAPHY. London: Weidenfield and Nicolson, 1959.

The standard biography. Critical judgments are not very trustworthy. Contains the first documentary evidence of JC's Marseilles suicide attempt. Extracts reprinted in 23038, 23046, 23065, 25138, and 25317.

22008 Blackburn, William. "Conrad and William Blackwood." In JOSEPH CONRAD: LETTERS TO WILLIAM BLACKWOOD AND DAVID S. MELDRUM. Pp. xiii-xxxiii. See 14003.

JC's relationship with, and ultimate estrangement from, Blackwood and his "Maga."

22009 Bojarski, Edmund A., and Harold R. Stevens. "Joseph Conrad and the FALCONHURST." JML, 1 (1970), 197-208.

Documents JC's previously unnoticed service on the FALCONHURST.

22010 Conrad, Borys. JOSEPH CONRAD'S HOMES IN KENT. Farnham, Engl.: Farnham Printing Co., 1974.

Brief commentaries on JC's residences.

22011 _____. MY FATHER: JOSEPH CONRAD. London: Calder and Boyar, 1970.

A valuable memoir. JC's wit and humanity are sympathetically portrayed.

*22012 Conrad, Jessie. JOSEPH CONRAD AND HIS CIRCLE. New York: Dutton, 1935.

Not very reliable, but an interesting memoir of JC's familial and literary relationships.

22013 _____. JOSEPH CONRAD AS I KNEW HIM. Garden City, N.Y.: Doubleday, 1926.

Entertaining collection of personal reminiscences.

22014 Conrad, John. "Some Reminiscences of My Father." CONRAD ZYWY (THE LIVING CONRAD). Ed. Wit Tarnawski. London: Swiderski, 1957. Pp. 10-31. In English, with parallel Polish translation.

Only recorded memories of JC by his younger son.

22015 Coolidge, Olivia E. THE THREE LIVES OF JOSEPH CONRAD. Boston: Houghton Mifflin, 1972.

Commercial biography of little distinction.

22016 Curle, Richard. THE LAST TWELVE YEARS OF JOSEPH CONRAD. Garden City, N.Y.: Doubleday, Page, 1928.

JC's years of literary success as seen by a friend and early critic. Extract reprinted in 25068.

22017 _____. "The Story of a Remarkable Friendship." In CARAVANSARY AND CONVERSATION: MEMORIES OF PLACES AND PERSONS. New York: Stokes, 1937. Pp. 153-63.

The Conrad-Galsworthy friendship.

*22018 Ford, Ford Madox. JOSEPH CONRAD: A PERSONAL REMEMBRANCE. Boston: Little, Brown, 1924.

An unreliable, but "impressionistically" valid account of Ford's and JC's literary and personal relationships. Extract reprinted in 23046.

22019 _____. "Working with Conrad." In RETURN TO YESTERDAY. New York: Liveright, 1932. Pp. 186-201.

Discusses JC's and Ford's literary collaboration.

22020 Galsworthy, John. "Reminiscences of Conrad: 1924; Preface to Conrad's Plays: 1924." In CASTLES IN SPAIN AND OTHER SCREEDS. London: Heinemann, 1927. Pp. 101-26; 175-84.

Galsworthy had known JC long before his writing career, meeting him when JC was first mate on the TORRENS (1892).

22021 Garnett, Edward. "Introduction." In LETTERS FROM JOSEPH CONRAD. Pp. 1-28. See 14007.

JC's struggling early years as a writer. Extracts reprinted in 25063 and 25068.

22022 Gee, John A., and Paul J. Sturm. "Introduction." In LETTERS OF JOSEPH CONRAD TO MARGUERITE PORADOWSKA, 1890-1920. Pp. xiii-xix. See 14008.

Mme. Poradowska was JC's benefactress and literary confidante during the 1890s.

22023 Goldring, Douglas. "Enter Joseph Conrad." In THE LAST PRE-RAPHAELITE: THE LIFE AND WRITINGS OF FORD MADOX FORD. London: Macdonald, 1948. Pp. 60-90.

Recounts Ford's and JC's relationship.

22024 Gurko, Leo. THE TWO LIVES OF JOSEPH CONRAD. New York: Crowell, 1965.

"Biography for young readers."

22024a Heilbrun, Carolyn G. THE GARNETT FAMILY. New York: Macmillan, 1961. Pp. 107-32 and passim.

JC's relationship with the Garnetts.

22025 Karl, Frederick R. "Conrad and Pinker: Some Aspects of the Correspondence." JML, 5 (1976), 59-78.

JC's correspondence with his literary agent. Similar to below. Reprinted in 23064.

22026 ______. "Joseph Conrad, Norman Douglas, and the ENGLISH REVIEW." JML, 2 (1972), 342-56.

The course of JC's and Douglas's "flimsy" friendship (1905-16), amply documented from their correspondence.

22027 Krzyzanowski, Ludwik. "Joseph Conrad: Some Polish Documents." In JOSEPH CONRAD: CENTENNIAL ESSAYS. Ed. Krzyzanowski. Pp. 113-43. See 23036.

Polish letters and political records relating to JC.

*22028 Meyer, Bernard C. JOSEPH CONRAD: A PSYCHOANALYTIC BIOGRAPHY. Princeton, N.J.: Princeton Univ. Press, 1967.

Important "remote psychoanalysis" of JC which sheds considerable light on the author's many personal "hearts of darkness." Extracts reprinted in 23033 and 25187.

22029 Milosz, Czeslaw. "Apollo N. Korzeniowski: Joseph Conrad's Father." MOSAIC, 6, No. 4 (1973), 121-40.

Biographical summary and assessment of Korzeniowski's political and literary careers.

22030 Moser, Thomas. "Conrad, Marwood, and Ford: Biographical Speculations on the Genesis of THE GOOD SOLDIER." MOSAIC, 8, No. 1 (1974), 217-27.

Relationships among the Conrads, the Fords, and the Marwoods (mutual friends) reflected in THE GOOD SOLDIER. Reprinted in 23064.

22031 Najder, Zdzislaw. "Introduction." In CONRAD'S POLISH BACKGROUND. Ed. Najder. Pp. 1-31. See 14001.

22032 Randall, Dale B. JOSEPH CONRAD AND WARRINGTON DAWSON: THE RECORD OF A FRIENDSHIP. Durham, N.C.: Duke Univ. Press, 1970.

Biography of the American journalist and aspiring novelist, Francis Warrington Dawson, account of his relationship with JC, and collection of their largely unpublished correspondence.

22033 Rees, Richard. "The Unobscure Conrad." In FOR LOVE OR MONEY: STUDIES IN PERSONALITY AND ESSENCE. Carbondale: Southern Illinois Univ. Press, 1960. Pp. 124-29.

Memoir and general appreciation.

22034 Retinger, Joseph H. CONRAD AND HIS CONTEMPORARIES. London: Minerva, 1941.

Remembered conversations of slight value.

22035 Russell, Bertrand. "Joseph Conrad." In his PORTRAITS FROM MEMORY. Pp. 81-85. See G7208.

Russell's fundamental agreement with JC's world view.

22036 Safroni-Middleton, A. TROPIC SHADOWS: MEMORIES OF THE SOUTH SEAS, TOGETHER WITH REMINISCENCES OF THE AUTHOR'S SEA MEETINGS WITH JOSEPH CONRAD. London: Richards, 1927. Pp. 35-59.

Unreliable "autobiographical romance."

22037 Sherry, Norman. CONRAD AND HIS WORLD. London: Thames and Hudson, 1972.

Brief biography, generously illustrated. An entertaining introduction to JC's life.

22038 Sutherland, John G. AT SEA WITH JOSEPH CONRAD. Boston: Houghton Mifflin, 1922.

Recounts, at unnecessary length, a wartime (1916) submarine patrol in which JC participated.

22039 Watts, Cedric T. "Introduction." In JOSEPH CONRAD'S LETTERS TO R.B. CUNNINGHAME GRAHAM. Ed. Watts. Pp. 3-42. See 14006.

Surveys Graham's life and traces his unbroken friendship with JC (from 1897).

2.3 Book-Length Critical Studies and Essay Collections

Also see books and essay collections on the following individual works (in section 2.5 below): on HD: Aubry (25037), Bentley (25039), Curle (25047), Dean (25051), Harkness (25063), Kimbrough (25068), Walker (25092); on LJ: Beebe (25116), Kuehn (25138), Moser (25145), Tanner (25164); on NN: Palmer (25187); on N: McLauchlan (25217); on RESCUE: Liljegren (25242); on SA: Watt (25301); on SS: Harkness (25317), Walker (25325); on V: Secor (25398).

23001 Andreach, Robert J. THE SLAIN AND THE RESURRECTED GOD: CONRAD, FORD, AND THE CHRISTIAN MYTH. New York: New York Univ. Press, 1970.

JC's Christian heritage uniquely, if not persuasively, related to his fiction. The archetypal criticism yields interesting insights into the major works (e.g., HD, LJ, N, SA, UWE, and V), but proves more convincing in the discussions of Ford.

23002 Andreas, Osborn. JOSEPH CONRAD: A STUDY IN NON-CONFORMITY. New York: Philosophical Library, 1959.

Studies the relationship between the outcast, the nonconformist and society in forty-two works by JC. Generalized, commonplace, and, at times, absurd critiques.

23003 Bancroft, William W. JOSEPH CONRAD: HIS PHILOSOPHY OF LIFE. Philadelphia: Univ. of Pennsylvania Press, 1931.

Sophisticated attempt to induct and explicate a systematic philosophy from JC's work, stressing his conception of the universe as indifferent and his assertion of the affirmative value of "moral law" and "human solidarity." To establish a uniform philosophic worldview in JC, Bancroft necessarily sacrifices some of the complexity and diversity of the fiction.

23004 Bendz, Ernst. JOSEPH CONRAD: AN APPRECIATION. New York: Wilson, 1923.

Some interesting and enduring judgments of JC's achievement largely debilitated by a pretentious and obfuscating style.

23004a Berman, Jeffrey. JOSEPH CONRAD: WRITING AS RESCUE. New York: Astra Books, 1977.

JC presented as an "extremist" artist, who escapes from his "obsession with death in general and suicide in particular" (both central themes in his work), through his writing. Evidently absorbs Berman's article (24012 below). (Not seen--annotation paraphrased from publisher's advertisement.)

23005 Boyle, Ted E. SYMBOL AND MEANING IN THE FICTION OF JOSEPH CONRAD. The Hague: Mouton, 1965.

Weak traversal of the major fiction, to V. Too often Boyle's commentaries descend to the unimaginative, derivative, or commonplace. Extract reprinted in 25068.

23006 Bradbrook, Muriel C. JOSEPH CONRAD: POLAND'S ENGLISH GENIUS. Cambridge: At the Univ. Press, 1941.

Early statement of the three-phase development scheme for JC's career (maturation, achievement, and decline), with many fine individual judgments. Bradbrook offers particularly valuable readings of V and Rov, finding the latter novel a return to strength in JC's last years. Extracts reprinted in 23065, 25063, and 25068.

23007 Burgess, C.F. THE FELLOWSHIP OF THE CRAFT: CONRAD ON SHIPS AND SEAMEN AND THE SEA. Port Washington, N.Y.: Kennikat, 1976.

Examines JC's eleven sea tales and two memoirs "to determine precisely Conrad's thoughts and feelings about the sea [ambivalent], ships, seamen, and the invisible ties that bind seamen in what Conrad called the 'fellowship of the craft.'" (Quoted from publisher's advertisement--not seen.)

23008 Busza, Andrezej. CONRAD'S POLISH LITERARY BACKGROUND AND SOME ILLUSTRATIONS OF THE INFLUENCE OF POLISH LITERATURE ON HIS WORK. Rome and London: Institutum Historicum Polonicum Romae/Societas Polonica Scientiarum et Litterarum in Exteris, 1966.

Useful study of JC's Polish literary heritage, stressing the formative artistic influences of his father (the romantic), of his uncle (the realist), and the impact of his "vital cultural background" as a child. Examines "Karain," V, "Amy Foster," and "Prince Roman" in detail.

23009 Cooper, Christopher. CONRAD AND THE HUMAN DILEMMA. New York: Barnes and Noble, 1970.

The moral basis of JC's art, weakly argued from the three political novels (N, SA, UWE). Cooper limits himself to surveys of the "different moralities of the major protagonists" of the novels chosen, but fails to explain his limited selection of works for consideration, to define his terms (e.g., "morality" itself), or to suggest JC's fundamental views of morality.

23010 Cox, C.B. JOSEPH CONRAD: THE MODERN IMAGINATION. Totowa, N.J.: Rowman and Littlefield, 1974.

Traces the impact of JC's philosophic pessimism and suicidal depressions upon his fiction. His weaker novels are attributable to a turning away from or a failure to confront the darkness of his modern imagination.

23011 Crankshaw, Edward. JOSEPH CONRAD: SOME ASPECTS OF THE ART OF THE NOVEL. London: Lane, 1936.

Important early consideration of JC's narrative and structural techniques from a Jamesian critical perspective. Although Crankshaw presents a valuable discussion of JC's experimentation with time shifts and symbolic settings, his study is seriously weakened by his limited approach to JC's narrators (seen as subjective voices used to circumvent direct authorial commentary) and his narrow selection of works for analysis (the Marlow stories, including Ch and N). Extracts reprinted in 23065 and 25145.

23012 Curle, Richard. JOSEPH CONRAD: A STUDY. Garden City, N.Y.: Doubleday, Page, 1914.

The first book-length critical estimate; a useful but dated introduction to the man and his fiction.

23013 _____. JOSEPH CONRAD AND HIS CHARACTERS: A STUDY OF SIX NOVELS. London: Heinemann, 1957.

Unsatisfactory survey of JC's principal characters (in LJ, N, SA, UWE, Ch, and V). Appreciative commentaries rather than penetrating criticism.

23013a Cushwa, Frank W. AN INTRODUCTION TO CONRAD. Garden City, N.Y.: Doubleday, Doran, 1933.

A prep-school introduction to JC, for an anthology of his short works, which presents a severely flawed, literally autobiographical reading of the fiction.

*23014 Daleski, H.M. JOSEPH CONRAD: THE WAY OF DISPOSSESSION. New York: Holmes and Meier, 1977.

Close analyses of several of the major works (including NN, HD, LJ, "Typhoon," N, SA, SS, and UWE). Daleski maintains that an "unremitting self-possession" was JC's "primary 'article of creed,'" as a mariner and as an artist. In his best work, this theme of self-possession exists in a constant tension with the possibilities of dispossession, or loss of self, through passion, panic, spiritual disintegration, or suicide. Daleski provides a provocative and insightful design for the "main structure" of JC's fiction.

23015 Dowden, Wilfred S. JOSEPH CONRAD: THE IMAGED STYLE. Nashville: Vanderbilt Univ. Press, 1970.

Interesting study which unfortunately falls off into image analysis. Dowden traces the development of JC's imagery through several major and minor works, arguing that JC only gradually realized the value of his imagery for "the subliminal aspects of plot and characterization." By the time he reaches the later works, however, Dowden praises JC's technical mastery of image and symbol in works he acknowledges as imaginative failures. Several good observations on the less-discussed minor works. Extract reprinted in 25063.

*23016 Fleishman, Avrom. CONRAD'S POLITICS: COMMUNITY AND ANARCHY IN THE FICTION OF JOSEPH CONRAD. Baltimore: Johns Hopkins Univ. Press, 1967.

Wide-ranging and astute discussion of JC's political ideal of "organic community" in his fiction. Initially, Fleishman relates JC's liberal-humanitarian political views to the organicist ideas of Burke, Rousseau, Coleridge, Carlyle, and George Eliot, as prelude to his often illuminating and consistently insightful analyses of individual works (especially NN, N, SA, UWE, Rov). One of the few indispensible books on JC. Extracts reprinted in 25187 and 25301.

23017 Follett, Wilson. JOSEPH CONRAD: A SHORT STUDY. Garden City, N.Y.: Doubleday, Page, 1915.

Study of JC's "intellectual and emotional attitude toward his work" and brief discussion of his major fiction through 1915. Follett's book remains a valuable exposition of important Conradian attitudes.

23018 Gillon, Adam. CONRAD AND SHAKESPEARE, AND OTHER ESSAYS. New York: Astra Books, 1976.

Not seen. Evidently absorbs several of Gillon's previously published essays on JC (sections 2.4 and 2.5, below).

23019 _____. THE ETERNAL SOLITARY: A STUDY OF JOSEPH CONRAD. New York: Bookman Associates, 1960.

Consideration of the moral and thematic significance of "isolation" in JC's fiction, seriously weakened by careless organization. Some useful information about JC's Polish critical reputation.

23020 Glassman, Peter J. LANGUAGE AND BEING: JOSEPH CONRAD AND THE LITERATURE OF PERSONALITY. New York: Columbia Univ. Press, 1976.

Methodologically unsound brief psychobiography of the young JC, followed by autobiographical readings of the works, through LJ, based on the tenuous psychological assumptions of the biography. For example, Glassman draws conclusions from semantic evidence in translated material and from notoriously unreliable retrospective comments by JC himself. Sketchily documented childhood traumas are exaggerated, and so on.

*23021 Gordan, John Dozier. JOSEPH CONRAD: THE MAKING OF A NOVELIST. Cambridge: Harvard Univ. Press, 1940.

Excellent and thoroughly documented study of JC's fictional maturation (to LJ). Gordan generally focuses upon the writer's stylistic development as illustrated by his manuscript revisions, but also offers important observations on his use of sources and his working methods. Gordan is the first critic to demonstrate JC's conscious artistry. Extract reprinted in 23065.

*23022 Graver, Lawrence. CONRAD'S SHORT FICTION. Berkeley and Los Angeles: Univ. of California Press, 1969.

The standard study of the short stories and most of the novellas. Graver traces throughout JC's variations upon the themes of egoism and altruism, from his years of apprenticeship (to Daudet, Maupassant, Flaubert, and Kipling), to his period as mastercraftsman (c. 1900) and, later, in his years as writer of magazine-formula potboilers. Includes several of the best commentaries on individual tales and appends a useful chronology of the stories. Ample bibliography.

*23023 Guerard, Albert J. CONRAD THE NOVELIST. Cambridge: Harvard Univ. Press, 1958.

Expansion of Guerard's earlier volume (JOSEPH CONRAD [New York: New Directions, 1947]). The psychological "journey within" is postulated as the key symbolic and technical characteristic of JC's fiction. Although all the works are discussed, a decided preference is shown for the novels and stories of JC's decade of "achievement" (c. 1898-1908). Many of the individual analyses are superlative, yet Guerard has a tendency to underrate works which do not conform to the Jungian psychological archetype. Still the best single critical study of JC. Extracts reprinted in 23033, 23046, 23065, 25039, 25051, 25063, 25068, 25092, 25138, 25145, 25187, 25301, and 25317.

23024 Gurko, Leo. JOSEPH CONRAD: GIANT IN EXILE. New York: Macmillan, 1962.

Interpretations of individual works often rewarding, but much unnecessary biographical summary. Gurko concentrates his criticism on JC's theme of exile and his philosophic pessimism. Extracts reprinted in 25068 and 25092.

23025 Haugh, Robert F. JOSEPH CONRAD: DISCOVERY IN DESIGN. Norman: Univ. of Oklahoma Press, 1957.

Study of the major works which explores JC's impressionistic technique from NN to V. Haugh concentrates on JC's use of <u>progression d'effect</u>, those technical devices which contribute to the "growth, movement, [and] heightening of all elements of the story." Thus, the works are classified and discussed in terms of their design, from the simple sea fiction to the more complex tales of the "shallows." Numerous provocative readings. Extracts reprinted in 23040 and 25068.

23026 Hay, Eloise Knapp. THE POLITICAL NOVELS OF JOSEPH CONRAD: A CRITICAL STUDY. Chicago: Univ. of Chicago Press, 1963.

A lesser book than Fleishman's study (see 23016, above). The complexities of JC's radical-conservative political views are persuasively related to his Polish-English heritage and his romantic-realist technique. Fine discussions of LJ, RESCUE, HD, N, SA, and UWE.

23027 Hewitt, Douglas. CONRAD: A REASSESSMENT. 1952. 3rd ed. Totowa, N.J.: Rowman and Littlefield, 1975.

Interesting and penetrating discussions of the realistic and symbolic levels of JC's appeal, arguing that JC's most successful fiction maintains a consistent counterpoint between surface details and their representative significance. Extracts reprinted in 23046, 23065, 25063, and 25138.

23028 Hodges, Robert R. THE DUAL HERITAGE OF JOSEPH CONRAD. The Hague: Mouton, 1967.

Uninspired biographical and critical study of JC's self-divided nature and its impact on his fiction. For a similar, but far more sophisticated study of the tensions in JC's heritage, see Busza (23008). The impact of JC's Polish background is expertly discussed by Morf (23042).

23029 Hoffman, Stanton de Voren. COMEDY AND FORM IN THE FICTION OF JOSEPH CONRAD. The Hague: Mouton, 1969.

Stresses the moral and technical significance of the rarely acknowledged comic vision in JC (largely limited to HD and LJ).

23029a Jablkowska, Roza, ed. JOSEPH CONRAD COLLOQUY IN POLAND, 5-12 SEPTEMBER, 1972. CONTRIBUTIONS. Wroclaw: Polish Academy of Sciences Neophilological Committee, 1975.

Texts of six papers delivered at the 1972 conference by a group of distinguished Conradians (E.K. Hay, G. Morf, T. Moser, U. Mursia, R. Rapin, and I. Watt). Received too late for itemized annotation in this guide. Includes 25024.

*23030 Johnson, Bruce M. CONRAD'S MODELS OF MIND. Minneapolis: Univ. of Minnesota Press, 1971.

On the important development of JC's psychological models for character, from the conventional nineteenth-century types of the early works, to the nearly existential conception of the major fiction. Johnson sees JC's maturation as a psychologist in his abandonment of static conceptions of personality, or concrete "models of mind," for the more amorphous, flexible conception of "self-image" (e.g., HD, LJ). The weaker, later works show the "exhaustion" of this self-image model.

23031 JOSEPH CONRAD. Garden City, N.Y.: Doubleday, Page, 1926.

Pamphlet (about 60 p.). Publisher's testimonial and introduction to JC's work for the first collected edition in America.

23032 Karl, Frederick R. A READER'S GUIDE TO JOSEPH CONRAD. 1960. Rev. ed. New York: Noonday, 1969.

Valuable opening chapters on JC's technique, followed by introductory essays on the individual works. A good, if not especially distinguished guide. Extracts reprinted in 23033 and 25138.

23033 _____, ed. JOSEPH CONRAD: A COLLECTION OF CRITICISM. New York: McGraw-Hill, 1975.

Reprints six essays on the major works, a discussion of JC's aesthetics, and Palmer's bibliographical note on the "achievement and decline" debate (see Palmer's JOSEPH CONRAD'S FICTION, 23051). Also includes 24061, 25229, 25292, 25390, and extracts from the following books: 22028, 23023, and 23032.

23034 Keating, George T., ed. A CONRAD MEMORIAL LIBRARY: THE COLLECTION OF GEORGE T. KEATING. Garden City, N.Y.: Doubleday, Doran, 1929.

Brief appreciative essays on the major novels and tales by various hands. Significant items annotated separately: see 25152, 25236, 25245, 25247, 25296, 25334, 25343, 25356, 25415, and 25422.

23035 Kirschner, Paul. CONRAD: THE PSYCHOLOGIST AS ARTIST. Edinburgh: Oliver and Boyd, 1968.

A generally unimpressive survey of JC's "psychological" themes. Although Kirschner offers occasional insights into JC's images of the self, most of his criticism is pedestrian.

23036 Krzyzanowski, Ludwik, ed. JOSEPH CONRAD: CENTENNIAL ESSAYS. New York: Polish Institute of Arts and Sciences in America, 1960.

Seven reprinted essays on JC's Polish heritage. Includes 22027, 23045 (extract), 25134, and 25239.

23037 Lee, Robert F. CONRAD'S COLONIALISM. The Hague: Mouton, 1969.

Mechanical survey of the "white man's burden" theme in JC which is marred by Lee's own racial arrogance.

23038 LONDON MAGAZINE. 4 (Nov. 1957), 21-49. "Joseph Conrad: A Critical Symposium."

Seven essays on JC and his work. Includes 22007 (extract), 24044, 24064, 24151, 24154, 25369.

23039 Megroz, Rodolphe L. JOSEPH CONRAD'S MIND AND METHOD: A STUDY OF PERSONALITY IN ART. London: Faber, 1931.

Pleasant memoir and critical overview. Curious, unreliable, and dated commentaries.

23040 MODERN FICTION STUDIES. 1, No. 1 (1955), 2-45. "Joseph Conrad Number."

23041 MODERN FICTION STUDIES. 10 (1964), 3-106. "Joseph Conrad Number."

Two special JC issues containing a number of valuable articles as well as Beebe's bibliographical checklists of JC scholarship. Includes 21001, 23025 (extract), 24020, 24085, 24115, 24164, 25010, 25026, 25108, 25216, 25227, 25277, 25326, and 25389.

*23042 Morf, Gustav. THE POLISH HERITAGE OF JOSEPH CONRAD. New York: Smith, 1930.

Still the standard discussion of JC's Polish background and its impact on his fiction. Morf finds LJ and N symbolic externalizations of JC's sense of the Polish-English dualism within himself, while he sees "Amy Foster," V and Rov as characteristic reflections of the exile's insecurities. Several additional observations of value include a commentary on the linguistic influence of Polish on JC's English writing style. Extracts reprinted in 23065 and 25145.

23043 _____. THE POLISH SHADES AND GHOSTS OF JOSEPH CONRAD. New York: Astra Books, 1976.

Not seen.

*23044 Moser, Thomas. JOSEPH CONRAD: ACHIEVEMENT AND DECLINE. Cambridge: Harvard Univ. Press, 1957.

Invaluable and influential statement of the "decline" theory for JC's career. Moser's chapters on the early works discuss JC's complex morality and his variations upon the test of character. Moser attributes JC's weaker later fiction to his movement from these psychological themes to romance, his "uncongenial subject." Even JC's reputed "later affirmation" can be seen as an evasion of "moral responsibility," as the test of character is subordinated to the fatalistic acceptance of chance (Ch, V, SL, RESCUE). Extracts reprinted in 23046, 23065, and 25063.

23045 Mroczkowski, Przemyslaw. CONRADIAN COMMENTARIES. Cracow: Jagiellonian Univ. Press, 1970.

A penetrating running commentary, in the nature of a "reader's guide," on "The Lagoon," HD, and LJ, concentrating on the structure of the works, but not to the exclusion of general interpretation. Extract reprinted in 23036.

*23046 Mudrick, Marvin, ed. CONRAD: A COLLECTION OF CRITICAL ESSAYS. Englewood Cliffs, N.J.: Prentice-Hall, 1966.

Important collection of reprinted essays which emphasizes JC's achievement in his shorter works. Contains extracts from the following books: 22007, 22018, 23023, 23027, 23044, 23073; and the following articles: 24010, 24108, 25079, 25295, 25308, and 25375.

23047 Nettels, Elsa. JAMES AND CONRAD. Athens: Univ. of Georgia Press, 1977.

Absorbs several previously published articles on JC (see sections 2.4 and 2.5 below). (Seen in page proofs.)

23048 Newhouse, Neville H. JOSEPH CONRAD. London: Evans, 1966.

Fine introduction for the beginning student.

23049 O'Flaherty, Liam. JOSEPH CONRAD: AN APPRECIATION. London: Lahr, 1930.

Pamphlet (11 p.). An appreciation stressing JC's imperial and romantic idealism.

23050 Ordonez, Elmer A. THE EARLY JOSEPH CONRAD: REVISIONS AND STYLE. Quezon City: Univ. of the Philippines Press, 1969.

Detailed dissertation on JC's stylistic development which retraces much of the ground already covered by Gordon (23021).

*23051 Palmer, John A. JOSEPH CONRAD'S FICTION: A STUDY IN LITERARY GROWTH. Ithaca, N.Y.: Cornell Univ. Press, 1968.

Close readings of the major novels paired with general critical commentaries on the lesser fiction. Palmer sees JC's career in four phases: the early works, through LJ, are preoccupied with "dilemmas of private honor and individual fidelity"; the more mature fiction, N through UWE, explores the relation of the individual to society; the masterworks, Ch and V, are concerned with the "metaphysical bases of any moral commitment"; the "affirmative" last works only appear a decline in strength because they have fewer of the "moral and philosophic perplexities that had motivated his fiction from the beginning." Extract reprinted in 23033.

23052 POLISH REVIEW. 20, Nos. 2-3 (1975), 5-222. "Joseph Conrad: Commemorative Essays."

Nineteen comparative, textual, and critical essays on JC. Received too late for itemized listing. Note: This same collection has been announced for book publication (Boston: Hall, 1977), under the editorship of Adam Gillon and Ludwik Krzyzanowski.

23053 Price, Arthur J. AN APPRECIATION OF JOSEPH CONRAD. London: Simpkin, Marshall, 1931.

A cursory review of JC's life, followed by separate discussions of his "intensity," his "language," his "spirit of romance," his "teaching," and his "short stories." Largely dated.

*23054 Rosenfield, Claire. PARADISE OF SNAKES: AN ARCHETYPAL ANALYSIS OF CONRAD'S POLITICAL NOVELS. Chicago: Univ. of Chicago Press, 1967.

Full archetypal readings of N, SA, and UWE, under the acknowledged influence of Frye's theories of myth, Campbell's analysis of the hero-type, and Guerard's exploration of the Jungian quest motif in JC. Rosenfield does not justify the limitation of her study to the three political novels, but within this restricted compass she manages to say a great deal about JC's uses of myths and types. Some excesses, but frequently exciting and interesting criticism.

23055 Roussel, Royal. THE METAPHYSICS OF DARKNESS: A STUDY IN THE UNITY AND DEVELOPMENT OF CONRAD'S FICTION. Baltimore: Johns Hopkins Univ. Press, 1971.

Poorly written study which investigates the philosophic implications of the Conradian rite de passage.

23056 Ryf, Robert S. JOSEPH CONRAD. New York: Columbia Univ. Press, 1970.

Good brief introduction.

23057 Said, Edward W. JOSEPH CONRAD AND THE FICTION OF AUTOBIOGRAPHY. Cambridge: Harvard Univ. Press, 1966.

Critique of JC's correspondence and heavily autobiographical readings of the short fiction. JC's spiritual self-discovery in his work is as much obscured as clarified.

23058 Saveson, John E. CONRAD: THE LATER MORALIST. Amsterdam: Rodopi, 1974.

23059 ______. JOSEPH CONRAD: THE MAKING OF A MORALIST. Amsterdam: Rodopi, 1972.

Companion studies of the impact of nineteenth-century psychological theories upon JC's fiction. Organized, argued, and written poorly. For a far more penetrating commentary on JC's use of psychological models, see Johnson (23030).

23060 Selzer, Leon F. THE VISION OF MELVILLE AND CONRAD: A COMPARATIVE STUDY. Athens: Ohio Univ. Press, 1970.

Studies similarities in theme and technique between the two authors, ultimately relating both to modern existentialist thought.

*23061 Sherry, Norman. CONRAD'S EASTERN WORLD. Cambridge: At the Univ. Press, 1966.

See below.

*23062 ______. CONRAD'S WESTERN WORLD. Cambridge: At the Univ. Press, 1971.

Two impressive studies which fully detail the backgrounds to JC's Eastern and Western fiction. Sherry pursues JC's fictional sources in his personal experience, observation, hearsay, and reading (categories derived from Gordan's study, 23021 above), concentrating on LJ, AF, OI, and SL among the "Eastern" works, and HD, N and SA among the "Western" works. In many ways Sherry's most valuable contributions are his final chapters, both of which emphasize the remarkable accuracy and synthetic brilliance of JC's assimilative imagination. It need only be added that Sherry is gifted with the ability to make complex data easily comprehensible and inherently dry material compellingly interesting. Extract of CONRAD'S WESTERN WORLD reprinted in 25301.

*23063 ______, ed. CONRAD: THE CRITICAL HERITAGE. London: Routledge, 1973.

Compendium of reviews and early critical statements concerning JC. Excellent guide to JC's contemporary reputation. Includes 21010, 24043, 24047 (extracts), 25021, and 25238.

23064 _____, ed. JOSEPH CONRAD: A COMMEMORATION. London: Macmillan, 1976.

Seventeen essays, from the international JC conference, Canterbury, 1974. Includes papers on JC's individual works, his aesthetic theory, literary relationships, political views, language, and critical reputation (in Poland). Received too late for itemized listing in this guide. Includes the following in revised or expanded form: 22025, 22030, 24050, and 24061.

*23065 Stallman, Robert W., ed. THE ART OF JOSEPH CONRAD: A CRITICAL SYMPOSIUM. East Lansing: Michigan State Univ. Press, 1960.

Generous compilation of more than thirty previously published essays on JC's fiction, including several primarily symbolic studies of individual works. Much of the best critical interpretation of JC (to 1960) is available here. Includes, 24036, 24105, 24132, 24166, 24174, 25028, 25054, 25055, 25056, 25059, 25085, 25088, 25108, 25165, 25196, 25232, 25278, 25292, 25324; and extracts from the following books and article: 22007, 23006, 23011, 23021, 23023, 23027, 23042, 23044, 23073, and 24080.

23066 Stauffer, Ruth M. JOSEPH CONRAD: HIS ROMANTIC-REALISM. Boston: Four Seas, 1922.

Early study, preoccupied with categorization. Stauffer defines and demonstrates the conflicting "romantic" and "realistic" elements of JC's art. His dualist aesthetic is both credited for creating a fertile ambiguity in his work and blamed for occasionally obfuscating his meaning.

23067 Stewart, J.I.M. JOSEPH CONRAD. New York: Dodd, 1968.

Well-written introduction for the general reader or the beginning student.

23068 Symons, Arthur. NOTES ON JOSEPH CONRAD WITH SOME UNPUBLISHED LETTERS. London: Myers, 1925.

Pamphlet (31 p.). Symons notes the exoticism and subtlety of JC's prose.

23068a Thomas, Claude, ed. STUDIES IN JOSEPH CONRAD. Cahiers d'Etudes et de Recherches Victoriennes et Edouardiennes, No. 2. Montpellier: Universite Paul-Valery, 1975.

Fifteen essays (in English) on JC's life and works, several from a French perspective. (Not seen.)

*23069 Thorburn, David. CONRAD'S ROMANTICISM. New Haven, Conn.: Yale University Press, 1974.

Finds JC's minor work representative of a continuing, anti-apocalyptic, romantic tradition. Thorburn argues that the major fiction has been recognized chiefly for its modern vision of the waste land, not for its romantic antecedents. This important reexamination of JC's overall achievement reasonably and persuasively argues his transitional role as a "modern and Romantic simultaneously."

23069a Tucker, Martin. JOSEPH CONRAD. New York: Ungar, 1976.

Extremely inadequate, hack-work introduction to JC. Best ignored.

23070 Visiak, Edward H. THE MIRROR OF CONRAD. London: Laurie, 1955.

Weak study which seeks the autobiographical basis of JC's art--with a vengeance.

23071 Walpole, Hugh. JOSEPH CONRAD. 1916. Rev. ed. New York: Holt, 1924.

Study of JC under four headings: "Biography," "The Novelist," "The Poet," and "Romance and Realism." Although largely dated, Walpole's discussion of JC's lyricism ("The Poet") remains perceptive.

23072 Warner, Oliver. JOSEPH CONRAD. 1951. 3rd ed. London: Longmans, 1960.

Introductory pamphlet on the "writer and his work."

*23073 Wiley, Paul L. CONRAD'S MEASURE OF MAN. Madison: Univ. of Wisconsin Press, 1954.

A three-phase thematic study of JC's career, centering on the development of his characters from isolated "Hermits," through self-destructive "Incendiaries," to disillusioned "Knights." Well written and insightful. Extracts reprinted in 23046, 23065, 25068, 25138, and 25187.

23074 Wright, Walter F. ROMANCE AND TRAGEDY IN JOSEPH CONRAD. Lincoln: Univ. of Nebraska Press, 1949.

JC's fiction divided into two arbitrary categories--romances and tragedies. Some fine analyses, but considerable padding. Extracts reprinted in 25063 and 25317.

23075 Yelton, Donald C. MIMESIS AND METAPHOR: AN INQUIRY INTO THE GENESIS AND SCOPE OF CONRAD'S SYMBOLIC IMAGERY. The Hague: Mouton, 1967.

Definition and illustration of JC's uses of symbols (in light of the French Symbolistes) and metaphors. Many of the individual readings deteriorate into image hunts. Extract reprinted in 25145.

23076 Zyla, Wolodymyr T., and Wendell M. Aycock, eds. JOSEPH CONRAD: THEORY AND WORLD FICTION. PROCEEDINGS OF THE COMPARATIVE LITERATURE SYMPOSIUM. Vol. 7. Lubbock: Texas Tech. Press, 1974.

Collects eleven original essays on JC's art and his place in world literature. Includes 24045, 24052, 24058, 24110, 24119, 24128, 24133, 24149, 25183, 25289.

2.4 General Critical Articles, or Chapters on JC

24001 Adams, Richard P. "The Apprenticeship of William Faulkner." TSE, 12 (1962), 113-56.

JC's influence on Faulkner.

24002 Allen, Mary. "Melville and Conrad Confront Stillness." RS, 40 (1972), 122-30.

"Becalmed at sea" as a test of character in the short fiction of JC and Melville.

24003 Allen, Walter. THE ENGLISH NOVEL. Pp. 361-74. See G2201.

High praise for the early fiction, and JC's creation of a "sense of 'indefinable' evil."

24004 ______. "Joseph Conrad." In SIX GREAT NOVELISTS. London: Hamilton, 1955. Pp. 154-82.

Biography and critique.

24005 Baker, Ernest A. "Conrad, the Teller of Tales" and "Conrad, the Novelist, with His Next of Kin." In THE HISTORY OF THE ENGLISH NOVEL. X, 11-44, 45-104. See G2203.

Literary history, with some critical commentary.

24006 Bantock, G.H. "Conrad and Politics." ELH, 25 (1958), 122-36.

JC's political skepticism a result of his own experience in positions of authority.

24007 _____. "The Two 'Moralities' of Joseph Conrad." EIC, 3 (1953), 125-42.

JC's fidelity to ideals of both public and private morality.

24008 Bates, Herbert E. "Thomas Hardy and Joseph Conrad." In THE ENGLISH NOVELISTS. Ed. Derek Verschoyle. Pp. 231-44. See G3150.

Stresses vast differences between the two writers.

24009 Beach, Joseph Warren. "Impressionism: Conrad." In his THE TWENTIETH-CENTURY NOVEL. Pp. 337-65. See G3004.

JC contributed to the "deformalization" of the novel. Extracts reprinted in 25092.

*24010 Beerbohm, Max. "The Feast, by J*s*ph C*nr*d." In A CHRISTMAS GARLAND. London: Heinemann, 1912. Pp. 127-34.

Parody of "Conradese" stylistic excesses (see Bross, 24016). Reprinted in 23046.

24011 Bender, Todd K. "Fictional Time and the Problem of Free Will." WISCONSIN STUDIES IN LITERATURE, No. 5 (1968), pp. 12-22.

Bergsonian time and the literary impressionism of JC and Ford.

24012 Berman, Jeffrey. "Writing as Rescue: Conrad's Escape from the Heart of Darkness." L&P, 25 (1975), 65-78.

JC's dependence upon art as an escape from the terrors of life.

*24013 Bonney, William W. "Joseph Conrad and the Discontinuous Point of View." JNT, 2 (1972), 99-115.

JC's apparently inconsistent narrative techniques are purposeful.

24014 Braybrooke, Patrick. "Joseph Conrad: Master Novelist." In SOME VICTORIAN AND GEORGIAN CATHOLICS, THEIR ART AND OUTLOOK. London: Burnes, Oates and Washbourne, 1932. Pp. 137-68.

JC's ideal of faithfulness reflects his religious heritage. JC is, however, mistakenly viewed here as an orthodox Catholic.

24015 Bridges, Horace J. "Joseph Conrad: A Memorial Tribute/The Genius of Joseph Conrad." In THE GOD OF FUNDAMENTALISM AND OTHER STUDIES. Chicago: Covici, 1925. Pp. 297-319.

A pleasant but uncritical appreciation

24016 Bross, Addison C. "Beerbohm's 'The Feast' and Conrad's Early Fiction." NCF, 26 (1971), 329-36.

Beerbohm's parody (see 24010) exploits several elements of JC's early style.

24017 Brown, Douglas. "From 'Heart of Darkness' to NOSTROMO: An Approach to Conrad." In THE MODERN AGE. Ed. Boris Ford. Pp. 119-37. See G2110.

JC's ambiguous skeptical affirmations.

24018 Brown, Edward K. "James and Conrad." YR, 35 (1945), 265-85.

Both novelists concerned primarily with character.

24019 Burkhart, Charles. "Conrad the Victorian." ELT, 6 (1963), 1-8.

JC a transitional novelist who reveals essentially Victorian ideas of character and morality.

24020 Carroll, Wesley. "The Novelist as Artist." MFS, 1, No. 1 (1955), 2-8.

JC's symbolism impressionistic. See 23040.

24021 Cassell, Richard A. "Ford's Theory of Fiction." In FORD MADOX FORD: A STUDY OF HIS NOVELS. Baltimore: Johns Hopkins Univ. Press, 1962. Pp. 37-72.

Discusses JC's influence.

24022 Cecil, David. "Joseph Conrad." In THE FINE ART OF READING, AND OTHER LITERARY STUDIES. Indianapolis, Ind.: Bobbs-Merrill, 1957. Pp. 179-215.

JC's fascination with moral dilemmas.

24023 Chattopadhyaya, Sisir [also Chatterjee, Sisir]. THE TECHNIQUE OF THE MODERN ENGLISH NOVEL. Pp. 98-109. See G3022.

Stresses narrative technique.

24024 Clemens, Florence. "Conrad's Favorite Bedside Book." SAQ, 38 (1939), 305-15.

JC's several debts to A.R. Wallace's THE MALAY ARCHIPELAGO for details in his fiction.

24025 Collins, Arthur S. "Conrad." In his ENGLISH LITERATURE OF THE TWENTIETH CENTURY. Pp. 185-92. See G2105.

JC in relation to modern literary movements.

24026 Cook, Albert S. "Plot as Discovery: Conrad. . . ." In his THE MEANING OF FICTION. Pp. 203-8. See G3026.

Thematic and structural significance of "detection" in JC's fiction.

24027 Cox, Brian. "Introduction." In "YOUTH," "HEART OF DARKNESS," "THE END OF THE TETHER." London: Dent, 1974. Pp. vii-xxii. "Notes" (added 1975), pp. 340-53.

24028 Crews, Frederick C. "The Power of Darkness." PR, 34 (1967), 507-25.

Questions "whether Conrad himself grasped the deeper consistencies of his art."

24029 Cross, Wilbur J. "The Illusions of Joseph Conrad." YR, 17 (1928), 464-82.

A review of the collected works and Aubry's early biography leads to a discussion of JC's idealism, his view of the world as composed of illusions, and its effects on his fiction.

24030 _____. "Joseph Conrad." In his FOUR CONTEMPORARY NOVELISTS. Pp. 9-60. See G3029.

On the theme of illusion.

24031 Curle, Richard. "Joseph Conrad: Ten Years After." VQR, 10 (1934), 420-35.

Brief reminiscence and memorial critical tribute.

*24032 Daiches, David. "Joseph Conrad." In THE NOVEL AND THE MODERN WORLD. Pp. 25-62. See G3030.

Isolation as a thematic and a structural device. Extract reprinted in 25138.

*24033 Davidson, Donald. "Joseph Conrad's Directed Indirections." SR, 33 (1925), 163-77.

JC's techniques create a higher realism.

24034 Drew, Elizabeth A. "Joseph Conrad." In her THE MODERN NOVEL. Pp. 223-40. See G3035.

JC's aesthetic and practice.

24035 Edgar, Pelham. "Joseph Conrad." In his THE ART OF THE NOVEL. Pp. 184-95. See G2205.

Critical history.

24036 Fernandez, Ramon. "The Art of Conrad." Trans. Charles Owen. In ART OF JOSEPH CONRAD. Ed. Robert W. Stallman. Pp. 8-13. See 23065.

JC's impressionism.

24037 Fernando, Lloyd. "Conrad's Eastern Expatriates: A New Version of His Outcasts." PMLA, 91 (1976), 78-91.

JC's Malaysian experiences and his symbolic use of the expatriate figure.

24037a Firchow, Peter. "Conrad, Goethe, and the German Grotesque." CLS, 13 (1976), 60-74.

Discusses the principal German characters in JC's fiction (e.g., Schomberg, the "Goethean" Stein).

*24038 Fleishman, Avrom. "Conrad." In his THE ENGLISH HISTORICAL NOVEL. Pp. 212-32. See G3042.

Considers N, Rov, and SUSPENSE.

24039 Ford, Ford Madox. "Decennial (It is ten years on the day of writing since the last book of Joseph Conrad's writing was posthumously published in New York)." LONDON MERCURY, 32 (1935), 223-31.

JC's greatest achievement his memoirs and his nonsea works. Absorbed into 24041 below.

24040 _____. "In the Last Quarter of a Century." In THE ENGLISH NOVEL: FROM THE EARLIEST DAYS TO THE DEATH OF JOSEPH CONRAD. London: Constable, 1930. Pp. 135-42.

James, Crane, and JC share a similar "Gallic origin" as novelists and the common ambition to make the reader "see" and "feel" their subjects.

24041 _____. "Joseph Conrad." In PORTRAITS FROM LIFE. Boston: Houghton Mifflin, 1937. Pp. 57-69.

Memoir and critique. Reprinted in 25051 and 25068 (extract). Also, see 24039.

*24042 _____. "Mr. Joseph Conrad and Anglo-Saxondom." In THUS TO REVISIT. New York: Dutton, 1921. Pp. 79-101.

JC's Englishness and universality.

*24043 Forster, E.M. "Joseph Conrad: A Note." 1921. In ABINGER HARVEST. New York: Harcourt, 1936. Pp. 136-41.

JC's failure to disclose his "general philosophic statement about the universe." Reprinted in 23063.

24044 Freislich, Richard. "Marlow's Shadow Side." LONDON MAGAZINE, 4 (Nov. 1957), 31-36.

Marlow's (and JC's) tendency to identify with his subject's darker side. See 23038.

24045 Friedman, Alan W. "Conrad's Picaresque Narrator: Marlow's Journey from 'Youth' through CHANCE." In JOSEPH CONRAD: THEORY AND WORLD FICTION. Ed. Wolodymyr T. Zyla and Wendell M. Aycock. Pp. 17-39. See 23076.

Marlow as the "developing," and not always trustworthy, center of a larger episodic fiction ("Youth," HD, LJ and Ch).

24046 Garnett, Edward. "Conrad's Place in English Literature." In CONRAD'S PREFACES TO HIS WORKS. Pp. 3-34. See 13004.

JC England's first continental writer.

24047 _____. "Mr. Joseph Conrad." 1898, 1904, 1921. In FRIDAY NIGHTS. New York: Knopf, 1922. Pp. 83-101.

Collects previously published essays on JC's lyric and realistic qualities (one of the first general articles on JC), on his "psychology of scene" in N, and on his "artistic veracity" (a review of NOTES ON LIFE AND LETTERS). First two parts reprinted in 23063.

*24048 Garrett, Peter K. "Joseph Conrad: Intrinsic Significance." In his SCENE AND SYMBOL. Pp. 160-80. See G3048.

JC's use of symbolic setting.

24049 Geddes, Gary. "Conrad and the Darkness before Creation." AntigR, No. 7 (1971), pp. 92-104.

JC's characteristically anguished state of mind before creation.

24050 Gillon, Adam. "Conrad in Poland." PolR, 19, Nos. 3-4 (1974), 3-28.

Up-to-date review of JC's Polish critical reputation. Reprinted in 23064.

24051 _____. "Cosmopolitanism in Conrad's Work." In PROCEEDINGS OF THE IVth CONGRESS OF THE INTERNATIONAL COMPARATIVE LITERATURE ASSOCIATION (FRIBOURG, 1964). Ed. Francois Jost. The Hague: Mouton, 1967. I, 94-99.

JC a product of several literary traditions (stresses his middle-European background).

24052 _____. "Joseph Conrad: Polish Cosmopolitan." In JOSEPH CONRAD: THEORY AND WORLD FICTION. Ed. Wolodymyr T. Zyla and Wendell M. Aycock. Pp. 41-69. See 23076.

JC's "cosmopolitanism stems from his psychological awareness of being an emigre."

24053 _____. "Joseph Conrad and Shakespeare." CONRADIANA, 1, Nos. 1-3 (1968-69), 19-25, 15-22, 7-27.

Shakespeare allusions in JC.

24054 _____. "Polish and Russian Literary Elements in Joseph Conrad." In ACTES DU Ve CONGRES DE L'ASSOCIATION INTERNATIONALE DE LITTERATURE COMPAREE (BELGRADE, 1967). Amsterdam: Swets and Zeitlinger, 1969. Pp. 685-94.

The relationship of JC's "Russian strains" (e.g., UWE) to his Polish origins.

24055 _____. "Some Polish Literary Motifs in the Works of Joseph Conrad." SEEJ, 10 (1966), 424-39.

JC's themes, rather than his subjects, show impact of his Polish heritage.

24056 Goldknopf, David. "Marlow's Mighty Lie: The I-Narrator in Joseph Conrad." In his THE LIFE OF THE NOVEL. Pp. 79-99. See G3053.

Conflict between JC and his narrators.

24057 Green, Jesse D. "Diabolism, Pessimism, and Democracy: Notes on Melville and Conrad." MFS, 8 (1962), 287-305.

Comparative study.

24058 Harkness, Bruce. "Conrad, Graham Greene, and Film." In JOSEPH CONRAD: THEORY AND WORLD FICTION. Ed. Wolodymyr T. Zyla and Wendell M. Aycock. Pp. 71-87. See 23076.

Discusses the failure of screen adaptations of JC's works.

24059 _____. "Conrad on Galsworthy: The Time Scheme of FRATERNITY." MFS, 1, No. 2 (1955), 12-18.

JC's influence on Galsworthy's use of time in FRATERNITY.

24060 Häusermann, Hans Walter. "Joseph Conrad's Literary Activities in Geneva." In THE GENEVESE BACKGROUND: STUDIES OF SHELLEY, FRANCIS DANBY, MARIA EDGEWORTH, RUSKIN, MEREDITH, AND JOSEPH CONRAD IN GENEVA, WITH HITHERTO UNPUBLISHED LETTERS. London: Routledge, 1952. Pp. 199-213.

Geneva treated badly in JC's fiction (e.g., UWE) because of his unfortunate experiences in the city.

24061 Hay, Eloise Knapp. "Joseph Conrad and Impressionism." JAAC, 34 (1975), 137-44.

JC came to accept the "stigma" of "impressionist" in reaction against the abuses (to him) of depth psychology in fiction. Reprinted in 23033 and 23064.

24062 Heimer, Jackson W. "Patterns of Betrayal in the Novels of Joseph Conrad." BSUF, 8, No. 3 (1967), 30-39.

24063 Hollingsworth, Alan M. "Freud, Conrad, and the Future of an Illusion." L&P, 5 (1955), 78-83.

Illusion as a form of deathwish. Reprinted in 25068.

24064 Hopkinson, Tom. "The Short Stories." LONDON MAGAZINE, 4 (Nov. 1957), 36-41.

JC's novellas his finest achievements. See 23038.

*24065 Howe, Irving. "Conrad: Order and Anarchy." In his POLITICS AND THE NOVEL. Pp. 76-113. See G6203.

Marxist examination of JC's politics. Extract reprinted in 25301.

*24066 Huneker, James G. "The Genius of Joseph Conrad." In IVORY APES AND PEACOCKS. New York: Scribner's, 1915. Pp. 1-21.

Perceptive early commentary. Argues that JC combines the adventure appeal of a sea romancer and the artistic quality of the French novelists (see Walt, 24152).

24067 Joseph, Edward D. "Identity and Joseph Conrad." PSYCHOANALYTIC QUARTERLY, 32 (1963), 549-72.

JC's fiction as auto-therapy.

24068 Kaplan, Harold J. "Character as Reality: Joseph Conrad." In his THE PASSIVE VOICE. Pp. 131-57. See G3079.

The only reality for JC found in character.

24069 Karl, Frederick R. "Conrad, Ford, and the Novel." MIDWAY, 10, No. 2 (1969), 17-34.

JC's and Ford's correspondence illuminates their relationship and their motives for collaboration.

24070 _____. "Conrad, Wells, and the Two Voices." PMLA, 88 (1973), 1049-65.

Wells the scientist, JC the humanist, and their views of each other's work.

24071 _____. "The Letters of Joseph Conrad: Textual and Editing Problems." CONRADIANA, 5, No. 3 (1973), 28-36.

24072 Karl, Frederick R., and Marvin Magalaner. "Joseph Conrad." In their A READER'S GUIDE TO GREAT TWENTIETH-CENTURY ENGLISH NOVELS. Pp. 42-99. See G3082.

Biography and introductory survey (especially on LJ, N, UWE, and V).

24073 Kenner, Hugh. "Conrad and Ford." In his GNOMON. Pp. 162-70. See G3083.

Comparisons among N, UWE, and THE GOOD SOLDIER.

24074 Keppler, Carl F. THE LITERATURE OF THE SECOND SELF. Tucson: Univ. of Arizona Press, 1972. Pp. 45-50, 86-91, 112-15.

The double in JC's V, LJ, and SS.

24075 Kerf, Rene. "Ethics versus Aesthetics: A Clue to the Deterioration of Conrad's Art." RLV, 31 (1965), 240-49.

JC's decline attributable to his growing ethical emphasis.

24076 Kirschner, Paul. "Conrad and the Film." QFRT, 11 (1957), 343-53.

JC's use of cinematic techniques in his fiction.

24077 Knight, Grant C. THE NOVEL IN ENGLISH. Pp. 305-13. See G2207.

Survey and brief critique.

24078 Kreisel, Henry. "Joseph Conrad and the Dilemma of the Uprooted Man." TamR, 7 (1958), 78-85.

Recurrent themes of alienation, or dispossession, in JC.

24079 Krieger, Murray. "Joseph Conrad: Action, Inaction, and Extremity." In his THE TRAGIC VISION. Pp. 154-94. See G3089.

Confrontations with the "darkness" in JC (HD, LJ, V). Extract reprinted in 25145.

*24080 Leavis, Frank R. "Joseph Conrad." In THE GREAT TRADITION. Pp. 173-226. See G3091.

An indispensible essay placing JC within the tradition of moral earnestness in English fiction. Leavis finds N and SA JC's finest novels, his most concrete realizations of his moral themes. Extracts reprinted in 23065, 25092, 25138, and 25301.

24081 Lerner, Laurence. "Conrad the Historian." LISTENER, 73 (1965), 554-56.

JC, like James, an "historian of fine consciences."

24082 Levin, Gerald H. "The Skepticism of Marlow." TCL, 3 (1958), 177-84.

The development of Marlow.

24083 Lilliard, R.G. "Irony in Hardy and Conrad." PMLA, 50 (1935), 316-22.

Comparisons and contrasts.

24083a Lincoln, Kenneth R. "Conrad's Mythic Humor." TSLL, 17 (1975), 635-51.

24084 Long, Robert E. "THE GREAT GATSBY and the Tradition of Joseph Conrad." TSLL, 8 (1966), 257-76, 407-22.

JC and Fitzgerald.

24085 Lorch, Thomas M. "The Barrier between Youth and Maturity in the Works of Joseph Conrad." MFS, 10 (1964), 73-80.

The "test" motif. See 23041.

24086 Lovett, Robert M., and Helen S. Hughes. "Joseph Conrad (1857-1924)." In their THE HISTORY OF THE NOVEL IN ENGLAND. Pp. 401-11. See G2209.

Survey of career, stressing JC's impressionistic style.

24087 Lynd, Robert. "Mr. Conrad at Home." In BOOKS AND AUTHORS. London: Cobden-Sanderson, 1922. Pp. 175-83.

JC's modesty, reticence, and critical views.

24088 _____. "Mr. Joseph Conrad." In OLD AND NEW MASTERS. London: Unwin, 1919. Pp. 212-23.

Perceptively notes the quality of mystery in JC's fiction.

24089 McIntyre, Allan O. "Conrad on Conscience and the Passions." UR, 31 (1964), 69-74.

JC's handling of passion.

*24090 _____. "Conrad on the Functions of the Mind." MLQ, 25 (1964), 187-97.

An important study of JC's epistemology.

*24091 MacShane, Frank. "Conrad Collaboration." In THE LIFE AND WORK OF FORD MADOX FORD. New York: Horizon, 1965. Pp. 36-54.

Excellent critical study of JC's and Ford's personal and literary relationships.

24092 Martin, Joseph J. "Edward Garnett and Conrad's Plunge into the 'Destructive Element.'" TSLL, 15 (1973), 517-36.

Garnett influenced JC's adoption of the "objective method."

24093 _____. "Edward Garnett and Conrad's Reshaping of Time." CONRADIANA, 6 (1974), 89-105.

Argues Garnett (rather than Ford) influenced JC's experimentations with time.

24094 Martin, W.R. "Beginnings and Endings in Conrad." CONRADIANA, 5, No. 1 (1973), 43-51.

24095 Masback, Fredric J. "Conrad's Jonahs." CE, 22 (1961), 328-33.

Use of Book of Jonah in NN and SL.

24096 Maser, Frederick E. "The Philosophy of Joseph Conrad." HJ, 56 (1957), 69-78.

General description.

24097 Maurois, Andre. "Joseph Conrad." In his PROPHETS AND POETS. Pp. 177-211. See G3102.

JC expresses in fiction the stoic philosophy of life of the "British man of action" (surveys life and works).

*24098 Meixner, John A. "Ford and Conrad." CONRADIANA, 6 (1974), 157-69.

Asserts Ford's influence on JC and defends Ford's version of his relationships with JC as essentially trustworthy. Ford has "been done a serious injustice by people of the Conrad persuasion."

24099 Mencken, H.L. "Joseph Conrad." In A BOOK OF PREFACES. New York: Knopf, 1917. Pp. 11-64.

Admiring and insightful early critique. Reprinted in 25068.

24100 Messenger, William E. "Conrad and His 'Sea Stuff.'" CONRADIANA, 6 (1974), 3-18.

JC's early sea fiction was, as he later seemed to feel, an abdication of artistic responsibility in a "quest for popularity."

24101 Meyers, Jeffrey. "Joseph Conrad: The Meaning of Civilization." In his FICTION AND THE COLONIAL EXPERIENCE. Pp. 57-78. See G6206.

Political context of HD and N.

24102 Michel, Laurence. "Conrad: Romance and Tragedy." In THE THING CONTAINED: A THEORY OF THE TRAGIC. Bloomington: Indiana Univ. Press, 1970. Pp. 86-106.

The tragic action in JC (cf. Shakespeare and Faulkner).

24103 Michel, Lois A. "The Absurd Predicament in Conrad's Political Novels." CE, 23 (1961), 131-36.

Existentialist readings.

*24104 Miller, J. Hillis. "Joseph Conrad." In POETS OF REALITY. Pp. 13-67. See G3106.

JC's "leap into the abyss" of nihilism. Extract reprinted in 25301.

24105 Milosz, Czeslaw. "Joseph Conrad in Polish Eyes." In THE ART OF JOSEPH CONRAD. Ed. Robert W. Stallman. Pp. 35-45. See 23065.

JC "irremediably" the product of <u>Western</u> civilization.

24106 Morris, Robert L. "The Classical Reference in Conrad's Fiction." CE, 7 (1946), 312-18.

JC's use of classical allusions, chiefly in LJ and V.

24107 Mudrick, Marvin. "Conrad and the Terms of Criticism." HudR, 7 (1954), 419-26.

JC's stronger work avoids symbolic paradigms. Reprinted in 25063 (extract) and 25317.

*24108 ______. "The Originality of Conrad." HudR, 11 (1958), 545-53.

JC's synthesis of realism and symbolism. Reprinted in 23046 and 25068.

24109 Muller, Herbert J. "Joseph Conrad." In his MODERN FICTION. Pp. 244-61. See G3111.

JC as pessimist.

24110 Najder, Zdzislaw. "Conrad and the Idea of Honor." In JOSEPH CONRAD: THEORY AND WORLD FICTION. Ed. Wolodymyr T. Zyla and Wendell M. Aycock. Pp. 103-14. See 23076.

JC in the "gentry" tradition of the ethos of honor (via his Polish heritage and conscious choice).

24111 ______. "Conrad in His Historical Perspective." ELT, 14 (1971), 157-66

Disappointingly slight essay.

24112 Nettels, Elsa. "The Grotesque in Conrad's Fiction." NCF, 29 (1974), 144-63.

Grotesque as symbol of a "dislocated and bizarre" sense of the world in JC (especially in SA and UWE).

24113 ______. "James and Conrad on the Art of Fiction." TSLL, 14 (1972), 529-43.

Comparative survey.

24114 Paterson, John. "Joseph Conrad: To Make You See." In his THE NOVEL AS FAITH. Pp. 69-106. See G3118.

JC as moralist and realist.

24115 Perry, John Oliver. "Action, Vision, or Voice: The Moral Dilemmas in Conrad's Tale-Telling." MFS, 10 (1964), 3-14.

The search for meaning, by JC and by his characters. See 23041.

24116 Phelps, Gilbert. THE RUSSIAN NOVEL IN ENGLISH FICTION. Pp. 125-32, 176-79. See G3120.

Influence of Turgenev and Dostoevsky on JC.

24117 Phelps, William L. THE ADVANCE OF THE ENGLISH NOVEL. Pp. 193-217. See G3122.

Stresses JC's "ethical value."

24118 Pritchett, Victor S. "Conrad." In his THE LIVING NOVEL. Pp. 190-99. See G3125.

General appreciation.

24119 Pulc, I.P. "The Imprint of Polish on Conrad's Prose." JOSEPH CONRAD: THEORY AND WORLD FICTION. Ed. Wolodymyr T. Zyla and Wendell M. Aycock. Pp. 117-39. See 23076.

Polish rhetorical habits, prose rhythms, and idioms in JC.

24120 Rajiva, Stanley F. "The Singular Person: An Essay on Conrad's Use of Marlow as Narrator." LCrit, 8, No. 2 (1967), 35-45.

Unoriginal study of JC's use of Marlow to achieve distance from his material.

24121 Ramsey, Roger. "The Available and the Unavailable 'I': Conrad and James." ELT, 14 (1971), 137-45.

Influence of "The Turn of the Screw" on JC's fiction (e.g., HD), especially in the use of a frame tale.

24122 Rapin, René. "Reality and Imagination in the Works of Joseph Conrad." CONRADIANA, 4, No. 3 (1972), 22-33; 5, No. 3 (1973), 46-59.

Introductory lecture on JC, of slight critical value.

24123 Raskin, Jonah. THE MYTHOLOGY OF IMPERIALISM. Pp. 126-221. See G6208.

JC as imperialist, from a Marxist perspective. Reductive.

24124 Reilly, Joseph J. "The Shorter Stories of Joseph Conrad." In OF BOOKS AND MEN. New York: Messner, 1942. Pp. 79-92.

JC's concern with moral and ethical problems of character. Surveys stories.

24125 Renner, Stanley. "The Garden of Civilization: Conrad, Huxley, and the Ethics of Evolution." CONRADIANA, 7 (1975), 109-20.

JC's life-long concern with the evolutionary struggle of civilization vs. savagery (cf. T.H. Huxley).

24126 Rogers, Robert. "The Secret Sharer." In A PSYCHOANALYTIC STUDY OF THE DOUBLE IN LITERATURE. Detroit: Wayne State Univ. Press, 1970. Pp. 40-59.

A general view of the double in JC, Kafka, and others.

24127 Rose, Alan M. "Conrad and the Sirens of the Decadence." TSLL, 11 (1969), 795-810.

JC's fin de siecle aestheticism.

24128 Rude, Donald W. "Conrad as Editor: The Preparation of THE SHORTER TALES." In JOSEPH CONRAD: THEORY AND WORLD FICTION. Ed. Wolodymyr T. Zyla and Wendell M. Aycock. Pp. 189-96. See 23076.

JC "deeply involved" in the planning of the posthumously published anthology of his shorter works (1924).

24129 Said, Edward W. "Conrad: The Presentation of Narrative." NOVEL, 7 (1974), 116-32.

JC's fictional technique.

24130 Sandison, Alan. "Joseph Conrad: A Window on to Chaos." In THE WHEEL OF EMPIRE: A STUDY OF THE IMPERIAL IDEA IN SOME LATE NINETEENTH- AND EARLY TWENTIETH-CENTURY FICTION. New York: St. Martin's, 1967. Pp. 120-48.

JC's equivocal imperialism.

24131 Schneider, Daniel J. "The Dream and the Knitting Machine: Joseph Conrad's Symbolism." In SYMBOLISM: THE MANICHEAN VISION. A STUDY IN THE ART OF JAMES, CONRAD, WOOLF, AND STEVENS. Lincoln: Univ. of Nebraska Press, 1975. Pp. 40-61.

JC's dualistic symbolism.

24132 Shand, John. "Some Notes on Joseph Conrad." In THE ART OF JOSEPH CONRAD. Ed. Robert W. Stallman. Pp. 13-19. See 23065.

Stylistic weaknesses in JC's later work.

24133 Sherry, Norman. "The Essential Conrad." E&S, 27 (1974), 98-113.

JC's realistic and atmospheric use of significant detail. Reprinted in 23076.

24134 Smoller, Sanford J. "A Note on Joseph Conrad's Fall and Abyss." MFS, 15 (1969), 261-64.

The gradual disappearance of catastrophic images in JC's fiction shows his movement toward guarded optimism.

24135 Solomon, Eric. STEPHEN CRANE IN ENGLAND: A PORTRAIT OF THE ARTIST. Columbus: Ohio State Univ. Press, 1964. Pp. 91-118.

JC and Crane.

24136 Stallman, Robert W. "Conrad and THE GREAT GATSBY." TCL, 1 (1955), 5-12.

Gatsby is to Nick as both Kurtz and Jim are to Marlow.

*24137 _____. "Fiction and Its Critics: A Reply to Mr. Rahv." KR, 19 (1957), 290-99.

Defense of symbolic criticism (e.g., in JC).

24138 Stavrou, C.N. "Conrad, Camus, and Sisyphus." AUDIENCE, 7 (1960), 80-96.

Existentialism in JC.

24139 Stawell, F. Melian. "Conrad." E&S, 6 (1920), 88-111.

Perceptive early general critique.

24140 Stein, William B. "Conrad's East: Time, History, Action, and Maya." TSLL, 7 (1965), 265-83.

JC and Eastern thought.

24141 _____. "The Eastern Matrix of Conrad's Art." CONRADIANA, 1, No. 2 (1968), 1-14.

Social and historical realities of JC's Eastern tales.

24142 Stewart, J.I.M. "Conrad." In his EIGHT MODERN WRITERS. Pp. 184-222, 656-65. See G3143.

Briefer survey and introduction than Stewart's critical study (23067).

24143 Swinnerton, Frank. THE GEORGIAN LITERARY SCENE. Pp. 115-23 and passim. See G2364.

Biographical and critical summary.

*24144 Tanner, Tony. "Mountains and Depths--An Approach to Nineteenth-Century Dualism." REL, 3, No. 4 (1962), 51-61.

JC's dualistic world view.

24145 Thomson, George H. "Conrad's Later Fiction." ELT, 12 (1969), 165-74.

JC's conventional late fiction seems a retreat from art.

*24146 Tindall, William York. "Apology for Marlow." In FROM JANE AUSTEN TO JOSEPH CONRAD. Ed. Robert Rathburn and Martin Steinmann, Jr. Minneapolis: Univ. of Minnesota Press, 1958. Pp. 274-85.

Marlow not entirely JC's voice. Reprinted in 25063.

24147 _____. FORCES IN MODERN BRITISH LITERATURE. Passim. See G2122.

Notes JC's relation to modern literary movements.

24148 Ure, Peter. "Character and Imagination in Conrad." CAMBRIDGE JOURNAL, 3 (1950), 727-40.

JC's characters as artist types.

24149 Vidan, Ivo. "Conrad's Legacy: The Concern with Authenticity in Modern Fiction." In JOSEPH CONRAD: THEORY AND WORLD FICTION. Ed. Wolodymyr T. Zyla and Wendell M. Aycock. Pp. 167-86. See 23076.

Adequacy in a vocation (e.g., JC and seamanship) has become a test of character in recent fiction.

24150 Wagenknecht, Edward. "Values and Joseph Conrad." In CAVALCADE OF THE ENGLISH NOVEL. Pp. 423-40. See G3151.

Criticism and literary history.

24151 Wain, John. "The Test of Manliness." LONDON MAGAZINE, 4 (Nov. 1957), 23-26.

The code of honor in JC's heroes. See 23038.

24152 Walt, James. "Conrad and James Huneker." CONRADIANA, 6 (1974), 75-88.

Sketches biography and assesses criticism of a perceptive and influential early American admirer of JC.

24153 Ward, Alfred C. "Joseph Conrad." In TWENTIETH-CENTURY ENGLISH LITERATURE. Pp. 47-55. See G2123.

Critical history.

24154 Warner, Oliver. "The Sea Writer." LONDON MAGAZINE, 4 (Nov. 1957), 21-23.

Reaffirms JC's excellence as a sea writer. See 23038.

*24155 Watt, Ian. "Joseph Conrad: Alienation and Commitment." In THE ENGLISH MIND: STUDIES IN THE ENGLISH MORALISTS PRESENTED TO BASIL WILLEY. Ed. Hugh S. Davies and George Watson. Cambridge: At the Univ. Press, 1964. Pp. 257-78.

The affirmative ideal of community in JC. An important essay.

24156 Weinstein, Arnold L. "Enclosed Vision: Conrad, Ford, and James." In VISION AND RESPONSE IN MODERN FICTION. Ithaca, N.Y.: Cornell Univ. Press, 1974. Pp. 50-90.

Epistemological problems in the depiction of and response to the seen, and the suspected "unseen," in JC (HD, LJ, UWE, V), Ford, and James.

24157 Weygant, Cornelius. "The Pageant of Joseph Conrad." In his A CENTURY OF THE ENGLISH NOVEL. Pp. 369-79. See G2214.

JC restores "romance" to recent English fiction.

24158 Whitehead, Lee M. "Conrad's 'Pessimism' Re-examined." CONRADIANA, 2, No. 3 (1970), 25-38.

JC's pessimism has been overemphasized.

24159 Whiting, George W. "Conrad's Revision of Six of His Short Stories." PMLA, 48 (1933), 552-57.

Study of revisions confirms JC's "remarkable word sense."

24160 Widmer, Kingsley. "Conrad's Pyrrhonistic Conservatism: Ideological Melodrama Around 'Simple Ideas.'" NOVEL, 7 (1974), 133-42.

JC withdraws from nihilism through his faith in a few "simple ideas."

24161 Williams, Raymond. "Joseph Conrad." In his THE ENGLISH NOVEL. Pp. 140-54. See G3156.

Isolation is man's response to a changing community.

24162 Woolf, Virginia. "Joseph Conrad; Mr. Conrad: A Conversation." 1924; 1923. In her COLLECTED ESSAYS. Ed. L. Woolf. New York: Hogarth, 1966. I, 302-8; 309-13.

Memorial tribute, and imaginary conversation concerning JC's greatness.

24163 Wright, Edgar. "Joseph Conrad and Bertrand Russell." CONRADIANA, 2, No. 1 (1970), 7-16.

Revealing study of Russell's attitude toward JC.

24164 Wright, Walter F. "'The Truth of My Own Sensations.'" MFS, 1, No. 1 (1955), 26-29.

JC's aesthetic. See 23040.

24165 Young, Vernon. "Joseph Conrad: Outline for a Reconsideration." HudR, 2 (1949), 5-19.

Survey's JC's critical reputation.

24166 _____. "Lingard's Folly: The Lost Subject." KR, 15 (1953), 522-39.

The Lingard novels as a possible trilogy (AF, OI, RESCUE). Reprinted in 23065.

*24167 Zabel, Morton Dauwen. "Conrad in His Age." In his CRAFT AND CHARACTER. Pp. 207-27. See G3162.

JC's modernity.

24168 _____. "Editor's Introduction." In THE PORTABLE CONRAD. Ed. Zabel. Pp. 1-47. See 13007.

Good general survey and criticism. Extracts reprinted in 25051.

24169 _____. "Introduction." In "THE SHADOW LINE" AND TWO OTHER TALES: "TYPHOON"/"THE SECRET SHARER." Garden City, N.Y.: Doubleday, 1959. Pp. 1-27.

The theme of "command."

24170 _____. "Introduction." In TALES OF HEROES AND HISTORY. Garden City, N.Y.: Doubleday, 1960. Pp. vii-xlv.

JC's concern with social themes after 1902.

24171 _____. "Introduction." In TALES OF THE EAST. Garden City, N.Y.: Doubleday, 1961. Pp. 9-39.

JC's knowledge of and sympathy for the East.

24172 _____. "Introduction." In TALES OF THE EAST AND WEST. Garden City, N.Y.: Hanover House, 1958. Pp. ix-xxx.

JC's imaginative world of "international dimensions."

24173 _____. "Introduction." In "YOUTH: A NARRATIVE" AND TWO OTHER STORIES: "HEART OF DARKNESS"/"THE END OF THE TETHER." Garden City, N.Y.: Doubleday, 1959. Pp. 1-25.

The tales related to the chief concerns of the novels.

*24174 _____. "Joseph Conrad: Chance and Recognition." SR, 53 (1945), 1-22.

Seminal essay on the nature of JC's "tests" of character in his fiction. Absorbed into "Conrad in His Age," above (24167). Reprinted in 23065.

24175 Zabierowski, Stefan. "Conrad's Polish Career, 1896-1968." Trans. I. P. Pulc. CONRADIANA, 6 (1974), 197-213.

Summarizes JC's uniform critical esteem and extraordinary popularity in Poland.

24176 Zeller, Leonard. "Conrad and Dostoevsky." In THE ENGLISH NOVEL IN THE NINETEENTH CENTURY: ESSAYS ON THE LITERARY MEDIATION OF HUMAN VALUES. Ed. George Goodin. Urbana: Univ. of Illinois Press, 1972. Pp. 214-23.

JC's ambivalence toward Dostoevsky, and general parallels between them (beyond UWE).

2.5 Studies of Individual Works

The following section is subdivided into two parts: i. Fiction (alphabetically by title) and ii. Miscellaneous Writings. Many of the full-length studies of JC consider individual works in detail. Alone among the biographers, Baines (22007 above) offers (mostly superficial) critiques. The books by the following authors generally devote most of their contents to work-by-work commentaries (2.3 above): Boyle (23005), Daleski (23014), Fleishman (23016), Graver (23022), Guerard (23023), Gurko (23024), Haugh (23025), Karl (23032), Moser (23044), Palmer (23051), Stallman (ed.) (23065), Wiley (23073), and Wright (23074). Critical articles (2.4 above) by Cox (24027), Leavis (24080), Whiting (24159), and Zabel (24167-24174) offer valuable comments on individual works.

i. FICTION

ALMAYER'S FOLLY (1895)

25001 Altick, Richard D. "The Search for Sambir." In THE SCHOLAR ADVENTURERS. New York: Macmillan, 1950. Pp. 289-97.

Story of the search for JC's sources.

25001a Eddleman, Floyd E., and David L. Higdon. "The Typescript of Conrad's ALMAYER'S FOLLY." TSLL, 18 (1976), 98-123.

Stresses importance and examines significance of JC's revisions.

25002 Eddleman, Floyd E., David L. Higdon, and Robert W. Hobson. "The First Editions of Joseph Conrad's ALMAYER'S FOLLY." PROOF, 4 (1975), 83-108.

Differences between the first English edition (revised in proof) and the first American edition (set from uncorrected proofs).

*25003 Hicks, John H. "Conrad's ALMAYER'S FOLLY: Structure, Theme, and Critics." NCF, 19 (1964), 17-31.

AF's structure determined by its theme of fidelity.

25003a O'Connor, Peter D. "The Function of Nina in ALMAYER'S FOLLY." CONRADIANA, 7 (1975), 225-32.

JC establishes Nina as the "moral and psychological norm" in the novel.

25004 Stein, William B. "ALMAYER'S FOLLY: The Terrors of Time." CONRADIANA, 1, No. 1 (1969), 27-34.

Structural and thematic significance of time.

*25005 Watt, Ian. "ALMAYER'S FOLLY: Memories and Models." MOSAIC, 8, No. 1 (1974), 165-82.

JC's transmutation of experience into art.

"Amy Foster" (1901)

25006 Andreach, Robert J. "The Two Narrators of 'Amy Foster.'" SSF, 2 (1965), 262-69.

JC experiments importantly with first person and with limited narration.

25007 Beidler, Peter G. "Conrad's 'Amy Foster' and Chaucer's Prioress." NCF, 30 (1975), 111-15.

Chaucer as a source for the characters of Amy and Yanko.

*25008 Herndon, Richard. "The Genesis of Conrad's 'Amy Foster.'" SP, 57 (1960), 549-66.

Source study.

THE ARROW OF GOLD (1919)

25009 Begnal, Michael H. "The Ideals of Despair: A View of Joseph Conrad's THE ARROW OF GOLD." CONRADIANA, 3, No. 3 (1971-72), 37-40.

JC offers no solution to his view of meaningless existence in the novel.

25010 Kirschner, Paul. "Conrad's Strong Man." MFS, 10 (1964), 31-36.

JC sublimated the guilt of his suicide attempt in the duels in "Gaspar Ruiz" and AG. See 23041.

25011 Mansfield, Katherine. NOVELS AND NOVELISTS. Ed. J.M. Murry. New York: Knopf, 1930. Pp. 60-64.

Admiring review of AG.

25012 Toliver, Harold E. "Conrad's ARROW OF GOLD and Pastoral Tradition." MFS, 8 (1962), 148-58.

JC uses tradition and the rhetoric of passion to voice an affirmation in the midst of cataclysm.

CHANCE (1913)

25013 Birdseye, Lewis. "CHANCE: Conrad's Modern Novel." STC, No. 15 (1975), pp. 77-94.

JC's "modernist" use of Marlow as a narrator-artist.

25014 Cagle, William R. "The Publication of Joseph Conrad's CHANCE." BC, 16 (1967), 305-22.

Ch's early publishing history.

25015 Fleischmann, Wolfgang B. "Conrad's CHANCE and Bergson's LAUGHTER." RENASCENCE, 14 (1962), 66-71.

Comic elements in the novel.

25016 Geddes, Gary. "The Structure of Sympathy: Conrad and the CHANCE That Wasn't." ELT, 12 (1969), 175-88.

Elaborate "machinery" of the novel closely related to the theme of "imaginative sympathy."

25017 Grabo, Carl. THE TECHNIQUE OF THE NOVEL. Pp. 66-71. See G3058.

Summary discussion of point of view in Ch.

*25018 Harkness, Bruce. "The Epigraph of Conrad's CHANCE." NCF, 9 (1954), 209-22.

Novel affirms order, not chance.

25019 Hough, Graham. "Chance and Joseph Conrad." In his IMAGE AND EXPERIENCE. Pp. 211-22. See G3071.

Theme of isolation in JC, including Ch as an example.

25020 Hudspeth, Robert N. "Conrad's Use of Time in CHANCE." NCF, 21 (1966), 283-89.

Thematic and structural uses of time.

*25021 James, Henry. "Joseph Conrad." 1914. In THE FUTURE OF THE NOVEL: ESSAYS ON THE ART OF FICTION. Ed. Leon Edel. New York: Random House, 1956. Pp. 275-86.

On the technical complexity of Ch. Reprinted in 23063.

25022 Johnson, J.W. "Marlow and CHANCE: A Reappraisal." TSLL, 10 (1968), 91-105.

Comedy and parody elements in the novel.

25023 Levin, Gerald H. "An Allusion to Tasso in Conrad's CHANCE." NCF, 13 (1958), 145-51.

Captain Anthony's "chivalrous idealism" derived from JERUSALEM DELIVERED.

*25024 Moser, Thomas C. "Conrad, Ford, and the Sources of CHANCE." CONRADIANA, 7 (1975), 207-24.

Ch the most "Fordian" of JC's novels and in many ways a prefiguration of THE GOOD SOLDIER. Finds several sources for Ch in the Victorian, Pre-Raphaelite, and Edwardian artistic circles. Reprinted in 23029a.

*25025 Watt, Ian. "Conrad, James, and CHANCE." In IMAGINED WORLDS. Ed. Maynard Mack and Ian Gregor. Pp. 301-22. See G3097.

Studies their personal and literary relationships.

25026 Zuckerman, Jerome. "Contrapuntal Structure in Conrad's CHANCE." MFS, 10 (1964), 49-54.

Counterpointed themes of command and self-discovery. See 23041.

"The Duel" (1908)

25027 Ferguson, J. Delaney. "The Plot of Conrad's 'The Duel.'" MLN, 50 (1935), 385-90.

Circumstances of the tale and many of its details derived from a newspaper story.

"The End of the Tether" (1902)

25027a Bruss, Paul S. "'The End of the Tether': Teleological Diminishing in Conrad's Early Metaphor of Navigation." SSF, 13 (1976), 311-20.

25028 Moynihan, William T. "Conrad's 'The End of the Tether': A New Reading." MFS, 4 (1958), 173-77.

Whalley an ironic-tragic hero in the Conradian "struggle." Reprinted in 23065.

25029 Schwarz, Daniel R. "'A Lonely Figure Walking Purposefully': The Significance of Captain Whalley in 'The End of the Tether.'" CONRADIANA, 7 (1975), 165-73.

Themes of aging and mutability in the story.

25030 Young, Gloria L. "Chance and the Absurd in Conrad's 'The End of the Tether' and 'Freya of the Seven Isles.'" CONRADIANA, 7 (1975), 253-61.

Both stories explore the ironies of a protagonist who believes in a providential order while living in "a world of flux and chance."

"Falk" (1903)

25031 Johnson, Bruce M. "Conrad's 'Falk': Manuscript and Meaning." MLQ, 26 (1965), 267-84.

Analysis of the story's failures.

25032 Kehler, Joel R. "The Centrality of the Narrator in Conrad's 'Falk.'" CONRADIANA, 6 (1974), 19-30.

Story's strength lies in the "complex psychology of the narrator."

25033 Ordonez, Elmer A. "Notes on the 'Falk' Manuscript." In TWENTY-SEVEN TO ONE. Ed. B. Broughton. Ogdensburg, N.Y.: Ryan Press, 1970. Pp. 45-51.

Examines JC's additions and deletions in the autograph manuscript.

25034 Schwarz, Daniel R. "The Significance of the Narrator in Conrad's 'Falk: A Reminiscence.'" TSL, 16 (1971), 103-10.

The middle-aged narrator's struggle to apprehend and communicate his experience.

"Freya of the Seven Isles" (1912)

25035 Young, Gloria L. "Chance and the Absurd in Conrad's 'The End of the Tether' and 'Freya of the Seven Isles.'" CONRADIANA, 7 (1975), 253-61.

See above, 25030.

"Gaspar Ruiz" (1906)

25036 Kirschner, Paul. "Conrad's Strong Man." MFS, 10 (1964), 31-36.

See above, 25010.

"Heart of Darkness: (1899)

Note: Also see A CONCORDANCE TO JOSEPH CONRAD'S "HEART OF DARKNESS," comp. Jacobson et al. (15002).

25037 Aubry, Georges Jean-. JOSEPH CONRAD IN THE CONGO. London: Bookman's Journal Office, 1926.

Detailed biographical study of JC's Congo experience, illustrating "to what extent his life and his work are merged together."

25038 Baum, Joan. "The 'Real' Heart of Darkness." CONRADIANA, 7 (1975), 183-87.

Reasserts the significance and continued validity of the realistic surface in HD.

25038a Benson, Donald R. "'Heart of Darkness': The Grounds of Civilization in an Alien Universe." TSLL, 7 (1966), 339-47.

HD about the "origins of civilization" in the post-Darwinian "alien universe" of scientific and philosophical naturalism. Reprinted in 25068.

25039 Bentley, Roy, ed. STUDENTS' SOURCES FOR SHAKESPEARE'S "HAMLET," SHAW'S "SAINT JOAN," CONRAD'S "HEART OF DARKNESS." Agincourt, Ont.: Book Society of Canada, 1966.

Collects six previously published essays. Includes 12001, 23023 (extract), 25040, 25047, 25059, and 25088.

25040 Brady, Marion B. "Conrad's Whited Sepulcher." CE, 24 (1962), 24-29.

HD's themes united in sepulcher image. Reprinted in 25039.

25041 Bross, Addison C. "The Unextinguishable Light of Belief: Conrad's Attitude toward Woman." CONRADIANA, 2, No. 3 (1970), 39-46.

Marlow's view of women related to HD's themes.

25042 Bruffee, Kenneth A. "The Lesser Nightmare: Marlow's Lie in 'Heart of Darkness.'" MLQ, 25 (1964), 322-29.

Marlow falls and is redeemed, ironically, through his lie. Reprinted in 25068.

25043 Burgess, C.F. "Conrad's Pesky Russian." NCF, 18 (1963), 189-93.

"Russian in motley" a thematically and technically important figure. Reprinted in 25068.

25044 Canario, John W. "The Harlequin in 'Heart of Darkness.'" SSF, 4 (1967), 225-33.

Marlow's developing insight into the young Russian parallels his other discoveries. Reprinted in 25068.

25045 Collins, Harold R. "Kurtz, the Cannibals, and the Second-Rate Helmsman." WHR, 8 (1954), 299-310.

Both the natives and Kurtz lose their integrity. Reprinted in 25051 and 25092.

25046 Conrad, Jessie. "Joseph Conrad and the Congo." LONDON MERCURY, 22 (1930), 261-63.

Letters and documents on JC's personal experience in the Congo. Reprinted in 25051.

*25047 Curle, Richard, ed. JOSEPH CONRAD'S DIARY OF HIS JOURNEY UP THE VALLEY OF THE CONGO IN 1890. London: Privately printed, 1926.

Documents the autobiographical elements of Marlow's journey. Reprinted in 25039.

25048 Dahl, James C. "Kurtz, Marlow, Conrad and the Human Heart of Darkness." SLitI, 1, No. 2 (1968), 33-40.

Man's therapeutic discovery of his shadow-self (cf. Jung).

25049 Daiches, David. "Experience and the Imagination: The Background of 'Heart of Darkness.'" In WHITE MAN IN THE TROPICS: TWO MORAL TALES. Ed. D. Daiches. New York: Harcourt, 1962. Pp. 3-16.

Man's need for "deep inward moral resources" to face the darkness.

25050 Dean, Leonard F. "Tragic Pattern in Conrad's 'Heart of Darkness.'" CE, 6 (1944), 100-104.

HD not a true tragedy because the moral discovery is not made by its chief protagonist, Marlow.

*25051 _____, ed. JOSEPH CONRAD'S "HEART OF DARKNESS": BACKGROUNDS AND CRITICISMS. Englewood Cliffs, N.J.: Prentice-Hall, 1960.

Text, reprinted documents related to JC's Congo experience, and several critical notes. Includes 24041, 25045, 25046, 25071, 25088; and extracts from the following works: 12001, 23023, and 24168.

25052 Edwards, Paul. "Clothes for the Pilgrimage: A Recurrent Image in 'Heart of Darkness.'" MOSAIC, 4, No. 3 (1971), 67-74.

25053 Emmett, Victor J. "Carlyle, Conrad, and the Politics of Charisma: Another Perspective on 'Heart of Darkness.'" CONRADIANA, 7 (1975), 145-53.

HD a criticism of Carlylean "hero worship."

25054 Evans, Robert O. "Conrad's Underworld." MFS, 2 (1956), 56-62.

Dantean reading. Reprinted in 23065, 25063, and 25068.

25055 _____. "Further Comment on 'Heart of Darkness.'" MFS, 3 (1957), 358-60.

Multiple levels of allusion in the story. Reprinted in 23065 and 25068.

*25056 Feder, Lillian. "Marlow's Descent into Hell." NCF, 9 (1955), 280-92.

Symbolism of the traditional voyage into Hades. Reprinted in 23065 and 25068.

25057 Gertzman, Jay A. "Commitment and Sacrifice in 'Heart of Darkness': Marlow's Response to Kurtz." SSF, 9 (1972), 187-96.

Kurtz's heroic dimension never admitted by Marlow, although his response to him is ambiguous.

25058 Gross, Harvey. "Aschenbach and Kurtz: The Cost of Civilization." CentR, 6 (1962), 131-43.

Mann and JC.

25059 Gross, Seymour L. "A Further Note on the Function of the Frame in 'Heart of Darkness.'" MFS, 3 (1957), 167-70.

Role of the story's first narrator. Reprinted in 23065, 25039, 25063, and 25068.

25060 Guetti, James L. "'Heart of Darkness': The Failure of Imagination." In THE LIMITS OF METAPHOR: A STUDY OF MELVILLE, CONRAD, AND FAULKNER. Ithaca, N.Y.: Cornell Univ. Press, 1967. Pp. 46-68.

Story and Marlow's search ultimately meaningless.

25061 Hardy, John Edward. "'Heart of Darkness': The Russian in Motley." In his MAN IN THE MODERN NOVEL. Pp. 17-33. See G3063.

On the significance of the Russian.

25062 Harkness, Bruce. "Textual Note." In his CONRAD'S "HEART OF DARKNESS" AND THE CRITICS. Pp. 161-68. See below.

Describes varying states of the story's text and the principles followed in preparing the collated edition.

*25063 ______, ed. CONRAD'S "HEART OF DARKNESS" AND THE CRITICS. San Francisco: Wadsworth, 1960.

Excellent corrected text, background information, and eleven critical papers. Includes 12001, 24146, 25054, 25059, 25062, 25085; and extracts from the following books and articles: 22005, 22021, 23006, 23015, 23023, 23027, 23044, 23074, and 24107.

25064 Harper, George M. "Conrad's Knitters and Homer's Cave of the Nymphs." ELN, 1 (1963), 53-57.

Classical allusion in HD.

25065 Hopwood, Alison L. "Carlyle and Conrad: PAST AND PRESENT and 'Heart of Darkness.'" RES, 23 (1972), 162-72.

HD an ironic critique of Carlyle.

25066 Kam, Rose Sallberg. "Silverberg & Conrad: Explorers of Inner Darkness." EXTRAPOLATION, 17 (1975), 18-28.

Influence of HD on recent science fiction.

25067 Ketterer, David A. "'Beyond the Threshold' in Conrad's 'Heart of Darkness.'" TSLL, 11 (1969), 1013-22.

Symbol and character study.

*25068 Kimbrough, Robert, ed. "HEART OF DARKNESS": AN AUTHORITATIVE TEXT, BACKGROUNDS AND SOURCES, ESSAYS IN CRITICISM. 1963. Rev. ed. New York: Norton, 1971.

Corrected and annotated text, a variety of background information, and a selection of critical essays. Includes 24108, 25054, 25055, 25056, 25059, 25085, 25088, 25098, 25099; and extracts from the following books and articles: 22016, 22021, 23006, 23023, 23024, 23025, 23073, and 24041. First edition (only) also includes 24010, 24063, 24099, 25078 (extract), and 25100. Second edition (only) also includes 23005 (extract), 25038a, 25042, 25043, 25044, and selections from the manuscript of HD.

25069 Levine, Paul. "Joseph Conrad's Blackness." SAQ, 63 (1964), 198-206.

"Symbolic blackness and white guilt" in JC's HD and NN, with reference to Melville.

25070 Lincoln, Kenneth R. "Comic Light in 'Heart of Darkness.'" MFS, 18 (1972), 183-97.

Comic elements in story.

25071 Lütkin, Otto. "Joseph Conrad in the Congo." LONDON MERCURY, 22 (1930), 40-43, 350-51.

HD based in part on JC's own experience, yet much is "pure fiction." Reprinted in 25051.

25072 McConnell, Daniel J. "'Heart of Darkness' in T.S. Eliot's THE HOLLOW MEN." TSLL, 4 (1962), 141-53.

JC's influence on Eliot's themes and images.

25073 Martin, David M. "The Diabolic Kurtz: The Dual Nature of His Satanism." CONRADIANA, 7 (1975), 175-77.

JC's mixed orthodox and romantic images for Kurtz (fiend and hero).

25074 Mellard, James M. "Myth and Archetype in 'Heart of Darkness.'" TSL, 13 (1968), 1-15.

Overall pattern for the story's symbolism supplied by the archetypal "rite of passage."

25075 Meyers, Jeffrey. "Savagery and Civilization in THE TEMPEST, ROBINSON CRUSOE, and 'Heart of Darkness.'" CONRADIANA, 2, No. 3 (1970), 171-79.

Variations on the theme of the savage vs. the "civilized" man.

25076 Nettels, Elsa. "'Heart of Darkness' and the Creative Process." CONRADIANA, 5, No. 2 (1973), 66-73.

Marlow's journey a "symbolic expression of the creative process."

25077 Ober, Warren U. "'Heart of Darkness': 'The Ancient Mariner' a Hundred Years Later." DR, 45 (1965), 333-37.

Coleridge's theme inverted from a post-Darwinian perspective.

25078 Owen, Guy. "A Note on 'Heart of Darkness.'" NCF, 12 (1957), 168-69.

Story's allusion to the Arthurian round table. Extract reprinted in 25068.

*25079 Reid, Stephen A. "The 'Unspeakable Rites' in 'Heart of Darkness.'" MFS, 9 (1963-64), 347-56.

Significance of Kurtz's crimes. Reprinted in 23046.

25080 Ridley, Florence H. "The Ultimate Meaning of 'Heart of Darkness.'" NCF, 18 (1963), 43-53.

Marlow and Kurtz in opposition.

25081 Ruthven, K.K. "The Savage God: Conrad and Lawrence." CritQ, 10 (1968), 39-54.

JC as _fin de siecle_ "decadent."

25082 Stark, Bruce R. "Kurtz's Intended: The Heart of 'Heart of Darkness.'" TSLL, 16 (1974), 535-55.

Structural and thematic centrality of HD's final scene.

25083 Stein, William B. "Buddhism and 'Heart of Darkness.'" WHR, 11 (1957), 281-85.

Marlow's consecutive Buddha postures.

25084 ______. "'Heart of Darkness': A Bodhisattva Scenario." CONRADIANA, 2, No. 2 (1970), 39-52.

Impact of Eastern myth and religion on Marlow's journey to enlightenment.

25085 ______. "The Lotus Posture and 'Heart of Darkness.'" MFS, 2 (1956), 235-37.

Buddah symbolism in the story. Reprinted in 23065, 25063, and 25068.

25086 Stephens, R.C. "'Heart of Darkness': Marlow's 'Spectral Moonshine.'" EIC, 19 (1969), 273-84.

Both Kurtz and Marlow deluded.

25087 Sugg, Richard P. "The Triadic Structure of 'Heart of Darkness.'" CONRADIANA, 7 (1975), 179-82.

Three stages of HD reflect the processes of the creative imagination (reason, passion, and imagination).

*25088 Thale, Jerome. "Marlow's Quest." UTQ, 24 (1955), 351-58.

Grail motif in HD. Reprinted in 23065, 25039, 25051, and 25068.

25089 ______. "The Narrator as Hero." TCL, 3 (1957), 69-73.

Reflective narrator-hero in HD and THE GREAT GATSBY.

*25090 Tindall, William York. THE LITERARY SYMBOL. Pp. 86-92. See G3146.

JC's manipulation of surface and symbol.

25091 Unger, Leonard. "Laforgue, Conrad, and T.S. Eliot." In THE MAN IN THE NAME: ESSAYS ON THE EXPERIENCE OF POETRY. Minneapolis: Univ. of Minnesota Press, 1956. Pp. 190-242.

Substantial impact of HD on Eliot's major poetry.

25092 Walker, Franklin, ed. "HEART OF DARKNESS" AND "THE SECRET SHARER": THE COMPLETE TEXTS AND A COMPREHENSIVE STUDY SUPPLEMENT. New York: Bantam, 1969.

Poor alternative to the other available casebooks. Texts of the two stories, sparse background materials, and five critical essays. Includes 25045; and extracts from the following books and articles: 23023, 23024, 24009, and 24080.

25093 Wasserman, Jerry. "Narrative Presence: The Illusion of Language in 'Heart of Darkness.'" SNNTS, 6 (1974), 327-38.

JC and Marlow concerned with truth of "transverbal experience."

25094 Watts, Cedric T. "'Heart of Darkness': The Covert Murder Plot and the Darwinian Theme." CONRADIANA, 7 (1975), 137-43.

Covert plot to "accelerate" the death of the "unfit" Kurtz in HD.

25095 Welsh, Alexander. "The Allegory of Truth in English Fiction." VS, 9 (1965), 7-28.

HD (pp. 22-24) within the proverbial tradition of the allegorical conflict between truth and falsehood.

25096 Whitehead, Lee M. "The Active Voice and the Passive Eye: 'Heart of Darkness' and Nietzsche's THE BIRTH OF TRAGEDY." CONRADIANA, 7 (1975), 121-35.

Marlow's function comparable to that of the Greek tragic chorus (viz. Nietzsche on tragedy).

25097 Whittemore, Reed. "The Fascination of the Abomination--Wells, Shaw, Ford, Conrad." In THE FASCINATION OF THE ABOMINATION. New York: Macmillan, 1963. Pp. 129-66.

Marlow's vicarious interest in Kurtz's decadence.

25098 Wilcox, Stewart C. "Conrad's 'Complicated Presentations' of Symbolic Imagery in 'Heart of Darkness.'" PQ, 39 (1960), 1-17.

JC's complex symbolic patterns. Reprinted in 25068.

25099 Wiley, Paul L. "Conrad's Skein of Ironies." In "HEART OF DARKNESS." Ed. Robert Kimbrough. Pp. 223-27. See 25068.

Kurtz, the "crowning irony" of the tale, the center of an intricate complex of ironies that leads Marlow to his moral discovery.

25100 Williams, George W. "The Turn of the Tide in 'Heart of Darkness.'" MFS, 9 (1963), 171-73.

Turn of the story and the change in the narrator's "vision" reinforced by the change of the tide. Reprinted in 25068.

25101 Yarrison, Betsy C. "The Symbolism of Literary Allusion in 'Heart of Darkness.'" CONRADIANA, 7 (1975), 155-64.

Reader's search for meaning in JC's allusions parallels Marlow's search for meaning in his experience.

25102 Zak, William F. "Conrad, F.R. Leavis, and Whitehead: 'Heart of Darkness' and Organic Holism." CONRADIANA, 4, No. 1 (1972), 5-24.

Disputes Leavis's criticism of the obscurities in HD. See 24080.

"The Idiots" (1896)

25103 Chaikin, Milton. "Zola and Conrad's 'The Idiots.'" SP, 52 (1955), 502-7.

Influence of at least two Zola novels on the tale.

"Il Conde" (1908)

25104 Hagopian, John V. "'Il Conde.'" In INSIGHT II. Eds. John Hagopian and Martin Dolch. Pp. 62-70. See G5007.

Summary, critique, and questions for study.

25105 Hughes, Douglas A. "Conrad's 'Il Conde': 'A Deucedly Queer Story.'" CONRADIANA, 7 (1975), 17-25.

Ambiguities of story attributable to an unreliable narrator.

25106 Schwarz, Daniel R. "The Self-Deceiving Narrator of Conrad's 'Il Conde.'" SSF, 6 (1969), 187-93.

Story's unreliable narrator the count's "secret sharer."

25107 Steinmann, Theo. "Il Conde's Uncensored Story." CONRADIANA, 7 (1975), 83-86.

Count's half-truths attributable to his sexual neuroses.

25108 Wills, John H. "Adam, Axel, and 'Il Conde.'" MFS, 1, No. 1 (1955), 22-25.

Allegorical motifs. See 23040. Reprinted in 23065.

"The Informer" (1906)

25109 Culbertson, Diana. "'The Informer' as Conrad's Little Joke." SSF, 11 (1974), 430-33.

Relationship with story's narrator reflects Conrad's own relation to his credulous magazine audience.

25110 Hagopian, John V. "'The Informer.'" In INSIGHT II. Eds. John Hagopian and Martin Dolch. Pp. 58-62 See G5007.

Summary, critique (of narrative technique), and questions for study.

25111 Walton, James H. "Mr. X's 'Little Joke': The Design of Conrad's 'The Informer.'" SSF, 4 (1967), 322-33.

Story epitomizes social themes of JC's greatest fiction.

"The Inn of the Two Witches" (1913)

25112 Solomon, Barbara H. "Conrad's Narrative Material in 'The Inn of the Two Witches.'" CONRADIANA, 7 (1975), 75-82.

JC's "qualities of structure and effect" stand out in comparison to his source, Wilkie Collins.

"Karain: A Memory" (1897)

25113 Johnson, Bruce M. "Conrad's 'Karain' and LORD JIM." MLQ, 24 (1963), 13-20.

See 25135 below.

"The Lagoon" (1897)

25114 Rice, Thomas J. "Conrad's 'The Lagoon': Malay and Pharisee." C&L, 25, No. 4 (1976), 25-33.

Archetypal reading.

LORD JIM (1900)

Note: Also see A CONCORDANCE TO CONRAD'S "LORD JIM," comp. Bender et al. (15001).

25115 Bass, Eben. "The Verbal Failure of LORD JIM." CE, 26 (1965), 438-44.

Jim's inarticulateness suggests his confusion and alienation.

25116 Beebe, Maurice. A CRITICAL STUDY GUIDE TO CONRAD'S "LORD JIM." Totowa, N.J.: Littlefield, Adams, 1968.

Fine introduction and plot summary.

25117 Brady, Marion B. "The Collector-Motif in LORD JIM." BuR, 16, No. 2 (1968), 66-85.

JC's use of motifs in the novel.

25118 Bruss, Paul S. "LORD JIM and the Metaphor of Awakening." STC, No. 14 (1974), 69-89.

JC's use of metaphor qualifies our view of Jim's success or failure in Patusan.

25119 ______. "Marlow's Interview with Stein: The Implication of the Metaphor." SNNTS, 5 (1973), 491-503.

Recognizing the complexity of Marlow's attitude toward Stein alters our view of their interview and of Stein's role in the novel.

25120 Burstein, Janet. "On Ways of Knowing in LORD JIM." NCF, 26 (1972), 456-68.

Novel both presents and embodies epistemological problems.

25121 Davis, Edward. "LORD JIM." In his READINGS IN MODERN FICTION. Pp. 190-204. See G3031.

LJ as a classic tragedy.

25122 Drew, Elizabeth A. "Joseph Conrad: LORD JIM." In her THE NOVEL. Pp. 156-72. See G3036.

Fine discussion of JC's primary themes and literary technique.

25123 Engleberg, Edward. "Lord Jim's 'Romantic Conscience.'" In THE UNKNOWN DISTANCE: FROM CONSCIOUSNESS TO CONSCIENCE. GOETHE TO CAMUS. Cambridge: Harvard Univ. Press, 1972. Pp. 172-85.

Jim's defective conscience.

25124 Epstein, Harry S. "LORD JIM as a Tragic Action." SNNTS, 5 (1973), 229-47.

25125 Freund, Philip. THE ART OF READING THE NOVEL. Pp. 89-100, 171-78. See G3044.

Autobiographical elements and fictional technique of the novel.

*25126 Gose, Elliott B., Jr. "LORD JIM." In IMAGINATION INDULGED: THE IRRATIONAL IN THE NINETEENTH-CENTURY NOVEL. Montreal: McGill-Queen's Univ. Press, 1972. Pp. 141-66.

LJ's two parts reflect the egoist's attempts to cope with, and his "satanic" withdrawal from, the world.

25127 Gossman, Ann M., and George W. Whiting. "The Essential Jim." NCF, 16 (1961), 75-80.

Argues the consistency of Jim's development.

25128 Hay, Eloise Knapp. "LORD JIM: From Sketch to Novel." CL, 12 (1960), 289-309.

LJ evolved through JC's therapeutic self-analysis. Reprinted in 25138 and 25145.

25129 Heilman, Robert B. "Introduction." In JC's LORD JIM. New York: Rinehart, 1957. Pp. v-xxv.

The isolated hero and his crime against community JC's two chief themes. Reprinted in 25138.

25130 Heimer, Jackson W. "Betrayal, Guilt, and Attempted Redemption in LORD JIM." BSUF, 9, No. 2 (1968), 31-43.

Jim's fated betrayal of his ideal is JC's critique of a standard of conduct based not on the human bond but on a code of "semi-military ethics."

25131 Hodges, Robert R. "The Four Fathers of Lord Jim." UR, 31 (1964), 103-10.

Jim's search for a father surrogate.

25132 Hoffmann, Richard. "Proportion and Incident in Joseph Conrad and Arnold Bennett." SR, 32 (1924), 79-92.

Bennett (e.g., CLAYHANGER) concerned with the immediate nature of life, while JC (e.g., LJ) more interested in the metaphysical implications of events.

25133 Hunt, Kellogg W. "LORD JIM and THE RETURN OF THE NATIVE: A Contrast." EJ, 49 (1960), 447-56.

LJ philosophically and technically more "effective."

25134 Janta, Alexander. "A Conrad Family Heirloom at Harvard." PolR, 2 (1957), 41-64.

Describes and reprints early sketch for LJ, "Tuan Jim." Reprinted in 23036.

25135 Johnson, Bruce M. "Conrad's 'Karain' and LORD JIM." MLQ, 24 (1963), 13-20.

Parallels between the works. Reprinted in 25145.

25136 Kohler, Dayton. "Introduction." In JC's LORD JIM. New York: Harper, 1965. Pp. xii-xix.

Jim's dilemma that of modern man faced with the "confusion and crisis of the twentieth century."

25137 Kramer, Dale. "Marlow, Myth, and Structure in LORD JIM." CRITICISM, 8 (1966), 263-79.

Conflicts between Marlow and Jim.

*25138 Kuehn, Robert E., ed. TWENTIETH-CENTURY INTERPRETATIONS OF "LORD JIM": A COLLECTION OF CRITICAL ESSAYS. Englewood Cliffs, N.J.: Prentice-Hall, 1969.

Collects twelve previously published commentaries and a selection of background materials. Includes 25128, 25163, 25165; and extracts from the following books and articles: 22007, 23023, 23027, 23032, 23073, 24032, 24080, 25129, and 25167.

25139 McCann, Charles J. "Lord Jim vs. The Darkness: The Saving Power of Human Involvement." CE, 27 (1965), 240-43.

Novel offers the hope that man may be able to surmount the impasse of his own divided nature.

25140 McCullough, Bruce. "The Impressionistic Novel: LORD JIM." In his REPRESENTATIVE ENGLISH NOVELISTS. Pp. 336-48. See G3096.

JC "sees his subject as something shifting and somewhat illusory."

*25141 Malbone, Raymond Gates. "'How to Be': Marlow's Quest in LORD JIM." TCL, 10 (1965), 172-80.

Marlow's development as the novel's center.

25142 Miller, J. Hillis. "The Interpretation of LORD JIM." In THE INTERPRETATION OF NARRATIVE. Ed. Morton W. Bloomfield. Pp. 211-28. See G4011.

LJ presents special critical problems in interpretation.

25143 Moore, Carlisle. "Conrad and the Novel as Ordeal." PQ, 42 (1963), 55-74.

Author and narrator similarly struggle to reconstruct reality in LJ.

25144 Moseley, Edwin M. "Christ as Tragic Hero: Conrad's LORD JIM." In his PSEUDONYMS OF CHRIST IN THE MODERN NOVEL. Pp. 15-35. See G6309.

LJ illustrates man's fall and redemption.

*25145 Moser, Thomas, ed. "LORD JIM": AN AUTHORITATIVE TEXT, BACKGROUNDS, SOURCES, ESSAYS IN CRITICISM. New York: Norton, 1968.

Best available text of LJ, together with an excellent casebook containing background materials (ed. N. Sherry), correspondence, and twelve previously published essays. Includes 25128, 25135, 25158, 25163, 25265; and extracts from the following books and articles: 23011, 23023, 23042, 23075, and 24079.

25146 Najder, Zdzislaw. "LORD JIM: A Romantic Tragedy of Honor." CONRADIANA, 1, No. 1 (1968), 1-7.

Slight.

25147 Nelson, Carl. "The Ironic Allusive Texture of LORD JIM: Coleridge, Crane, Milton, and Melville." CONRADIANA, 4, No. 2 (1972), 47-59.

JC's literary allusions provide ironic contrast.

25148 Nettels, Elsa. "Vision and Knowledge in THE AMBASSADORS and LORD JIM." ELT, 18 (1975), 181-93.

JC's and James's comparable use of centers of consciousness.

25149 Newell, Kenneth B. "The Destructive Element and Related 'Dream' Passages in the LORD JIM Manuscript." JML, 1 (1970), 31-44.

Seeks interpretation of Stein's speech from the manuscript.

25150 _____. "The Yellow-Dog Incident in Conrad's LORD JIM." SNNTS, 3 (1971), 26-33.

Yellow-dog incident a microcosm of Marlow's relationship with Jim.

25151 Paris, Bernard J. "The Dramatization of Interpretation: LORD JIM." In A PSYCHOLOGICAL APPROACH TO FICTION: STUDIES IN THACKERAY, STENDAHL, GEORGE ELIOT, DOSTOEVSKY, AND CONRAD. Bloomington: Indiana Univ. Press, 1974. Pp. 215-74.

Psychological interpretations of Jim and Marlow.

25152 Powys, T.F. "LORD JIM." In A CONRAD MEMORIAL LIBRARY. Ed. George T. Keating. Pp. 65-70. See 23034.

Praises JC's achievement and describes his fatalism.

25153 Reichard, Hugo M. "The Patusan Crises: A Revaluation of Jim and Marlow." ES, 49 (1968), 547-52.

The distortion of Marlow's view of Jim's Patusan career.

25154 Sadoff, Ira. "Sartre and Conrad: LORD JIM as Existentialist Hero." DR, 49 (1969), 518-25.

25155 Schwarz, Daniel R. "The Journey to Patusan: The Education of Jim and Marlow in Conrad's LORD JIM." SNNTS, 4 (1972), 442-58.

Jim and Marlow as complementary opposites.

25156 Seltzer, Alvin J. "The Rescued Fragment: Elusiveness of Truth in Conrad's LORD JIM." In his CHAOS IN THE NOVEL. Pp. 80-91. See G4083.

JC's exploitation of form to express a philosophically inconclusive but aesthetically whole (chaotic) vision.

25157 Sherry, Norman. "Introduction" and "Notes." In JC's LORD JIM. London: Dent, 1974. Pp. vii-xix, 309-27.

Derived from his CONRAD'S EASTERN WORLD (see 23061).

25158 ______. "Sources: Introduction; The Pilgrim-Ship Episode; The Bornean River and Its People." In LORD JIM. Ed. Thomas Moser. Pp. 308-56. See 25145.

Essays on the Eastern backgrounds and sources drawn from Sherry's CONRAD'S EASTERN WORLD (see 23061).

25159 Stegner, Wallace. "Variations on a Theme by Conrad." YR, 39 (1950), 512-23.

Echoes of LJ in Fitzgerald and Hemingway.

25160 Steinmann, Theo. "Lord Jim's Progression through Homology." ARIEL, 5, No. 1 (1974), 81-93.

JC's use of counterpointed character to illustrate Jim's progress toward an "ambiguous catharsis."

25161 Stevenson, Richard C. "Stein's Prescription of 'How to Be' and the Problem of Assessing Lord Jim's Career." CONRADIANA, 7 (1975), 233-43.

Stein's paradoxical statements "logically imperfect" by intention. His "primary function in LJ is to sum up the paradoxical nature" of human experience.

25162 Tanner, J.E. "The Chronology and the Enigmatic End of LORD JIM." NCF, 21 (1967), 369-80.

Marlow's shifting attitudes toward Jim.

*25163 Tanner, Tony. "Butterflies and Beetles--Conrad's Two Truths." ChiR, 16 (1963), 123-40.

Dualistic symbolism in LJ. Reprinted in 25138 and 25145.

25164 ______. CONRAD: "LORD JIM." London: Arnold, 1963.

Useful, but elementary introduction, summary, and critique.

*25165 Van Ghent, Dorothy. "On LORD JIM." In her THE ENGLISH NOVEL. Pp. 229-44, 440-54. See G3149.

Jim's failure to achieve greatness. Contains "study questions." Reprinted without study questions in 23065, 25138, and 25145.

25166 Whiting, George W. "Conrad's Revision of LORD JIM." EJ, 23 (1934), 824-32.

Textual examination.

*25167 Zabel, Morton Dauwen. "Introduction." In JC's LORD JIM. Boston: Houghton Mifflin, 1958. Pp. v-xxxvii.

Stresses importance of the "test" motif. Extract reprinted in 25138.

THE NIGGER OF THE "NARCISSUS" (1897)

25168 Bernard, Kenneth. "Conrad's Fools of Innocence in THE NIGGER OF THE 'NARCISSUS.'" CONRADIANA, 2, No. 1 (1970), 49-57.

NN a fable of the loss of innocence.

25169 Bonney, William W. "Semantic and Structural Indeterminancy in THE NIGGER OF THE 'NARCISSUS': An Experiment in Reading." ELH, 40 (1973), 564-83.

Narrator's "interpretational struggle" with his experience.

25170 Burgess, C.F. "Of Men and Ships and Mortality: Conrad's THE NIGGER OF THE 'NARCISSUS.'" ELT, 15 (1972), 221-31.

Highly derivative essay on the relationship between Wait and the ship.

25171 Daleski, H.M. "Hanging On and Letting Go: Conrad's THE NIGGER OF THE 'NARCISSUS.'" HUSL, 2, No. 2 (1974), 171-96.

Absorbed into Daleski's book-length study (see 23014).

*25172 Davis, Kenneth W., and Donald W. Rude. "The Transmission of the Text of THE NIGGER OF THE 'NARCISSUS.'" CONRADIANA, 5, No. 2 (1973), 20-45.

On the seven states of the novel's textual evolution.

25173 Echeruo, M.J.C. "James Wait and THE NIGGER OF THE 'NARCISSUS.'" ESA, 8 (1965), 166-80.

JC's uses of racial and metaphoric darkness.

25174 Foulke, Robert. "Postures of Belief in THE NIGGER OF THE 'NARCISSUS.'" MFS, 17 (1971), 249-62.

JC's ironic exploitation of romance motifs.

25175 Friedman, Norman. FORM AND MEANING IN FICTION. Pp. 335-39. See G4029.

Tests the symbolic interpretations of the two trials (the storm and Wait's death) in NN.

25176 Gallagher, Michael P. "THE NIGGER OF THE 'NARCISSUS': Two Worlds of Perspective." CONRADIANA, 3, No. 1 (1970-71), 51-60.

JC's narrative technique.

25177 Hammes, Kenneth W. "Melville, Dana, and Ames: Sources for Conrad's THE NIGGER OF THE 'NARCISSUS.'" PolR, 19, Nos. 3-4 (1974), 29-33.

Describes three additional sources for NN.

25178 Johnson, Bruce M. "Joseph Conrad and Crane's RED BADGE OF COURAGE." PMASAL, 48 (1963), 649-55.

The complex relationship between NN and THE RED BADGE OF COURAGE.

25179 Kaplan, Morton, and Robert Kloss. "Fantasy of Immortality: Conrad's THE NIGGER OF THE 'NARCISSUS.'" In THE UNSPOKEN MOTIVE. Pp. 47-61. See G2349.

Wait's and the crew's unspoken (unconscious) conspiracy to deny the inevitability of death.

25180 Kinney, Arthur F. "Jimmy Wait: Joseph Conrad's Kaleidoscope." CE, 26 (1965), 475-78.

Wait "the embodiment of several characters, individually, at their chief moments of recognition."

25181 Levine, Paul. "Joseph Conrad's Blackness." SAQ, 63 (1964), 198-206.

See 25069 above.

25182 Martin, W.R. "The Captain of the NARCISSUS." ESA, 6 (1963), 191-97.

The archetype of the fall of man in the novel centers upon the god-captain figure.

25183 Michael, Marion C. "James Wait as Pivot: Narrative Structure in THE NIGGER OF THE 'NARCISSUS.'" In JOSEPH CONRAD: THEORY AND WORLD FICTION. Eds. Wolodymyr T. Zyla and Wendell M. Aycock. Pp. 89-102. See 23076.

JC's dual narrative technique creates irony and reflects Wait's paradoxical knowledge and self-deception.

*25184 Miller, James E., Jr. "THE NIGGER OF THE 'NARCISSUS': A Reexamination." PMLA, 66 (1951), 911-18.

Important full study. Reprinted in 25187.

25185 Morgan, Gerould. "Narcissus Afloat." HAB, 15 (1964), 45-57.

Myth in the novel.

*25186 Mudrick, Marvin. "The Artist's Conscience and THE NIGGER OF THE 'NARCISSUS.'" NCF, 11 (1957), 288-97.

NN a flawed novel. Reprinted in 25187.

*25187 Palmer, John A., ed. TWENTIETH CENTURY INTERPRETATIONS OF "THE NIGGER OF THE 'NARCISSUS'": A COLLECTION OF CRITICAL ESSAYS. Englewood Cliffs, N.J.: Prentice-Hall, 1969.

Reprints ten of the best essays and chapters on NN. Includes 25184, 25186, 25189, 25193, 25195, 25196; and extracts from the following books: 22028, 23016, 23023, and 23073.

25188 Pulc, I.P. "Two Portrayals of a Storm: Some Notes on Conrad's Descriptive Style in THE NIGGER OF THE 'NARCISSUS' and 'Typhoon.'" STYLE, 4 (1970), 49-57.

Storm in NN far more forceful and immediate in its appeal to the senses than in the "almost total failure" of "Typhoon."

25189 Scrimgeour, Cecil. "Jimmy Wait and the Dance of Death: Conrad's NIGGER OF THE 'NARCISSUS.'" CritQ, 7 (1965), 339-52.

Danse macabre motif. Reprinted in 25187.

25190 Sherry, Norman. "Introduction" and "Notes." In JC's THE NIGGER OF THE "NARCISSUS." London: Dent, 1974. Pp. v-xvii, 279-96.

Backgrounds and sources.

25191 Smith, David R. "'One Word More' about THE NIGGER OF THE 'NARCISSUS.'" NCF, 23 (1968), 201-16.

Also on JC's "Preface."

25192 Torchiana, Donald. "THE NIGGER OF THE 'NARCISSUS': Myth, Mirror and Metropolis." WascanaR, 2, No. 2 (1967), 29-41.

Associates the story with Ovid's version of the Narcissus myth.

*25193 Watt, Ian. "Conrad Criticism and THE NIGGER OF THE 'NARCISSUS.'" NCF, 12 (1958), 257-83.

Reaction against overly symbolic readings of JC. Reprinted in 25187.

25194 Wiley, Paul L. "Two Tales of Passion." CONRADIANA, 6 (1974), 189-95.

JC's and Ford's adaptation of the oral-tale form (NN, THE GOOD SOLDIER).

*25195 Yates, Norris W. "Social Comment in THE NIGGER OF THE 'NARCISSUS.'" PMLA, 79 (1964), 183-85.

Topical background to the novel. Reprinted in 25187.

*25196 Young, Vernon. "Trial by Water: Joseph Conrad's THE NIGGER OF THE 'NARCISSUS.'" ACCENT, 12 (1952), 67-81.

Symbolic reading. Reprinted in 23065 and 25187.

25197 Zabel, Morton Dauwen. "Conrad: The East and the Sea, THE NIGGER OF THE 'NARCISSUS.'" In his CRAFT AND CHARACTER. Pp. 168-86. See G3162.

NN's descriptive passages intended to make the reader "see."

NOSTROMO (1904)

25198 Adicks, Richard. "Conrad and the Politics of Morality." HAB, 23, No. 2 (1972), 3-7.

The moral basis of JC's politics (e.g., N).

25199 Brewster, Dorothy, and Angus Burrell. "NOSTROMO: Thirty Years After." In their MODERN FICTION. Pp. 63-83. See G3014.

N a novel of "modern life."

25200 Bufkin, E.C. "Conrad, Grand Opera and NOSTROMO." NCF, 30 (1975), 206-14.

Influence of opera on N.

25201 Croft-Cooke, Rupert. "Introduction." In JC's NOSTROMO. New York: Heritage Press, 1961. Pp. ix-xvii.

N expands JC's theme of betrayal from the individual to a complex, diverse society.

25202 Davis, Edward. "NOSTROMO." In his READINGS IN MODERN FICTION. Pp. 205-21. See G3031.

Equivocal evaluation.

25203 Emmett, Victor J. "The Aesthetics of Anti-Imperialism: Ironic Distortions of the Vergilian Epic Mode in Conrad's NOSTROMO." SNNTS, 4 (1972), 459-72.

JC inverts the Vergilian epic mode in N.

25204 Freeman, Rosemary. "Conrad's NOSTROMO: A Source and Its Use." MFS, 7 (1961), 317-26.

JC's use of Dumas's MEMOIRES DE GARIBALDI.

*25205 Friedman, Alan W. "Joseph Conrad: 'The End, Such As It Is.'" In his THE TURN OF THE NOVEL. Pp. 75-105. See G3045.

Technique of the open ending in N.

25206 Gillon, Adam. "The Merchant of Esmeralda--Conrad's Archetypal Jew." PolR, 9, No. 4 (1964), 3-20.

Study of Hirsch.

25207 Haltresht, Michael. "The Gods of Conrad's NOSTROMO." RENASCENCE, 24 (1972), 207-12.

Religious elements in N.

25208 Halverson, John, and Ian Watt. "The Original Nostromo: Conrad's Source." RES, 10 (1959), 45-52.

Source of the stolen silver idea.

25209 Harris, Wendell V. "Of Time and the Novel." BuR, 16, No. 1 (1968), 114-29.

General consideration of the varieties of time in fiction (N, with DAVID COPPERFIELD and THE SOUND AND THE FURY).

25210 Heimer, Jackson W. "Betrayal, Confession, Attempted Redemption, and Punishment in NOSTROMO." TSLL, 8 (1967), 561-79.

Patterns of betrayal in Gould, Decoud, Monygham, and Nostromo.

*25211 Hoffman, Frederick J. THE MORTAL NO. Pp. 57-64. See G3070.

N's concern with social violence and political force.

*25212 Kettle, Arnold. "Joseph Conrad: NOSTROMO (1904)." In his AN INTRODUCTION TO THE ENGLISH NOVEL. II, 67-81. See G3088.

Marxist interpretation.

25213 Kimpel, Ben, and T.C. Duncan Eaves. "The Geography and History in NOSTROMO." MP, 56 (1958), 45-54.

Accuracy and consistency of JC's geography and history.

25214 Leavis, Frank R. "Foreword." In JC's NOSTROMO. New York: New American Library, 1960. Pp. vi-xi.

Praises the sustained ironic tone, the "close patterned structure" and the range of N (derived largely from his THE GREAT TRADITION, see 24080).

25215 Leech, Clifford. "The Shaping of Time: NOSTROMO and UNDER THE VOLCANO." In IMAGINED WORLDS. Eds. Maynard Mack and Ian Gregor. Pp. 323-41. See G3097.

Time and structure compared in the two novels.

25216 Lynskey, Winifred. "The Role of the Silver in NOSTROMO." MFS, 1, No. 1 (1955), 16-21.

Silver as a corrosive force. See 23040.

*25217 McLauchlan, Juliet. CONRAD: "NOSTROMO." London: Arnold, 1969.

Excellent critical introduction and analysis.

25218 Maclennan, D.A.C. "Conrad's Vision." ESA, 7 (1964), 195-201.

JC's vision, as illustrated in N, ultimately nihilistic.

25219 McMillan, Dougald. "NOSTROMO: The Theology of Revolution." In THE CLASSIC BRITISH NOVEL. Ed. Howard M. Harper and Charles Edge. Pp. 166-82. See G3064.

Christian reading.

25220 Marten, Harry. "Conrad's Skeptic Reconsidered: A Study of Martin Decoud." NCF, 27 (1972), 81-94.

Decoud's ambiguous nature.

25221 Mueller, William R. "Joseph Conrad: NOSTROMO and the Orders of Creation: An Ontological Argument." In his CELEBRATION OF LIFE. Pp. 77-97. See G6310.

N concerns the conflict between man and nature.

25221a Oates, Joyce Carol. "'The Immense Indifference of Things': The Tragedy of Conrad's NOSTROMO." NOVEL, 9 (1975), 5-22.

25222 Overton, Grant. "Joseph Conrad: NOSTROMO." In his THE PHILOSOPHY OF FICTION. Pp. 161-84. See G4069.

N an exemplary modern novel of character (much summary).

25223 Said, Edward W. "Conrad/NOSTROMO: Record and Reality." In APPROACHES TO THE TWENTIETH CENTURY NOVEL. Ed. John Unterecker. Pp. 108-52. See G3148.

Only the "true artist and the man of immensely honest intellect" can distinguish between reality and the illusory sense of history.

25224 Saunders, William S. "The Unity of NOSTROMO." CONRADIANA, 5, No. 1 (1973), 27-36.

JC's consistent detachment unifies N.

25225 Sherry, Norman. "Introduction" and "Notes." In JC's NOSTROMO. London: Dent, 1972. Pp. vi-xi, 567-81.

N's technical complexity. Notes contain information on sources.

25226 Smith, David R. "NOSTROMO and the Three Sisters." SEL, 2 (1962), 497-508.

Symbols and archetypes in the novel.

*25227 Tick, Stanley. "The Gods of NOSTROMO." MFS, 10 (1964), 15-26.

Religion as a theme in N. See 23041.

25228 Tillyard, E.M.W. "Conrad: NOSTROMO" and "Conrad's Costaguana." In his THE EPIC STRAIN IN THE ENGLISH NOVEL. Pp. 126-67, 199-203. See G3145.

On N's epic dimensions and the book's setting.

*25229 Van Ghent, Dorothy. "Introduction." In JC's NOSTROMO. New York: Holt, Rinehart and Winston, 1961. Pp. vii-xxv.

Archetypal critique. Reprinted in 23033.

25230 Vidan, Ivo. "One Source of Conrad's NOSTROMO." RES, 7 (1956), 287-93.

Political situation in Sulaco influenced by G.F. Masterman's SEVEN EVENTFUL YEARS IN PARAGUAY.

25231 Vidan, Ivo, and Juliet McLauchlan. "The Politics of NOSTROMO." EIC, 17 (1967), 392-406.

Two brief articles asserting the sophistication of JC's political themes. Responses to Wilding's first article (25235).

*25232 Warren, Robert Penn. "NOSTROMO." SR, 59 (1951), 363-91.

Important general assessment. Stresses JC's achievement in N and his ideal of the human community. Reprinted in 23065.

25233 Whitehead, Lee M. "NOSTROMO: The Tragic 'Idea.'" NCF, 23 (1969), 463-75.

N embodies JC's "sense of the tragedy of man's social nature."

25234 Whiting, George W. "Conrad's Revision of 'The Lighthouse' in NOSTROMO." PMLA 52 (1937), 1183-90.

JC revised to clarify and vitalize N's final section.

25235 Wilding, Michael. "The Politics of NOSTROMO." EIC, 16 (1966), 441-56; and 18 (1968), 234-36.

N a moral fable, not a political novel per se. See 25231.

AN OUTCAST OF THE ISLANDS (1896)

25236 Clifford, Hugh. "AN OUTCAST OF THE ISLANDS." In A CONRAD MEMORIAL LIBRARY. Ed. George T. Keating. Pp. 14-21. See 23034.

A general, unenthusiastic commentary on the book.

25237 Gekoski, R.A. "AN OUTCAST OF THE ISLANDS: A New Reading." CONRADIANA, 2, No. 3 (1970), 47-58.

Lingard, not Willems, the novel's central character.

25238 Wells, H.G. "AN OUTCAST OF THE ISLANDS." SatR (London), 81 (1896), 509-10.

JC's friendship with Wells followed this early, favorable review. Reprinted in 23063.

"Prince Roman" (1911)

*25239 Krzyzanowski, Ludwik. "Joseph Conrad's 'Prince Roman': Fact and Fiction." PolR, 1, No. 4 (1956), 22-62.

Exhaustive background study. Reprinted in 23036.

THE RESCUE (1920)

25240 Geddes, Gary. "THE RESCUE: Conrad and the Rhetoric of Diplomacy." MOSAIC, 7, No. 3 (1974), 107-25.

Theme of "diplomacy" and its impact on JC's style.

25241 Howarth, Herbert. "Conrad and Imperialism: The Difference of THE RESCUE." OhR, 13, No. 1 (1971), 62-72.

JC's political and social themes.

25242 Liljegren, Sten Bodvar. JOSEPH CONRAD AS A PROBER OF FEMININE HEARTS. NOTES ON THE NOVEL "THE RESCUE." Upsala, Sweden: Lundesquistska, 1968.

Monograph survey of JC's characterization.

25243 Mansfield, Katherine. NOVELS AND NOVELISTS. Ed. J.M. Murry. New York: Knopf, 1930. Pp. 222-26.

JC's sensitivity in THE RESCUE.

*25244 Moser, Thomas. "'The Rescuer' Manuscript: A Key to Conrad's Development and Decline." HLB, 10 (1956), 325-55.

Investigates unique development of JC's novel.

25245 Munro, Neil. "THE RESCUE." In A CONRAD MEMORIAL LIBRARY. Ed. George T. Keating. Pp. 288-93. See 23034.

General commentary and appreciation.

25246 Wright, Walter F. "Conrad's THE RESCUE from Serial to Book." RS, 13 (1945), 203-24.

Textual study.

THE ROVER (1923)

25247 Aubry, Georges Jean-. "THE ROVER." In A CONRAD MEMORIAL LIBRARY. Ed. George T. Keating. Pp. 326-36. See 23034.

Important biographical reverberations in the novel.

25248 Higdon, David L. "Conrad's THE ROVER: The Grammar of a Myth." SNNTS, 1 (1969), 17-26.

Christian and classical archetypes in JC's fiction.

*25249 Howarth, Herbert. "The Meaning of Conrad's THE ROVER." SoR, 6 (1970), 682-97.

Rov as valedictory novel.

25250 Knight, Grant C. "The Greatest Hero." In SUPERLATIVES. New York: Knopf, 1925. Pp. 167-87.

In Peyrol, JC demonstrates "the highest type of human valor, the debonair defiance of death, the refusal to be conquered, the victory of spirit over matter."

25251 Laine, Michael. "Conrad's THE ROVER: The Rejection of Despair." QQ, 80 (1973), 246-55.

Rov a serious attempt "to provide an answer to life, an affirmative view which denies despair."

25252 Lehmann, John. "On Rereading THE ROVER." In THE OPEN NIGHT. New York: Harcourt, 1952. Pp. 54-62.

Praises Rov's atmosphere and the character of Peyrol.

25253 Lippincott, H.F. "Sense of Place in Joseph Conrad's THE ROVER." CONRADIANA, 6 (1974), 106-12.

Novel's strengths are its realistic and symbolic landscapes.

25254 Martin, W.R. "Allegory in Conrad's THE ROVER." ESA, 10 (1967), 186-94.

Enumerates a grab-bag of archetypal symbols, but finds no coherent allegory in the novel.

25255 Wright, Elizabeth Cox. "The Defining Function of Vocabulary in Conrad's THE ROVER." SAQ, 59 (1960), 265-77.

The "Frenchness" of JC's style.

THE SECRET AGENT (1907)

25256 Cheney, Lynne. "Joseph Conrad's THE SECRET AGENT and Graham Greene's IT'S A BATTLEFIELD: A Study in Structural Meaning." MFS, 16 (1970), 117-31.

SA's broken structure involves reader in the detective process (cf. Greene).

25257 Davis, Harold E. "Conrad's Revisions of THE SECRET AGENT: A Study in Literary Impressionism." MLQ, 19 (1958), 244-54.

Technical significance of JC's revision.

*25258 Fradin, Joseph I. "Anarchist, Detective, and Sanit: The Possibilities of Action in THE SECRET AGENT." PMLA, 83 (1968), 1414-22.

Forms of moral action in the novel.

25259 ______. "Conrad's Everyman: THE SECRET AGENT." TSLL, 11 (1969), 1023-38.

Existentialist reading.

25260 Fradin, Joseph I., and Jean W. Creighton. "The Language of THE SECRET AGENT: The Art of Non-Life." CONRADIANA, 1, No. 2 (1968), 23-35.

JC's language appropriately "destructive."

25261 Gilmore, Thomas B. "Retributive Irony in Conrad's THE SECRET AGENT." CONRADIANA, 1, No. 3 (1969), 41-50.

Good study of the quality of JC's irony.

*25262 Gose, Elliott B., Jr. "'Cruel Devourer of the World's Light': THE SECRET AGENT." NCF, 15 (1960), 39-51.

Light and darkness symbolism.

25263 Hagan, John. "The Design of Conrad's THE SECRET AGENT." ELH, 22 (1955), 148-64.

JC's structure reflects the moral and social chaos of the community.

25264 Haltresht, Michael. "Disease Imagery in Conrad's THE SECRET AGENT." L&P, 21 (1971), 101-5.

Disease a metaphor for social, psychic, and emotional illness in the novel.

25265 ______. "The Dread of Space in Conrad's THE SECRET AGENT." L&P, 22 (1972), 89-97.

Fears of confinement and of open spaces evident in the spatial imagery of SA.

25266 Heimer, Jackson. "Betrayal in THE SECRET AGENT." CONRADIANA, 7 (1975), 245-51.

Part of a continuing series of essays on patterns of betrayal in the novels.

25267 Hertz, Robert. "The Scene of Mr. Verloc's Murder in THE SECRET AGENT: A Study of Conrad's Narrative and Dramatic Method." Person, 43 (1962), 214-25.

JC's methods for building tension.

*25268 Hoffman, Frederick J. THE MORTAL NO. Pp. 50-57. See G3070.

SA the "first true novel of violence."

25269 Holland, Norman N. "Style as Character: THE SECRET AGENT." MFS, 12 (1966), 221-31.

25270 Jacobs, Robert G. "Comrade Ossipon's Favorite Saint: Lombroso and Conrad." NCF, 23 (1968), 74-84.

Lombroso's theory of physiognomy influenced JC.

25271 Johnston, John H. "THE SECRET AGENT and UNDER WESTERN EYES: Conrad's Two Political Novels." WVUPP, 17 (1970), 57-71.

SA and UWE inferior as political novels because of their unsophisticated social vision.

25272 Jones, Charles. "Varieties of Speech Presentation in Conrad's THE SECRET AGENT." LINGUA, 20 (1968), 162-76.

Deplorably jargon-laden attempt to describe JC's use of dialect.

25273 Knoepflmacher, U.C. "THE SECRET AGENT: The Irony of the Absurd." In LAUGHTER AND DESPAIR: READINGS IN TEN NOVELS OF THE VICTORIAN ERA. Berkeley and Los Angeles: Univ. of California Press, 1971. Pp. 240-73.

JC distances the reader from despair.

25274 Kubal, David L. "THE SECRET AGENT and the Mechanical Chaos." BuR, 15, No. 3 (1967), 65-77.

SA's unresolved tension between chaos (the anarchists) and the machine (the police) an emblem of modern society.

25275 Langbaum, Robert. "Thoughts for Our Time: Three Novels on Anarchism." ASch, 42 (1973), 227-50.

James (PRINCESS CASSAMASSIMA), JC (SA), and Dostoevsky

(POSSESSED) negate revolutionary political values for traditional moral values.

25276 Lee, Robin. "THE SECRET AGENT: Structure, Theme, Mode." ESA, 11 (1968), 185-93.

SA terrifies, because it shows man's fate beyond his control.

25277 Luecke, Jane M. "Conrad's Secret and Its Agent." MFS, 10 (1964), 37-48.

Finds JC's world view affirmative. See 23041.

*25278 Mann, Thomas. "Conrad's THE SECRET AGENT." 1926. Trans. H.T. Lowe-Porter. In THE ART OF JOSEPH CONRAD. Ed. Robert W. Stallman. Pp. 227-34. See 23065.

Originally a German introduction to the novel. Sensitive to the political backgrounds and implications of SA. Reprinted in 25301.

25279 Marsh, D.R.C. "Moral Judgments in THE SECRET AGENT." ESA, 3 (1960), 57-70.

Ego and illusion corrupt characters' judgment in SA.

25280 Matlaw, Ralph E. "Dostoevskij and Conrad's Political Novels." In AMERICAN CONTRIBUTIONS TO THE FIFTH INTERNATIONAL CONGRESS OF SLAVISTS. SOFIA, SEPTEMBER 1963. The Hague: Mouton, 1963. II, 213-30.

JC's indebtedness to and reaction against Dostoevsky (SA and UWE).

25281 Michael, Marion C. "Conrad's 'Definite Intention' in THE SECRET AGENT." CONRADIANA, 1, No. 1 (1968), 9-17.

Evolution of the novel's text.

25282 Morley, Patricia A. "Conrad's Vision of the Absurd." CONRADIANA, 2, No. 1 (1970), 59-68.

25283 Mukerji, N. "THE SECRET AGENT: Anarchy and Anarchists." CalR, 172 (1964), 138-48.

SA is JC's attack on anarchists and revolutionaries.

25284 Nash, Christopher. "More Light on THE SECRET AGENT." RES, 20 (1969), 322-27.

Sir Robert Anderson's SIDELIGHTS ON THE HOME RULE MOVEMENT a source for the novel.

25285 O'Grady, Walter. "On Plot in Modern Fiction: Hardy, James, and Conrad." MFS, 11 (1965), 107-15.

Comparative study of TESS, AMBASSADORS, and SA.

25286 Pritchett, Victor S. "An Emigre." In BOOKS IN GENERAL. New York: Harcourt, 1953. Pp. 216-22.

JC's sense of isolation. Reprinted in 25301.

25287 Shadoian, Jack. "Irony Triumphant: Verloc's Death." CONRADIANA, 3, No. 2 (1971-72), 82-86.

JC's comic grotesque tone in his treatment of Verloc's murder.

25288 Sherry, Norman. "Introduction" and "Notes." In JC's THE SECRET AGENT. London: Dent, 1974. Pp. vii-xx, 312-29.

Derived from Sherry's CONRAD'S WESTERN WORLD (see 23062).

25289 Smitten, Jeffrey R. "Faubert and the Structure of THE SECRET AGENT: A Study in Spatial Form." In JOSEPH CONRAD: THEORY AND WORLD FICTION. Ed. Wolodymyr T. Zyla and Wendell M. Aycock. Pp. 151-66. See 23076.

JC's fragmentation and juxtaposition of his materials to achieve "spatial form."

25290 Spector, Robert D. "Irony as Theme: Conrad's THE SECRET AGENT." NCF, 13 (1958), 69-71.

Ultimate unity of SA in its ironic mode. Reprinted in 25301.

*25291 Stallman, Robert W., comp. "Checklist of Some Studies of Conrad's THE SECRET AGENT Since 1960." CONRADIANA, 6 (1974), 31-45.

Lists, annotates, and evaluates seventy-three publications on SA.

*25292 ______. "Time and THE SECRET AGENT." TSLL, 1 (1959), 101-22.

Space and time symbolism. Reprinted in 23033 and 23065.

25293 Sullivan, Walter. "The Dark Beyond the Sunrise: Conrad and the Politics of Despair." SoR, 8 (1972), 507-19.

Ironic tone and moral center of SA lacking in UWE.

25294 _____. "Irony and Disorder: THE SECRET AGENT." SR, 81 (1973), 124-31.

Ironic method makes JC's skepticism "abundantly clear."

25295 Tillyard, E.M.W. "THE SECRET AGENT Reconsidered." EIC, 11 (1961), 309-18.

SA flawed in point of view. Reprinted in 23046.

25296 Walpole, Hugh. "THE SECRET AGENT." In A CONRAD MEMORIAL LIBRARY. Ed. George T. Keating. Pp. 159-64. See 23034.

JC a master storyteller and an excellent creator of character. Reprinted in 25301.

25297 Walton, James H. "Conrad and Naturalism: THE SECRET AGENT." TSLL, 9 (1967), 289-301.

JC's use of naturalistic devices (especially with Winnie Verloc).

25298 _____. "Conrad and THE SECRET AGENT: The Genealogy of Mr. Vladimir." PolR, 12, No. 3 (1967), 28-42.

Sources for Mr. Vladimir.

25299 _____. "Conrad, Dickens, and the Detective Novel." NCF, 23 (1969), 446-62.

JC's indebtedness to Dickens (cf. BLEAK HOUSE).

25300 Watt, Ian. "The Political and Social Background of THE SECRET AGENT." In his THE SECRET AGENT. Pp. 229-51. See below.

Stresses JC's imaginative exploration of his raw materials.

25301 _____, ed. CONRAD: "THE SECRET AGENT": A CASEBOOK. London: Macmillan, 1973.

An excellent compilation of background materials, correspondence, reviews, textual commentary, and eleven reprinted critical essays. Indexed. Includes 25278, 25286, 25290, 25296, 25300; and extracts from the following books and articles: 23016, 23023, 23062, 24065, 24080, and 24104.

25302 Wiesenfarth, Joseph. "Stevie and the Structure of THE SECRET AGENT." MFS, 13 (1967), 513-17.

Stevie the novel's compositional center.

25303 Zuckerman, Jerome. "The Motif of Cannibalism in THE SECRET AGENT." TSLL, 10 (1968), 295-99.

JC's metaphors of "human selfishness."

"The Secret Sharer" (1910)

25304 Benson, Carl. "Conrad's Two Stories of Initiation." PMLA, 69 (1954), 46-56.

SL and SS. Reprinted in 25317.

25305 Bidwell, Paul. "Leggatt and the Promised Land: A New Reading of 'The Secret Sharer.'" CONRADIANA, 3, No. 2 (1971-72), 26-34.

Parallels between Leggatt and Moses.

25306 Brown, P.L. "'The Secret Sharer' and the Existential Hero." CONRADIANA, 3, No. 3 (1971-72), 22-30.

25307 Burjorjee, Dinshaw M. "Comic Elements in Conrad's 'The Secret Sharer.'" CONRADIANA, 7 (1975), 51-61.

Comic "relief" traced especially in JC's caricatures and dialogue.

*25308 Curley, Daniel. "Legate of the Ideal." In CONRAD'S "SECRET SHARER" AND THE CRITICS. Ed. Bruce Harkness. Pp. 75-82. See 25317.

An important corrective reading. Leggatt a positive ideal for the young Captain. Reprinted in 23046.

25309 _____. "The Writer and His Use of Material: The Case of 'The Secret Sharer.'" MFS, 13 (1967), 179-84.

JC's creative methods.

25310 Day, Robert A. "The Rebirth of Leggatt." L&P, 13 (1963), 74-81.

Captain's initiation complemented by Leggatt's rebirth.

25311 Dussinger, Gloria R. "'The Secret Sharer': Conrad's Psychological Study." TSLL, 10 (1969), 599-608.

SS simply a psychological study of the young captain, not a social or moral tract.

25312 Evans, Frank B. "The Nautical Metaphor in 'The Secret Sharer.'" CONRADIANA, 7 (1975), 3-16.

A "definitive explanation" of the ship maneuver and a story interpretation.

25313 Foye, Paul F., Bruce Harkness, and Nathan L. Marvin. "The Sailing Maneuver in 'The Secret Sharer.'" JML, 2 (1971), 119-23.

Explicates the maneuver.

25314 Gettmann, Royal A., and Bruce Harkness. "Morality and Psychology in 'The Secret Sharer.'" In CONRAD'S "SECRET SHARER" AND THE CRITICS. Ed. Bruce Harkness. Pp. 125-32. See 25317.

Significance of SS psychological, not moral.

*25315 Harkness, Bruce. "The Secret of 'The Secret Sharer' Bared." CE, 27 (1965), 55-61.

Fine parody of interpretive excesses.

25316 _____. "Textual Note." In CONRAD'S "SECRET SHARER" AND THE CRITICS. Ed. Bruce Harkness. Pp. 151-61. See below.

Describes the manuscript, serial, and printed versions of the story and explains the basis for the corrected text.

*25317 _____, ed. CONRAD'S "SECRET SHARER" AND THE CRITICS. Belmont, Calif.: Wadsworth, 1962.

Corrected text, background materials, and nine essays (two original). Includes 24107, 25304, 25308, 25314, 25316, 25319, 25324; and extracts from the following books: 22007, 23023, and 23074.

25318 Hoffmann, Charles G. "Point of View in 'The Secret Sharer.'" CE, 23 (1962), 651-54.

JC's alternating points of view.

25319 Leiter, Louis H. "Echo Structures: Conrad's 'The Secret Sharer.'" TCL, 5 (1960), 159-75.

Symbols of doubleness reinforce the doppelganger theme. Reprinted in 25317.

25320 O'Brien, Justin. "Camus and Conrad: An Hypothesis." In CONTEMPORARY FRENCH LITERATURE: ESSAYS. Ed. L.S. Roudiez. New Brunswick, N.J.: Rutgers Univ. Press, 1971. Pp. 210-14.

Influence of SS on Camus.

25321 Ryan, Alvan S. "'The Secret Sharer.'" In INSIGHT II. Ed. John V. Hagopian and Martin Dolch. Pp. 70-76. See G5007.

Story summary, critique (stressing "command" theme), and study questions.

25322 Schenck, Mary-Low. "Seamanship in Conrad's 'The Secret Sharer.'" CRITICISM, 15 (1973), 1-15.

Leggatt initiates Captain into full command of his vessel.

25323 Simmons, J.L. "The Dual Morality in Conrad's 'The Secret Sharer.'" SSF, 2 (1965), 209-20.

Moral ambiguity as central theme of SS.

*25324 Stallman, Robert W. "Conrad and 'The Secret Sharer.'" In THE ART OF JOSEPH CONRAD. Ed. Robert W. Stallman. Pp. 275-95. See 23065.

Captain gains self-knowledge and self-confidence. Reprinted in 25317.

25325 Walker, Franklin, ed. "HEART OF DARKNESS" AND "THE SECRET SHARER": THE COMPLETE TEXTS AND A COMPREHENSIVE STUDY SUPPLEMENT. See 25092.

25326 Williams, Porter. "The Brand of Cain in 'The Secret Sharer.'" MFS, 10 (1964), 27-30.

Cain story "a precise symbol of Leggatt's predicament." See 23041.

25327 _____. "The Matter of Conscience in Conrad's 'The Secret Sharer.'" PMLA, 79 (1964), 626-30.

Captain must experience evil (Leggatt) to know good (the "code").

25328 Wills, John H. "Conrad's 'The Secret Sharer.'" UKCR, 28 (1961), 115-26.

Summarizes the captain's maturation.

*25329 Wright, Walter F. "Ambiguity of Emphasis in Joseph Conrad." In ON STAGE AND OFF: EIGHT ESSAYS IN ENGLISH LITERATURE. Ed. J.W. Ehrstine, J.R. Elwood, and R.C. McLean. Pullman: Washington State Univ. Press, 1968. Pp. 90-96.

Ambiguities in JC attributable to his desire to present the multiple facets of reality with equal fidelity and emphasis (e.g., Leggatt's role in SS).

25330 Wyatt, Robert D. "Joseph Conrad's 'The Secret Sharer': Point of View and Mistaken Identities." CONRADIANA, 5, No. 1 (1973), 12-26.

Captain Archbold the story's moral center, Leggatt its villain, and the captain an unreliable narrator.

A SET OF SIX (1908)

25331 Bross, Addison C. "A SET OF SIX: Variations on a Theme." CONRADIANA, 7 (1975), 27-44.

Six stories explore variations upon JC's "single great theme," the act of belief.

25332 Cuthbertson, Gilbert M. "Freedom, Absurdity, and Destruction: The Political Theory of Conrad's A SET OF SIX." CONRADIANA, 6 (1974), 46-52.

JC organizes the collection upon the three existential themes of this article's title.

THE SHADOW LINE (1917)

25333 Benson, Carl. "Conrad's Two Stories of Initiation." PMLA, 69 (1954), 46-56.

SL and SS. See 25304.

25334 Bone, David W. "THE SHADOW LINE." In A CONRAD MEMORIAL LIBRARY. Ed. George T. Keating. Pp. 255-61. See 23034.

SL simple autobiography.

*25335 Leavis, Frank R. "Joseph Conrad." SR, 66 (1958), 179-200.

Stresses importance of SL.

*25336 Watt, Ian. "Story and Idea in Conrad's THE SHADOW LINE." CritQ, 2 (1960), 133-48.

Important critical analysis of JC's chief ideas.

25337 Waugh, Arthur. "Mr. Joseph Conrad and the Discipline of Fear." In TRADITION AND CHANGE. New York: Dutton, 1919. Pp. 276-84.

The importance of the ordeal in JC's novels, and his skillful creation of an atmosphere of fear (e.g., SL).

25338 Zabel, Morton Dauwen. "Introduction." In "THE SHADOW LINE" AND TWO OTHER TALES: "TYPHOON"/"THE SECRET SHARER." Garden City, N.Y.: Doubleday, 1959. Pp. 1-27.

Theme of "command."

25339 Zuckerman, Jerome. "The Architecture of THE SHADOW LINE." CONRADIANA, 3, No. 2 (1971-72), 87-92.

Integration of the themes of self-knowledge and command.

THE SISTERS (1928)

25340 Ford, Ford Madox. "Introduction." In JC's THE SISTERS. Pp. 1-16. See 11015.

Story abandoned because of its too sensitive incest theme.

"A Smile of Fortune" (1911)

25341 Lafferty, William. "Conrad's 'A Smile of Fortune': The Moral Threat of Commerce." CONRADIANA, 7 (1975), 63-74.

The young Captain fails to resolve a moral conflict between his codes of seamanship and the codes of commercial life.

25342 Zuckerman, Jerome. "'A Smile of Fortune': Conrad's Interesting Failure." SSF, 1 (1964), 99-102.

Story embodies a number of JC's characteristic themes, but fails because of its flawed form.

SUSPENSE (1925)

25343 Aubry, Georges Jean-. "SUSPENSE." In A CONRAD MEMORIAL LIBRARY. Ed. George T. Keating. Pp. 351-57. See 23034.

General background information on JC's interest in Napoleonic material and on his probable intentions for the unfinished novel.

"The Tale" (1917)

25344 Harrington, David V., and Carol Estness. "Aesthetic Criteria and Conrad's 'The Tale.'" DISCOURSE, 7 (1964), 437-45.

True "organic unity" of the story.

25345 Williams, Porter. "Story and Frame in Conrad's 'The Tale.'" SSF, 5 (1968), 179-85.

Parts of story linked by common themes of conflict, doubt, and betrayal.

"Typhoon" (1902)

25346 Bruss, Paul S. "'Typhoon': The Initiation of Jukes." CONRADIANA, 5, No. 2 (1973), 46-55.

Jukes seen as story's center.

25347 Hussey, William R.M. "'He Was Spared that Annoyance.'" CONRADIANA, 3, No. 2 (1971-72), 17-25.

Weak character study of MacWhirr.

25348 Pulc, I.P. "Two Portrayals of a Storm: Some Notes on Conrad's Descriptive Style in THE NIGGER OF THE 'NARCISSUS' and 'Typhoon.'" STYLE, 4 (1970), 49-57.

See 25188, above.

25349 Rice, Thomas J. "'Typhoon': Conrad's Christmas Story." CITHARA, 14, No. 2 (1975), 19-35.

Allegorical reading.

25350 Ward, Alfred C. "Joseph Conrad: 'Typhoon.'" In his ASPECTS OF THE MODERN SHORT STORY. Pp. 145-57. See G5010.

Discusses JC's cosmopolitanism in the TYPHOON AND OTHER STORIES volume (see 11020) and the wholeness of JC's portrait of MacWhirr.

25351 Webster, H.T. "Conrad's Changes in Narrative Conception in the Manuscripts of TYPHOON AND OTHER STORIES and VICTORY." PMLA, 64 (1949), 953-62.

Studies variants between manuscripts and published versions.

25352 Wegelin, Christof. "MacWhirr and the Testimony of the Human Voice." CONRADIANA, 7 (1975), 45-50.

The captain's voice becomes symbolic of the absurd hero's act of self-assertion.

25353 Weiand, Hermann. "'Typhoon.'" In INSIGHT II. Ed. John V. Hagopian and Martin Dolch. Pp. 49-58. See G5007.

JC endorses simplicity.

25354 Wills, John H. "Conrad's 'Typhoon': A Triumph of Organic Art." NDQ, 30 (1962), 62-70.

The "ironic victory of modern society over a world it cannot understand," the neglected theme of the novel.

UNDER WESTERN EYES (1911)

25355 Adams, Barbara B. "Sisters under Their Skins: The Women in the Lives of Raskolnikov and Razumov." CONRADIANA, 6 (1974), 113-24.

Further evidence of JC's indebtedness to Dostoevsky is their parallel symbolic development of women (UWE and CRIME AND PUNISHMENT).

25356 Canby, Henry Seidel. "UNDER WESTERN EYES." In A CONRAD MEMORIAL LIBRARY. Ed. George T. Keating. Pp. 187-93. See 23034.

Praises JC's insight into the Russian mind and character.

25357 Eagleton, Terry. "Joseph Conrad and UNDER WESTERN EYES." In EXILES AND EMIGRES. Pp. 21-32. See G3039.

UWE builds a tension between passion and the detachment of alienation.

25358 Fries, Maureen. "Feminism--Antifeminism in UNDER WESTERN EYES." CONRADIANA, 5, No. 2 (1973), 56-65.

JC more sympathetic to the feminist position in the book than in his personal comments.

25359 Goodin, George. "The Personal and the Political in UNDER WESTERN EYES." NCF, 25 (1970), 327-42.

Razumov becomes a political symbol for Russia.

25360 Hagan, John. "Conrad's UNDER WESTERN EYES: The Question of Razumov's 'Guilt' and 'Remorse.'" SNNTS, 1 (1969), 310-22.

Razumov's moral development.

25361 Heimer, Jackson W. "The Betrayer as Intellectual: Conrad's UNDER WESTERN EYES." PolR, 12, No. 4 (1967), 57-68.

Razumov ("Reason") represents intellectual isolation.

25362 Izsak, Emily K. "UNDER WESTERN EYES and the Problems of Serial Publication." RES, 23 (1972), 429-44.

JC's harried composition.

25363 Johnston, John H. "THE SECRET AGENT and UNDER WESTERN EYES: Conrad's Two Political Novels." WVUPP, 17 (1970), 57-71.

See 25271, above.

25364 Kaye, Julian B. "Conrad's UNDER WESTERN EYES and Mann's DOCTOR FAUSTUS." CL, 9 (1957), 60-65.

UWE a source for Mann.

25365 Kelley, Robert E. "'This Chance Glimpse': The Narrator in UNDER WESTERN EYES." UR, 37 (1971), 285-90.

Purposeful limitations of the narrator.

25366 Martin, W.R. "Compassionate Realism in Conrad and UNDER WESTERN EYES." ESA, 17 (1974), 89-100.

Subject of UWE "the condition and nature of man in the light of his own vision."

25367 Matlaw, Ralph E. "Dostoevskij and Conrad's Political Novels." In AMERICAN CONTRIBUTIONS TO THE FIFTH INTERNATIONAL CONGRESS OF SLAVISTS. SOFIA, SEPTEMBER 1963. The Hague: Mouton, 1963. II, 213-30.

See 25280, above.

25368 Pritchett, Victor S. "An Emigre." In BOOKS IN GENERAL. New York: Harcourt, 1953. Pp. 216-22.

See 25286, above.

25369 Robson, W.W. "The Politics of Solitude." LONDON MAGAZINE, 4 (Nov. 1957), 26-31.

Theme of alienation between East and West still timely.
See 23038.

25370 Secor, Robert. "The Function of the Narrator in UNDER WESTERN EYES." CONRADIANA, 3, No. 1 (1970-71), 27-38.

Parallel and contrast between narrator and Razumov.

25371 Sullivan, Walter. "The Dark beyond the Sunrise: Conrad and the Politics of Despair." SoR, 8 (1972), 507-19.

See 25293, above.

25372 Swanson, Donald R. "The Observer Observed: Notes on the Narrator of UNDER WESTERN EYES." In RENAISSANCE AND MODERN. Ed. Murray J. Levith. Syracuse, N.Y.: Syracuse Univ. Press, 1976. Pp. 109-18.

Reflections on JC's intentions in his use of the narrator.

*25373 Tanner, Tony. "Nightmare and Complacency: Razumov and the Western Eye." CritQ, 4 (1962), 197-214.

Razumov's self-division.

25374 Viswanathan, Jacqueline. "Point of View and Unreliability in Bronte's WUTHERING HEIGHTS, Conrad's UNDER WESTERN EYES, and Mann's DOKTOR FAUSTUS." OL, 29 (1974), 42-60.

JC's use of a limited narrator (cf. Bronte and Mann).

*25375 Zabel, Morton Dauwen. "Introduction." In JC's UNDER WESTERN EYES. Garden City, N.Y.: Doubleday, 1963. Pp. ix-lviii.

Full reading of UWE as the finest political novel of the century. Reprinted in 23046.

VICTORY (1915)

25376 Beebe, Maurice. IVORY TOWERS AND SACRED FOUNTS. Pp. 165-71. See G3005.

Heyst and the isolated artist archetype.

25377 Bluefarb, Sam. "Samburan: Conrad's Mirror Image of Eden." CONRADIANA, 1, No. 3 (1969), 89-94.

Inverted Eden archetype in the novel.

25378 Bonney, William W. "Narrative Perspective in VICTORY: The Thematic Relevance." JNT, 5 (1975), 24-39.

JC's skillful manipulation of inconsistent narrative technique for thematic purposes.

25379 Butler, Richard E. "Jungian and Oriental Symbolism in Joseph Conrad's VICTORY." CONRADIANA, 3, No. 2 (1971-72), 36-54.

Novel's symbols of dualism.

25380 Dike, Donald A. "The Tempest of Axel Heyst." NCF, 17 (1962), 95-113.

Theme of illusion and reality.

25381 Gatch, Katherine H. "Conrad's Axel." SP, 48 (1951), 98-106.

Influence of Villiers de l'Isle-Adam's AXEL.

25382 Gillon, Adam. "Joseph Conrad and Shakespeare: A New Reading of VICTORY." CONRADIANA, 7 (1975), 263-81.

V reveals the "overwhelming impact of Shakespeare on Conrad" (cites echoes from and allusions to the plays--first of a two-part essay to be completed in 1976.

*25383 Goens, Mary B. "The 'Mysterious and Effective Star': The Mythic World-View in Conrad's VICTORY." MFS, 13 (1967), 455-63.

Dualism in character, theme, and structure.

25384 Greenberg, Robert A. "The Presence of Mr. Wang." BUSE, 4 (1960), 129-37.

Wang as a foil to Heyst.

25385 Gross, Seymour L. "The Devil in Samburan: Jones and Ricardo in VICTORY." NCF, 16 (1961), 81-85.

Demonic imagery in V.

25386 Heimer, Jackson W. "'Look On--Make No Sound': Conrad's VICTORY." STUDIES IN THE HUMANITIES, 1, No. 1 (1969), 8-13.

V is JC's attack on the philosophic detachment of the impotent intellectual.

25387 Hollahan, Eugene. "Beguiled into Action: Silence and Sound in VICTORY." TSLL, 16 (1974), 349-62.

The "complex motif" of silence and sound adds "force and meaning" to the novel.

25388 Howell, Elmo. "The Concept of Evil in Conrad's VICTORY." BSUF, 12, No. 2 (1971), 76-79.

JC obsessed with the omnipresence of evil.

*25389 Kaehele, Sharon, and Howard German. "Conrad's VICTORY: A Reassessment." MFS, 10 (1964), 55-72.

An antisentimental reading. See 23041.

25390 Lewis, R.W.B. "The Current of Conrad's VICTORY." In TWELVE ORIGINAL ESSAYS ON GREAT ENGLISH NOVELS. Ed. Charles Shapiro. Pp. 203-31. See G3134.

Novel moves toward nihilism. Reprinted in 23033.

25391 Lodge, David. "Conrad's VICTORY and THE TEMPEST: An Amplification." MLR, 59 (1964), 195-99.

Shakespeare echoes.

25392 Lordi, R.J. "The Three Emissaries of Evil: Their Psychological Relationship in Conrad's VICTORY." CE, 23 (1961), 136-40.

Shifting relations among Jones, Ricardo, and Pedro.

25393 Page, Norman. "Dickensian Elements in VICTORY." CONRADIANA, 5, No. 1 (1973), 37-42.

Unimaginative parallels to DOMBEY AND SON.

25393a Park, Douglas B. "Conrad's VICTORY: The Anatomy of a Pose." NCF, 31 (1976), 150-69.

V an analysis and critique of Heyst's "hollow" pose of "skeptical detachment," a pose often shared by JC himself and other characters in his fiction.

25394 Raphael, Alice. "Joseph Conrad's Faust." In GOETHE THE CHALLENGER. New York: Cape and Ballou, 1932. Pp. 39-83.

Heyst and Faust.

25395 Reinecke, George F. "Conrad's VICTORY: Psychomachy, Christian Symbols, and Theme." In EXPLORATIONS OF LITERATURE. Ed. Rima D. Reck. Baton Rouge: Louisiana State Univ. Press, 1966. Pp. 70-80.

Systematic symbolic reading.

25396 Roberts, Mark. "Joseph Conrad and the Springs of Action: A Study of VICTORY." In THE TRADITION OF ROMANTIC MORALITY. London: Macmillan, 1973. Pp. 259-87.

V a "most intelligent and thoughtful" discussion of "Romantic morality" (i.e., "energy" of means justifies ends).

25397 Schwab, Arnold T. "Conrad's American Speeches and His Reading From VICTORY." MP, 62 (1965), 342-47.

Reprints JC's notes for a speech and for his readings from V.

25398 Secor, Robert. THE RHETORIC OF SHIFTING PERSPECTIVES: CONRAD'S "VICTORY." University Park: Pennsylvania State Univ. Press, 1971.

A monograph which focuses on JC's use of various points of view to unify his complex novel.

25399 Stallman, Robert W. "The Structure and Symbolism of Conrad's VICTORY." WR, 13 (1949), 146-57.

Search for JC's "secret meaning."

25400 Webster, H.T. "Conrad's Changes in Narrative Conception in the Manuscripts of TYPHOON AND OTHER STORIES and VICTORY." PMLA, 64 (1949), 953-62.

See 25351, above.

25401 Whalen, Terry. "Heyst's Moral Oddity: A Reading of VICTORY." CONRADIANA, 3, No. 1 (1970-71), 39-49.

Vagueness of V attributable to Heyst's (and JC's) confused moral and sexual sensibilities.

25402 Whitehead, Lee M. "Alma Renamed Lena in Conrad's VICTORY." ELN, 3 (1965), 55-57.

Heyst redeems "Alma" (Turkish for courtesan) and renames her "Lena" (Magdalen).

25403 Widmer, Kingsley. "Conrad's Pyrrhic VICTORY." TCL, 5 (1959), 123-30.

V's title ironic. Novel's ending a skeptic's vision of despair.

"Youth" (1898)

25404 Bruss, Paul S. "Conrad's 'Youth': Problems in Interpretation." COLLEGE LITERATURE, 1 (1974), 218-29.

General problems in reading and teaching "Youth."

25405 Emmett, Victor J. "'Youth': Its Place in Conrad's Oeuvre." ConnR, 4, No. 1 (1970), 49-58.

Marlow qualified by his initiation in "Youth" to judge Kurtz and Jim.

25406 Gonzalez, N.V.M. "Time as Sovereign: A Reading of Joseph Conrad's 'Youth.'" LITERARY APPRENTICE, 17 (1954), 106-22.

"Youth's" moral and aesthetic values.

25407 Krieger, Murray. "Conrad's 'Youth': A Naive Opening to Art and Life." CE, 20 (1959), 275-80.

JC fails to capitalize on the story's dual perspective.

25408 Mathews, James W. "Ironic Symbolism in Conrad's 'Youth.'" SSF, 11 (1974), 117-23.

JC's irony and the story's complexity arise not from the narrator, but from the symbols of the tale.

25409 Owen, Guy. "Crane's 'The Open Boat' and Conrad's 'Youth.'" MLN, 73 (1958), 100-102.

Notable resemblances between Crane's and JC's stories.

25410 Smith, J. Oates. "The Existential Comedy of Conrad's 'Youth.'" RENASCENCE, 16 (1963), 22-28.

Absurd comedy in story.

25411 Weston, John Howard. "'Youth': Conrad's Irony and Time's Darkness." SSF, 11 (1974), 399-407.

Ironic relation between JC and Marlow.

*25412 Wills, John H. "A Neglected Masterpiece: Conrad's 'Youth.'" TSLL, 4 (1963), 591-601.

Praises novella's organic unity.

ii. MISCELLANEOUS WRITINGS

25413 Brebach, Raymond T. "The Making of ROMANCE, Part Fifth." CONRADIANA, 6 (1974), 171-81.

Novel's stages of development largely attributable to Ford.

25414 Esslinger, Pat M. "A Theory and Three Experiments: The Failure of the Conrad-Ford Collaboration." WHR, 22 (1968), 59-67.

Failure attributable to their lack of a theory of collaboration.

25415 Ford, Ford Madox. "THE INHERITORS." In A CONRAD MEMORIAL LIBRARY. Ed. George T. Keating. Pp. 74-83. See 23034.

Ford emphasizes his importance in establishing JC's career.

25416 Geddes, Gary. "Conrad and the Fine Art of Understanding." DR, 47 (1967-68), 492-503.

Critical essay on the miscellaneous prose.

25417 Greene, Graham. "Remembering Mr. Jones." 1937. In THE LOST CHILDHOOD AND OTHER ESSAYS. New York: Viking, 1952. Pp. 98-99.

JC's prefaces, unlike James's, are for readers, not novelists.

*25418 Hynes, Samuel. "Conrad and Ford: Two Rye Revolutionists." In his EDWARDIAN OCCASIONS. Pp. 48-53. See G2345.

Ford and JC as impressionistic critics and memoirists.

25419 Kertzer, J.M. "Conrad's Personal Record." UTQ, 44 (1975), 290-303.

JC moralizes his life "by ordering its main events in a pattern based," like his fiction, on a few simple values.

25420 Kleiner, Elaine L. "Joseph Conrad's Forgotten Role in the Emergence of Science Fiction." EXTRAPOLATION, 15 (1973), 25-34.

THE INHERITORS as an early attempt at the genre of science fiction (Ford's role ignored).

25421 Meixner, John A. "ROMANCE: Collaborating with Conrad." In FORD MADOX FORD'S NOVELS: A CRITICAL STUDY. Minneapolis: Univ. of Minnesota Press, 1962. Pp. 27-39.

Studies individual roles of Ford and JC in the collaboration.

25422 Riesenberg, Felix. "THE MIRROR OF THE SEA." In A CONRAD MEMORIAL LIBRARY. Ed. George T. Keating. Pp. 151-53. See 23034.

JC's romantic perspective and his melancholic temperament result from his maritime career.

25423 Rose, Charles. "ROMANCE and the Maiden Archetype." CONRADIANA, 6 (1974), 183-88.

The character of Seraphina, Ford's conception.

25424 Smith, David R. "Conrad's Manifesto: Preface to a Career." In CONRAD'S MANIFESTO. Pp. 47-79. See 13003.

Evolution of the Preface to NN. Also see 25191.

25425 Tarnawski, Wit. "Conrad's A PERSONAL RECORD." CONRADIANA, 1, No. 2 (1969), 55-59.

A PERSONAL RECORD marks the "catharsis" of JC's "Polish complex."

*25426 Watt, Ian. "Conrad's Preface to THE NIGGER OF THE 'NARCISSUS.'" NOVEL, 7 (1974), 101-15.

JC's undoctrinaire theory of fiction.

25427 Worth, George J. "Conrad's Debt to Maupassant in the 'Preface' to THE NIGGER OF THE 'NARCISSUS.'" JEGP, 54 (1955), 700-704.

JC's preface compared to Maupassant's preface for PIERRE ET JEAN.

25428 Wright, Walter F. "Introduction: Conrad's Critical Perspectives." In JOSEPH CONRAD ON FICTION. Pp. ix-xiv. See 13006.

JC's criteria for critical judgment, notably his views of realism and symbolism.

25429 _____. "Joseph Conrad's Critical Views." RS, 12 (1944), 155-75.

Draws from letters, essays and fiction.

25430 Zabel, Morton Dauwen. "Introduction." In "THE MIRROR OF THE SEA" AND "A PERSONAL RECORD." Garden City, N.Y.: Doubleday, 1960. Pp. ix-xlix.

JC's subjective approach to the past.

"Baron Corvo." See Frederick Rolfe in vol. 2.

[GEORGE] NORMAN DOUGLAS (1868-1952)

1. PRIMARY BIBLIOGRAPHY

Books available in recent paperback printings are denoted by "(P)."

1.1 Fiction

All works are novels unless otherwise noted.

11001 IN THE BEGINNING. Florence: Privately printed, 1927. New York: Day, 1928. First complete Engl. ed. London: Folio Society, 1953.

Fantasy parable of the creation of man and the emergence of religion, suffused with ND's humanistic skepticism.

11002 SOUTH WIND. London: Secker, 1917. New York: Dodd, Mead, 1918. (P).

Often-imitated prototype of the witty discussion novel, intended by ND to illustrate the relativity of morals: "How to make murder palatable to a bishop: that is the plot."

11003 THEY WENT. London: Chapman and Hall, 1920. New York: Dodd, Mead, 1921.

Fantasy, set in the court of a mythical kingdom in druidic Brittany, which examines the conflict of "beauty _versus_ betterment."

11004 UNPROFESSIONAL TALES. [Stories]. London: Unwin, 1901. No Amer. ed.

Exceedingly rare collection of sixteen stories, written in association with his wife and published under the pseudonym

Normyx. Six tales were revised and collected in EXPERIMENTS (12003). "Nerinda," in revised form, was also separately published (Florence: Orioli; New York: Day, 1929).

1.2 Miscellaneous Writings

Included here are all of ND's nonfiction writings which relate directly to his fiction, his life, and his social and critical views. The reader should be aware that ND also published widely on a variety of scientific topics--for example, zoology, herpetology, ornithology, Darwinian theory, and archeology--as well as on topics as diverse as London street games and aphrodisiacs. For more information, see Woolf's bibliography (21004).

12001 ALONE. London: Chapman and Hall, 1921. New York: McBride, 1922.

Although ostensibly a travel essay (Italy), contains much autobiographical information and provocative reflections on history, the arts, and other topics.

12002 D.H. LAWRENCE AND MAURICE MAGNUS: A PLEA FOR BETTER MANNERS. Florence: Privately printed, 1924.

Reasoned attack on Lawrence's ill-mannered denigration of their mutual acquaintance, Magnus, which Lawrence published as an introduction to Magnus's posthumous MEMOIRS OF THE FOREIGN LEGION (see 22013). ND's pamphlet reprinted in the English and American editions of EXPERIMENTS, below.

12003 EXPERIMENTS: A MISCELLANY. London: Chapman and Hall; New York: McBride, 1925.

Critical essays on various authors (including Poe), revised and original tales, reviews, and essays. Includes D.H. LAWRENCE AND MAURICE MAGNUS, above.

12004 FOUNTAINS IN THE SAND: RAMBLES AMONG THE OASES OF TUNISIA. London: Secker, 1912. New York: Dodd, Mead, 1921.

Like ALONE, discursive essays in the form of a travel narrative.

12005 GOODBYE TO WESTERN CULTURE. See HOW ABOUT EUROPE? (below).

12006 HOW ABOUT EUROPE? SOME FOOTNOTES ON EAST AND WEST. Florence: Privately printed, 1929. London: Chatto and Windus, 1930. Published as GOODBYE TO WESTERN CULTURE. New York: Harper, 1930.

Highly polemical compendium of ND's social and political views.

12007 LATE HARVEST. London: Drummond, 1946. No Amer. ed.

Autobiographical commentaries on ND's own books (their origin, publication, and other background information) and reprinting of SUMMER ISLANDS (descriptive travel essays--1931).

12008 LOOKING BACK: AN AUTOBIOGRAPHICAL EXCURSION. London: Chatto and Windus; New York: Harcourt, Brace, 1933.

Discursive autobiography, composed largely of reminiscences occasioned by reviewing the numerous calling cards collected from acquaintances over the years.

12009 OLD CALABRIA. London: Secker; Boston: Houghton Mifflin, 1915.

Like ALONE, discursive essays in the form of a travel narrative.

12010 SIREN LAND. London: Dent; New York: Dutton, 1911.

Like ALONE, discursive essays in the form of a travel narrative (Sorrentine peninsula and Capri).

12011 TOGETHER. London: Chapman and Hall; New York: McBride, 1923.

Like ALONE, discursive essays in the form of a travel narrative (Tyrol, 1919-20).

1.3 Collected and Selected Works

13001 AN ALMANAC. Lisbon: Privately printed, 1941. London: Chatto and Windus, Secker and Warburg, 1945.

Anthology of quotations for every day of the year, drawn from ND's own work. Reminiscent of a nineteenth-century keepsake volume.

13002 NORMAN DOUGLAS: A SELECTION FROM HIS WORKS. Ed. D.M. Low. London: Chatto and Windus, Secker and Warburg, 1955.

Generous selections from ND's nonfiction (including reminiscences, travel, science, and sociology) and excerpts from SOUTH WIND. See 24006.

13003 "SIREN LAND" AND "FOUNTAINS IN THE SAND." London: Secker and Warburg; New York: Macmillan, 1957.

1.4 Letters

Also see Aldington (22002) and Karl (22012), below.

14001 Aubry, Georges Jean-. JOSEPH CONRAD: LIFE AND LETTERS. Garden City, N.Y.: Doubleday, Page, 1927. II, passim.

Prints texts of nine letters from Conrad to ND, plus several letters mentioning ND and his work (see Aubry's index).

14002 Palmer, Arnold. "Some Norman Douglas Letters." REL, 6, No. 3 (1965), 81-92.

Seventeen letters (1937-47), with commentary.

2. SECONDARY BIBLIOGRAPHY

2.1 Bibliographies

21001 Holloway, Mark. "The Norman Douglas Collection at Yale." YULG, 50 (1975), 1-14.

Describes the extensive holdings of ND's manuscripts, letters, and personal papers at Yale.

21002 McDonald, Edward D., ed. A BIBLIOGRAPHY OF THE WRITINGS OF NORMAN DOUGLAS. Philadelphia: Centaur Book Shop, 1927.

Full collations, with descriptive notes (and some additional notes contributed by ND), of fifteen monographs (chiefly scientific) and ten books, with briefer notes on ND's contributions to books and periodicals. Complete through 1925. Also contains brief lists of books and periodical articles concerning ND and his work.

21003 Wiley, Paul L., comp. "Norman Douglas (1868-1952)." In THE BRITISH NOVEL. Comp. Wiley. Pp. 32-33. See G1419.

Brief checklist.

*21004 Woolf, Cecil, ed. A BIBLIOGRAPHY OF NORMAN DOUGLAS. London: Hart-Davis, 1954.

Collates first and early editions of 39 books and pamphlets, 9 contributions to books and 6 translations, and lists 174 contributions to periodicals. Many items with additional bibliographical annotation (e.g., collected publication of articles). Indexed.

2.2 Biographies, Memoirs, Reminiscences

22001 Acton, Harold. "'Uncle Norman.'" In GRAND MAN. Comp. Nancy Cunard. Pp. 236-42. See 23001.

First (Florence, 1923) and last meetings with ND (1951).

22002 Aldington, Richard. PINORMAN: PERSONAL RECOLLECTIONS OF NORMAN DOUGLAS, PINO ORIOLI, AND CHARLES PRENTICE. London: Heinemann, 1954.

Memories and notes, for a "future biographer," concerning ND, Pino Orioli, and Prentice (of Chatto and Windus--publisher for Aldington, ND, and Orioli). Considerable detail on ND's lifestyle and character in Italy during the thirties.

22003 Cunard, Nancy. "Letter to Norman." In GRAND MAN. Comp. Cunard. Pp. 59-228. See 23001.

A highly personal memoir, in the form of a letter, reflecting on Cunard's friendship with ND (1923 and after).

22004 Cunard, Victor. "Norman Douglas: 1868-1952." In GRAND MAN. Comp. Nancy Cunard. Pp. 231-35. See 23001.

Obituary memories of ND in Italy (1920s) and England (1940s).

22005 Davenport, John. "Norman Douglas." ATLANTIC MONTHLY, 194 (Sept. 1954), 69-74.

Memoir and admiring commentary on ND's works.

22006 Duff, Charles. "A Letter about Norman Douglas." In GRAND MAN. Comp. Nancy Cunard. Pp. 243-47. See 23001.

Memories of ND and his opinions (London, 1940s).

22007 FitzGibbon, Constantine. NORMAN DOUGLAS: A PICTORIAL RECORD. New York: McBride, 1953.

Collection of sixteen photographs of ND (and one Beerbohm caricature), prefaced by a brief memoir, biographical summary, and critical appreciation.

22008 ______. "Norman Douglas: Memoir of an Unwritten Biography." ENCOUNTER, 43 (Sept. 1974), 23-37.

An expanded version of the prefatory memoir and commentary above.

22009 Golding, Louis. SUNWARD. New York: Knopf, 1924. Passim.

Memories and impressions of ND, among others.

22010 Holloway, Mark. NORMAN DOUGLAS: A BIOGRAPHY. London: Secker and Warburg, 1976.

"Depicts the long, varied and on many occasions scandalous life of Douglas." (Quoted from publisher's advertisement. Not seen. To appear late 1976.)

22011 Johnson, Arthur. "Douglas on Capri." In GRAND MAN. Comp. Nancy Cunard. Pp. 248-53. See 23001.

ND's antimystical, classical temperament.

22012 Karl, Frederick R. "Joseph Conrad, Norman Douglas, and the ENGLISH REVIEW." JML, 2 (1972), 342-56.

The course of Conrad's and ND's "flimsy" friendship (1905-16), amply documented from their correspondence.

22013 Lawrence, D.H. "Introduction to MEMOIRS OF THE FOREIGN LEGION." 1924. In PHOENIX II: UNCOLLECTED, UNPUBLISHED, AND OTHER PROSE WORKS. Ed. Warren Roberts and Harry T. Moore. New York: Viking, 1968. Pp. 303-61.

Although not concerned with ND himself, Lawrence's controversial, condescending treatment of their mutual acquaintance prompted ND's rejoinder in D.H. LAWRENCE AND MAURICE MAGNUS: A PLEA FOR BETTER MANNERS (see 12002).

22014 ______. "The Late Mr. Maurice Magnus: A Letter." 1926. In PHOENIX: THE POSTHUMOUS PAPERS OF D.H. LAWRENCE. Ed. Edward D. McDonald. New York: Viking, 1936. Pp. 806-7.

Lawrence's response to ND's D.H. LAWRENCE AND MAURICE MAGNUS.

22015 Lowenfels, Walter. "Remembering Norman Douglas (for Nancy Cunard)." LITERARY REVIEW, 5 (1962), 336-48.

Memoir, written in the same gushing, impressionistic style that mars Cunard's work.

22016 Macpherson, Kenneth. "A Day." In GRAND MAN. Comp. Nancy Cunard. Pp. 254-64. See 23001.

Memorial reconstruction of activities and conversation on a typical day with ND.

22017 ______. OMNES EODEM COGIMUR: SOME NOTES WRITTEN FOLLOWING THE DEATH OF NORMAN DOUGLAS, 9 FEBRUARY 1952. Turin, Italy: Privately printed, 1953.

Notes, impressions, and reminiscences. A 23-page pamphlet.

22018 Moore, Harry T. THE PRIEST OF LOVE: A LIFE OF D.H. LAWRENCE. New York: Farrar, Straus and Giroux, 1974. Passim.

Details on the Lawrence-Douglas acquaintance and the controversy over Maurice Magnus.

22019 Weintraub, Stanley. REGGIE: A PORTRAIT OF REGINALD TURNER. New York: Braziller, 1965. Pp. 189-211 and passim.

Account of ND and Turner's "strange" and mercurial relationship.

2.3 Book-Length Critical Studies and Essay Collections

23001 Cunard, Nancy, comp. GRAND MAN: MEMORIES OF NORMAN DOUGLAS. London: Secker and Warburg, 1954.

A strange composite of critical essays, bibliographical notes, and reminiscences. The greater part of the volume, a memoir of Cunard's friendship and travels with ND (1923 and after, see 22003), is bracketed by Cunard's critical essay on ND emphasizing his humor and humanism) and by five appreciations by several hands (see 22001, 22004, 22006, 22011, and 22016). Cunard's final section, a brief descriptive survey of ND's books, is a useful, though effusive, introduction to the work.

*23002 Dawkins, Richard M. NORMAN DOUGLAS. 1933. 2nd ed. London: Hart-Davis, 1952. Originally published under the pseudonym Richard MacGillivray.

Balanced review of ND's ideas and opinions, stressing the consistency of his humanism, skepticism, antiasceticism, and "Mediterranean" view of nature. Dawkins's brief, perceptive commentary on the three novels finds them chiefly philosophic studies of religion (IN THE BEGINNING), beauty (THEY WENT), and morals (SOUTH WIND), "the True, the Beautiful and the Good."

23003 Greenlees, Ian. NORMAN DOUGLAS. London: Longmans, 1957.

Brief biographical survey and critical assessment which rates the travel writings as ND's best work (especially OLD CALABRIA). Also includes a commentary on SOUTH WIND as a distillation of ND's "philosophy of life." A 33-page pamphlet.

23004 Leary, Lewis. NORMAN DOUGLAS. New York: Columbia Univ. Press, 1968.

Useful and balanced critical introduction. Leary devotes several pages of his brief essay to a critical commentary on SOUTH WIND. A 45-page pamphlet.

*23005 Lindeman, Ralph D. NORMAN DOUGLAS. New York: Twayne, 1965.

Excellent brief biography and critical introduction. Lindeman presents full chapters on ND's attitudes and values (e.g., dilletantism, hedonism, individualism), his writing methods (chiefly the travel work), his novels (analyses) and his style (fine close analysis). The final chapter, on ND's reputation, valuably assesses ND's influence upon and relation to modern literature. Lindeman's judgments are fortunately untainted by the overly enthusiastic admiration found too often among ND's critics.

23006 Tomlinson, Henry M. NORMAN DOUGLAS. 1931. 2nd ed. London: Chatto and Windus, 1952.

Critical introduction to ND's works and ideas, with special praise reserved for the essays and travel books. Tomlinson views SOUTH WIND equivocally as a destructively "diabolic [yet] sprightly disclosure of the bankruptcy of our social, artistic, and moral values." (Second edition slightly enlarged and revised.)

2.4 General Critical Articles, or Chapters on ND

24001 Davenport, John. "Norman Douglas." TWENTIETH CENTURY, 151 (1952), 359-67.

Biographical summary and brief critiques of the major works.

*24002 Flint, R.W. "Norman Douglas." KR, 14 (1952), 660-68.

ND an accomplished and attractive dilettante.

24003 Flory, Evelyn A. "Norman Douglas and the Scientific Spirit." ELT, 14 (1971), 167-77.

Notes on ND's scientific and "quasi-scientific" writings.

24004 Ford, Ford Madox. "A Haughty and Proud Generation." YR, 11 (1922), 703-17.

Brief critique of ND (pp. 710-12) as one of the writers in the second rank of moderns.

24005 Greene, Graham. "Norman Douglas." 1952. In his COLLECTED ESSAYS. New York: Viking, 1969. Pp. 362-65.

ND's "open, tolerant, and unashamed" life. Obituary remarks.

24006 Low, D.M. "Introduction." In NORMAN DOUGLAS: A SELECTION FROM HIS WORKS. Pp. 9-24. See 13002.

General summary of ND's views, with special emphasis on SOUTH WIND's "sustained challenge to the foundations of modern morality and manners."

24007 Lynd, Robert. "Mr. Norman Douglas's Dislikes." In BOOKS AND AUTHORS. London: Cobden-Sanderson, 1922. Pp. 256-62.

ND's outspoken opinions. Includes a review of ALONE, a "book of hatred" tempered with laughter.

*24008 McDonald, Edward D. "The Early Work of Norman Douglas." BOOKMAN (New York), 66 (1927), 42-46.

Discussion of ND's treatises and creative writing prior to SOUTH WIND.

*24009 Pritchett, Victor S. "Norman Douglas: 1868-1952." NEW STATESMAN AND NATION, 43 (1952), 307-8.

The note of the ex-Puritan in ND's hedonism. Important obituary critique.

24010 Stevenson, Lionel. THE HISTORY OF THE ENGLISH NOVEL. XI, 158-59. See G2212.

Brief commentary on ND as a representative "Edwardian exquisite" in fiction.

24011 Swan, Michael. "The Living Dead--II. Norman Douglas and the Southern World." LONDON MAGAZINE, 3 (June 1956), 49-55.

ND's weaknesses and self-division as an artist.

24012 Swinnerton, Frank. THE GEORGIAN LITERARY SCENE. Pp. 129-34. See G2364.

ND a desultory and fitful writer, a hedonist in life and a dilettante in art.

*24013 Webster, H.T. "Norman Douglas: A Reconsideration." SAQ, 49 (1950), 226-36.

Drastic eclipse in ND's reputation due in part to his diversity. Balanced survey.

24014 Wheatley, Elizabeth D. "Norman Douglas." SR, 40 (1932), 55-67.

Excessively admiring overview of ND's three classes of work--scientific, critical, and creative--stressing his imposing erudition.

24015 Wilson, Edmund. "The Nietzschean Line." 1930. THE SHORES OF LIGHT. Pp. 485-91. See G2376.

ND's "diluted and inconsistent Nietzscheanism" in his attacks on Western civilization (e.g., GOODBYE TO WESTERN CULTURE).

2.5 Studies of Individual Works

The following section is subdivided into two parts: i. Fiction, and ii. Miscellaneous Works. Each of the critical studies on ND (2.3, above) contains some commentary on the individual works.

i. FICTION

SOUTH WIND (1917)

25001 Brewster, Dorothy. EAST-WEST PASSAGE. Pp. 204-6. See G2312.

ND's satire of Russian characters and themes in SOUTH WIND.

25002 Frierson, William C. THE ENGLISH NOVEL IN TRANSITION. Pp. 249-53. See G3047.

Notes on the "'dialogue' or 'ventriloquial'" SOUTH WIND and its influence on the "Sophisticate" fiction of the twenties.

25003 Irwin, W.R. THE GAME OF THE IMPOSSIBLE. Pp. 120-23. See G6417.

SOUTH WIND a typical fantasy of an "impossible society."

25004 Mais, Stuart P.B. "Norman Douglas." In BOOKS AND THEIR WRITERS. New York: Dodd, Mead, 1920. Pp. 27-36.

Appreciation of SOUTH WIND's humor and satiric brilliance.

25005 Matthews, Jack. "Norman Douglas's SOUTH WIND." In REDISCOVERIES: INFORMAL ESSAYS IN WHICH WELL-KNOWN NOVELISTS REDISCOVER NEGLECTED WORKS OF FICTION BY ONE OF THEIR FAVORITE AUTHORS. Ed. David Madden. New York: Crown, 1971. Pp. 191-96.

Admirer's plea for a revaluation of SOUTH WIND.

25006 Scarborough, Dorothy. "Introduction." In SOUTH WIND. New York: Macmillan, 1929. Pp. v-xiii.

Brief appreciation and commentary (many factual errors).

ii. MISCELLANEOUS WRITINGS

25007 Aldington, Richard. "Norman Douglas and Calabria." ATLANTIC MONTHLY, 163 (1939), 757-60.

Special praise for OLD CALABRIA as "one of the few genuine solid books of travel of this century."

25008 Davenport, John. "Introduction." In OLD CALABRIA. New York: Harcourt, 1956. Pp. vii-xvi.

Excellent survey of the backgrounds to and the origin and composition of OLD CALABRIA.

[ARTHUR ANNESLEY] RONALD FIRBANK (1886-1926)

1. PRIMARY BIBLIOGRAPHY

Books available in recent paperback printings are denoted by "(P)."

1.1 Fiction

All works are novels unless otherwise noted. COUNT FANNY'S NUPTIALS, by "Simon Arrow" (1907), a short novel in RF's manner, has been attributed to RF on hearsay evidence.

11001 THE ARTIFICIAL PRINCESS. London: Duckworth, 1934. New York: Coward-McCann, 1935 (in EXTRAVAGANZAS, see 13002).

> Early work (begun c. 1906-10) published posthumously. A variation on the Salome myth. See 25001.

11002 CAPRICE. London: Richards, 1917. New York: Brentano's, 1929 (in WORKS, vol. II, see 13007).

> Exploits of the young heroine in London's social and theatrical worlds.

11003 CONCERNING THE ECCENTRICITIES OF CARDINAL PIRELLI. London: Richards, 1926; New York: Brentano's, 1929 (in WORKS, vol. V, see 13007).

> The Cardinal's bizarre activities, in the Spanish town of Clemeza, including dog baptisms (and funerals) and pursuits of choir boys.

11004 THE FLOWER BENEATH THE FOOT: BEING A RECORD OF THE EARLY LIFE OF ST. LAURA DE NAZIANZI AND THE TIMES IN WHICH SHE LIVED. London: Richards, 1923. New York: Brentano's, 1924.

Often hilarious social novel, set in the court of the King of "Pisuerga" and its environs, and dealing in general with the frustrated love of Laura de Nazianzi and her withdrawal to a convent.

11005 INCLINATIONS. London: Richards, 1916. New York: Brentano's, 1929 (in WORKS, vol. II, see 13007).

Mabel Collins's "inclinations" (e.g., travel to Greece, illegitimate child) the slight substance of this dialogue-novel. Editions after 1925 include a revised chapter.

11006 "ODETTE D'ANTREVERNES" AND "A STUDY IN TEMPERAMENT." [Stories]. London: Mathews, 1905.

Two early pieces, a fairy tale and a London sketch. First work revised and published as ODETTE: A FAIRY TALE FOR WEARY PEOPLE (London: Richards, 1916) and collected in the WORKS (see 13007). A STUDY IN TEMPERAMENT was reprinted in THE NEW RYTHUM (1962), see 13003.

11007 PRANCING NIGGER. New York: Brentano's, 1924. Published as SORROW IN SUNLIGHT. London: Brentano's, 1924.

Fantastic satire of the middle-class aspirations of a provincial Cuban family (the "Mouths"), on the move to the big city.

11008 SANTAL. London: Richards, 1921. New York: Brentano's, 1929 (in WORKS, vol. IV, see 13007).

An ornately exotic Eastern tale of an innocent Arab boy in North Africa.

11009 SORROW IN SUNLIGHT. See PRANCING NIGGER (11007).

11010 VAINGLORY. London: Richards, 1915. New York: Brentano's, 1925.

RF's first full-length work. A crowded novel of late-Edwardian London society.

11011 VALMOUTH: A ROMANTIC NOVEL. London: Richards, 1919. New York: Brentano's, 1929 (in WORKS, vol. III, see 13007).

A satire of the rural novel, dealing with the loves and liaisons of several characters (some centenarians) at a country estate.

1.2 Miscellaneous Writings

Note: Some fragments of RF's unfinished works have been published in THE NEW RYTHUM, AND OTHER PIECES (see 13003). Benkovitz also notes some early essays which were published in fugitive journals (see her bibliography, 21002).

12001 THE PRINCESS ZOUBAROFF: A COMEDY. London: Richards, 1920. New York: Brentano's, 1929 (in WORKS, vol. III, see 13007).

A play, RF's only major departure from fiction.

1.3 Collected and Selected Works

13001 THE COMPLETE RONALD FIRBANK. London: Duckworth; Norfolk, Conn.: New Directions, 1961.

Single-volume reprint of the works. See 24017.

13002 EXTRAVAGANZAS: CONTAINING "THE ARTIFICIAL PRINCESS" AND "CONCERNING THE ECCENTRICITIES OF CARDINAL PIRELLI." New York: Coward-McCann, 1935.

Includes first American issue of THE ARTIFICIAL PRINCESS.

13003 THE NEW RYTHUM, AND OTHER PIECES. London: Duckworth, 1962. Norfolk, Conn.: New Directions, 1963.

Collects "A Study in Temperament" (1905), "Lady Appledore's Mesalliance" (unpublished), "The New Rythum" (unfinished novel c. 1925), with "Extracts from the Notebooks" and "A Miscellany of Short Passages from Unpublished Writings." See 21001 and 24013.

13004 "LA PRINCESSE AUX SOLEILS" AND "HARMONIE." Trans. Edgell Rickword. Berkeley, Calif.: Enitharmon, 1974.

Collected issue of RF's first two published sketches (1904, 1905), translated from the original French.

13005 TWO EARLY STORIES BY RONALD FIRBANK. Ed. Miriam J. Benkovitz. New York: Albondocani, 1971.

Collected publication of "The Wavering Disciple: A Fantasy" (1906) and "A Study in Opal" (1907), two undergraduate pieces.

13006 TWO NOVELS: "THE FLOWER BENEATH THE FOOT" AND "PRANCING NIGGER." Norfolk, Conn.: New Directions, 1962. (P).

Also includes "Chronology of Ronald Firbank" by Miriam J. Benkovitz (pp. 351-56).

13007 THE WORKS OF RONALD FIRBANK. 5 vols. London: Duckworth; New York: Brentano's, 1929.

First collected edition. English edition, only, expanded to six volumes in 1934 with the addition of THE ARTIFICIAL PRINCESS. See 24022.

13008 THE WORKS OF RONALD FIRBANK: OMNIBUS EDITION. 2 vols. London: Duckworth, 1949-50. Published as FIVE NOVELS and THREE NOVELS: VAINGLORY; INCLINATIONS; CAPRICE. Norfolk, Conn.: New Directions, 1949, 1951.

The eight novels, collected into two volumes. See 22011 and 24014.

1.4 Letters

There has been no separate publication of RF's correspondence, but most of the important letters to publishers, to his sister, and to his mother, are available within the text of Benkovitz's biography (see 22002). Also see 21001, below.

2. SECONDARY BIBLIOGRAPHY

2.1 Bibliographies

21001 "Appendix: The Manuscripts and Correspondence of Ronald Firbank." In THE NEW RYTHUM AND OTHER PIECES. Pp. 127-35. See 13003.

Reprint of the 1961 Sotheby sale catalog.

*21002 Benkovitz, Miriam J., ed. A BIBLIOGRAPHY OF RONALD FIRBANK. London: Hart-Davis, 1963.

Full descriptive bibliography of RF's books and pamphlets (20 items to 1962), with briefer listings of RF's nine contributions to periodicals and his manuscript and typescript locations. Benkovitz supplements the descriptions with generous notes and commentaries on the publishing histories of the works.

*21003 Davis, Robert M., comp. "Ronald Firbank: A Selected Bibliography of Criticism." BB, 26 (1969), 108-11.

Lists over 150 reviews, notes, and articles on RF.

21004 Wiley, Paul L., comp. "Ronald Firbank (1886-1926)." In THE BRITISH NOVEL. Comp. Wiley. Pp. 36-37. See G1419.

Brief primary and secondary checklist.

2.2 Biographies, Memoirs, Reminiscences

Also see 23003.

22001 Benkovitz, Miriam J. "Notes toward a Chapter of Biography: Lord Alfred Douglas and Ronald Firbank." BNYPL, 67 (1963), 143-51.

RF's brief correspondence with Douglas during his formative years as a writer (1905-9).

*22002 ______. RONALD FIRBANK: A BIOGRAPHY. New York: Knopf, 1969.

Extensively documented biography, unburdened by a thesis. Benkovitz draws widely from the unpublished manuscripts, notebooks, and, most significantly, from the letters, to present an unbiased portrait of a far more serious and complex RF than his semimythical reputation would suggest.

22003 Berners, Lord. "Ronald Firbank." In RONALD FIRBANK: A MEMOIR. Comp. Ifan K. Fletcher. Pp. 145-50. See 22006.

Brief memoir, including an account of RF's death in Rome.

22004 Brophy, Brigid. PRANCING NOVELIST: A DEFENSE OF FICTION IN THE FORM OF A CRITICAL BIOGRAPHY IN PRAISE OF RONALD FIRBANK. New York: Barnes and Noble, 1973.

Arrogant and pretentious "defense of fiction" (including a self-comparison with Shelley and Sidney), as well as a biographical and critical study of RF and a "chapter in the history of ideas." Brophy's multiple aims create a muddle of confused notions and blanket assertions. Within the impressionistic critical chapters, Brophy offers some tantalizing comments on RF's approximation of musical form in his fiction, but little else that is original or noteworthy. Her biography does contain some useful additional information about RF's life and could be read as a supplement to Benkovitz.

22005 Cunard, Nancy. THOUGHTS ABOUT RONALD FIRBANK. New York: Albondocani, 1971.

Memories and impressions of RF (1919-25). Brief pamphlet (9 pages of text).

*22006 Fletcher, Ifan K. RONALD FIRBANK: A MEMOIR. London: Duckworth, 1930.

Compilation of five distinct memoirs, the longest by Fletcher (pp. 13-100), who has accumulated a considerable amount of factual detail on RF's lineage, early reading, travels, associations, and other background. Supplementary reminiscences provide further information on RF's character and an account of his death. Includes 22003, 22007, 22008, and 22011.

22007 Holland, V.B. "Ronald Firbank." In RONALD FIRBANK: A MEMOIR. Comp. Ifan K. Fletcher. Pp. 101-12. See above.

Memories of a fellow Cambridge student.

22008 John, Augustus. "Ronald Firbank." In RONALD FIRBANK: A MEMOIR. Comp. Ifan K. Fletcher. Pp. 113-15. See above.

Brief personal reminiscences of RF's portraitist.

22009 Nicolson, Harold. SOME PEOPLE. London: Constable, 1927. Pp. 55-78.

Semifictional, satiric portrait of RF as "Lambert Orme," drawn from meetings with RF in Spain (1905).

22010 Richards, Grant. AUTHOR HUNTING. New York: Coward-McCann, 1934. Pp. 248-60.

Patronizing account of Richards' dealings, as publisher, with the childlike RF.

22011 Sitwell, Osbert. "Ronald Firbank." 1929. In NOBLE ESSENCES, OR COURTEOUS REVELATIONS. London: Macmillan, 1950. Pp. 68-88.

Memoir of meetings with RF (1917 and after), noting, with some astonishment, RF's abilities as a businessman. Expanded version appeared in Fletcher's RONALD FIRBANK: A MEMOIR (22006). Also appeared as the introduction to FIVE NOVELS (1949); see 13008.

2.3 Book-Length Critical Studies and Essay Collections

*23001 Brooke, Jocelyn. RONALD FIRBANK. New York: Roy, 1951.

Still the best introduction to RF's life, works, style, and place in literary history. Brooke finds a "curious ambivalence . . . a perpetual conflict between his ninetyish sensibility and a cynical self-mockery" in the novels and argues that the resolution of this conflict, in RF's best work, "gives his writing its unique quality." Most of Brooke's commentaries on the works "present" rather than criticize.

23002 _____. RONALD FIRBANK AND JOHN BETJEMAN. London: Longmans, 1962.

Brief introductory essay (24 pp.), bound together with Brooke's separate study of Betjeman. Brooke's book-length study, above, of which this essay is a radical condensation, is a far better introduction to RF.

23003 Horder, Mervyn, ed. RONALD FIRBANK: MEMOIRS AND CRITIQUES. London: Duckworth, 1977.

Not seen.

23004 Kiechler, John Anthony. THE BUTTERFLY'S FRECKLED WINGS: A STUDY OF STYLE IN THE NOVELS OF RONALD FIRBANK. Bern, Switzerland: Francke, 1969.

Specialized dissertation-study of the technical and verbal characteristics of RF's literary style. Some aspects are given detailed analyses in individual chapters: "Local Colour," "Reported Speech," "Dialogue," and "Imagery." Kiechler devotes his final chapters to a critical overview of RF's originality and achievement as a stylist.

23005 Merritt, James D. RONALD FIRBANK. New York: Twayne, 1969.

Close technical and thematic analysis of RF's novels, with marginal comment on the life. Merritt contends that RF began as a writer firmly within "the fin de siecle or Decadent tradition who modified and eventually reshaped that tradition into thoroughly original novels and stories." Also includes discussions of RF's only play and fragmentary remains (THE NEW RYTHUM AND OTHER PIECES), and a brief bibliography.

23006 Potoker, Edward M. RONALD FIRBANK. New York: Columbia Univ. Press, 1969.

Chronological survey of the works, describing RF's ambiguous views, ironic technique, absurdist vision, and eccentricities of style. Good introductory pamphlet (46 pp.).

2.4 General Critical Articles, or Chapters on RF

24001 Auden, W.H. "Ronald Firbank and an Amateur World." LISTENER, 65 (1961), 1004-5, 1008.

Intriguing and humorous view of RF's idiosyncratic fantasy world.

24002 Baker, Ernest A. THE HISTORY OF THE ENGLISH NOVEL. Vol. 9. THE DAY BEFORE YESTERDAY. New York: Barnes and Noble, 1939. Pp. 240-42.

RF a "belated straggler" from the rear guard of the aesthetic movement. Brief critique.

24003 Benkovitz, Miriam J. "On 'An Early Flemish Painter' by Ronald Firbank." BNYPL, 72 (1968), 653-55.

Note on RF's "only excursion into the world of journalism," an article on Jan Grossaert (1907).

24004 ______. "Ronald Firbank in New York." BNYPL, 63 (1959), 247-59.

Surveys RF's interest in New York, and New York's interest in RF (critical reviews and other notices).

24005 Braybrooke, Neville. "Ronald Firbank: 1886-1926." DR, 42 (1962), 38-49.

RF's comedy a deliberate defense against a harsh view of the realities of life (reviews novels).

24006 ______. "Thorns and Vanities: Ronald Firbank Revisited." ENCOUNTER, 31, No. 3 (1968), 66-74.

General biographical and critical summary.

*24007 Connolly, Cyril. "Anatomy of Dandyism." In his ENEMIES OF PROMISE. Pp. 33-39. See G3025.

Equivocal critique of RF as a literary "dandy," an impressionistic stylist who has tapped the vein of "inconsequence." Dismisses RF's sexual frivolity as vulgar.

*24008 Davis, Robert M. "From Artifice to Art: The Technique of Firbank's Novels." STYLE, 2 (1968), 33-47.

Traces the development of RF's complex structural use of pictorial and dramatic techniques.

*24009 _____. "'Hyperaesthesia with Complications': The World of Ronald Firbank." RENDEZVOUS, 3, No. 1 (1968), 5-15.

Fine description and assessment of RF's unique view of the world.

24010 Dickinson, Patric. "A Note on Ronald Firbank (1886-1915-1926)." WINDMILL, 1, No. 3 (1946), 26-36.

Biographical and critical appreciation of the "original, unique, uninfluenced, absolute" RF. Several fine observations.

*24011 Forster, E.M. "Ronald Firbank." 1929. In his ABINGER HARVEST. New York: Harcourt, 1936. Pp. 115-21.

Benevolent appreciation, asserting RF's lack of moral seriousness. See Hafley (below).

*24012 Hafley, James. "Ronald Firbank." ArQ, 12 (1956), 161-71.

Important definition of the "quality of high-seriousness" or "moral awareness" in RF's work, written in response to Forster (above).

24013 Harris, Alan. "Introduction." In THE NEW RYTHUM, AND OTHER PIECES. Pp. 9-17. See 13003.

Notes on RF's unpublished writings and on the illustrations included in THE NEW RYTHUM.

24014 Jones, Ernest. "Introduction." In RF's THREE NOVELS. Pp. vii-xx. See 13008.

RF's comic mask, romantic irony, and serious artistry (cf. Joyce and Woolf).

24015 Long, Richard A., and Iva G. Jones. "Towards a Definition of the 'Decadent Novel.'" CE, 22 (1961), 245-49.

Art versus life in various novelists (RF passim).

24016 McCormick, John. CATASTROPHE AND IMAGINATION. Pp. 298-300. See G3095.

RF's work a "dated and enervated" giggle at civilization.

24017 Powell, Anthony. "Preface." In THE COMPLETE RONALD FIRBANK. Pp. 5-16. See 13001.

Brief biographical summary and appreciation of the works.

24018 Pritchett, Victor S. "Firbank." In BOOKS IN GENERAL. London: Chatto and Windus, 1953. Pp. 229-34.

RF good fun in his "wild satires and fairy tales," but tiring in large doses.

24019 Stevenson, Lionel. THE HISTORY OF THE ENGLISH NOVEL. XI, 159-63. See G2212.

RF the "most effete" Edwardian exquisite, a novelist of both laborious craftsmanship and frivolity.

*24020 Tyler, Parker. "The Prince Zoubaroff: Praise of Ronald Firbank." PROSE, Nos. 1-2 (1970-71), pp. 135-52, 155-69.

Important, though frequently impressionistic critique of RF's prose style.

24021 Van Vechten, Carl. "Ronald Firbank." In EXCAVATIONS: A BOOK OF ADVOCACIES. New York: Knopf, 1926. Pp. 170-76.

Composite of three appreciative essays, placing RF in a _fin de siecle_ context. Absorbs Van Vechten's preface to PRANCING NIGGER (1924).

24022 Waley, Arthur. "Introduction." In THE WORKS OF RONALD FIRBANK. I, 1-11. See 13007.

RF "the first and almost the only Impressionist in English fiction." Summary of career.

*24023 Waugh, Evelyn. "Ronald Firbank." LIFE AND LETTERS, 2 (1929), 191-96.

RF's humor and exquisite technique. Important appreciation.

*24024 Wilson, Edmund. "A Revival of Ronald Firbank." 1949. In his CLASSICS AND COMMERCIALS. Pp. 486-502. See G2375.

RF "one of the finest English writers of his period and one of those most likely to become a classic." High praise for RF's densely textured art.

24025 Woodward, A.G. "Ronald Firbank." ESA, 11 (1968), 1-9.

RF's "toughness" and moral vision belied by his eccentric, "hot-house flower" reputation.

2.5 Studies of Individual Works

Brophy's biography (22004) and the critical studies by Brooke and Merritt (23001, 23005) offer substantial commentaries on the individual novels. For comments on one of RF's few works of nonfiction, see Benkovitz (24003).

THE ARTIFICIAL PRINCESS (1934)

25001 Kennard, Coleridge. "Introduction." In RF's THE ARTIFICIAL PRINCESS. Pp. vii-x. See 11001.

Describes briefly the history and eventual publication of the manuscript.

CONCERNING THE ECCENTRICITIES OF CARDINAL PIRELLI (1926)

25002 Davis, Robert M. "On Firbank." In his MODERN BRITISH SHORT NOVELS. Glenview, Ill.: Scott, Foresman, 1972. Pp. 153-58.

Brief commentary on RF and CARDINAL PIRELLI, with textual note and bibliographical checklist.

25003 Wilson, Edmund. "Firbank and Beckford." 1926. In his THE SHORES OF LIGHT. Pp. 264-66. See G2376.

Praise for CARDINAL PIRELLI, with a comparison to Beckford's VATHEK.

THE FLOWER BENEATH THE FOOT (1923)

25004 Irwin, W.R. THE GAME OF THE IMPOSSIBLE. Pp. 114-19 and passim. See G6417.

RF's use of fantasy style and the "impossible society" device in THE FLOWER BENEATH THE FOOT.

25005 Wilson, Edmund. "Late Violets from the Nineties." 1923. In his THE SHORES OF LIGHT. Pp. 68-72. See G2376.

Van Vechten and RF (FLOWER BENEATH THE FOOT) last survivors of the _fin de siecle_.

VAINGLORY (1915)

*25006 Davis, Robert M. "The Ego Triumphant in Firbank's VAINGLORY." PLL, 9 (1973), 281-96.

Close structural analysis of the novel's "meaningful pattern."

25007 ______. "The Text of Firbank's VAINGLORY." PBSA, 63 (1969), 36-41.

Egregious textual errors in THE COMPLETE RONALD FIRBANK reprinting of VAINGLORY (see 13001).

VALMOUTH (1919)

25008 Alford, Norman W. "Seven Notebooks of Ronald Firbank." LCUT, 8, No. 3 (1967), 33-39.

Describes, with some transcription and illustration, the mosaic-like VALMOUTH notebooks.

FORD MADOX FORD (1873-1939)

A note on Ford's name: In 1919 FMF officially changed his name from "Ford Madox Hueffer" to "Ford Madox Ford." For the purposes of this guide he will be referred to consistently as Ford or Ford Madox Ford with one exception: whenever the earlier form of his name has been used in a title, it will be retained.

1. PRIMARY BIBLIOGRAPHY

Abbreviations of titles used in this bibliography (if any) are noted at the end of the entry. Books available in recent paperback printing are denoted by "(P)."

1.1 Fiction

This section is divided into two parts: i. Novels and Story Collections, and ii. Collaborations. All works are novels unless otherwise noted.

i. NOVELS AND STORY COLLECTIONS (first collected publication)

11001 THE BENEFACTOR: A TALE OF A SMALL CIRCLE. London: Brown, Langham, 1905. No Amer. ed.

Disasters befall a talented but too altruistic young writer.

11002 A CALL: THE TALE OF TWO PASSIONS. London: Chatto and Windus, 1910. No Amer. ed.

Jamesian treatment of a love quadrangle (an "affair").

11003 AN ENGLISH GIRL: A ROMANCE. London: Methuen, 1907. No. Amer. ed.

Conflicts between money and morality, American and English values.

11004 THE FIFTH QUEEN: AND HOW SHE CAME TO COURT. London: Alston Rivers, 1906. New York: Vanguard, 1963.

First novel of the Tudor trilogy THE FIFTH QUEEN, concerning Katherine Howard, Henry VIII's fifth queen. See 13001.

11005 THE FIFTH QUEEN CROWNED: A ROMANCE. London: Nash, 1908. New York: Vanguard, 1963.

Third novel in the Tudor trilogy THE FIFTH QUEEN. See 13001.

11006 THE GOOD SOLDIER: A TALE OF PASSION. London and New York: Lane, 1915. (P). Abbreviated as GS.

Love quadrangle told with fascinating narrative complexity.

11007 THE "HALF MOON": A ROMANCE OF THE OLD WORLD AND THE NEW. London: Nash; New York: Doubleday, Page, 1909.

First and only novel of a proposed historical trilogy, set in early America.

11008 HENRY FOR HUGH: A NOVEL. Philadelphia and London: Lippincott, 1934.

Companion novel to THE RASH ACT (11023). A doppelganger tale set in the depression.

11009 LADIES WHOSE BRIGHT EYES: A ROMANCE. London: Constable, 1911. New York: Doubleday, Page, 1912. Rev. ed. Philadelphia and London: Lippincott, 1935.

Historical novel of medieval England.

11010 LAST POST. London: Duckworth; New York: Literary Guild of America, 1928. (P).

Final novel in Tietjens tetralogy PARADE'S END (13004). See SOME DO NOT, 11027.

11011 A LITTLE LESS THAN GODS: A ROMANCE. London: Duckworth; New York: Viking, 1928.

Historical novel of romance and intrigue, set in Napoleonic times.

11012 A MAN COULD STAND UP--A NOVEL. London: Duckworth; New York: Boni, 1926. (P).

Third novel in the Tietjens tetralogy PARADE'S END (13004). See SOME DO NOT, 11027.

11013 THE MARSDEN CASE: A ROMANCE. London: Duckworth, 1923. No Amer. ed.

FMF's first attempt to describe the personal, social, and cultural impact of the war.

11014 MR. APOLLO: A JUST POSSIBLE STORY. London: Methuen, 1908. No Amer. ed.

Serious fantasy of god's (Apollo's) trials in the modern world.

11015 MR. FLEIGHT. London: Latimer, 1913. No Amer. ed.

Extraordinarily scarce novel concerning politics and scandals.

11016 THE NEW HUMPTY-DUMPTY. London and New York: Lane, 1912.

Satire of international politics, published under the pseudonym Daniel Chaucer.

11017 NO ENEMY: A TALE OF RECONSTRUCTION. New York: Macaulay, 1929. No English ed.

Slightly fictionalized war experiences.

11018 NO MORE PARADES: A NOVEL. London: Duckworth; New York: Boni, 1925. (P).

Second novel in the Tietjens tetralogy PARADE'S END (13004). See SOME DO NOT, 11027.

11019 THE PANEL: A SHEER COMEDY. London: Constable, 1912. Rev. and expanded American ed. titled RING FOR NANCY: A SHEER COMEDY. Indianapolis: Bobbs-Merrill; New York: Grosset and Dunlap, 1913.

Comic novel in the style of, and parodying a devotee of Henry James.

11020 PARADE'S END. See 13004, below.

11021 THE PORTRAIT. London: Methuen, 1910. No Amer. ed.

Comic historical novel, set in the eighteenth century.

11022 PRIVY SEAL: HIS LAST VENTURE. London: Alston Rivers, 1907. New York: Vanguard, 1963.

Second novel of the Tudor trilogy THE FIFTH QUEEN. See 13001.

11023 THE RASH ACT: A NOVEL. London: Cape; New York: Long and Smith, 1933.

Earlier of the two companion novels on the doppelganger theme (see HENRY FOR HUGH, 11008).

11024 RING FOR NANCY. See THE PANEL (11019).

11025 THE SHIFTING OF THE FIRE. London: Unwin; New York: Putnam, 1892.

FMF's first novel. Concerns, as many of his works do, the trials of the gentleman of honor.

11026 THE SIMPLE LIFE LIMITED. London and New York: Lane, 1911.

Satire of socialism, published under the pseudonym Daniel Chaucer.

11027 SOME DO NOT . . ., A NOVEL. London: Duckworth; New York: Seltzer, 1924. (P).

First of the Tietjens tetralogy PARADE'S END (13004). The four novels develop the character of Christopher Tietjens, the "last English Tory," a gentleman of honor, who is faced with the postwar disintegration of his culture.

11028 VIVE LE ROY: A NOVEL. Philadelphia: Lippincott, 1936. London: Allen and Unwin, 1937.

Mystery novel, against the background of intrigue and revolution in present-day France.

11029 WHEN THE WICKED MAN. New York: Liveright, 1931. London: Cape, 1932.

Moral conflicts faced by an Englishman in charge of an American publishing house.

11030 THE YOUNG LOVELL: A ROMANCE. London: Chatto and Windus, 1913. No Amer. ed.

Romantic historical novel of medieval England.

11031 ZEPPELIN NIGHTS: A LONDON ENTERTAINMENT. [Stories]. London and New York: Lane, 1915.

DECAMERON-style story collection, written in slight collaboration with Violet Hunt. The stories are probably all by FMF, the bridge passages largely by Hunt.

ii. COLLABORATIONS

11032 THE INHERITORS: AN EXTRAVAGANT STORY (with Joseph Conrad). London: Heinemann; New York: McClure, Phillips, 1901.

First collaboration with Conrad.

11033 THE NATURE OF A CRIME (with Joseph Conrad). London: Duckworth; Garden City, N.Y.: Doubleday, Page, 1924.

Short novel originally published serially in 1909.

11034 ROMANCE: A NOVEL (with Joseph Conrad). London: Smith, Elder, 1903. New York: McClure, Phillips, 1904.

The most important (and successful) of their novel collaborations.

1.2 Miscellaneous Writings

Of FMF's "Miscellaneous Writings" special note is made here of his literary criticism, his memoirs (arguably some of his finest work), and his periodical editorships. Harvey's bibliography (21003) should be consulted for information on FMF's numerous other publications, ranging from fairy tales and war propaganda to sociological "impressions" of England, Germany, France, and America. Harvey also lists nearly five hundred contributions by FMF to books by others and to periodicals, of which only the most significant have been noted here.

12001 ANCIENT LIGHTS AND CERTAIN NEW REFLECTIONS: BEING THE MEMORIES OF A YOUNG MAN. London: Chapman and Hall, 1911. Published as MEMORIES AND IMPRESSIONS: A STUDY IN ATMOSPHERES. New York: Harper, 1911.

Memories and criticisms, chiefly of the Pre-Raphaelites.

12002 THE CRITICAL ATTITUDE. London: Duckworth, 1911. No Amer. ed.

Essays in literary criticism collected from the ENGLISH REVIEW. See 12004.

12003 THE ENGLISH NOVEL: FROM THE EARLIEST DAYS TO THE DEATH OF JOSEPH CONRAD. Philadelphia: Lippincott, 1929. London: Constable, 1930.

Critical history, intended for college students. The English edition adds a preface.

12004 THE ENGLISH REVIEW. London, 1908-9.

Influential literary periodical established by FMF, and edited by him for its first year. (The REVIEW afterwards languished under other hands.) The REVIEW published several of the most prominent Edwardians (including Conrad, Galsworthy, Wells) and is credited with the "discovery" of Norman Douglas, D.H. Lawrence, and Wyndham Lewis. Its impact on the avant-garde literary movements is noted by Wees (see 24043).

12005 FORD MADOX BROWN: A RECORD OF HIS LIFE AND WORK. London and New York: Longmans, 1896.

Biography of FMF's grandfather (and guardian), the Pre-Raphaelite painter.

12006 HANS HOLBEIN, THE YOUNGER: A CRITICAL MONOGRAPH. London: Duckworth; New York: Dutton, 1905.

Biography and art criticism.

12007 HENRY JAMES: A CRITICAL STUDY. London: Secker, 1913. New York: Boni, 1915.

The "Subjects," "Temperaments," and "Methods" of the "greatest of living writers."

12008 "Introduction." In Ernest Hemingway's A FAREWELL TO ARMS. New York: Modern Library, 1932. Pp. ix-xx.

FMF and Hemingway in Paris.

12009 "Introduction." In Joseph Conrad's THE SISTERS. New York: Crosby, Gaige, 1928. Pp. 1-16.

Speculative discussion of Conrad's novel fragment.

12010 "Introduction." In TRANSATLANTIC STORIES. Ed. Ford. London: Duckworth; New York: Dial, 1926. Pp. vii-xxxi.

Introduction to collection of stories originally published in the TRANSATLANTIC REVIEW. Includes Djuna Barnes, Dos Passos, Hemingway, and Dorothy Richardson. See 12022.

12011 IT WAS THE NIGHTINGALE. Philadelphia: Lippincott, 1933. London: Heinemann, 1934.

Memoirs, 1918-33.

12012 JOSEPH CONRAD: A PERSONAL REMEMBRANCE. London: Duckworth; Boston: Little, Brown, 1924.

An unreliable, but "impressionistically" valid account of FMF's and Conrad's literary and personal relationships.

12013 THE MARCH OF LITERATURE: FROM CONFUCIUS' DAY TO OUR OWN. New York: Dial Press, 1938. Published as THE MARCH OF LITERATURE: FROM CONFUCIUS TO MODERN TIMES. London: Allen and Unwin, 1939.

FMF's last complete work--a sadly neglected critical survey.

12014 MEMORIES AND IMPRESSIONS. See ANCIENT LIGHTS (12001).

12015 MIGHTIER THAN THE SWORD. See PORTRAITS FROM LIFE, below.

12016 PORTRAITS FROM LIFE. Boston: Houghton Mifflin, 1937. Published as MIGHTIER THAN THE SWORD: MEMORIES AND CRITICISMS. London: Allen and Unwin, 1938.

Includes memoirs of Conrad, Galsworthy, Lawrence, and Wells, among others.

12017 THE PRE-RAPHAELITE BROTHERHOOD: A CRITICAL MONOGRAPH. London: Duckworth; New York: Dutton, 1907.

Art criticism.

12018 RETURN TO YESTERDAY. London: Gollancz, 1931. New York: Liveright, 1932. Original English title: REMINISCENCES 1894-1914: RETURN TO YESTERDAY (1931). (P).

Memories and criticisms.

12019 "Rive Gauche." In Jean Rhys's THE LEFT BANK & OTHER STORIES. New York and London: Harper, 1927. Pp. 7-27.

Memoir and introduction.

12020 ROSSETTI: A CRITICAL ESSAY ON HIS ART. London: Duckworth; New York: Dutton, 1902.

Biography and art criticism.

12021 THUS TO REVISIT: SOME REMINISCENCES. London: Chapman and Hall; New York: Dutton, 1921.

Memories and criticisms. Includes Conrad, James, Pound, the imagists, and others.

12022 THE TRANSATLANTIC REVIEW. Paris, 1924.

This ambitious literary magazine was founded and edited by FMF, at the insistence of Ezra Pound. Although short-lived, several of the "lost generation" of Americans were published here, as well as the earliest portions of Joyce's FINNEGANS WAKE and contributions by FMF himself.

12023 "ULYSSES and the Handling of Indecencies." ENGLISH REVIEW, 35 (1922), 538-48.

FMF's ambivalent response to Joyce.

12024 WOMEN AND MEN. Paris: Three Mountains Press, 1923.

Reprinted essays on "undistinguished people."

1.3 Collected and Selected Works

13001 THE BODLEY HEAD FORD MADOX FORD. 5 vols. London: Bodley Head, 1962-63, 1971.

A useful selection of FMF's major works edited by Graham Greene (vols. 1-4) and Michael Killigrew (vol. 5; see YOUR MIRROR TO MY TIMES, 13006). Contents: vol. 1, THE GOOD SOLDIER (1915) and "Selected Memories"; vol. 2, THE FIFTH QUEEN TRILOGY: THE FIFTH QUEEN (1906), PRIVY SEAL (1907), THE FIFTH QUEEN CROWNED (1908); vols. 3-4, PARADE'S END: SOME DO NOT (1924), NO MORE PARADES (1925), A MAN COULD STAND UP (1926) [note LAST POST omitted]; vol. 5, MEMORIES AND IMPRESSIONS (1911). Also see 13004 and 24016.

13002 COLLECTED POEMS. New York: Oxford Univ. Press, 1936.

FMF achieved some distinction as a poet, especially in the teens and early twenties.

13003 THE CRITICAL WRITINGS OF FORD MADOX FORD. Ed. Frank MacShane. Lincoln: Univ. of Nebraska Press, 1964. (P).

Collects FMF's major critical statements under a variety of headings: "The Traditions of the Novel," "Impressionism and Fiction," "Novelists and Novels," "Impressionism and Poetry," and "A Summary Statement." See 25074.

13004 PARADE'S END. New York: Knopf, 1950. (P). Abberviated as PE.

First collected publication of the Tietjens tetralogy: SOME DO NOT (1924), NO MORE PARADES (1925), A MAN COULD STAND UP (1926), and LAST POST (1928). Most FMF critics consider the four novels as a whole, although Graham Greene has argued for the removal of LAST POST. See THE BODLEY HEAD FORD MADOX FORD above and 24016. Also see 25055 and 25061.

13005 SELECTED POEMS. Ed. Basil Bunting. Cambridge, Mass.: Pym-Randall Press, 1971.

Includes additional poems not found in the 1936 collected edition.

13006 YOUR MIRROR TO MY TIMES: THE SELECTED AUTOBIOGRAPHIES AND IMPRESSIONS OF FORD MADOX FORD. Ed. Michael Killigrew. New York: Holt, 1971. Published in England as vol. 5 of THE BODLEY HEAD FORD MADOX FORD (13001).

Selects and arranges a wealth of material from the memoirs, criticism, and travel works. See 25071.

1.4 Letters

Also see Hynes (25050), Karl (24026), and MacShane (21005).

14001 THE LETTERS OF FORD MADOX FORD. Ed. Richard M. Ludwig. Princeton, N.J.: Princeton Univ. Press, 1965.

Includes brief editorial commentaries.

2. SECONDARY BIBLIOGRAPHY

2.1 Bibliographies

An annotated bibliography of FMF studies is presently in preparation. The volume will be a companion to the several "Annotated Secondary Bibliographies" already published by Northern Illinois University Press (general editor Helmut Gerber). For information on its availability, check a recent issue of ELT.

*21001 Beebe, Maurice, and Robert G. Johnson, comps. "Criticism of Ford Madox Ford: A Selected Checklist." MFS, 9 (1963), 94-100.

Good first stop for FMF bibliography, though now somewhat dated. Includes separate checklists for GS and PE. See 23012.

21002 Gerber, Helmut, et al., eds. "Ford Madox Ford: An Annotated Checklist of Writings About Him." EFT [now ELT], 1, No. 2 (1958), 2-19 and continuing.

Brief abstracts of studies, appearing irregularly. See G1404.

*21003 Harvey, David Dow, ed. FORD MADOX FORD, 1873-1939: A BIBLIOGRAPHY OF WORKS AND CRITICISM. Princeton, N.J.: Princeton Univ. Press, 1962.

An excellent and indispensible listing of FMF's books (with full bibliographical data), his contributions to books, his manuscripts, and his contributions to periodicals. The secondary section, which gathers articles and books mentioning FMF, includes brief extracts from the studies, though it avoids evaluative commentary. Most sections arranged chronologically.

21004 MacShane, Frank. "Introduction." FORD MADOX FORD: THE CRITICAL HERITAGE. Ed. MacShane. Pp. 1-16. See 23010.

Excellent summary of FMF's critical reputation.

21005 ______, comp. "Ford Madox Ford: Collections of His Letters, Collections of His Manuscripts, Periodical Publications by Him, His Introductions, Prefaces and Miscellaneous Contributions to Books by Others." EFT [now ELT], 4, No. 2 (1961), 11-18.

Much of this information has been superseded and supplemented by Harvey (21003, above).

21006 Naumburg, Edward, Jr., comp. "A Catalogue of a Ford Madox Ford Collection." PULC, 9 (1948), 134-65.

An extensive list of FMF first editions, now replaced by Harvey (see 21003). Also, see 23015.

21007 Wiley, Paul L., comp. "Ford Madox Ford (1873-1939)." In THE BRITISH NOVEL. Comp. Wiley. Pp. 37-40. See G1419.

Brief primary and secondary checklist.

2.2 Biographies, Memoirs, Reminiscences

Although FMF's will stipulated that there be no biography, his varied career as novelist, collaborator, editor, teacher, and memoirist himself, in England, France, and America, has prompted an enormous memoir-literature. The following entries are a generous (but far from complete) sampling of this biographical material. FMF's own reminiscences should also be examined (especially 12001, 12011, 12012, 12016, 12018, and 12021).

22001 Aldington, Richard. LIFE FOR LIFE'S SAKE: A BOOK OF REMINISCENCES. New York: Viking, 1941. Pp. 149-59.

Sympathetic recollections of FMF and Hunt in the early years of their liaison.

22002 Baines, Jocelyn. JOSEPH CONRAD: A CRITICAL BIOGRAPHY. London: Weidenfeld and Nicolson, 1959. Passim.

Excellent, balanced account of the Conrad-Ford friendship and collaboration.

*22003 Bowen, Stella. DRAWN FROM LIFE: REMINISCENCES. London: Collins, 1941.

Memoirs of FMF during the twenties by his mistress. On the whole a sympathetic portrait.

22004 Bradbury, Malcolm. "THE ENGLISH REVIEW." LONDON MAGAZINE, 5 (Aug. 1958), 46-57.

Favorable assessment of FMF's editorship.

22005 Chambers, Jessie [Wood]. "Debut." In D.H. LAWRENCE: A PERSONAL RECORD BY E.T. 1935. Ed. J.D. Chambers. 2nd ed. New York: Barnes and Noble, 1965. Pp. 155-77.

The Lawrence-Ford meeting and relationship recounted by the original of Miriam in SONS AND LOVERS.

22006 Conrad, Jessie. JOSEPH CONRAD AND HIS CIRCLE. New York: Dutton, 1935. Passim.

Rather hostile reminiscences of Conrad's relationship with FMF.

22007 _____. JOSEPH CONRAD AS I KNEW HIM. Garden City, N.Y.: Doubleday, Page, 1926. Passim.

More of Mrs. Conrad's anecdotes of the Conrad-Ford friendship.

22008 Ellmann, Richard. JAMES JOYCE. New York: Oxford Univ. Press, 1959. Passim.

Joyce's contacts with FMF and the TRANSATLANTIC REVIEW during the Paris years.

22009 Garnett, David. THE GOLDEN ECHO. New York: Harcourt, 1954. Passim.

Garnett's humorous and pathetic encounters with FMF, from childhood on.

22010 Goldring, Douglas. THE LAST PRE-RAPHAELITE: THE LIFE AND WRITINGS OF FORD MADOX FORD. London: Macdonald, 1948. Amer. title: TRAINED FOR GENIUS: THE LIFE AND WRITINGS OF FORD MADOX FORD. New York: Dutton, 1949.

Largely anecdotal biography by an outspoken admirer, drawn from personal acquaintance with FMF and from the memoirs of Bowen and Hunt. Goldring concentrates on FMF's English and Parisian years, but does not attempt more than a brief survey of the later life in America. Supplements but does not incorporate his memoir, SOUTH LODGE (below).

*22011 _____. SOUTH LODGE: REMINISCENCES OF VIOLET HUNT, FORD MADOX FORD, AND THE "ENGLISH REVIEW" CIRCLE. London: Constable, 1943.

A sympathetic portrait of FMF and Hunt, an account of the various scandals and controversies about them, and a memoir of the ENGLISH REVIEW years. Goldring previously published a substantial amount of this material in other formats.

22012 Gorman, Herbert S. "Ford Madox Ford: A Portrait in Impressions." BOOKMAN (New York), 67 (1928), 56-60.

Lively account of FMF in Paris. Reprinted in 23010.

22013 _____. "Ford Madox Ford: The Personal Side." PULC, 9 (1948), 119-22.

FMF in Paris during the twenties. See 23015.

22014 Harris, Markham. "A Memory of Ford Madox Ford." PrS, 19 (1955), 252-63.

FMF and the TRANSATLANTIC REVIEW.

22015 Huddleston, Sisley. PARIS SALONS, CAFES, STUDIOS. Philadelphia: Lippincott, 1928. Pp. 116-21, 219.

FMF and Joyce among others in Paris.

*22016 Hunt, Violet. THE FLURRIED YEARS. London: Hurst and Blackett, 1926. Rev. Amer. ed. published as I HAVE THIS TO SAY: THE STORY OF MY FLURRIED YEARS. New York: Boni and Liveright, 1926.

Memoir of her relationship with FMF (1908-15) and the ENGLISH REVIEW circle generally.

22017 McAlmon, Robert. BEING GENIUSES TOGETHER: 1920-1930. 1938. Rev. ed. Garden City, N.Y.: Doubleday, 1968. Passim.

Reminiscences of FMF in Paris during the twenties.

22018 Macauley, Robie. "The Dean in Exile: Notes on Ford Madox Ford as Teacher." SHENADOAH, 4 (1953), 43-48.

By a former student at Olivet college.

*22019 MacShane, Frank. THE LIFE AND WORK OF FORD MADOX FORD. New York: Horizon, 1965.

The standard biography of FMF. MacShane has not attempted a definitive biography. (Goldring should be consulted for supplemental information.) Although private papers were withdrawn from him, he has managed, nonetheless, to present a "coherent account of Ford's career as a literary figure and to discuss, in this context, his development as an artist and thinker." MacShane's criticism of the major works also deserves close attention.

22020 Marshall, Archibald. OUT AND ABOUT. London: Murray, 1933. Passim.

One of FMF's former publishers attacks him for willful distortion in his reminiscences.

22021 Mizener, Arthur. "The Lost Papers of Violet Hunt." CLJ, 3 (1967), 1-6.

Describes the recently acquired Hunt correspondence collection at Cornell (materials used by Mizener in his biography).

22022 _____. THE SADDEST STORY: A BIOGRAPHY OF FORD MADOX FORD. New York: World, 1971.

Biography of FMF which is more impressive for its size than for its portrait of the novelist. Mizener's book is handicapped by its essentially unsympathetic view of its subject. Moreover, little of substance is added to the story of FMF found in MacShane's earlier biography. Mizener does provide a very helpful appendix-discussion of FMF's lesser-known novels.

22023 Moore, Harry T. THE PRIEST OF LOVE: A LIFE OF D.H. LAWRENCE. Rev. ed. New York: Farrar, Straus and Giroux, 1974. Pp. 105-10 and passim.

The Ford-Lawrence relationship.

22024 Moser, Thomas. "From Olive Garnett's Diary: Impressions of Ford Madox Ford and His Friends, 1890-1906." TSLL, 16 (1974), 511-33.

22025 Naumburg, Edward, Jr. "A Collector Looks at Ford Madox Ford." PULC, 9 (1948), 105-18.

Memoir. See 23015.

*22026 Poli, Bernard J. FORD MADOX FORD AND THE "TRANSATLANTIC REVIEW." Syracuse, N.Y.: Syracuse Univ. Press, 1967.

Fine account of FMF's unsuccessful attempt to edit a "little magazine" for a large, international audience. Despite its publication of significant writings by the American "exiles" in Paris, as well as by Joyce and FMF himself, the TRANSATLANTIC REVIEW (1924) failed to satisfy either the avant-garde or the traditional readers.

22027 Price, Lawrence M. "Ford Madox Ford." UNIVERSITY OF CALIFORNIA CHRONICLE, 27 (1925), 346-65.

Describes visits with FMF.

22028 Putnam, Samuel. "The 'Dean of English Novelists' (Ford Madox Ford)." In PARIS WAS OUR MISTRESS: MEMOIRS OF A LOST & FOUND GENERATION. New York: Viking, 1947. Pp. 118-27.

FMF in the twenties.

22029 Schneidau, Herbert N. EZRA POUND: THE IMAGE AND THE REAL. Baton Rouge: Louisiana State Univ. Press, 1969. Passim.

FMF's and Pound's literary and personal relationships.

22030 Scott-James, Rolfe A. "Ford Madox Ford When He Was Hueffer." SAQ, 57 (1958), 236-53.

Reminiscences by an acquaintance of FMF and a fellow editor of literary periodicals.

22031 Soskice, Juliet. CHAPTERS FROM CHILDHOOD. New York: Harcourt, 1922. Passim.

Slight memories of FMF by his sister.

22032 Webb, Max. "Ford Madox Ford and the Baton Rouge Writers' Conference." SoR, 10 (1974), 892-903.

FMF's "ultimately beneficial" relationships with southern American writers, including Gordon, Tate, and Warren.

2.3 Book-Length Critical Studies and Essay Collections

23001 Andreach, Robert J. THE SLAIN AND THE RESURRECTED GOD: CONRAD, FORD, AND THE CHRISTIAN MYTH. New York: New York Univ. Press, 1970.

An archetypal analysis of Conrad's and FMF's use of the religious "quest" and the Beatrix-figure as divine "mediatrix." FMF moves from the parody of myth in his early fiction (e.g., THE INHERITORS) to an affirmative revitalization of the archetypes in his later works (especially GS and PE). Overly systematic readings.

*23002 Cassell, Richard A. FORD MADOX FORD: A STUDY OF HIS NOVELS. Baltimore: Johns Hopkins Univ. Press, 1962.

One of the two best comprehensive studies of FMF's fiction (with Wiley). Cassell's excellent readings of GS and PE are supported by his pioneering examination of the developing technical methods and major themes of the lesser fiction. The early chapters survey FMF's biography, theories of art and fiction, and the early work. Separate chapters on GS, PE, and "Last Novels" conclude the book. Cassell's criticisms and evaluations are admirably judicious throughout.

*23003 _____, ed. FORD MADOX FORD: MODERN JUDGEMENTS. London: Macmillan, 1972.

Superb collection of twelve essays and a poem on FMF (by W.C. Williams), most previously published. Cassell's introduction is an excellent survey of FMF's reputation. Includes 24012, 24035, 24047, 25002, 25016, 25030, 25046, 25059, 25062, 25070; and extracts from the following books: 23009 and 23011.

23004 Gordon, Ambrose, Jr. THE INVISIBLE TENT: THE WAR NOVELS OF FORD MADOX FORD. Austin: Univ. of Texas Press, 1964.

An exercise in critical analysis which limits itself to FMF's seven "war" novels: NO ENEMY, THE MARSDEN CASE, GS, and the PE tetralogy. Separate chapters stress the scenic and pictoral qualities (FMF's impressionism) and the technical complexities of the works, as well as their French heritage and fairy tale elements. Gordon's eclectic approach leads to many fine individual insights, but also to an overall diffuseness in his study. Extract originally appeared in 23012.

23005 Gordon, Caroline. A GOOD SOLDIER: A KEY TO THE NOVELS OF FORD MADOX FORD. Davis: Univ. of California Library, Davis, 1963.

The archetypal woman-goddess and the passive hero in FMF's fiction. A lecture-pamphlet, with brief bibliography, compiled by H. Gerber. Reprinted in 23010.

23006 Hoffmann, Charles G. FORD MADOX FORD. New York: Twayne, 1967.

Valuable general survey, although limited to FMF's fiction. Hoffmann devotes an opening essay to the analysis of the techniques, themes, and characters of the impressionistic Conrad collaborations, which he follows with individual chapters on the early novels, GS, PE, and the late novels.

Hoffmann finds patterns of development in the early writings, culminating in the master works. The last novels are neither an advance, nor a decline, but a continuation of the early fiction. Only GS and PE are discussed in detail.

*23007 Huntley, H. Robert. THE ALIEN PROTAGONIST OF FORD MADOX FORD. Chapel Hill: Univ. of North Carolina Press, 1970.

Behind FMF's fiction lies the deterministic assumption that Western man is in the last phase of a four-fold historical cycle of achievement and decline. This version of reverse evolution was derived by FMF from his later-nineteenth century Hegelian/Darwinian heritage. To emphasize this larger process, FMF characteristically depicts his heroes/heroines as alienated figures, supportive of values in conflict with their age. Huntley draws impressively from the fiction and nonfiction to document FMF's views and support his thesis, although his study generally concentrates on the early fiction (through GS).

23008 Leer, Norman. THE LIMITED HERO IN THE NOVELS OF FORD MADOX FORD. East Lansing: Michigan State Univ. Press, 1966.

A specialized study of FMF's use and modification of the hero/heroine figure in his fiction. FMF is seen developing from an emphasis on the ineffectuality of heroism in his early fiction (especially the satires and historical fiction), to a recognition of the distinction between public and private heroism, between the epical hero and the limited hero (e.g., GS). PE shows the movement toward the ideal of limited heroism which persists into the late works.

23009 Lid, R.W. FORD MADOX FORD: THE ESSENCE OF HIS ART. Berkeley and Los Angeles: Univ. of California Press, 1964.

FMF's "essence" is found in GS and PE. Lid's opening two chapters are a biographical summary and a survey of the early fiction. Several chapters are devoted to close thematic and technical analyses of GS and the Tietjens tetralogy. Lid is best in his discussion of FMF's narrative strategies. Extract reprinted in 23003.

*23010 MacShane, Frank, ed. FORD MADOX FORD: THE CRITICAL HERITAGE. London: Routledge, 1972.

Impressive and useful collection of reviews, criticisms, and general assessments of FMF and his work by his contemporaries. MacShane's introduction (21004) is an excellent survey of FMF's reputation. Includes 22012, 23005, 23013 (extracts), 24012, 24015, 24019, 24035, 24047 (extracts), and 25062.

*23011 Meixner, John A. FORD MADOX FORD'S NOVELS: A CRITICAL STUDY. Minneapolis: Univ. of Minnesota Press, 1962.

A comprehensive and often incisive critical study of FMF's fiction. Meixner opens his book with a valuable survey of FMF's ideals and intentions for the novel. The balance of the volume divides the work into groups for critical analysis: historical novels, social satires, the novels of "small circles" (including GS), the expansive social novels (including PE), and the unsatisfactory late works. Extract reprinted in 23003.

23012 MODERN FICTION STUDIES, 9 (1963), 3-100. "Ford Madox Ford Number." Includes "THE GOOD SOLDIER: A Symposium," pp. 39-93.

Seven critical articles, a survey of FMF's reputation, and a general checklist of FMF studies. Includes 21001, 23004 (extract), 24017, 24023, 25007, 25024, 25029, 25038, and 25046.

23013 NEW DIRECTIONS: NUMBER SEVEN. "Homage to Ford Madox Ford--A Symposium." Norfolk, Conn.: New Directions, 1942. Pp. 443-94.

Memoirs, appreciations, and criticisms of FMF (some reprinted), plus a checklist of his work. Twenty-four items in all. Now rather dated and not generally accessible. Includes reprint of 24019. Extracts reprinted in 23010.

*23014 Ohmann, Carol. FORD MADOX FORD: FROM APPRENTICE TO CRAFTSMAN. Middletown, Conn.: Wesleyan Univ. Press, 1964.

Traces FMF's "slow and difficult moral and psychological discovery" in the early fiction culminating in the masterly achievements of GS and PE. The later novels are seen as the sentimentalized restatements of the ethical values most fully articulated in the five masterworks (over half of Ohmann's study is devoted to GS and the tetralogy). While GS elliptically presents FMF's individual value system through his ironic narrative perspective, PE reflects his larger (and somewhat less successful) efforts to record and to evaluate the life and moral values of his times. Excellent readings.

23015 PRINCETON UNIVERSITY LIBRARY CHRONICLE, 9 (1948), 105-65. "Ford Madox Ford Symposium."

Collects two memoirs, two critical essays, and a brief primary bibliography. Includes 21006, 22013, 22025, 24007, and 25030.

*23016 Smith, Grover. FORD MADOX FORD. New York: Columbia Univ. Press, 1972.

An excellent brief survey of FMF's life, work (chiefly GS), and character. On this last subject, Smith presents an objective portrait of FMF as an impressionist with facts (such as his memoirs), as well as with his fiction, whose intention was to reveal the "truth au fond, the meaning hidden under appearances."

23017 Stang, Sondra J. FORD MADOX FORD. New York: Ungar, 1977.

A "Modern Literature Monograph." (Not seen.)

*23018 Wiley, Paul L. NOVELIST OF THREE WORLDS: FORD MADOX FORD. Syracuse, N.Y.: Syracuse Univ. Press, 1962.

One of the two best comprehensive studies of FMF's fiction (with Cassell). Wiley sees FMF's progressive formal development culminating in his perfection in GS of his "formula" for recording contemporary experience, the "Affair." Wiley's consideration of FMF's total output includes the most enthusiastic and penetrating discussions of the historical fiction and the most favorable assessment of the last novels. Fine chapters on the Conrad collaboration and FMF's impressionism enhance the already considerable value of Wiley's study.

23019 Young, Kenneth. FORD MADOX FORD. 1956. 2nd ed. London: Longmans, 1970.

Brief introduction to FMF's biography and his fiction, stressing the Tudor novels, GS and PE. Slight bibliography.

2.4 General Critical Articles, or Chapters on FMF

24001 Allen, Walter. THE ENGLISH NOVEL. Pp. 364-66, 394-99. See G2201.

FMF's and Conrad's impressionism, and a brief discussion of GS and PE.

24002 ______. THE MODERN NOVEL. Pp. 33-36. See G2202.

Abbreviated version of above critique. GS "formally perfect," but PE weakened by the unconvincing goodness of Tietjens.

24003 Beach, Joseph Warren. THE TWENTIETH CENTURY NOVEL. Passim. See G3004.

FMF, Conrad, and modern fictional techniques. FMF generally slighted.

24004 Bender, Todd K. "Fictional Time and the Problem of Free Will." WISCONSIN STUDIES IN LITERATURE, No. 5 (1968), pp. 12-22.

Bergsonian time and the literary impressionism of Conrad and FMF.

24005 Bergonzi, Bernard. HEROES' TWILIGHT. Pp. 175-82 and passim. See G2308.

FMF's reflection of his war experience, from his patriotic poems to his equivocal views in PE.

24006 _____. "The Reputation of Ford Madox Ford." In his THE TURN OF THE CENTURY. Pp. 139-46. See G2309.

The highs and lows of FMF's English reputation.

*24007 Blackmur, R.P. "The King over the Water: Notes on the Novels of F.M. Hueffer." PULC, 9 (1948), 123-27.

As FMF's characters are devoted to causes "known to be lost," so also is FMF a facile technician, devoted to the lost cause of Jamesian art fiction. See 23015.

*24008 Borowitz, Helen O. "The Paint beneath the Prose: Ford Madox Ford's Pre-Raphaelite Ancestry." MFS, 21 (1975), 483-98.

FMF's inheritances from his Pre-Raphaelite associations (particularly his grandfather, Ford Madox Brown), and the enduring influence of the visual arts on his fictional techniques.

24009 Bradbury, Malcolm. POSSIBILITIES. Pp. 133-39. See G3012.

FMF's transmission of the techniques of modernism to the second generation of twentieth-century novelists.

24010 Braybrooke, Neville. "The Walrus and the Windmill: A Study of Ford Madox Ford." SR, 74 (1966), 810-31.

FMF's Roman Catholic perspective. Essentially the same article has also appeared in MONTH and DUBLIN MAGAZINE.

24011 Cassell, Richard A. "Images of Collapse and Reconstruction: Ford's Vision of Society." ELT, 19 (1976), 265-82.

FMF's views of the world's situation while writing GS and PE.

24012 Crankshaw, Edward. "Ford Madox Ford." NATIONAL REVIEW, 131 (1948), 160-67.

Review article and general estimate. Some valuable commentary on the novels. Reprinted in 23003 and 23010.

24013 Esslinger, Pat M. "A Theory and Three Experiments: The Failure of the Conrad-Ford Collaboration." WHR, 22 (1968), 59-67.

FMF and Conrad lacked an effective theory of collaboration.

24014 Gill, Richard. HAPPY RURAL SEAT. Pp. 98-100, 126-32, and passim. See G2330.

The country house as symbol in FMF.

24015 Greene, Graham. "Ford Madox Ford." 1939. In THE LOST CHILDHOOD, AND OTHER ESSAYS. New York: Viking, 1951. Pp. 89-91.

Obituary tribute. Reprinted in 23010.

*24016 _____. "Introduction." In THE BODLEY HEAD FORD MADOX FORD, I, 7-12; III, 5-8. See 13001.

Introductions to FMF's GS, historical fiction and memoirs, and to his PE, respectively. Latter essay defends the omission of LAST POST from the tetralogy. See Griffith, 25046, and Kashner, 25051, below.

*24017 Harvey, David Dow. "Pro Patria Mori: The Neglect of Ford's Novels in England." MFS, 9 (1963), 3-16.

FMF's neglect attributable to the amount and variety of his works, as well as to a vituperative campaign by a group of adversary critics (documented). See 23012.

24018 Herndon, Richard. "The Genesis of Conrad's 'Amy Foster.'" SP, 57 (1960), 549-66.

Emphasizes FMF's role in the story's genesis.

24019 Hicks, Granville. "Ford Madox Ford--A Neglected Contemporary." BOOKMAN (New York), 72 (1930), 364-70.

Argues for a revaluation of FMF as an outstanding psychological and impressionistic novelist. Reprinted in 23010 and 23013.

24020 Homberger, Eric. "Pound, Ford and 'Prose': The Making of a Modern Poet." JAmS, 5 (1971), 281-92.

Role of FMF in Pound's poetic development, 1910-14.

24021 Howarth, Herbert. "Hewlett and Ford among Renaissance Women." JML, 5 (1976), 79-88.

FMF's modern approach to the historical "romance" (i.e., a movement toward historical "realism"), in the FIFTH QUEEN TRILOGY (cf. Hewlett's THE QUEEN'S CHAIR [1904]).

24022 Huntley, H. Robert. "Flaubert and Ford: The Fallacy of '_Le Mot Juste_.'" ELN, 4 (1967), 283-87.

The influence of, and FMF's borrowings from, Flaubert.

24023 Hynes, Samuel. "Ford and the Spirit of Romance." In his EDWARDIAN OCCASIONS. Pp. 71-79. See G2345.

Elements of the "romancing memory" in FMF's fiction (distinguishes between "romances" and "novels"). Reprinted from 23012.

*24024 _____. "Ford Madox Ford--The Conscious Artist." In his EDWARDIAN OCCASIONS. Pp. 62-70. See G2345.

The two phases of FMF's career: as conscious artist (to World War I) and as alien wanderer (after the war).

24025 Jones, A.R. "Notes toward a History of Imagism: An Examination of Literary Sources." SAQ, 60 (1961), 262-85.

Touches on FMF's role, and his misrepresentation of his role, in the evolution of the imagist movement (see 24032).

*24026 Karl, Frederick R. "Conrad, Ford, and the Novel." MIDWAY, 10 No. 2 (1969), 17-34.

Analysis of their relationship and motives for collaboration, based on their correspondence.

24027 _____. A READER'S GUIDE TO JOSEPH CONRAD. 1960. Rev. ed. New York: Noonday, 1969. Passim.

Especially insightful comments on FMF's role in the development of Conrad's literary theories.

24028 Kenner, Hugh. THE POETRY OF EZRA POUND. Norfolk, Conn.: New Directions, 1951. Pp. 264-72 and passim.

The relations between the imagists and the impressionists, such as FMF.

*24029 Ludwig, Richard M. "The Reputation of Ford Madox Ford." PMLA, 76 (1961), 544-51.

Unbiased attempt to see the various facets of FMF's personality "whole" (as editor, Pre-Raphaelite, artist, and English country gentleman).

*24030 Macauley, Robie. "The Good Ford." KR, 11 (1949), 269-88.

FMF's technical mastery most evident in GS and PE tetralogy. This essay was largely responsible for the revival in FMF's reputation in the fifties.

*24031 MacShane, Frank. "A Conscious Craftsman: Ford Madox Ford's Manuscript Revisions." BUSE, 5 (1961), 178-84.

Analysis of FMF's careful craftsmanship, chiefly concerned with SOME DO NOT and PROFESSOR'S PROGRESS (unfinished novel).

24032 ______. "'To Establish the Facts': A Communication on Mr. A.R. Jones and Ford Madox Ford." SAQ, 61 (1962), 260-65.

Attacks A.R. Jones (see 24025) for his distorted emphasis upon T.E. Hulme's role in the evolution of the imagist movement, at the expense of FMF.

*24033 Meixner, John A. "Ford and Conrad." CONRADIANA, 6 (1974), 157-69.

Asserts FMF's influence on Conrad and defends FMF's versions of his relationship with Conrad as essentially trustworthy. FMF has "been done a serious injustice by people of the Conrad persuasion."

24034 Mendilow, A.A. TIME AND THE NOVEL. Passim. See G4063.

FMF an important innovator with time.

24035 Pound, Ezra. "Ford Madox Ford; Obit." NINETEENTH CENTURY AND AFTER, 126 (1939), 178-81.

Tribute to FMF's artistic integrity. Reprinted in 23003 and 23010.

24036 Price, Lawrence M. "Ford Madox Hueffer." POET LORE, 31 (1920), 432-53.

General critique of FMF's work to 1920. Praises the poetry and historical fiction particularly.

24037 Ray, Paul C. THE SURREALIST MOVEMENT IN ENGLAND. Pp. 68-70. See G2356.

FMF's connection with French surrealists through the TRANSATLANTIC REVIEW.

24038 Solomon, Eric. STEPHEN CRANE IN ENGLAND: A PORTRAIT OF THE ARTIST. Columbus: Ohio State Univ. Press, 1964. Pp. 51-65 and passim.

Crane's relations with FMF and Conrad, among others.

24039 Stevenson, Lionel. THE HISTORY OF THE ENGLISH NOVEL. XI, 73-87 and passim. See G2212.

FMF's fictional career and contributions to an aesthetic for the novel.

24040 Swinden, Patrick. "Time and Motion: English Realism. Ford. Bennett. V.S. Naipaul." In UNOFFICIAL SELVES. Pp. 120-57. See G3144.

Impressionsim vs. naturalism in modern fiction, with a decided preference for the former (via FMF).

24041 Tindall, William York. FORCES IN MODERN BRITISH LITERATURE. Passim. See G2122.

FMF in relation to modern literary movements.

24042 Wagner, Geoffrey. "Ford Madox Ford: The Honest Edwardian." EIC, 17 (1967), 75-88.

FMF's reflection of and insight into his age (primarily GS and PE).

*24043 Wees, William C. "Ford and Hulme." VORTICISM AND THE ENGLISH AVANT-GARDE. Pp. 73-85 and passim. See G2374.

FMF's (and Hulme's) influence on avant-garde movements.

24044 Whigham, Peter. "Ford Madox Ford." EUROPEAN, 10 (1957), 212-18.

FMF as a modern "transmitter" of Pre-Raphaelite influence.

24045 Whittemore, Reed. "The Fascination of the Abomination--Wells, Shaw, Ford, Conrad." In THE FASCINATION OF THE ABOMINATION. New York: Macmillan, 1963. Pp. 129-66.

FMF and Conrad, versus Wells and Shaw, as "Hard-facts" realists.

24046 Wimsatt, William K., Jr., and Cleanth Brooks. LITERARY CRITICISM: A SHORT HISTORY. New York: Knopf, 1957. Pp. 682-85 and passim.

FMF's technical innovations (especially time) and critical theories.

24047 Zabel, Morton Dauwen. "Ford Madox Ford: Yesterday and After." In CRAFT AND CHARACTER. Pp. 253-63. See G3162.

FMF as a novelist of the transition to modernism. Partially reprinted in 23003 and 23010.

2.5 Studies of Individual Works

The following section is subdivided into two parts: i. Fiction (alphabetically by title) and ii. Miscellaneous Writings. Virtually all criticism of FMF's fiction is concentrated on the two major works: GS and PE, with the exception of a handful of critical books on FMF, noted in 2.3 above, which consider the lesser known works of fiction. See especially Cassell (23002), Ambrose Gordon (23004), Hoffmann (23006), Huntley (23007), Leer (23008), Meixner (23011), and Wiley (23018). These books, as well as the studies by Andreach (23001), Lid (23009), Ohmann (23014), and Smith (23016), should also be consulted for additional criticisms of GS and PE. Among the biographies (2.2 above), MacShane (22019), and Mizener (22022) contain useful commentaries on the individual works.

i. FICTION

THE GOOD SOLDIER (1915)

25001 Aswell, Duncan. "The Saddest Storyteller in Ford's THE GOOD SOLDIER." CLAJ, 14 (1970), 187-96.

The ironic and technical implications of FMF's original title: "The Saddest Story."

25002 Baerstein, Jo-Ann. "Image, Identity, and Insight in THE GOOD SOLDIER." Crit, 9, No. 1 (1966), 19-42.

Dowell's use of animal imagery and the theme of identity in GS. Reprinted in 23003.

*25003 Barnes, Daniel R. "Ford and the 'Slaughtered Saints': A New Reading of THE GOOD SOLDIER." MFS, 14 (1968), 157-70.

Religious framework of GS (especially the Albigensian heresy).

*25004 Bender, Todd K. "The Sad Tale of Dowell: Ford Madox Ford's THE GOOD SOLDIER." CRITICISM, 4 (1962), 353-68.

Dowell and Ashburnham together comprise a "double personality."

25005 Bort, Barry D. "THE GOOD SOLDIER: Comedy or Tragedy?" TCL, 12 (1967), 194-202.

GS a comedy of manners.

25006 Cohen, Mary. "THE GOOD SOLDIER: Outworn Codes." SNNTS, 5 (1973), 284-97.

GS exposes the moral dissolution of prewar England, especially in its use of the courtly love tradition.

25007 Cox, James Trammell. "The Finest French Novel in the English Language." MFS, 9 (1963), 79-93.

Direct and general parallels between GS and MADAME BOVARY. See 23012.

*25008 ______. "Ford's 'Passion for Provence.'" ELH, 23 (1961), 383-98.

FMF's tragicomic use of the courtly love tradition in GS.

25009 Gabbay, Lydia R. "The Four Square Coterie: A Comparison of Ford Madox Ford and Henry James." SNNTS, 6 (1974), 439-53.

FMF's developing "hatred" of James completed in his parody portrait through Ashburnham.

*25010 Gose, Elliott B., Jr. "The Strange Irregular Rhythm: An Analysis of THE GOOD SOLDIER." PMLA, 72 (1957), 494-509.

Dowell seen as a reliable narrator.

*25011 Hafley, James. "The Moral Structure of THE GOOD SOLDIER." MFS, 5 (1959), 121-28.

GS a novel about "faith" and threatened values.

25012 Hanzo, T.A. "Downward to Darkness." SR, 74 (1966), 832-55.

Mythical archetypes and their significance in GS.

25013 Henighan, T.J. "THE DESIRABLE ALIEN: A Source for Ford Madox Ford's THE GOOD SOLDIER." TCL, 11 (1965), 25-29.

Some major scenes and themes in GS grew from a Ford-Violet Hunt collaborative travel book (1913).

*25014 Hoffmann, Charles G. "Ford's Manuscript Revisions of THE GOOD SOLDIER." ELT, 9 (1966), 145-52.

Examines the three manuscripts of GS (two complete and one fragmentary).

25015 Huntley, H. Robert. "THE GOOD SOLDIER and DIE WAHLVERWANDTSCHAFTEN." CL, 19 (1967), 133-41.

Influence of Goethe on GS.

*25016 Hynes, Samuel. "The Epistemology of THE GOOD SOLDIER." In his EDWARDIAN OCCASIONS. Pp. 54-62. See G2345.

The epistemological implications of the question of Dowell's reliability. One of the best views of the narrational problem in GS. Reprinted in 23003.

25017 Isaacs, Neil D. "The Narrator of THE GOOD SOLDIER." ELT, 6 (1963), 14-15.

Note on the implicit ironies in Dowell's name.

25018 Johnson, Ann S. "Narrative Form in THE GOOD SOLDIER." Crit, 11, No. 2 (1969), 70-80.

Dowell's character and narrative reliability related to the novel's form.

25019 Jones, Lawrence W. "The Quality of Sadness in Ford's THE GOOD SOLDIER." ELT, 13 (1970), 296-302.

GS's modernist nihilism.

25020 Kenner, Hugh. "Conrad and Ford." In his GNOMON. Pp. 162-70. See G3083.

Comparisons among NOSTROMO, UNDER WESTERN EYES, and GS.

25021 Lehan, Richard. "Ford Madox Ford and the Absurd: THE GOOD SOLDIER." TSLL, 5 (1963), 219-31.

Dowell's failure to grasp the sense of his narration reflects the basic dilemma of the absurd character.

25022 Lentz, Vern B. "Ford's Good Narrator." SNNTS, 5 (1973), 483-90.

Dowell, who reflects FMF's own theories of narration, a totally reliable narrator of a quite complex situation.

25023 McCaughey, G.S. "The Mocking Bird and the Tomcat: An Examination of Ford Madox Ford's THE GOOD SOLDIER." HAB, 16 (1965), 49-58.

Examination of Dowell's role as narrator and his relationship to Edward.

*25024 McFate, Patricia, and Bruce Golden. "THE GOOD SOLDIER: A Tragedy of Self-Deception." MFS, 9 (1963), 50-60.

Dowell's confusion of time and fact used by FMF to indicate his general self-deception. See 23012.

25025 McLaughlin, Marilou B. "Adjusting the Lens for THE GOOD SOLDIER." EngR, 22, No. 3 (1972), 41-48.

GS's mode of narration an illustration of the "internal and external manipulations of perception."

25026 Moser, Thomas. "Conrad, Ford, and the Sources of CHANCE." CONRADIANA, 7 (1975), 207-24.

Considers CHANCE Conrad's most "Fordian" novel, surveys its sources (as below) in the lives of their acquaintances, and traces its influence on FMF's conception of GS.

25027 _____. "Conrad, Marwood, and Ford: Biographical Speculations on the Genesis of THE GOOD SOLDIER." MOSAIC, 8, No. 1 (1974), 217-27.

Relationships among the Fords, the Conrads, and the Marwoods (mutual friends) reflected in GS. With 25026, part of a forthcoming study of Conrad and FMF.

25028 Peirce, William P. "The Epistemological Style of Ford's THE GOOD SOLDIER." LANGUAGE AND STYLE, 8 (1975), 34-46.

*25029 Ray, Robert J. "Style in THE GOOD SOLDIER." MFS, 9 (1963), 61-66.

Close and perceptive analysis of FMF's uses of language and form. See 23012.

*25030 Schorer, Mark. "The Good Novelist in THE GOOD SOLDIER." PULC, 9 (1948), 128-33.

Important, often-reprinted critical analysis of GS which stresses Dowell's unreliability. Expanded version appears as "An Interpretation" in the Knopf and Vintage printings of GS (1951, 1957). Reprinted in 23003. Also see 23015.

25031 Schow, H. Wayne. "Ironic Structure in THE GOOD SOLDIER." ELT, 18 (1975), 203-11.

Structure of GS communicates its meaning--the irony of Dowell's sad storytelling.

25032 Siemens, Reynold. "The Juxtaposition of Composed Renderings in Ford's THE GOOD SOLDIER." HAB, 23, No. 3 (1972), 44-49.

FMF's expansion of meaning through juxtaposition.

25033 Stang, Sondra J. "A Reading of Ford's THE GOOD SOLDIER." MLQ, 30 (1969), 545-63.

GS a speculation about the value of a falling civilization.

25034 Thornton, Lawrence. "Escaping the Impasse: Criticism and the Mitosis of THE GOOD SOLDIER." MFS, 21 (1975), 237-41.

Argues a tragic reading of GS.

25035 ______. "Ford Madox Ford and THE GREAT GATSBY." FITZGERALD-HEMINGWAY ANNUAL (1975), pp. 57-74.

FMF's GS a stronger influence on Fitzgerald than the frequently suggested works by Conrad.

25036 Tytell, John. "The Jamesian Legacy in THE GOOD SOLDIER." SNNTS, 3 (1971), 365-73.

Impact of the "objective" Jamesian tradition in fiction on milieu, character, and structure of GS.

25037 Weinstein, Arnold L. "Enclosed Vision: Conrad, Ford, and James." VISION AND RESPONSE IN MODERN FICTION. Ithaca, N.Y.: Cornell Univ. Press, 1974. Pp. 50-90.

Epistemological problems in the depiction of and response to the seen, and the suspected "unseen," in Conrad, Ford (GS), and James.

*25038 Wiesenfarth, Joseph. "Criticism and the Semiosis of THE GOOD SOLDIER." MFS, 9 (1963), 39-49.

The uncertainty of Dowell's credibility makes GS an ultimately ambiguous novel. See 23012.

25039 Wiley, Paul L. "Two Tales of Passion." CONRADIANA, 6 (1974), 189-95.

Conrad's and FMF's adaptation of the oral-tale form (GS and THE NIGGER OF THE "NARCISSUS").

PARADE'S END (1950)--tetralogy including SOME DO NOT (1924), NO MORE PARADES (1925), A MAN COULD STAND UP (1926), and LAST POST (1928)

25040 Bradbury, Malcolm. "The Denuded Place: War and Form in PARADE'S END and U.S.A." In THE FIRST WORLD WAR IN FICTION. Ed. Holger Klein. London: Macmillan, 1976. Pp. 193-209.

PE and DosPassos's U.S.A. reflect the changes in culture, individual psychology, and the aesthetics of fiction, wrought by the war experiences.

25041 Core, George. "Ordered Life and the Abysses of Chaos: PARADE'S END." SoR, 8 (1972), 520-32.

PE deals with the conflict between the individual's ordered life and the chaos of modern society.

25042 Delbaere-Garant, Jeanne. "'Who shall inherit England?': A Comparison between HOWARDS END, PARADE'S END, and UNCONDITIONAL SURRENDER." ES, 50 (1969), 101-5.

Comparable themes of class change, social transformation, and inheritance in Forster, FMF, and Waugh.

25043 Firebaugh, Joseph J. "Tietjens and the Tradition." PACIFIC SPECTATOR, 6 (Winter 1952), 23-32.

PE concerns tradition and "social decay."

25044 Gordon, Caroline. "The Story of Ford Madox Ford." In HIGHLIGHTS OF MODERN LITERATURE. Ed. Francis Brown. New York: New American Library, 1954. Pp. 113-18.

FMF's fascination with the <u>femme fatale</u> figure (re: PE).

25045 Gose, Elliott B., Jr. "Reality to Romance: A Study of Ford's PARADE'S END." CE, 17 (1956), 445-50.

Autobiographical backgrounds.

*25046 Griffith, Marlene. "A Double Reading of PARADE'S END." MFS, 9 (1963), 25-38.

FMF's deft development of PE's social and psychological levels of meaning. Defends LAST POST's inclusion in the tetralogy. See Greene, 24016 above. Reprinted in 23003. Also, see 23012.

25047 Hays, Peter L. THE LIMPING HERO: GROTESQUES IN LITERATURE. New York: New York Univ. Press, 1971. Pp. 148-55.

The emasculated hero in FMF's PE.

25048 Heldman, James M. "The Last Victorian Novel: Technique and Theme in PARADE'S END." TCL, 18 (1972), 271-84.

As PE's themes move from a social to an individual focus, its technique modulates correspondingly to more modern forms.

25049 Henighan, T.J. "Tietjens Transformed: A Reading of PARADE'S END." ELT, 15 (1972), 144-57.

The changes in Tietjens through the tetralogy (especially the shift of psychic dominance from male to female) reflects FMF's view of the larger social changes in England.

*25050 Hynes, Samuel. "Ford Madox Ford: 'Three Dedicatory Letters to PARADE'S END' with Commentary and Notes." MFS, 16 (1970), 515-28.

FMF's changing attitude toward LAST POST reflected in the letters (reprinted here).

25051 Kashner, Rita J. "Tietjens' Education: Ford Madox Ford's Tetralogy." CritQ, 7 (1966), 150-63.

LAST POST necessary to the tetralogy for the completion of Tietjens' education. See Greene, 24016 above.

25052 Kennedy, Alan. "Tietjens' Travels: PARADE'S END as Comedy." TCL, 16 (1970), 85-95.

*25053 Kenner, Hugh. "Remember That I Have Remembered." In his GNOMON. Pp. 144-61. See G3083.

FMF the crucial figure in the introduction of French innovative techniques to the English literary scene. His work often more obsolete than his theories.

*25054 Levin, Gerald H. "Character and Myth in Ford's PARADE'S END." JML, 1 (1970), 183-96.

FMF uses myth in PE to suggest the deterioration of heroic ideals.

25055 Macauley, Robie. "Introduction." In FMF's PARADE'S END. Pp. v-xxii. See 13004.

Derived from his "The Good Ford." See 24030.

25056 McCormick, John. CATASTROPHE AND IMAGINATION. Pp. 217-21 and passim. See G3095.

FMF an influential, but not entirely successful war novelist (PE).

25057 Mizener, Arthur A. "Afterword." In FMF's PARADE'S END. New York: New American Library, 1964. I, 505-17; II, 337-50.

Background information and useful general critiques.

25058 Seiden, Melvin. "The Living Dead--VI. Ford Madox Ford and His Tetralogy." LONDON MAGAZINE, 6 (Aug. 1959), 45-55.

In the inherent contradictions of Tietjens, FMF embodies a vision of the tragicomic complexity of modern life.

25059 ______. "Persecution and Paranoia in PARADE'S END." CRITICISM, 8 (1966), 246-62.

Psychoanalysis of Tietjens's character. Reprinted in 23003.

25060 Solomon, Eric. "From Christ in Flanders to CATCH 22: An Approach to War Fiction." TSLL, 11 (1969), 851-66.

PE praised passim as the "finest English war novel."

25061 Strauss, Harold. FORD MADOX FORD: "PARADE'S END." THE STORY OF AN OLD BOOK NEWLY MADE. New York: Knopf, 1950.

Pamphlet account of the revival in FMF's reputation which led to the collected publication of PE. Strauss, the editor-in-chief of the Knopf project, quotes several "enthusiastic plaudits" from a number of FMF's admirers, for the reissue of the four novels. See 13004.

*25062 Williams, William Carlos. "PARADE'S END." In SELECTED ESSAYS OF WILLIAM CARLOS WILLIAMS. New York: Random House, 1954. Pp. 315-23.

High praise, especially for FMF's mastery of style. Reprinted in 23003 and 23010.

ii. MISCELLANEOUS WRITINGS

25063 Bornhauser, Fred. "Ford as Art Critic." SHENANDOAH, 4 (1953), 51-59.

Survey of FMF's art criticism.

25064 Brebach, Raymond T. "The Making of ROMANCE, Part Fifth." CONRADIANA, 6 (1974), 171-81.

Novel's stages of development attributed to FMF.

25065 Coffman, Stanley K., Jr. IMAGISM: A CHAPTER FOR THE HISTORY OF MODERN POETRY. Norman: Univ. of Oklahoma Press, 1951. Pp. 113-19, 138-51 and passim.

FMF's impressionist poetry and the imagist movement (especially Pound).

25066 Fairchild, Hoxie N. RELIGIOUS TRENDS IN ENGLISH POETRY. Vol. 5: 1880-1920. New York: Columbia Univ. Press, 1962. Pp. 428-30, 493-99.

FMF's role in the imagist movement and the "sentimental shapeless chitchat" of his poetry.

25067 Harmer, J.B. VICTORY IN LIMBO: IMAGISM, 1908-1917. London: Secker and Warburg, 1975. Pp. 83-90 and passim.

FMF among the imagists, and as an imagist poet.

*25068 Hynes, Samuel. "Conrad and Ford: Two Rye Revolutionists." In his EDWARDIAN OCCASIONS. Pp. 48-53. See G2345.

FMF and Conrad as impressionistic critics and memoirists.

25069 Keating, George T., ed. A CONRAD MEMORIAL LIBRARY: THE COLLECTION OF GEORGE T. KEATING. Garden City, N.Y.: Doubleday, Doran, 1929.

Brief appreciative essays and bibliographical descriptions of Conrad's works, including his collaborations with FMF. Also an essay by FMF on "The Inheritors" (pp. 74-83).

*25070 Kenner, Hugh. "The Poetics of Speech." In FORD MADOX FORD. Ed. Richard A. Cassell. Pp. 169-81. See 23003.

FMF, and his ideals of poetic diction, among Pound and Eliot.

25071 Killigrew, Michael. "Introduction." In FMF's YOUR MIRROR TO MY TIMES. Ed. Killigrew. Pp. ix-xxi. See 13006.

Notes FMF's impressionistic memoir technique and explains selection and arrangement of the anthology of FMF's memoirs, criticism, and travel works.

25072 Kleiner, Elaine L. "Joseph Conrad's Forgotten Role in the Emergence of Science Fiction." EXTRAPOLATION, 15 (1973), 25-34.

THE INHERITORS as early science fiction. (FMF's role in its composition ignored.)

25073 MacShane, Frank. "Ford Madox Ford and His Contemporaries: The Techniques of the Novel." EFT [now ELT], 4, No. 1 (1961), 2-11.

FMF's theories of fiction.

25074 _____. "Introduction." In THE CRITICAL WRITINGS OF FORD MADOX FORD. Ed. MacShane. Pp. ix-xiv. See 13003.

FMF's criticism the "by-product of his imaginative work." MacShane also contributes brief editorial commentaries throughout the anthology.

*25075 Pound, Ezra. "Mr. Hueffer and the Prose Tradition in Verse." POETRY, 4 (1914), 111-20.

Reprinted often. A significant defense of FMF as critic and prose-poet.

25076 Rose, Charles. "ROMANCE and the Maiden Archetype." CONRADIANA, 6 (1974), 183-88.

Seraphina FMF's conception.

25077 Silkin, Jon. OUT OF BATTLE: THE POETRY OF THE GREAT WAR. London: Oxford Univ. Press, 1972. Pp. 191-96.

Considers and questions the sincerity of FMF's patriotic poetry.

25078 Sisson, G.H. ENGLISH POETRY, 1900-1950: AN ASSESSMENT. London: Hart-Davis, 1971. Pp. 44-54.

Influence of prose techniques on FMF's verse.

25079 Stock, Noel. "Modern Poetry and the Norm of Language." TQ, 4 (1961), 134-44.

Especially good on FMF's role in the development of modern poetry.

25080 Sturgeon, Mary C. "F.M. Hueffer." In STUDIES OF CONTEMPORARY POETS. 1916. Rev. ed. London: Harrop, 1920. Pp. 122-36.

FMF's refreshing but unconventional beauties as a poet.

25081 Thorburn, David. CONRAD'S ROMANTICISM. New Haven, Conn.: Yale Univ. Press, 1974. Pp. 25-46 and passim.

FMF and Conrad compromised their aesthetic ideals in the unconvincing, escapist, adventure story ROMANCE.

EDWARD MORGAN FORSTER (1879-1970)

1. PRIMARY BIBLIOGRAPHY

Abbreviations of titles used in this bibliography are noted at the end of the entry. Books available in recent paperback printings are designated by "(P)."

1.1 Fiction

Brief fragments of unfinished fiction have been separately published over the years. Since they will shortly be collected in the ninth volume of the Abinger edition (see 13001, below), they are not listed here. For information on the fictional fragments, see Kirkpatrick's bibliography (21008). The following works are all novels unless otherwise noted. Also see 12002, below.

11001 THE CELESTIAL OMNIBUS, AND OTHER STORIES. [Stories]. London: Sidgwick and Jackson, 1911. New York: Knopf, 1923. (P).

"The Story of a Panic" (1904), "The Other Side of the Hedge" (1904), "The Celestial Omnibus" (1908), "Other Kingdom" (1909), "The Curate's Friend" (1907), "The Road from Colonus" (1904).

11002 THE ETERNAL MOMENT, AND OTHER STORIES. [Stories]. London: Sidgwick and Jackson; New York: Harcourt, 1928. (P).

"The Machine Stops" (1909), "The Point of It" (1911), "Mr. Andrews" (1911), "Co-Ordination" (1912), "The Story of the Siren" (1920), "The Eternal Moment" (1905).

11003 HOWARDS END. London: Arnold; New York: Putnam's, 1910. (P). Abbreviated as HE.

The tension between bourgeois and humanistic values and the attempts to reconcile or connect them. ("Only connect" is the novel's often quoted epigraph.)

11004 THE LIFE TO COME, AND OTHER STORIES. [Stories]. London: Arnold, 1972. New York: Norton, 1973.

Collects fourteen stories, only two of which have been previously published: "Albergo Empedocle" (1903) and "Three Courses and a Dessert" (1944).

11005 THE LONGEST JOURNEY. Edinburgh and London: Blackwood, 1907. New York: Knopf, 1922. (P). Abbreviated as LJ.

The early Forsterian hero, Rickie Elliot, is destroyed by his irreconcilable dual allegiances to art (Cambridge) and life (middle-class Sawston).

11006 THE MANUSCRIPTS OF "HOWARDS END." Ed. Oliver Stallybrass. London: Arnold, 1973.

A variorum companion to the Abinger edition of HE (see 13001).

11007 MAURICE. London: Arnold; New York: Norton, 1971. (P).

Exploration of the homosexual theme, published posthumously.

11008 A PASSAGE TO INDIA. London: Arnold; New York: Harcourt, 1924. (P). Abbreviated as PI.

EMF's acknowledged masterpiece. A novel of social and racial separation and the difficulties of transcending these differences, set in colonial India.

11009 A ROOM WITH A VIEW. London: Arnold, 1908. New York: Putnam's, 1911. (P). Abbreviated as RWV.

Light social comedy set in Italy and England.

11010 WHERE ANGELS FEAR TO TREAD. Edinburgh and London: Blackwood, 1905. New York: Knopf, 1920. (P). Abbreviated as WAFT.

Englishmen in Italy. EMF's first published novel.

1.2 Miscellaneous Writings

This section includes EMF's biography, criticism, travel, drama, and other nonfiction. Several brief pieces by EMF were published over the years in ephemeral, limited editions. No attempt is made to list these works here. For their titles the student may consult Kirkpatrick's bibliography (21008). These pamphlet-essays will eventually be collected in the forthcoming Abinger edition (see 13001).

12001 ABINGER HARVEST. London: Arnold; New York: Harcourt, 1936. (P).

Over eighty critical essays, articles, reviews, and reminiscences.

12002 ALBERGO EMPEDOCLE, AND OTHER EARLY WRITINGS. Ed. George H. Thomson. New York: Liveright, 1971.

Essays, satirical sketches, and reviews (1900-1915), published for the first time in collected form, and EMF's first published story, "Albergo Empedocle" (1903).

12003 ALEXANDRIA: A HISTORY AND A GUIDE. Alexandria, Egypt: Whitehead, Morris, 1922. Garden City, N.Y.: Doubleday, 1961.

Brief review of Alexandria's history and a travel guide to the city. A product of EMF's volunteer service experiences in Egypt during World War I.

12004 ASPECTS OF THE NOVEL. London: Arnold; New York: Harcourt, 1927. (P). Abbreviated by the short title ASPECTS.

Important theoretical study.

12005 BILLY BUDD: OPERA IN FOUR ACTS (with Eric Crozier). London: Boosey and Hawkes, 1951.

Opera libretto collaboration, for Benjamin Britten.

12006 ENGLAND'S PLEASANT LAND: A PAGEANT PLAY. London: Hogarth, 1940.

A patriotic, "save the countryside" drama, originally performed in 1938.

12007 GOLDSWORTHY LOWES DICKINSON. London: Arnold; New York: Harcourt, 1934. (P).

Biography of EMF's teacher and friend.

12008 THE HILL OF DEVI. London: Arnold; New York: Harcourt, 1953. (P).

Memoir of EMF's Indian experiences. Important background to PI.

12009 MARIANNE THORNTON, 1797-1887: A DOMESTIC BIOGRAPHY. London: Arnold; New York: Harcourt, 1956. (P).

Biography of EMF's grandaunt, which ends as an autobiography of his early years.

12010 NORDIC TWILIGHT. London: Macmillan, 1940.

Anti-Nazi war pamphlet.

12011 PHAROS AND PHARILLON. Richmond, Engl.: Hogarth; New York: Knopf, 1923.

Essays on Egypt and on the poetry of Cavafy.

12012 TWO CHEERS FOR DEMOCRACY. London: Arnold; New York: Harcourt, 1951. (P).

Various essays and broadcasts on politics, art, travel, and other topics. Includes "Anonymity: An Inquiry" (1925), "What I Believe" (1939), "Virginia Woolf" (1942).

1.3 Collected and Selected Works

13001 ABINGER EDITION OF E.M. FORSTER. Ed. Oliver Stallybrass. London: Arnold, 1972--

Corrected texts, notes and appendixes. Volumes 1-6 will include the novels; 7-8, the stories; 9, the fictional fragments; 10-17, the nonfiction; 18-20, previously unpublished nonfiction; 21, dramatic works. See 11006, 24095, and 25125.

13002 THE COLLECTED TALES OF E.M. FORSTER. New York: Knopf, 1947.

Combines CELESTIAL OMNIBUS and ETERNAL MOMENT volumes. Not complete.

13003 E.M. FORSTER: SELECTED WRITINGS. Ed. G.B. Parker. London: Heinemann, 1968.

Includes thirteen "Essays and Addresses," two stories, and four extracts from the novels. See 24079.

1.4 Letters

Also see Meyers (22009, below).

14001 E.M. FORSTER'S LETTERS TO DONALD WINDHAM. New York: S. Campbell, 1975.

Thirty-seven letters (1948-65) to a friend and fellow novelist.

2. SECONDARY BIBLIOGRAPHY

2.1 Bibliographies

Also see 23013.

21001 Beebe, Maurice, and Joseph Brogunier, comps. "Criticism of E.M. Forster: A Selected Checklist." MFS, 7 (1961), 284-92.

Now dated, but still useful secondary listing. See 23021.

*21002 Borrello, Alfred, ed. E.M. FORSTER: AN ANNOTATED BIBLIOGRAPHY OF SECONDARY MATERIALS. Metuchen, N.J.: Scarecrow Press, 1973.

Lists chronologically and annotates over 700 EMF items, through 1970. Unfortunately large number of errors and inaccuracies.

21003 Bradbury, Malcolm. "Forster." In THE ENGLISH NOVEL. Ed. A.E. Dyson. Pp. 314-33. See G1408.

Bibliographical essay and selected checklist.

21004 Gardner, Philip. "Introduction." In E.M. FORSTER: THE CRITICAL HERITAGE. Pp. 1-39. See 23011.

Fine survey of EMF's developing critical reputation, through the publication of MAURICE (1971).

21005 Gerber, Helmut, Frederick P.W. McDowell, et al., comps. "E.M. Forster: An Annotated Checklist of Writings about Him." EFT [now ELT], 2, No. 1 (1959), and continuing.

Abstracts of studies, appearing irregularly. Little critical evaluation. See G1404.

21006 Greiff, Louis K., comp. "E.M. Forster--A Bibliography." BB, 24 (1964), 108-11.

Primary bibliography.

21007 HEFFER CATALOGUE SEVEN: E.M. FORSTER. Cambridge, Engl.: Heffer, 1971.

Catalog for the sale of EMF's library.

*21008 Kirkpatrick, Brownlee Jean, ed. A BIBLIOGRAPHY OF E.M. FORSTER. 1965. Rev. ed. London: Hart-Davis, 1968.

Best primary bibliography, but recent additions to the EMF canon will necessitate a supplement.

*21009 McDowell, Frederick P.W., ed. E.M. FORSTER: AN ANNOTATED BIBLIOGRAPHY OF WRITINGS ABOUT HIM. DeKalb: Northern Illinois Univ. Press, 1975.

Chronologically arranged, with 1,913 entries and abstracts. Some evaluative comment. Five separate indexes. All students should be aware of this volume, but it is not intended as nor is it easy to use as a research guide.

21010 Wiley, Paul L., comp. "E.M. Forster (1879-1970)." In THE BRITISH NOVEL. Comp. Wiley. Pp. 40-44. See G1419.

Brief primary and secondary checklist.

2.2 Biographies, Memoirs, Reminiscences, Interviews

An authorized biography, by P.N. Furbank, has recently been published (see 22004).

22001 Ackerley, Joe R. E.M. FORSTER: A PORTRAIT. London: Ian Mckelvie, 1970.

Pamphlet memoir.

22002 Arlott, John. "Forster and Broadcasting." In ASPECTS OF E.M. FORSTER. Ed. Oliver Stallybrass. Pp. 87-92. See 23026.

EMF's World War II services for BBC.

22003 Fagan, B.W. "Forster and His Publishers." In ASPECTS OF E.M. FORSTER. Ed. Oliver Stallybrass. Pp. 93-98. See 23026.

Remarks by EMF's publishing agent.

22004 Furbank, P.N. E.M. FORSTER: A LIFE. Vol. 1. GROWTH OF THE NOVELIST, 1879-1914. London: Secker and Warburg, 1977.

Not seen. Second volume of this authorized biography was published late in 1978.

*22005 Furbank, P.N., and F.J.H. Haskell. "E.M. Forster." In WRITERS AT WORK: THE "PARIS REVIEW" INTERVIEWS. Ed. M. Cowley. New York: Viking, 1958. Pp. 23-35.

Interview discussion of EMF's working methods. Reprinted in 25046.

22006 Garnett, David. "Forster and Bloomsbury." In ASPECTS OF E.M. FORSTER. Ed. Oliver Stallybrass. Pp. 29-35. See 23026.

EMF's relation to Bloomsbury distant, but substantial.

22007 _____. "Some Writers I Have Known: Galsworthy, Forster, Moore, and Wells." TQ, 4, No. 2 (1961), 190-202.

22008 Lawrence, D.H. THE COLLECTED LETTERS OF D.H. LAWRENCE. Ed. Harry T. Moore. New York: Viking, 1962. I, 315-20 and passim.

Lawrence's relationship with and views of EMF.

22009 Meyers, Jeffrey. "E.M. Forster and T.E. Lawrence: A Friendship." SAQ, 69 (1970), 205-16.

Discusses their responses to each other's work and their correspondence.

22010 Natwar-Singh, K., ed. E.M. FORSTER: A TRIBUTE, WITH SELECTIONS FROM HIS WRITINGS ON INDIA. New York: Harcourt, 1964.

Collects six recollections of EMF by Indian admirers, and reprints twelve selections from his Indian writings.

22011 O'Connor, William Van. "Toward a History of Bloomsbury." SWR, 40 (1955), 36-52.

Touches on EMF.

22012 _____. "A Visit with E.M. Forster." WR, 19 (1955), 215-19.

EMF and Bloomsbury.

22013 Plomer, William. "Forster as a Friend." In ASPECTS OF E.M. FORSTER. Ed. Oliver Stallybrass. Pp. 99-105. See 23026.

Reminiscences.

22014 Randall, Alec. "Forster in Rumania." In ASPECTS OF E.M. FORSTER. Ed. Oliver Stallybrass. Pp. 51-60. See 23026.

Memoir of an EMF visit.

22015 Roerick, William. "Forster and America." In ASPECTS OF E.M. FORSTER. Ed. Oliver Stallybrass. Pp. 61-72. See 23026.

Recounts two visits to America.

22016 Shahane, V.A. "A Visit to Mr. E.M. Forster." QUEST, 53 (1967), 42-46.

Much comment on PI.

22017 Wilkinson, Patrick. "Forster and Kings." In ASPECTS OF E.M. FORSTER. Ed. Oliver Stallybrass. Pp. 13-28. See 23026.

EMF and Cambridge.

22018 Wilson, Angus. "A Conversation with E.M. Forster." ENCOUNTER, 9 (Nov. 1957), 52-57.

Comments on EMF's personality and fiction.

2.3 Book-Length Critical Studies and Essay Collections

Also see books and essay collections on the following individual works: on HE: Wakefield (25022), Widdowson (25024); on PI: Boulton (25043), Bradbury (25046), Colmer (25052), Levine (25074), Mason (25079), Moody (25082), Rutherford (25094), Shahane (25097, 25098); and on the miscellaneous writings: Joseph (25117).

*23001 Beer, J.B. THE ACHIEVEMENT OF E.M. FORSTER. London: Chatto and Windus, 1962.

A reading of the novels, with passing mention of the other prose, which concentrates on EMF's romantic sense of dualism. The early novels (RWV and WAFT) are social comedies, while LJ marks a transition to spiritual themes which is completed in HE. PI presents a picture of social and individual dualisms in conflict. Reconciliation and survival are possible only through the powers of love and imagination. Fine analyses. Extract reprinted in 25046.

23002 Borrello, Alfred, comp. AN E.M. FORSTER DICTIONARY. Metuchen, N.J.: Scarecrow, 1971.

Summaries of EMF's works with their publication data, and lists of all his characters, geographical locations, and sites.

23003 ______, comp. AN E.M. FORSTER GLOSSARY. Metuchen, N.J.: Scarecrow, 1972.

An alphabetical listing and identification of all EMF's allusions to writers, artists, musicians, works of art, mythological and historical figures, events, and places. Cross-referenced. Culled from the fiction and the major prose.

*23004 Bradbury, Malcolm, ed. FORSTER: A COLLECTION OF CRITICAL ESSAYS. Englewood Cliffs, N.J.: Prentice-Hall, 1966.

A fine collection of outstanding essays on EMF, his ideas, his heritage, and his fiction. Includes 24024, 24061, 24066, 24088, 24090, 24091, 24105, 24106, 25007, 25026, 25048, 25088; extracts from the following books: 23007, 23029; and a good biographical-critical introduction by the editor (see 24016).

23005 Brander, Laurence. E.M. FORSTER: A CRITICAL STUDY. London: Hart-Davis, 1968.

Mostly routine summary of the major works, with occasional critical commentary. Brander devotes more than customary attention to the biographies (which he values rather highly) and the essays.

23006 Colmer, John. E.M. FORSTER: THE PERSONAL VOICE. London: Routledge, 1975.

Study of EMF's intellectual development (using his unpublished essays and memoranda) and close textual analysis of the novels.

*23007 Crews, Frederick C. E.M. FORSTER: THE PERILS OF HUMANISM. Princeton, N.J.: Princeton Univ. Press, 1962.

One of the few indispensible books on EMF. Crews traces in detail the biographical, religious, and educational foundations of EMF's liberal humanism. Finding EMF primarily a novelist of ideas, Crews sees the five novels as developments and refinements of his philosophic position. EMF moves from a questioning of the "perils" of the humanistic position to an "embracing of the ironies and disappointments inherent in humanism" (his "dominant theme"). The individual analyses are often brilliant and supportive of, rather than subordinate to his main thesis. Extracts reprinted in 23004, 25046, and 25094.

23008 Das, G.K. E.M. FORSTER'S INDIA. Totowa, N.J.: Rowman and Littlefield, 1977.

Study of "the whole corpus of Forster's writings about India, published and unpublished, including the accounts in his personal letters and diaries . . . [in part] based on personal interviews with Forster himself." (Quoted from publisher's advertisement--not seen.)

23009 ENGLISH LITERATURE IN TRANSITION, 16 (1973), 245-306. "Seminar on E.M. Forster."

Includes Stallybrass's description of the forthcoming Abinger edition (24095) and three essays on EMF's craft. Includes 23010 (extract), 24047, and 24107.

23010 Finkelstein, Bonnie B. FORSTER'S WOMEN: ETERNAL DIFFERENCES. New York: Columbia Univ. Press, 1975.

Traces through the six novels (MAURICE included) EMF's sympathetic interest in "the gentle and sensitive outsider . . . regardless of the actual physical sex of the protagonists." EMF appears to hold an "androgynous ideal" for personal relations (via Bloomsbury) which, by dismissing simple sexual distinctions between characters, heightens the sense of "eternal differences" between individual human beings. Extract originally appeared in 23009.

23011 Gardner, Philip, ed. E.M. FORSTER: THE CRITICAL HERITAGE. London: Routledge, 1973.

Contemporary criticism of EMF's fiction, chiefly from 1905 to 1928, with a selection of more recent items. Gardner also reprints commentaries on the later nonfiction and several reviews of MAURICE. Includes 21004, 24011 (extract), 24021, 24084, 24102, 24109, 25113, and 25127.

23012 Godfrey, Denis. E.M. FORSTER'S OTHER KINGDOM. Edinburgh: Oliver and Boyd, 1968.

An attempt to emphasize, describe, and suggest the impact of the visionary element of EMF's fiction. Godfrey cites the manifestations of the "other world" through the short fiction and novels, but shows scant judgment in his commentary.

23013 Gowda, H.H.A., ed. A GARLAND FOR E.M. FORSTER. Mysore, India: THE LITERARY HALF-YEARLY, 1969.

A gathering of appreciations, letters, brief comments, reviews of EMF criticism, a few critical essays, and a checklist of criticism on PI. (Expanded from a LITERARY HALF-YEARLY special issue). Includes 23023 (extract), 24075, 24082, 24100, and 25009.

23014 Gransden, K.W. E.M. FORSTER. 1962. Rev. ed. Edinburgh: Oliver and Boyd, 1970.

Fine critical introduction to the short fiction, novels, and essays, concentrating on EMF's relation to the English literary tradition (especially Austen and Butler) and his developing treatment of personal relations. Extract reprinted in 25098.

23015 Kelvin, Norman. E.M. FORSTER. Carbondale: Southern Illinois Univ. Press, 1967.

A pedestrian and frequently peculiar reading of the fiction which stresses EMF's concern for form, his symbolism, and his humanistic themes. The final chapter on the nonfiction prose is useful.

23016 Macaulay, Rose. THE WRITINGS OF E.M. FORSTER. London: Hogarth, 1938.

First book-length study. Macaulay, a professional novelist herself, considers the stories, novels, travel books, criticism, biography, and essays in individual brief chapters. Although more appreciation than literary criticism, her book still offers considerable insight into EMF's work. Her commentaries emphasize his liberal humanism and its background, while her readings of the novels stress his gifts as a social satirist.

*23017 McConkey, James. THE NOVELS OF E.M. FORSTER. Ithaca, N.Y.: Cornell Univ. Press, 1957.

One of the finest, and earliest, critical studies of EMF. McConkey sees personal relationships and "transcendant realities" as EMF's two chief fictional concerns. EMF tries to "connect" these themes through his authorial voice and symbolism. EMF's manipulation of myth and fantasy in the stories and early fiction develops into a prophetic synthesis of real and ideal in HE and PI. His rhythmic use of symbolism similarly develops through his fiction to become a vitally important connection between the reality of his fiction and its transcendant implications. Extracts reprinted in 25046 and 25098.

*23018 McDowell, Frederick P.W. E.M. FORSTER. New York: Twayne, 1969.

One of the best studies of EMF. Although primarily intended as a general introduction to the man and his works, McDowell's study offers an excellent brief summary of EMF's intellectual backgrounds and beliefs, followed by incisive commentaries on the fiction. The final chapter on the nonfiction prose is an admirably concise survey. Extract originally appeared in 23021.

23019 Martin, John Sayre. E.M. FORSTER: THE ENDLESS JOURNEY. Cambridge: At the Univ. Press, 1976.

Critical introduction ot EMF's long and short fiction, including the posthumous works. Martin assesses EMF's use of the theme of travel, the implicit and explicit homosexuality of his fiction, and his relationship to other moderns.

23020 Martin, Richard. THE LOVE THAT FAILED: IDEAL AND REALITY IN THE WRITINGS OF E.M. FORSTER. The Hague: Mouton, 1974.

A competent study of the intellectual backgrounds of EMF's liberal idealism (from Mill, Moore, et al.) and his "constant attempt to adapt ideal to reality" in his art. The fiction is surveyed, through PI, to demonstrate EMF's developing admission of defeat. A final chapter on the prose, however, shows EMF's modifications of this view and a return to tentative affirmation.

23021 MODERN FICTION STUDIES. 7 (1961), 207-92. "E.M. Forster Number."

Typically first-class editorial presentation by Maurice Beebe. Includes six essays, concentrating on individual novels, and a checklist of criticism. Includes 21001, 24005, 25016, 25055; and extracts from the following books: 23018 and 23028

23022 Moore, Harry T. E.M. FORSTER. New York: Columbia Univ. Press, 1965.

Balanced essay evaluation of the nonfiction, stories, and novels. Moore stresses EMF's concern with man's failure to communicate, his inability to establish satisfactory relationships. Each of the works receives brief consideration.

23023 Oliver, Harold J. THE ART OF E.M. FORSTER. Melbourne: Melbourne Univ. Press, 1960.

Brief interpretations of the minor fiction and full studies of HE and PI. Oliver's analyses are governed by his belief that EMF's one subject is "the supreme importance of personal relationships" and that EMF's brilliant use of the omniscient method gives his novels a technical unity. Extract reprinted in 23013.

23024 Rose, Martial. E.M. FORSTER. London: Evans, 1970.

Competent and useful short introduction to the fiction, essays, and biography. Rose's study, unlike most introductions, offers brief commentaries on EMF's literary criticism and biographies.

23025 Shusterman, David. THE QUEST FOR CERTITUDE IN E.M. FORSTER'S FICTION. Bloomington: Indiana Univ. Press, 1965.

A weak study of the stories and novels by a critic somewhat exasperated by the ambiguities, inconsistencies, and "muddle" of EMF. Shusterman asserts that EMF's art is a "violent pursuit of personal order, of certainty, of meaning" and that his artistic and personal dilemmas arose from his failure to achieve a "unified vision." This thesis is pursued with unfortunate violence to the works. Extract reprinted in 25098.

23026 Stallybrass, Oliver, ed. ASPECTS OF E.M. FORSTER: ESSAYS AND RECOLLECTIONS WRITTEN FOR HIS NINETIETH BIRTHDAY, JANUARY 1, 1969. New York: Harcourt, 1969.

An excellent compilation of memoirs and criticism, most published here for the first time. Includes 22002, 22003, 22006, 22013, 22014, 22015, 22017, 24012, 24018, 24075, 24094, 24097, 25045, 25101, and 25126.

*23027 Stone, Wilfred. THE CAVE AND THE MOUNTAIN: A STUDY OF E.M. FORSTER. Stanford, Calif.: Stanford Univ. Press, 1966.

The largest and most comprehensive book on EMF. Stone partly reduplicates the findings of others (e.g., Crews' discussion of the intellectual backgrounds), but his commentaries on the rarely treated biographies, the essays and criticism, and the fiction all deserve close attention. His critical analyses observe the traditional dualisms of EMF's world view (e.g., prose and poetry, Benthamite and Coleridgean) and follow through the works EMF's pursuit of the "objective" work of art.

*23028 Thomson, George H. THE FICTION OF E.M. FORSTER. Detroit: Wayne State Univ. Press, 1967.

An archetypal reading of EMF's stories and novels which emphasizes his powers as symbolist and visionary mythmaker. EMF writes romances, not novels or realistic fictions in the traditional sense. Thomson argues persuasively for a revision of the standard view of EMF as a realistic and philosophic novelist. Contains excellent studies of HE and PI. Extract originally appeared in 23021. Extract reprinted in 25098.

*23029 Trilling, Lionel. E.M. FORSTER: A STUDY. 1943. Rev. ed. London: Hogarth, 1967.

The most influential study of EMF. Trilling defines the special qualities of EMF's liberal imagination: his intellectual support of the ideals of the liberal tradition (progress, collectivism, and humanitarianism), and his imaginative distrust of such idealism. While EMF's books consistently examine the intense conflicts between opposed forces (e.g., good and evil), EMF's "comic manner" transcends conflict and suggests reconciliation. This higher, "moral realism" and the political libertarianism are traced through the short and longer fiction. (HE is found to be the "masterpiece.") EMF's distrust of absolutes and categories, however, makes his literary criticism impressionistic. Extracts reprinted in 23004, 25046, and 25094.

23030 Warner, Rex, and John Morris. E.M. FORSTER. 1950. Rev. ed. London: Longmans, 1970.

Overview of EMF's place and reputation, and analyses of the novels. Brief but insightful criticism of the works. Revised edition includes Morris's more recent assessment of EMF's critical reputation.

*23031 Wilde, Alan. ART AND ORDER: A STUDY OF E.M. FORSTER. New York: New York Univ. Press, 1964.

Valuable developmental reading of the fiction and prose. Wilde sees "everywhere in Forster's novels a sense of opposition and twoness." Each novel portrays a war of oppositions (e.g., art and life), with a tentative solution which is in turn tested in the next novel. The pessimistic admission of chaos and futility in PI causes EMF to turn to his nonfiction where he can "ignore . . . the horror of the world."

2.4 General Critical Articles, or Chapters on EMF

24001 Allen, Walter. THE ENGLISH NOVEL. Pp. 400-409. See G2201.

Brief survey.

24002 ______. THE MODERN NOVEL. Pp. 33-39 and passim. See G2202.

EMF a traditional novelist.

24003 Armand, Laura M. "Forster's Fallible Narrator." EA, 28 (1975), 269-80.

EMF's purposeful use of the "pompous" narrative voice in the Edwardian novels.

24004 Ault, Peter. "Aspects of E.M. Forster." DUBLIN REVIEW, 219 (1946), 109-34.

Ethical and religious perspective.

24005 Austin, Don. "The Problem of Continuity in Three Novels of E.M. Forster." MFS, 7 (1961), 217-28.

LJ, RWV, WAFT. The homestead and the family elder are forces for continuity between the older and younger generations. See 23021.

24006 Baker, James R. "Forster's Voyage of Discovery." TQ, 18, No. 2 (1975), 99-118.

EMF's fiction and essays seen as a "diary or log" of his quest for and abandonment of humanistic ideals.

24007 Beaumont, Ernest. "Mr. E.M. Forster's Strange Mystics." DUBLIN REVIEW, 225 (1951), 41-51.

Mrs. Wilcox (HE) and Mrs. Moore (PI), transcendental figures.

24008 Bedient, Calvin. ARCHITECTS OF THE SELF: GEORGE ELIOT, D. H. LAWRENCE, AND E.M. FORSTER. Berkeley and Los Angeles: Univ. of California Press, 1972. Pp. 183-265.

EMF, unlike Eliot or Lawrence, finds a "new principle of significance" for man in the connection between the social and the private selves.

24009 Belgion, Montgomery. "The Diabolism of Mr. E.M. Forster." CRITERION, 14 (1934), 54-73.

EMF's attitude toward life centers on the disparity between man's values and reality.

24010 Bentley, Phyllis. "The Novels of E.M. Forster." CE, 9 (1948), 349-56.

EMF's "brilliant" humanism evidenced in the five novels.

24011 Bowen, Elizabeth. "E.M. Forster." 1936; 1938. In COLLECTED IMPRESSIONS. New York: Knopf, 1950. Pp. 119-26.

Conflates two essays on "our great novelist" (reviews of EMF's ABINGER HARVEST [12001] and Rose Macaulay's WRITINGS OF E.M. FORSTER [23016]). First essay reprinted in 23011.

24012 ______. "A Passage to E.M. Forster." In ASPECTS OF E.M. FORSTER. Ed. Oliver Stallybrass. Pp. 1-12. See 23026.

Appreciation and criticism.

24013 Bowen, Roger. "A Version of Pastoral: E.M. Forster as Country Guardian." SAQ, 75 (1976), 36-54.

EMF's "guardianship of a pastoral island heritage" reflected in his nonfiction and, prominently, in LJ and HE.

24014 Boyle, Alexander. "Novels of E.M. Forster." IRISH MONTHLY, 78 (1950), 405-15.

The first three novels discover and the final two explore EMF's unbelief.

24015 Bradbury, Malcolm. "E.M. Forster as Victorian and Modern: HOWARDS END and A PASSAGE TO INDIA." In his POSSIBILITIES. Pp. 91-120. See G3012.

Drawn from two previously published essays. See 25007, 25045

24016 ______. "Introduction." In FORSTER. Ed. Bradbury. Pp. 1-14. See 23004.

Fine survey of EMF's critical reputation.

24017 Brewer, D.S. "E.M. Forster and Sawston: The Divided Mind." In PROTEUS: STUDIES IN ENGLISH LITERATURE. Tokyo: Kenkyusha, 1958. Pp. 198-232.

Cultural and symbolic significance of middle-class Sawston in EMF's fiction.

24018 Britten, Benjamin. "Some Notes on Forster and Music." In ASPECTS OF E.M. FORSTER. Ed. Oliver Stallybrass. Pp. 81-86. See 23026.

EMF's lyric qualities as a writer and his musical intelligence.

24019 Brower, Reuben A. "Beyond E.M. Forster: Part I--The Earth." FOREGROUND, 1 (1946), 164-74.

EMF's lyricism obscures his philosophic confusion.

*24020 ______. "Beyond E.M. Forster: The Unseen." ChiR, 2 (1948), 102-12.

Myth of the "unseen" in HE and PI.

24021 Brown, Edward K. "E.M. Forster and the Contemplative Novel." UTQ, 3 (1934), 349-61.

The chasm between the outer world and the world of ideas bridged by the contemplative mind (e.g., Mrs. Wilcox, Mrs. Moore). Reprinted in 23011.

24022 _____. "The Revival of E.M. Forster." YR, 33 (1944), 668-81.

EMF's revival in the forties a recognition of his subtlety as a novelist of ideas.

24023 Bullett, Gerald. MODERN ENGLISH FICTION. Pp. 70-85. See G3018.

Balanced early survey.

*24024 Burra, Peter. "The Novels of E.M. Forster." NINETEENTH CENTURY AND AFTER, 116 (1934), 581-94.

Perceptive critical study which uses EMF's own criteria in ASPECTS to judge his work. Reprinted in 23004 and 25046.

24025 Cecil, David. "Virginia Woolf and E.M. Forster" and "E.M. Forster." In POETS AND STORY-TELLERS. New York: Macmillan, 1949. Pp. 155-59; 181-201.

A comparison of Woolf and EMF, and an essay on EMF's moral purpose.

24026 Collins, Arthur S. ENGLISH LITERATURE OF THE TWENTIETH CENTURY. Pp. 193-203. See G2105.

General overview and comparison with Lawrence.

24027 Connolly, Cyril. "The Art of Being Good: A Note on Maugham and Forster." In THE CONDEMNED PLAYGROUND: ESSAYS: 1927-1944. New York: Macmillan, 1946. Pp. 250-59.

EMF as moralist.

24028 Cox, C.B. "E.M. Forster's Island." In THE FREE SPIRIT. Pp. 74-102. See G3028.

EMF in the tradition of liberal humanism. Extract reprinted in 25094.

24029 Craig, David. "Fiction and the Rising Industrial Classes." EIC, 17 (1967), 64-74.

Social themes in Dickens, George Eliot, and EMF (HE and PI).

24030 Dobree, Bonamy. "E.M. Forster." In THE LAMP AND THE LUTE: STUDIES IN SEVEN AUTHORS. 1929. 2nd ed. London: Cass, 1963. Pp. 65-81.

EMF's concern with human relationships and the problems of life.

24031 Doughty, Howard N. "The Novels of E.M. Forster." BOOKMAN (New York), 75 (1932), 542-49.

EMF's novels lack integration.

24032 Echeruo, M.J.C. "E.M. Forster and the 'Undeveloped Heart.'" ESA, 5 (1962), 151-55.

Warfare between the heart and misplaced values in EMF's characters.

24033 Ellen, Elizabeth W. "E.M. Forster's Greenwood." JML, 5 (1976), 89-98.

EMF's recurrent use of the "greenwood," the "refuge from the cultural and intellectual life," in his early fiction.

24034 Evans, B. Ifor. ENGLISH LITERATURE BETWEEN THE WARS. Pp. 27-39. See G2324.

EMF an influential innovator as well as a traditionalist.

24035 Fraser, G.S. THE MODERN WRITER AND HIS WORLD. Pp. 90-95. See G2111.

EMF's place in literary history.

*24036 Friedman, Alan W. "E.M. Forster: 'Expansion. Not Completion.'" In his THE TURN OF THE NOVEL. Pp. 106-29. See G3045.

Rhythmic expansion and contraction of form in EMF (RWV, WAFT, PI).

24037 Frierson, William C. THE ENGLISH NOVEL IN TRANSITION. Pp. 168-72. See G3047.

EMF's attack on materialism (cf. Lawrence).

24038 Garnett, David. "E.M. Forster and John Galsworthy." REL, 5 (1964), 7-18.

Memoir and critical comparison.

24039 Gill, Richard. HAPPY RURAL SEAT. Passim. See G2330.

The country house as symbol in EMF.

24040 Gilomen, W. "Fantasy and Prophecy in E.M. Forster's Work." ES, 27 (1946), 97-112.

Supernatural and symbolic elements in EMF's fiction.

24041 Goldman, Mark. "Virginia Woolf and E.M. Forster: A Critical Dialogue." TSLL, 7 (1966), 387-400.

Woolf's and EMF's views of their own and each other's art.

24042 Hall, James. "Family Reunions: E.M. Forster." In his THE TRAGIC COMEDIANS. Pp. 11-30. See G3061.

The liberal humanist's conservative view of the family.

24043 Hampshire, Stuart N. "E.M. Forster." In his MODERN WRITERS, AND OTHER ESSAYS. Pp. 47-55. See G2335.

EMF's philosophy is of the nineteenth century, but his doubts are modern.

24044 Hannah, Donald. "The Limitations of Liberalism in E.M. Forster's Work." EM, 13 (1962), 165-78.

In PI, EMF overcomes the contrived liberalism of the earlier fiction.

24045 Hardy, Barbara. THE APPROPRIATE FORM. Pp. 73-82 and passim. See G3062.

EMF's dogmatic use of fate, and form (cf. Defoe, C. Bronte, and Hardy). Reprinted in 25094.

24046 Heilbrun, Carolyn G. TOWARDS ANDROGYNY. Pp. 97-101. See G2336.

EMF's androgynous heroes and heroines.

24047 Heine, Elizabeth. "The Significance of Structure in the Novels of E.M. Forster and Virginia Woolf." ELT, 16 (1973), 289-306.

See 23009.

24048 Hoare, Dorothy M. "E.M. Forster." In her SOME STUDIES IN THE MODERN NOVEL. Pp. 68-96. See G3069.

The balance of romantic and ironic in EMF.

24049 Holt, Lee Elbert. "E.M. Forster and Samuel Butler." PMLA, 61 (1946), 804-19.

EMF a "disciple" of Butler.

24050 Howarth, Herbert. "E.M. Forster and the Contrite Establishment." JGE, 17 (1965), 196-206.

EMF's contrition for his socially, intellectually, and economically elite position expressed throughout his fiction.

24051 Hynes, Samuel. "E.M. Forster. a. The Old Man at King's: Forster at 85; b. An Obituary; c. Forster's Cramp." In his EDWARDIAN OCCASIONS. Pp. 104-11; 111-14; 114-22. See G2345.

Collects three previously published essays.

24052 Irwin, W.R. THE GAME OF THE IMPOSSIBLE. Pp. 39-43 and passim. See G6417.

EMF's statements on the theory of fantasy and his uses of fantasy and the supernatural in his fiction.

24053 _____. "The Survival of Pan." PMLA, 76 (1961), 159-67.

Pan myth in Hawthorne, Lawrence, and EMF.

24054 Johnson, Elaine H. "The Intelligent Mr. E.M. Forster." Person, 35 (1954), 50-58.

EMF intelligent and humane, but emotionally limited.

24055 Johnson, Reginald Brimley. "E.M. Forster." In his SOME CONTEMPORARY NOVELISTS (MEN). Pp. 173-81. See G3076.

Jamesian qualities in the fiction (to HE).

*24056 Johnstone, J.K. THE BLOOMSBURY GROUP. Pp. 63-77, 100-113, 159-266, and passim. See G2348.

Exposition of EMF's aesthetic, a critique of his work, and a survey of his Bloomsbury relationships.

24057 _____. "E.M. Forster (1879-1970)." In THE POLITICS OF TWENTIETH-CENTURY NOVELISTS. Ed. George A. Panichas. Pp. 15-29. See G6207.

Assessment of EMF's political views, drawn chiefly from HE and PI.

24058 Jones, E.B.C. "E.M. Forster and Virginia Woolf." In THE ENGLISH NOVELISTS. Ed. Derek Verschoyle. Pp. 261-76. See G3150.

EMF both a traditional and an experimental novelist.

24059 Jones, W.S. Handley. "The Priest and the Siren." In his THE PRIEST AND THE SIREN. Pp. 1-12. See G6306.

Influence of the "Clapham" sect's views of religion and art on EMF, among others.

24060 Karl, Frederick R., and Marvin Magalaner. "E.M. Forster." In their A READER'S GUIDE TO GREAT TWENTIETH-CENTURY ENGLISH NOVELS. Pp. 100-124. See G3082.

Brief biography and critical commentary concentrating on WAFT, HE, and PI.

*24061 Kermode, Frank. "The One Orderly Product (E.M. Forster)." In his PUZZLES AND EPIPHANIES. Pp. 79-85. See G3086.

EMF as a symbolist. Reprinted in 23004 and 25046.

24062 Klingopulos, G.D. "E.M. Forster's Sense of History: and Cavafy." EIC, 8 (1958), 156-65.

EMF's sense of history in his essays and fiction.

24063 _____. "Mr. Forster's Good Influence." In THE MODERN AGE. Ed. Boris Ford. Pp. 245-56. See G2110.

EMF's growth of a genuine sensibility of "intellectual shrewdness, delicacy, and responsibility," exceptional among moderns.

24064 Lakshmi, Vijay. "Virginia Woolf and E.M. Forster: A Study of Their Critical Relations." LHY, 12, No. 2 (1971), 39-49.

EMF's and Woolf's critical views of each other.

24065 Langbaum, Robert. "A New Look at E.M. Forster." In THE MODERN SPIRIT: ESSAYS ON THE CONTINUITY OF NINETEENTH AND TWENTIETH CENTURY LITERATURE. New York: Oxford Univ. Press, 1970. Pp. 127-46.

Review essay, commenting upon EMF's intellectual milieu and his "two masterpieces": WAFT and PI.

*24066 Leavis, Frank R. "E.M. Forster." SCRUTINY, 7 (1938), 185-202.

EMF's gift for social comedy like Austen's but his preoccupation with the theme of emotional vitality (cf. Lawrence) inappropriate to the distanced comic mode. Important assessment. Reprinted in 23004.

24067 Liddell, Robert. A TREATISE ON THE NOVEL. Pp. 64-70 and passim. See G3093.

EMF as humanist, with qualifications.

24068 Lovett, Robert M., and Helen S. Hughes. "E.M. Forster (1879)." In their THE HISTORY OF THE NOVEL IN ENGLAND. Pp. 416-21. See G2209.

Brief survey. Notes EMF's "sharp originality" beneath the "semblance of conformity" to traditional fictional techniques.

24069 Macaulay, Rose. "E.M. Forster." In LIVING WRITERS. Ed. Gilbert Phelps. Pp. 94-105. See G3121.

A critique on EMF's own terms (cf. ASPECTS).

24070 MacDonald, Alastair A. "Class-Consciousness in E.M. Forster." UKCR, 27 (1971), 235-40.

To the detriment of his fiction, EMF shares the values of the class he dissects.

24071 McLuhan, H. Marshall. "Kipling and Forster." SR, 52 (1944), 332-43.

Compared as cultural "neurotics."

24072 Merivale, Patricia. PAN THE GOAT-GOD: HIS MYTH IN MODERN TIMES. Cambridge: Harvard Univ. Press, 1969. Pp. 180-91 and passim.

Allusions to Pan in EMF's fiction.

24073 Morton, Arthur Leslie. "E.M. Forster and the Classless Society." In LANGUAGE OF MEN. London: Cobbett Press, 1945. Pp. 78-88.

EMF writes for a society ("classless") which does not yet exist.

24074 Müllenbrock, Heinz-Joachim. "Modes of Opening in the Work of E.M. Forster: A Contribution to the Poetics of His Novels." MP, 70 (1973), 216-29.

Stylistic and thematic significance of EMF's openings (LJ, HE, PI).

24075 Natwar-Singh, K. "Only Connect . . . : Forster and India." In ASPECTS OF E.M. FORSTER. Ed. Oliver Stallybrass. Pp. 37-50. See 23026.

EMF's attitudes to India, and the Indian response to his work. Reprinted in 23013 and 25097.

24076 Nicholson, Norman. MAN AND LITERATURE. Pp. 157-60. See G2353.

EMF a "supreme" satirist of the modern "liberal" and "natural" conceptions of man found in Wells and Lawrence.

24077 Nierenberg, Edwin. "The Prophecy of E.M. Forster." QQ, 71 (1964), 189-202.

EMF's essentially Christian ethos.

24078 Panichas, George A. "E.M. Forster and D.H. Lawrence: Their Views on Education." In RENAISSANCE AND MODERN ESSAYS. Ed. George R. Hibbard. London: Routledge, 1966. Pp. 199-213.

EMF and Lawrence often embody their social themes within their views of modern education.

24079 Parker, G.B. "Introduction." In E.M. FORSTER: SELECTED WRITINGS. Ed. Parker. Pp. ix-xv. See 13003.

EMF's championing of the "cause of individual freedom" in his fiction and nonfiction.

24080 Pritchett, Victor S. "Mr. Forster's Birthday." In his THE LIVING NOVEL AND LATER APPRECIATIONS. Pp. 244-50. See G3125.

Appreciation of EMF's moral impact.

24081 Putt, Samuel Gorley. "The Strength of Timid Hearts: E.M. Forster." In SCHOLARS OF THE HEART. London: Faber, 1962. Pp. 35-42.

EMF's attitudes toward the heart and the mind.

24082 Rajiva, Stanley F. "E.M. Forster and Music." In A GARLAND FOR E.M. FORSTER. Ed. H.H.A. Gowda. Pp. 55-68. See 23013.

EMF's musical interests and use of music in his work.

24083 Raleigh, John Henry. "Victorian Morals and the Modern Novel." PR, 25 (1958), 241-64.

Butlerian echoes in EMF and D.H. Lawrence.

24084 Ransom, John Crowe. "E.M. Forster." KR, 5 (1943), 618-23.

EMF in relation to the liberal tradition. Reprinted in 23011.

24085 Raskin, Jonah. THE MYTHOLOGY OF IMPERIALISM. Pp. 222-71, 286-93, and passim. See G6208.

Marxist reading of EMF's imperialistic themes.

24086 Rawlings, Donn. "E.M. Forster, 'Prophecy,' and the Subversion of Myth." PAUNCH, No. 30 (1967), pp. 17-36.

The use of and attitudes toward myth in the fiction.

24087 Reed, John R. "Made in England: The Gentleman Abroad." In OLD SCHOOL TIES: THE PUBLIC SCHOOLS IN BRITISH LITERATURE. Syracuse, N.Y.: Syracuse Univ. Press, 1964. Pp. 124-56 and passim.

EMF as critic of the public-school ethos.

*24088 Richards, I.A. "A Passage to Forster: Reflections on a Novelist." FORUM, 78 (1927), 914-20.

EMF's "elusive weakness" attributed to his "odd" assumptions and alien sense of values. Reprinted in 23004.

24089 Routh, Harold V. ENGLISH LITERATURE AND IDEAS IN THE TWENTIETH CENTURY. Pp. 58-62. See G2119.

EMF in the context of modern literary history.

24090 Savage, Derek S. "E.M. Forster." In his THE WITHERED BRANCH. Pp. 44-69. See G3129.

Search for the "significant pattern" (the "liberal dilemma") which underlies EMF's work and his silence. Reprinted in 23004.

24091 Smith, H.A. "Forster's Humanism and the Nineteenth Century." In FORSTER. Ed. Malcolm Bradbury. Pp. 106-16. See 23004.

EMF's links to enlightenment, romantic, and Victorian humanist traditions.

24092 Spender, Stephen. "English Threnody, American Tragedy; Elegies for England: E.M. Forster." In LOVE-HATE RELATIONS: ENGLISH AND AMERICAN SENSIBILITIES. New York: Random House, 1974. Pp. 222-33.

A constant theme in EMF's novels is the "ritualistic murdering of the ancient, beautiful and unspoiled, the tolerant and benignant England."

24093 ______. "Personal Relations and Public Powers." In his THE CREATIVE ELEMENT. Pp. 77-91. See G3135.

EMF as visionary.

24094 Sprott, W.J.H. "Forster as a Humanist." In ASPECTS OF E.M. FORSTER. Ed. Oliver Stallybrass. Pp. 73-80. See 23026.

EMF's humanism evaluated in the light of his own definition.

*24095 Stallybrass, Oliver. "The Abinger Edition of E.M. Forster." ELT, 16 (1973), 245-56.

Explanation of the scope and editorial policy of the Abinger edition. See 13001 and 23009.

24096 Stevenson, Lionel. THE HISTORY OF THE ENGLISH NOVEL. XI, 87-102. See G2212.

Surveys EMF's career as an "Earnest Realist."

24097 Stone, Wilfred. "Forster on Love and Money." In ASPECTS OF E. M. FORSTER. Ed. Oliver Stallybrass. Pp. 107-21. See 23026.

Especially on the significance of money in EMF's work.

24098 Swinnerton, Frank. THE GEORGIAN LITERARY SCENE. Pp. 303-12. See G2364.

Brief critical commentary emphasizing EMF's craft and "coldness."

24099 Thomson, George H. "E.M. Forster and Howard Sturgis." TSLL, 10 (1968), 423-33.

Influence study.

24100 Thorpe, Michael. "E.M. Forster's Short Stories." In A GARLAND FOR E.M. FORSTER. Ed. H.H.A. Gowda. Pp. 69-75. See 23013.

General survey and critique.

24101 Tindall, William York. FORCES IN MODERN BRITISH LITERATURE. Passim. See G2122.

EMF's relation to modern literary movements.

24102 Traversi, D.A. "The Novels of E.M. Forster." ARENA, No. 1 (1937), pp. 28-40.

EMF's pessimism. Reprinted in 23011.

24103 Turk, Jo M. "The Evolution of E.M. Forster's Narrator." SNNTS, 5 (1973), 428-40.

Developmental pattern in EMF's apparently paradoxical use of his narrative voices.

24104 Voorhees, Richard J. "The Novels of E.M. Forster." SAQ, 53 (1954), 89-99.

Discursive survey of EMF's themes.

24105 Waggoner, Hyatt Howe. "Exercises in Perspective: Notes on the Uses of Coincidence in the Novels of E.M. Forster." CHIMERA, 3 (Summer 1945), 3-14.

EMF's use of coincidence to arrange multiple perspectives enlarges our vision. Reprinted in 23004.

*24106 Warren, Austin. "E.M. Forster." 1937. In RAGE FOR ORDER: ESSAYS IN CRITICISM. Ann Arbor: Univ. of Michigan Press, 1959. Pp. 119-41.

EMF in the tradition of the nineteenth-century commentator novelists. Reprinted in 23004.

24107 Wilde, Alan. "Depths and Surfaces: Dimensions of Forsterian Irony." ELT, 16 (1973), 257-74.

See 23009.

24108 Woodward, A.G. "The Humanism of E.M. Forster." THEORIA, 20 (1963), 17-33.

Humanistic world view and humanists in EMF.

*24109 Woolf, Virginia. "The Novels of E.M. Forster." 1927. In her COLLECTED ESSAYS. Ed. L. Woolf. London: Hogarth, 1966-67. I, 342-51.

EMF part art-novelist, part teacher. Reprinted in 23011 and 25046 (extract).

24110 Zabel, Morton Dauwen. "E.M. Forster: The Trophies of the Mind." In his CRAFT AND CHARACTER. Pp. 228-52. See G3162.

General survey of EMF's world view and assessment of his fiction.

24111 Zwerdling, Alex. "The Novels of E.M. Forster." TCL, 2 (1957), 171-81.

The later works move away from novels of manners to more profound social and symbolic fictions.

2.5 Studies of Individual Works

The following section is subdivided into two parts: i. Fiction (alphabetically by title), and ii. Miscellaneous Writings. Virtually every full-length study of EMF considers the individual novels in detail. For discussions of the miscellaneous writings, see section 2.3 above, particularly Beer (23001), Brander (23005), Kelvin (23015), Macaulay (23016), Martin (23020), Rose (23024), Stone (23027), and Trilling (23029).

i. FICTION

"Albergo Empedocle" (1903)

25001 Malek, James S. "Forster's 'Albergo Empedocle': A Precursor of MAURICE." SSF, 11 (1974), 427-30.

"Implicit homosexuality" of the story.

"The Celestial Omnibus" (1908)

25002 Wilcox, Stewart C. "The Allegory of Forster's 'The Celestial Omnibus.'" MFS, 2 (1956), 191-96.

Story embodies an allegory of innocence.

"The Eternal Moment" (1905)

25003 Hagopian, John V. "'The Eternal Moment.'" In INSIGHT II. Ed. John Hagopian and Martin Dolch. Pp. 122-30. See G5007.

Summary, critique and study questions.

HOWARDS END (1910)

25004 Armstrong, Paul. "E.M. Forster's HOWARDS END: The Existential Crisis of the Liberal Imagination." MOSAIC, 8, No. 1 (1974), 183-99.

The liberal imagination raises questions which only the existential imagination can answer.

25005 Bensen, Alice R. "E.M. Forster's Dialectic: HOWARD'S END." MFS, 1, No. 2 (1955), 17-22.

EMF attempts a synthesis of clashing forces in HE.

25006 Berland, Alwyn. "James and Forster: The Morality of Class." CAMBRIDGE JOURNAL, 6 (1953), 259-80.

Comparative study of PRINCESS CASAMASSIMA and HE.

*25007 Bradbury, Malcolm. "HOWARD'S END." In FORSTER. Ed. Bradbury. Pp. 128-43. See 23004.

HE blends both of EMF's chief modes: social comedy and visionary fiction.

25008 Churchill, Thomas. "Place and Personality in HOWARD'S END." Crit, 5 (1962), 61-73.

The connectedness of place and tradition reflects the social theme of connection between personalities.

25009 Colmer, John. "HOWARD'S END Revisited." In A GARLAND FOR E.M. FORSTER. Ed. H.H.A. Gowda. Pp. 9-22. See 23013.

HE a structurally and thematically rhythmic novel.

25010 Delany, Paul. "Lawrence and E.M. Forster: Two Rainbows." DHLR, 8 (1975), 54-62.

EMF's and Lawrence's similar use of rainbow symbolism (HE and THE RAINBOW).

25011 Delbaere-Garant, Jeanne. "'Who shall inherit England?': A Comparison between HOWARD'S END, PARADE'S END and UNCONDITIONAL SURRENDER." ES, 50 (1969), 101-5.

Comparable themes of class change, social transformation, and inheritance in EMF, Ford, and Waugh.

25012 Gillen, Francis. "HOWARD'S END and the Neglected Narrator." NOVEL, 3 (1970), 139-52.

Narrator makes connections and acts as an "exemplum" of how connection can be made.

25013 Green, Robert. "Messrs. Wilcox and Kurtz, Hollow Men." TCL, 14 (1969), 231-39.

Dealing with the ruling class, HE is as much a novel of empire as Conrad's "Heart of Darkness."

25014 Hagopian, John V., and Anne Beltran. "HOWARD'S END." In INSIGHT II. Ed. Hagopian and Martin Dolch. Pp. 130-41. See G5007.

Summary, brief critical commentary and study questions.

25015 Hardy, John Edward. "HOWARD'S END: The Sacred Center." In MAN IN THE MODERN NOVEL. Pp. 34-51. See G3063.

The integral structure and theme of integrity in HE.

*25016 Hoffman, Frederick J. THE MORTAL NO. Pp. 79-87. See G3070.

Novel examines the inadequacies of the philistine's linear view of progress ("the bogey of progress"), and the intellectual's sterile antiprogressivism. Originally appeared in 23021.

*25017 Hoy, Cyrus. "Forster's Metaphysical Novel." PMLA, 75 (1960), 126-36.

EMF's systematic attempt to reconcile opposites.

25018 McGurk, E. Barry. "Gentlefolk in Philistia: The Influence of Matthew Arnold on E.M. Forster's HOWARD'S END." ELT, 15 (1972), 213-19.

25019 Maskell, Duke. "Style and Symbolism in HOWARD'S END." EIC, 19 (1969), 292-308.

Deficiencies of language and symbol in HE.

25020 Roby, Kinley E. "Irony and the Narrative Voice in HOWARD'S END." JNT, 2 (1972), 116-24.

Technical analysis.

25021 Rueckert, William H. KENNETH BURKE AND THE DRAMA OF HUMAN RELATIONS. Minneapolis: Univ. of Minnesota Press, 1963. Pp. 179-90 and passim.

Analysis of the wych-elm symbol in the light of Burke's critical theories.

25022 Wakefield, George P. "HOWARD'S END" (E.M. FORSTER). Oxford: Blackwell, 1968.

Introduction to the novel's style, themes, and characters, and model analyses of two chapters.

25023 Westburg, Barry R. "Forster's Fifth Symphony: Another Aspect of HOWARD'S END." MFS, 10 (1964), 359-65.

EMF's use of musical allusion and symbolism.

25024 Widdowson, Peter. E.M. FORSTER'S "HOWARD'S END": FICTION AS HISTORY. Sussex, Engl.: Sussex Univ. Press, 1977.

Not seen.

THE LONGEST JOURNEY (1907)

25025 Hanquart, Evelyne. "The Manuscript of Forster's THE LONGEST JOURNEY." RES, 25 (1974), 152-62.

Reading of manuscript and comparison to published version.

*25026 Harvey, John. "Imagination and Moral Theme in E.M. Forster's THE LONGEST JOURNEY." EIC, 6 (1956), 418-33.

The novel's failure is attributable to EMF's inability to give imaginative life to its moral and thematic center, "the Real." Reprinted in 23004.

25027 Heine, Elizabeth. "Rickie Elliot and the Cow: The Cambridge Apostles and THE LONGEST JOURNEY." ELT, 15 (1972), 116-34.

LJ's symbolism and philosophic background.

*25028 Magnus, John. "Ritual Aspects of E.M. Forster's THE LONGEST JOURNEY." MFS, 13 (1967), 195-210.

EMF's use of ritual for structure, symbol, and character development.

25029 Paul, David. "Time and the Novelist." PR, 21 (1954), 636-49.

LJ among other works, departs from Victorian narrative conventions.

25030 Seward, Barbara. THE SYMBOLIC ROSE. Pp. 132-33. See G3133.

Rose symbolism in LJ.

25031 Shahane, V.A. "THE LONGEST JOURNEY." LCrit, 4 (Dec. 1960), 1-8.

LJ a moral fable of appearance and reality.

"The Machine Stops" (1909)

25032 Berman, Jeffrey. "Forster's Other Cave: The Platonic Structure of 'The Machine Stops.'" EXTRAPOLATION, 17 (1976), 172-81.

25033 Hillegas, Mark R. THE FUTURE AS NIGHTMARE: H.G. WELLS AND THE ANTI-UTOPIANS. Pp. 83-95 and passim. See G6415.

"The Machine Stops" the first major anti-Utopian work.

MAURICE (1971)

Also see 23011.

*25034 Bolling, Douglass. "The Distanced Heart: Artistry in E.M. Forster's MAURICE." MFS, 20 (1974), 157-67.

Favorable evaluation of MAURICE within the contexts of EMF's work and the Edwardian conventions for fiction.

25035 Hotchkiss, Joyce. "Romance and Reality: The Dualistic Style of E.M. Forster's MAURICE." JNT, 4 (1974), 163-75.

EMF's "tension-creating" and "dissonant" style.

25036 McDowell, Frederick P.W. "Second Thoughts on E.M. Forster's MAURICE." VWQ, 1, No. 1 (1972), 46-59.

Analysis of the novel.

25037 Malek, James S. "Forster's 'Albergo Empedocle': A Precursor of MAURICE." SSF, 11 (1974), 427-30.

See 25001.

25038 Rising, C. "E.M. Forster's MAURICE: A Summing Up." TQ, 17, No. 1 (1974), 84-96.

Despite weaknesses, MAURICE an important summation of several EMF themes.

25039 Spender, Stephen. "Forster's Queer Novel." PR, 39 (1972), 113-17.

Review essay consideration of the homosexual themes in MAURICE.

A PASSAGE TO INDIA (1924)

Also see 23013.

*25040 Allen, Glen O. "Structure, Symbol, and Theme in E.M. Forster's A PASSAGE TO INDIA." PMLA, 70 (1955), 934-54.

PI a fully "integrated experience." Its themes, symbols, and structure provide a unified, but complex whole. Reprinted in 25098.

25041 Austin, Edgar A. "Rites of Passage in A PASSAGE TO INDIA." OW, 9, No. 3 (1964), 64-72.

Ritualistic life and death initiations in PI.

25042 Bell, Vereen M. "Comic Seriousness in A PASSAGE TO INDIA." SAQ, 66 (1967), 606-17.

Emphasis on the social and psychological comedy of the novel.

25043 Boulton, J.A. NOTES ON E.M. FORSTER'S "A PASSAGE TO INDIA." Bath, Engl.: James Brodie, 1966.

Chapter-by-chapter summary, general critical commentary, and a conjectural map of the novel. Introductory in nature.

25044 Boyle, Ted E. "Adela Quested's Delusion: The Failure of Rationalism in A PASSAGE TO INDIA." CE, 26 (1965), 478-80.

Adela's sexual frustration is EMF's indictment of her sterile rationalism. Reprinted in 25098.

*25045 Bradbury, Malcolm. "Two Passages to India: Forster as Victorian and Modern." In ASPECTS OF E.M. FORSTER. Ed. Oliver Stallybrass. Pp. 123-42. See 23026.

EMF's divided sensibility. Reprinted in 25046. Also see 24015.

*25046 ______, ed. "A PASSAGE TO INDIA": A CASEBOOK. London: Macmillan, 1970.

Collects four commentaries on PI's composition, five contemporary responses (including D.H. Lawrence's) to the novel, and eleven "more recent" critical studies. Indexed. Includes 22005, 24024, 24061, 25045, 25047, 25048, 25101, 25106; and extracts from the following books and articles: 23001, 23007, 23017, 23029, and 24109.

*25047 Brower, Reuben A. "The Twilight of the Double Vision: Symbol and Irony in A PASSAGE TO INDIA." In THE FIELDS OF LIGHT: AN EXPERIMENT IN CRITICAL READING. New York: Oxford Univ. Press, 1951. Pp. 182-98.

PI ("Temple") fails to reconcile the ironic tension between the symbolic dualisms of the "Mosque" and the "Caves." Reprinted in 25046.

*25048 Brown, Edward K. "Rhythm in E.M. Forster's A PASSAGE TO INDIA." In his RHYTHM IN THE NOVEL. Pp. 87-115. See G3015.

EMF's own rhythmic ideas (see ASPECTS) applied to his use of leitmotif in the novel. Reprinted in 23004 and 25046.

25049 Burke, Kenneth. "Social and Cosmic Mystery: A PASSAGE TO INDIA." In LANGUAGE AS SYMBOLIC ACTION: ESSAYS ON LIFE, LITERATURE, AND METHOD. Berkeley and Los Angeles: Univ. of California Press, 1966. Pp. 223-39.

Considers, among several theoretical concerns, EMF's creation of " a mood of ironically sympathetic contemplation."

25050 Cammarota, Richard S. "Musical Analogy and Internal Design in A PASSAGE TO INDIA." ELT, 18 (1975), 38-46.

PI's musical structure.

25051 Chaudhuri, Nirad C. "Passage To and From India." ENCOUNTER, 2 (1954), 19-24.

Political impact of PI. Reprinted in 25094 and 25098.

*25052 Colmer, John. E.M. FORSTER: "A PASSAGE TO INDIA." London: Arnold, 1967.

An excellent introduction to the novel's principal themes, its philosophical implications, and EMF's fictional technique.

25053 _____. "Form and Design in the Novel." In APPROACHES TO THE NOVEL. Ed. J. Colmer. Edinburgh: Oliver and Boyd, 1967. Pp. 1-16.

On the relation of art to life, with PI as the chief example.

25054 Daleski, H.M. "Rhythmic and Symbolic Patterns in A PASSAGE TO INDIA." HUSL, 17 (1966), 259-79.

EMF's "rhythm" achieved through symbolic patterning.

25055 Dauner, Louise, "What Happened in the Cave? Reflections on A PASSAGE TO INDIA." MFS, 7 (1961), 258-70.

Archetypal psychoanalysis of the cave experience. See 23021. Reprinted in 25098.

25056 Deacon, Andrew. "A PASSAGE TO INDIA: Forster's Confidence." CR, 14 (1971), 125-36.

25057 Eaglestone, Arthur A. [Roger Dataller]. THE PLAIN MAN AND THE NOVEL. Pp. 165-69. See G3038.

PI a "satire of contrasts" with a promise of reconciliation.

25058 Enright, D.J. "To the Lighthouse or to India?" In THE APOTHECARY'S SHOP: ESSAYS ON LITERATURE. London: Secker and Warburg, 1957. Pp. 168-86.

Comparison of Woolf and EMF.

*25059 Fleischman, Avrom. "Being and Nothing in A PASSAGE TO INDIA." CRITICISM, 15 (1973), 109-25.

Three distinct levels of being embodied in the novel (existentialist).

25060 Fussell, Paul. "E.M. Forster's Mrs. Moore: Some Suggestions." PQ, 32 (1953), 388-95.

Comparison of Mrs. Moore as a prophetic figure with Mrs. Wilcox (HE) and Madame Blavatsky.

25061 Gish, Robert. "Forster as Fabulist: Proverbs and Parables in A PASSAGE TO INDIA." ELT, 15 (1972), 245-56.

25062 Goonetilleke, D.C.R.A. "Colonial Neuroses: Kipling and Forster." ARIEL, 5, No. 4 (1974), 56-68.

Racial and cultural fear in Kipling and PI.

25063 Hale, Nancy. "A Passage to Relationship." AR, 20 (1960), 19-30.

Novel's theme is human relationships.

25064 Henderson, Philip. "Bloomsbury: E.M. Forster." In his THE NOVEL TODAY. Pp. 91-96. See G3067.

Although the sentiments of PI are enlightened and admirable, EMF never grasps the hard realities of colonialism (Marxist).

25065 Hollingsworth, Keith. "A PASSAGE TO INDIA: The Echoes in the Marabar Caves." CRITICISM, 4 (1962), 210-24.

Symbol analysis. Reprinted in 25098.

25066 Horowitz, Ellin. "The Communal Ritual and the Dying God in E.M. Forster's A PASSAGE TO INDIA." CRITICISM, 6 (1964), 70-88.

EMF's synthesis of social and mythical concerns.

25067 Hunt, John Dixon. "Muddle and Mystery in A PASSAGE TO INDIA." ELH, 33 (1966), 497-517.

"Muddle" both PI's theme and its impact on the reader.

25068 Italia, Paul G. "On Miss Quested's Given Name, in E.M. Forster's A PASSAGE TO INDIA." ELN, 11 (1973), 118-20.

Name symbolism.

25069 Kain, Richard M. "Vision and Discovery in E.M. Forster's A PASSAGE TO INDIA." In TWELVE ORIGINAL ESSAYS ON GREAT ENGLISH NOVELS. Ed. Charles Shapiro. Pp. 253-75. See G3134.

General critical reading of PI.

25070 Keir, Walter A.S. "A PASSAGE TO INDIA Reconsidered." CAMBRIDGE JOURNAL, 5 (1952), 426-35.

PI not a tract or a philosophic essay, but a work of art. Reprinted in 25094.

25071 Kennard, Jean E. "A PASSAGE TO INDIA and Dickinson's Saint at Benares." SNNTS, 5 (1973), 417-27.

Source study.

25072 Kettle, Arnold. "E.M. Forster: A PASSAGE TO INDIA (1924)." In his AN INTRODUCTION TO THE ENGLISH NOVEL. II, 152-63. See G3088.

EMF's greatness lies in his undertaking of large issues, rather than in the solutions he might propose. Reprinted in 25094.

25073 Lebowitz, Naomi. "A PASSAGE TO INDIA: History as Humanist Humor." In HUMANISM AND THE ABSURD IN THE MODERN NOVEL. Evanston, Ill.: Northwestern Univ. Press, 1971. Pp. 67-83.

The ordering of life in fiction (e.g., PI) consoles EMF in his confrontation with the absurdity of existence.

*25074 Levine, June P. CREATION AND CRITICISM: "A PASSAGE TO INDIA." Lincoln: Univ. of Nebraska Press, 1971.

An excellent and thorough study of PI's backgrounds (biographical, political, cultural, and philosophic), manuscript development, and critical reputation. Levine also offers her own full interpretation of the novel.

25075 McDonald, Walter R. "The Unity of A PASSAGE TO INDIA." CEA, 36, No. 1 (1973), 38-42.

Unities of action, character, and style make PI a "textbook" novel.

25076 Maclean, Hugh. "The Structure of A PASSAGE TO INDIA." UTQ, 22 (1953), 157-71.

PI suggests an optimistic resolution of differences. Reprinted in 25098.

25077 Mahood, M.M. "Amristar to Chandrapore: E.M. Forster & the Massacre." ENCOUNTER, 41, No. 3 (1973), 26-29.

Political comparison between EMF's Chandrapore affair and the Amristar Massacre (1919).

25078 Martin, John Sayre. "Mrs. Moore and the Marabar Caves: A Mythological Reading." MFS, 11 (1965), 429-33.

The Greek archetype of the Cumaean Sibyl and the cave scene.

25079 Mason, W.H. "A PASSAGE TO INDIA." New York: Barnes and Noble, 1963.

An introduction to PI for the undergraduate student. Mason offers chapters on the "significance," style, and characterization of the novel.

25080 Mendilow, A.A. "The Triadic World of E.M. Forster." HUSL, 17 (1966), 280-91.

Triadic patterns in the novel.

*25081 Meyers, Jeffrey. "E.M. Forster: A PASSAGE TO INDIA." In his FICTION AND THE COLONIAL EXPERIENCE. Pp. 29-53. See G6206.

Interrelationship of political events, political ideas, and moral ideas in PI.

25082 Moody, Phillipa. A CRITICAL COMMENTARY ON E.M. FORSTER'S "A PASSAGE TO INDIA." New York: St. Martin's Press, 1968.

A student's study guide. General chapters on PI's cultural backgrounds and EMF's liberal imagination bracket useful critical commentaries on the three sections of the novel.

25083 Morley, Patricia A. "E.M. Forster's 'Temple': Eclectic or Visionary." UTQ, 39 (1970), 229-41.

Role of the "Temple" section in the novel as a whole.

25084 Moseley, Edwin M. "Christ as One Avatar: Forster's PASSAGE TO INDIA." In his PSEUDONYMS OF CHRIST IN THE MODERN NOVEL. Pp. 153-62. See G6309.

Religious and cross-cultural mythic patterns in PI.

25085 Naslund, Sena Jeter. "Fantasy, Prophecy, and Point of View in A PASSAGE TO INDIA." SNNTS, 7 (1975), 258-76.

Relationships among the fantastic and prophetic passages, and EMF's point of view in the novel.

25086 Nierenberg, Edwin. "The Withered Priestess: Mrs. Moore's Incomplete Passage to India." MLQ, 24 (1964), 198-204.

Mrs. Moore fails to find fulfillment, but indicates the necessary ideal of ethical humanism. Reprinted in 25098.

25087 Overton, Grant. "E.M. Forster: A PASSAGE TO INDIA." In his THE PHILOSOPHY OF FICTION. Pp. 315-25. See G4069.

EMF, like Tolstoy, transcends documentary realism to suggest the "riddle of the universe."

25088 Parry, Benita. "Passage to More Than India." In FORSTER. Ed. Malcolm Bradbury. Pp. 160-74. See 23004.

The Indian experience becomes a challenge to the alien's accepted notions of belief. Reprinted in 25098.

25089 Pedersen, Glenn. "Forster's Symbolic Form." KR, 21 (1959), 231-49.

While PI realistically documents cultural divisions, its symbolism suggests a transcendant unity.

25090 Pradhan, S.V. "A 'Song' of Love: Forster's A PASSAGE TO INDIA." CentR, 17 (1973), 297-320.

PI's latent spiritual content.

25091 Price, Martin. "People of the Book: Character in Forster's A PASSAGE TO INDIA"; "The Logic of Intensity: More on Character." CRITICAL INQUIRY, 1 (1975), 605-22; 2 (1975), 369-79.

EMF and the theoretical aspects of characterization.

25092 Rantavaara, Irma. VIRGINIA WOOLF AND BLOOMSBURY. Helsinki: Annales Academiae Fennicae, 1953. Pp. 42-48, 126-36 and passim.

EMF's relation to ideas and figures of Bloomsbury.

25093 Rau, Santha Rama. A PASSAGE TO INDIA: A PLAY. New York: Harcourt, 1961.

Dramatic adaptation.

*25094 Rutherford, Andrew, ed. TWENTIETH CENTURY INTERPRETATIONS OF "A PASSAGE TO INDIA": A COLLECTION OF CRITICAL ESSAYS. Englewood Cliffs, N.J.: Prentice-Hall, 1970.

Collects six critical and interpretive essays on PI, two briefer comments on EMF, a study of the novel's composition, and the editor's introduction (pp. 1-16). Includes 24045, 25051, 25070, 25072, 25101, 25106; and extracts from the following books and articles: 23007, 23029, and 24028.

25095 Scott, P. "India: A Post-Forsterian View." EDH, 36 (1970), 113-32.

Personal experience confirms EMF's prophetic view of Anglo-Indian relations in PI.

25096 Shahane, V.A. "Symbolism in A PASSAGE TO INDIA: 'Temple.'" ES, 44 (1963), 423-31.

Final section of PI symbolizes reconciliation and harmony. Ending realistic, not defeatist. Reprinted in 25098.

25097 _____, ed. FOCUS ON FORSTER'S "A PASSAGE TO INDIA": INDIAN ESSAYS IN CRITICISM. London: Longmans, 1975.

Collects thirteen "part academic, part personal, part critical" essays, focused on various aspects of PI, which, together, testify to the continued high regard for EMF among Indian scholars. Received too late for itemized annotation in this guide. Includes 24075.

*25098 _____, ed. PERSPECTIVES ON E.M. FORSTER'S "A PASSAGE TO INDIA": A COLLECTION OF CRITICAL ESSAYS. New York: Barnes and Noble, 1968.

Reprints fourteen articles on PI (mostly symbolic readings), plus the editor's introduction to its critical reputation. Includes 25040, 25044, 25051, 25055, 25065, 25076, 25086, 25088, 25096, 25106; and extracts from the following books: 23014, 23017, 23025, and 23028.

25099 Singh, Bhupal. A SURVEY OF ANGLO-INDIAN FICTION. London: Oxford Univ. Press, 1934. Pp. 221-33.

Praises EMF's objectivity and insight.

25100 Spencer, Michael. "Hinduism in E.M. FORSTER'S A PASSAGE TO INDIA." JASt, 27 (1968), 281-95.

25101 Stallybrass, Oliver. "Forster's 'Wobblings': The Manuscripts of A PASSAGE TO INDIA. In ASPECTS OF E.M. FORSTER. Ed. Stallybrass. Pp. 143-54. See 23026.

Describes and discusses the complex state of the manuscripts. Reprinted in 25046 and 25094.

25102 Tindall, William York. THE LITERARY SYMBOL. Pp. 142-44, 189-90. See G3146.

The caves as a central symbol.

25103 Wagner, Roland C. "The Excremental and the Spiritual in A PASSAGE TO INDIA." MLQ, 31 (1970), 359-71.

Dualistic thesis.

25104 Webner, Helene L. "E.M. Forster's Divine Comedy." RENASCENCE, 23 (1971), 98-110.

Parallels to Dante.

25105 Werry, Richard R. "Rhythm in Forster's A PASSAGE TO INDIA." In STUDIES IN HONOR OF JOHN WILCOX. Ed. A. Dayle Wallace and Woodburn O. Ross. Detroit: Wayne State Univ. Press, 1958. Pp. 227-37.

Analyzes the two dimensions of rhythmic development in PI (using EMF's own definitions from ASPECTS).

*25106 White, Gertrude M. "A PASSAGE TO INDIA: Analysis and Revaluation." PMLA, 68 (1953), 641-57.

Dialectical theme and structure in PI. Reprinted in 25046, 25094, and 25098.

"The Road from Colonus" (1904)

25107 Hagopian, John V. "The Road from Colonus." In INSIGHT II. Ed. Hagopian and Martin Dolch. Pp. 117-22. See G5007.

Summary, critique, and study questions.

25108 Lee, L.L. "'Oedipus at Colonus': The Modern 'Vulgarizations' of Forster and Cicellis." SSF, 8 (1971), 561-67.

EMF inverts the traditional myth of regeneration into frustration.

A ROOM WITH A VIEW (1908)

*25109 Lucas, John. "Wagner and Forster: PARSIFAL and A ROOM WITH A VIEW." ELH, 33 (1966), 92-117.

A close study of PARSIFAL analogues in RWV.

25110 Meyers, Jeffrey. "Giotto and A ROOM WITH A VIEW." In his PAINTING AND THE NOVEL. Pp. 38-45. See G3105.

EMF's use of models from painting to develop the symbolism, characters, and themes of RWV.

25111 ______. "'Vacant Heart and Hand and Eye': The Homosexual Theme in A ROOM WITH A VIEW." ELT, 13 (1970), 181-92.

25112 Tait, Stephan, and Kenneth Allot. A ROOM WITH A VIEW. London: Arnold, 1951.

Dramatic adaptation of novel.

"The Story of the Siren" (1920)

25113 Mansfield, Katherine. "Throw Them Overboard!" In NOVELS AND NOVELISTS. Ed. J.M. Murry. New York: Knopf, 1930. Pp. 237-39.

EMF's leisurely style. Reprinted in 23011.

25114 Missey, James Lawrence. "Forster's Redemptive Siren." MFS, 10 (1964), 383-85.

Siren an affirmative symbol.

WHERE ANGELS FEAR TO TREAD (1905)

25115 Delbaere-Garant, Jeanne. "The Call of the South: WHERE ANGELS FEAR TO TREAD and THE LOST GIRL." RLV, 29 (1963), 336-57.

Sexual, class, and cultural confrontations in EMF and Lawrence.

25116 Meyers, Jeffrey. "Ghirlandaio and WHERE ANGELS FEAR TO TREAD." In his PAINTING AND THE NOVEL. Pp. 31-38. See G3105.

EMF's use of models from painting to develop the symbolism, characters, and themes of WAFT.

ii. MISCELLANEOUS WRITINGS

25117 Joseph, David I. THE ART OF REARRANGEMENT: E.M. FORSTER'S "ABINGER HARVEST." New Haven, Conn.: Yale Univ. Press, 1964.

Argues the significant reflection of EMF's chief fictional themes in ABINGER HARVEST, and the essential coherence of the essay collection.

25118 Leavis, Q.D. "Mr. E.M. Forster." In A SELECTION FROM "SCRUTINY." Ed. Frank R. Leavis. I, 134-38. See G2351.

Review essay on ABINGER HARVEST.

25119 McDowell, Frederick P.W. "E.M. Forster and Goldsworthy Lowes Dickinson." SNNTS, 5 (1973), 441-56.

Backgrounds to and limitations of EMF's biography of Dickinson.

*25120 _____. "E.M. Forster's Conception of the Critic." TSL, 10 (1965), 93-100.

*25121 _____. "E.M. Forster's Theory of Literature." CRITICISM, 8 (1966), 19-43.

Important essay (with above) on EMF's critical perspective.

25122 Muir, Edwin. THE STRUCTURE OF THE NOVEL. Pp. 134-46. See G4065.

Critique of EMF's discussion of character in ASPECTS.

25123 Schmerl, Rudolf B. "Fantasy as Technique." VQR, 43 (1967), 644-56.

On the views of fantasy in ASPECTS.

25124 Shaheen, M.Y. "Forster on Meredith." RES, 24 (1973), 185-91.

EMF's indecisive views of Meredith.

*25125 Stallybrass, Oliver. "Introduction." In GOLDSWORTHY LOWES DICKINSON AND RELATED WRITINGS. London: Arnold, 1974. Pp. xi-xix.

Valuable backgrounds to the biography. See 13001.

25126 Thomson, George H. "A Forster Miscellany: Thoughts on the Uncollected Writings." In ASPECTS OF E.M. FORSTER. Ed. Oliver Stallybrass. Pp. 155-75. See 23026.

Argues for the collected publication of these works (over 200 items).

*25127 Woolf, Virginia. "The Art of Fiction." 1927. In her COLLECTED ESSAYS. Ed. L. Woolf. London: Hogarth, 1966. II, 51-55.

Important review of ASPECTS. Reprinted in 23011.

JOHN GALSWORTHY (1867-1933)

1. PRIMARY BIBLIOGRAPHY

Books available in recent paperback printings are designated by "(P)."

1.1 Fiction

All works are novels unless otherwise noted. JG's novels and stories were collected and reprinted in a number of different arrangements during his career. First editions of the novels and first collected issues of the stories alone are noted here. See section 1.3, below, for later collected publications.

11001 THE APPLE TREE. See FIVE TALES (11010).

11002 AWAKENING. [Story]. London: Heinemann; New York: Scribner's 1920.

Brief Forsyte tale, later reprinted as an interlude between the second and third novels in THE FORSYTE SAGA (13007).

11003 BEYOND. London: Heinemann; New York: Scribner's, 1917. Rev. and abridged ed., 1923.

A self-confessed "bad" novel of "love" and an unhappy marriage.

11004 THE BURNING SPEAR, BEING THE EXPERIENCES OF MR. JOHN LAVENDER IN TIME OF WAR. RECORDED BY A.R. P--M. London: Chatto and Windus, 1919. Published as THE BURNING SPEAR, BEING THE EXPERIENCES OF MR. JOHN LAVENDER IN TIME OF WAR. RECORDED BY JOHN GALSWORTHY. New York: Scribner's 1923.

A quixotic "comedic satire" of war mania.

11005 CAPTURES. [Stories]. London: Heinemann; New York: Scribner's, 1923.

Sixteen stories, all of which are reprinted in CARAVAN: THE ASSEMBLED TALES (13003).

11006 CARAVAN: THE ASSEMBLED TALES. See 13003.

11007 THE COUNTRY HOUSE. London: Heinemann; New York: Putnam's, 1907.

Second of JG's social novels of the "upper crust," treating the affairs of a country squire and his family (the "Pendyces"). See MAN OF PROPERTY (11023). Also see 11013.

11008 THE DARK FLOWER. London: Heinemann; New York: Scribner's, 1913.

A "novel of love," chronicling the three melancholy passions of one character: in youth, in young manhood, and in maturity. See 22013.

11009 END OF THE CHAPTER. See 13005.

11010 FIVE TALES. London: Heinemann; New York: Scribner's, 1918. Retitled THE APPLE TREE, AND OTHER TALES in later revised editions. (P).

Four tales reprinted in CARAVAN: THE ASSEMBLED TALES (13003). The important interlude, "Indian Summer of a Forsyte," reappears as a bridge-story between the first and second novels of THE FORSYTE SAGA (13007).

11011 FLOWERING WILDERNESS. London: Heinemann; New York: Scribner's, 1932.

Second novel of JG's posthumous trilogy, END OF THE CHAPTER (13005). A story of frustrated love, set, like its companion novels in the last trilogy, within the colonial service stratum of society.

11012 THE FORSYTE SAGA. See 13007.

11013 FORSYTES, PENDYCES, AND OTHERS. [Stories and essays]. London: Heinemann; New York: Scribner's, 1935.

Ten previously uncollected stories and sixteen essays, including "Notes on Fellow-Writers Past and Present" (includes Conrad). One story, "Danae," is the original opening of THE COUNTRY HOUSE (11007).

11014 FRATERNITY. London: Heinemann; New York: Putnam's, 1909.

Third of JG's social novels of the "upper crust," counterpointing the intellectual elite and the impoverished masses of London. See MAN OF PROPERTY (11023).

11015 THE FREELANDS. London: Heinemann; New York: Scribner's, 1915.

Like FRATERNITY, a counterpointing of the affluent and the poor, but placed in a rural setting and highlighting agrarian problems.

11016 FROM THE FOUR WINDS. [Stories]. London: Unwin, 1897. No Amer. ed.

Ten stories published under the early pseudonym John Sinjohn, and later regretted by JG.

11017 IN CHANCERY. London: Heinemann; New York: Scribner's, 1920.

Second novel of the Forsyte chronicles, collected in THE FORSYTE SAGA (13007). Soames's divorce from Irene, his remarriage, and Irene's remarriage to his cousin Jolyon highlight the family's affairs.

11018 THE ISLAND PHARISEES. London: Heinemann; New York: Putnam's, 1904. Rev. ed., 1908.

Partly autobiographical tale of a young man's search for the meaning of life.

11019 JOCELYN. London: Duckworth, 1898. No Amer. ed.

Published under the early pseudonym John Sinjohn; a self-confessed "bad" novel of love in Monte Carlo.

11020 THE LITTLE MAN, AND OTHER SATIRES. [Stories]. London: Heinemann; New York: Scribner's, 1915.

Twenty-one "satires," seven of which reappear in CARAVAN: THE ASSEMBLED TALES (13003) and in ABRACADABRA (13001).

11021 MAID IN WAITING. London: Heinemann; New York: Scribner's, 1931.

First novel in JG's posthumous trilogy END OF THE CHAPTER (13005). The trials of a young officer in the colonial service.

11022 A MAN OF DEVON. [Stories]. Edinburgh and London: Blackwood, 1901. New York: Grosset and Dunlap, 1906.

Four tales of infatuation published under the early pseudonym John Sinjohn. Collected in subsequent publications with VILLA RUBEIN (11035) and reprinted in CARAVAN: THE ASSEMBLED TALES (13003).

11023 THE MAN OF PROPERTY. London: Heinemann; New York: Scribner's, 1906. (P).

First novel in the Forsyte chronicles, collected in THE FORSYTE SAGA (13007). The story of Soames Forsyte, his marriage, and its dissolution. Also first of a four-novel sequence dissecting the English "upper crust" in ascending order of station: the bourgeois "man of property," the country squire (see COUNTRY HOUSE, 11007), the intellectual elite (see FRATERNITY, 11014), and the aristocracy (see PATRICIAN, 11028).

11024 A MODERN COMEDY. See 13009.

11025 A MOTLEY. [Stories]. London: Heinemann; New York: Scribner's, 1910.

Twenty-eight stories, half of which are reprinted in CARAVAN: THE ASSEMBLED TALES (13003).

11026 ON FORSYTE 'CHANGE. [Stories]. London: Heinemann; New York: Scribner's, 1930.

Collects nineteen "apocryphal Forsyte tales," several having appeared in earlier separate publication (e.g., FOUR FORSYTE STORIES, 1929).

11027 OVER THE RIVER. London: Heinemann, 1933. Published as ONE MORE RIVER. New York: Scribner's, 1933.

Final novel in JG's posthumous trilogy, END OF THE CHAPTER (13005), concerning a divorce scandal in the colonial service.

11028 THE PATRICIAN. London: Heinemann; New York: Scribner's, 1911.

Fourth of JG's social novels of the "upper crust," dealing with the aristocracy and their loves. See MAN OF PROPERTY (11023).

11029 SAINT'S PROGRESS. London: Heinemann; New York: Scribner's, 1919.

Involved tale of love, religion, bigotry, and the war, set in the family of an Anglican clergyman.

11030 THE SILVER SPOON. London: Heinemann; New York: Scribner's, 1926.

Fifth novel of the Forsyte chronicles, collected in A MODERN COMEDY (13009). Fleur's further misadventures projected against a topical social and political background of the twenties.

11031 SWAN SONG. London: Heinemann; New York: Scribner's, 1928.

Sixth and final novel of the Forsyte chronicles, collected in A MODERN COMEDY (13009). The death of Soames concludes the otherwise uninspired continuation of Fleur's affairs.

11032 TATTERDEMALION. [Stories]. London: Heinemann; New York: Scribner's, 1920.

Twenty-three stories of "war-time" and "peace-time." Fourteen reappear in CARAVAN: THE ASSEMBLED TALES (13003).

11033 TO LET. London: Heinemann; New York: Scribner's, 1921.

Third of the Forsyte chronicles, collected in THE FORSYTE SAGA (13007). The development and frustration of a love affair (c. 1920) between Soames's daughter, Fleur, and Irene's son, Jon, and Fleur's rebound marriage to Michael Mont.

11034 TWO FORSYTE INTERLUDES: A SILENT WOOING; PASSERS-BY. [Stories]. London: Heinemann, 1927. New York: Scribner's, 1928.

Separate publication of two brief stories later incorporated as bridge passages between the three novels of A MODERN COMEDY (13009).

11035 VILLA RUBEIN: A NOVEL. London: Duckworth, 1900. New York: Putnam's, 1908. Rev. ed. Published as VILLA RUBEIN, AND OTHER STORIES. London: Duckworth, 1909. New York: Scribner's, 1926.

Love story set in the Tirol. First edition appeared under the early pseudonym John Sinjohn. Subsequent editions include the stories originally published as A MAN OF DEVON (11022).

11036 THE WHITE MONKEY. London: Heinemann; New York: Scribner's, 1924.

Fourth novel of the Forsyte chronicles, collected in A MODERN COMEDY (13009). Fleur's dissipation and love affair treated with little sympathy.

1.2 Miscellaneous Writings

In his nonfictional writings JG directed his attention to an immense variety of topics, ranging from pamphlets on the war effort, or on cruelty to animals, to travel works, political commentary, and literary criticism. JG's complementary career as a dramatist is beyond the scope of this guide, and his plays are not noted here. Marrot's bibliography or the collected editions of the drama (see 21004 or 13010, below) may be consulted for information on the occasional writings or the plays. The following is a checklist of JG's writings which relate directly to the social ideas and literary values which inform his fiction.

12001 ADDRESSES IN AMERICA, 1919. London: Heinemann; New York: Scribner's, 1919.

Seven speech transcripts from JG's 1919 American tour.

12002 ANOTHER SHEAF. London: Heinemann; New York: Scribner's, 1919.

Twelve essays on society, travel, and other topics.

12003 CASTLES IN SPAIN, AND OTHER SCREEDS. London: Heinemann; New York: Scribner's, 1927.

Fourteen essays and addresses, several on literary topics. Two articles (a reminiscence of Conrad and a preface to Conrad's plays) were drawn from this collection for the privately printed TWO ESSAYS ON CONRAD (1930).

12004 A COMMENTARY. London: Richards; New York: Putnam's, 1908.

Twenty prose sketches on such varied topics as fashion and sport, collected from JG's articles in the NATION.

12005 GLIMPSES AND REFLECTIONS. London: Heinemann, 1937. No Amer. ed.

Miscellaneous uncollected papers and correspondence, arranged topically.

12006 THE INN OF TRANQUILLITY: STUDIES AND ESSAYS. London: Heinemann; New York: Scribner's, 1912.

Essays on "life" (18) and "letters" (8). JG's reminiscences of his dog, "Memories," was later published separately (1914). Two of the studies of life were reprinted as stories in CARAVAN: THE ASSEMBLED TALES (13003).

12007 "Notes on Fellow-Writers Past and Present." In FORSYTES, PENDYCES, AND OTHERS. See 11013.

12008 A SHEAF. London: Heinemann; New York: Scribner's 1916.

Twenty-six essays on diverse social topics, from the position of women to the war.

1.3 Collected and Selected Works

13001 ABRACADABRA, AND OTHER SATIRES. London: Heinemann, 1924. No Amer. ed.

Re-collected satires and essays.

13002 CANDELABRA: SELECTED ESSAYS AND ADDRESSES. London: Heinemann, 1932. New York: Scribner's, 1933.

13003 CARAVAN: THE ASSEMBLED TALES OF JOHN GALSWORTHY. London: Heinemann; New York: Scribner's, 1925.

Collects fifty-six stories written through 1923, gathered from CAPTURES, FIVE TALES, INN OF TRANQUILLITY, LITTLE MAN, MAN OF DEVON, MOTLEY and TATTERDEMALION.

13004 COLLECTED POEMS. Ed. Ada Galsworthy. London: Heinemann; New York: Scribner's, 1934.

13005 END OF THE CHAPTER. New York: Scribner's, 1934. London: Heinemann, 1935.

Volume title for the posthumous trilogy of novels concerned with the Colonial Service: MAID IN WAITING (1931), FLOWERING WILDERNESS (1932), OVER THE RIVER (1933).

13006 "The Forsyte Chronicles."

Omnibus title for the six Forsyte novels and four interludes collected in THE FORSYTE SAGA and A MODERN COMEDY (see below). Sometimes extended to include the indirectly related novels of END OF THE CHAPTER, above.

13007 THE FORSYTE SAGA. London: Heinemann; New York: Scribner's, 1922.

Volume title for the first trilogy of the Forsyte chronicles: includes THE MAN OF PROPERTY (1906), IN CHANCERY (1920), TO LET (1921) and two special interludes, "Indian Summer of a Forsyte" and "Awakening," which form transitions between the novels.

13008 THE GALSWORTHY READER. Ed. Anthony West. New York: Scribner's, 1968.

Collects five stories, THE MAN OF PROPERTY, two plays, and extracts from three novels. See 24068.

13009 A MODERN COMEDY. London: Heinemann; New York: Scribner's, 1929.

Volume title for the second trilogy in the Forsyte chronicles: includes THE WHITE MONKEY (1924), THE SILVER SPOON (1926), SWAN SONG (1928), and the two interludes, "A Silent Wooing" and "Passers By," which form transitions between the novels.

13010 THE PLAYS OF JOHN GALSWORTHY. London: Duckworth, 1929. No complete Amer. ed.

The only complete edition of the twenty-one full-length and six short plays. Various American editions (New York: Scribner's, 1928 and after) lack from two to three of the last plays.

13011 THE WINTER GARDEN: FOUR DRAMATIC PIECES. London: Duckworth, 1935. No Amer. ed.

Two fragments and two previously uncollected short pieces.

13012 THE WORKS OF JOHN GALSWORTHY: "COMPACT EDITION." 7 vols. New York: Scribner's, 1931-34.

A selective edition. Includes six volumes of novels and tales and a one-volume edition of the plays. Reissued (1934) as the "Nobel Prize Edition."

13013 THE WORKS OF JOHN GALSWORTHY: "MANATON EDITION." 30 vols. New York: Scribner's, 1922-36; London: Heinemann, 1923-35.

Supersedes earlier twenty-one-volume edition. Volumes 1-14: novels and tales; 15-17: essays; 18-22: plays;

23-30: later fiction (includes MODERN COMEDY and END OF THE CHAPTER), plays, poetry, and miscellaneous writings. Prefaces provided by JG himself and Ada Galsworthy.

1.4 Letters

Also see Croft-Cooke (22004), Karl (22011), Morris (22013), and Reynolds (22016), below.

14001 AUTOBIOGRAPHICAL LETTERS OF GALSWORTHY: A CORRESPONDENCE WITH FRANK HARRIS, HITHERTO UNPUBLISHED. New York: English Book Shop, 1933.

Pamphlet (14-page) issue of a slight correspondence (two letters).

14002 JOHN GALSWORTHY'S LETTERS TO LEON LION. Ed. Asher B. Wilson. The Hague: Mouton, 1968.

A detailed historical survey of JG's dramatic career (see 25049) and an account, illustrated by the correspondence, of JG's relationship "to the London theatre of the nineteen twenties in the person of one theatrical producer, Leon Lion."

14003 LETTERS FROM JOHN GALSWORTHY, 1900-1932. Ed. Edward Garnett. London: Cape; New York: Scribner's, 1934.

Collects 25 letters to and 122 letters from JG, concerning both personal and literary matters. See 24031.

14004 THE LIFE AND LETTERS OF JOHN GALSWORTHY. Ed. H.V. Marrot. London: Heinemann, 1935. New York: Schribner's, 1936.

Marrot's biography relies extensively upon JG's letters and journals throughout its narrative. Supplementary letters are collected in the final section of the volume (pp. 657-804). See 22012.

2. SECONDARY BIBLIOGRAPHY

2.1 Bibliographies

An annotated bibliography of JG studies is presently in preparation. The volume will be a companion to the several "Annotated Secondary Bibliographies" already published by Northern Illinois University Press (general editor Helmut Gerber). For information on its availability, check a recent issue of ELT. Also see 23012.

21001 Bennett, JoAnn W. "Galsworthy and H.G. Wells." YULG, 28 (1954), 33-43.

Brief biographical summary and description of the Yale JG collection (pp. 33-37).

21002 Fabes, Gilbert H., comp. JOHN GALSWORTHY: HIS FIRST EDITIONS, POINTS AND VALUES. London: Foyle, 1932.

Pamphlet listing of first editions (supplements Marrot, 21004).

21003 Gerber, Helmut, et al., comps. "John Galsworthy: An Annotated Checklist of Writings about Him." EFT [now ELT], 1, No. 3 (1958), 7-29 and continuing.

Brief abstracts of studies, appearing irregularly. See G1404.

*21004 Marrot, H.V., ed. A BIBLIOGRAPHY OF THE WORKS OF JOHN GALSWORTHY. New York: Scribner's, 1928.

Still the standard primary bibliography of JG, though complete only to 1928. Lists first English and American publication of the novels, plays, poetry, essays, pamphlets, collected editions, periodical appearances, and occasional publications, and translations. Also includes sections on critical essays and books on JG, and JG "Iconography." Indexed.

21005 Mikhail, E.H., comp. JOHN GALSWORTHY THE DRAMATIST: A BIBLIOGRAPHY OF CRITICISM. Troy, N.Y.: Whitston, 1971.

Of peripheral value to the student of JG's fiction.

21006 Wiley, Paul L., comp. "John Galsworthy (1867-1933)." In THE BRITISH NOVEL. Comp. Wiley. Pp. 44-46. See G1419.

Brief primary and secondary checklist.

2.2 Biographies, Memoirs, Reminiscences

22001 Barker, Dudley. THE MAN OF PRINCIPLE: A VIEW OF JOHN GALSWORTHY. London: Heinemann, 1963.

Popular biography. Barker does not attempt to add to the factual information about JG's life already published by Marrot (22012); rather, as his subtitle indicates, he offers a psychological interpretation of his subject, relying principally on JG's unfulfilling relationships with his parents, his disenchantment with their class, and his love affair with his future wife Ada. An interesting "view" of JG, but Marrot must still be consulted for the fuller story of the life.

22002 Clark, Barrett H. "John Galsworthy." In INTIMATE PORTRAITS. New York: Dramatists Play Service, 1951. Pp. 29-44.

Memoir of JG in Chicago (1912).

22003 Core, George. "Author and Agency: Galsworthy and the Pinkers." LCUT, 6 (1973), 61-73.

Summarizes JG's relations with his agents.

22004 Croft-Cooke, Rupert. "Grove Lodge." CORNHILL MAGAZINE, 173 (Autumn 1962), 50-59.

JG's generosity to the author as a young poet (prints three letters).

22005 Curle, Richard. "The Story of a Remarkable Friendship." In CARAVANSARY AND CONVERSATION: MEMORIES OF PLACES AND PERSONS. New York: Stokes, 1937. Pp. 153-63.

Traces JG's and Conrad's literary and personal relationships.

22006 Dupre, Catherine. JOHN GALSWORTHY: A BIOGRAPHY. London: Collins, 1976.

The third major biography of JG, unencumbered either by the systematic thesis of Barker (22001), or by the copious documentation of Marrot (22012). Dupre's balanced and readable story of the life gives due attention to the recently revealed love affair with Margaret Morris. Unfortunately, little commentary on JG's writings.

22007 Galsworthy, Ada. OUR DEAR DOGS. London: Heinemann, 1935.

Contains more information on the dogs than on the Galsworthys.

*22008 ______. OVER THE HILLS AND FAR AWAY. London: Hale, 1937.

Travel reminiscences of JG's wife. Since the Galsworthys spent an awesome amount of time together travelling about the world (Europe, Africa, North and South America), this memoir presents a much broader picture of their private lives than might initially appear to be the case.

22009 Garnett, David. THE GOLDEN ECHO. New York: Harcourt, 1954. Pp. 70-72.

Reminiscence. Suggests Bossiney's character (MAN OF PROPERTY) based on Edward Garnett.

22010 ______. "Some Writers I Have Known: Galsworthy, Forster, Moore, and Wells." TQ, 4, No. 2 (1961), 190-202.

Memoir, again discussing Bossiney's origins.

22011 Karl, Frederick R. "Conrad--Galsworthy: A Record of Their Friendship in Letters." MIDWAY, 9, No. 2 (1968), 87-106.

JG's "quondam" apprenticeship to Conrad, and their fundamental sympathy for each other's work.

*22012 Marrot, H.V. THE LIFE AND LETTERS OF JOHN GALSWORTHY. London: Heinemann, 1935.

The standard biography, commissioned and supervised by JG's wife and extensively documented by JG's correspondence and diaries. Marrot avoids critical commentary (besides an occasional quotation from reviews) and glosses over some aspects of JG's life and relationship with Ada. See Barker (22001) and Morris (below) for supplementary views.

22013 Morris, Margaret. MY GALSWORTHY STORY. London: Owen, 1967.

Documents an unconsummated romance between the actress-dancer Morris and JG (1910-13) which was fictionalized in JG's DARK FLOWER. Prints sixty-seven letters from JG.

*22014 Mottram, Ralph H. FOR SOME WE LOVED: AN INTIMATE PORTRAIT OF ADA AND JOHN GALSWORTHY. London: Hutchinson, 1956.

Memoir-biography of the Galsworthys and criticism of the writings by a long-time acquaintance (1890s on). Although most of Mottram's comments on the works are limited to biographical sources and publishing backgrounds, his interpretive insights are frequently superior to those found in the several critical books on JG.

22015 Ould, Hermon. JOHN GALSWORTHY. London: Chapman and Hall, 1934.

A "purely personal appreciation" of JG, consisting largely of remembered conversations and assertions of JG's views (e.g., "man versus society," conscience: "a terrible and fierce thing"). Ould draws chiefly from the drama when he seeks illustrations from JG's work. Although Ould does offer some slight criticism, his book's chief interest is its memoir-portrait of JG.

22016 Reynolds, M.E. MEMORIES OF JOHN GALSWORTHY, BY HIS SISTER. London: Hale, 1936.

Personal reminiscences of JG, from childhood to his death. Prints eighty-seven miscellaneous JG letters to various correspondents, to illustrate "points of character."

22017 Sauter, Rudolf. GALSWORTHY THE MAN: AN INTIMATE PORTRAIT. London: Owen, 1967.

Memoir of JG (c. 1905 on) at home as artist, and as fellow traveller, compiled from memory and contemporary notes by JG's nephew. Among several appendixes to his book, Sauter includes a useful calendar of JG's travels (1891-1932) and the locations of JG's manuscripts.

2.3 Book-Length Critical Studies and Essay Collections

Four of the twelve works listed below are studies concentrating on JG's drama. They are entered here, rather than in section 2.5 below, "Studies of Individual Works: Miscellaneous Writings," because their commentaries on JG's "naturalist" drama are generally relevant to his fiction. Also see Fisher, 25012 below (re: FORSYTE SAGA).

23001 BOOKMAN (London), 83 (1933), 473-79, 485-87, 506-7. "In Commemoration."

Obituary issue. Includes a survey of the career, comments on JG as a "novelist" and "internationalist," three brief memoirs, and a brief essay on JG's first editions.

23002 Choudhuri, Asoke Dev. GALSWORTHY'S PLAYS: A CRITICAL SURVEY. Calcutta: Orient Longmans, 1961.

Critical interpretation of the dramas, with scarce reference to the fiction. On occasion Choudhuri offers valuable general remarks on JG's social views.

23003 Coats, R.H. JOHN GALSWORTHY AS A DRAMATIC ARTIST. New York: Scribner's, 1926.

A full study of JG's plays through 1926 which, insofar as it discusses major themes and concerns of JG in his work (e.g., family relationships, social injustice, and caste feeling), has value for the student of the fiction.

23004 Croman, Natalie. JOHN GALSWORTHY: A STUDY IN CONTINUITY AND CONTRAST. Cambridge: Harvard Univ. Press, 1933.

Brief study of JG's development through THE FORSYTHE SAGA and A MODERN COMEDY. Written as a Radcliffe honors thesis.

23005 Dupont, V. JOHN GALSWORTHY: THE DRAMATIC ARTIST. Paris and Toulouse: Didier, 1942.

Extensive and detailed study of JG's symbolic, naturalistic, and experimental dramas. Although Dupont scarcely refers to the novels, his demonstrations of JG's "philosophical sincerity," "artistic conscientiousness," and "profound humanity" are equally relevant to the fiction.

23006 JOHN GALSWORTHY: AN APPRECIATION. London: Heinemann, n.d. [c. 1928].

Anonymous publisher's pamphlet (16 pp.) occasioned by the publication of the Grove edition of JG's works. Contains a brief survey of the novels with general appreciative commentary.

23007 Kaye-Smith, Sheila. JOHN GALSWORTHY. London: Nisbets, 1916.

Mid-career survey of the plays, the novels, and the sketches, concluding with a brief essay entitled "Galsworthy the Artist." Kaye-Smith generally summarizes the works with some critical remarks. The novels are considered inferior to the drama in social and literary merit (perhaps true as of 1916), although MAN OF PROPERTY and FRATERNITY are highly regarded. Little here of permanent value.

23008 Marrot, H.V. A NOTE ON JOHN GALSWORTHY, DRAMATIST. London: Matthews and Marrot, 1928.

Pamphlet (14 pp.) commentary.

23009 Mottram, Ralph H. JOHN GALSWORTHY. 1953. 2nd ed. London: Longmans, 1963.

Pamphlet survey of the life and the work, concentrating on the fiction. Mottram divides the novels into two groups, the early "period" works (to 1920), and the later "affirmative" trilogies, which he finds different in nature and intention.

*23010 Schalit, Leon M. JOHN GALSWORTHY: A SURVEY. New York: Scribner's, 1929.

The most complete study of JG's work (to 1929), though neither original nor profound in its insights. Shalit considers the novels, stories, poems, and plays in order, in brief essays. Each work is summarized, with occasional critiques of characterization, theme, imagery, or other literary aspects. The study is prefaced by two brief chapters on JG's ideas and biography.

23011 Smit, J. Henry. THE SHORT STORIES OF JOHN GALSWORTHY. Rotterdam, Netherlands: Van Sijn and Zonen, 1947.

A peculiar book of little value, written in the style of a grade school primer and rarely remarking anything beyond the obvious. Smit surveys the history of short fiction (from 3459 B.C.!) in four pages, and moves on to discuss JG's tales under several topical headings (e.g., poetic element, pessimism, or sentimentality).

23012 Takahashi, Genji. STUDIES IN THE WORKS OF JOHN GALSWORTHY. WITH SPECIAL REFERENCE TO HIS VISIONS OF LOVE AND BEAUTY. 1954. 3rd ed. Tokyo: Shinozaki Shorin, 1973.

Four extended essays, on JG's "quixotic" characters and their "vision of love," on JG's mystical "vision of beauty," on the posthumous works (OVER THE RIVER and after), and on select members of the JG circle (added 1970). Takahashi's commentaries on JG's vision entail rather vague surveys of the works, written in an awkward, nonidiomatic English. Includes a bibliography of Japanese translations and studies.

2.4 General Critical Articles, or Chapters on JG

24001 Aiken, Conrad. "John Galsworthy." In A REVIEWER'S ABC. New York: Meridian, 1958. Pp. 213-17.

JG's failure to get inside his characters.

24002 Allen, Walter. THE ENGLISH NOVEL. Pp. 310-12. See G2201.

Brief critique. THE MAN OF PROPERTY JG's only enduring work.

24003 Austin, H.P. "John Galsworthy." DUBLIN REVIEW, 189 (1931), 95-106.

Praises JG's portrayal of upper-middle-class, Forsyte values.

24004 Baker, Ernest A. THE HISTORY OF THE ENGLISH NOVEL. X, 319-44. See G2203.

Surveys the life and the work. Little critical commentary.

24005 Beach, Joseph Warren. "Variations: Galsworthy." In his THE TWENTIETH-CENTURY NOVEL. Pp. 246-62. See G3004.

Although JG superficial, his development of the modern sequence-novel is significant.

*24006 Bellamy, William. THE NOVELS OF WELLS, BENNETT, AND GALSWORTHY. Pp. 88-102, 165-204 and passim. See G3007.

The transition from fin de siecle fiction, which concerns itself largely with the "post-Darwinian cultural crisis" (JG's JOCELYN), to the "utopianization" of experience in the Edwardian fiction. Wells, Bennett, and JG emerge, rather strangely, as modern existentialists who have assimilated Darwinism, "learning to live with human animality" (JG's MAN OF PROPERTY, COUNTRY HOUSE, and FRATERNITY).

24007 Bergonzi, Bernard. "Man as Property." In his THE TURN OF THE CENTURY. Pp. 134-38. See G2309.

JG's revolt against materialistic, Victorian conventions in life and in fiction.

24008 Bjorkman, Edwin. "John Galsworthy: An Interpreter of Modernity." In IS THERE ANYTHING NEW UNDER THE SUN? London: Swift, 1913. Pp. 183-200.

JG a social realist as well as an impressionistic artist.

24009 Bloor, R.H.U. THE ENGLISH NOVEL FROM CHAUCER TO GALSWORTHY. London: Nicholson and Watson, 1935. Pp. 242-46.

JG's novels an "epilogue" to the Victorian age.

24010 Brash, W. Bardsley. "John Galsworthy." LQHR, 160 (1935), 460-71.

Balanced evaluation, praising the short fiction.

24011 Bullett, Gerald. "John Galsworthy." In his MODERN ENGLISH FICTION. Pp. 46-53. See G3018.

Brief critical survey noting JG's dramatic use of overemphasis.

24012 Chevalley, Abel. "John Galsworthy." In his THE MODERN ENGLISH NOVEL. Pp. 175-80. See G3023.

General overview.

24013 Chevrillon, Andre. "John Galsworthy." In THREE STUDIES IN ENGLISH LITERATURE: KIPLING, GALSWORTHY, SHAKESPEARE. Trans. F. Simmonds. New York: Doubleday, Page, 1923. Pp. 153-219.

JG questions in his fiction the "prejudices, beliefs and traditions" of his culture. Praises JG's psychological penetration.

24014 Colenutt, R. "The World of Mr. Galsworthy's Fiction." CORNHILL MAGAZINE, 149 (1934), 55-64.

Place and time in JG.

24015 Collins, Arthur S. "Galsworthy." In his ENGLISH LITERATURE OF THE TWENTIETH CENTURY. Pp. 176-84. See G2105.

General estimate of JG's place in literary history.

24016 Cooper, Frederic Taber. "John Galsworthy." In his SOME ENGLISH STORY TELLERS. Pp. 177-205. See G3027.

Interesting mid-career assessment.

*24017 Cross, Wilbur J. "John Galsworthy." In his FOUR CONTEMPORARY NOVELISTS. Pp. 101-53. See G3029.

Full survey of JG's career and chief fictional concerns.

24018 Cunliffe, J.W. "John Galsworthy (1867-1933)." In his ENGLISH LITERATURE IN THE TWENTIETH CENTURY. Pp. 163-84. See G2106.

Survey, stressing JG's social vision and artistic integrity.

24019 Curle, Richard. "John Galsworthy." BOOKMAN (London), 45 (1913), 91-97.

JG's moral and literary "fervor" unifies his writings.

*24020 Daiches, David. "John Galsworthy." In THE NOVEL AND THE MODERN WORLD. 1st ed. Chicago: Univ. of Chicago Press, 1939. Pp. 33 47.

JG as the last Victorian novelist. This essay dropped from the second edition (1960).

*24021 Drew, Elizabeth A. "John Galsworthy." In her THE MODERN NOVEL. Pp. 155-73. See G3035.

Valuable, balanced general assessment of the work. JG's vision and craft distinguished, but his achievement falls short of greatness.

24022 Eaker, J. Gordon. "Galsworthy and the Modern Mind." PQ, 29 (1950), 31-48.

JG's novels shed contemporary light on the transition from Victorian to modern values.

24023 Elwin, Malcolm. "Galsworthy and the Forsytes." In OLD GODS FALLING. New York: Macmillan, 1939. Pp. 363-90.

JG's later work fails as he becomes "enslaved" to his popularity (biographical and critical survey).

24024 Ervine, St. John G. "John Galsworthy." In SOME IMPRESSIONS OF MY ELDERS. New York: Macmillan, 1922. Pp. 113-60.

Runs counter to contemporary enthusiasm for JG. A reasoned, unfavorable assessment of the fiction and drama.

24025 _____. "John Galsworthy, 1867-1933." In GREAT DEMOCRATS. Ed. A. Barratt Brown. London: Nicholson and Watson, 1934. Pp. 277-95.

JG's lack of control over his material. Derogatory.

24026 Follett, Helen Thomas, and Wilson Follett. "John Galsworthy." In their SOME MODERN NOVELISTS. Pp. 264-88. See G3043.

JG's economy and restraint in fiction the product of his dramatic career.

*24027 Ford, Ford Madox. "A Man of Infinite Pity (John Galsworthy)." In YOUR MIRROR TO MY TIMES. Ed. M. Killigrew. New York: Holt, 1971. Pp. 323-38.

Memories and critique of JG drawn from several earlier publications.

24028 Freeman, James C. "Whyte-Melville and Galsworthy's 'Bright Beings.'" NCF, 5 (1950-51), 85-100.

JG's characterization of his bright young men influenced by Whyte-Melville.

24029 Frierson, William C. THE ENGLISH NOVEL IN TRANSITION. Pp. 161-68. See G3047.

JG's "dogged determination" to write serious novels of character.

24030 Garnett, David. "E.M. Forster and John Galsworthy." REL, 5 (1964), 7-18.

Memoir and critical evaluation (Forster and JG as Edwardian "angry young men").

24031 Garnett, Edward. "Introduction." In LETTERS FROM JOHN GALSWORTHY. Pp. 5-16. See 14003.

Briefly recounts his personal and literary relationship with JG, attributes JG's maturation to his discovery of Turgenev (through Constance Garnett's translation), and praises JG's insight into the "English types he knew so well."

24032 Gettmann, Royal A. TURGENEV IN ENGLAND AND AMERICA. Urbana: Univ. of Illinois Press, 1941. Pp. 178-80.

JG favorably compared to Turgenev.

24033 Gill, Richard. HAPPY RURAL SEAT. Pp. 113-20 and passim. See G2330.

The country house as symbol in JG's writings.

24034 Gindin, James. "Ethical Structures in John Galsworthy, Elizabeth Bowen, and Iris Murdoch." In FORMS OF MODERN BRITISH FICTION. Ed. Alan W. Friedman. Pp. 15-41. See G3046.

Discusses the continuity of traditional fiction with a social and "ethical focus," rather than an individual and metaphysical orientation, in JG, Bowen, and Murdoch.

24035 Gould, Gerald. "John Galsworthy as a Novelist." BOOKMAN (London), 65 (1923), 131-35.

JG's claim to immortality rests on THE FORSYTE SAGA (surveys works).

24036 Guedalla, Philip. "Mr. John Galsworthy." In A GALLERY. New York: Putnam's, 1924. Pp. 85-97.

JG suffers as a novelist from "the defects of his qualities" as a dramatist (e.g., superficial characterization).

24037 Hamilton, Robert. "John Galsworthy: A Humanitarian Prophet." QR, 291 (1953), 72-80.

JG an admirable craftsman, but lacking in depth and purpose.

24038 Hawkes, Carol A. "Galsworthy: The Paradox of Realism." ELT, 13 (1970), 288-95.

JG paradoxically evokes "the familiar world" through realism "as an instrument of revulsion from the [material] values on which that world was built."

24039 Henderson, Philip. "Philistines: John Galsworthy." In his THE NOVEL TODAY. Pp. 103-9. See G3067.

JG's sentimental and hypocritical sensualism.

*24040 Hynes, Samuel. THE EDWARDIAN TURN OF MIND. Pp. 72-86 and passim. See G2346.

JG's criticism of social injustice related to the changing attitudes of Edwardian England.

24041 Jones, W.S. Handley. "John Galsworthy and the Dilemma of Liberalism." In his THE PRIEST AND THE SIREN. Pp. 96-113. See G6306.

JG's tendency to see both sides of a question diminishes the social and religious impact of his fiction.

24042 Kain, Richard M. "Galsworthy, The Last Victorian Liberal." MADISON QUARTERLY, 4 (1944), 84-94.

JG's retreat from "liberalism" after the war.

24043 Knight, Grant C. THE NOVEL IN ENGLISH. Pp. 320-26. See G2207.

Survey and brief critique.

*24044 Lawrence, D.H. "John Galsworthy." 1928. PHOENIX: POSTHUMOUS PAPERS. Ed. Edward D. McDonald. New York: Viking, 1936. Pp. 539-50.

Lawrence's celebrated attack on JG's ineffectual satire and sentimentality. Focuses chiefly on FORSYTE SAGA.

24045 Lovett, Robert M., and Helen S. Hughes. "John Galsworthy (1867)." In their THE HISTORY OF THE NOVEL IN ENGLAND. Pp. 382-88. See G2209.

Brief survey of JG as the "most distinguished" modern British novelist.

24046 MacCarthy, Desmond. "Galsworthy, 1933." In MEMORIES. New York: Oxford Univ. Press, 1953. Pp. 55-60.

JG's deterioration as a satirist (obituary critique).

*24047 Mann, Thomas. "An Impression of John Galsworthy." VQR, 6 (1930), 114-16.

Highly qualified critical appreciation of the man and the work.

24048 Martin, Dorothy. "Mr. Galsworthy as Artist and Reformer." YR, 14 (1924), 126-39.

JG more effective as artist when less immediately involved in social questions.

24049 Moses, Montrose J. "John Galsworthy." NORTH AMERICAN REVIEW, 235 (1933), 537-45.

JG's "acute realization" of the Edwardian English period and its characters, his strength as well as his limitation as a novelist.

24050 Myers, Walter L. THE LATER REALISM. Pp. 114-18 and passim. See G3112.

JG's experimentation with and refinement of realistic methods of characterization, dialogue, and other literary techniques.

24051 Overton, Grant. "Mr. Galsworthy's Secret Loyalties." In AMERICAN NIGHTS ENTERTAINMENT. New York: Appleton, Doran, Doubleday and Scribner's, 1923. Pp. 13-33.

JG's concern for conflicts between equally just "loyalties" in his fiction and his drama.

24052 Pallette, Drew B. "Young Galsworthy: The Forging of a Satirist." MP, 56 (1959), 178-86.

"Emotional turmoil" of JG's frustrated passion for Ada developed his powers as a satirist of the emotional sterility of his own class.

24053 Phelps, Gilbert. THE RUSSIAN NOVEL IN ENGLISH FICTION. Pp. 112-25 and passim. See G3120.

Comparison of Turgenev and JG.

24054 Phelps, William L. THE ADVANCE OF THE ENGLISH NOVEL. Pp. 217-23. See G3122.

JG's powers greatest in his satires of hypocrisy.

24055 Priestley, John B. "John Galsworthy." EJ, 14 (1925), 347-55.

Decline of JG's powers and influence.

24056 Reilly, Joseph J. "John Galsworthy: An Appraisal." In OF BOOKS AND MEN. New York: Messner, 1942. Pp. 108-16.

JG ultimately fails as a novelist.

24057 ______. "John Galsworthy and His Short Stories." In DEAR PRUE'S HUSBAND AND OTHER PEOPLE. New York: Macmillan, 1932. Pp. 45-67.

JG's sentimentality (review of CARAVAN).

24058 Ross, Woodburn O. "John Galsworthy: Aspects of an Attitude." In STUDIES IN HONOR OF JOHN WILCOX. Ed. A. Dayle Wallace and Woodburn O. Ross. Detroit: Wayne State Univ. Press, 1958. Pp. 195-208.

JG's use of the love triangle and defense of the socially repressed derived from personal experience.

24059 Scott-James, Rolfe A. "Bennett and Galsworthy." In his FIFTY YEARS OF ENGLISH LITERATURE. Pp. 34-46. See G2121.

Bennett and JG (pp. 42-46), unlike Wells, both concerned with the craft of their fiction.

24060 Shanks, Edward. "Mr. John Galsworthy." In SECOND ESSAYS ON LITERATURE. London: Collins, 1927. Pp. 41-61.

Equivocal study of JG as a critic of the institutions of modern life in his drama and fiction.

*24061 Stevens, Earl E. "John Galsworthy." In BRITISH WINNERS OF THE NOBEL LITERARY PRIZE. Ed. Walter E. Kidd. Norman: Univ. of Oklahoma Press, 1973. Pp. 130-67.

Biographical summary and valuable balanced critique. Stevens offers a perceptive discussion of JG's aesthetic and working methods.

24062 Swinnerton, Frank. THE GEORGIAN LITERARY SCENE. Pp. 153-59. See G2364.

Remarks JG's rare quality of gentility.

24063 Wagenknecht, Edward. "Pity, Irony, and John Galsworthy." In his CAVALCADE OF THE ENGLISH NOVEL. Pp. 477-93. See G3151.

Summarizes the Forsyte novels, the "novels of social criticism," and the "novels of passion," and offers a general, admiring critique of JG's artistic and social ideas.

24064 Walpole, Hugh. "John Galsworthy." In THE POST VICTORIANS. London: Nicholson and Watson, 1933. Pp. 175-85.

JG's failure to develop as a novelist and his overly simplified treatment of injustice.

24065 Ward, Alfred C. "John Galsworthy." In his TWENTIETH-CENTURY ENGLISH LITERATURE. Pp. 41-47. See G2123.

Biographical summary and brief survey.

24066 _____. "Wells; Bennett; Galsworthy." In his THE NINETEEN-TWENTIES. Pp. 30-37. See G2373.

"Between 1920 and 1930 the three senior English novelists published little that is likely to take a permanent place in literature."

24067 Watkin, E.I. "Galsworthy: In Darkness and the Shadow of Death." In MEN AND TENDENCIES. London: Sheed, 1937. Pp. 18-28.

JG's lack of an integrating personal philosophy.

24068 West, Anthony. "Introduction." In THE GALSWORTHY READER. Pp. vii-xxi. See 13008.

JG's mastery of the storyteller's art.

24069 West, Rebecca. "Uncle Bennett." In THE STRANGE NECESSITY. Garden City, N.Y.: Doubleday, Doran, 1928. Pp. 215-31.

JG (with Bennett, Shaw, and Wells) as a generous "Uncle ot the English-speaking world." Praises JG's attacks on the middle-class "infections of materialism and self-righteousness and narrowness."

24070 Weygant, Cornelius. "John Galsworthy, Gentleman." In his A CENTURY OF THE ENGLISH NOVEL. Pp. 380-90. See G2214.

JG's plays have sapped his vitality as a novelist.

*24071 Woolf, Virginia. "Mr. Bennett and Mrs. Brown." In her COLLECTED ESSAYS. Ed. L. Woolf. London: Hogarth, 1966-67. I, 319-37.

Includes JG, along with Wells and Bennett as obsolete realists.

2.5 Studies of Individual Works

The following section is subdivided into two parts: i. Fiction (alphabetically by title) and ii. Miscellaneous Writings. Along among the critical books on JG (section 2.3 above), Schalit (23010), and Takahashi (23012) consider individual works in some detail, and Smit (23011) could be consulted for commentary on the short stories. Also see Mottram's memoir (22014).

i. FICTION

"The Apple Tree" (1917)

25001 Fisher, John C. "Mythical Concepts in 'The Apple Tree.'" CE, 23 (1962), 655-56.

Archetypal reading.

25002 Gesner, Carol. "Galsworthy's 'Apple Tree' and the Longus Tradition." STC, No. 9 (1972), pp. 83-88.

Greek elements in the story (cf. Longus and Euripides).

25003 Linn, James W., and H.W. Taylor. A FOREWORD TO FICTION. New York: Appleton, 1935. Pp. 81-85.

Textbook analysis of "The Apple Tree."

25004 Zumwalt, Eugene E. "The Myth of the Garden in Galsworthy's 'The Apple Tree.'" RS, 27 (1959), 129-34.

Classical and Christian archetypes.

"The Forsyte Chronicles." Includes two trilogies: THE FORSYTE SAGA (1922), which contains THE MAN OF PROPERTY (1906), IN CHANCERY (1920), and TO LET (1921); and A MODERN COMEDY (1929), which contains THE WHITE MONKEY (1924), THE SILVER SPOON (1926), and SWAN SONG (1928).

25005 Auchincloss, Hugh. "Afterword." In THE MAN OF PROPERTY. New York: New American Library, 1967. Pp. 293-99.

The SAGA deteriorates as JG becomes increasingly involved in his story at the expense of his themes.

25006 Burgum, Edwin B. THE NOVEL AND THE WORLD'S DILEMMA. Pp. 53-55. See G3020.

JG's and Mann's comparable handling of the kunstler vs. burger theme in THE FORSYTE SAGA.

25007 Conrad, Joseph. "John Galsworthy." 1906. In his LAST ESSAYS. London: Dent, 1926. Pp. 125-31.

Summarizes MAN OF PROPERTY, admires JG's style, and praises his entertainment value.

*25008 Davies, S.H. "Galsworthy the Craftsman: Studies in the Original Manuscripts of the Forsyte Chronicles." BOOKMAN (London), 85 (1933), 18-20; 86 (1934), 12-16.

Argues JG's "conscious" artistry from examinations of the manuscripts. Reproduces valuable information from JG's notes (e.g., characters' ages, genealogy, architectural diagrams).

*25009 Dooley, D.J. "Character and Credibility in THE FORSYTE SAGA." DR, 50 (1970), 373-77.

Reasserts the credibility of JG's traditional, realistic, external handling of character (cites the popular acceptance of the TV "Forsyte Saga").

25010 Duffin, Henry C. "The Rehabilitation of Soames Forsyte." CORNHILL MAGAZINE, 68 (1930), 397-406.

Soames's character transforms and comes alive, as the SAGA progresses, through his love for his daughter Fleur.

25011 Edgar, Pelham. "John Galsworthy." In his THE ART OF THE NOVEL. Pp. 206-16. See G2205.

Summarizes THE FORSYTE SAGA, praising JG's "surer" artistry, in comparison to Bennett and Wells, and his more "reliable" view of human nature.

25012 Fisher, John C. THE WORLD OF THE FORSYTES. New York: Universe Books, 1976.

Social history of the English upper-middle class, 1886-1926, tied to JG's SAGA, but ranging far beyond the novels for illustration.

25013 Frazer, June M. "Galsworthy's Narrative Technique in THE MAN OF PROPERTY." ELT, 19 (1976), 15-24.

JG's "complex," "effective," and modern narrative techniques.

25014 Grove, Frederick P. "Morality in THE FORSYTE SAGA." UTQ, 15 (1945-46), 54-64.

JG's shifting moral values through the novels.

25015 Hamilton, Robert. "THE FORSYTE SAGA." QR, 204 (1966), 431-41.

Singles out most successful of the Forsyte tales for high praise.

25016 Harris, Wendell V. "Molly's 'Yes': The Transvaluation of Sex in Modern Fiction." TSLL, 10 (1968), 107-18.

Sex an affirmation of life. Uses FORSYTE SAGA as an example.

25017 Hart, John E. "Ritual and Spectacle in THE MAN OF PROPERTY." RS, 40 (1972), 34-43.

Examines the "archetypal" pattern of confrontation between passion and property.

25018 Hutchinson, Percy. "Introduction." In JG's THE FORSYTE SAGA. New York: Scribner's, 1933. Pp. xv-xxxv.

JG a traditional, objective novelist.

25019 James, Stanley B. "A Contrast in Sagas: Sigrid Undset and John Galsworthy." MONTH, 159 (1933), 520-26.

*25020 Kettle, Arnold. "John Galsworthy: THE MAN OF PROPERTY." In his AN INTRODUCTION TO THE ENGLISH NOVEL. II, 95-100. See G3088.

Alone among JG's "middle-brow" fiction, THE MAN OF PROPERTY "has its core of seriousness, its spark of genuine insight" in the conflict between "humanity and property."

25021 McCullough, Bruce. "The Novelist as Social Critic: John Galsworthy: THE FORSYTE SAGA." In his REPRESENTATIVE ENGLISH NOVELISTS. Pp. 320-35. See G3096.

Surveys life and summarizes novels, with sparse critical commentary.

25022 Mansfield, Katherine. NOVELS AND NOVELISTS. Ed. J.M. Murry. New York: Knopf, 1930. Pp. 316-20.

Approving review of IN CHANCERY (and Wharton's AGE OF INNOCENCE).

*25023 Marchant, Peter. "THE FORSYTE SAGA Reconsidered: The Case of the Common Reader versus Literary Criticism." WHR, 24 (1970), 221-29.

The "unconscious meaning" of FORSYTE SAGA is found in its presentation of the sexual substratum of modern behavior (cf. Richardson's PAMELA).

25024 Muir, Edwin. THE STRUCTURE OF THE NOVEL. Pp. 116-24. See G4065.

The chronicle, or period novel, "not essentially an aesthetic form." Uses FORSYTE SAGA, among other works, as an example.

*25025 Muller, Herbert J. "Realism of the Center: John Galsworthy." In his MODERN FICTION: A STUDY OF VALUES. Pp. 232-40. See G3111.

FORSYTE SAGA JG's only critically respectable work, yet too "refined" and "melancholic" to be considered a tragedy.

25026 Pritchett, Victor S. "The Forsytes." In his THE LIVING NOVEL AND LATER APPRECIATIONS. Pp. 282-88. See G3125.

JG's "lukewarm" imagination and "jog-trot realism."

25027 Routh, Harold V. ENGLISH LITERATURE AND IDEAS IN THE TWENTIETH CENTURY. Pp. 43-48. See G2119.

JG's insight into his own class in MAN OF PROPERTY.

25028 Stevenson, Lionel. "Introduction." In THE MAN OF PROPERTY. New York: Scribner's, 1949. Pp. vii-xviii.

FORSYTE SAGA portrays the end of an economic era and "the end of a literary genre which concurrently flourished."

25029 Thody, Philip. "The Politics of the Family Novel: Is Conservatism Inevitable?" MOSAIC, 3, No. 1 (1969), 87-101.

Movement "from criticism to defense of family values" in FORSYTE SAGA (cf. Zola, Mann, and others).

25030 Tilby, A. Wyatt. "The Epic of Property." EDINBURGH REVIEW, 241 (1925), 271-85.

Glowing review of FORSYTE SAGA and WHITE MONKEY, praising JG's "quality" fiction in an age of "quantity" publication. Summary and critique of the works.

25031 Van Egmond, Peter. "Naming Techniques in John Galsworthy's THE FORSYTE SAGA." NAMES, 16 (1968), 371-79.

Names of JG's characters have both symbolic and etymological significance.

25032 Wagenknecht, Edward. "The Selfish Heroine: Thackeray and Galsworthy." CE, 4 (1942-43), 293-98.

Comparison of Fleur Forsyte and Beatrix (HENRY ESMOND).

FRATERNITY (1909)

25033 Findlater, J.H. "Three Sides to a Question." LIVING AGE, 264 (1910), 603-12.

JG's attack upon the "cultivated middle classes" in FRATERNITY (cf. Wells and Stephen Reynolds).

25034 Harkness, Bruce. "Conrad on Galsworthy: The Time Scheme of FRATERNITY." MFS, 1, No. 2 (1955), 12-18.

Conrad's influence on JG's use of time.

*25035 Stevens, Harold R. "Galsworthy's FRATERNITY: The Closed Door and the Paralyzed Society." ELT, 19 (1976), 283-98.

Images of frustration and paralysis in the social vision of the novel. Close and thorough reading.

"The Japanese Quince" (1910)

25036 Ramsey, Roger. "Another Way of Looking at Blackbird." RS, 39 (1971), 152-54.

Critical explication of the story.

JOCELYN (1898)

25037 Dupre, Catherine. "Introduction." In JG's JOCELYN. London: Duckworth/Sidgwick and Jackson, 1976. Pp. 7-13.

Biographical backgrounds to the melodramatic and uneven, but "very personal" first novel.

SAINT'S PROGRESS (1919)

25038 Mansfield, Katherine. NOVELS AND NOVELISTS. Ed. J.M. Murry. New York: Knopf, 1930. Pp. 99-104.

Approving review and summary of SAINT'S PROGRESS.

ii. MISCELLANEOUS WRITINGS

25039 Archer, William. THE OLD DRAMA AND THE NEW: AN ESSAY IN REVALUATION. Boston: Small, Maynard, 1923. Passim.

JG's achievement in the drama.

25040 Beatty, Richmond C. "Galsworthy as Poet." SR, 44 (1936), 100-102.

JG a "disappointing" poet (review of COLLECTED POEMS).

25041 Nicholson, Norman. "Galsworthy and the Realist Drama." In his MAN AND LITERATURE. Pp. 32-39. See G2353.

In his plays JG approached nearer to his aim of presenting a "complete picture of man in relation to society."

25042 Nicoll, Allardyce. BRITISH DRAMA. 1925. 5th ed. New York: Barnes and Noble, 1963. Pp. 254-58.

JG and the modern realistic drama of "social situation" (rather than of character).

25043 Phelps, William L. "John Galsworthy." In ESSAYS ON MODERN DRAMATISTS. New York: Macmillan, 1921. Pp. 99-141.

Survey of plays (to 1921), praising JG's appeal to reason: "his vitality is the vitality of the mind rather than of the passions."

25044 Scheick, William J. "Chance and Impartiality: A Study Based on the Manuscript of Galsworthy's LOYALTIES." TSLL, 17 (1975), 653-72.

Textual and critical study of JG's play LOYALTIES (1922).

*25045 Scrimgeour, Gary J. "Naturalist Drama and Galsworthy." MD, 7 (1964), 65-78.

JG's "drama enmeshed in staginess and [his] philosophy trapped in dubious theory."

25046 Skemp, Arthur R. "The Plays of Mr. John Galsworthy." E&S, 4 (1913), 151-71.

Perceptive early study of JG's dramatic strengths and weaknesses.

25047 Waugh, Arthur. "Mr. John Galsworthy." In TRADITION AND CHANGE: STUDIES IN CONTEMPORARY LITERATURE. New York: Dutton, 1919. Pp. 285-91.

JG as a "pleader and a moralist" in his essays (review of A SHEAF).

25048 Wells, Arvin R. "The Skin Game." In INSIGHT II. Ed. John V. Hagopian and Martin Dolch. Pp. 142-47. See G5007.

Play summary, critique, and study questions.

*25049 Wilson, Asher B. "Introduction." In JOHN GALSWORTHY'S LETTERS TO LEON LION. Ed. A.B. Wilson. Pp. 11-86. See 14002.

Thoroughly assesses JG's role in the London theatre, before and after the war, and describes his development as a dramatist.

HENRY GREEN (1905-73)
[Pseud. of Henry Vincent Yorke]

1. PRIMARY BIBLIOGRAPHY

Books available in recent paperback printings are denoted by "(P)."

1.1 Fiction

HG published several as yet uncollected shorter works and extracts from forthcoming books in the new writing journals of the forties: FOLIOS OF NEW WRITING, NEW WRITING AND DAYLIGHT, and PENGUIN NEW WRITING. The following works are novels, unless otherwise noted.

11001 BACK: A NOVEL. London: Hogarth, 1946. Published without subtitle. New York: Viking, 1950.

> Painful return and emotional rebirth of a prisoner of war in postwar London.

11002 BLINDNESS. London: Dent; New York: Dutton, 1926.

> HG's first novel, the diary and stream-of-consciousness of a newly blinded young man.

11003 CAUGHT: A NOVEL. London: Hogarth, 1943. New York: Viking, 1950.

> Personal life of a member of the Auxiliary Fire Service and "evocation" of the blitzed London of 1940.

11004 CONCLUDING: A NOVEL. London: Hogarth, 1948. New York: Viking, 1951.

> Stream of thought of an aged, distinguished scientist, firmly entrenched at a girls' school in a welfare state of the not-too-distant future.

11005 DOTING: A NOVEL. London: Hogarth, 1952. Published without subtitle. New York: Viking, 1952.

Light tale of the protagonist's middle-aged dalliance with the eighteen-year-old daughter of a friend.

11006 LIVING: A NOVEL. London: Hogarth, 1929. St. Clair Shores, Mich.: Scholarly Press, 1971.

Stylistically experimental, yet realistic tale of life among Birmingham foundry workers.

11007 LOVING: A NOVEL. London: Hogarth, 1945. Published without subtitle. New York: Viking, 1949.

Relationships among a group of household servants at an Irish estate, in the first years of World War II.

11008 NOTHING: A NOVEL. London: Hogarth, 1950. Published without subtitle. New York: Viking, 1950.

Satiric comedy of manners, concerning the shadow of incest and, more seriously, the empty morality in two modern families.

11009 PARTY GOING: A NOVEL. London: Hogarth, 1939. New York: Viking, 1951.

Social interactions among a group of rich young party-goers, awaiting the departure of the boat-train to France.

11010 "An Unfinished Novel." LONDON MAGAZINE, 6 (Apr. 1959), 11-17.

HG describes and quotes from a derivative early novel in the manner of Woolf (MOOD [late twenties]), which he found "impossible" to finish.

1.2 Miscellaneous Writings

12001 "Before the Great Fire." LONDON MAGAZINE, 7 (Dec. 1960), 12-27.

Extract from HG's work-in-progress, a documentary history of London firefighters during World War II, LONDON AND FIRE, 1940. Also printed, in a modified form, as "Fire-fighting," TQ, 3, No. 4 (1960), 105-20.

12002 "The English Novel of the Future." CONTACT, 1 (July-Aug. 1950), 20-24.

12003 "A Fire, a Flood, and the Price of Meat." LISTENER, 46 (1951), 293-94.

12004 "A Novelist to His Readers." LISTENER, 44 (1950), 505-6; 45 (1951), 425-27.

Together with the two articles above, a series of conversational and theoretical essay-commentaries on the state of the novel and on HG's own "nonrepresentational" fiction.

12005 PACK MY BAG: A SELF-PORTRAIT. London: Hogarth, 1940. No Amer. ed.

Autobiographical account of HG's childhood and education, through 1927 (when he voluntarily left Oxford for work in a Birmingham factory).

1.3 Collected and Selected Works

Note: Penguin-Viking (Harmondsworth, Engl. and Baltimore, Md.) has recently published (1978) a single-volume reissue of three HG novels: LIVING, LOVING, and PARTY GOING, with an introduction by John Updike (received too late for entry in this guide).

1.4 Letters

HG's letters have not been made public.

2. SECONDARY BIBLIOGRAPHY

2.1 Bibliographies

21001 Wiley, Paul L., comp. "Henry Green (pseud. Henry Vincent Yorke). (1905--)." In THE BRITISH NOVEL. Comp. Wiley. Pp. 52-54. See G1419.

Brief primary and secondary checklist.

2.2 Biographies, Memoirs, Reminiscences, Interviews

22001 Dennis, Nigel. "The Double Life of Henry Green." LIFE, 4 Aug. 1952, pp. 83-94.

Brief biographical and critical commentary (with photographs).

22002 Lambourne, David. "'No Thundering Horses': The Novels of Henry Green." SHENANDOAH, 26, No. 4 (1975), 57-71.

Interview with HG, including slight comment on the works.

22003 Ross, Alan. "Green, with Envy: Critical Reflections and an Interview." LONDON MAGAZINE, 6 (Apr. 1959), 18-24.

Review of Stokes's NOVELS OF HENRY GREEN (23005) and interview discussion of the study with HG himself.

*22004 Russell, John. "There It Is." KR, 26 (1964), 433-65.

Impressions of HG's character and accounts of his conversation, based on a fortnight's visit. Includes remarks on HG's work-in-progress, LONDON AND FIRE, 1940.

*22005 Southern, Terry. "The Art of Fiction, XXII-Henry Green." PARIS REVIEW, No. 19 (1958), pp. 60-77.

Delightful interview with the witty, elusive, and hard-of-hearing novelist.

2.3 Book-Length Critical Studies and Essay Collections

23001 Bassoff, Bruce. TOWARD "LOVING": THE POETICS OF THE NOVEL AND THE PRACTICE OF HENRY GREEN. Columbia: Univ. of South Carolina Press, 1975.

A theoretical study of two chief trends in novel criticism (formalism and ethical criticism) and examination of HG's practice in light of these theories (especially his "poetic tendencies"). Bassoff's final chapter concentrates on LOVING as a test case for the close formal analysis of poetic fiction. Includes an appendix: "Plot Summaries of Green's Novels."

23002 LONDON MAGAZINE, 6 (Apr. 1959), 7-35.

Special number on HG. Includes editor's foreword, HG's comments on his unfinished novel MOOD (see 11010), an interview (22003), and a critical article (25007).

*23003 Russell, John. HENRY GREEN: NINE NOVELS AND AN UNPACKED BAG. New Brunswick, N.J.: Rutgers Univ. Press, 1960.

An able complement to Stokes's book (below), a study comprised of chapter-length analyses of the individual works. Russell opens with a "sequential account" of the novels and the autobiography, and with brief essays on HG's titles, his relation to modern writers, and his views on "thoery, technique, style," as a prelude to his close readings of theme and method in the fiction.

23004 Ryf, Robert S. HENRY GREEN. New York: Columbia Univ. Press, 1967.

Sensible introductory pamphlet (46 pp.). Ryf summarizes the nine novels and autobiography with brief critical commentaries.

*23005 Stokes, Edward. THE NOVELS OF HENRY GREEN. London: Hogarth Press, 1959.

The first book-length study of HG. Stokes considers each of the novels in turn, under general thematic and technical headings: "Proletarians and Plutocrats" (characters), "Methods and Techniques," "Stories and Structures," "Themes and Symbols," and "Styles and Manners." Frequently perceptive and helpful readings despite the piecemeal approach.

23006 Weatherhead, A. Kingsley. A READING OF HENRY GREEN. Seattle: Univ. of Washington Press, 1961.

Narrowly defined but perceptive study of the theme of "self-creation" in the novels. Weatherhead disavows all intentions of relating his subject to any context outside itself, thus somewhat limiting his work's value. Interesting observations throughout.

2.4 General Critical Articles, or Chapters on HG

24001 Allen, Walter. "Henry Green." PENGUIN NEW WRITING, 25 (1945), 144-55.

HG a unique technician and "the only pure artist among the novelists of the thirties." Expanded version of earlier essay (1941).

24002 ______. THE MODERN NOVEL. Pp. 214-19 and passim. See G2202.

Brief summary and appreciation of the works, concentrated on the most successful novels: LIVING, PARTY GOING, CAUGHT, and LOVING.

24003 Bain, Bruce. "Henry Green: The Man and His Work." WORLD REVIEW, No. 3 (May 1949), pp. 55-58, 80.

HG's work "distinctive" among modern novelists for its social range, personal style, and vigorous development.

24004 Gill, Richard. HAPPY RURAL SEAT. Pp. 191-93 and passim. See G2330.

The country house as symbol in HG.

*24005 Hall, James. "Paradoxes of Pleasure-and-Pain: Henry Green." In his THE TRAGIC COMEDIANS. Pp. 66-81. See G3061.

For HG, unlike most comic writers, "continuing conflict rather than struggle-and-resolution is the pattern of experience."

24006 Johnson, Bruce M. "Henry Green's Comic Symbolism." BSUF, 6, No. 3 (1965), 29-35.

HG's "peculiar wedding of symbolism and comedy."

*24007 Karl, Frederick R. "Normality Defined: The Novels of Henry Green." In his A READER'S GUIDE TO THE CONTEMPORARY ENGLISH NOVEL. Pp. 183-200. See G3081

Survey, stressing HG's comic vision and his fascination with language and communication (though questioning his dialogue technique).

*24008 Melchiori, Giorgio. "The Abstract Art of Henry Green." In THE TIGHTROPE WALKERS. Pp. 188-212. See G3103.

Time and memory in HG's fiction.

24009 Newby, Percy H. THE NOVEL, 1945-1950. Pp. 31-32. See G3113.

Praise for HG's unique "personal vision," his recognition of complexity in simple people, and his skill with conversation.

*24010 Phelps, Robert. "The Vision of Henry Green." HudR, 5 (1953), 614-20.

HG "dramatizes our attempts, largely by speech, to make contact with each other, and the hazard and failure for the most part sustained."

24011 Prescott, Orville. IN MY OPINION. Pp. 92-98. See G3124.

Attacks HG as an "artificially mannered" coterie writer.

24012 Stevenson, Lionel. THE HISTORY OF THE ENGLISH NOVEL. XI, 323-33. See G2212.

HG's amalgam of social realism and impressionistic method. Stevenson surveys HG's works.

24013 Taylor, Donald S. "Catalytic Rhetoric: Henry Green's Theory of the Modern Novel." CRITICISM, 7 (1965), 81-99.

Assesses HG's theoretical statements on the "non-representational novel."

24014 Tindall, William York. FORCES IN MODERN BRITISH LITERATURE. Passim. See G2122.

HG in relation to modern movements in the arts (especially the symbolic novel).

24015 ______. THE LITERARY SYMBOL. Pp. 92-97. See G3146.

HG as symbolic novelist (LIVING, LOVING, and PARTY GOING).

*24016 Toynbee, Philip. "The Novels of Henry Green." PR, 16 (1949), 487-97.

HG's experimentation with language.

24017 Turner, Myron. "The Imagery of Wallace Stevens and Henry Green." WSCL, 8 (1967), 60-77.

Imagery in both writers a "vivid transfiguration of surface reality into something unreal yet tangible." Comparative surveys.

*24018 Unterecker, John. "Fiction at the Edge of Poetry: Durrell, Beckett, Green." In FORMS OF MODERN BRITISH FICTION. Ed. Alan W. Friedman. Pp. 165-99. See G3046.

Use of cinematic techniques to present an altered modern perspective on "the complexity of reality." Discusses HG, among others.

24019 Weatherhead, A. Kingsley. "Structure and Texture in Henry Green's Latest Novels." ACCENT, 19 (1959), 111-22.

HG's "conception of the novel as a panorama of percepts and phenomena [texture] uncommodated to a comprehensive organization," or structure, in CONCLUDING, NOTHING, and DOTING.

*24020 Welty, Eudora. "Henry Green: Novelist of the Imagination." TQ, 4, No. 3 (1961), 246-56.

HG "the most interesting and vital imagination in English fiction in our time." Excellent critical overview.

2.5 Studies of Individual Works

The book-length studies by Bassoff (23001), Russell (23003), Stokes (23005), and Weatherhead (23006) contain lengthy commentaries on the individual novels.

BACK (1946)

25001 Shapiro, Stephen A. "Henry Green's BACK: The Presence of the Past." Crit, 7, No. 1 (1964), 87-96.

Study of novel "from the point of view of depth psychology."

DOTING (1952)

25002 Pritchett, Victor S. "Green on Doting." NEW YORKER, 17 May 1952, pp. 137-42.

HG belongs to the "mad" tradition in English literature (review of DOTING).

LOVING (1945)

25003 Churchill, Thomas. "LOVING: A Comic Novel." Crit, 4, No. 2 (1961), 29-38.

Stresses the light-hearted comedy of LOVING, in reaction to Labor's overly solemn reading, below.

*25004 Davidson, Barbara. "The World of LOVING." WSCL, 2, No. 1 (1961), 65-78.

Novel's tension between realism and fantasy, the visual and the abstract.

25005 Labor, Earle. "Henry Green's Web of Loving." Crit, 4, No. 1 (1961), 29-40.

Novel's chief theme the corrosive effect of "loving" on the senses of duty and responsibility.

25006 Lehmann, Rosamond. "An Absolute Gift." TLS, 6 Aug. 1954, p. xli.

LOVING and LIVING the masterworks of "this distinguished, poetic and grimly realistic, witty and melancholy, amorous and austere voluptuary."

25007 Quinton, Anthony. "A French View of LOVING." LONDON MAGAZINE, 6 (Apr. 1959), 25-35.

Summary of and commentary on a French existentialist criticism of LOVING (by Vinaver, in LETTRES NOUVELLES, 1953).

25008 Schorer, Mark. "Introduction to Henry Green's World." NYTBR, 9 Oct. 1949, pp. 1, 22.

HG's mixture of naturalism and mystery (review of LOVING).

NOTHING (1950)

25009 Gill, Brendan. "Something." NEW YORKER, 25 Mar. 1950, pp. 111-12.

Praise for HG's wit and humor (review of NOTHING).

PARTY GOING (1939)

*25010 Hart, Clive. "The Structure and Technique of PARTY GOING." YES, 1 (1971), 185-99.

HG's detachment, his "abnegation of authorial control" on the surface of the novel, in tension with his ordered use of images and symbols.

*25011 Kettle, Arnold. "Henry Green: PARTY GOING." In his AN INTRODUCTION TO THE ENGLISH NOVEL. II, 190-97. See G3088.

Novel captures and brilliantly illuminates the "social situation" of the party-goers. Fine, balanced evaluation of PARTY GOING and HG's work generally.

LESLIE POLES HARTLEY (1895-1972)

1. PRIMARY BIBLIOGRAPHY

1.1 Fiction

All works are novels unless otherwise noted. For itemized contents of the story collections, to 1954, see Bien's "A L.P. Hartley Bibliography" (21001).

11001 THE BETRAYAL: A NOVEL. London: Hamilton, 1966. No Amer. ed.

Sequel to THE BRICKFIELD (see below). The narrator's homosexual relationship with his secretary disintegrates as he continues to probe and reexamine his traumatic adolescence.

11002 THE BOAT. London: Putnam, 1949. Garden City, N.Y.: Doubleday, 1950.

Depressing and isolated life of a repressed late-middle-aged bachelor, during the war.

11003 THE BRICKFIELD. London: Hamilton, 1964. No Amer. ed.

Traumatic adolescent sexual encounter, recounted by an aged narrator to his secretary. (Also see THE BETRAYAL, above.)

11004 THE COLLECTIONS. London: Hamilton, 1972. No Amer. ed.

Farce, concerning an elderly art collector whose private hoard is threatened by his own niece.

11005 EUSTACE AND HILDA. London: Putnam, 1947. Published with THE SHRIMP AND THE ANEMONE and THE SIXTH HEAVEN. New York: British Book Centre, 1958.

Eustace ultimately destroyed by his dominant sister. Concluding volume of the "Eustace and Hilda" trilogy. See 13003.

11006 FACIAL JUSTICE. London: Hamilton, 1960. Garden City, N.Y.: Doubleday, 1961.

Fantasy-satire of the modern welfare state and religion, set in a futuristic, benevolent dictatorship.

11007 THE GO-BETWEEN. London: Hamilton, 1953. New York: Knopf, 1954.

Nostalgic memorial reconstruction of the loss of innocence of a young boy, the go-between in a "Lawrencean" lady-and-gamekeeper affair. LPH's most admired novel.

11008 THE HARNESS ROOM. London: Hamilton, 1971. No Amer. ed.

Tragic short novel about a homosexual relationship between a chauffeur and his employer's son.

11009 THE HIRELING. London: Hamilton, 1957. New York: Rinehart, 1958.

Frustration of a car-hire driver's love for an aristocratic young war widow.

11010 THE KILLING BOTTLE. [Stories]. London and New York: Putnam, 1932.

Eight stories. Several reprinted in later story collections.

11011 THE LOVE-ADEPT: A VARIATION ON A THEME. London: Hamilton, 1969. No Amer. ed.

Farcial novel-within-a-novel, concerning a novelists's attempts to finish his novel.

11012 MRS. CARTERET RECEIVES, AND OTHER STORIES. [Stories]. London: Hamilton, 1971. No Amer. ed.

Ten tales.

11013 MY FELLOW DEVILS. London: Barrie, 1951. New York: British Book Centre, 1959.

Melodramatic tale of a serious, highly moral woman's discovery of evil in her husband.

11014 MY SISTERS' KEEPER. London: Hamilton, 1970. No Amer. ed.

Complex relationships of a passive middle-aged bachelor with his three sisters and their families.

11015 NIGHT FEARS, AND OTHER STORIES. [Stories]. London and New York: Putnam's, 1924.

Seventeen early stories collected from previous periodical publication. Several reprinted in later collections.

11016 A PERFECT WOMAN. London: Hamilton, 1955. New York: Knopf, 1956.

The disintegration of a stable, "perfect," modern marriage into two secretive affairs.

11017 POOR CLARE. London: Hamilton, 1968. No Amer. ed.

Seriocomic love triangle among mediocre middle-aged artists.

11018 THE SHRIMP AND THE ANEMONE. London: Putnam, 1944. Published as THE WEST WINDOW. Garden City, N.Y.: Doubleday, 1945.

Loving re-creation of the childhood world of nine-year-old Eustace, a delicate boy who is dominated by his beautiful sister Hilda. First volume of the "Eustace and Hilda" trilogy (with THE SIXTH HEAVEN and EUSTACE AND HILDA). See 13003.

11019 SIMONETTA PERKINS. London: Putnam, 1925. New York: Putnam's, 1926. 2nd ed. London: Barrie, 1952.

Jamesian nouvelle dealing with an American (Bostonian) girl in Venice.

11020 THE SIXTH HEAVEN. London: Putnam, 1946. Garden City, N.Y.: Doubleday, 1947.

Covers Eustace's years at Oxford and Hilda's work in a children's clinic. Second volume of the "Eustace and Hilda" trilogy (with THE SHRIMP AND THE ANEMONE and EUSTACE AND HILDA). See 13003.

11021 THE TRAVELLING GRAVE, AND OTHER STORIES. [Stories]. Sauk City, Wis.: Arkham House, 1948. London: Barrie, 1951.

Twelve tales, nine reprinted from THE KILLING BOTTLE (11010) and NIGHT FEARS (11015).

11022 TWO FOR THE RIVER, AND OTHER STORIES. [Stories]. London: Hamilton, 1961. No Amer. ed.

Fourteen tales.

11023 THE WEST WINDOW. See THE SHRIMP AND THE ANEMONE (11018).

11024 THE WHITE WAND, AND OTHER STORIES. [Stories]. London: Hamilton, 1954. No Amer. ed.

Fourteen tales, six reprinted from THE KILLING BOTTLE (11010) and NIGHT FEARS (11015).

11025 THE WILL AND THE WAY. London: Hamilton, 1973. No Amer. ed.

Posthumously published novel depicting the impact of a contested will upon a family.

1.2 Miscellaneous Writings

LPH wrote regular literary columns in SPECTATOR (1923-24), SATURDAY REVIEW (London, 1925-30), SKETCH (1929-47), WEEK-END REVIEW (1930-33), OBSERVER (1935-42), LIFE AND LETTERS TODAY (1943-46), and TIME AND TIDE (1946-54). See Bien's discussion of LPH's criticism (23002, below). Only a small sampling of these essays has been collected (THE NOVELIST'S RESPONSIBILITY, below).

12001 THE NOVELIST'S RESPONSIBILITY. London: Hamilton, 1967. No Amer. ed.

An ecclectic collection of thirteen reprinted critical essays, touching at points on the novelist's responsibility (commitment) as illustrated by a number of writers.

1.3 Collected and Selected Works

13001 THE COLLECTED SHORT STORIES. London: Hamilton, 1968. No Amer. ed.

See below.

13002 THE COMPLETE SHORT STORIES OF L.P. HARTLEY. London: Hamilton, 1973. No Amer. ed.

Supersedes above volume, but still is <u>not</u> complete. Reprints SIMONETTA PERKINS (1925) and four story collections: THE TRAVELLING GRAVE (1948), THE WHITE WAND (1954), TWO FOR THE RIVER (1961), and MRS. CARTERET RECEIVES (1971), but lacks nine early tales originally collected in NIGHT FEARS (1924). See 24004.

13003 EUSTACE AND HILDA: A TRILOGY. London: Putnam; New York: British Book Centre, 1958.

Collects THE SHRIMP AND THE ANEMONE (1944), a bridge story: "Hilda's Letter" (1950; also in THE WHITE WAND, 1954), THE SIXTH HEAVEN (1946), and EUSTACE AND HILDA (1947).

1.4 Letters

LPH's correspondence has not been published. Bien, however, quotes from several letters sent to him by LPH in his L.P. HARTLEY (23002).

2. SECONDARY BIBLIOGRAPHY

2.1 Bibliographies

*21001 Bien, Peter, comp. "A L.P. Hartley Bibliography." ADAM INTERNATIONAL REVIEW, 29, Nos. 294-96 (1961), 63-70.

Lists first and subsequent editions of LPH's books to 1961 (with itemized contents of the story collections) and LPH's contributions to books and periodicals. Partial reprint in Bien's L.P. HARTLEY (23002).

21002 Wiley, Paul L., comp. "L.P. Hartley (1895--)." In THE BRITISH NOVEL. Comp. Wiley. Pp. 58-59. See G1419.

Brief primary and secondary checklist.

2.2 Biographies, Memoirs, Reminiscences, Interviews

Note: There are to date (1977) no significant biographical materials on LPH. The critical studies in section 2.3 do have brief biographical sections, which should be consulted. The following items are interviews.

22001 Firchow, Peter, ed. THE WRITER'S PLACE: INTERVIEWS ON THE LITERARY SITUATION IN CONTEMPORARY BRITAIN. Minneapolis: Univ. of Minnesota Press, 1974. Pp. 163-72.

LPH comments on the situation of the modern British novelist and notes the influence of Americans (especially Hawthorne and James) on his fiction.

22002 "The Novelist L.P. Hartley Talks about His Childhood to Derek Parker." LISTENER, 88 (1972), 274-75.

Brief conversation.

2.3 Book-Length Critical Studies and Essay Collections

23001 ADAM INTERNATIONAL REVIEW, 29, Nos. 294-96 (1961), 2-70.

Special LPH issue including four brief tributes (in French and English), a French translation of "The Novelist's Responsibility," two stories by LPH ("The Face" and "A Very Present Help"), and a primary bibliography (by Bien, see 21001).

*23002 Bien, Peter. L.P. HARTLEY. University Park: Pennsylvania State Univ. Press, 1963.

Excellent critical study. Bien finds in LPH a synthesis of social realism and symbolism, of moral earnestness and self-conscious artistry. After a general overview of LPH's "moral instinct" and "aesthetic," Bien closely examines the "Eustace and Hilda" trilogy (psychological analysis), THE BOAT (sources and biographical implications), and THE GO-BETWEEN ("new critical" reading), with briefer essays on the remaining novels, on fantasy in the works, and on LPH as a critic. Brief bibliography.

23003 Bloomfield, Paul. L.P. HARTLEY. 1962. Rev. ed. London: Longmans, 1970.

Pamphlet introduction (33 pp.) to LPH's life and work. Bloomfield comments insightfully on LPH's chronicles of upper-middle-class life, through MY SISTERS' KEEPER (1970), but has too little room for extended analysis. (Expanded version of earlier essay which had been bound with Bergonzi's study of Anthony Powell.)

23004 Mulkeen, Anne. WILD THYME, WINTER LIGHTNING: THE SYMBOLIC NOVELS OF L.P. HARTLEY. London: Hamilton, 1974.

Formulary critical study which "plugs" LPH into the archetypal-symbolist circuit. LPH "gives us a unique kind of 'double vision' whereby characters and objects and events are seen as at once themselves . . . and as suggestions of, embodiments of universals, essences, archetypes." Mulkeen energetically pursues the symbolic patterns and keys in the short fiction, the trilogy, THE BOAT, THE GO-BETWEEN, and seven later novels.

2.4 General Critical Articles, or Chapters on LPH

*24001 Allen, Walter. THE MODERN NOVEL. Pp. 253-57. See G2202.

LPH's narrow range and his constant theme: "the relationship of man to his conscience, his sense of right and wrong, and right behaviour." Praises the "Eustace and Hilda" trilogy.

24002 Athos, John. "L.P. Hartley and the Gothic Infatuation." TCL, 7 (1962), 172-79.

LPH's fascination with the supernatural, viewed within the romantic, "gothic" tradition.

24003 Atkins, John. "L.P. Hartley: Tarnished Glamour." In his SIX NOVELISTS LOOK AT SOCIETY. Pp. 77-111. See G3003.

LPH's reflection of various social themes and attitudes (e.g., antimodernism, money, and class relationships).

24004 Cecil, David. "Introduction." In LPH's THE COMPLETE SHORT STORIES. Pp. vii-x. See 13002.

LPH's originality and "intense moral vision."

24005 Closs, August. "L.P. Hartley." NS, 6 (1957), 39-42.

Not seen.

*24006 Hall, James. "Games of Apprehension: L.P. Hartley." In his THE TRAGIC COMEDIANS. Pp. 111-28. See G3061.

LPH as a modern comic writer with an undertone of terror.

24007 Karl, Frederick R. A READER'S GUIDE TO THE CONTEMPORARY ENGLISH NOVEL. Pp. 277-78. See G3081.

Admires LPH's craft, "within the limitations he places on his novels."

24008 McCormick, John. CATASTROPHE AND IMAGINATION. Passim. See G3095.

LPH influenced by James as a novelist of manners.

*24009 Melchiori, Giorgio. "The English Novelist and the American Tradition (1955)." SR, 68 (1960), 502-15.

LPH's indebtedness "in narrative method, style, textual analogy and even moral problems to a typically American tradition" (especially Hawthorne).

24010 Newby, Percy H. THE NOVEL, 1945-1950. Pp. 35-36. See G3113.

LPH's originality, charm, and literary distinction (especially in the "Eustace and Hilda" trilogy).

24011 Phelps, Gilbert. "The Novel Today." In THE MODERN AGE. Ed. Boris Ford. Pp. 475-95. See G2110.

LPH (pp. 481-83) strongest in his detached explorations of childhood (e.g., in THE SHRIMP AND THE ANEMONE and THE GO-BETWEEN).

24012 Stevenson, Lionel. THE HISTORY OF THE ENGLISH NOVEL. XI, 370-72. See G2212.

Brief survey. Sees LPH as "chronicler of reticent upper class mores."

24013 Tindall, William York. FORCES IN MODERN BRITISH LITERATURE. Pp. 293-95. See G2122.

LPH as symbolic novelist.

*24014 Webster, Harvey Curtis. "L.P. Hartley: Diffident Christian." In his AFTER THE TRAUMA. Pp. 152-67. See G3154.

LPH a "varyingly distinguished" novelist. Full critical survey.

24015 Willmott, Michael B. "'What Leo Knew': The Childhood World of L.P. Hartley." ENGLISH, 24 (1975), 3-10.

LPH's movement in his fiction from the world of the child to the world of the adult.

2.5 Studies of Individual Works

Also see the full-length critical studies of Bien (23002) and Mulkeen (23004) for commentaries on most of the individual novels (section 2.3, above). Many of the general critical articles, in section 2.4 above, draw their illustrations from the novels in the "Eustace and Hilda" trilogy and THE GO-BETWEEN.

FACIAL JUSTICE (1960)

25001 Sorensen, Knud. "Language and Society in L.P. Hartley's FACIAL JUSTICE." OL, 26 (1971), 68-78.

LPH's integration of experimental language into the society of his Utopia.

THE GO-BETWEEN (1953)

25002 Gordon, Lois. "THE GO-BETWEEN--Hartley by Pinter." KanQ, 4, No. 2 (1972), 81-92.

Pinter's reaction to and film adaptation of THE GO-BETWEEN. Chiefly on Pinter.

25003 Grossvogel, David I. "Under the Sign of Symbols: Losey and Hartley." DIACRITICS, 4, No. 3 (1974), 51-56.

Comparison of symbols in the novel and the film.

25004 Jones, Edward T. "Summer of 1900: A la recherche of THE GO-BETWEEN." LFQ, 1 (1973), 154-60.

On the film adaptation of the novel.

*25005 Moan, Margaret A. "Setting and Structure: An Approach to Hartley's THE GO-BETWEEN." Crit, 15, No. 2 (1973), 27-36.

LPH's use of setting and structure to "underscore" the drastic changes in his narrator-protagonist.

A PERFECT WOMAN (1955)

25006 Kreutz, Irving. "L.P. Hartley, Who are U? or: Luncheon in the Lounge." KR, 25 (1963), 150-54.

Speech-usage and social station in LPH's A PERFECT WOMAN.

THE SHRIMP AND THE ANEMONE (1944)

25007 D'Arcy, Patricia. "Commentary; Notes." In L.P.H.'s THE SHRIMP AND THE ANEMONE. London: Bodley Head, 1967. Pp. 213-32; 235-54.

Elementary commentary on character, plot, symbolism, background, and other literary aspects. The notes, keyed to the text, are critical as well as explanatory.

ALDOUS HUXLEY (1894-1963)

1. PRIMARY BIBLIOGRAPHY

Abbreviations of titles used in this bibliography (if any) are noted at the end of the entry. Books available in recent paperback printings are designated by "(P)."

1.1 Fiction

All works are novels unless otherwise noted. For the complete contents of the short story collections, and any uncollected works, consult the Eschelbach and Shober bibliographies (21004, 21005), and Clareson's and Davis's supplements (21001 and 21002). Also see Laura A. Huxley's THIS TIMELESS MOMENT (22010) for the first publication of the opening pages of AH's unfinished, "hypothetical," autobiographical novel, and backgrounds to its composition.

11001 AFTER MANY A SUMMER. London: Chatto and Windus, 1939. Published as AFTER MANY A SUMMER DIES THE SWAN. New York: Harper, 1939. (P).

Fantasy satire of materialism, Hollywood style.

11002 AFTER THE FIREWORKS. Reissue title for Amer. ed. of BRIEF CANDLES (see 11006).

11003 ANTIC HAY. London: Chatto and Windus; New York: Doran, 1923. (P).

The picaresque adventures of Theodore Gumbril, loose among the social set in London.

11004 APE AND ESSENCE. London: Chatto and Windus; New York: Harper, 1948. (P).

Pessimistic fantasy of a future scientific expedition (2108 A.D.), examining the ruins of North American civilization.

11005 BRAVE NEW WORLD. London: Chatto and Windus; Garden City, N.Y.: Doubleday, Doran, 1932. (P). Abbreviated as BNW.

AH's best-known novel, an antiutopian satire of a future, totally mechanized, totalitarian civilization.

11006 BRIEF CANDLES: STORIES. [Stories]. London: Chatto and Windus; Garden City, N.Y.: Doubleday, Doran, 1930.

Four stories (including "After the Fireworks").

11007 CROME YELLOW. London: Chatto and Windus, 1921. New York: Doran, 1922. (P).

AH's first novel. A light satire of modern life through the microcosm of the country house.

11008 EYELESS IN GAZA. London: Chatto and Windus; New York: Harper, 1936. (P).

Sprawling novel, covering the characters' childhood and maturity (1902-35) and dealing prominently with the political polarizations of the thirties.

11009 THE GENIUS AND THE GODDESS. London: Chatto and Windus; New York: Harper, 1955. (P).

Unique menage a trois dramatizes the conflicts between the intellect and the sexual life force.

11010 ISLAND. London: Chatto and Windus; New York: Harper, 1962. (P).

Psychedelic fantasy paradise visited by the corrupt modern man.

11011 LIMBO. [Stories]. London: Chatto and Windus; New York: Doran, 1920.

Seven short stories.

11012 LITTLE MEXICAN, AND OTHER STORIES. [Stories]. London: Chatto and Windus, 1924. Published as YOUNG ARCHIMEDES, AND OTHER STORIES. New York: Doran, 1924.

Six tales.

11013 MORTAL COILS. [Stories]. London: Chatto and Windus; New York: Doran, 1922.

Four tales and a play. The most famous story, "The Gioconda Smile," has also been published separately (1938).

11014 POINT COUNTER POINT. London: Chatto and Windus; Garden City, N.Y.: Doubleday, Doran, 1928. (P). Abbreviated as PCP.

AH's most successful novel. A satiric analysis of modern society through the complex relationships of a group of Londoners.

11015 THOSE BARREN LEAVES. London: Chatto and Windus; New York: Doran, 1925.

Like CROME YELLOW, a novel of conversations and love affairs, set in an Italian (rather than English) country house.

11016 TIME MUST HAVE A STOP. New York: Harper, 1944. London: Chatto and Windus, 1945. (P).

Saints and sinners, politics and conversation, in England and Italy of the twenties.

11017 TWO OR THREE GRACES, AND OTHER STORIES. [Stories]. London: Chatto and Windus; New York: Doran, 1926.

Four tales.

11018 YOUNG ARCHIMEDES, AND OTHER STORIES. See LITTLE MEXICAN (11012).

1.2 Miscellaneous Writings

AH wrote widely on a variety of literary and nonliterary topics. The works listed below all relate closely to his views on art, philosophy, religion, and perception. For information on AH's travel essays, drama, and poetry, consult the Eschelbach and Shober bibliographies (21004, 21005), and Clareson's and Davis's supplements (21001 and 21002).

12001 ADONIS AND THE ALPHABET, AND OTHER ESSAYS. London: Chatto and Windus, 1956. Published as TOMORROW AND TOMORROW AND TOMORROW, AND OTHER ESSAYS. New York: Harper, 1956.

Seventeen essays, several on literary topics.

12002 BRAVE NEW WORLD REVISITED. London: Chatto and Windus; New York: Harper, 1958. (P).

Analysis of the varied forms of mind and thought control, persuasion and propaganda, and their threat to modern man's freedoms.

12003 THE DEVILS OF LOUDON. London: Chatto and Windus; New York: Harper, 1952. (P).

Fascinating account of an episode of witchcraft and demonology in seventeenth-century France.

12004 THE DOORS OF PERCEPTION. London: Chatto and Windus; New York: Harper, 1954. (P).

Documents AH's experiences with mind-altering drugs.

12005 DO WHAT YOU WILL: ESSAYS. London: Chatto and Windus; Garden City, N.Y.: Doubleday, Doran, 1929.

Twelve essays on literature, philosophy, and religion. Includes "Wordsworth in the Tropics" and "Pascal." See 12010.

12006 ENDS AND MEANS: AN ENQUIRY INTO THE NATURE OF IDEALS AND INTO THE METHODS EMPLOYED FOR THEIR REALIZATION. London: Chatto and Windus; New York: Harper, 1937.

Philosophic essay.

12007 ESSAYS NEW AND OLD. London: Chatto and Windus, 1926. New York: Doran, 1927.

Twenty-eight essays, some previously published.

12008 GREY EMINENCE: A STUDY IN RELIGION AND POLITICS. London: Chatto and Windus; New York: Harper, 1941.

Biography of Father Joseph, Richelieu's chief-of-staff for foreign affairs.

12009 HEAVEN AND HELL. London: Chatto and Windus; New York: Harper, 1956. (P).

Essay on the nature of visionary experience.

12010 HOLY FACE, AND OTHER ESSAYS. London: Fleuron, 1929.

Six essays, five of which also appear in DO WHAT YOU WILL (12005).

12011 "Introduction." In THE LETTERS OF D.H. LAWRENCE. Ed. A. Huxley. London: Heinemann; New York: Viking, 1932. Pp. ix-xxxiv.

Excellent critique and memoir, also collected in THE OLIVE TREE (12015) and frequently reprinted.

12012 JOYCE, THE ARTIFICER: TWO STUDIES OF JOYCE'S METHOD (with S. Gilbert and J. Schwartz). London: Privately printed, 1952.

Pamphlet essays (one by AH) on Joyce's fictional technique.

12013 LITERATURE AND SCIENCE. London: Chatto and Windus; New York: Harper, 1963.

A plea for literary men to understand and accept science.

12014 MUSIC AT NIGHT, AND OTHER ESSAYS. London: Chatto and Windus; Garden City, N.Y.: Doubleday, Doran, 1931.

Twenty-five essays, some on literary topics.

12015 THE OLIVE TREE, AND OTHER ESSAYS. London: Chatto and Windus, 1936. New York: Harper, 1937.

Sixteen essays, most on literary subjects. Includes "D.H. Lawrence" (see 12011).

12016 ON THE MARGIN, NOTES AND ESSAYS. London: Chatto and Windus; New York: Doran, 1923.

Twenty-eight essays, several on art and poetry.

12017 THE PERENNIAL PHILOSOPHY. New York: Harper, 1945. London: Chatto and Windus, 1946. (P).

Philosophic essay.

12018 PROPER STUDIES. London: Chatto and Windus, 1927. Garden City, N.Y.: Doubleday, Doran, 1928.

Twelve essays, chiefly on religion.

12019 SCIENCE, LIBERTY, AND PEACE. New York: Harper, 1946. London: Chatto and Windus, 1947.

Essay on role of science and scientists in modern society.

12020 TEXTS AND PRETEXTS: AN ANTHOLOGY WITH COMMENTARIES. London: Chatto and Windus, 1932. New York: Harper, 1933.

Anthology, largely of poetry, arranged under topical headings (e.g., marriage, magic, God, death), with AH's critical, reflective, or evaluative commentaries.

12021 THEMES AND VARIATIONS. London: Chatto and Windus; New York: Harper, 1950.

Seven essays on art and philosophy.

12022 TOMORROW AND TOMORROW AND TOMORROW, AND OTHER ESSAYS. See ADONIS AND THE ALPHABET (12001).

12023 VULGARITY IN LITERATURE: DIGRESSIONS FROM A THEME. London: Chatto and Windus, 1930. No separate Amer. ed.

Lawrencean defense of frankness ("physiology") in literature. First American publication in RETROSPECT (13007).

1.3 Collected and Selected Works

13001 THE COLLECTED ESSAYS. New York: Harper, 1959. London: Chatto and Windus, 1960.

Reprints the forty-six most important essays on art, literature, music, travel, psychology, society, and other topics.

13002 THE COLLECTED POETRY OF ALDOUS HUXLEY. Ed. Donald J. Watt. London: Chatto and Windus; New York: Harper, 1971.

Collects the four published volumes of AH's poetry: THE BURNING WHEEL (1916), THE DEFEAT OF YOUTH (1918), LEDA (1920), and THE CICADAS (1931). See 25075.

13003 THE COLLECTED SHORT STORIES. London: Chatto and Windus; New York: Harper, 1957. (P).

Not complete. Reprints twenty-one tales. Includes "The Gioconda Smile."

13004 THE COLLECTED WORKS OF ALDOUS HUXLEY. 35 vols. London: Chatto and Windus, 1946.

Although most of AH's best known works are available in America from Harper and Row, only his English publishers have issued a "collected" edition. A new COLLECTED EDITION OF THE WORKS OF ALDOUS HUXLEY was begun by Chatto and Windus in 1968.

13005 THE GREAT SHORT WORKS OF ALDOUS HUXLEY. Ed. Bernard Bergonzi. New York: Harper, 1970.

Includes three novels (CROME YELLOW, APE AND ESSENCE, THE GENIUS AND THE GODDESS), plus selected stories and essays. See 24007.

13006 ON ART AND ARTISTS. Ed. Morris Philipson. London: Chatto and Windus; New York: Harper, 1960.

Collects thirty-four essays on architecture, art, literature, and music. See 25091.

13007 RETROSPECT: AN OMNIBUS OF ALDOUS HUXLEY'S BOOKS. Garden City, N.Y.: Doubleday, Doran, 1933.

Anthology of stories, essays, poetry, and a complete novel (CROME YELLOW).

13008 ROTUNDA: A SELECTION FROM THE WORKS OF ALDOUS HUXLEY. London: Chatto and Windus, 1932.

Anthology of stories, essays, poetry, and a complete novel (THOSE BARREN LEAVES).

13009 SELECTED ESSAYS. Ed. Harold Raymond. London: Chatto and Windus, 1961.

Twenty-three reprinted essays and extracts from thirteen of the essay collections (1923-59). Good selection. See 25096.

13010 STORIES, ESSAYS, AND POEMS. London: Dent, 1937.

Everyman Library anthology of stories, novel excerpts, essays, and poetry.

13011 TWICE SEVEN: FOURTEEN SELECTED STORIES. [Stories]. London: Reprint Society, 1944.

Reprinted tales.

13012 THE WORLD OF ALDOUS HUXLEY: AN OMNIBUS OF HIS FICTION AND NON-FICTION OVER THREE DECADES. Ed. Charles J. Rolo. New York: Harper, 1947.

Anthology. Includes stories, essays, poetry, novel extracts, and a complete novel (ANTIC HAY). See 24079.

1.4 Letters

Also see Wickes (21009), below.

14001 LETTERS OF ALDOUS HUXLEY. Ed. Grover Smith. London: Chatto and Windus; New York: Harper, 1969.

Contains 943 letters (1899-1963). Well annotated.

2. SECONDARY BIBLIOGRAPHY

2.1 Bibliographies

21001 Clareson, Thomas D., and Carolyn S. Andrews, comps. "Aldous Huxley: A Bibliography, 1960-1964." EXTRAPOLATION, 6 (1964), 2-21.

Supplements Eschelbach and Shober (21004).

21002 Davis, Dennis D., comp. "Aldous Huxley: A Bibliography, 1965-1973." BB, 31 (1974), 67-70.

Updated checklist of works by and about AH.

21003 Duval, Hanson R., ed. ALDOUS HUXLEY: A BIBLIOGRAPHY. New York: Arrow, 1939.

The only descriptive primary bibliography of AH's books, pamphlets, and "miscellanea." Contains forty-two items, English and American editions through September 1939. Also contains briefer listings of his prefaces, introductions, and contributions to books and periodicals.

*21004 Eschelbach, Claire J., and Joyce Lee Shober [Marthaler], comps. ALDOUS HUXLEY: A BIBLIOGRAPHY, 1916-1959. Berkeley and Los Angeles: Univ. of California Press, 1961.

Full listing of works by AH, to 1959, and checklist of books, dissertations, and articles on and reviews of AH's work. Supplemented by Clareson (21001), Davis (21002), and Eschelbach (below).

21005 Eschelbach, Claire J., and Joyce [Lee] S[hober]. Marthaler, comps. "Aldous Huxley: A Bibliography, 1914-1964 (A Supplementary Listing)." BB, 28 (1971), 114-17.

Supplements Eschelbach and Shober (above).

21006 Farmer, David R. "The Bibliographical Potential of a Twentieth-Century Literary Agent's Archives: The Pinker Papers." LCUT, 2 (1970), 27-35.

Describes papers of importance on AH and others, recently acquired by the University of Texas.

21007 Lash, Barry, comp. BY AND ABOUT ALDOUS HUXLEY: A BIBLIOGRAPHY OF THE ALDOUS HUXLEY COLLECTION AT MILNE LIBRARY. Geneseo, N.Y.: Milne Library, 1973.

Catalogs the primary and secondary AH collections of the Milne Library at the State University of New York college.

*21008 Watt, Donald J. "Introduction." In ALDOUS HUXLEY: THE CRITICAL HERITAGE. Ed. Watt. Pp. 1-36. See 23021.

A fine survey of AH's career and critical reputation.

21009 Wickes, George, ed. ALDOUS HUXLEY AT UCLA: A CATALOGUE OF THE MANUSCRIPTS IN THE ALDOUS HUXLEY COLLECTION, WITH THE TEXTS OF THREE UNPUBLISHED LETTERS. Los Angeles: Univ. of California Library, 1964.

Lists and describes the UCLA collection of letters and literary manuscripts (nine typescripts and holographs).

21010 Wiley, Paul L., comp. "Aldous Huxley (1894-1963)." In THE BRITISH NOVEL. Comp. Wiley. Pp. 60-63. See G1419.

Brief primary and secondary checklist.

2.2 Biographies, Memoirs, Reminiscences, Interviews

22001 "Aldous Huxley on Thought Control." LISTENER, 60 (1958), 373-74.

Shortened transcript of a television interview with Mike Wallace.

*22002 Bedford, Sybille. ALDOUS HUXLEY: A BIOGRAPHY. Vol. 1, 1894-1939; vol. 2, 1939-1963. New York: Knopf, 1973-74. 1-vol. ed., 1974.

The most comprehensive and detailed biographical study of AH. Bedford generously illustrates her account with exhaustive references to AH's personal papers and work. The individual novels are considered, largely for their biographical relevance, in separate subsections. Index unfortunately limited to proper names and titles.

22003 Beerman, Hans. "An Interview with Aldous Huxley." MQ, 5 (1964), 223-30.

Brief interview (1960) discussion of AH's ideas on freedom, education, love, and other topics.

22004 Cary, Richard. "Aldous Huxley, Vernon Lee and the Genius Loci." CLQ, Series 5 (1960), pp. 128-41.

The friendship and comparable gifts for travel writing of AH and Violet Paget ("Vernon Lee").

22005 Clark, Ronald W. THE HUXLEYS. New York: McGraw-Hill, 1968.

Primarily a historical and biographical study, concentrating on Thomas Henry Huxley and his two illustrious grandsons, Julian Huxley and AH, with incidental consideration of other family members. Clark is most valuable for presenting AH's intellectual backgrounds and formation. For a fuller biography or for close criticism and evaluation of AH's work, the reader should look to Bedford (22002) or the critical studies (section 2.3, below).

22006 A CONVERSATION WITH ALDOUS HUXLEY: A 1963 DISCUSSION WITH THE RENOWNED NOVELIST AND PHILOSOPHER. North Hollywood, Calif.: Center for Cassette Studies, 1972.

Twenty-eight-minute interview on cassette tape.

22007 Craft, Robert. "With Aldous Huxley." ENCOUNTER, 25, No. 5 (1965), 10-16.

Memories of the Huxleys and the Stravinskys in the early fifties.

*22008 Huxley, Julian S., ed. ALDOUS HUXLEY, 1894-1963: A MEMORIAL VOLUME. New York: Harper, 1965.

Twenty-seven memorial tributes (mostly brief memoirs) by a distinguished list of contributors (including Julian Huxley, Kenneth Clark, T.S. Eliot, Yehudi Menuhin), and a previously unpublished essay by AH entitled "Shakespeare and Religion."

22009 Huxley, Laura Archera. THIS TIMELESS MOMENT: A PERSONAL VIEW OF ALDOUS HUXLEY. New York: Farrar, Straus and Giroux, 1968.

Memoir concentrating on the years 1948-63. AH's second wife offers valuable information on the later years, the experimentations with mind-altering drugs and mystical experience, as well as the backgrounds to the last works (especially ISLAND). A thirty-page fragment of AH's unfinished novel-in-progress is also included. See 25089 and 25094.

*22010 "Huxley Brothers." LIFE, 24 Mar. 1947, pp. 53ff.

Intersting photographic essay, concerned with Julian Huxley and AH.

22011 Powell, Lawrence C., et al. ALDOUS HUXLEY, 1894-1963: ADDRESSES AT A MEMORIAL MEETING HELD IN THE SCHOOL OF LIBRARY SERVICE, FEBRUARY 27, 1964. Los Angeles: Univ. of California, 1964.

A 10-page pamphlet.

22012 Sitwell, Edith. "Maria and Aldous Huxley." In TAKEN CARE OF. New York: Atheneum, 1965. Pp. 98-105.

Remembered conversations and parties with the Huxleys.

*22013 Wickes, George, and R.A.H. Frazer. "Aldous Huxley." In WRITERS AT WORK: THE PARIS REVIEW INTERVIEWS, 2ND SERIES. Comp. George Plimpton. New York: Viking, 1963. Pp. 193-214.

Composite of two interview-discussions of AH's views, working methods, and past and forthcoming work (ISLAND).

2.3 Book-Length Critical Studies and Essay Collections

Also see Calder, 25013 below (re: BNW).

23001 Atkins, John. ALDOUS HUXLEY: A LITERARY STUDY. 1956. Rev. ed. New York: Orion, 1967.

Thematically organized study of AH's ideas. Atkins considers such miscellaneous topics as AH's persona, his preoccupation with flesh and corruption, his detachment, cynicism, mysticism, and pacifism, in separate chapters, but generally fails either to show the evolution of AH's thought or to relate coherently the ideas and the works. The revised edition includes a lengthy, equally miscellaneous introduction.

23002 Birnbaum, Milton. ALDOUS HUXLEY'S QUEST FOR VALUES. Knoxville: Univ. of Tennessee Press, 1971.

Study of AH's shifting and developing views of the "traditional sources of value" (art, education, politics, love, nature, science, and religion). Birmbaum synthesizes these views from the novels and major nonfiction and traces throughout the pattern of AH's quest for value and meaning in the world and in man. The organization of this book by theme, however, prevents full critical analysis of the individual works. (Considerable portions published previously.) Extract reprinted in 23013.

*23003 Bowering, Peter. ALDOUS HUXLEY: A STUDY OF THE MAJOR NOVELS. New York: Oxford Univ. Press, 1969.

Critical commentaries (with some source study) on the intellectual and moral significance of nine novels (APE AND ESSENCE and THE GENIUS AND THE GODDESS omitted), prefaced by essays on AH's "Novel of Ideas" and "Moral Dilemma." Bowering's final chapter, "The Moralist and the Artist," argues for a higher estimation of AH's fiction as art. Valuable and well-written study. Extract reprinted in 23013.

23004 Brander, Laurence. ALDOUS HUXLEY: A CRITICAL STUDY. Lewisburg, Pa.: Bucknell Univ. Press, 1970.

On the whole, a rather superficial survey of the fiction, essays, philosophy, travel books, biographies, and other writings. Most of Brander's criticism is limited to appreciative comments on and summaries of the works.

23005 Brooke, Jocelyn. ALDOUS HUXLEY. 1954. Rev. ed. London: Longmans, 1963.

Good general introduction to AH's life and work. Includes a brief bibliography.

23006 Chatterjee, Sisir [also Chattopadhyaya, Sisir]. ALDOUS HUXLEY: A STUDY. 1955. 2nd ed. Calcutta: Mukhopadhyay, 1966.

Study (written c. 1940) of AH's evolution from cynical Pyrrhonist to Vedantic mystic, with evidence drawn from the essays and novels (to AFTER MANY A SUMMER). Chatterjee's Postscript for the second edition qualifies his youthful enthusiasm for AH's work.

23007 Firchow, Peter. ALDOUS HUXLEY: SATIRIST AND NOVELIST. Minneapolis: Univ. of Minnesota Press, 1972.

Reading of the fiction which considers AH primarily as a satirist who also happened to be a novelist ("satire is an attitude and not a form"). Firchow's best chapters, therefore, deal with the major satires (PCP, BNW and APE AND ESSENCE). Throughout, Firchow emphasizes the objects of AH's satire (e.g., the "American dream") rather than his form or technique (cf. Meckier, 23016). The survey-chapters devoted to the early and late novels are less satisfactory. Extract reprinted in 23013.

*23008 Ghose, Sisirkumar. ALDOUS HUXLEY: A CYNICAL SALVATIONIST. Bombay: Asia Publishing House, 1962.

Study of the "neo-Brahmin" AH's evolving "Weltanschauung," from the perspective of Indian philosophy. Ghose usefully charts the four stages of AH's development, from materialism to Vedantic mysticism and, under a separate heading, surveys the evidence from the novels (to 1945, the date of this study's composition). A useful attempt to discover the systematic basis of AH's conversion from cynic to salvationist.

23009 Henderson, Alexander. ALDOUS HUXLEY. London: Chatto and Windus, 1935.

The first book-length study. Henderson attempts to dispose of several inaccurate contemporary notions about AH (his inhumanity, skepticism, and immorality) through a close reading of the novels (to BNW) and an examination of AH's ideas derived from the essays, criticism, travel books, and other nonfiction. Perceptive and interesting commentaries.

23010 Hines, Bede. THE SOCIAL WORLD OF ALDOUS HUXLEY. 1957. 3rd ed. Loretto, Pa.: Mariale Press, 1962.

Highly moralistic view of AH's fiction and biographies, organized under several broad thematic headings (e.g., "Literary Artifice," "Pointless Living"). AH's point of view is seen developing from a humanistic perspective in the early works, to a vision of God as "the Absolute seen through man."

*23011 Holmes, Charles M. ALDOUS HUXLEY AND THE WAY TO REALITY. Bloomington: Indiana Univ. Press, 1970.

Analytical study of AH's works and, in a larger sense, his "long, complicated and anguished mental journey" toward the resolution of personal, moral, and intellectual conflicts. A more useful book than most volumes on AH, principally for Holmes's perceptive discussion of AH's poetry, short fiction, essays, biographies, and philosophical essays, in close relation to his excellent analyses of the novels. Extract reprinted in 23013.

23012 Jog, D.V. ALDOUS HUXLEY THE NOVELIST. Bombay: Book Centre, 1966.

Ill-written, impressionistic doctoral thesis, containing simplified summaries of AH's "intellectual milieu" and "ideological content" and brief commentaries on the novels. Pedestrian chapters on AH's characterization ("mirroring") and style do little to strengthen Jog's study.

23013 Kuehn, Robert E., ed. ALDOUS HUXLEY: A COLLECTION OF CRITICAL ESSAYS. Englewood Cliffs, N.J.: Prentice-Hall, 1974.

Reprints fifteen critical essays on AH's views, techniques, and individual works, together with the editor's brief introduction. Includes 23014, 24006, 24041, 24059, 25053; and extracts from the following books: 23002, 23003, 23007, 23011, 23016 and 23022.

23014 LONDON MAGAZINE. 2 (Aug. 1955), 51-64. "A Critical Symposium on Aldous Huxley."

Five appreciative commentaries on the fiction (through AFTER MANY A SUMMER) and essays. Includes 24098, 25004, 25009, 25039, and 25092. Reprinted in 23013 and 23021.

*23015 May, Keith M. ALDOUS HUXLEY. London: Elek, 1972.

Close critical reading of AH as a traditional novelist, which explores his uses of structure, character, language, setting, and theme. May divides the novels chronologically and thematically into two groups: CROME YELLOW through EYELESS IN GAZA as works "Seeking Reconciliation of the Absolute and the Relative" and AFTER MANY A SUMMER through ISLAND as works "Seeking Perfection of the Life and the Work." Although this division oversimplifies AH's development and reduces the possibility of comparative criticism among the works, May's readings are consistently substantial and rewarding.

*23016 Meckier, Jerome. ALDOUS HUXLEY: SATIRE AND STRUCTURE. New York: Barnes and Noble, 1969.

A fine though somewhat rigid critical study of the novels. Meckier vigorously disputes the prevalent critical notion of AH's technical shortcomings as a novelist, arguing that in his refinement of the structural device of counterpoint as a vehicle for his satire, AH has discovered an ideal fusion of design and meaning. Meckier's opening definition of the contrapuntal nature of satire in AH's work, suggesting the ideal of integration through the counterpoint of dualisms, is amplified in a six-chapter analysis of the satire and structure of the eleven novels. Extract reprinted in 23013.

23017 Ramamurty, K. Bhaskara. ALDOUS HUXLEY: A STUDY OF HIS NOVELS. Bombay: Asia Publishing House, 1974.

A well-written analysis of the novels, though occasionally effusive. Ramamurty defines AH's chief concern with the schism between the physical and spiritual ("ape" and "essence") in modern man and traces his progressive quest for synthesis in the eleven novels, emphasizing the final statement in ISLAND ("The Summing Up"). Ramamurty's discussions of AH's "Life-Theory" ("How Not to be a Hamlet"), his relationship to D.H. Lawrence, and his development of the novel of ideas are particularly valuable.

23018 Savage, David S. MYSTICISM AND ALDOUS HUXLEY: AN EXAMINATION OF HEARD-HUXLEY THEORIES. New York: Baradinsky, 1947.

Pamphlet (23 pp.) analyzing AH's and Heard's "chimerical" attempt to articulate a vision which integrates scientific reality and values (faith) through mysticism. "Would 'wishful thinking' be too harsh a description of it?"

23019 Scales, Derek P. ALDOUS HUXLEY AND FRENCH LITERATURE. Sydney: Sydney Univ. Press, 1969.

Detailed examination of the influence of French writers on AH's work, as well as AH's critical views of French literature. Special emphasis is placed on AH's relations with Pascal and Baudelaire. A comprehensive though narrow study.

23020 Thody, Philip. ALDOUS HUXLEY: A BIOGRAPHICAL INTRODUCTION. London: Studio Vista, 1973.

Useful complement to Watts's primarily critical introduction to AH's fiction (see 23022). A study of AH's life and the evolution of his ideas with wide reference to the nonfiction as well as the fiction. Thody focuses on AH's attempts to reconcile science and religion and, less convincingly, on the biographical sources of his obsessions with pain, disease, and the tragic conflict between ideals and reality.

*23021 Watt, Donald J., ed. ALDOUS HUXLEY: THE CRITICAL HERITAGE. London: Routledge, 1975.

Reprints selected contemporary reviews of the fiction, poetry, biographies, and essays. Watt's introduction (pp. 1-36) is an excellent survey of AH's career and critical reputation. Includes 21008, 23014, 24052, 25055, 25070, 25074; and extracts from the following articles: 24015, 24021, 24038, 24049, 24073, 24078, 25048, 25076, 25081, and 25083.

*23022 Watts, Harold H. ALDOUS HUXLEY. New York: Twayne, 1969.

Fine introduction to AH's thought and fiction. Watts devotes separate chapters to AH's "mind" (a valuable survey of AH's ideas), BNW, ISLAND, and the biographies. The remaining novels are examined in two lengthy chapters. Brief, annotated bibliography. Extract reprinted in 23013.

23023 Weaver, Raymond, et al. ALDOUS HUXLEY, SATIRIST AND HUMANIST: BEING A COLLECTION OF CRITICAL AND BIOGRAPHICAL STUDIES. Garden City, N.Y.: Doubleday, Doran, n.d. [c. 1929].

Collects a sketchy bibliography of AH, five critical essays, and a selection of brief personal and critical comments from the press. A 72-page pamphlet. Includes extracts from the following articles: 24066 and 24073.

23024 Woodcock, George. DAWN AND THE DARKEST HOUR: A STUDY OF ALDOUS HUXLEY. New York: Viking, 1972.

Full reading of the fiction and nonfiction which traces the now familiar pattern of disillusion and affirmation in AH's thought. Woodcock relies extensively on metaphors of darkness and light to characterize AH's progress from negativism to enlightment. Although his overview is unoriginal, many of Woodcock's analyses are fresh and perceptive (especially on BNW and EYELESS IN GAZA, AH's "best novel").

23025 Zahner, Lilly. DEMON AND SAINT IN THE NOVELS OF ALDOUS HUXLEY. Bern, Switzerland: Francke, 1975.

Study of the dichotomy between good and evil in AH's novels and histories, observing the gradual "blurring" of polarities and eventual attempt at synthesis in the late works. A considerable portion of Zahner's commentary is preoccupied with routine summary of the books, leaving scant space for analysis or discussion of the continuing thesis.

2.4 General Critical Articles, or Chapters on AH

24001 Allen, Walter. THE MODERN NOVEL. Pp. 41-44. See G2202.

AH's developing seriousness and retreat into mysticism detrimental to his art.

24002 Armytage, W.H. "The Disenchanted Mecanophobes in Twentieth Century England." EXTRAPOLATION, 9 (1968), 33-60.

AH as an antiutopian, along with Orwell, Lawrence, and others.

24003 Bald, R.C. "Aldous Huxley as a Borrower." CE, 11 (1950), 183-87.

Although cultured, AH lacks the "creative concentration of the artist." Suggests AH's "borrowing" amounts to plagiarism.

24004 Bartlett, Norman. "Aldous Huxley and D.H. Lawrence." AusQ, 36, No. 1 (1964), 76-84.

"Huxley was always trying to justify intellectually D.H. Lawrence's instinctive religion of sensuality."

24005 Bentley, Joseph. "Aldous Huxley's Ambivalent Responses to the Ideas of D.H. Lawrence." TCL, 13 (1967), 139-53.

Concentrates on the Lawrencean and anti-Lawrencean ideas in the novels of the twenties. Contains several misreadings.

*24006 ______. "The Later Novels of Huxley." YR, 59 (1970), 507-19.

AH's movement from outrageousness to moral affirmation. Reprinted in 23013.

24007 Bergonzi, Bernard. "Aldous Huxley: 'A Novelist of Talent and an Essayist of Genius.'" In THE GREAT SHORT WORKS OF ALDOUS HUXLEY. Ed. Bergonzi. Pp. vii-xv. See 13005.

AH not primarily a literary artist, but a "remarkable personality" and a distinguished man of letters.

24008 ______. "The Huxley Line." In his THE TURN OF THE CENTURY. Pp. 162-70. See G2309.

AH's "intellectual brilliance" and distinguished family heritage.

24009 Bradbury, Malcolm. POSSIBILITIES. Pp. 151-53. See G3012.

AH's "complex blend of involvement and disguise" in his comic novels of the twenties (cf. Wyndham Lewis and Evelyn Waugh).

24010 Buck, Philo M. "Sight to the Blind: Aldous Huxley." In DIRECTIONS IN CONTEMPORARY LITERATURE. New York: Oxford Univ. Press, 1942. Pp. 169-91.

AH's value as a critic of modern life and society.

24011 Bullough, Geoffrey. "Aspects of Aldous Huxley." ES, 30 (1949), 233-43.

The changes in AH's belief, from modernist negativism and satire to affirmation.

24012 Burgum, Edwin B. "Aldous Huxley and His Dying Swan." In his THE NOVEL AND THE WORLD'S DILEMMA. Pp. 140-56. See G3020.

AH's decadence and flagging powers as a novelist.

24013 Butts, Mary. "Aldous Huxley." In SCRUTINIES. Comp. Edgell Rickword. London: Wishart, 1928. II, 74-98.

AH mirrors the misery, failure, and "idiocy of our age."

24014 Chase, Richard V. "The Huxley-Heard Paradise." PR, 10 (1943), 143-58.

AH (an "unoriginal" thinker) and Heard as prophets of a new spiritualism (cf. Comte's positivism).

24015 Chesterton, G.K. "The End of the Moderns." 1933. In THE COMMON MAN. London: Sheed and Ward, 1950. Pp. 196-205.

AH (and D.H. Lawrence) seen, not as a sexual revolutionists, but as "last figures of a defeated anarchist army." Extracts reprinted in 23021.

*24016 Church, Margaret. "Aldous Huxley: Perennial Time." In her TIME AND REALITY. Pp. 102-19. See G3024.

AH's development from an absolute concept of time in his early fiction (as opposed to a psychological sense of "inner time") to a mystical timelessness in the later work.

24017 Collins, Arthur S. ENGLISH LITERATURE OF THE TWENTIETH CENTURY. Pp. 231-43. See G2105.

General overview (cf. J.C. Powys).

*24018 Conner, Frederick W. "'Attention!': Aldous Huxley's Epistemological Route to Salvation." SR, 81 (1973), 282-308.

Traces the "history and logic" of AH's stress on the importance of attention to or full realization of immediate experience (cf. Croce, Bergson, Russell).

24019 Conolly, Cyril. ENEMIES OF PROMISE. Pp. 52-54. See G3025.

Examination of AH's "mandarin" (romantic) prose.

24020 Cunliffe, J.W. "Georgian Novelists: Aldous Huxley (1894--)." In his ENGLISH LITERATURE IN THE TWENTIETH CENTURY. Pp. 239-45, 257. See G2106.

Critical survey and brief bibliography.

24021 Daiches, David. "Aldous Huxley." In THE NOVEL AND THE MODERN WORLD. 1st ed. Chicago: Univ. of Chicago Press, 1939. Pp. 188-210.

AH's development from "frustrated romantic," who "would like to believe in love and progress and spirituality," to a satisfied mystic and unsuccessful novelist. This essay omitted from second edition (1960). Extracts reprinted in 23021.

*24022 Dyson, A.E. "Aldous Huxley and the Two Nothings." In his THE CRAZY FABRIC. Pp. 166-86. See G3037.

AH's ambiguous irony, from CROME YELLOW to AFTER MANY A SUMMER.

24023 Eaton, Gai. "Monk at Large: Aldous Huxley." In THE RICHEST VEIN: EASTERN TRADITION AND MODERN THOUGHT. London: Faber, 1949. Pp. 166-82.

AH's use of Eastern doctrine to justify his "hatred of life."

24024 Edgar Pelham. "Aldous Huxley." In his THE ART OF THE NOVEL. Pp. 278-93. See G2205.

Like Voltaire, AH fuses his skeptical irony with humanitarian ardor (surveys CROME YELLOW to BNW).

24025 Ellis, Geoffrey U. TWILIGHT ON PARNASSUS. Pp. 256-86 and passim. See G3040.

AH as moralist and artist.

24026 Evans, B. Ifor. "Aldous Huxley." In ENGLISH LITERATURE BETWEEN THE WARS. Pp. 58-67. See G2324.

AH, like H.G. Wells in the previous generation, a representative of the writers of his time.

24027 Frierson, William C. THE ENGLISH NOVEL IN TRANSITION. Pp. 258-65. See G3047.

Brief review of AH's conception of fiction (the novel of ideas) and his place in postwar English literature.

24028 Gerber, Richard. UTOPIAN FANTASY. Passim. See G6414.

The literary values of and the views of science and society in AH (especially APE AND ESSENCE and BNW).

24029 Gill, Richard. HAPPY RURAL SEAT. Passim. See G2330.

The country house as symbol in AH's fiction.

*24030 Glicksberg, Charles I. "Aldous Huxley: Art and Mysticism." PrS, 27 (1953), 344-53.

AH's abandonment of the art of fiction for "mystical propaganda."

24031 ______. "Aldous Huxley: Sex and Salvation." In THE SEXUAL REVOLUTION IN MODERN ENGLISH LITERATURE. Pp. 118-39. See G3051.

AH's transformation from skeptical hedonist to antisensual mystic. Surveys AH's views of sensuality in his fiction.

24032 ______. "Huxley: The Experimental Novelist." SAQ, 52 (1953), 98-110.

Remarkably similar to "Aldous Huxley: Art and Mysticism," above.

24033 ______. "The Intellectual Pilgrimage of Aldous Huxley." DR, 19 (1939), 165-78.

General overview of AH's ideas as intellectual novelist and thinker.

24034 ______. "The Literary Struggle for Selfhood." Person, 42 (1961), 52-65.

AH among Proust, Sartre, Gide, and other writers.

24035 Greenblatt, Stephen Jay. THREE MODERN SATIRISTS: WAUGH, ORWELL, AND HUXLEY. New Haven, Conn.: Yale Univ. Press, 1965. Pp. 77-101, 105-17 and passim.

AH's detachment, his failure to adopt a distinguishable point of view, weakens his satiric force. Discusses CROME YELLOW, ANTIC HAY, PCP, and BNW.

24036 Hays, Peter L. THE LIMPING HERO: GROTESQUES IN LITERATURE. New York: New York Univ. Press, 1971. Pp. 79-82 and passim.

The emasculated hero in AH, especially in PCP.

24037 Heard, Gerald. "The Poignant Prophet." KR, 27 (1965), 49-70.

AH's poignant sense of the irrational, ludicrous, and absurd pretentiousness of mankind.

24038 Henderson, Philip. "Aldous Huxley." In his THE NOVEL TODAY. Pp. 118-30. See G3067.

AH's "emotional immaturity." Extracts reprinted in 23021.

24039 Hillegas, Mark R. THE FUTURE AS NIGHTMARE: H.G. WELLS AND THE ANTI-UTOPIANS. Pp. 111-23. See G6415.

Varieties of the utopian ideal in BNW, ISLAND, and other works.

24040 Hoffmann, Charles G. "The Change in Huxley's Approach to the Novel of Ideas." Person, 42 (1961), 85-90.

AH's departure from an allegorical approach to the novel of ideas toward direct philosophic discourse in his later fiction (BNW and after).

*24041 Hoffman, Frederick J. "Aldous Huxley and the Novel of Ideas." In FORMS OF MODERN FICTION. Ed. William Van O'Connor. Pp. 189-200. See G3114.

Defines and illustrates AH's use of the "novel of ideas." Reprinted in 23013.

24042 Houston, P.H. "The Salvation of Aldous Huxley." AMERICAN REVIEW, 4 (1934), 209-32.

Sees AH as the spokesman of his age and potential "guide" out of the depth of its despair.

24043 Joad, C.E.M. "Aldous Huxley and the Dowagers." In RETURN TO PHILOSOPHY: BEING A DEFENSE OF REASON, AN AFFIRMATION OF VALUES, AND A PLEA FOR PHILOSOPHY. 1935. 2nd ed. London: Faber, 1945. Pp. 78-94.

AH's "confused" attack on rationalistic philosophy (re: "Pascal").

24044 Jones, Rufus M. "The Way of Affirmation." In THE LUMINOUS TRAIL. New York: Macmillan, 1947. Pp. 9-26.

Questions AH's assumption, in PERENNIAL PHILOSOPHY, that the "way of negation" is the right way to reality.

24045 Jones, W.S. Handley. "The Modern Hamlet." In his THE PRIEST AND THE SIREN. Pp. 127-41. See G6306.

AH's main preoccupation with questions of "faith and morals."

24046 Karl, Frederick R., and Marvin Magalaner. "Aldous Huxley." In their A READER'S GUIDE TO GREAT TWENTIETH-CENTURY ENGLISH NOVELS. Pp. 254-84. See G3082.

Survey of AH as a "novelist of ideas" ("to apply literary standards to AH's fiction is often futile"). Examines CROME YELLOW, ANTIC HAY, PCP, BNW, and EYELESS IN GAZA.

24047 Ketser, G. "Aldous Huxley: A Retrospect." RLV, 30 (1964), 179-84.

Obituary and general critique.

*24048 King, Carlyle. "Aldous Huxley and Music." QQ, 70 (1963), 336-51.

Adduces from the fiction AH's "wide ranging musical culture" and fundamentally good taste.

*24049 ______. "Aldous Huxley's Way to God." QQ, 61 (1954), 80-100.

Asserts the consistency of AH's "quest for values" in his fiction, from CROME YELLOW on, in opposition to the usual two-phase view of AH's career. Extract reprinted in 23021.

24050 Kirkwood, M.M. "The Thought of Aldous Huxley." UTQ, 6 (1937), 189-98.

Despite his verbal pyrotechnics and wit, AH a thinker of high seriousness (notes AH's conversion from skepticism).

24051 Kolek, Leszek. "Music in Literature--Presentation of Huxley's Experiment in 'Musicalization of Fiction.'" ZRL, 14, No. 2 (1972), 111-22.

Traces AH's attempt to approximate musical form in his early fiction.

*24052 Lalou, Rene. "The Ends and Means of Aldous Huxley." 1938. Trans. and ed. Clementine Robert and Nina Lavroukine. In ALDOUS HUXLEY: THE CRITICAL HERITAGE. Ed. Donald J. Watt. Pp. 294-303. See 23021.

Disputes AH's reputation as a skeptic and asserts his moral earnestness.

24053 Legates, Charlotte. "Huxley and Brueghel." WHR, 29 (1975), 365-71.

AH's attraction to Brueghel the Elder's view of life, and comparable vision in the novels of the twenties.

24054 Lovett, Robert M., and Helen S. Hughes. "Aldous Leonard Huxley (1894--)." In their THE HISTORY OF THE NOVEL IN ENGLAND. Pp. 453-55. See G2209.

AH representative of the modern, postwar bitterness in fiction.

24055 MacCarthy, Desmond. "Aldous Huxley." In CRITICISM. London: Putnam, 1932. Pp. 235-46.

The strengths and limitations of AH's fiction, to BRIEF CANDLES (1930).

24056 McCormick, John. CATASTROPHE AND IMAGINATION. Pp. 284-89 and passim. See G3095.

AH an "obsessed satirist who turns to allegory" in his later work.

24057 Macdermott, Doireann. "The Zoologist of Fiction: Aldous Huxley." FMod, 9, No. 37 (1969), 27-45.

AH's fascination with man's relation to the animal world and with the parallels between animal and human behavior.

*24058 Marovitz, Sanford E. "Aldous Huxley and the Visual Arts." PLL, 9 (1973), 172-88.

AH's transformation as a novelist reflected in his changing

view of the visual arts, from a form of intellectual exercise to a recognition of their religious and visionary implications. Reviews AH's art criticism.

*24059 _____. "Aldous Huxley's Intellectual Zoo." PQ, 48 (1969), 495-507.

AH's animal imagery increasingly archetypal as his view of human nature expands from a simple dualism of mind and body to a mystical trinity of mind, body, and spirit. Reprinted in 23013.

24060 Matson, Floyd W. "Aldous and Heaven Too: Religion among the Intellectuals." AR, 14 (1954), 293-309.

AH epitomizes the modern intellectual's turn toward religion.

24061 Maurois, Andre. "Aldous Huxley." In his PROPHETS AND POETS. Pp. 287-312. See G3102.

Survey, stressing AH's "encyclopaedist" qualities.

24062 Meckier, Jerome. "The Case of the Modern Satirical Novel: Huxley, Waugh, and Powell." STC, No. 14 (1974), pp. 21-42.

Argues the modern satirical novel is "a recognizable genre," and describes its characteristics.

24063 _____. "Housebreaking Huxley: Saint versus Satirist." MOSAIC, 5, No. 4 (1972), 165-77.

Useful survey of AH's critical reputation (and review of six recent books).

24064 _____. "Shakespeare and Aldous Huxley." SHAKESPEARE QUARTERLY, 22 (1971), 129-35.

Technical and structural patterns in Shakespeare's work are similar to AH's own.

24065 Misra, G.S.P., and Nora Satin. "The Meaning of Life in Aldous Huxley." MQ, 9 (1968), 351-63.

Influence of Indian mysticism on AH's concern for the destiny of man in a "supra-technical world."

24066 Muir, Edwin. "Aldous Huxley." In his TRANSITION. Pp. 101-13. See G3110.

AH's novels a "loose frame for his intellectual fantasies." Extracts reprinted in 23023.

24067 Muller, Herbert J. MODERN FICTION: A STUDY OF VALUES. Pp. 383-95. See G3111.

AH's cynicism and his eventual discovery of faith by the time of EYELESS IN GAZA (cf. Hemingway).

24068 Nagarajan, S. "Religion in Three Recent Novels of Aldous Huxley." MFS, 5 (1959), 153-65.

AFTER MANY A SUMMER, TIME MUST HAVE A STOP, and THE GENIUS AND THE GODDESS religious novels embodying the search for "self-transcendance."

24069 Nazareth, Peter. "Aldous Huxley and His Critics." ESA, 7 (1964), 65-81.

AH a successful satirist (cf. Swift and Jonson), but a "minor" writer and a lesser genius.

*24070 Nicholson, Norman. "Aldous Huxley." In his MAN AND LITERATURE. Pp. 94-103. See G2353.

AH's exploration of the Lawrencean concept of the "natural" man in his fiction.

24071 O'Faolain, Sean. "Huxley and Waugh, or 'I do not think, therefore I am.'" In his THE VANISHING HERO. Pp. 33-69. See G3116.

A war of ideas in AH's own mind confuses the meaning of his novels.

24072 Olney, James. "'Most Extraordinary': Sybille Bedford and Aldous Huxley." SAQ, 74 (1975), 376-86.

AH and his ideal biographer, Bedford, share the sense of life's strangeness, marvelousness, and mysteriousness.

24073 Overton, Grant. "The Twentieth Century Gothic of Aldous Huxley." In CARGOES FOR CRUSOES. New York: Appleton, 1924. Pp. 97-113.

Early and emphatic recognition of the moral, rather than aesthetic, values of AH's work. Extracts reprinted in 23021 and 23023.

24074 Quennell, Peter. "Aldous Huxley." In LIVING WRITERS. Ed. Gilbert Phelps. Pp. 128-36. See G3121.

AH's unrestrained facility of invention detrimental to any sense of aesthetic unity in his works.

24075 _____. "D.H. Lawrence and Aldous Huxley." In THE ENGLISH NOVELISTS. Ed. Derek Verschoyle. Pp. 247-57. See G3150.

Intellectual and artistic contrasts and a fundamental similarity (their disdain for form) between Lawrence and AH.

24076 Quina, James H. "The Philosophical Phases of Aldous Huxley." CE, 23 (1962), 636-41.

AH's development from philosophic negation to mystical affirmation.

24077 Roberts, John H. "Huxley and Lawrence." VQR, 13 (1937), 546-57.

AH's conversion to Lawrence's ideals in PCP and after.

*24078 Rogers, Winfield H. "Aldous Huxley's Humanism." SR, 43 (1935), 262-72.

Argues perceptively the unity of thought, intellectual acumen, humanity, and morality of AH's philosophy. Extracts reprinted in 23021.

24079 Rolo, Charles J. "Introduction." In THE WORLD OF ALDOUS HUXLEY. Ed. Rolo. Pp. vii-xxv. See 13012.

AH a "great comic artist who is, always and inescapably, a passionately serious thinker."

24080 Savage, Derek S. "Aldous Huxley." In his THE WITHERED BRANCH. Pp. 129-55. See G3129.

AH's change from "sophisticated hedonist" to contemplative mystic signals the end of his art.

24081 Schall, James V. "Buber and Huxley: Recent Developments in Philosophy." MONTH, 19 (1958), 97-102.

For AH, the experience of language "keeps man from his own true self" (AH's and Buber's similar views of language).

*24082 Schmerl, Rudolf B. "Aldous Huxley's Social Criticism." ChiR, 13, No. 1 (1959), 37-58.

AH's views oscillate from "varied calls" to social action, to bitter descriptions of society in decline.

24083 Simons, John D. "The Grand Inquisitor in Schiller, Dostoevsky and Huxley." NZSJ, No. 8 (1971), pp. 20-31.

Comparative study.

24084 Slochower, Harry. "Bourgeois Bohemia: Aldous Huxley and Ernest Hemingway." In his NO VOICE IS WHOLLY LOST. Pp. 32-40. See G2360.

AH's and Hemingway's incomplete revolts against their middle-class materialism and rationalism.

24085 Stevenson, Lionel. THE HISTORY OF THE ENGLISH NOVEL. XI, 183-98 and passim. See G2212.

AH a fundamentally uncreative novelist and satirist. Survey.

*24086 Stewart, Douglas H. "Aldous Huxley--Mysticism." In his THE ARK OF GOD. Pp. 44-70. See G3142.

AH considers mysticism "the vital soul of all religious experience which can be . . . presented in a pure form as the way of salvation." Distinguished analysis from a Christian perspective.

24087 Swinnerton, Frank. THE GEORGIAN LITERARY SCENE. Pp. 339-45. See G2364.

AH an "interwar" pessimist (biographical and critical survey).

24088 Tindall, William York. "The Trouble with Aldous Huxley." ASch, 11 (1942), 452-64.

AH's "decline" as a novelist attributed to his mysticism (and the influence of Heard).

24089 Vann, Gerald. "The Polytheism of Mr. Aldous Huxley." In ON BEING HUMAN: ST. THOMAS AND MR. ALDOUS HUXLEY. London: Sheed and Ward, 1933. Pp. 99-110.

Appendix to a study of St. Thomas's synthesis of humanism and spiritualism. Despite AH's objections to monotheism, his "life-worship theory" is very similar to Aquinas's philosophy.

*24090 Vitoux, Pierre. "Aldous Huxley and D.H. Lawrence: An Attempt at Intellectual Sympathy." MLR, 69 (1974), 501-22.

AH's interest in the dissociated personality and his successive responses to the "balanced" personality of Lawrence.

24091 Ward, Alfred C. "Aldous Huxley." In his THE NINETEEN-TWENTIES. Pp. 115-19. See G2373.

AH reveals rather than condemns the decadent spectacle of modern society.

24092 Watkin, E.I. "Aldous Huxley: A Philosophy of Moods." In MEN AND TENDENCIES. London: Sheed, 1937. Pp. 29-48.

AH and Pascal as philosophic pessimists (occasioned by AH's essay "Pascal").

24093 Webster, H.T. "Aldous Huxley: Notes on a Moral Evolution." SAQ, 45 (1946), 372-83.

AH's works reflect his generation's struggle to adjust to an apparently hostile society.

24094 Webster, Harvey Curtis. "Aldous Huxley: Sceptical Mystic." In his AFTER THE TRAUMA. Pp. 31-50. See G3154.

AH's novels reflect "the physical and psychical disgust" of the postwar generation.

24095 ______. "Facing Futility: Aldous Huxley's Really Brave New World." SR, 42 (1934), 193-208.

AH's development toward a saner, "more hopeful philosophy," from CROME YELLOW to BNW.

24096 Wilson, Colin. "Existential Criticism and the Work of Aldous Huxley." In his THE STRENGTH TO DREAM. Pp. 213-38. See G3159.

AH has "stood still as a creator."

24097 Woodcock, George. "Mexico and the English Novelist." WR, 21 (1956), 21-32.

AH's disillusionment with primitivism and his Mexican experiences.

24098 Wyndham, Francis. "The Teacher Emerges." LONDON MAGAZINE, 2 (Aug. 1955), 56-58.

The increasing didacticism of AH's fiction (especially PCP, MORTAL COILS and EYELESS IN GAZA) makes his works less satisfactory ("slightly indigestible"). See 23014. Reprinted in 23013 and 23021.

24099 Yoder, Edwin M. "Aldous Huxley and His Mystics." VQR, 42 (1966), 290-94.

AH a "qualified" mystic who never lost his belief in the value of sensory experience.

2.5 Studies of Individual Works

The following section is subdivided into two parts: i. Fiction (alphabetically by title), and ii. Miscellaneous Writings. Many of the full-length studies of AH consider the individual novels in detail. The books by the following authors (in section 2.3, above) generally devote most of their contents to work-by-work commentaries: Bowering (23003), Brander (23004), Firchow (23007), Henderson (to BNW) (23009), Holmes (23011), May (23015), Meckier (23016), Watts (23022), and Woodcock (23024). Brander, Holmes, and Woodcock also offer analyses of the poetry, biographies, and essays. Also see Bedford's biography (22002).

i. FICTION

AFTER MANY A SUMMER (1939)

25001 Powell, Lawrence C. "AFTER MANY A SUMMER." In CALIFORNIA CLASSICS. Los Angeles: Ward Ritchie, 1971. Pp. 357-70.

25002 Spencer, Theodore. "Aldous Huxley: The Latest Phase." ATLANTIC MONTHLY, 165 (1940), 407-9.

Novel praised as a forceful satire, despite its weaknesses in point of view. A review essay.

25003 Wagner, Linda W. "Satiric Masks: Huxley and Waugh." SNL, 3 (1966), 160-62.

AH abandons the satiric mask in AFTER MANY A SUMMER, while Waugh maintains objective detachment in THE LOVED ONE.

25004 Wain, John. "Tracts against Materialism." LONDON MAGAZINE, 2 (Aug. 1955), 58-61.

In BNW and AFTER MANY A SUMMER, AH a pseudonovelist, writing antimaterialist tracts. See 23014. Reprinted in 23013 and 23021.

ANTIC HAY (1923)

25005 Enroth, Clyde. "Mysticism in Two of Aldous Huxley's Early Novels." TCL, 6 (1960), 123-32.

Argues AH's sustained interest in mysticism throughout his career (illustrated from ANTIC HAY and BNW).

25006 Green, Martin. "Introduction." In "ANTIC HAY" AND "THE GIOCONDA SMILE." New York: Harper, 1963. Pp. vii-xix.

AH's strengths and weaknesses as one of the "clever" satirists of the twenties.

25007 Hall, James. "The Appeal to Grandfathers: Aldous Huxley." In his THE TRAGIC COMEDIANS. Pp. 31-44. See G3061.

ANTIC HAY, AH's only important comic novel, tests the validity of the postwar generation's nihilism.

25008 Karl, Frederick R. "The Play within the Novel in ANTIC HAY." RENASCENCE, 13 (1961), 59-68.

Play the focal point and symbolic center of the novel.

25009 Waugh, Evelyn. "Youth at the Helm and Pleasure at the Prow." LONDON MAGAZINE, 2 (Aug. 1955), 51-53.

AH's later work loses the "frivolous and sentimental and perennially delightful" qualities of ANTIC HAY. See 23014. Reprinted in 23013 and 23021.

APE AND ESSENCE (1948)

*25010 Schmerl, Rudolf B. "The Two Future Worlds of Aldous Huxley." PMLA, 77 (1962), 328-34.

Technique and satiric message in BNW and APE AND ESSENCE.

BRAVE NEW WORLD (1932)

25011 Berneni, Marie L. "Huxley: BRAVE NEW WORLD." In her JOURNEY THROUGH UTOPIA. Pp. 316-17. See G6405.

Comparison with Zamyatin.

25012 Bloomfield, Paul. "The Year 632 A.F." In his IMAGINARY WORLDS. Pp. 253-68. See G6407.

Summary and critique of BNW as utopia.

*25013 Calder, Jenni. HUXLEY AND ORWELL: "BRAVE NEW WORLD" AND "NINETEEN EIGHTY-FOUR." London: Arnold, 1977.

Close comparative reading of BNW and 1984, concentrated on their origins, object, plots and people, views of human nature, and political visions. Both a fine introduction to and a sophisticated assessment of the works.

25014 Clareson, Thomas D. "The Classic: Aldous Huxley's BRAVE NEW WORLD." EXTRAPOLATION, 2 (1961), 33-40.

BNW as science fiction.

25015 Coleman, D.C. "Bernard Shaw and BRAVE NEW WORLD." ShawR, 10 (1967), 6-8.

AH's attacks on Shaw in BNW.

25016 Enroth, Clyde. "Mysticism in Two of Aldous Huxley's Early Novels." TCL, 6 (1960), 123-32.

See 25005, above.

25017 Firchow, Peter. "Science and Conscience in Huxley's BRAVE NEW WORLD." ConL, 16 (1975), 301-16.

The scientific accuracy and the continuing relevance of BNW's prophecies.

25018 _____. "Wells and Lawrence in Huxley's BRAVE NEW WORLD." JML, 5 (1976), 260-78.

BNW seen as an ill-informed response to Wells's utopianism, influenced by AH's assimilation of Lawrencean ideas.

25019 Green, Martin. "Introduction." In "BRAVE NEW WORLD" AND "BRAVE NEW WORLD REVISITED." New York: Harper, 1965. Pp. v-xii.

Stresses both AH's humor and his ultimate high seriousness.

25020 Grushow, Ira. "BRAVE NEW WORLD and THE TEMPEST." CE, 24 (1962), 42-45.

Ironic relationship between the themes of the two works.

25021 Hacker, Andrew. "Dostoevsky's Disciples: Man and Sheep in Political Theory." JOURNAL OF POLITICS, 17 (1955), 590-613.

BNW (pp. 600-602) presents a theoretical society which has abandoned the principle of individual autonomy (cf. Dostoevsky and B.F. Skinner).

25022 Jones, Joseph. "Utopia as Dirge." AMERICAN QUARTERLY, 2 (1950), 214-26.

BNW a "mechanical" dystopia (cf. Orwell's 1984 and Twain's CONNECTICUT YANKEE).

25023 Jones, William M. "The Iago of BRAVE NEW WORLD." WHR, 15 (1961), 275-78.

Othello pattern in novel (Savage as Othello, Shakespeare as his Iago).

25024 Kessler, Martin. "Power and the Perfect State: A Study in Disillusionment as Reflected in Orwell's NINETEEN-EIGHTY FOUR and Huxley's BRAVE NEW WORLD." PSQ, 72 (1957), 565-77.

To AH and Orwell, the cause and the effect of totalitarianism are the denial of the individual's right to hold "apolitical" views (e.g., morality).

25025 Miles, O. Thomas. "Three Authors in Search of a Character." Person, 46, (1965), 65-72.

Society created by man (BNW) versus man created by society (Miller's DEATH OF A SALESMAN and Camus's EXILE AND THE KINGDOM).

25026 New, Melvyn. "Ad nauseam: A Satiric Device in Huxley, Orwell, and Waugh." SNL, 8 (1970), 24-28.

Use of nausea imagery to reflect the satirist's ultimate disgust with human folly (BNW, 1984, and VILE BODIES).

25027 Richards, D. "Four Utopias." SEER, 40 (1962), 220-28.

Compares ideologies in BNW, 1984, and utopian fictions by Zamyatin and Dostoevsky.

25028 Rolo, Charles J. "Introduction." In "BRAVE NEW WORLD" AND "BRAVE NEW WORLD REVISITED." New York: Harper, 1960. Pp. vii-xvi.

AH's mystical philosophy of "nonattachment" inspires BNW and all his subsequent works.

25029 Ross, Julian L. PHILOSOPHY IN LITERATURE. Syracuse, N.Y.: Syracuse Univ. Press, 1949. Pp. 97-99.

BNW as a satiric parody of the ideal utopia.

*25030 Schmerl, Rudolf B. "The Two Future Worlds of Aldous Huxley." PMLA, 77 (1962), 328-34.

See 25010, above.

25031 Wain, John. "Tracts against Materialism." LONDON MAGAZINE, 2 (Aug. 1955), 58-61.

See 25004, above.

25032 Weber, Eugene. "The Anti-Utopia of the Twentieth Century." SAQ, 58 (1959), 440-47.

The dystopia a peculiarly modern form, arising out of the disillusionment with the possible "omnipotence of human reason" (BNW, among others).

25033 Wells, Arvin R. "BRAVE NEW WORLD." In INSIGHT II. Ed. John V. Hagopian and Martin Dolch. Pp. 176-85. See G5007.

Plot summary, critique, and study questions.

25034 Westlake, J.H.J. "Aldous Huxley's BRAVE NEW WORLD and George Orwell's NINETEEN EIGHTY-FOUR: A Comparative Study." NS, 71 (1972), 94-102.

Notes elementary similarities and differences of tone and purpose between the works.

25035 Wilson, Robert H. "BRAVE NEW WORLD as Shakespeare Criticism." SHAKESPEARE ASSOCIATION BULLETIN, 21 (1946), 99-107.

Implicit social, ethical, and literary criticism of Shakespeare in BNW.

25036 ______. "Versions of BRAVE NEW WORLD." LCUT, 8, No. 4 (1968), 28-41.

Textual study.

25037 Wing, George. "The Shakespearian Voice of Conscience in BRAVE NEW WORLD." DR, 51 (1971), 153-64.

AH's attack on sexual permissiveness and the decline of human dignity reflected in his use of "the intensest expressions of Shakespearian guilt in the matter of sexual incontinence" in BNW.

CROME YELLOW (1921)

25038 Farmer, David R. "A Note on the Text of Huxley's CROME YELLOW." PBSA, 63 (1969), 131-33.

Collation of first American and British texts.

*25039 Wilson, Angus. "The House Party Novels." LONDON MAGAZINE, 2 (Aug. 1955), 53-56.

CROME YELLOW and THOSE BARREN LEAVES endure not so much for their ideas or influence, but for their pastoral "sense of material pleasure in the natural world." See 23014. Reprinted in 23013 and 23021.

EYELESS IN GAZA (1936)

*25040 Bentley, Phyllis. "The Structure of EYELESS IN GAZA." EJ, 26 (1937), 127-32.

Analysis of the jumbled structure of the novel reveals "a highly significant design."

25041 Estrich, H.W. "Jesting Pilate Tells the Answer." SR, 47 (1939), 63-81.

AH's new "cosmology" in ENDS AND MEANS reflected in EYELESS IN GAZA.

25042 Gunn, Drewey W. AMERICAN AND BRITISH WRITERS IN MEXICO, 1556-1973. Austin: Univ. of Texas Press, 1974. Pp. 160-63.

Peripheral influence of AH's Mexican sojourn on BEYOND THE MEXIQUE BAY and EYELESS IN GAZA.

*25043 Vitoux, Pierre. "Structure and Meaning in Aldous Huxley's EYELESS IN GAZA." YES, 2 (1972), 212-24.

AH's complex, "jumbled" structure suggests the "climactic" rather than evolutionary development of his characters and reveals a sophisticated conception of time in fiction.

"The Gioconda Smile" (1921)

25044 Green, Martin. "Introduction." In "ANTIC HAY" AND 'THE GIOCONDA SMILE'. New York: Harper, 1963. Pp. vii-xix.

See 25006, above.

25045 Watt, Donald J. "The Absurdity of the Hedonist in Huxley's 'The Gioconda Smile.'" SSF, 7 (1970), 328-30.

Huxley's chief theme in his fiction, the absurdity of life without "genuine purpose," traced in "The Gioconda Smile."

ISLAND (1962)

25046 Choudhary, Nora S. "ISLAND: Huxley's Attempt at Practical Philosophy." LITERATURE EAST AND WEST, 16 (1972), 1155-67.

Traces elements of Indian and Oriental belief in novel. Slight.

25047 Elliott, Robert C. THE SHAPE OF UTOPIA. Pp. 137-53. See G6413.

Comparative readings of ISLAND and B.F. Skinner's WALDEN TWO as "anti-anti-Utopias."

*25048 Kennedy, Richard S. "Aldous Huxley: The Final Wisdom." SWR, 50 (1965), 37-47.

ISLAND AH's attempt at final, affirmative synthesis in his work. Extract reprinted in 23021.

25049 Leeper, Geoffrey. "The Happy Utopias of Aldous Huxley and H.G. Wells." MEANJIN, 24 (1965), 120-24.

ISLAND and Wells's MEN LIKE GODS share a confidence in "the good possibilities of science."

25050 McMichael, Charles T. "Aldous Huxley's ISLAND: The Final Vision." SLitI, 1, No. 2 (1968), 73-82.

ISLAND a culminating statement of AH's ideas on man, mysticism, and society.

25051 Meckier, Jerome. "Cancer in Utopia: Positive and Negative Elements in Huxley's ISLAND." DR, 54 (1974-75), 619-33.

AH embraces both the positive and the negative elements of existence for his utopian vision in ISLAND.

25052 Stewart, Douglas H. "Aldous Huxley's ISLAND." QQ, 70 (1963), 326-35.

Speculates on the social as well as the personal significance of AH's movement from dystopia (BNW) to utopia.

*25053 Watt, Donald J. "Vision and Symbol in Aldous Huxley's ISLAND." TCL, 14 (1968), 149-60.

AH's vision of man's inward search for salvation embodied in his symbols (e.g., island, mountains). Reprinted in 23013.

POINT COUNTER POINT (1928)

*25054 Baker, Robert S. "Spandrell's 'Lydian Heaven': Moral Masochism and the Centrality of Spandrell in Huxley's POINT COUNTER POINT." CRITICISM, 16 (1974), 120-35.

Spandrell the center of AH's "ruthless scrutiny" of modern man's disordered relationships (with parent, lover, death, and God).

*25055 Baldanza, Frank. "POINT COUNTER POINT: Aldous Huxley on 'The Human Fugue.'" SAQ, 58 (1959), 248-57.

AH's use of musical structure (the fugue) in PCP. Reprinted in 23021.

25056 Beach, Joseph Warren. "Counterpoint: Huxley." In his THE TWENTIETH-CENTURY NOVEL. Pp. 458-69. See G3004.

Similarities between AH and Gide as technicians and novelists of ideas (e.g., PCP and THE COUNTERFEITERS).

25057 Brewster, Dorothy, and Angus Burrell. MODERN FICTION. Pp. 248-59. See G3014.

PCP a sophisticated novel of the "thinking class in a civilized community [which] is disillusioned and skeptical in temper" (cf. Gide).

25058 Glicksberg, Charles I. MODERN LITERARY PERSPECTIVISM. Pp. 23-27 and passim. See G3050.

AH and the relativity of perception (e.g., PCP).

25059 Kettle, Arnold. "Aldous Huxley: POINT COUNTER POINT." In AN INTRODUCTION TO THE ENGLISH NOVEL. II, 167-70. See G3088.

Novel never comes to life.

25060 Meckier, Jerome. "Quarles among the Monkeys: Huxley's Zoological Novels." MLR, 68 (1973), 268-82.

AH's animal imagery (especially PCP), and a possibly influential source (THE HERMIT, 1727 [anonymous]).

25061 Patty, James S. "Baudelaire and Aldous Huxley." SAB, 3, No. 4 (1968), 5-8.

Briefly traces Baudelaire's influence, especially in the creation of the diabolic Spandrell in PCP.

25062 Ross, Julian L. PHILOSOPHY IN LITERATURE. Syracuse, N.Y.: Syracuse Univ. Press, 1949. Pp. 24-32.

AH documents the hedonistic ethics of the twenties in PCP.

25063 Watson, David S. "POINT COUNTER POINT: The Modern Satiric Novel a Genre?" SNL, 6, No. 2 (1969), 31-35.

PCP a successful "modern satire" (defines and illustrates).

25064 Watt, Donald J. "The Criminal-Victim Pattern in Huxley's POINT COUNTER POINT." SNNTS, 2 (1970), 42-51.

AH's use of "colliding temperaments," or counterpoint, in PCP (e.g., extrovert-introvert, aggressive-passive).

THOSE BARREN LEAVES (1925)

25065 Aiken, Conrad. "Aldous Huxley." In A REVIEWER'S ABC. New York: Meridian, 1958. Pp. 225-30.

AH's "best work," the "sharpest single advance that he has made."

25066 Garman, Douglas. "THOSE BARREN LEAVES." In TOWARDS STANDARDS OF CRITICISM: SELECTIONS FROM THE "CALENDAR OF MODERN LETTERS," 1925-27. Ed. F.R. Leavis. London: Wishart, 1933. Pp. 43-46.

AH's mastery of characterization and movement toward a more creative form of satire. A review essay.

25067 Harris, Wendell V. "Molly's 'Yes': The Transvaluation of Sex in Modern Fiction." TSLL, 10 (1968), 107-18.

Sex as an affirmation of life (e.g., AH's THOSE BARREN LEAVES, among others).

*25068 Wilson, Angus. "The House Party Novels." LONDON MAGAZINE, 2 (Aug. 1955), 53-56.

See 25039, above.

TIME MUST HAVE A STOP (1944)

25069 Lebowitz, Martin. "The Everlasting Mr. Huxley." In THE KENYON CRITICS: STUDIES IN MODERN LITERATURE FROM THE "KENYON REVIEW." Ed. J[ohn] C[rowe] Ransom. Cleveland: World, 1951. Pp. 289-93.

TIME MUST HAVE A STOP a "parable" of AH's own development as a novelist.

*25070 Wilson, Edmund. "Aldous Huxley in the World beyond Time." In CLASSICS AND COMMERCIALS. Pp. 209-14. See G2375.

TIME MUST HAVE A STOP in its way a brilliant "dismal" book. Reprinted in 23021.

ii. MISCELLANEOUS WRITINGS

Also see Green (25019), Joad (24043), Jones (24044), Marovitz (24058), and Rolo (25028), above.

25071 Aldington, Richard. "Aldous Huxley." 1929. In SELECTED CRITICAL WRITINGS, 1928-1960. Ed. A. Kershaw. Carbondale: Southern Illinois Univ. Press, 1970. Pp. 19-23.

Admires AH's attempt to "say something positive" about life in DO WHAT YOU WILL.

*25072 Barzun, Jacques. "The Anti-Modern Essays of Aldous Huxley." LONDON MAGAZINE, 4 (Aug. 1957), 51-55.

AH's miscellaneous essays (e.g., ADONIS AND THE ALPHABET) unified by his vision of modern man's "warped" spirit, blunted senses, and irreverence for the powers of the word.

25073 Bedoyere, Michael de la. "Aldous Huxley's Challenge." DUBLIN REVIEW, 202 (1938), 13-26.

Catholic response to AH's "challenge" to Christian philosophy in ENDS AND MEANS.

25074 Bowen, Elizabeth. "Mr. Huxley's Essays." 1936. In COLLECTED IMPRESSIONS. New York: Knopf, 1950. Pp. 146-48.

The clever "prodigy" enters sober, earnest middle age (re: THE OLIVE TREE, AND OTHER ESSAYS). Reprinted in 23021.

25075 Church, Richard. "Introduction." In THE COLLECTED POETRY OF ALDOUS HUXLEY. Ed. Donald Watt. Pp. 7-12. See 13002.

AH's social and mystical "vision."

25076 Day-Lewis, C. WE'RE NOT GOING TO DO NOTHING: A REPLY TO ALDOUS HUXLEY'S "WHAT ARE YOU GOING TO DO ABOUT IT?" London: LEFT REVIEW, 1936.

Pamphlet response to AH's plea for pacifism, arguing for active resistence to fascism (1936). Extracts reprinted in 23021.

25077 Estrich, H.W. "Jesting Pilate Tells the Answer." SR, 47 (1939), 63-81.

See 25041, above.

25078 Fairchild, Hoxie N. RELIGIOUS TRENDS IN ENGLISH POETRY. Vol. 5. 1880-1920. New York: Columbia Univ. Press, 1962. Pp. 620-26.

Survey of AH's poetry (to 1920), noting his early interest in mysticism and his indebtedness to Laforgue.

25079 Fletcher, John G. "Two Travelers." AMERICAN REVIEW, 3 (1934), 530-36.

Judging from BEYOND MEXIQUE BAY, AH "does not know what to make of his dip into primitivism" (review, with DosPassos's IN ALL COUNTRIES).

25080 Gunn, Drewey W. AMERICAN AND BRITISH WRITERS IN MEXICO, 1556-1973. Austin: Univ. of Texas Press, 1974. Pp. 160-63.

See 25042, above.

*25081 Häusermann, Hans Walter. "Aldous Huxley as a Literary Critic." PMLA, 48 (1933), 908-18.

AH's critical views arise from his search for a "scientific integrity" or its literary equivalent (summarizes his criticism). Extracts reprinted in 23021.

25082 Hazlitt, Henry. "ENDS AND MEANS." In A PREFACE TO LITERATURE. Ed. Edward Wagenknecht. New York: Holt, 1954. Pp. 356-60.

AH's "dubious metaphysics" in support of his ethical beliefs. A review of ENDS AND MEANS.

*25083 Inge, W.R. "Discussion: THE PERENNIAL PHILOSOPHY." PHILOSOPHY, 22 (1947), 66-70.

Despite its flirtations with parapsychology, PERENNIAL PHILOSOPHY is "probably the most important treatise on mysticism" in many years. Extracts reprinted in 23021.

25084 Lothian, John M. "Wordsworth North of Forty-Nine." ABERDEEN UNIVERSITY REVIEW, 33 (1950), 245-51.

Corrects AH's distortion of the romantic view of nature (in "Wordsworth in the Tropics").

25085 MacCarthy, Desmond. "The Stage and the Spirits." In HUMANITIES. New York: Oxford Univ. Press, 1954. Pp. 99-104.

AH's "remarkable talent for the stage" (re: THE WORLD OF LIGHT: A COMEDY IN THREE ACTS, 1931).

25086 McCormack, Arthur. "Mr. Huxley and Overpopulation." MONTH, 22 (1959), 84-91.

Argues the falsehoods in AH's pessimistic view of the world population problem in BRAVE NEW WORLD REVISITED.

25087 Mais, Stuart P.B. "The Poems of Aldous Huxley." In WHY WE SHOULD READ. London: Richards, 1921. Pp. 88-96.

AH's "cleverness" and "perversity of intellect."

25088 Martin, Kingsley. "The Pacifist's Dilemma To-Day." POLITICAL QUARTERLY, 9 (1938), 155-72.

Detailed consideration of AH's "historical and utilitarian" arguments for pacifism in ENDS AND MEANS.

*25089 Meckier, Jerome. "The Hippopotamian Question: A Note on Aldous Huxley's Unfinished Novel." MFS, 16 (1970), 505-14.

Examination of the fragment of AH's last, unfinished novel (printed in Laura Huxley's THIS TIMELESS MOMENT, 22010), suggests he was heading in some new technical and philosophical directions.

25090 Pakenham, Frank. "GREY EMINENCE and Political Morality." POLITICAL QUARTERLY, 13 (1942), 407-13.

Disputes AH's fatalistic contention that "there is no place for a man of virtue" in the political world.

25091 Philipson, Morris. "Introduction." In ON ART AND ARTISTS. Ed. Philipson. Pp. 9-14. See 13006.

AH's search for a world view which could comprehend both the sciences and the arts.

25092 Quennell, Peter. "Electrifying the Audience." LONDON MAGAZINE, 2 (Aug. 1955), 62-64.

Notes the dexterity, erudition, and wit of AH's essays (in MUSIC AT NIGHT and BEYOND MEXIQUE BAY), as well as their occasional disturbing superficiality. See 23014. Reprinted in 23013 and 23021.

25093 Vickery, John B. "Three Modes and a Myth." WHR, 12 (1958), 371-78.

AH's use of myth in his poem "Leda" (1919. Cf. Graves and Yeats).

25094 Wajc-Tenenbaum, R. "Aesthetics and Metaphysics: Aldous Huxley's Last Novel." RLV, 37 (1971), 160-75.

Full description and critique of the unfinished novel fragment. See 22010.

25095 Watt, Donald J. "The Meditative Poetry of Aldous Huxley." MODERN POETRY STUDIES, 6 (1975), 115-28.

Readings of several AH poems, in the light of Louis Martz's definition of "meditative" poetry.

25096 Whitehead, Frank. "Introduction." In SELECTED ESSAYS. Ed. Harold Raymond. Pp. 7-14. See 13009.

AH's "power to educate is due to the extraordinary range and diversity of his interests."

25097 Woods, Richard D. "SANGRE PATRICIA and THE DOORS OF PERCEPTION." RomN, 12 (1971), 302-6.

Similarities between AH's essay and a Venezuelan novel.

25098 Zaehner, Robert C. MYSTICISM, SACRED AND PROFANE: AN INQUIRY INTO SOME VARIETIES OF PRAETERNATURAL EXPERIENCE. Oxford: Clarendon Press, 1957. Pp. 1-29 and passim.

AH's mysticism and belief in mescalin's powers as a "religion surrogate" (re: DOORS OF PERCEPTION).

INDEXES

AUTHOR INDEX

This index includes all authors, compilers, editors, and translators cited in this volume. Those entry numbers prefixed by the letter "G" refer to items appearing in the General Bibliography section of this guide. All other entries refer to the individual author sections of this guide and, for ease in location, are prefixed by two or three-letter author abbreviations. See the Introduction for an explanation of the volume's numbering system and a table of author abbreviations.

Throughout this index the order of the entry numbers, for multiple appearances in the volume, follows the order of appearance in the volume, with the following major exception: For ready reference, the entry numbers for the primary bibliographies of the authors who are the subjects of this guide are given preceding their appearances as authors elsewhere in the volume. (See, for example, Elizabeth Bowen, below.)

A

B

C

E

F

G

H

K

M

N

O

P

Q

R

S

TITLE INDEX

This index includes the titles of all books, essay collections, and pamphlets entered in this guide. Article titles are omitted. In all cases of identical titles, the author's name has been placed in brackets after the title. Those entry numbers prefixed by the letter "G" refer to items appearing in the General Bibliography section of this guide. All other entries refer to the individual author sections of this guide and, for ease in location, are prefixed by two or three-letter author abbreviations. See the Introduction for an explanation of the volume's numbering system and a table of author abbreviations. The entry number(s) indicates the first, or, in a few cases, each complete listing of the title with full publishing data. For subsequent short-title, cross-referenced entries of many of these titles, consult the appropriate author in the author index. For subsequent references to the title as subject, consult the subject index.

A

D

E

F

G

H

J

K

L

N

O

P

Q

R

S

T

U

V

W

Y

Z

SUBJECT INDEX

Those entry numbers prefixed by the letter "G" refer to items appearing in the General Bibliography section of this guide. All other entries refer to the individual author sections of this guide and, for ease in location, are prefixed by two or three-letter author abbreviations. See the Introduction for an explanation of the volume's numbering system and a table of author abbreviations.

This index differs slightly from the author and title indexes in including subjects that appear in the headnotes used throughout the author sections of this guide. Such references will include the author abbreviation and the section number where the headnote appears (e.g., MB1.2 refers to the headnote for section 1.2, Miscellaneous Writings, in the Max Beerbohm section).

Throughout this index the order of multiple entry numbers follows their order of appearance in the volume, with the following major exceptions: For ready reference, when a subject, an author, or a work is the primary subject of an entire section or subsection of this guide, the appropriate entry numbers are listed first.

A

B

D

E

F

G

H

M

N

S

T

U

V

W